ROMANS

THE IVP NEW TESTAMENT COMMENTARY SERIES

GRANT R. OSBORNE

GRANT R. OSBORNE, SERIES EDITOR

D. STUART BRISCOE AND HADDON ROBINSON,
CONSULTING EDITORS

IVP Academic
An imprint of InterVarsity Press
Downers Grove, Illinois

InterVarsity Press
P.O. Box 1400, Downers Grove, IL 60515-1426
World Wide Web: www.ivpress.com
E-mail: email@ivpress.com

*InterVarsity Press® is the book-publishing division of InterVarsity Christian Fellowship/USA®, a
movement of students and faculty active on campus at hundreds of universities, colleges and
schools of nursing in the United States of America, and a member movement of the International
Fellowship of Evangelical Students. For information about local and regional activities, write
Public Relations Dept., InterVarsity Christian Fellowship/USA, 6400 Schroeder Rd., P.O. Box 7895,
Madison, WI 53707-7895, or visit the IVCF website at <www.intervarsity.org>.*

Design: Cindy Kiple
Images: *Einzug in Jerusalem—Entry into Jerusalem by Wilhelm Morgner at Museum am Ostwall,
Dortmund, Germany. Erich Lessing/Art Resource, NY.*

ISBN 978-1-84474-456-5

Printed in the United kingdom by 4edge Limited

Library of Congress Cataloging-in-Publication Data

Osborne, Grant R.
  Romans/Grant R. Osborne.
    p. cm.—(The IVP New Testament commentary series; 6)
Includes bibliographical references.
  ISBN 0-8308-1806-5
  1. Bible. N.T. Romans—Commentaries. I. Title. II. Series.
  BS2665.53R66 2003
  227'.107—dc21
                                                                    2003013829

P 17 16 15 14 13 12 11 10 9 8 7 6 5 4 3 2 1
Y 24 23 22 21 20 19 18 17 16 15 14 13 12 11 10

In Memoriam
William L. Lane
scholar, teacher, friend

General Preface

In an age of proliferating commentary series, one might easily ask why add yet another to the seeming glut. The simplest answer is that no other series has yet achieved what we had in mind—a series to and from the church that seeks to move from the text to its contemporary relevance and application.

No other series offers the unique combination of solid, biblical exposition and helpful explanatory notes in the same user-friendly format. No other series has tapped the unique blend of scholars and pastors who share both a passion for faithful exegesis and a deep concern for the church. Based on the New International Version of the Bible, one of the most widely used modern translations, the IVP New Testament Commentary Series builds on the NIV's reputation for clarity and accuracy. Individual commentators indicate clearly whenever they depart from the standard translation as required by their understanding of the original Greek text.

The series contributors represent a wide range of theological traditions, united by a common commitment to the authority of Scripture for Christian faith and practice. Their efforts here are directed toward applying the unchanging message of the New Testament to the ever-changing world in which we live.

Readers will find in each volume not only traditional discussions of authorship and backgrounds, but useful summaries of principal themes and approaches to contemporary application. To bridge the gap between commentaries that stress the flow of an author's argument but skip over exegetical nettles and those that simply jump from one difficulty to another, we have developed our unique format that expounds the text in uninterrupted form on the upper portion of each page while dealing with other issues underneath in verse-keyed notes. To avoid clutter we have also adopted a social studies note system that keys references to the bibliography.

We offer the series in hope that pastors, students, Bible teachers and small-group leaders of all sorts will find it a valuable aid—one that stretches the mind and moves the heart to ever-growing faithfulness and obedience to our Lord Jesus Christ.

Author's Preface

Have you ever been given an assignment that seemed too daunting for you, too far beyond your meager abilities? Such was the case when I was asked to do Romans for this series by InterVarsity Press. Paul's letter to the Romans is clearly the deepest theological treatise in the New Testament, indeed of Scripture as a whole. It was written by one of the great geniuses of the early church under the inspiration of the Holy Spirit. Who am I to try to unpack such a work, perhaps the greatest of history? My fear is that inadvertently I might obscure some of the deep truths of this book. Moreover, many of the greatest debates in the history of the church have stemmed from attempts to interpret it. I asked the Lord why he did not spare Bill Lane, my good friend whom I had originally asked to do this project. He was far more able than I! When the Lord took Bill home, InterVarsity asked if I would take the project. It is a great honor to read Romans, let alone interpret it, so I said yes. This work is dedicated to the memory of this great man.

Yet a valid question arises: Do we need another commentary on Romans? After all, some of the greatest minds in the church have already produced one—Chrysostom, Calvin, Godet, Sanday and Headlam, Barth, Lagrange, Michel, Käsemann, Cranfield, Barrett, Bruce, Wilckens, Moo, Dunn, Schreiner. No doubt, we in the West have published too much, while churches in the rest of the world have been unable to publish what they need. Yet many Western commentaries, for the most part, are too technical for many pastors and nearly all laypersons. Others are too shallow and miss the meaning of the text. There still needs to be a work that will make all the deep insights of the critical commentaries accessible and understandable to those without technical training, and that will show the way to apply these truths to modern life. This balance—deeply committed to the God-intended meaning of Romans and yet at the same time relevant for the daily life of the Christian—is somewhat rare in a commentary. This is one of my primary purposes for this work on Romans. The reader will have to judge how well I succeed.

I cannot begin to say how humbly grateful to the Lord I am for enabling me to produce this work. I feel I have been blessed more and more at each level of the Christian life. The joy of being a child of God is something none of us deserves, and then the honor of being called to be a leader in the church, given to God's people as the Lord's "grace-gift" (Eph 4:8, 11) is something we could never begin to imagine. As Paul says, "How beautiful are the feet of those who bring good news" (Rom 10:15 from Is 52:7 TNIV), and the inestimable privilege not only of proclaiming the truths of Scripture so that God's people can walk rightly before him but also of providing information to help pastors and others engaged in serious Bible study to understand the text more deeply is a joy beyond compare. To have the honor of writing a commentary on the only eternal truth the world will ever know is mind-boggling to say the least. Much prayer has gone into this volume, and I can only trust the Lord to use it for his glory and the church's benefit!

Introduction

Have you ever thought about writing the perfect letter, a letter so profound that the reader could only sigh with awe at its incredible truths? Paul has written just that letter, one that is so deep that Calvin said, "I fear, lest through my recommendations falling far short of what they ought to be, I should do nothing but obscure its merits," and then added, "when any one gains a knowledge of this Epistle, he has an entrance opened to him to all the most hidden treasures of Scripture" (Calvin 1979:xxix). It is generally agreed that this is the most important book in the New Testament from the standpoint of the meaning of salvation and the Christian life. It was Martin Luther's study of Romans that led to his discovery of justification by faith alone and thus to the Reformation. In every generation a Romans commentary has stood out as a landmark work, from Calvin in 1540 to Sanday and Headlam in 1895 to Karl Barth in 1919 to C. E. B. Cranfield in 1975 to Douglas Moo in 1996. Each has had a profound effect on theological reflection and on the understanding of Scripture in general. It is difficult to overstate the importance of this epistle for the church. The issues discussed in it are at the core of what it means to be a Christian.

☐ Authorship, Date and Situation

Hardly anyone doubts that this letter was written by Paul. In fact, the universal acceptance of Pauline authorship has always been one of the assured results of modern scholarship. Most also agree it was written between A.D. 54 and 58. One of the keys to dating New Testament events is the appointment of Gallio as proconsul of Corinth, which we know, because of existing inscriptions, occurred in A.D. 51-52. Paul was tried by him in Corinth (Acts 18:12) at the end of his second missionary journey and then stayed in Corinth a while (Acts 18:18). Afterward he went to Jerusalem and on to Antioch, where he stayed a short time and then began his third missionary journey (Acts 18:22-23). He spent the majority of it in Ephesus, where he stayed about two and a half years before going to Macedonia and Greece (staying three months), from which the epistle was written. Based on these facts, it is common to assign A.D. 57-58 as the probable date for his writing of Romans (so Sanday and Headlam 1902; M. Black 1973; Fitzmyer 1993b; Byrne 1996; Moo 1996).

This has to be one of the greatest periods of creative activity of any person who ever lived. It was at the end of Paul's third missionary journey (he wrote 1-2 Corinthians and Romans at this time) as he returned to Jerusalem with a delegation from the Gentile churches in Asia Minor, Macedonia and Achaia to deliver a collection for the poor Jewish Christians. We know this on the basis of 15:23-33, where Paul says he is leaving Greece on his way to Jerusalem to deliver the collection for the poor and that he then plans to visit Rome on his way to Spain. Paul mentions only Macedonia and Achaia in 15:26, for that is where he had been ministering at that time. However, there were representatives from Derbe (Galatia, Acts 14:20-21) and the province of Asia (the western half of Asia Minor, where Ephesus was located) mentioned in Acts 20:4, and they were the official delegation taking the gift for the poor in Jerusalem from the Gentile churches.

Paul wrote this letter to Rome while staying three months in Greece (Acts 20:1-4), probably at Corinth, where he stayed at the home of Gaius (see the discussion at 16:21-23), who had been baptized there (1 Cor 1:14). He had written 1 Corinthians about a year earlier after hearing very bad news regarding opposition against him in the Corinthian church as he ministered at Ephesus. During that time he actually wrote three letters (a "previous letter" [1 Cor 5:9-11], 1 Corinthians and a "severe letter" [2 Cor 2:6-9, 7:12]) and visited the church once (the "painful visit" [2 Cor 2:1; 12:14, 21; 13:1-2]; see Harris 1976:302-3; for a somewhat different order, see Gilchrist 1988:47-69), culminating in 2 Corinthians, probably written just a month or two before coming to Corinth and writing this letter. Much of the trouble he had experienced from the opponents in Corinth was over, and this was a happy time for him. Romans 16 seems to show an untroubled situation in Corinth and may mean the that strong admonitions of 2 Corinthians 10—13 had worked. Still, he was worried about two things—opposition from the Jews when he reached Jerusalem, and how the Jewish Christians would receive the collection for the poor (15:31). The second turned out positively. However, the first turned out badly from a human perspective when he was arrested, was taken prisoner by the Romans, and went first to Caesarea (for two years) and then to Rome in chains. Still, as Paul realized later (Acts 21:4, 10-14), this was indeed the will of God.

☐ The Church at Rome

The origin of the Roman church is unknown. The ancient belief that it was founded by Peter and Paul (Irenaeus *Against Heresies* 3.1.2) is certainly wrong, for there is no historical evidence either in the New Testament or in external sources. Moreover, if it had been founded by an apostle, Paul would not have laid claim to it on the grounds that he was "apostle to the Gentiles" (1:6, 14; so Sanday and Headlam 1902:xxvi). It originated fairly early, for the emperor Claudius expelled the Jews and Christians in A.D. 49 because of riots between the Jews and Christians (see Suetonius *Life of Claudius* 25.2), indicating that it was a well-established movement by then. Most believe it was founded by Jewish Christians (perhaps returning from the Pentecost of Acts 2, but also traveling merchants and others), who may have witnessed in the synagogues that the Messiah had come (so Murray 1968; Dunn 1988a; Schreiner 1998). Rome had a sizable population of Jews, estimated at forty to fifty thousand (Dunn 1988a:xlvi), almost the size of Jerusalem itself! In this sense the coming of Christ was a "fulfillment of time" because of the tremendous mobility of people in the Roman Empire. There had never been so many traveling from one city to another. The strategy of preaching in the synagogues was also practiced by Paul on his missionary journeys, and the pattern of preaching the gospel followed by conflict and riots also occurred frequently (Acts 13:50; 14:4-7, 19; 17:5-8, 13; 18:6; 19:9, 23-24).

The history of this church was probably strongly influenced by Claudius's expulsion of Jews from Rome. Before that time Jewish Christians dominated, but after their expulsion the Gentiles had to develop their own leadership. Many had been originally converted from the synagogues themselves, from the many "God-fearers" that worshiped as Jews but had been unwilling to undergo circumcision (see Acts 10:2, 22; 13:16, 26). It is often thought that they were the major source of converts from the synagogues. They in turn would have evangelized their own countrymen. During the ensuing years the Gentile church grew, and when many of the Jewish Christians returned after the death of Claudius (A.D. 54), the Gentiles were in the majority and were leaders in the Roman church, causing further tension with the returning Jews and their different lifestyle. So when Paul wrote this letter the Gentiles may have been in the majority (so Murray 1968; Cranfield 1975; Dunn 1988a; Moo 1996; Schreiner 1998). They are directly addressed in 11:13-32 and 15:7-12, and Paul tended to side with them in the dispute even while arguing that they should live in unity and respect one another's opinions.

□ Genre, Purposes and Themes of the Letter

There have been several who have believed Romans was not really addressed to the situation at Rome but was a treatise written for the church as a whole, summarizing Paul's gospel. Nygren (1949:7-8) said that Paul was writing to recount his own "life problem," his own salvation from works, and so he summarized "the new way of salvation, the way of faith, and the way in which the people of God had hitherto walked, the way of works." In fact, Bornkamm (1991:12-14) called Romans Paul's "last will and testament," his legacy reflecting his experiences and struggles and seeking to sum up all Paul had learned into a universally valid compendium of his message. These commentators argue that the opening salutation and the closing greetings were added later to Paul's treatise on the meaning of the gospel (1:16—11:36 or perhaps 1:16—15:13 with 14:1—15:13 reflecting Corinth as well as Rome). There is very little explicit mention of the Roman situation in the body of the text, even in 14:1—15:13 (see Karris 1991:65-84). However, this scenario is unlikely because everything in the text can be shown to address the situation in Roman. It is an epistle, though like Ephesians it does seem to go beyond the purely Roman situation and sum up the Pauline gospel (see below). As Moo says (1996:14), "these specifics have not played a large role in Paul's presentation, but they have the agenda of theological and practical issues with which Paul deals." There are simply too many issues he would have included if this were indeed his "last will and testament" (eschatology [e.g., the parousia and resurrection of the body] and ecclesiology [the "in Christ" motif, the church as the "body" or "temple"]). So it is first an epistle and second has aspects of a treatise as Paul goes beyond the needs of Rome to present a detailed summary of his gospel. Certainly it does have a rhetorical function in drawing the Roman readers into Paul's vision for the true Christian life and mission (see Crafton 1990:317-39), but it also addresses specific issues faced by the Roman church.

Morris (1988:8-17) reviews twelve different possibilities for the genre and occasion of Romans as suggested by commentators over the years. The letter could be: (1) "a compendium of Christian teaching," meaning a summary of the church's theology (Nygren 1949); (2) "Paul's mature thinking on essential Christianity," that is, his personal reflections after years of ministry (Bornkamm 1991:16-28); (3) Paul's discussion of the state of the church as he had finished his eastern ministry and prepared to go west, showing that all believers were incorporated into the church via the Abrahamic promises (Leenhart 1961); (4) a circular letter of fourteen or fifteen chapters, with "to Rome" added later, containing a manifesto of his theology (Manson 1991); (5) a draft intended for the Jerusalem church containing a defense of his gospel and collection for the poor there (Jervell 1991); (6) Paul's personal claim to apostolic authority in light of challenges by opponents (Käsemann 1980); (7) Paul's attempt to provide his "authentic apostolic stamp" to a church that had not been founded by an apostle (G. Klein 1991:29-43); (8) his admonition of the "weak" Jewish Christians and the "strong" Gentile Christians to live in peace (Donfried 1991); (9) an attempt to win to Paul's gospel an influential church still mired in the law (D. A. Black 1989); (10) a rhetorical letter (demonstrative/epideictic [Wuellner 1991] or ambassadorial [Jewett 1988]) designed to inculcate Paul's views on the Roman church; (11) Paul's dialogue with the Jews to answer their questions about the Christian gospel (Beker 1980:77); (12) preparation for his visit to Rome to minister there and gain support for his proposed trip to Spain (especially since he was highly criticized) (Morris 1988). Several are probably wrong (numbers 1-7), but the others are more or less correct, though none are *the* genre or purpose (see below).

Byrne (1996:2-3) believes we cannot discover the provenance or purpose of Romans because we can only study the text. However, while he is correct that all such conclusions can never be decisive, he is too skeptical. As is the case with every New Testament epistle, the purpose of a letter can only be discovered by looking at its internal statements and ascertaining what situation lay behind them. Paul's intention was to come to Rome as soon as he finished delivering the collection to Jerusalem. Many have stated that he considered Rome just a short stop on his way to Spain, but actually it was more than that. He planned to spend some time in Rome to strengthen the church (1:11-12) and *have a harvest* of souls by proclaiming the gospel there (1:13, 15). He also wanted to enlist Rome as a major sponsor of his ministry in Spain and the western half of the empire (15:24). He had finished his ministry in the eastern half (15:23) and had planted significant churches in Arabia (possibly, compare Gal 1:17-18), Cilicia (Tarsus, his hometown, Acts 11:25-26), Galatia (Pisidian Antioch, Iconium, Lystra and Derbe), Mysia (Troas), Macedonia (Philippi, Thessalonica, Berea) and Achaia (Corinth, possibly Athens). Paul felt he had completed his ministry and it was time for pastors to enter and "water" those churches he had "planted" (like Apollos in Corinth, 1 Cor 3:6). His calling was to *preach the gospel where Christ was not known* so as not to build on anyone else's *foundation* (15:20). Therefore, he thought he had finished his work there, and it was time to start the second half of his life's work, namely the western half of the Roman empire. He wanted Rome to have the same place in that ministry that Antioch had in his three missionary journeys to the eastern cities (Acts 13:1-3), that is, to be the sending church. As Fitzmyer (1993b:79) says, "He writes this essay-letter to introduce himself to the Roman Christians." But it is more than this: one of his purposes in explaining his gospel with such detail might be what Moo (1996:17) calls "a letter of introduction" designed to explain his theology in such a way as to get the Romans to commend him to others and to realize that he was completely orthodox.

Second, he wanted prayer for himself as he went to Jerusalem, both for protection from his Jewish enemies and for the churches in Palestine, that they might accept the gift (15:31). Paul considered the collection for the poor not just a gift the Gentile churches were sending to the Jewish churches in Palestine but also (and perhaps more importantly) a means of forging unity between Jewish and Gentile Christians throughout the church. So in his arguments in the letter, he certainly used conclusions he had made when writing Galatians and Corinthians, but with a milder tone because he was not addressing false teaching but rather a different outlook regarding the place of the law in the Christian life.

A third purpose of the letter is to bring unity to a church in conflict. It is valid to ask how he could have known all this when he had never visited the Roman church. Yet Paul had many friends in Rome (like Priscilla and Aquila as well as others mentioned in Rom 16) who would have been in touch with him regarding the problems there. They would have told him that the Jews and the Gentiles were split over issues regarding the place of the law in the Christian life. The Jewish Christians were judging the Gentile Christians for failing to keep the food laws and the holy days, and the Gentiles were filled with contempt for the Jews for their failure to realize that Christ had freed believers from the law. Marcus (1989:68-70) says that the primary problem in the church was the conflict between law-observant Jewish Christians ("the weak") and law-free Gentile Christians ("the strong"). It is important at the outset to understand that these Jewish Christians were not the Judaizers who had replaced the cross with the law (as in Galatians, Corinthians and Philippians). This was not heresy, as Paul's tone in Romans 14:1—15:13 shows, but rather centered on the Christian life and its observance. Paul himself participated in the sacrifices (Acts 21:24-26) and vows (Acts 18:18) occasionally, but he agreed with the "strong" Gentile Christians that the demand of the Jewish Christians showed they were "weak in faith" (Rom 14:2). Still, he commanded the Gentiles to accept the "weaker" Christians and not to "put any stumbling block" in their way by trying to force them to eat that meat which was offensive to them, for in doing so they could destroy the faith of the weaker Christians entirely (14:13-15). Paul wanted both sides to understand that God expects each Christian to live at the level of his or her faith and to forge a unity out of differences, thus bringing peace to the church (14:17, 19; 15:5-7). Haacker (1990), noting Paul's use of "peace" in virtually every section of the book, believes Romans constitutes a plea for peace at every level—between self and God, between Jew and Gentile, and within ourselves. In this sense the lengthy exposition of the gospel in 3:21—8:39 and the salvation-historical discussion of God's faithfulness in removing many Jews from the olive tree and grafting in the Gentiles was intended as a message to the Jewish Christians that the grace of God in Christ had replaced the law as the center point of the Christian life and also a message to the Gentiles that God's turning to them was still part of his plan to bring the Israelites back to him (compare 11:13-32).

Still, as several commentators point out (Stuhlmacher 1988:31-44; Moo 1996; Schreiner 1998), the discussion in these chapters goes beyond the needs of the Roman church and takes on an internal force of its own, turning the local situation into a treatise on the heart of the gospel and on the salvation-historical work of God. Paul most likely intends to communicate this message to Christians everywhere, not just to Roman Christians. The difficulties between Jewish and Gentile Christians at Rome were similar to those in Jerusalem, Galatia, Corinth, Ephesus and Philippi. Paul wanted to tell both groups that he was not against the law (see 7:7, 12-14, 16; 8:4) and that he believed it was valid for Jewish Christians to live as they did (14:5-7) because it was an expression of their level of faith (14:23). Although it was a weaker level of faith (14:1-2), God honored their conscience so long as their trust was in the cross rather than the law. In other words, legal observance was viable (though not preferable) so long as their true faith was in Christ and it was an expression of their worship of him. This is the difference between the Jewish Christian living by the law and the Judaizer, who made the law a requirement for salvation. This latter view was heretical, for the law virtually replaced the cross in their beliefs. In this sense Romans provides an important model for Christians today who differ in their theological framework and worship style. Unity and understanding are needed as much in the church today as in Paul's day.

So while Romans is highly theological, Paul did not write it to be a compendium of his systematic theology, as some have said. It was a letter to a historical church and was addressing problems in that church. It is true that in it Paul summarizes his doctrine of salvation in a deeper way than in any other epistle, but Paul did so to solve existing problems in the Roman church. Still, it is certainly likely that he went beyond the situation in Rome in order to summarize the gospel for all who read it. Most of the book does not address the Roman Christians as directly as his other epistles address their audiences. Therefore, while he was addressing the Roman church, he intended it to sum up the issues regarding the gospel truth for all churches.

This leads us to the issue of the themes of the letter. Since Luther it has been common to think that the central theme is that of justification by faith. Nygren (1949:17) speaks of "a great unbroken unity in this letter, an inner consistency . . . centering throughout in our new righteousness through God, and revealing the single, central theme of justification by faith." But this has been challenged of late, for it is central to the first five chapters rather than to the whole. Others have centered on chapters 5—8 and the Spirit-filled life, or chapters 9—11 and the great theme of election, or chapters 14—15 and the unity of Jew and Gentile. However, any discussion of theme (or themes) must tie the whole of the epistle together. All these themes—justification, the Spirit, divine election, church unity—are central components of the book but hardly a unifying theme. Moo (1996:25-30) suggests three: (1) Christology, with God's salvific action in Christ as the core of the book (cf. 1:3-4; 3:21-26; 5:12-21); (2) salvation-history, meaning that God has brought about his redemptive work in human history and thus transferred the believer from the realm of sin and death to the realm of justification and life in the Spirit, inaugurating the new age in Christ; and (3) primarily the gospel as a whole, central in the frame of the letter (introduction: 1:1, 2, 9, 15; conclusion: 15:16, 19) and also in Paul's statement of the theme (1:16-17, "I am not ashamed of the gospel"). Paul is summarizing the contents and meaning of the gospel. This certainly comes the closest, although I wonder if Paul would say any one theme unifies the whole of his letter. Still, if we consider that Paul includes all of these under the rubric of "gospel," that may well tie the letter together.

□ Unity and Integrity

Nearly all scholars agree that the letter is a unity (see Schreiner 1998:5 for some who have divided Romans into two or three letters). However, there are several questions regarding its integrity. First, "in Rome" in 1:7 is missing in a few manuscripts (C 1739[mg] 1908[mg] Origen), as is "to you who are at Rome" in 1:15 (G, the Latin translation of Origen). However, the vast majority of manuscripts contain the two phrases, and it is generally agreed that the destination was removed in some manuscripts to make the epistle a general letter applicable to all churches (Metzger 1971:505-6; Schreiner 1998). Second, there are several theories that Romans 15—16 or 16 alone was added later to an original letter. This speculation results partly from text-critical difficulties. Romans 15:1—16:23 is missing in several manuscripts of the Latin Vulgate (1648, 1792, 2089), Marcion, Tertullian, Irenaeus and Cyprian. So some have said that Paul wrote Romans as a general letter for churches not founded by him and then added the material in 1:7, 15 and chapters 15—16 in order to send it to Rome. However, this is unlikely because there is material pointing to Rome in 1:8-13 (Paul wanted to come many times but had been prevented from doing so, which would not fit many other cities), and 14:23 ("everything that does not come from faith is sin") does not provide a suitable ending (see Cranfield 1975:7). Manson (1991:3-15) believes that chapter 16 was added to the letter to Rome in order to send it to Ephesus. Noting that in the papyrus p[46] the doxology (16:25-27) follows chapter 15, Manson conjectures that Paul could not have been acquainted with twenty-six people in Rome (he had never been there) while he would have easily known that many in Ephesus (he had just spent over two years there). Moreover, Priscilla and Aquila went to Ephesus with Paul in Acts 18:18-19 and were seemingly still there years later in 2 Timothy 4:19. Therefore, it is certainly possible that chapter 16 reflects an Ephesian provenance. However, several factors lead us to pause. (1) Even in p[46] chapter 16 follows the doxology. There is simply no manuscript evidence that chapters 1—15 ever constituted a separate unit. (2) Priscilla and Aquila were originally in Rome until they were forced out during the expulsion of Claudius in A.D. 49. There is no reason they would not have moved back to Rome after Claudius died. Leather workers/tent makers by their very trade often moved from place to place, thus accounting for their moves from Rome to Corinth to Ephesus to Rome to Ephesus. (3) There is no reason that Paul could not have known or been aware of that many people in Rome, because of the incredible mobility of Roman society and the insular nature of the Christian community in the empire. When we realize how the church at Troas was willing to stay up until midnight to hear Paul, probably delivering news about other churches as well as a sermon, it is understandable how deeply Christians cared about each other back then. Paul would have met many and heard about others. (4) Paul greeted so many (far more than in any other letter) because he had never visited the Roman church and wanted to establish a personal relationship. In his later letter to Ephesus he greets no single person by name, for he knew them well. So the very number of greetings indicates an unusual situation. In short, Romans is a unified epistle written to the church at Rome.

Outline of Romans

COMMENTARY

PAUL INTRODUCES HIS MISSION AND THE GOSPEL (1:1-17)
What do you say to a church you have never met but one that is facing a serious situation and desperately needs your help? How do you introduce yourself and your intentions in a way that will gain their trust and get their attention? Of course, Paul was undoubtedly well known to the Roman Christians by reputation, but he had not visited the church and had to win their trust. So he spends more time than usual introducing himself (1:1-5), expressing his desire to visit the Roman church (1:8-15) and summarizing the theme of his message (1:16-17). Du Toit (1989:192-209) argues that Paul is trying to do more than just introduce himself, that he has a rhetorical purpose in trying to persuade the Roman Christians of the centrality of his gospel message.

☐ **He Greets Them and Describes His Mission (1:1-7)**
One of the strange aspects of life is the way our best friends often do not remain close over the years. It is frequently the secondary friends who are still close years later. It all depends on their willingness to write letters. I remember one family who did many things with us, but we have not seen or heard from them in over twenty years since we moved: out of sight, out of mind. Paul was the opposite; he was a letter writer, and that was one of the keys to success in his ministry. Here he writes a letter to a church he did not even know! This demonstrates his deep love and concern. Yet it was a church he deeply cared about, and

it had a problem he could not ignore—conflict between two different "congregations" in the same church, namely, Jewish and Gentile factions. The solution he sees here lies in promise (v. 2) and obedience (v. 5) (see Anderson 1993:25-40).

As in his other letters, Paul generally follows the normal Greek custom for writing letters, introducing himself first and then addressing his readers. But the normal Greek letter was quite simple: "____ to ____, greetings." Paul's introductions were far more complex, and the one in Romans is the lengthiest of all, containing the most complex description of himself and his ministry. The reason: He is describing to them his gospel, the subject of much of this letter, as well as reminding them of his credentials.

The Prescript (1:1) Paul typically begins with a statement of his office but here breaks the pattern by first emphasizing his Lord and Master, calling himself "a slave of Christ Jesus." This should not be watered down to NIV's *servant of Christ Jesus,* for Paul is alluding to the fact of slavery in the Roman empire (it is estimated that 85 to 90 percent of the population of Rome and Italy were slaves or of slave origin; see Rupprecht 1993:881) as well as to the metaphor of slavery in the Old Testament. After the people of Israel were liberated from slavery in Egypt, it became common for them to call themselves "slaves of God" (Lev 25:55 [NIV, "servants"]) as a title of honor designating their new allegiance. Many of the leaders of Israel (Abraham, Moses, Joshua, David and Elijah) called themselves God's slaves. Since Jesus has become both Lord and God, now Paul is the slave of *Christ Jesus,* with emphasis on the messianic office, i.e., Messiah Jesus. Paul is saying not only that he belongs to Christ but also that this is a privileged state. In the Roman world slaves were protected and even paid by their owner; they were members of the owner's extended family and often had higher social status as slaves than they did after gaining their freedom. So Paul considers this a badge of honor, as should all believers.

Apostle is Paul's more typical self-designation and has two basic

---

1:1 See Bartchy (1992:66), who points to several differences between first-century slavery and that practiced in America: racial factors had no place; education was preferred, and often the slaves were more educated than the owners; slaves often had

meanings—a church representative or missionary (2 Cor 8:23; Phil 2:25), and one of those *called* or chosen by God to be founding agents and leaders of the churches. We know some of them, beginning with the Twelve (called apostles from the beginning, Mk 3:14) but probably including also Barnabas (Acts 14:4), James (1 Cor 15:7), and perhaps Andronicus and Junias (Rom 16:7). The normal criteria for that high office included walking with the Lord as well as seeing the risen Lord (Acts 1:21-22), but Paul was included on the basis of his having "seen" the Lord in the Damascus Road vision (1 Cor 9:1; 15:8). Paul was especially "chosen" to be God's envoy to the Gentiles (Acts 9:15; 22:21), giving him authority (cf. Gal 1:1) that afforded this letter special weight as an official communication from God through Paul his chosen instrument.

Finally, he has been *set apart for the gospel.* This is a further definition of what it means to be called, specifying that Christ has chosen him to take the gospel to the Gentiles. In Galatians 1:15 Paul says that he was "set apart . . . from my mother's womb," an allusion to the call of Jeremiah (Jer 1:5), and this may be alluded to here as well. Moo (1996:42-43) says that *gospel* here refers not only to the gospel message and its proclamation but also to the very events by which the gospel came to be, God sending his Son as the sacrifice that produced salvation. Thus *by Jesus Christ and God* should be seen as indicating origin; that is, this gospel came from God. Lohse (1995:127-40) notes that *the gospel of God* frames the letter (1:1-17; 15:14-21), which especially centers on the proclamation of justification in Christ. The gospel is central to Paul's purpose in writing this letter.

Defining the Gospel (1:2-4) Paul now describes the gospel he has been sent to proclaim, noting three characteristics. First, he tells us it was *promised beforehand* in the Old Testament. Throughout Romans, Paul will be anchoring his theological points in Old Testament truth. This statement in verse 2 establishes the promise-fulfillment pattern that will dominate his use of the Old Testament. The verb is made up

---

very responsible positions; they could own property and receive salaries; they had the same religious and cultural traditions as the free people; and they could expect to be emancipated by the time they were thirty.

of two parts, *promise* and *before,* with the latter drawing out the main aspect of the promise, that it was given ahead of time through the *prophets.* The idea of promise is frequent in the New Testament (especially in the writings of Paul, who employs it twenty-two of the fifty-two times it is used in the New Testament) to describe the blessings of salvation (e.g., Gal 3:22; 2 Cor 7:1; Heb 4:1; 10:23). Cranfield (1975:56-57, from Barth [1959:12-13]) points out how this idea dominates the letter. Anchoring these truths in the previous revelation by God in the Old Testament gives Paul's message special credence, providing a perfect introduction for an apostle the church had not yet met. The prophets here are undoubtedly not just those of the latter part of the Old Testament but would also include Moses (Acts 3:22) and David (Acts 2:30). It is important for us to realize that the Bible as a whole, and not just the New Testament, forms the *gospel.*

Second, the heart of the gospel is the Son of God as descended from David. Actually, there are two points in verse 3: his preexistence and his earthly existence. His preexistence is seen in that the Son "came into being" *(genomenou*—NIV, *was)* as a human. His earthly existence shows his royal messianic status. This is part of a movement from *descendant of David* (v. 3) to *Son of God* (v. 4). In fact, many believe that verses 3-4 stem from an earlier creedal statement. Yet the Davidic status of Jesus' messiahship is also important (cf. also Rom 15:7-9). The idea goes back to 2 Samuel 7:12-16, where David was promised an eternal throne. This led to the idea of a Davidic Messiah who would deliver the nation (Ps 89:3-4; Is 11:1; Jer 23:5-6; Ezek 34:23-24), an idea recognized both in Judaism (*Psalms of Solomon* 17—18; Qumran: 1QM 11:1-8; 4QFlor 1:11-14) and in the early church (Mt 1:1-16; Mk 10:47; 12:35-37; Jn 7:42; 2 Tim 2:8). Jesus then is the royal Messiah who has come to assume his throne.

1:3-4 For a good balanced treatment, concerning whether these verses stem from an earlier creedal statement, see Schreiner (1998:39-40). The balanced parallelism of the phrasing in verses 3 and 4 as well as the high Christology and non-Pauline language employed could point to an early pre-Pauline creed (so especially Käsemann 1980:10-13), but there are several cautions necessary, one of which is the speculative nature of the arguments. Proponents have to do a redactional study of those aspects coming from pre-Pauline tradition and those added by Paul himself. Paul could also be writing in a high prose style. Either way, however, this is a significant passage

Third, the gospel centers on God's *designation* (better than NIV's *declared*) of Jesus as his divine Son. The verb is similar in meaning to other terms signifying "appoint" or "assign" (Louw and Nida 1988:483). This has led some to an adoptionistic theology, claiming that Jesus was not the Son until "adopted" at his baptism or (here) at his resurrection. But that would be an overly literal interpretation of Paul here, and this merely says that at his resurrection God *designated* him Son. Jesus is also designated Son at his baptism (Mk 1:11 and parallels), and sonship defines his entire earthly existence. Moreover, I have already commented on his preexistence as Son in verse 3, so this simply means God has shown him to be Son in a new way at his resurrection. Schreiner (1998:42) notes that *his Son* in verse 3 refers to Jesus' "messianic kingship as the descendent of David," while in verse 4 *Son of God* refers to his enthronement as messianic King and Lord of all. It is better to take *in power* with the noun rather than the verb (contra NIV's *declared with power*), meaning Christ has been designated "Son-of-God-in-power" (so most recent commentaries). As Nygren points out (1949:51, in Stott 1994:50), "So *the resurrection is the turning point in the existence of the Son of God.* Before that he was the Son of God in weakness and lowliness. Through the resurrection he becomes the Son of God in power" (italics his). His sonship is now defined in terms of cosmic Lord with authority over heaven and earth (Mt 28:19). So the idea of *power* is important to the message, and it prepares for verse 5, where the gospel to the Gentiles is inaugurated by the "Son-of-God-in-power." It is also connected with the later statement that the gospel is "the power of God for salvation" (1:16).

The basis of this new status is *the Spirit of holiness.* There is a certain "flesh-Spirit" dualism between verses 3 and 4, in which Jesus' earthly nature leads to (rather than "is contrasted with," see above) his Spirit-

---

pointing back to early Christian tradition.

1:3 See Hurtado (1999:226-27) for the positive meaning of this, contra Dunn (1988a). The idea moves from Jesus' earthly status as Davidic Son to his heavenly status as divine Son.

1:4 Dunn (1988a:12) speaks of "antithetical parallelism" here, as if the Davidic sonship was somehow contrasted with the divine sonship. However, it would be better to speak of step parallelism: Paul is showing that Jesus is not only the Davidic Messiah but is also the Son of God.

given office. Some (e.g., Sanday and Headlam 1902:9) have taken *spirit* to mean Jesus' divine spirit rather than the Holy Spirit, but there are two problems with this view: flesh-spirit dualism in Paul normally refers to the Holy Spirit, and the *Spirit of holiness* is a more natural phrase for the Holy Spirit. From this standpoint, the Holy Spirit is the turning point from the earthly messianic ministry of Jesus to the eschatological lordship of Jesus as Son of God. There is a natural link between the resurrection of Jesus and the Holy Spirit. Romans 8:11 entitles the third member of the Trinity "the Spirit of him who raised Jesus from the dead," and it is the resurrection that is the turning point from the age of Jesus to the age of the Spirit (Lk 24:49; Acts 1:8). Yet the strange phrase *Spirit of holiness* (occurring only here in the New Testament) may be more than a Semitic equivalent of "Holy Spirit." It might also mean that the Spirit "set Jesus apart" (the meaning of *holiness*) as cosmic Lord of all. *Jesus Christ our Lord* culminates verses 3-4 and concludes the christological movement from Son to seed of David to Son of God to Messiah to Lord. This incredible passage tells us that the Gospel is all about Jesus—Messiah, Son of God and Lord of all creation. To paraphrase J. B. Phillips's famous book, we must say that for most Christians "your Jesus is too small." We need to see Jesus not just as our friend and helper but also as God and Lord of all.

Defining Paul's Mission (1:5-6) The gospel is all about mission. Paul rejoices in the ministry to the Gentiles that Christ has graciously given him. The verse (in the Greek text) is framed by two prepositional phrases showing that Christ the Lord is both the instrument *(through him)* and the recipient *(for his name's sake)* of Paul's ministry. The Lord is the means and the focus of the gospel proclamation. Paul's goal is to honor and glorify the name of Christ. He gave Paul two things, *grace and apostleship,* which should be combined to indicate that Paul's apostolic commission as apostle to the Gentiles (Acts 9:15; 22:21; Rom 11:13; 15:16; Gal 2:8-9) was an undeserved gift of grace from Christ. Paul was always amazed that God had chosen him, the worst of sinners (1 Tim 1:15-16), to be his chosen instrument. That call was first to *all the Gentiles.* That this could mean "nations" and include the Jews is exemplified in Romans 1:16 ("first for the Jew, then for the Gentile") and Paul's constant practice on his missionary journeys of beginning in the synagogues and then going to the Gentiles (so Stott 1994:51). But the term itself more often refers to Paul's Gentile ministry, and that is likely here (so Cranfield 1975:67; Moo 1996:53).

Paul's purpose is to bring them to *the obedience of faith,* a phrase that could mean "obedience to the faith" (objective genitive), "believing faith" (adjectival genitive), "the obedience that comes from faith" (genitive of source) or "the obedience that is faith" (genitive of apposition). While the first is unlikely (there is no article with *faith*), Dunn (1988a:17-18) is probably correct in saying that the latter two are probably both part of the meaning here. Obedience is the natural result of a faith relationship with Christ, and faith always produces obedience. They are interchangeable aspects of a proper relationship with Christ (similarly, see Garlington 1990b:209-13, arguing that the adjectival use preserves this deliberate ambiguity). Obedience also occurs in Romans 5:19; 6:12, 16, 17; 10:16; 15:18; and 16:19, 20, and is a central theme in any enumeration of the responsibilities of the Christian life. This phrase would also define the task of every church today—evangelism (faith) and discipleship (obedience) as inseparable aspects of a true New Testament church. To center upon one aspect and neglect the other is to be unbalanced and unbiblical.

Paul then includes the Roman Christians among the Gentile converts (v. 6). As several point out (Godet 1969; Cranfield 1975; Dunn 1988a; Moo 1996), Paul is subtly reminding them that even though he did not establish their church, they are still part of his apostolic commission. Thus he can address them with authority from God. Moreover, they are also *called to belong to Jesus Christ;* they join Paul (1:1) as chosen by Christ. The debate over whether this means the Romans were predominantly Gentile (so Sanday and Headlam 1902; Dunn 1988a; Moo 1996) or simply geographically existed among the Gentile nations (Cranfield 1975; Käsemann 1980) is difficult to know for certain (Bruce 1985 believes both are part of the meaning). *Among those who are called* could indicate either, but the former is slightly more probable in view of the likelihood that the Roman church was mainly Gentile (see Introduction).

The Greeting (1:7) In most of Paul's epistles the greeting is part of the prescript and occurs with it, but here he has inserted a lengthy discussion of his gospel in order to anchor his right to address the church. So now Paul returns to epistolary convention and addresses the Roman church. He is writing to *all in Rome,* probably all the house churches in the city. His usual practice is to greet "the church" in the city, so this unusual form may indicate that there are too many to meet in one place and perhaps that he is addressing the factions in the city as a whole group (so Dunn 1988a:19). The believers are described as *loved by God and called to be saints.* One of the great truths of Scripture is that in spite of our sinfulness and rebellion, we are the objects of God's divine love (Rom 5:8). That is the basis of our love for one another (Rom 12:19). The idea of the divine call has already been seen twice (vv. 1, 6) and is a major theme of this epistle, reminiscent of Israel as God's elect (Is 49:1; 50:2; Jer 7:13). Here as in 8:29 ("predestined to be conformed to the likeness of his Son") the election is primarily ethical and spiritual: they are *called to be saints* or set apart for him alone, pulled out from this world to serve him. Paul is calling us to recognize our special allegiance to the God who loves us and to begin acting upon it as his special people.

Paul's greetings have always combined the Greek ("grace") and Hebrew ("peace") greetings, but they are also theologized as an eschatological promise that the Christian experiences God's *grace* and the *peace* in an entirely new way as a result of what God and Christ have done. What the Greeks and Hebrews symbolically sought in their greetings has now been actualized in Christ. Finally, we can truly experience God's grace and find peace. The reason is that God is our *Father,* establishing a whole new intimacy in our relationship with him, and Christ has become our *Lord* as a result of his resurrection (see especially v. 4 above).

□ Thanksgiving for Their Faith and a Prayer to Visit Them (1:8-15)

The typical Greek letter contained a brief thanksgiving and prayer (usually formulaic), but Paul always expands this form to develop a

---

1:8 Note the direction of the thanksgiving. It is first to *my God,* expressing the deeply intimate relationship between Paul and his Father (cf. Pss 3:7; 5:2; 7:1 and so on). Second, it occurs *through Jesus Christ,* noting Christ not just as the means of the

theological message. In fact, it has long been recognized that his opening prayer often contains the basic thesis of his epistle (see O'Brien 1977). However, this paragraph does not so much contain the theme of the epistle as establish Paul's close relationship with the receivers. Paul was a man of deep love and concern, and that is reflected here. He also was God's apostle to the Gentiles, so as Schreiner points out (1998:48) the anticipated visit was not just personal but was the formal or official arrival of Paul as the emissary of Christ.

Thanksgiving (1:8) Paul rejoices primarily because all the world has learned about the Christians in Rome. While some (Hodge 1950; Barrett 1957) believe this means that their faith was so extraordinary that it was known everywhere, it is more likely that this refers not so much to the quality of their faith as to the fact of it (Bruce 1985; Cranfield 1975; Moo 1996; Schreiner 1998). Rome was the hub of the world, and as such the Roman church would be known everywhere. Paul was thankful that God had established his church there and that it had an effect everywhere. As Nygren says (1949:59), it was "a fountain of joy that the Gospel had been received with faith in the very capital of the world." There is a bit of hyperbole in *all over the world,* for it does not mean every single person has heard the report; it probably does mean all the churches and unbelievers everywhere (at least in the Roman world). The growth of the Gospel in Rome would have widespread repercussions. Paul rejoices as we rejoice in the successful evangelization of cities like Seoul, Hong Kong, Mexico City, Moscow and Beijing.

Prayer (1:9-15) Have you ever wanted to make a trip so badly that there was almost an ache in your heart? My wife and I have always wanted to visit Australia and New Zealand. I keep waiting for that invitation to speak, but it just has not come. This prayer shows a similar ache in Paul to visit Rome. This is occasioned by two things: the situation in Rome that needs his attention, and his desire to go on to Spain

---

thanks but as the one through whom such worship is made possible (so Cranfield 1975; Käsemann 1980; Moo 1996).

to continue his pioneer missionary work (Rom 15:24, 28). Paul introduces his prayer with a solemn oath (*God . . . is my witness*) by which Paul attests the truth of what he is saying (2 Cor 1:23; Gal 1:20; Phil 1:8). He wants the Romans to know beyond a shadow of a doubt that he continually holds them up in prayer. By adding the further description that he *serve[s] (God) with [his] whole heart in preaching the gospel of his Son,* he places these prayers in the larger arena of his service to God. *Serve* is a particularly strong verb used in the LXX (Greek Old Testament) for worshipful service to God. Paul's preaching the Gospel as well as his prayer life were aspects of his worship. He did it all for the glory of God. What a model for us Paul provides! His activity and his prayer life were at all times focused upon God; what he did and how he prayed were alike aspects of his worship.

Paul moves from the general to the concrete in verses 9-10. Generally, he prays for them constantly. This is emphasized by two terms, *constantly* and *at all times.* This means not that he prayed at every moment but rather that he regularly held them up before the Lord. For us it could mean a prayer journal to help us not to forget others. Specifically, he prayed that the *way may be opened* for him to visit the Roman church. Yet he recognizes that he can only come if it is *God's will.* This does not mean that Paul was hesitant or tentative in his plans, as some have said. Rather, it recognizes the sovereignty of God in all such endeavors. Paul is trusting the Lord for the privilege of visiting Rome soon.

The purpose of this visit is specified in verses 11-12. Paul's desire is to *impart . . . some spiritual gift* to them. It is difficult to know for certain what Paul means by this. Are those general spiritual gifts as in Romans 12 or 1 Corinthians 12 (Barrett 1957:25, but those are always given by Christ, not Paul) or Paul's own apostolic gifts, namely, his doctrinal teaching as seen in this letter (Stott 1994:57) or the gift of the gospel to the Gentiles (Schreiner 1998:54)? Or does Paul mean it more generally as a "blessing or benefit" to be given by God through himself

---

1:9 This is literally "in my spirit," and it could mean "in prayer" (Cranfield 1975:77, as Paul's inward activity), the Holy Spirit (Fee [1994:485-86] says it is the Holy Spirit at work in Paul's spirit), or Paul's wholehearted service to God (Michel 1966:46-47;

(Cranfield 1975:79) or perhaps a God-given "insight or ability" that Paul will "share" with them (Moo 1996:60). Since Paul says he wants to impart *some* gift to them, we cannot easily exclude any of these. In this context, it should be linked to the gospel proclamation in some way, so Stott and Schreiner are probably closest. This is a wonderful way for all of us to think of our ministries as sharing our spiritual gifts with others. Paul's purpose is to *make [the church] strong*. Paul may have thought that the divisive controversies in Rome weakened the church's spiritual fiber, or perhaps he was concerned for the general tenor of the church as a whole. The latter is more likely in terms of the clarification in verse 12.

Paul wanted to strengthen the Roman church through mutual encouragement. In a sense he is qualifying verse 11 by saying there will be mutual benefit from his presence with them. He is not coming just to help them but wants also to be helped by them. If more Christian leaders had this humble philosophy of servanthood ministry, the church would have far fewer problems. *Encouragement* is actually a more general term for "exhortation" and so may include both encouragement and admonition. As Paul challenges them, he expects to be challenged by them. Still, the view of most scholars that comfort is primary is seen in the fact that their mutual *faith* produces this sharing. Because they have the same *faith* (the Greek has *faith, both yours and mine*) and that faith brings a common purpose to their interaction, they will indeed *encourage* one another in the faith.

Paul further clarifies his desire to visit them by telling them in 1:13 that he had *planned many times to come,* but those plans kept being thwarted (also 15:22). He has obviously been worried that they might think his failure to visit them earlier showed a lack of concern. He had not only wanted to come (vv. 10-11) but had actually made plans to do so. Most likely, the plans had been set aside by urgent ministries elsewhere as exemplified in the missionary journeys (remember that this is being written toward the end of the third journey). Trocmé (1992:44)

Moo 1996:58). This latter is the best interpretation, designating the inward depth of Paul's service to God.

points to Acts 13—19 as showing both the importance of Rome to Paul's mission and the barriers that kept Paul from making it to Rome. His desire then and now is to *have a harvest among* them, both in proclaiming the gospel to the lost and in strengthening the Christians, in other words, both evangelism and discipleship. The word *harvest* (literally "fruit") is used in Philippians 1:22 for the rewards of his apostolic "labor" and here probably has a similar thrust. Paul is often seen as a pure evangelist, one whose whole concern is for the unsaved. That is not true. To be sure, he was primarily a pioneer missionary, taking the gospel to the unreached. However, all his epistles demonstrate his tremendous concern for the spiritual life of his churches. Neither he nor anyone else in the early church would have made the type of dichotomy between evangelism and discipleship that exists today. It needs to be remembered by most of us that the Great Commission said, "Go and *make disciples* of all nations" (Mt 28:19).

Since Rome was part of the larger Gentile world that God had placed in Paul's care, he then speaks of his larger obligations in 1:14. He wants them to know that his field of God-given ministry goes beyond Rome to the larger Gentile world, and that is why he was *prevented* from coming to them earlier (see also 1 Cor 9:16). Since God had "called" (1:1) him to the Gentiles, he is duty-bound to minister to them. He divides the Gentile world into two pairs—*Greeks and non-Greeks* (literally "barbarians") as well as *wise and foolish*. Both pairs are inclusive of the pagan world as a whole (so also Col 3:11). The barbarians are not primitives but rather those peoples who did not speak the Greek language and so were considered to be inferior and uncultured. *Wise and foolish* is probably another way of saying the same thing from the vantage point of the Gentile world, that is, those who thought they were wise and those considered by the Greeks to be foolish. Paul is saying he ministers to everyone, the elite and the downtrodden, the intellectuals as well as the ignorant. Christianity is a religion for every-

---

1:13 Kruger (1987:167-70) restricts the "fruit" to Paul's collection for the poor in Jerusalem (15:22-29). While this is certainly part of the fruit Paul hoped to harvest in Rome, it is unlikely that it exhausts Paul's purpose. In fact, it is likely that Paul is reporting the collection in 15:25-27 rather than asking for a contribution from Rome, for he took the collection to Jerusalem on his way to Rome. At best, he is planting

one, not just those with status in this world.

So as a result Paul is also *eager* [or "filled with desire"] *to preach the gospel . . . at Rome* as part of his larger ministry to the Gentiles. Paul is very careful to qualify his ministry in Rome sufficiently, because he was not the founder of the church there and so does not wish to come across too strongly. So his language throughout 1:8-15 has been cautious. Moreover, preaching the gospel here most likely includes not just evangelistic ministry to the pagan community but also a teaching ministry in the churches. Once more, it is important to realize that *gospel* in the New Testament included discipleship as well as evangelism.

☐ **Theme of the Letter—Righteousness from God (1:16-17)**
In four short clauses Paul summarizes what his letter will be arguing, that salvation is not a humanly controlled phenomenon but comes entirely from God. Since the clauses center on a causal link (*gar* twice in v. 16 and once in v. 17 [NIV omits the first instance and renders the other two *because* and *for*]) with verse 15, Paul is clarifying further what he means by "preach the gospel" to the Gentiles, namely, that it is a gospel about God's *righteousness* given to humankind. Let's consider these one at a time:

1. Paul says that he wants to preach in Rome (v. 15) because he is *not ashamed of the gospel* (v. 16). There are two aspects of *not ashamed:* first, the fearless proclamation of the gospel in difficult circumstances (= not afraid to proclaim it) and, second, the positive confession of the saving power of God to the world (Käsemann 1980:21-22 wrongly rejects the psychological aspect of the former and stresses only the latter as a "fixed confessional formula"). The difficulty of shame for the gospel caused by fear of the negative repercussions occurred in the first century as well as today. Jesus warned the disciples against being ashamed of him (Mk 8:38), and because of Timothy's timidity in condemning the false teachers (2 Tim 1:7-8), Paul had to

---

seeds in Rome for the future.
1:14 Paul would not be including the Jewish people in this since this is about his ministry among the Gentiles, but they would certainly be considered "barbarians" (NIV *non-Greeks*) by the Greeks.

challenge him not to be *ashamed* of the Lord or of Paul. The problem of timidity that is in effect shame of the gospel is a great problem today as well. Watts (1999:22-23) connects this shame further with the larger theodicy question in Romans: how do you demonstrate the justice of the gospel when it means the setting aside of Israel as the people of God? So Paul stresses that the gospel centers on the righteous judgment of God and is "the revelation of Yahweh's faithful exercise of his power in effecting salvation.

2. Paul is not ashamed because this gospel is *the power of God for . . . salvation.* Divine power produces salvation, not human effort. In 1 Corinthians 1:18, 24 he says, "for us who are being saved it is the power of God" and is based on "Christ the power of God" (paralleling 1:4 where Christ is designated "Son of God in power"). The gospel is a powerful force that carries with it the divine call to salvation. Nearly one-third of the appearances of *power* in the New Testament are in Paul, and all three members of the Godhead are connected with this divine *power . . . for . . . salvation.* It is quite clear that God is sovereign in salvation. At the heart *salvation* means "deliverance," with the imagery stemming from Israel's deliverance from Egypt at the Exodus. It connotes "liberation from evil powers, and in the ultimate sense deliverance in the decisive final judgment and accordingly eschatological salvation" (Schelke 1993:327). Here there is both a present and a future dimension comprising liberation from the power of sin, reconciliation with the God of salvation and deliverance from the final judgment.

This power is especially seen in the fact that salvation is given to *everyone who believes,* that is, each one who comes to God in faith and accepts his offer of salvation. The verb *believe* and its cognate, the noun *faith,* occur four times in these two verses. The act of belief involves surrender to God, mental assent and the commitment of the will. The call to faith and the power to achieve it come from God; the surrender of the will to him is our part. But cognitive belief in Jesus is

---

1:16-17 Achtemeier (1985:35-36) argues that 1:16-17 is not the theme of the letter because it is subordinate to verse 15 and part of Paul's discussion of his Roman ministry. However, this type of clause can often carry more weight, and the message of it along with its link to 3:21-26 shows that it is indeed the theme of the epistle (see

only one aspect. The commitment of the will is a major aspect; one does not know Jesus as Savior until beginning the process of Lordship. But this is not a "work" (Eph 2:8, 9), for it is the power of God alone that makes it possible.

Strangely, Paul goes on to define *everyone* further as *first for the Jew, then for the Gentile*. It is difficult to understand this demarcation, but it must in some way be connected to Paul's own practice during his missionary journeys, when he went to the synagogues before ministering to the Gentiles (e.g., Acts 13:5, 14; 14:1; 17:1, 10, 17). Since the Jewish people were the chosen ones of God (see Rom 9) and since they still have a future (see Rom 11:26-27), they must be given some priority in the proclamation of the gospel. In a sense this anticipates Paul's lengthier discussion of the place of the Jewish people in God's salvation in chapters 9—11. It is debated how extensively this priority of Jewish evangelism is binding on the church today. But the reasoning behind Paul's statement here still applies in our day, so this priority should still stand. It does not mean, however, that every Christian is to go to the synagogue first. Rather, Jewish mission must have visibility and emphasis in the mission of the church worldwide, in terms both of prayer and of action.

3. As 1:16 gave the reason *for* Paul's mission to the Gentiles, so verse 17 gives the reason that the gospel is indeed the power of salvation. In the gospel *a righteousness [of] God is revealed* (says *from God*, but see the following discussion). The term *revealed* is significant, referring to a near-apocalyptic (the transliteration of the term in English) event, the disclosure of God's plan of salvation in human history. Moo (1996:69, following Ridderbos 1975:47) emphasizes the historical dimension of the concept, that it does not just speak of a cognitive revealing of knowledge but "actually makes manifest, or brings into existence, the 'righteousness of God.'" The major debate, however, is on the meaning of *righteousness of God*. The importance of this phrase

Dunn 1988a:38; Schreiner 1998:59). Schreiner sums up the theme this way: "The gospel is the saving power of God in which the righteousness of God is being revealed."

is seen in that it is central to the two thesis sections of the book, 1:16-17 and 3:21-26. There are three major views of this phrase: *(a) Of God* could be possessive, thus indicating that *righteousness of God* refers to an attribute of God describing his character, either his justice or his faithfulness, perhaps both (so Williams 1979:241-90). *(b) Of God* could be subjective, referring to God's activity in making people righteous. This gives a spiritual or moral dimension to the concept, describing God's saving power in bringing people to himself and transforming them. Käsemann (1980:25-30) speaks of his "covenant faithfulness" in drawing a fallen world to himself (see also Dodd 1932:38-39; Dunn 1988a:40-42).*(c) Of God* can refer to source or origin, giving the phrase a forensic or legal aspect referring to God's judicial decision to "declare us righteous" on the basis of Christ's sacrifice on the cross for our sins. In this way God imparts a new status to believers, namely, that they are now the children of God. This was Luther's view, and it has been highly influential in Protestantism (so Bultmann 1964b:12-16; Cranfield 1975:95; Stott 1994:63-64).

While the balance of interpretation rests solidly on the side of the forensic approach, it is becoming increasingly apparent that this is not really an either-or situation (see Moo 1996:71-75; Schreiner 1998:63-70). Moo (1996:79-89) has an excellent excursus on "righteousness language" in the Old Testament and Paul, centering on his definition that it refers to "the act by which God brings people into right relationship with himself" (1996:74). In the Old Testament the terms clearly point to the active side, as God intervenes on behalf of his people and delivers them (Ps 51:14; Mic 6:5; 7:9; Is 46:13; 51:5-8). Micah and Isaiah especially connect this with God's eschatological deliverance, and other texts connect this liberation with God's righteous character (Ps 31:1; 35:24; Is 38:19; 63:7). In Paul *righteousness* is expressed through a noun, an adjective and a verb. With the verb especially, the forensic aspects predominate, as shown ably by Morris (1965:224-74) and Schrenk (1964:215-16), referring to the justification of the repentant sinner (Rom 3:22; 4:5; 8:33). When God justifies, he makes a legal acquittal and a declaration of innocence. The picture is of God sitting on his judgment seat accepting the believer as free from guilt. It is also clear in Paul that this is based not on works but on the faith of the sinner. It is a gift from

God (Eph 2:8, 9), called in Romans 5:17 "the gift of righteousness." The noun and the adjective can refer to the forensic or nonforensic (ethical righteousness) aspects depending on the context. In short, the primary force of *righteousness* in Paul and here centers on the legal act of God whereby the repentant sinner is declared right by God and brought into a right relationship with him, resulting in right living.

This righteousness is further defined as *from faith to faith* (as in the NIV margin), a clarification of the statement in verse 16 that the gospel is for *everyone who believes.* This is another phrase with multiple understandings—from the faith of the Old Testament to the faith of the New Testament; from God's (or Christ's) faithfulness to our faith; or faith as God's gift to us; or faith shared from one believer to another; or simply a metaphor for a high degree of faith. This latter is best, simply stating that faith and only faith is the central basis for righteousness (so Murray 1968; Cranfield 1975; Ziesler 1972; Moo 1996; Schreiner 1998).

4. Paul anchors this with a quote from Habakkuk 2:4. This is interesting because of the movement from the Hebrew Old Testament to the Greek Old Testament (LXX) to Paul. The Hebrew Old Testament includes a pronoun, centering on the individual: "the righteous will live by *his* faith." In Habakkuk there is a contrast between the one who trusts only in self, and the *righteous* one who trusts entirely in God. The Greek Old Testament includes a different pronoun, thus centering on God: "the righteous shall live by *my* faithfulness." Paul (here and in Gal 3:11) has the most generic: *the righteous shall live by faith.* Paul, by omitting both pronouns, seems to seek a middle ground. Yet what does he mean, and how does it fit the context? As one would expect, there are many interpretations. We can discard those theories that say God or Christ is the subject. The entire context is the righteousness of the person, not of the Godhead. But an important issue is identification of the word that *by faith* modifies: does it refer to the noun (*the one who is righteous through faith will live;* so Nygren 1949; Barrett 1957; Bruce 1985, Cranfield 1975; Stott 1994; Moo 1996) or to the verb (*the one who is righteous will live by faith;* so Godet 1969; Sanday and Headlam 1902; Michel 1966; Murray 1968; Schreiner 1998)? Or should we see here a deliberate ambiguity and a thrust in both directions (Dunn 1988a)? In the immediate context the connection between *right-*

eous and *faith* is so great that it seems likely that *by faith* modifies the noun, but yet we must remember that Paul is being deliberately ambiguous, so the double meaning is viable. Paul would be saying that those whose righteousness is expressed in faith (i.e., absolute trust in God, not just lives of faithfulness) will truly find life. In other words, they live by faith and therefore find life. There is also double meaning in *live:* both life now and eternal life, i.e., salvation now as well as final salvation. Finally, Watts (1999:21) sees a further ambiguity in which the "faithfulness of God" (Hab 2:4 LXX) leads to our *faith*.

THE UNIVERSALITY OF HUMAN SINFULNESS (1:18—3:20)

It is impossible to pick up a history book or watch the evening news without realizing once again the utter depravity of humankind. The ability of people to mock others or savagely mistreat them is beyond comprehension, as the 9/11 tragedy has so horribly demonstrated. The ease with which national leaders plunge their nations into war and guarantee the death of thousands of their youth over pure greed boggles my mind. Yet at the same time I also get discouraged about my own sinful tendencies, at the constant struggle I have with pride and self-centeredness. This is what Paul is talking about. The one factor that unites "me and them" is our total depravity. Paul therefore begins with the sinfulness of the Gentiles (1:18-32), then turns to the sinfulness of the Jews (2:1-3:8), and finally concludes with the universal sinfulness of all humankind (3:9-20). Paul's basic purpose in this section is to tell all people that they cannot find the righteousness of God until they recognize their depravity, whether they are Jew or Gentile. Only then can they turn to God in faith and discover his saving power. Yet, as several have argued (Bruce 1985; Moo 1996; Schreiner 1998), the Jewish people are the special objects here. Gentile depravity was commonly understood, even by the Gentiles themselves, and Paul summarizes that here. Greater space and effort go into showing Jewish guilt, for they had too little awareness of their actual position before God.

1:18-32 There is another possible outline that focuses more on the progression of thought than on the formula *exchange/gave them over*. This moves from the introductory rejection of God's revelation (vv. 18-20) to a chiastic emphasis on their

They were the covenant people and therefore, they believed, exempt in some fashion from his wrath. Paul shows that that is not the case. He does this by anchoring everything he says in the Jewish Scriptures (see the excellent discussion of this rhetorical strategy in Tobin 1993).

☐ God's Wrath Against the Gentiles (1:18-32)

Cranfield (1975:105) and Dunn (1988a:53) exemplify a recent trend to see this section as a general indictment of all humankind rather than a specific condemnation of the Gentiles. Paul refers to *men* rather than Gentiles in 1:18, and the language is reminiscent of the Adam story in Genesis 2—3. Also, in 1:23 Paul refers to Psalm 106:20 and Jeremiah 2:11, both detailing Israel's idolatry. So Paul could move from the general (the sinfulness of all humanity) to the specific (the sinfulness of the Jews). But there is no way any Jewish person reading this would have understood this passage as aimed at himself. The sins mentioned— idolatry, immorality, homosexuality—were part of Jewish polemics against the Gentiles in the first century. It is true that Paul implicitly includes the Jewish people in places (e.g., v. 23, Gen 2—3 imagery and the idolatry into which Israel fell throughout its history), but in 1:18-32 he is preparing the reader for chapter 2, where he explains that the sinfulness of the Gentiles is replicated in the sinfulness of the Jews.

The section itself falls into three subsections: the introductory part (vv. 18-20) detailing how humankind has rejected God's revelation and thus incurred his wrath, the central section (vv. 21-31) dealing with divine retribution for their depraved acts, and a conclusion (v. 32) showing their deliberate sin in spite of their knowledge that such sins *deserve death*. In discussing the central section, Moo (1996:96, following Klostermann 1933:1-6) speaks of "three parallel 'retribution' sequences": verses 21-24 (when people *exchanged* God's truth for idols, God *gave them over*); verses 25-26 (when people *exchanged* God's truth for a lie, God *gave them over*); and verses 26-31 (when people *exchanged* natural sexual practices for unnatural ones, God again *gave them over*).

---

mindset (vv. 21-23, 28-31) and their immoral actions (vv. 24-25, 26-27), with a progression in the latter pair from general immorality to homosexuality.

Rejection of God's Revelation (1:18-20) The *wrath of God* stands over against his "righteousness" (1:16-17) as the two parts of his nature—love and justice. His righteousness must react to human depravity with wrath. Of course, some (e.g., Dodd 1932:47-50; MacGregor 1960-1961:101-9) find God's anger to be merely the cause-and-effect process by which his love and mercy bring people to himself. But his wrath against sin is too comprehensive in Scripture to allow such a reinterpretation. It is part of his very nature—the holiness of God demands wrath against the sinner and mercy toward the repentant. This could almost sum up the message of both testaments. The book of Judges, for instance, describes the cycle of wrath when Israel fell into sin followed by blessing when they turned back to God. Here God's wrath *is being revealed,* paralleling the revelation of his righteousness in 1:17. While this could refer to the last judgment (a futuristic present, "is going to be revealed"), when his anger will manifest itself in eternal punishment, the present tense should be understood in a more natural sense (as indeed it was in 1:17). God's anger is kindled against depraved humanity now (so Rom 3:5; 4:15; 5:9, though final wrath is described in 2:5, 8; 3:5; 9:22). Moreover, it is revealed *from heaven,* referring to a sovereign act of judgment from the very throne of God. This adds a definite apocalyptic air, but that does not mean only a future judgment. There is an inaugurated aspect: the wrath of God now is a harbinger of final judgment to come.

This wrath is caused by *all the godlessness and wickedness* displayed in humankind. Since the first refers generally to religious sins and the second to moral sins, it is possible to separate them and see them as reflecting the two tables of the Decalogue, where the first four of the ten commandments refer to sins against God and the rest to ethical sins (so Michel 1966:61-62). This would fit the rest of the chapter with its distinction between idolatry and immorality. However, as Moo points out (1996:102 n.) the terms are usually synony-

---

1:18 Sovereign judgment is better than Cranfield's interpretation (1975:107-11) that *from heaven* simply underlines that it is *God's* wrath and that this is revealed in the preaching of the gospel. He removes the vertical element, i.e., God's feeling of wrath, and subsumes it entirely under a proclamation event, the preaching of the gospel.

mous and refer to sins against God in general. This is seen in the added comment that they *suppress the truth by their wickedness,* repeating the second of the two terms. To *suppress* means to "hinder" the truth of God by opposing it. As Cranfield says (1975:112), people attempt to "bury it out of sight, obliterate it from memory." The end result of wickedness is to bury the truths of God under a mountain of rationalization and evil behavior. This is seen in the recent rash of immoral behavior among Christian leaders. The process of rationalization is so powerful that many of them refuse to admit that they have done wrong and even go so far as to say, "I have never been so close to God as I am now."

Yet it is clear that all such sinful deeds are deliberate. Paul says that the Gentiles have always known the truth and thus are responsible before God for their actions. So God is justified in his wrath against them. Knowledge of God refers to the process by which one comes to know God rather than knowing God in any absolute sense. Isaiah 55:8-9 says "my thoughts are not your thoughts . . . my ways are higher than your ways." So this undoubtedly means *what may be known about God,* as the phrase is translated in the TNIV. Nevertheless, God has made himself *plain* (visible) through creation. The term is similar in meaning to "revealed" (special revelation) above but speaks of natural revelation. This can also be seen in Paul's messages to the Gentiles at Lystra and Derbe (Acts 14:15-17) and at Athens (Acts 17:22-31), both of which centered on God's revelation through nature rather than through his Word (there was no reference to Scripture in either speech). This is an excellent example of redemptive analogies. Since the Gentiles did not have revealed truth, God convicted them through nature.

Natural revelation is explicitly explained in 1:20. God has revealed himself *since the creation of the world.* Even in the Garden of Eden God was disclosing himself to Adam and Eve through nature. So the Gentiles, even without God's Word, have known of *God's invisible*

1:20 Moo (1996:104-5) points out the deliberate oxymoron between God who "cannot be seen" and his attributes here that are *clearly seen.* The latter verb denotes more physical perception than mental understanding. That is, they understand somewhat, but until they believe they cannot understand fully.

qualities. These invisible things are his divine attributes, for God cannot be seen (Jn 1:18), is "spirit" (Jn 4:24) and so is "invisible" (Col 1:15; 1 Tim 1:17). Thus humankind can only know those aspects of his being that he has revealed in his creation (Ps 19:1; Is 6:3). This is not saving knowledge, of course, for this entire passage centers on depravity, the absence of salvation. Paul spells out which attributes are indeed revealed by nature—*his eternal power and divine nature.* Creation first demonstrates the power of God. That is easily proven by the vastness of the universe, the power of a supernova, indeed the power in a single atom (i.e., atomic fusion). At the same time, these also evidence the reality and necessity of his deity. The odds of all the perfection of the natural world happening by chance are so infinitesimally small as to be virtually nil. When one understands how DNA works, how cells function, indeed how a perfect baby comes into being through sperm and an egg, the reality of God becomes *clearly seen,* as Paul says. Stott (1994:74) adds, "Anthropologists have also found a worldwide moral sense in human beings so that, although conscience is of course to some extent conditioned by culture, it still testifies to everybody everywhere both that there is a difference between right and wrong, and that evil deserves to be punished."

Since the created order has indeed helped all people understand something of the reality of God, it then follows that everyone is *without excuse.* Of course, we have already seen in verse 19 how human beings *suppress* that knowledge, but that deliberate rejection of God's self-disclosure is the basis of their guilt. God has indeed manifested himself to the world, and the inhabitants have perceived the reality, no matter how hardened their hearts and evil their minds. So they stand before God guilty and without excuse. This is law court language—God has just pronounced them guilty, and all that is left is the sentence.

Divine Retribution for Human Depravity (1:21-32)

The Depravity of Their Minds in Idolatry (1:21-24) This passage explains why *(for)* the unsaved are without excuse (v. 20). God has indeed revealed himself in nature, but human minds have been darkened by sin. They *knew God,* but the question is, how much knowledge did they have? This is hardly the biblical sense of a knowledge of God that leads to belief and surrender to him (1 Cor 1:21; Gal 4:9; Phil 3:7-10; 1 Jn 4:7-8). Rather, they only knew what nature revealed, namely, his power and deity (1:20). But this knowledge led neither to glorifying him as God nor to giving thanks to him. Neither worship nor gratitude resulted. How can a person walk through the woods on a gorgeous spring day without giving thanks to the God who created all this beauty? Or study the glory of his creation without acknowledging the Creator as God? Dunn (1988a:59) speaks of "thanksgiving as characteristic of a whole life, as the appropriate response of one whose daily experience is shaped by the recognition that he stands in debt to God, that his very life and experience of living is a gift from God."

But the problem is that depraved human beings in *their thinking became futile;* that is, their ability to reason from cosmos to Creator became empty of content. Their rational thought was perverted by sin and emptied itself of all truth, so that their *foolish hearts were darkened.* In reality, the *heart* in Scripture refers to the mental processes (see Osborne 1984:55-70), so this is clarifying the futility of the mind further. First their hearts and minds are *foolish,* a term meaning devoid of understanding (cf. Mk 7:18; Rom 1:31, 10:19). Second, they are *darkened,* meaning they have deliberately rejected the light of God. They believe they are wise (v. 22), but in reality the foolishness of this world's thinking has darkened their counsel, exactly as it did Job (Job 38:2; 42:3) and the foolish leaders at Corinth (1 Cor 1:18—2:5). The antithesis of 1 Corinthians is illuminating here: the wisdom of the cross is foolishness to the world, while the wisdom of the world is foolishness with God. Choose you this day which you will serve!

As in 1 Corinthians 1, the Gentiles *claimed to be wise.* This is especially true of the Greeks, who developed the greatest concentration of philosophical "wisdom" in history in the midst of one of the most depraved cultures in the ancient world. But worldly wisdom is not divine truth, so in reality they *became fools.* Their mental depravity became dementia, as their pretension to earthly wisdom led them to prove themselves to be fools. The proof of this folly is seen in their idolatry (v. 23). This begins the series of divine retributions (see the introduction to this section). *Exchange* stems from the Greek word for *another* and means to substitute one thing for another. Here they are substituting idols for *the glory of the immortal God*. There is an allusion here to Psalm 106:20 and Jeremiah 2:11, though in both places it is Israel's glory that is exchanged for worthless idols. Here it is the divine *glory*, a term often used of the Shekinah or glorious presence of God in his sanctuary (Ex 40:34-35; 1 Kings 8:10-11; 2 Chron 7:1; Ps 26:8). Nearly half the New Testament occurrences are in Paul's writings, with sixteen in Romans alone. It connotes the splendor, majesty and honor due God alone by his earthly creatures. God's creation has manifested the glory of his deity, giving the world the knowledge (1:20) that he is indeed *immortal God*. But they have exchanged that knowledge for the foolishness of finite idols.

This foolishness is especially seen in that their idolatry centers on the images of *mortal man* (note the contrast with *immortal God*) as well as *birds and animals and reptiles*. Several (Barrett 1957; Käsemann 1980; Dunn 1988a; Moo 1996; Schreiner 1998) have noted that *images made to look like* is a redundant phrase that emphasizes the inferiority and weakness of these worthless idols. The list of human and animal idols comes from Deuteronomy 4:15-18, where God prohibits images of man, animal, bird, reptile or fish (cf. Ex 20:3-4; Deut 5:7-8). The major thrust, of course, is upon the worship of God alone, and the idol represents the tendency of sinful humanity to reject the heavenly reality and embrace only the earthly, that is, to exchange the eternal for the temporary. This was not just an ancient problem. In many parts of the world idolatry is just as predominant as it was in the Roman Empire. In the West, where there are few physical idols, another type of idolatry predominates (even more dangerous because it is not identified as such): the idolatry of self that is manifested in possessions, status in society and sex.

Because of this idolatry, the divine *lex talionis* (the "law of retribution" that predominated in the jurisprudence of the ancient world) led

---

1:24 Schreiner (1998:90) argues that verse 24 begins a section (vv. 24-32) delineating the consequences of refusing to worship God (vv. 18-23). He says the "therefore" that introduces verse 24 draws an inference from verses 18-23 and that verse 24 is more closely related to verse 25, saying God gave them over to sexual sin (v. 24) because they worshiped idols (v. 25). This is possible, but the threefold pattern of *ex-*

God to hand them over to the results of their sin (1:24). The verb for *gave them over* means to "deliver" them for their punishment; as Cranfield (1975:120) notes, it refers to a judicial act on God's part. This is superior to Dodd's (1932:52-53) view that this is not divine judgment but rather the natural outworking of "the moral rottenness of pagan society." Since the Gentiles have refused to acknowledge God, he has handed them over to the *impurity* they have chosen, a term that often refers to sexual immorality (2 Cor 2:21; Gal 5:19; Eph 4:19; 5:3). This does not mean that God forced them to commit such acts; rather it means that he allowed their sin to run full course, according to *the sinful desires of their hearts*. God simply gave them up to the lustful depravity of their natural selves. Moreover, because they did not honor (the other meaning of *glory* in v. 23) God, he handed them over so that they would dishonor their bodies through sexual depravity. It does not take much analysis of the moral state of the Roman Empire or of our world today to see the extent to which sexual license dishonors the body. Without moral standards, sex is degraded to animal behavior. There is an emptiness and an incredible sadness behind the state of our world without God.

Exchanging the Truth of God for a Lie (1:25-26) Not only did they exchange God's glory for idols (v. 23), but they also substituted human lies for divine truth. The meanings of these two are quite similar. *Truth of God* does not mean the "truth about God" as proclaimed by his people; rather it is the truth that God has revealed of himself, that is, the knowledge that has come via natural revelation regarding his power and deity (vv. 20-21). Dunn (1988a:63) believes that *truth* would also contain ideas of God's "reliability and trustworthiness" to any Jewish Christian. Instead, they have chosen a *lie,* which Paul defines as having *worshiped and served created things rather than the Creator.* The two verbs probably imply pagan cultic worship in idolatrous temples. Idols were lies in the sense that false gods were given

---

change/gave them over in 1:21-31 (see the introduction to this section) makes the organization used here more likely. The "therefore" in verse 24 draws an inference from verse 23: people preferred idols (v. 23), and so God *gave them over* to sexual sin (v. 24).

creaturely form as statues, and people believed they represented living gods. To choose the creature over the Creator is the essence of idolatry.

There are only three places where Paul adds a benediction (here, Rom 9:5, and 2 Cor 11:31). Following Jewish precedent (the phrase *who is forever praised* is used often in rabbinic literature) he adds his praise to the idea of the Creator. He is so horrified at the desecration of the name of God in pagan idolatry that he feels he must bless the name of God. The concluding *amen* (see also 9:5; 11:36; 15:33) adds a note of affirmation and solemn commitment (see Schlier 1964:335-37).

As a result of their choosing the *lie,* God then hands them over (as in v. 24) to their *shameful lusts. Shameful* means "dishonorable" and looks back to the *impurity* that causes the *degrading of their bodies* (v. 24). The connection between idolatry and immorality has been long recognized. In many of the ancient temples there were sacred prostitutes, and fornication there was considered an act of worship. Moo (1996:111) alludes to Wisdom of Solomon 14:12: "the idea of making idols was the beginning of fornication, and the invention of them was the corruption of life." So these terrible sins are interconnected. In one sense immorality is idolatry, for it is the illicit worship of another person's body.

Exchanging Natural Sexual Relations for Unnatural Ones (1:26-31) While this is in one sense a separate section based on the threefold exchange-hand over formula (as outlined above), it is also the primary example of God's delivery of them to shameful passions in the first half of verse 26, as seen in the introductory *even.* Now God's judicial punishment is to give them over to homosexual practices, as *women exchanged natural relations for unnatural ones.* The key term here and in the debate today is *nature* (Greek *physis*). Paul uses both the adjective *natural* and the noun *unnatural ones* to emphasize that homosexual practices are against God's created order. The term itself was used in the Old Testament and Jewish world to speak of the cre-

---

1:26-27 Paul does not use the normal terms for *women (gynē)* and *men (anēr)* but two terms *(thēlys* and *arsēn)* that may well allude to God's created order, as they are used in the LXX of the creation account, "male and female he created them" (Gen

ated order. By the first century it was seen as a divinely given power that controlled the way things are supposed to be (e.g., Philo and Josephus; see Harder 1976:658-59; De Young 1988:429-41). So Paul is saying not just that this is not the natural way of having sexual relations but that this is against what God intended in creation (see France 1999:249).

It is common today to challenge this interpretation. Some scholars argue that *natural* should be understood as it is used in the Hellenistic world as a reference to what is the custom from the culture or natural tendencies of the individual (pointing to passages in Paul where *physis* does not refer to divine intentionality: Rom 2:14; 11:21, 24; Gal 2:15; 4:8; Eph 2:3). In this sense Paul would be saying that homosexuality is wrong only when the culture prohibits it or when the individual does not have that sexual proclivity (so Scroggs 1983:116-28; Mollenkott and Scanzoni 1978:61-66). Since the Greek culture strongly embraced homosexual practices, Paul would only be prohibiting it in these restricted areas. But this would only be true if Paul were writing from a Hellenistic perspective and not a Jewish one. The entire tone of this passage is Jewish, and in verse 27 Paul condemns homosexual practices entirely, evidencing a strong Jewish tone. *Natural* here refers not to what is natural in the culture but to God's created order. The Old Testament contains many condemnations of homosexual practices (Gen 19:5, 8; Lev 18:22; 20:13; Deut 23:17-18; Judg 19:22-24; 1 Kings 14:24; 15:12; 2 Kings 23:7; Is 1:9; 3:9; Lam 4:6), and these are continued in intertestamental writings (Wisdom of Solomon 14:26; *2 Enoch* 10:1-5; 34:1-3; *Sibylline Oracles* 3:184-86, 596-600; *Testament of Levi* 17:11; *Testament of Naphtali* 3:4-5; Philo *On the Life of Abraham* 135-37) and the New Testament (1 Cor 6:9; 1 Tim 1:10; Jude 7). In short, Paul is writing as a Jewish Christian and is in complete agreement with the tradition of which he is a part (see also Boughton 1992:141-53).

Paul continues this diatribe in 1:27. Here he turns from female to male homosexuality, pointing out three perversions: abandoning *natu-*

1:27 LXX; cf. also Mk 10:6; Mt 19:4). Thus the terms also emphasize the sexual distinctiveness of male and female (so Cranfield 1975; Moo 1996; Schreiner 1998).

ral relations with women, that is, God's intention that sex be restricted to male with female; *inflamed with lust for one another,* with strong language describing them as burning up with desire; and committing *indecent acts with other men,* stressing the shameful or dishonorable nature of what they have done. Again, it is common for revisionist writers today to reinterpret this. Some (e.g., Scroggs 1983:122) say Paul condemns only pederasty, i.e., men having sex with boys. But De Young (2000:158-59) argues strongly that 1:26-27 is far more general since Paul has men with men (not boys) in verse 27, includes lesbianism (there is no evidence for female pederasty then), and discusses the *natural* order, all of which center on adult relationships. In other words, all types of homosexual relationships are included. Countryman (1988:109-17) believes the issue is not morality but purity. So they are not sinful but only unclean in a Jewish setting. But this is impossible, for the entire context of 1:18-32, let alone the context of 1:18—3:8, centers on the depravity of humanity. There is no mention of purity issues here, only sin. France (1999:249-51) concludes that Paul unambiguously follows biblical precedent and teaches that "homosexuality . . . runs counter to the way God has designed human sexuality." In short, we must say with Hurtado (1996:13-19) that the issue is one of biblical authority. Even when the command runs counter to the current cultural norm, the true Christian must obey God's command rather than the demands of political correctness.

The *penalty,* then, is exactly what is *due . . . for their perversion,* with the idea that their reward (here in the negative sense of *penalty*) is divinely necessary. Because they have perverted the sexuality God gave them, God will now force them to pay the price. But it is debated whether the penalty is homosexuality itself (Cranfield 1975; Dunn 1988a; Schreiner 1998) or eternal punishment as in 1 Corinthians 6:8-10 (not to "inherit the kingdom of God," so Michel 1966; Murray 1968; Moo 1996). Since nothing is specified here, the context makes the former more likely. God has abandoned them to terrible sexual degradation, a punishment in itself.

Paul returns to the issue of the *knowledge of God* (1:19, 21) in 1:28. It is debated whether the conjunction here *(kathōs)* means "because" (so Cranfield 1975; Käsemann 1980; and NRSV "since") or "just as" (Godet 1969; Murray 1968; Dunn 1988a; Moo 1996). The causal would make sense in light of a similar construction in 1:24, 26. However, "just as" is by far the more common meaning (Moo 1996:117 challenges the evidence for "because"), so it is more likely that a correlation is made here between the sin and the consequence. The one leads naturally to the other. The literal translation of the clause here is, "they did not see fit to have God in knowledge." The first part means that they tested God and disqualified him as worthy of their attention. It emphasizes the deliberate nature of their rejection. In the first century, "ignorance" meant active rejection and not just lack of knowledge. As Dunn says (1988a:66), "they gave God their consideration and concluded that God was unnecessary for their living . . . an 'unnecessary hypothesis,' an infantile projection no longer needed by man 'come of age.'" The second part reinforces this, as knowledge implies not just intellectual understanding but the kind of knowledge that is experienced in right conduct (Hackenburg 1991:25). In other words, it refers to the practical understanding that results from cognitive knowledge. Putting this together with 1:19 and 21, they have received *knowledge of God* from creation, tested it and found it unworthy of affecting their conduct. They have totally refused to consider God in their daily lives.

In the same way that they have rejected God, God has handed them over to the folly of their sins. In verses 24 and 26 this judicial delivery to punishment took the form of immorality. This is more basic; God yields them to a *depraved* [worthless or disqualified] *mind*. They have rejected the possibility of knowing God, so God now gives them over to that mindset. There is a wordplay here in that they have tested God's worth (Greek *edokimasan*) and rejected him, so God yields them to a mind that has failed the test, or is worthless (Greek *adokimon*). As a result, they do *what ought not to be done*. The idea of proper conduct was especially emphasized by the Stoic philosophers. Here it describes the kind of mindset that is completely unable to make the right decisions (see 1:21, *their thinking became futile and their foolish hearts were darkened*). It describes so well the depraved mind, choosing always the path that leads to dissolution. Once more, this fits modern life as clearly as it did the Roman world.

Paul now turns to a vice list (1:29-31) to sum up the sins that result from such a worthless mind. Such lists were common in both the Jewish and Hellenistic worlds to depict human depravity (cf. Wisdom of Solomon 14:25-26; in Paul see also Gal 5:19-21; 1 Cor 6:9-10; Eph 4:25-32; 5:3-5; Col 3:5, 8; 1 Tim 1:9-10; 2 Tim 3:2-4; Tit 3:3). It is probably best to organize these into three groups:

1. The first four are general sins that introduce the list—*filled with every kind of wickedness, evil, greed and depravity.* The language describes them as vessels filled to the brim with evil. Three of the four are synonyms that describe the wicked nature of the depraved person, giving great emphasis to the depths of their sin. *Greed* is in the list because it is one of the basic manifestations of evil, namely, the self-centered desire to take everything for yourself. Paul elsewhere calls greed idolatry (Eph 5:5; Col 3:5) because it places the accumulation of possessions above God.

2. The next five follow *filled with* and describe a desire to mistreat others—*envy, murder, strife, deceit and malice. Envy* is the natural outgrowth of *greed* and leads into those that follow. When one is filled with desire for what belongs to someone else, it can lead to *murder* or *strife* (Moo 1996:119 points out that several ancient writers linked envy with "acts of violence such as 'murder'"). To show the relevance of this, one could survey how many churches have split over the strife that results from envy. *Deceit* and *malice* are at the top of the vice list in 1 Peter 2:1 because they are so basic to the theme of man's inhumanity to man. The desire to take things from others by tricking them or to get them to believe a lie is one of the basic sins. And the desire to hurt others deeply is one the basic areas of human depravity.

3. The final twelve can be further divided into sins of the tongue (*gossips, slanderers*), sins of pride (*God-haters, insolent, arrogant and boastful*), summary sins (*they invent ways of doing evil; they disobey their parents*) and negative sins (*senseless, faithless, heartless and ruthless*).The first two make a natural pair. The Greek word for *gossip* refers to one who whispers the slander to someone else. In a very real sense gossip is passive slander. In fact, it is worse than slander in the sense

---

1:30 Lenski (1945:121) sees four groups of pairs here—"god-hated insolents," "slanderous whisperers," "arrogant boasters" and "inventors of cruelties." But this is too

that slander is more honest; that is, it is intended to hurt the person. The gossip does not care enough about the person to worry about whether he or she is hurt. The next sin is interesting because the term could mean "hated by God" or "hating God." In light of the whole emphasis on their rejection of God, the latter is more likely here. The three terms for pride are fairly similar in meaning, though *insolent* implies the possibility of violence, *arrogant* is used to describe an attitude, and *boastful* words place oneself above others.

The two following sins are linked mostly by the fact that each is two words rather than one. Those who *invent ways of doing evil,* literally "invent evil," look for more and more creative ways to commit their terrible sins. Those who *disobey . . . parents,* or are rebellious toward their parents, are castigated often in Scripture (Deut 21:18; Prov 30:11, 17; 2 Tim 3:2). In Leviticus 20:9 cursing one's parents was considered punishable by death!

The final four are connected only by the fact that they all begin with the negative particle *a-*. They do function, however, as summaries of the section. Those who are *senseless* possess the depraved mind of 1:19-21, 28. Creation has communicated the fact of God to them, and the Holy Spirit has proven to them their guilt before God (Jn 16:8-11). Yet they have neglected that voice of God in every instance. This is not a passive ignorance but a willful rejection, building on the picture of the fool in the Old Testament (Ps 53:1; 74:22; Prov 10:14, 21, 23; 15:14). The *faithless* will break all promises to God or those around them. They cannot be trusted to do anything except live for themselves. The term is used in Jeremiah 3:7-11 of those who broke God's covenant. Those who are *heartless* especially lack family love. People without natural affection care only for themselves. Cranfield (1975:132-33) refers to the widespread Greco-Roman practice of "exposing," where parents would take unwanted babies (usually girls) and put them on the trash heap to die by the weather or wild animals. The *ruthless* have feelings for no one. Godet (1969:111) alludes to the bloodthirsty Roman preoccupation with gladiatorial combats and pictures the people

---

artificial and unnecessary to the context.

"gloating over the dying agonies of the vanquished combatant."

Conclusion (1:32) The willful nature of the depravity of the Gentile world provides a fitting conclusion to this section. At the deepest level of their being, sinners *know* (the fourth time this is emphasized after 1:19-21, 28, 31) *God's righteous decree,* undoubtedly referring to the divine requirement that people must get right with God. In 2:26; 8:4 this is the law, but here it is more general, referring to creation and the personal conscience. As 2:15 brings out, this realization was "written on their hearts." In 1:20 and 21 this decree was positive, speaking of natural revelation. Here it is negative, speaking of the fact that *those who do such things* [namely the sins of 1:28-31] *deserve death.* Not only was God's deity and power revealed in nature (1:21), but the folly and consequences of sin were also known. At the core of their being they realized that such moral outrages are worthy of death. As Dunn brings out (1988a:69), this may well allude to the Genesis 2—3 story of the death penalty for sin, especially since most of the sins in the vice list of verses 29-31 were not worthy of death. The main point is that every human being has been given by God a deep awareness of two things: (1) the existence and power of God and (2) each person's general guilt before God because of sin.

The rest of verse 32 is difficult. It sounds like Paul is saying that consent to evil is more condemnable than the actual practice of it. In fact, many ancient scribes rearranged the verse to avoid this supposition. Yet in a very real sense Paul is correct. The person who commits sin is certainly guilty before God, but the one who applauds such acts has even more guilt because that person encourages many others to join in the depraved actions. Hodge says (1950:44), "This is the lowest point of degradation. To sin, even in the heat of passion, is evil; but to delight in the sins of others shows that men are of set purpose and fixed preference, wicked."

2:1-16 Several scholars (Barrett 1957; Käsemann 1980; Dunn 1988a; Cranfield 1975) believe this section should be 2:1-11 and that 2:12-16 is separate on the grounds that it introduces the law. However, the diatribe style moves from second person in verses 1-5 to third person in verses 6-16 and then back to second person in verses 17-27. It seems more likely that verses 12-16 join verses 6-11 in explaining God's just judgment of the Jews.

2:1 Some (e.g., Stott 1994:81) believe that Paul here addresses not just the Jewish

□ God's Wrath Against the Jews (2:1—3:8)

Most people find a certain satisfaction in reading about other people's sins because it makes them feel better about themselves. So the Jewish Christians must have enjoyed reading Paul's condemnation of the Gentiles. But now Paul turns to the guilt of the Jews and uses even stronger language. It is commonly agreed that Paul uses the diatribe form here, establishing an imaginary dialogue with his opponents with rhetorical questions to expose their presumptions and inconsistencies. This can especially be seen in the switch from the third-person style in 1:18-32 to the second-person style of 2:1-5, 17-27. While God's wrath was turned against "them" (the Gentiles) in chapter 1, now it addresses *you,* the Jews. It is clear here that the Jewish people cannot escape condemnation by calling themselves the elect people. Their sins, if anything, are greater than the Gentiles because they sin even while *under the law* (2:12) and so sin with knowledge. They have all the advantages of being the recipients of God's revelation and law and therefore stand all the more guilty before him. There are three parts to Paul's argument: the truthfulness of God's judgment on the Jews (2:1-16), the inadequacy of the Law for salvation (2:17-29) and God's faithfulness toward Israel (3:1-8).

The Truthfulness of God's Judgment (2:1-16) Here Paul develops a three-part argument regarding the guilt of the Jewish people before God. First (2:1-5), in second-person style he shows that the Jewish condemnation of the Gentiles turns upon them because they commit the same sins. Second (2:6-11), he switches back to third-person style to explain that God will judge each person on the basis of their works, and so God's impartial judgment must fall on everyone alike. Third (2:12-16), he shows that having the Mosaic law gives the Jews no advantage, for God demands that they obey the law. Therefore, Jew and Gentile stand before God equally condemned.

people but all self-conscious moralizers "who presume to pass moral judgments on other people." But Bruce (1985:86-87), from whom Stott draws much of his data, admits that in the context Paul is thinking primarily of Jewish critics, as seen in the repetition of "first for the Jew, then for the Gentile" in 1:16; 2:9-10). He says "the Jews are the first to receive the judgment of God as well as the first to receive the good news of his saving grace."

God's Wrath on Those Who Pass Judgment (2:1-5) Paul now creates an imaginary foe who apparently considers the condemnation of the Gentiles in 1:18-32 to be his own work (so Dunn 1988a:78; Carras 1992:191-93 calls him the "critic" around whom Paul develops his case throughout the chapter). In Greek Paul addresses him as "you, . . . O man, who . . ." (reduced to "you" in NIV) in order to make the hypocrisy of the Jews more rhetorically powerful. He begins with the fact that they *have no excuse,* repeating the condemnation of the Gentiles in 1:20. Morris (1988:109) calls this a legal concept, meaning they are "without reasoned defense." The Jewish people are just as guilty before God as the Gentiles. The first basis of their guilt is the fact that they *pass judgment on* the Gentiles without considering their own duplicity in the issue. This is similar to Christ's condemnation of judging others, voiced in Matthew 7:1-5, where he also states that the sin is not so much in the admonition but in the failure to consider one's own sins (cf. also Gal 6:1). Scripture clearly tells us to admonish each other when we are caught up in sin (also Mt 18:15-18; Heb 3:13), but we do so as an act of love rather than judgmentalism, and we must be certain to consider our own spiritual state. The Jews were too smug in their condemnation, and thus they *condemn* themselves because they *practice the same things.* This does not mean that the Jewish people with their highly developed moral stance committed all the sins of 1:26-29 (e.g., homosexuality, idolatry or hating God—Dunn 1988a; Moo 1996; Schreiner 1998 believe the sins of 1:29-31 are particularly in mind here). But they committed many of them and so stood before God with *no excuse.*

In fact, Paul goes on to say (2:2), *God's judgment* in such matters is always *based on truth.* When God condemns sin, he always does so justly and fairly. Paul says that *we know* this, referring to commonly held assumptions on the part of his readers (cf. 3:19; 7:14; 8:22, 28). The justice and fairness of God was accepted by everyone. *Truth* (see also 1:18) could refer to God's reliability and commitment to Israel (so Dunn 1988a:80-81), but it more likely refers to the factual evidence. Divine judgment is completely just because it is always based on the true facts of the matter. In other words, God is always impartial and correct in all his judgments.

On the basis of God's just and impartial judgments, Paul then reiterates the basic error of the Jews (2:3), namely, their passing judgment on the Gentiles while committing many of the same sins themselves. There is an ABA pattern in verses 1-3 in which the guilt of the self-righteous Jews (1:1, 3) is ratified by the impartial Judge (v. 2). The message for us is inescapable. Like the Jewish people, we must never look down upon or judge others when we ourselves are not right with God. We are all alike sinners before God, and in our condemnation of others we indict ourselves.

As Cranfield points out (1975:144) the *or* in 1:4 introduces not an alternative idea for verse 3 but an intensification of the same idea. When the Jews ignore the justice of God in their judgmentalism (vv. 1-3), they actually *show contempt for* his goodness and mercy. The verb means to "despise or heap scorn on" a thing, to regard it as having no value. Paul names three things they are scorning, all introduced by the idea of God's *riches,* a strong phrase expressing the overwhelming abundance of the blessings he has poured out upon his people. The first area of abundance is God's *kindness* or goodness. The particular term here is used only by Paul in the New Testament (ten times, half of which are found in Romans [2:4; 8:12; three times in 11:22, where it contrasts the "kindness" and "sternness" of God]). Morris (1988:112 n., following Shedd) believes it connotes not the abstract quality of God's goodness but the acts of goodness by which his gracious benevolence are felt by people. More likely, however, it refers to both, as in the LXX (e.g., Ps 25:7; 69:16; 100:5), where it describes God's "kind and merciful disposition or actions (including the resulting gifts of fortune and redemption)" (Zmijewski 1993:475). The second area of abundance is God's *tolerance,* referring to God's postponing his judgment and giving people time to repent (so also 3:26). The third area is quite similar, God's *patience* or "longsuffering" as he puts up with sinners, "not wanting anyone to perish, but everyone to come to repentance" (2 Pet 3:9).

Paul's purpose is to show God's incredible compassion with sinners as contrasted to the Jewish self-righteous condemnation of sinners. However, they do not realize (again, deliberate rejection of truth rather than ignorance; cf. 1:19, 21) the actual purpose of God, that his *kindness leads you towards repentance.* Note the implicit message, that repentance is not just for the Gentile but also for *you,* the Jew.

Repentance means not just a turning away from sin but also a turning to God. It is a key component in experiencing God's salvation. Without a remorse for sin as well as a commitment to God, salvation is not possible. Many scholars (e.g., Moo 1996:133) have noted the influence of Wisdom of Solomon 11—15 on this passage, indeed on 1:18-32 as well. Wisdom of Solomon 15:1-2 says after a condemnation of Gentile idolatry, "But thou, our God, art kind and true, patient, and ruling all things in mercy. For even if we sin we are thine, knowing thy power." The number of parallels with 2:4 here are remarkable. The Jewish people thought of themselves as completely secure in the covenant, but Paul is correcting this error and telling them that they must repent as well.

Yet it must be understood that God's forbearance and patience are not eternal. God gives the sinner a chance, but judgment will result when that opportunity is spurned. The Jews' *stubbornness and . . . unrepentant heart* will bring down upon them God's wrath (v. 5). Here they are the basis (Greek *kata*) of God's wrath. Paul uses strong language to make his point, centering on the hardness-of-heart theme found so often in Scripture (Deut 9:27; 10:16; 31:27 as well as passages on Pharaoh's hardened heart and the hardness of the Pharisees [Mk 3:5] and the disciples [Mk 6:52; 8:17]). In Romans 11:25 the Jews are described as hardened, and in Ephesians 4:18 the Gentiles are hardened toward God. Morris (1988:115 n., following Earle) notes that the Greek term is behind *arteriosclerosis,* hardening of the arteries, and so calls this "'spiritual sclerosis,' the 'hardening of the spiritual arteries.'"

This spiritual hardness accompanied by impenitence causes them to store up wrath, a metaphor drawn from commerce for accumulating wealth, literally "storing treasure." The picture here is the progressive accumulation of sin throughout one's lifetime that will end with the final judgment before God's judgment seat, called *the day of God's wrath.* This is the flip side of the love of God, as his holiness also demands justice, and so sin must be punished. As sin accumulates, so does the divine

---

2:5 Several scholars (Murray 1968; Stott 1994; Morris 1988) place verse 5 with the following section (vv. 1-4, 5-11) rather than with verses 1-4. Whenever scholars debate whether a verse goes with the preceding or the following sections, that is usually a good indication that it provides a transition from one to the other. That is certainly the case here. It concludes verses 1-4 on the judgment of God against the

wrath, and "day of wrath" is a technical phrase for the final judgment (Ps 110:5; Zeph 1:15; Rev 6:17; cf. Joel 1:15; 2:1-2; Rev 16:14) as described in Revelation 20:11-15. Yet Paul carefully clarifies that this is not just a day of wrath but also a day of revelation, and in this case it is God's *righteous judgment* that is *revealed*. In 1:17 God's "righteousness" was revealed, and in 1:18 his "wrath" was revealed. Both aspects are combined here, but while in 1:17, 18 the time of revelation was now, 2:5 describes the final revelation at the eschaton, when history will end and the final judgment occur. Clearly, God's wrath is part of his righteousness, and his justice is the basis of it all. This prepares for chapters 9—11, when Paul will address in detail the issue of God's justice in removing the Jews from their place as God's chosen people.

The Impartiality of Divine Judgment (2:6-11) Grobel (1964:255-61) and Moo (1996:135-36) correctly see a chiastic arrangement in this section (see figure 1). The purpose of chiasm is to highlight the themes

---

A God judges everyone fairly (v. 6).

   B Those doing good gain eternal life (v. 7).

      C Those following evil gain wrath (v. 8).

      C′ There will be trouble for those doing evil (v. 9).

   B′ Those doing good gain glory (v. 10).

A′ God does not show favoritism (v. 11).

Figure 1. A chiastic diagram of Romans 2:6-11

by reversing the order in the second half. It is clear what Paul is trying to do here, namely, demonstrate divine justice by showing how God judges fairly with both Gentiles and Jews. The emphasis throughout centers upon what the Romans called *lex talionis,* Latin for "the law of retribution." In a sense it describes the basic New Testament ethic—what we do to others we are doing to God, since they are made in his

---

self-righteous judgmentalism of the Jews, and it leads into verses 6-11 on the impartial nature of divine judgment. Grammatically it leads more closely into verse 6, which begins with a relative clause modifying *God* in verse 5. However, thematically it is more closely related to the divine judgment of verses 1-4, and so we have placed it in that section.

image—and God will turn those deeds back upon our heads. When we perform good deeds, we will receive a reward, and when we do evil we will be punished, both in accordance with what we have done.

Paul begins with his basic theme, that God *"will give to each person in accordance with what he has done"* (quoting Ps 62:12). The verb means to "return, render, recompense" and signifies equal pay for equal work. This does not contradict Paul's emphasis on the free gift of salvation (e.g., Eph 2:8-9). It relates not to our justification but to our Christian life—we are saved by grace but judged by works. Moreover, it is a major biblical theme, frequent in the Old Testament (2 Chron 6:23; Job 34:11; Ps 28:4; 62:12; Prov 24:12; Eccles 12:14; Jer 17:10; Ezek 18:20; Hos 12:2), Jewish literature (*1 Enoch* 41:1-2; *Psalms of Solomon* 2:16; 17:8; *4 Ezra* 7:35; 8:33; *2 Baruch* 14:12), and the New Testament (Mt 16:27; Rom 2:6; 14:12; 1 Cor 3:12-15; 2 Cor 5:10; 11:15; 2 Tim 4:14; 1 Pet 1:17). In Revelation it refers to both believers (Rev 2:23; 11:18; 14:13; 20:12; 22:12) and unbelievers (Rev 18:6; 11:18; 20:13). We all will stand before the Lord and give account for our lives. We will be rewarded for the good we have done and judged for the evil (including the sins of omission, Jas 4:17, those things we should have done and did not). The idea of ethical responsibility and its consequences is too often ignored in modern preaching and needs to be given more attention.

In verses 7-8 this theme of divine recompense is illustrated by contrasting good and evil works. Paul applies this theme first to those who show *persistence in doing good*. This means that good works are the

---

2:7, 10 Scholars have developed a whole series of hypotheses to explain the seeming discrepancy between the works theology of verses 6-11 and the teaching of Paul elsewhere that we are saved only by grace (combining the discussions in Cranfield 1975; Moo 1996; Schreiner 1998): (1) Paul is inconsistent, sometimes saying we will be justified by faith and here by works; (2) this referred to Jews and moral Gentiles before Christ (most often found in the patristic period); (3) Paul is speaking hypothetically of the situation if there had been no Christ and the law was the only medium of salvation; (4) Paul is speaking of those who do not hear the Gospel but live up to the "light they have received"; so as long as it is God's grace that makes this possible, there is no contradiction with salvation by faith alone; (5) Paul refers to Christians and actually means that the *doing good* here is "faith," so verses 7 and 10 refer to salvation by faith; (6) this is a true offer of salvation for those who do good works, but because of total depravity no human being can possibly gain salvation

defining characteristic of a person's life. The eschatological reward is seen in the fact that believers *seek glory, honor and immortality* by their good works. These three rewards refer to the gifts that God will bestow on the faithful at the final judgment when he *will give eternal life* to those who have so lived. These three define the meaning of eternal life for the faithful. However, this is not works righteousness, for Paul clearly throughout his teaching makes it clear that salvation is not based on works (Gal 3:2-5, 11; Rom 3:20; 4:2; 2 Tim 1:9; Tit 3:5). So Paul is describing here not the process of regeneration but the obligation of Christian living (see Schreiner 1993a:131-58 for more on this issue). Moreover, this is in keeping with another basic theme that is found in Jesus' challenge that the saints seek treasures in heaven rather than treasures on earth (Mt 6:9-21) and Paul's exhortation to seek and think heavenly rather than earthly things (Col 3:1-2). The purpose of the Christian life is to work for eternal rather than earthly glory.

In contrast, those who are characterized by self-centeredness, disobedience and evil will receive divine *wrath and anger.* The *self-seeking* is "selfish ambition" in Philippians 2:3 and James 3:14, 16, but here it probably means more simply "selfishness" and describes the basic self-centered attitude that produces disobedience and evil (see Giesen 1991:52). Since they have rejected and disobeyed *the truth* (namely the truth about God and the gospel) and have pursued evil (equating them with the Gentiles in 1:18-32), they too will face divine wrath. As Cranfield points out (1975:149), *wrath* could refer to God's inner feeling and *anger* to its outward expression, but they are more likely syn-

this way; (7) Paul is writing only about Christians in verses 7 and 10, and this refers not to works that bring about salvation but works that result from salvation. There is no need to accept the first view unless all the other attempts to harmonize this with salvation by grace alone fail. The second and third are unlikely because the whole context shows Paul is speaking of an actual situation in his own time, namely, the Jew-Gentile controversy. Also, there is no hint that Paul is thinking here of those who have not heard the gospel but "live up to the light" God has given them; that would have to become a form of works-righteousness for Paul. The fifth is similarly weak because there is no hint that Paul is equating *doing good* with faith. Paul clearly teaches that "faith" is not a "work" (Eph 2:8, 9). The sixth is very possible and held by many (e.g., Hodge 1950; Murray 1968; Moo 1996), but I do not see any evidence in verses 6-11 that Paul has this in mind; in reality it is another type of hypothetical interpretation. The seventh is problematic because Paul is describing all

onyms, with the second strengthening the first.

The contrast between the terrible future for the sinner and the glorious future for the saint is further emphasized in verses 9-10. Those practicing (literally "producing") evil are now promised *trouble and distress*. The Greek actually has "every soul of a person" in order to emphasize again the absolute fairness of God; every single person will receive exactly what they have earned. While this could mean trials and difficulties in this life, it more likely refers to suffering at the final judgment in this context (see vv. 7-8). The two terms here correspond to *wrath and anger* in verse 8 and like them probably intensify one another rather than connoting inner and outward suffering (contra Godet 1969; Cranfield 1975; Moo 1996). In contrast, those doing good works will have *glory, honor and peace*, repeating the list in verse 7 but with *peace* (stressing eternal tranquility and bliss; see 1:7; 5:1) replacing *immortality*. Those who live for doing good will have eternal glory and those who live for doing evil will have eternal punishment. Paul emphasizes in both verses 9 and 10 that this punishment will be *first for the Jew, then for the Gentile*. As the Jewish people were the recipients of divine revelation and the Torah, and as they have priority in evangelism (1:16), so they will also have priority in both judgment and reward. As Jesus said in Luke 12:48 (NLT), "Much is required from those to whom much is given, and much more is required from those to whom much more is given."

The final point restates the truth of verse 6, *God does not show favoritism*. The Greek phrase communicating "impartiality" here is an interesting one; the components mean literally "does not r eceive according to face" or on the basis of favoritism. The Jewish background for this is "receive by face" in the LXX of Psalm 80:2 and Malachi 1:8. Often in the Old Testament there are warnings against this type of partiality (Lev 19:15; Job 13:8, 10; Prov 18:5; 28:21; Mal 2:9), and God is described as never showing such favoritism (Deut 10:17; 2 Chron 19:7; Job 34:19; Acts 10:34; Gal 2:6; Eph 6:9; Col 3:25; 1 Pet 1:17). Faber

---

people, Christian and non-Christian alike, in verses 6-11. However, there is a contrast between saint and sinner in the passage, and the whole passage relates to the final judgment when all will be judged on the basis of their works. This means that

(1995:304-5) shows that this term has a legal thrust here, pointing to God's eschatological judgment (i.e., retribution for people's deeds) and meaning that he is always impartial when dispensing justice. God will always judge or reward both Jew and Gentile fairly. Neither has any advantage over the other. This is a fitting conclusion to this important section and a very real warning to all of us who think God will prefer us because of race, pedigree or status in the church.

God's Impartial Judgment with or Without the Law (2:12-16) Paul now introduces the Mosaic law for the first time, an issue that will be prominent in the rest of the letter. The point is that if judgment comes by works (vv. 6-11), then all will be judged by the same impartial criteria, whether they are Jews with the Mosaic law or Gentiles apart from it (but still having a law written on their hearts by God). The theme of God's impartial judgment in verse 11 is explained further (vv. 12, 13 and 14 all begin with *gar, for*) in terms of its effect on those without the law (v. 12) and with the law (vv. 12-13). All stand equally guilty before God, for those who have the Mosaic law fail to keep it (v. 13) and those who do not have that law still have God's law written on their hearts (vv. 14-15).

The Jews and Gentiles are separated in verse 12 as those outside the Mosaic law and those within it. Those outside *will perish* without it, but those inside *will be judged* by it. The first half is common Jewish diatribe against Gentiles (the fact that they were not the recipients of the Torah was the heart of Jewish contempt for them), but the second half is Paul's rejoinder regarding their equal guilt before God. The key is that both have equally sinned, one outside and the other inside the law, and so both must suffer the consequences of that depravity. Since the Gentiles have sinned outside the Mosaic law, they will be judged accordingly, for they have still sinned against God. But the Jews have sinned from inside the law and so will by judged *by the law*. The parallelism between *perish* and *be judged* is obvious. Here the judgment of the Jews leads to a death sentence similar to that for

the saint could be the subject of verses 7 and 10 and the sinner the subject of verses 8 and 9. So the seventh view seems most likely (so also Cranfield 1975; Schreiner 1998).

the Gentiles at the last judgment (2:2, 5, 8-9, 16). There is no distinction, and the Jewish people have no final advantage. Today this is an important message to many churchgoers who think being active gives them a distinct advantage before God. Many will have the terrible shock of Matthew 7:23 when they too hear, "I never knew you. Away from me, you evildoers!"

Verse 13 tells why the Jewish people are condemned in their sin. It is not enough to be mere hearers of the law; one must be a doer of it (found only here in Paul but see Jas 1:22-25; 4:11) in order to be declared righteous or just before God. Here Paul introduces the important verb "justify" *(dikaiōthēsontai)*, which is part of the discussion in 1:17 and means that God makes a legal decision, declaring repentant sinners righteous or innocent as a result of the sacrifice of Christ for them. Yet this is problematic because it seems to link justification with obeying the law, something that Paul rejects in 3:20 ("no one will be declared righteous [justified] in his sight by observing the law"). It could be that Paul is not thinking of present justification but of final justification at the last judgment (so Dunn 1988a; Schreiner 1998); more likely Paul is writing from the standpoint of the Jew under the law, for whom the heart of the matter was obedience and not just hearing (so Barrett 1957; Murray 1968; Stott 1994; Morris 1988; Moo 1996). Of course, none could ever be truly justified by keeping the law, but Jews standing before God are held accountable for their actions.

While the Jews have the law, the Gentiles do not. However, Paul argues that they do have a kind of *law* that God has *written on their hearts* (vv. 14-15). While some have argued that these are Gentile Christians on the grounds that they are the justified of verse 13 (so Cranfield 1975:155-56, following Barth), it is better to see these as pagan Gentiles in keeping with Paul's use throughout chapters 1—3. Paul is saying that even though they do not have the Mosaic law, they do have an internal "law" in the sense of a moral conscience that allows them to understand God's basic requirements, so that they *do by nature things required by*

2:14 Stuhlmacher (1994:44) says, "Paul adopts the view of the early Jewish wisdom theology, according to which God created the world through his creative word (which is identical with wisdom) and thus imprinted all of his creation with a sense

the law. By nature (see also 1:26) is used in accordance with "the typically Stoic thought of the moral law found in nature," a view also seen in Philo and Josephus (Harder 1976:600; cf. also Martens 1994:55-67). Calvin (1974:97-98) called this "common grace," and it means that the Gentiles had a certain innate sense of right and wrong that allowed them at times to do that which was required in God's law. They do not know God, but they have an internal barometer that enables them to know when they are doing wrong in his sight. As Stott says (1994:86), "Not all human beings are crooks, blackguards, thieves, adulterers, and murderers. On the contrary, some honor their parents, recognize the sanctity of human life, are loyal to their spouses, practice honesty, speak the truth and cultivate contentment, just as the last six of the ten commandments require." In this sense the Gentiles become *a law for themselves,* that is, they possess a God-given form of the divine law, a form that is in keeping with the Mosaic law. Paul's point is that the Jews have no true advantage over the Gentiles by having the law, for the Gentiles have their own form of it.

The Gentiles have the law because the law's demands (literally "the work of the law") are *written on their hearts.* The Jews had the law written on stone tablets, while the Gentiles have the law written on their hearts. In other words, both stand before God on an equal footing. We must not be fooled into thinking Paul is saying the Gentiles will be justified by their works. He could not be more clear than in 1:18-32 when he says the works of the Gentiles lead to divine judgment. This will in fact be addressed in the next verse. The point here is that the Gentiles stand alongside the Jews before God. This could allude to the new covenant prophecy of Jeremiah 31:33, "I will put my law in their minds and write it on their hearts." However, Paul is writing not about the new covenant established in the church (cf. Heb 8:8-12) but rather about the conscience of the Gentiles. The idea of *conscience* stems more from Greek than Jewish thought and refers to that inner awareness of right and wrong (see previous paragraph) *bearing*

---

of God and of that which he desires (cf. Prov 8:12-36; Job 28; Sir 24:1-6; Wis 7:15-8:1; 9:1-3)."

witness (along with the law above) to the Gentile regarding proper actions. In other words, the conscience attests to the individual the rightness of a proposed action. As Moo indicates (1996:152 n.), this is both prospective as well as retrospective; that is, it both points out the proper choice and convicts when the wrong path is taken. This witness also has a judicial function, for it is *accusing* or excusing individuals in the midst of their *thoughts* regarding the validity of their choices. That is, their minds form a type of law court in which actions are judged. However, as many point out, the accusations predominate (note that it says *now even defending*), for the Gentiles stand guilty before God.

Finally, this function of the inner law of the heart prepares for the final judgment. The relationship of verse 16 to verses 12-15 is difficult because the previous verses discuss a present work of the conscience while verse 16 links it with the final judgment. Several different solutions have been proposed (see Cranfield 1975; Dunn 1988a; Moo 1996; Schreiner 1998): (1) Some believe it is a later addition, but there are no grounds for such. (2) Verse 16 might connote a present judgment in the mind (like v. 15), but Paul elsewhere uses "the day" for the Day of the Lord at the end of history (e.g., Rom 13:12; 1 Cor 1:8; 2 Cor 1:14; Eph 4:30; Phil 1:6, 10). (3) Both verses 15 and 16 could refer to the final judgment, with the conscience exercised at that final event, but that does not fit the present orientation of verses 14, 15. (4) The NIV places verses 14-15 in parentheses, with the result that verse 16 would go back to verse 13 and justification at the final judgment. However, there is too close a link between verse 15 and verse 16 for this. (5) Verse 16 might sum up the whole paragraph with its emphasis on both present and final judgment. This is partially correct, but the introductory *on the day when* that opens verse 16 points to a special relationship with verse 15. (6) The best option is to see the present activity of the conscience as finding its culmination in the final judgment. In this sense verse 16 is in inclusio with verse 12, both referring to that final consummation when God *will judge [everyone's] secrets*, that is, when all

---

2:22 Moo (1996:164-65) discusses why Paul chose three sins committed infrequently by the Jewish people to demonstrate their failure to live the law. While some say this should be understood in light of Jesus' "deepening" of the law in Matthew 5:21-48, so that everyone has in a sense broken these commandments, there is no hint of that

the things hidden from others will be brought to light by God (1 Sam 16:7; Ps 139:1-2; Mk 4:22 par.; Lk 12:2-3). This is similar to 1 Peter 1:17, where God is described as "a Father who judges each man's work impartially"; that is, he both refuses to play favorites and judges on the basis of the totality of one's actions.

The Jewish Failure to Keep the Law (2:17-29) It is human nature to think we are somehow better than others. We all tend to point to something in our pedigree that makes us stand above the commoners around us, perhaps a successful relative or a moment of victory in the past. For the Jews it was their family tree. They thought that being the recipients of the law placed them above others and gave them a special status before God. In 2:1-16 Paul explained that Jew and Gentile stand equally before God as guilty of sin, and therefore neither can be justified by keeping the law. Now he turns to the other side of the issue. The Jewish people knew they were sinners but believed that they had a special privilege because they were the people of the covenant. Now Paul bursts that bubble as well. He points out first that being the recipients of the law brings them no advantage because they do not truly obey it (vv. 17-24). Then he turns to the covenant and its sign, circumcision, arguing that it does them no good either because they are lawbreakers (vv. 25-29). In this section also, Paul returns to the diatribe style of 2:1-5, challenging *you Jews* (just *you* in NIV) to think seriously about their relationship to God and the law.

The Law and Lawbreakers (2:17-24) Paul discusses the situation of the Jewish people relative to the law in two parts. First (vv. 17-20), he addresses their self-understanding in relation to the law. They thought they had a privileged place because they had the law (vv. 17-18) and therefore were placed in this world to guide the blind and the foolish around them (vv. 19-20). Second (vv. 21-24), he points out to them the basic problem—they had the law but failed to keep it (vv. 21-22). That they transgress their law obviates all the advantages of being

---

here. More likely Paul is using these sins to show that a great gulf exists between their claims and their conduct. The Jews are equally as guilty as the Gentiles because they too have failed to keep God's laws.

the covenant people because they actually dishonor God by breaking the law (vv. 23-24).

The section begins by listing five claims to special privilege (2:17-18). It is commonly assumed that this list is entirely positive, and that Paul is describing the value of the law in Jewish life. That is certainly correct, but in the context Paul also intends to show how they rely on these things too much, and that centering on the law without obeying it leads to hypocrisy and guilt before God.

1. They are Jews, they have the law, and they thus have a special relationship with God. Paul introduces them with a conditional particle, *if,* that recognizes that they make these claims. However, there is no evident *then* clause to draw the conclusion. Most likely Paul intends the rest of the paragraph to answer their claims. Their first claim focuses on their identification as *Jews.* Gutbrod (1965:369-71) says that the term became the normal term used for the Hebrew people by pagans and was then adopted by the Jewish people for themselves, giving the term both national and religious connotations. In the Synoptic Gospels the term is rare, but John frequently uses it to denote the opponents of Jesus. Paul is unique in using the term without the article (as here) to denote the group or type of people who claim attachment to the law (e.g., Gal 2:13; 1 Cor 9:20). So when he says *you call yourself a Jew,* he recognizes that they choose to affirm a special status among the nations.

2. They *rely on the law,* meaning that they "rest upon" or "depend on" the law for their religious identity. Here is the heart of the matter. Of course, the statement in and of itself is positive. They should rely on the law in living their lives (so Ps 1:2; 19:7-11; 119:9-34). However, it was one thing to center on their need for the law but quite another to center on their possession of the law. Their reliance was not so much on their walk with God as it was on the law he gave them, and it gave them a false security. Because of this they felt they were justified in the sight of God and would not have to face judgment.

3. They *brag about [their] relationship to God.* Again, it is completely valid to glory in God and in a true relationship with him (see Ps 34:2; 44:8; Jer 9:23-24; Rom 5:11; 1 Cor 1:31). It is to one's credit to take pride in a right relationship with God. But here there is an absence of

humility that leads them to center on their status rather than on knowing God (contra Schreiner 1998:130, who argues that these statements are intended entirely positively). It is like the self-important elder in a church who walks around with piety as a badge of pride.

4. They *know his will.* Since they had the law, they assumed that in all things they knew what God wanted. Once more, this is positive on the surface and describes a proper use of the law to determine what God demands (Ps 40:8; 143:10; Heb 10:7, 9). Yet the context of the passage implies that the Jews relied on their superior knowledge and felt this in and of itself made them right with God. However, as Paul brings out later, it is one thing to know something and quite another thing to guide your life accordingly.

5. They *approve of what is superior* as they understand it on the basis of the law. There are two ways of understanding this. It could be translated, "approve the things that matter," that is, distinguish between right and wrong (so Godet 1969; Käsemann 1980; Cranfield 1975; Dunn 1988a on the grounds that the term means "the things that differ"), or it could read, "approve the things that are best," that is, that which is truly "excellent" (Murray 1968; Barrett 1957; Morris 1988; Moo 1996; Schreiner 1998). The latter is better because Paul would more likely intend the higher meaning. Also, the section centers on those things that made the Jews feel superior to the Gentiles. They discovered what is best because they were *instructed by the law,* meaning that the Mosaic law was the sole criterion for decisions (as it should have been).

After the list of Jewish "strengths," Paul then turns to a list of four things that describe how the Jews related to the Gentiles (2:19-20). That they were *convinced* of these shows that they considered them their personal prerogatives or rights. They believed that in the law they had the *embodiment of knowledge and truth.* While the Gentiles had knowledge through natural revelation, the Jews felt they personified all knowledge because in the law they had truth. As before, this is largely correct, for the law was divine revelation. But at the same time, if the Gentiles were "without excuse" because of their knowledge (1:20-21), then the Jews were all the more guilty before God. That is the theme of Romans 2. ·

When Paul calls them a *guide for the blind* and *a light for those who are in the dark,* he describes the Jewish mission to the Gentiles. Isaiah

42:6-7 called upon Israel to be "a light for the Gentiles, to open eyes that are blind" (also Is 49:6; Wisdom of Solomon 18:4, "the light of the law given by your sons"). Jesus described this activity in Matthew 23:15, "you (the Pharisees) travel over land and sea to win a single convert." However, there were very real differences within Judaism regarding this mission. Qumran considered the Gentiles predestined for wrath and ignored them. Most activity toward winning Gentiles occurred in the Diaspora (see McKnight 1991:74-77). Sirach 13:1-15 spoke of a "universal brotherhood," and there was interest in proselytes in 2 Esdras 6:26 and *1 Enoch* 48:4. But, for the most part, the conversion of Gentiles was thought to be a triumph for nationalism, and such activity was spasmodic. When Pharisees did "travel over land and sea," they went to the synagogues to talk the God-fearers into going the final step of circumcision in order to become full proselytes. Still, this was missionary activity, and they also thought of themselves as *instructor[s] of the foolish* as well as *teacher[s] of infants.* These are virtually synonymous phrases, and both the *foolish* and *infants* probably refer to the Gentiles, perhaps new converts. As Morris says (1988:134), "Since he had the law, the Jew saw himself as the teacher of the immature Gentiles, people with no knowledge of the living God."

But now Paul turns the tables on the Jewish people in a series of four rhetorical questions (2:21-22), following Jesus' example in the "woes" of Matthew 23 (see especially Mt 23:2-3). In so doing he exposes their hypocrisy—they fail to practice what they preach—and exposes the hypocrisy of all too many people today as well. Summarizing verses 19-20, the first asks the basic question, *you, who teach others, do you not teach yourself?* (v. 21). This parallels Jesus' charge in Matthew 23:15 to the Pharisees who go to the ends of the earth to make a convert: you "make him twice as much a son of hell as you are." It is right that those who have the law teach those who do not, but when they fail to teach themselves, that is, to live by the law they uphold, they obviate their right to teach others.

The other three questions demonstrate the validity of this by giving

2:23 The NIV follows those (Morris 1988; KJV; NRSV; TEV) who make the verse a question *(Do you dishonor God?),* but the change of grammar (from participles in vv. 21-22 to a relative clause in v. 23) makes it more likely that this is a statement and more

examples from the Ten Commandments (as Jesus did in the antitheses of Mt 5:21-48): stealing (the eighth), adultery (the seventh) and idolatry (the first and second); cf. Exodus 20:3-5, 14, 15. The third of these is debated. It is clear what Paul means by saying that they *abhor idols* since the idolatry that occurred so often in Israel according to the Old Testament was virtually unknown in the first century; the Jews were proud of their monotheism, and it was a symbol of their superiority over Gentiles. But it is difficult to see how the Jews would *rob temples*. Stealing from temples did commonly occur in the ancient world (see Josephus *Jewish Antiquities* 4.207), but the word itself can mean either "robbing temples" or "committing sacrilege or irreverent acts" against a temple (so Bauer et al. 1979:373). Therefore many believe that the sin is irreverence toward the Jerusalem temple, perhaps disregarding God by placing the law and themselves above God's will (Hodge 1950; Barth 1933; Barrett 1957; Cranfield 1975) or by magnifying the law so highly that they turn it into an idol (Garlington 1990a:142-51). But this seems an obscure offense to set alongside the Jewish abhorrence of idols. Others see this as stealing from the Jerusalem temple itself (e.g., Bruce 1985), but again this does not parallel idolatry very well. Thus, most likely this refers either to the actual robbery of pagan temples or to the misuse of articles and wealth originally belonging to such temples (Godet 1969; Murray 1968; Michel 1966; Käsemann 1980; Krentz 1990; Stott 1994; Moo 1996; Schreiner 1998), which would have been regarded as taking from the temples by Jews. Derrett (1994:558-71) believes the "robbery" was defrauding pagan temples, but literal robbery is a very real possibility as well. Paul is hardly saying that all Jews did this but rather that it was a well-known practice.

Paul concludes the section by charging the Jewish people with dishonoring the law (2:23-24). First he sums up verses 17-20 by stating that they *brag about the law*. Such boasting (the same term as in v. 17) would be viable if indeed they kept the law, but the problem is they are guilty of *breaking the law*, with the term referring to "transgression" or "violation" of the law (also 4:15; 5:14). Lawbreakers have no right to

closely linked with verse 24 than with verses 21-22 (so Dunn 1988a; Moo 1996; NLT; REB; NJB).

take pride in the law. Thus they *dishonor God* because of their hypocrisy. The whole purpose of the law was to help the Jewish people to honor God by keeping it. Thus they have brought him dishonor; the term also means to "disgrace" or "insult" someone. By their disobedience they have given the Gentiles a reason to heap scorn on God. Then Paul uses Isaiah 52:5 to anchor this charge. In Isaiah 40—66 the exile of Israel is seen as the result of national sin, which has caused the name of God to be mocked by the nations. So here too as a result of Israel's disobedience, *God's name is blasphemed among the Gentiles.* Those who believed they both glorified God and were completely superior to the Gentiles because they had the law were actually no better than the Gentiles. Both Jew and Gentile disobeyed the laws God had given each and so were guilty. In fact, the Jews were worse off because they caused the Gentiles to slander the name of God by their transgressions.

The Inadequacy of Circumcision (2:25-29) While the law was the essence of God's covenant at Sinai, circumcision was the sign of the Abrahamic covenant (Gen 17:9-14). Thus after Paul shows how the disobedience of the Jews has nullified the law (2:12-24), he shows that their transgressions have also nullified the value of circumcision. It is difficult to overstate the importance of this covenant obligation. The *for* (not present in the NIV) that begins this section probably implies a Jewish response that Paul is wrong about their relation to the law because they are the people of circumcision and so are the chosen people of God. In the intertestamental period, Antiochus Epiphanes banned circumcision (1 Maccabees 1:48, 60-61), and as a result it was made even more the single definitive sign of being Jewish (see Schreiner 1998:137). In the New Testament period it was the concluding rite when a Gentile became a Jew; and when the sages "went over land and sea to make a convert" (Mt 23:15), the emphasis was on talking God-fearers into taking the final step of circumcision.

So Paul begins by stating that circumcision only *has value if you observe the law.* The verb for *has value* means to "profit" in terms of their relationship to God. This is a point already made in verse 23, and it applies to their relation both to the law and to circumcision. Disobedience breaks all covenant relationships, so Israel has *become as though [it] had not been circumcised,* like the uncircumcised Gentiles. Thus they too stand under condemnation before God (v. 27). In Galatians 5:3 Paul tells all who are circumcised that they are "obligated to obey the whole law" (also Gal 3:10; 1 Cor 7:19; Jas 2:10). Since they have failed to do so, circumcision has no saving value. As Morris brings out (1988:140), "what is said here of circumcision applies with equal force to baptism." Those who think they are going to heaven because of being baptized but who are not committed to Christ face the same tragic consequence—they too are under God's wrath.

Next, Paul turns to the opposite issue (v. 26). If breaking the law makes the Jewish people "uncircumcised," then will not keeping *the law's requirements* make the Gentiles (the uncircumcised) *as though they were circumcised?* This is not really advocating works-righteousness, for Paul intends only to show that by obedience to the law Gentiles are on the same footing as Jews. This is furthered in verse 27. Not only is the presence of the law and circumcision of no value for the Jewish people, but the uncircumcised who obey the law *will condemn* the Jews on the day of judgment (more likely than present judgment). This is unusual, for normally in Scripture it is God who will be the final judge (Rev 20:11-15). But it was not unusual to state that the saints would also participate in the judgment over sinners (e.g., Wisdom of Solomon 3:8; *1 Enoch* 91:12; Mt 19:28; 1 Cor 6:2; Rev 3:21; 20:4). However, the Jews naturally thought it would be they who would condemn the Gentiles rather than the other way around. So here Paul goes beyond his earlier statements. Not only are Jew and Gentile equally guilty before God, but the Gentiles will actually stand in judgment over the Jews at the last judgment.

This last point is difficult and brings up the same issue as that in 2:7, 10. Is this a hypothetical point regarding Gentiles who may inadvertently obey some aspects of the law and in that way judge the Jews (probably in the sense that their faithfulness to the law stands as evidence against the unfaithfulness of the Jews), or is this a real situation? If so, Schreiner (1998:140-41) is probably correct when he argues that Paul has Christian Gentiles in mind because only they could actually keep the law and stand over the Jews at the last judgment. He finds evidence in their being called *circumcision* in verse 26, implying the community of the redeemed (compare Phil 3:3), and in the fact that they are *regarded* as circumcised, a verb used elsewhere of those in right relationship with God (Rom 3:28; eleven times in 4:3-24; 9:8). Note also the parallel with Romans 8:4, where believers fulfill "the righteous requirements of the law," as well as the concluding statements in verses 28-29 below. In short, this likely refers to Christians among the Gentiles who will fulfill the law in Christ and thus stand in judgment of unbelieving Jews at the eschaton.

Paul then tells why *(gar)* circumcision no longer makes one right with God by differentiating between a professing Jew and a true Jew (2:28-29). One cannot be in right relationship with God merely by possessing the covenant signs of the law and circumcision. Such are outward or external realities, and they no longer make one right with God. Since Christ has come, it is the *inward* or internal reality that matters. In other words, it is not the act of circumcision but *circumcision of the heart* that God demands. This was also demanded in the Old Testament, as in Deuteronomy 10:16 or Jeremiah 4:4 ("circumcise your hearts"); cf. also Jeremiah 9:25-26. Of course, Paul gives this an entirely new meaning, for this internal reality is now completely realized in Christ and made possible by the Spirit, and only in both can it occur. There are several contrasts here—*outwardly/inwardly, physical/of the heart, written code/Spirit, from men/from God*. Each is important. For instance, the *written code* is the Mosaic law, and the *Spirit* is not the human spirit (e.g., NRSV, "it is spiritual and not literal") but the Holy Spirit. As several commentators point out (Käsemann 1980; Moo 1996; Schreiner 1998), this is a salvation-historical switch—the Old Testament covenant centering on the law has now given way to the New Testament covenant centering on the age of the Spirit. Therefore, the true follower of God seeks praise not from people but *from God,* most likely again a reference to the final judgment (see 2:16). The message is just as important for our day as it was for Paul's. It is just as easy today to center on the external (church attendance, activity or external piety)

2:29 The contrast between the letter and the spirit has often been used (e.g., in the Alexandrian school of interpretation following Origen) to contrast interpreting the Bible "in the spirit" (i.e., in allegorical fashion) with interpreting "in the letter" (i.e.,

rather than on one's relationship with God. As Stott says (1994:94), "Human beings are comfortable with what is outward, visible, material and superficial. What matters to God is a deep, inward, secret work of the Holy Spirit in our hearts."

God's Faithfulness and Israel's Failure (3:1-8) The diatribe style of Romans 2 continues with the rhetorical questions of this section. There are two parts: 3:1-4 on the faithfulness of God and 3:5-8 answering objections to his righteousness. Moo (1996:179) is probably correct in saying that Paul focuses on the Jews throughout verses 1-8 rather than shifting to a general objection in verses 5-8. The basic issue is this: if there is no advantage in being Jewish, and if God can reject one of his covenant people, then how can it be said that God is faithful to his covenant promises? Paul's lengthier response in Romans 9—11 is anticipated here: God's response in judgment also constitutes being faithful to his promises. The covenant contained blessings and curses (= salvation and judgment here), and both are proper depending on the actions of the covenant people. So Paul's purpose is to demonstrate the justice of God in terms of Israel's unbelief. The people of Israel have brought about the situation, and God's righteousness is apparent at every point. Yet at the same time nearly all commentators agree with Godet's judgment (1969:131) that this is "one of the most difficult [portions], perhaps, in the epistle." The problem is the logic behind the questions and Paul's responses. I will try to make this logic plain as I discuss the passage.

The Faithfulness of God (3:1-4) This proceeds in two parts (1-2, 3-4), each introduced by a rhetorical question. In chapter 2 Paul argued that neither the law nor circumcision availed the Jewish people because they failed to obey the law; therefore Jew and Gentile stand before God equally as sinners. Thus the natural question arises, *What advantage, then, is there in being a Jew?* Throughout their history the Jews believed that since they possessed the law, they were the chosen people. If Paul was correct that there was no advantage whatsoever,

---

in literal fashion). But that has no place here, for Paul is clearly contrasting the *written code* of the law with the inner work of the Spirit.

then for instance *what value is there in circumcision?* If true circumcision is of the heart rather than physical circumcision (2:28-29), then the natural conclusion is that there is no profit whatsoever in being a member of the covenant people. Paul answers that there is *much* advantage *in every way,* meaning that there are a great number of advantages. Here we must remember that Paul never denied there was value in possessing the law; he only said that these advantages did not automatically give the Jews special privileges over the Gentiles. Both were to be judged at the *bēma* seat of God on the basis of their keeping the law, not on the basis of who possessed it. So Paul mentions the primary advantage—*they have been entrusted with the very words of God.* Because of Paul's introduction of this with *first of all,* one would expect a list of items to follow (as in 9:4-5—"the adoption of sons; . . . the divine glory, the covenants, the receiving of the law, the temple worship and the promises . . . the patriarchs"). However, there is only one item, so most likely this is akin to "foremost of all": the *words of God* are esteemed as the primary blessing God has given his people. In the Greek this is actually "the oracles of God" (the only time Paul uses this phrase in his writings), and some have seen this as the Mosaic law (as in Acts 7:38). Literally, the term refers to "sayings" or "pronouncements," and many have interpreted it here in terms of the divine promises to Israel that were behind his *faithfulness* (3:3). In a sense, both are correct, and it is best seen in its broadest sense: the entire Old Testament as the source of God's covenant promises to Israel.

Now Paul turns to the second difficulty, the faithfulness of God in light of Jewish unbelief. There are two questions in verse 3, and several ways to understand them (see Cranfield 1975:179-80; Moo 1996:183-84): (1) both questions voice objections to Paul's thesis; (2) both questions stem from Paul (with the primary question being *what then?* (not included in NIV); (3) the first is an objection and the second Paul's re-

---

3:2 Dodd (1932:68) calls this response "obscure" because Paul had already shown in chapter 2 that there was no advantage whatsoever in being a Jew. He believes Paul answers his own question and fudges on his answer because of his own Jewish heritage. However, this is a perfectly reasonable response in light of the purposes of this section and fits the logic of the whole of 2:1—3:8. The Jewish people had the advantage of possessing the law as the *words of God* but squandered it because of their disobedience.

sponse to it. While all three can make sense, the second is the most likely. Paul is saying in effect, "What then do we do with the fact of God's blessings upon Israel (3:2) in light of his judgment upon them for unbelief (2:2-3, 5, 12, 16, 25-27)?" His response then comes via two further questions: "What about some Jews who have not been faithful? Their unfaithfulness cannot nullify God's faithfulness, can it?" (the second question is written in such a way as to expect the answer "no"). God's covenant promises can never be *nullified,* a favorite term of Paul's (twenty-five times) that means to "render powerless" or even "wipe out" a thing (Bauer et al. 1979:417). In the covenant ceremony of Genesis 15:1-21 God had Abraham sacrifice a heifer, a goat, and a ram and then lay "the halves opposite each other." Then God caused a deep sleep to descend on him and sent a vision in which a "smoking firepot with a blazing torch" passed between the parts. Wenham (1987:332-33) states that this was a symbol of God walking between the parts, a covenant rite that was an "enacted curse," saying in effect, "May this happen to me if I do not fulfill this covenant" (see also Jer 34:18). In this sense God is guaranteeing his faithfulness in keeping his covenant. Nothing can invalidate his promises.

However, Israel can fail to keep its covenant promises and thus bring upon itself the covenant curse. That is exactly what Paul is talking about here. The irony is that for four hundred years Israel (for the first time in its history) had failed to fall into idolatry and had centered on the Torah. However, when they rejected God's Messiah (Cosgrove 1987b:96-98 believes the *lack of faith* is mainly unbelief in Christ), they failed at the core of the covenant, so they were now more apostate than before; indeed, the Jewish unbelievers have been removed from the olive tree (Rom 11:17-21). Yet this is also a lesson for us all, as Paul goes on to say in Romans 11:22, which warns that God's mercy will be experienced only by those who "continue in his kindness. Otherwise,

---

3:3 Morris (1988:154) notes the debate about whether it should be "were unfaithful" (NRSV; NLT; Moffatt; Hodge 1950; Bruce 1985; Dunn 1988a; Schreiner 1998; Moo 1996) or *did not believe* (NIV; NASB; Sanday and Headlam 1902; Murray 1968; Cranfield 1975). He points out correctly that the context (centering of the "faithfulness" of God) strongly supports the former. It is not so much unbelief in Christ as it is their failure to obey the Torah that is the chief issue in this section.

you also will be cut off." We must all examine ourselves constantly to
see where we really stand with God, not where we think we stand!

Paul's response to the question is stated emphatically in verse 4. *Not
at all!* is the famous "God forbid" of the KJV, the strongest possible negation of a question. Fitzmyer (1993b:327-28) calls it a negative oath
("Let it not be so!") and points to its use in the LXX (e.g., Gen 44:7, 17) to
translate the Hebrew "Far be it from me." Jewish unfaithfulness can
never cancel God's faithfulness. Instead, *let God be true and everyone a
liar.* Behind the term *true* is the Old Testament term for "faithful"
(emet), meaning God is true to his promises. Once more, this refers to
the covenant promises of the Old Testament, containing blessings for
the faithful and curses for the unfaithful. So God is *true* in judging Israel (as stated in Ps 45:4; 96:13; Neh 9:32-33; so Moo 1996:185). In contrast, every person is *a liar,* a likely allusion to Psalm 116:11, "And in
my dismay I said, 'All men are liars.'" The question here is whether
Paul is stretching the imagery to every human being or restricting it to
Israel in this context. These are not mutually exclusive. Israel is being
included in the totality of humanity as a *liar* or one unfaithful to the
covenant (that is, promising to obey and then failing to do so).

Paul then anchors this with a specific quotation (note *as it is written*
here) from Psalm 51:4, *so that you may be proved right when you speak
and prevail when you judge.* The quotation opens with a purpose
statement, *Let God be true . . . so that.* God's faithfulness and truth will
be vindicated in judging Israel (contra Käsemann 1980:81, who takes it
of justification). Psalm 51 is David's lament when he confesses his sin
of adultery with Bathsheba, and in Psalm 51:4 he says that because of
his evil act, any judgment God places on him will be just. Paul applies
this confession to Israel's sin, in effect saying that God's judgment on
the nation is also just. The key is that Israel did not believe they had
broken the covenant and so felt they should be exempt from such

---

3:5 Piper (1983:107-9) argues that the *righteousness* here must be saving rather than
punitive righteousness on the grounds that it makes better sense (how can my sin
shed light on God's judgment by making him unrighteous for punishing me?) and
fits the emphasis on God's salvation in verses 2-4. Schreiner (1998:156-57, following
Räisanen 1983) responds that the Jewish objection is actually that if humans are
completely unable to avoid sin, then God is unjust to punish them for it (see v. 7).
Paul then responds that God is indeed just when he punishes sin, for he is acting in

charges. Paul acts as a prosecuting attorney in telling them that they are wrong. God cannot be faithful to his covenant until he judges Israel; only then will he be *proved right* to his promises (and warnings).

Objections to God's Righteousness (3:5-8) While some call this a digression on the basis of a possible misunderstanding of Paul's argument (Cranfield 1975:183), the objections here are integral to the argument. Again, there are two parts (vv. 5-6, 7-8), and both stem from Paul's own paraphrasing of Jewish objections to his arguments in verses 1-4 (especially v. 4). If it is true that the *unrighteousness* (literally "wickedness") of the people of God (as above, this likely refers to Jewish sin more than to that of humanity in general) actually *brings out God's righteousness more clearly,* one could ask, "What should we conclude?" So Paul is asking what light wickedness can shed on divine righteousness. The second question is again phrased in such a way as to anticipate the answer "no": "God is not *unjust in bringing his wrath on us,* is he? As in chapter 2, this is the wrath of the last judgment, and the question once more is the justice of God in judging his people rather than saving them. The basic message is the same as in 2:1—3:4: when God judges his people, he is faithful to his covenant promises because evil works demand judgment. Finally, Paul adds that he is *using a human argument* to clarify that when he even raises the question of divine injustice, he does so from a purely human point of view (compare Gal 3:15; 1 Cor 9:8). Simple logic will acknowledge the rightness of God's judgment upon evil.

Paul's response to the second question of verse 5 is another strong negation (cf. v. 4): *Certainly not!* As Morris says (1988:159), "It is unthinkable that God could be unjust (cf. Abraham's question, Gen. 18:25, and that of Elihu, Job 34:17)." If that were the case, *how could God judge the world?* It is difficult to know whether this is present judgment (the verb is a present indicative) or the future final judgment (it could be a fu-

---

accord with his righteousness in doing so.
3:6 Inaugurated eschatology is the doctrine that with the coming of Christ the last days have begun (as in "inaugural address") but will not culminate until the second coming. Thus we are living in a time of tension between the "already" (the kingdom of God as present with us) and the "not yet" (the kingdom of God as yet to be consummated).

turistic present, "going to judge"). In light of the inaugurated eschatology of Paul, the two could well be intended together—judging the world now as an anticipation of final judgment. However, in light of the emphasis throughout chapters 2—3, the final thrust is predominant. This is a key doctrine of the Old Testament (see also Deut 32:4; Job 8:3; 2 Chron 19:7; Ezek 18:25), and Paul is saying in effect, "If God is unjust in judging the Jews, how can he judge the Gentiles as well?" (so Schreiner 1998:158). God's ability and right to judge are at stake.

The second part of the paragraph (vv. 7-8) repeats the basic Jewish objection of verse 5 another way, using the falsehood of verse 4: *If my falsehood enhances God's truthfulness and so increases his glory, why am I still condemned as a sinner?* The point is that if sin is used positively to bring glory to God for his righteousness, then the sinner should be applauded for doing so rather than punished. So if human lies highlight the truthfulness of God, they are a good thing. The emphasis is on the term *glory,* stemming from the Jewish concern for the glory of God. That is the highest pursuit of every person, so if my sin actually does bring glory to God, how then can it be worthy of judgment?

Their objection is furthered in verse 8 by their claim that Paul is in effect saying, *"Let us do evil that good may result."* This is so illogical that it scandalizes Paul. Most likely, this was a common charge made against Paul by his opponents in Rome and elsewhere (so Stuhlmacher 1994; Moo 1996; contra Dunn 1988a) and is the natural conclusion of the objections in verses 5, 7. If sin does highlight the righteousness of God (v. 5) and bring him glory (v. 7), then we should try to sin even more so as to bring even more good out of it (v. 8). Paul's response is twofold: first, the rumor spread about Paul's teaching is "blasphemy" (the other meaning of *slander* here; both aspects are probably intended) because the charge impugned both the character of God and the gospel he had given Paul. Second, *their condemnation is deserved.* This could mean that their argument should be condemned or that they

---

3:8 There is debate whether verse 8 should be taken as Paul's response to the objection of verse 7 (so Cranfield 1975; Stott 1994) or another part of the objections in verses 5 and 7 (so Murray 1968; Barrett 1957; Dunn 1988a; Morris 1988; Moo 1996). The former is viable because otherwise Paul never responds to this second objection. But the latter is favored both by the "and" (absent in NIV) introducing the verse

themselves (more likely all the objectors of vv. 5-8 and not just the slanderers of v. 8) should be condemned. The latter is far more likely in light of the emphasis throughout chapters 2—3, and the emphasis is upon the "justness" (the actual meaning of *deserved* here) of God's judgment. This is a fitting end for this section, concluding the basic point that God is righteous and just when he judges sinners, for his covenant demands that he do so.

☐ The Sinfulness of All Humanity (3:9-20)

One of the greatest powers of rationalization ever seen is the ability of people to explain away their sin. Our society finds all types of excuses, like poor parenting, social disadvantages, mistreatment by others and so on. Very few admit the truth: we are all guilty and accountable for our actions. Virtually all non-Christian religions assume that there is good in everyone and that everyone will be all right if he or she does more good than bad. Paul demonstrates the sinfulness of the Gentiles in 1:18-20 and the sinfulness of the Jews in 2:1—3:8. Now he concludes his discussion by emphasizing the guilt of all people under sin. There are three sections: an introductory rhetorical question and answer on the universal nature of sin (v. 9), a series of Old Testament quotations that demonstrate the extent of their depravity (vv. 10-18), and a concluding summary stating that the whole world is unrighteous and accountable to God (vv. 19-20).

The Universal Nature of Sin (3:9) The introductory *what . . . then* was also used in 3:1 and here probably should be read as a separate question as in the NIV, *What shall we conclude then?* Most likely it relates to all of 2:1—3:8 and not just to 3:1-8. The second question could be translated several ways since the verb can mean "make an excuse," "surpass," or "have an advantage" (see Cranfield 1975; Morris 1988; Moo 1996; Schreiner 1998): (1) "Should I (editorial 'we') make excuse

---

(indicating a connection between vv. 7 and 8) and by the fact that Paul claims he is slanderously accused of this very thing. Paul's response is implicit in the use of "blasphemy" (NIV, *slanderously*) to describe their claim and by the conclusion that *their condemnation is deserved.*

for the Jews?" (2) "Should we Jews make excuse for ourselves?" (3) "Are we Jews surpassed by them (i.e., inferior to them)?" (4) "Do we Jews have an advantage over them?" The first is problematic because the context points more to the Jews than to Paul as the subject. The first two are also difficult because the verb nearly always has an object when it means "make excuse" ("for something"). The third is based on an extremely rare use of the word and does not quite fit the context of 3:1-8 (where no true contrast between Jew and Gentile is developed). Most scholars today (contra Dunn 1988a:146, who prefers the second option) accept the fourth as the most likely, since it fits the context (3:1-2) and the message of verses 9-20. Yet this is also a rare use of the verb, for the middle voice employed by Paul here normally fits the first two options rather than the third. However, the middle voice in the New Testament period was in a state of flux, and there are many examples of middle verbs with active meanings. So the question relates to the basic issue of 2:1—3:8, the advantages of Jews over Gentiles as the covenant people of God.

Cranfield (1975:190) interprets *not at all* as "not altogether" or "not in every respect" on the basis of word order (literally "not in every way") and the connection with 3:2, where an advantage is listed. But more likely this is simply a variation of Paul's emphatic negatives in verses 4 and 6 and does mean "certainly not." The advantage of verse 2 (the Jews "have been entrusted with the very words of God") does not mean that they are not answerable for their sins. In fact, it is just the opposite; the words of God have shown their guilt before him. Paul has *already made the charge* in 1:18—2:29 that Jew and Gentile are equally *under sin*. Sin is personified here as a malignant force placing humanity "under" its power. Stott (1994:99) describes it as "a cruel tyrant who holds the human race imprisoned in guilt and under judgment. Sin is on top of us, weighs us down, and is a crushing burden." We will later note Paul's image of the two realms, that of sin and that of Christ. Here sin conquers all people and forces them to live under its power.

The Extent of Their Depravity (3:10-18) Paul introduces this catena or list of Old Testament passages (the rabbis called this "pearl-stringing," with one pearl after another being given) with his characteristic *as it is* *written.* The organization of the citations may well be topical, with the thesis of universal sin stated in verses 10-12 followed by specific acts of sin—sins of speech (vv. 13-14) and of murder and its results (vv. 15-17)—and finally by the religious aspect of sin: no fear of God (v. 18; note the inclusio with the end of v. 11). The first passage is Psalm 14:1-3 (also Ps 53:1-3), though verse 10 here deviates from the psalm and may well be a summary introduction to the whole (perhaps adapting Ps 14:1; compare Sirach 7:20). Of special importance is the statement that none are *righteous,* since that is the major theme of 1:18—3:20 (cf. 1:17, 32; 2:5, 13, 26; 3:4, 5, 8, 19, 20). In light of total depravity, every single person stands before God stripped of all pretensions to righteousness. This is developed further with two statements taken from Psalm 14 (the famous psalm that begins, "The fool says in his heart, 'There is no God'"), centering on the complete lack of understanding and of seeking God. This is not just passive ignorance but active rejection (as in 1:18-21), and it is closely connected with a refusal to seek God, a preference for the things of this world rather than the things of God (cf. Mt 6:19-21; Mk 8:33; Col 3:1-2). Total depravity by definition means that people want nothing to do with God; and in fact, whenever they choose between God and their selfish desires, they always choose against God. This is because they *have turned away* from God and thus have become absolutely *worthless,* as in the fool's denial of God in Psalm 14:1. Craigie (1983:147) defines the fool as one who "lives as if there were no covenant, and thus as if there were no God." This is not so much the atheist as the fool who simply has no place for God, no time for him. The conclusion is *there is no one who does good.* This is a natural outgrowth of the list thus far. Those who have no righteousness and reject God are certainly going to fail to do good. The self-centered, worldly person will do only that which is good for themselves, not for others or for God. The world's golden rule is, "Do unto others before they can do unto you!"

The sins of speech (3:13-14) combine three different Old Testament passages held together by the organs of speech—the throat, the tongue, the lips and the mouth. The first is taken from Psalm 5:9 and depicts the *throats* of the wicked as *open graves,* a particularly apt metaphor for that which continually produces unclean things (like a corpse). Coming out of it will be decay and death. It does not take much imagination to see the many connections between evil speech and the grave. Morris adds, "An open tomb may be thought of as a tomb ready to receive the dead; taken this way the words point to the murderous impulses of the wicked (cf. Luther, 'they devour the dead' . . .)" (1988:167). As such this would prepare for verses 15-17. The next three statements give illustrations of the deadly results of this. First, *their tongues practice deceit,* noting the treacherous trickery that always accompanies evil deeds. Second (from Ps 140:3), *the poison of vipers is on their lips,* referring to the destructive effects of the tongue, but even more to the desire to inflict harm on the other person. Sanday and Headlam (1902:79) note that the text actually says it is *under* their lips, the actual "position of the poison-bag of the serpent," possibly referring to the bite (Num 21:9; Prov 33:32) rather than the forked tongue. Third (from Ps 10:7), *their mouths are full of cursing and bitterness,* noting the habitual tendency of sinful human beings to complain and curse when they fail to get their way.

The sins of violence (3:15-17) are drawn from Isaiah 59:7-8, where they are part of a section describing the sinful corruption of Israel. Another part of the body, *their feet,* probably chosen to symbolize the direction of one's life, *are swift to shed blood* (see also Prov 1:16), a reference to the ease with which people hurt and kill each other. As in the image of *their mouths are full* (v. 14), so *their feet are swift* points to the frequency with which these terrible things occur. The results of these violent acts are seen in the other two statements: (1) *ruin and misery,* pointing to the destruction and sorrow that inevitably flow out of such violent occasions, and (2) the rejection of any *way of peace,* with *do not know* referring not to ignorance but to willful repudiation (as in 1:18-21; 3:11) of any possibility of peace. Their desire is to destroy others, not to establish peaceful relations.

Finally (v. 18), they have *no fear of God,* a phrase drawn from Psalm 36:1, where the sinfulness of humanity is contrasted to the righteousness of God. In Proverbs the "fear of God" is the basis of wisdom (Prov 1:7; 9:10; 15:33). As so often in Scripture, *fear* means not just reverence for

---

3:19 Some (e.g., Murray 1968; Hendriksen 1981) expand *those . . . under the law* to include Jews and Gentiles on the basis of the preceding context (the universality of sin). Hendriksen (1981:124) reasons, "Does not the law, God's word, have a mes-

God but terror of his judgment (cf. 1 Pet 1:17). In verse 18 the final part of the body is noted, namely, *their eyes,* probably referring to their outlook on life. The illogical extent to which people think only of the here and now and ignore eternity (or even deny the possibility of eternity) is a tragic byproduct of human self-centeredness. Even more illogical is the incredible effort people give to preparing for the few years of retirement and the corresponding total neglect of preparing for eternity. God is the final Judge who will determine where we spend eternity, and to refuse to give any thought to the ultimate future is the height of folly.

Conclusion Regarding the Universality of Sin (3:19-20) In reality 3:19-20 concludes not just chapter 3 but the whole section on the sinfulness of Gentile and Jew in 1:18—3:18. While the world does not know God (3:11), Paul says that *we know* certain things. As in 2:2, he appeals to a generally recognized truth to make his point. *The law* here refers to that just quoted in verses 10-18, namely, the whole Old Testament (the quotations are taken from the Psalms and Isaiah, not the Pentateuch) as well as the Mosaic law (the normal meaning of *the law*). Yet the Torah is still highlighted, for the statement that the law speaks primarily *to those who are under the law* certainly refers to the Jews under the Mosaic ordinances (though the Old Testament as a whole is probably included here as well; cf. 3:2). The twofold purpose of the Old Testament law is then given. First, *every mouth* must be *silenced.* The difficulty here is that the first half addresses only the Jewish people while the second half expands that to include everyone. This undoubtedly addresses the false security of the Jews who believed that the condemnation of the Old Testament was addressed primarily to the Gentiles while they were safe on the basis of being the covenant people. The Old Testament teaches that everyone comes under the judgment of God and thus that *the whole world,* Jew as well as Gentile, is *held accountable to God.* Moo (1996:205) sees a courtroom metaphor here. All are silenced because they have no defense as they stand before God, and they are "liable to persecution" (the meaning of *ac-*

sage for all? . . . And does it not concern all, without exception, whether they be Jews and Gentiles by race?" In one sense this is correct, but it is difficult to see how Paul's readers would think of anyone other than the Jews (see on 2:12).

countable) before God the Judge as he pronounces the verdict. The point is the universal guilt of all people, Jew and Gentile, before the righteous judgment seat of God.

Scholars are divided over whether *therefore* (Greek *dioti*) in verse 20 refers to a confirmation (Cranfield 1975; Moo 1996) or a reason (Sanday and Headlam 1902; Morris 1988; Schreiner 1998) for verse 19. In light of the subject matter, it is best to see it as a confirmation of the preceding, stating the same truth in slightly different form. Paul probably echoes Psalm 143:2 here: "no one living is righteous before you." The point is that no person can be "justified" or *declared righteous* by God on the basis of *observing the law*, or "works of the law." This means that the works of the law can never suffice to make a person acceptable to God; that is, no one can keep God's laws perfectly enough to get to heaven. It is clear that *observing the law* here refers to the requirements of the whole law (more the Old Testament law than God's law generally for all people). As often pointed out, this is fairly synonymous with "works" in general in 4:4-6 but viewed specifically from the perspective of the Jews. The point is that no one, Jew or Gentile, can find salvation by works. This is a fitting conclusion for chapter 2, which taught that the Jewish people would stand before God guilty because they transgressed the law. The true purpose of the law is not to "justify" but to force people to *become conscious of sin,* that is, to have "knowledge of sin." This does not mean that the law causes them to sin, but it causes them to be aware that their transgressions are indeed sin. In spite of the powers of rationalization to explain away sin, deep

---

3:20 The meaning of "works of the law" (NIV, *observing the law*) as attempts to be accepted by God has been challenged from several perspectives. German scholars in the Bultmann camp have said that anyone who tries to obey the law sins by definition, for such an attempt is idolatrous since salvation can only come by grace (so Bultmann 1955:52; Käsemann 1980:89). But this is clearly wrong, for Paul is not saying that keeping the law is sin. In fact, just the opposite: failing to keep the law is sin. The more important challenge comes from "the new perspective on Paul," a movement centered on E. P. Sanders and James D. G. Dunn. Sanders (1977) developed his view of "covenantal nomism," stating that for the Jews there was no issue of getting in the covenant but only of staying in it. Therefore, the law was for maintaining their relationship with God, and the "works of the law" were simply the means by which one remained in the covenant. This was modified by Dunn (1988a:153-54, 158; 1992b:99-117), who interpreted the "works of the law" as the

down all human beings are conscious of the evil within them and of the deeds that result from that depravity.

SALVATION FROM GOD ON THE BASIS OF FAITH (3:21—8:39)

How can a person be saved? That question has been the subject of two thousand years of discussion in church history. Nowhere in the Bible is the answer clearer than in this section of Romans. Those who think we participate in producing our salvation need to listen to the clarion call of the sovereignty of God in salvation. Those who believe we can earn it by our works must listen to the emphasis on the sacrifice of Christ as the only basis for salvation. Moreover, in this section we also learn that justification and sanctification are not two separate experiences but interconnected aspects of salvation (especially chap. 6). Justification is the first moment of sanctification. There are two major sections: (1) the righteousness of God in justification (3:21—4:25) and (2) the new life and hope provided for those in Christ (5:1—8:39).

☐ The Righteousness of God in Justification (3:21—4:25)

Paul has demonstrated beyond doubt the insufficiency of Jew and Gentile for achieving salvation on their own. The universal sinfulness of all humanity demands judgment (1:18—3:20). Is there any hope? Paul gives his resounding answer in this section, *But now a righteousness from God . . . has been made known* (3:21). This is in embryo the theme of the entire epistle—God has displayed his righteousness in providing the salvation humankind could not attain. What human beings could not do for

---

"boundary markers" that differentiated a Jew from a Gentile, "those acts prescribed by the law by which a member of the covenant people identified himself as a Jew and maintained his status within the covenant" (1988a:158). Therefore, Paul rejected the "works of the law" because it offered salvation to the Jews alone and excluded the Gentiles. This has rightly been challenged by Cranfield (1991:89-101), Moo (1996:206-17) and Schreiner (1998:171-74), who point out that such works were never "identity markers" or nationalistic indicators, and that chapter 2 clearly teaches that the Jewish people will be judged by God on the basis of their failure to keep the law. For Paul, transgressing the law is sin, and the problem is human inability to obey the law. As Moo says (1996:215-16), Sanders's very thesis that works for the Jews were a means of "staying in" indicates that at the final judgment works would play "a necessary and instrumental role in 'salvation.' " This in fact is the point of 3:20, that no one can be "justified" (NIV, *declared righteous*) on the basis of works.

themselves God has done for them. Over against the absolute depravity of the Gentiles and the legal self-righteousness of the Jews God has shown his grace—the sacrificial death of Christ has brought redemption out of hopelessness. Moreover, sinful humanity can experience this by responding in faith. But the key point is that faith is the only means of justification. There are three sections here: the thesis statement (of the whole epistle, building on 1:16-17) in 3:21-26; the centrality of righteousness by faith not by works in 3:27-31; and the supreme model of Abraham, who was justified by faith not works, in 4:1-25.

Thesis—The Righteousness of God and Justification (3:21-26)
This is the core of Romans and indeed of any discussion of the doctrine of salvation. Every aspect is here. Dominating the landscape is the phrase from 1:17, *righteousness from God* (3:21, 22, 25, 26), for his righteousness is the basis of salvation. Then come the primary Pauline terms that describe the process of salvation. Let me give them in logical order rather than in the order of this text. At the outset, Christ has given himself as the *sacrifice of atonement* or "propitiation" for our sins (v. 25), producing in his sacrificial death the atoning work that makes salvation possible. In so doing, then, he has provided *redemption* by making the "ransom" payment that has "freed" us from our sins (v. 24). Finally, as sinners respond by faith, they are *justified* or "declared righteous" by a just God (vv. 24, 26). As Moo suggests (1996:220-21), Paul may well reflect a set creedal tradition in what he says here; that is, it sums up the basic gospel as developed by the apostles themselves.

God's Righteousness Revealed (3:21) With *but now* Paul returns to the topic of 1:17, the *righteousness from God*. Obviously a change of tone from 3:9-20 has occurred, but is the change logical (concluding the teaching in 1:18—3:20) or temporal (moving from the old situation of Jews and Gentiles under sin to the new age of salvation inaugurated by Christ)? The latter is more likely, for Paul tells us here that as a result of Christ's sacrificial act a new era, one of salvation, has dawned. As Schreiner says (1998:180, building on Wilckens 1978), this indicates "a salvation-historical shift between the old covenant and the new." God's "saving righteousness" has been "actualized in history." As stated in 1:17, *righteousness from God* refers to his act of justifying sinners and making them right in his eyes. This divine act of righteousness has now been *made known* or "manifested" to humankind, referring to its revelation in Christ (cf. "revealed" in 1:17).

Summing up the emphasis of 2:1—3:8, Paul then adds that this must come *apart from the law.* In one sense this means that righteousness cannot come by "observing the law," i.e., "the works of the law" (v. 20; so Hodge 1950; Nygren 1949; Cranfield 1975), but in another sense this refers to the new era inaugurated by Christ, a new age of salvation in which God will deliver people *apart from* the law (so Moo 1996). The latter is better since *apart from the law* modifies *made known* more than it does *a righteousness from God* and so refers to the process by which it is revealed rather than to the way it is received by us. Moreover, Paul adds, this change is in keeping with the Old Testament; it is testified to or "witnessed to" by *the Law and the Prophets,* a frequent way of referring to the whole Old Testament (with *the Prophets* referring to the rest of the Old Testament apart from the Pentateuch; cf. Mt 11:13; Lk 16:16; Acts 24:14). This means that the Old Testament prepared for the age of justification, as seen especially in the "new covenant" prophecy of Jeremiah 31:31-34, "The time is coming . . . when I will make a new covenant . . . not like the covenant I made with their forefathers" (cf. Heb 8:8-12).

The Righteousness of God Received (3:22-23) The means by which (Greek *dia*) the repentant sinner receives this divine gift is *faith.* As Paul says in Ephesians 2:8-9, this faith does not constitute "works" because it is a "gift of God" rather than just an act of human volition. As the Holy Spirit opens the heart to God, faith is the passive acceptance of God's salvation. It is still a faith decision, but it is the human response to the Spirit's work. We do not control the process; God does. It is the universal convicting power of the Holy Spirit that allows the sinner to make a faith decision, that is, to accept God's offer of salvation or on the other hand to reject that offer. Michel (1975:599, 601-2) discusses the centrality of faith for Paul, noting that it is both saving faith called for in Gospel proclamation and a gift of divine grace. However, there is a great debate here as to whether *faith [of] Jesus Christ* (NIV has *in*) should be interpreted as "faith in Jesus Christ" (an objective genitive, the traditional view) or as "the faithfulness of Jesus Christ" (a subjective genitive, so Johnson 1982:77-90; B. W. Longenecker 1993:478-80; for an interesting historical survey see Pollard 1997). This latter would remove the repetitive nature of *faith . . . to all who believe* and allow the movement to be from the faithfulness of Christ to our faith. Moreover, there are examples of the subjective genitive in Romans (e.g., the "God's faithfulness" in 3:3 or the "faith of Abraham" in 4:12, 16). Nevertheless, while that would make sense, we must agree with the strong arguments of Moo (1996:225) and Schreiner (1998:182-86) that the objective genitive is more likely. There are many examples of an objective sense in the New Testament (e.g., Mk 11:22; Acts 3:16; Col 2:12; Jas 2:1; Rev 2:13; 14:12), and it fits the context here much better since throughout 3:21—4:25 *faith* speaks of belief in Christ (seventeen times!). Moreover, in the immediate context the contrast is between finding the *righteousness from God* via the law or via faith. Finally, there is no tautology between *faith* and *all who believe,* for the latter shows the all-inclusive nature of God's righteousness—it is for *all,* both Jews and Gentiles. As 2:1—3:8 has argued, there is only one way to experience God's saving righteousness—through faith not works—and it is available to all who put their faith in Christ.

Verses 22-23 explain the reason for the universal availability of this righteousness. Paul explains that *there is no difference* or "distinction" between Jew and Gentile, a point made throughout 1:18—3:20. Since both Gentile and Jew are guilty before God due to sin, they stand before him on equal footing. Thus Paul can summarize in that famous verse, *for all have sinned and fall short of the glory of God.* The verb *sinned* is global, referring to all the sins of the human race as a complete whole. All stand as sinners, guilty before God and deserving of judgment. None are worthy of his grace. The reason is that they *fall short,* a present tense that shows the present results of the fact of sin. They cannot meet the standard of God's righteousness on their own.

3:24 There has been considerable debate about whether verses 24-26 stem from creedal tradition (see Käsemann 1980:173 n.) or just verses 24-25 (see Dunn 1988a:163-64). This is decided on the basis of non-Pauline language (*presented, sacrifice of atonement, demonstrate, sins, committed beforehand, forbearance, present*), which is primarily in verse 25-26, with verse 24 possibly being pre-Pauline on the basis of the awkward participle "being justified" (NIV *and are justified*) that intro-

Stott (1994:109) quotes Bishop Handley Moule here: "The harlot, the liar, the murderer, are short of it [sc. God's glory]; but so are you. Perhaps they stand at the bottom of the mine, and you are on the crest of an Alp; but you are as little able to touch the stars as they." The *glory of God* here adds an eschatological element, referring to "that share of the divine glory, which, in Jewish thought, man possessed before he fell away from his true relationship to God and which will be restored in the eschatological future (cf. 5:2; 8:18, 21, 30)" (Cranfield 1975:204). As both Jews and Christians believed, the glory was lost in Adam. (In *Apocalypse of Moses* 21:6 Adam says to Eve, "You have deprived me of the glory of God.") While in one sense both unbelievers and believers lack this glory, the emphasis here is entirely on the unbeliever. Moreover, that glory is in the process of being restored to those who are in Christ (e.g., Heb 2:9-10: "But we see Jesus . . . crowned with glory and honor . . . bringing many sons to glory"). Thus it is only in Christ that the glory can be restored to sinners.

The Righteousness of God Achieved (3:24-26) What human beings could not procure on their own God secured for them via the sacrificial death of Christ. The introductory participle "being justified," translated in the NIV as *are justified,* most likely picks up on the "all" of verse 23 and reintroduces the theme of verses 21-22 (so Cranfield 1975:205), namely, that "all who believe" from among the sinners are then *justified* or declared right before God. The meaning of *justified* (see 1:17) is clear. On the basis of Jesus' atoning sacrifice God has legally declared the repentant sinner righteous. He has acquitted us from the guilt and penalty of our sins. As Moo says (1996:228), "This judicial verdict, for which one had to wait until the last judgment according to Jewish theology, is according to Paul rendered the moment a person believes." Moreover, God has done so *freely;* this verdict is a gift of God (so also Eph 2:9). The basis of this gift is *his grace,* a primary

---

duces that verse. However, other scholars (e.g., Piper 1983:116-20; Schreiner 1998:188) doubt this strongly, arguing that the presence of such terms is not comprehensive enough to warrant such a conclusion and that the theology of verses 24-26 is very Pauline. I agree. It is more likely that Paul does not quote from a pre-Pauline creed but simply uses such material in his own construction (see Moo 1996:227).

Pauline motif (occurring ninety-seven times in his writings) that describes the undeserved favor of God bestowed on the believer in salvation, seen especially in Ephesians 2:5, 8, "it is by grace you have been saved." Sinners have done nothing to merit such a gift, but God through his gracious character has justified those who come to him by faith.

This gracious verdict is achieved *through the redemption that came by Christ Jesus*. This is another major Pauline idea (seven of the ten New Testament occurrences), referring literally to the payment of a ransom in order to free a person from bondage. The idea of a payment is found in the fact that this free gift of salvation is effected *through the redemption* effected by Christ. The sacrificial death of Christ is the payment (see *blood* in v. 25) that has brought about our redemption or freedom from the bondage of sin. The terms for redemption were used often in the ancient world for the manumission of a slave or the freeing of a prisoner of war or a person in bondage due to debts. So Jesus' death is a ransom payment made to free the repentant person from the slavery of sin. There is no hint in any of the New Testament passages to identify the recipient of the payment. If an identification were made, however, it would also certainly be the Judge of all the earth rather than Satan, as some have believed. Still, there is no evidence in this passage for either view. Moreover, this occurred *in Christ Jesus* (better than *by Christ Jesus* of the NIV), the first appearance in Romans of a major Pauline theme (the "in Christ" motif) that occurs eighty-three times

---

3:24 Many have challenged the idea of a payment made in the *redemption* imagery (*lytron* and cognates; cf. Büchsel 1967:341-56, esp. 354-55; Hill 1967:58-80). Büchsel prefers the concept of substitution and liberation rather than ransom payment. While the payment idea was common in Greek literature, it is missing in the LXX (e.g., the LXX of Dan 4:32 and passages on liberation from Egypt: Deut 7:8; 9:26; and so on), where it means to be set free from bondage rather than to be bought out of slavery. Moreover, many New Testament passages contain no hint of a payment made to ransom people (Mk 10:45; Lk 21:28; 1 Cor 1:30; Eph 1:14; 4:30; Heb 9:15; 11:35). However, there are strong indications that a ransom payment was involved (see Morris 1965:16-55). In several New Testament passages the price (the blood of Christ) is clearly indicated (Eph 1:7; 1 Pet 1:18-19) and in others it is definitely implied (Mk 10:45 = Mt 20:28). Marshall (1974:153-69) shows that even though *price* is not always present, some aspect of cost is normally implied. Therefore, the student must allow the context to determine whether the *redemption* passage emphasizes the price paid

in his writings (with forty-seven more having "in the Lord"). We are redeemed "in Christ" (Rom 3:24; cf. 6:11) as well as "one body in Christ" (Rom 12:4-5) and "sanctified in Christ" (1 Cor 1:2). The concept refers both to our union in him and to our membership in his body (see Dunn 1998a:390-412). Here it means that God has brought about our redemption "in Christ" and could include not only what Christ has done but also our participation in it through faith (Dunn 1988a:170; Moo 1996:230).

To bring about this redemption, God *presented him as a sacrifice of atonement.* Moo (1996:231) makes a good case for understanding the verb not as "present" (which is the meaning of the active form rather than the middle form used here) but as "display publicly" (NASB), meaning that God has openly displayed Christ as an atoning sacrifice for sin. This has extraordinary implications, for God is seen as showing all humanity the solution for sin and the basis for liberation. This term for the atoning sacrifice (only here and in Heb 9:15 in the New Testament) is closely connected to the "mercy seat" in the Holy of Holies (see the strong argument of Fryer 1987:111-13, who would even translate it "mercy seat" here). It occurs twenty-one times in the Pentateuch for the mercy seat or cover over the ark. That was both where the blood was poured on the Day of Atonement (Lev 16:14) and where Yahweh was particularly present (Lev 16:2). Thus the mercy seat was the place of atonement, and Christ here is seen as the Old Testament counterpart, the means of atonement for all humanity. His blood then

---

to free the person or the liberation that is effected.

3:25 There has been considerable debate on the meaning of *sacrifice of atonement* (Greek *hilastērion*). Dodd (1931:352-60) argued strongly that the term never meant "propitiation" or the appeasing of God's wrath, calling that a pagan idea. Instead, it referred to "expiation," that is, God wiping away or forgiving sin. In other words, it is not God but sin that is the object of the word group. However, Morris (1965:144-213) and Ridderbos (1975:186-93) have shown that the concept of God's wrath is inherent in the word groups. That is especially true in the context of Romans 1—3, where God's wrath over sin is so predominant. Furthermore, this is not a pagan concept but at the very heart of God's holy reaction to sin. Jesus' sacrificial act atoned for sin and satisfied the holy wrath of God because it justified the sinner before God. In reality, of course, these two options are not disjunctive. Both the appeasing of divine wrath and the forgiveness of sins are part of the concept.

is the once-for-all sacrifice for sin, the only way atonement can be effected for sinful humanity. Christ's sacrifice accomplished two things: the wrath of God was appeased, and sins were forgiven. This is certainly one of the most important doctrines we have, for it is the means by which we can discover the reason God created humankind, to find a focus for his love. Through Christ's atoning sacrifice sinners can be reconciled to God, and only then can eternal fellowship begin. As the Westminster Confession says, God created humankind to "glorify God and enjoy him forever." This is realized only through the redemption Christ purchased with his blood.

Paul then follows this with a series of prepositional phrases (in the Greek) that define the significance of this atoning sacrifice. Once again *through faith* indicates how the sinner appropriates the effects of Christ's death (see on v. 22). Hay (1989:472-74) argues that this faith is both a subjective response and an objective "ground" or "pledge" to follow Christ, but the subjective side is certainly primary in this context. It is unlikely that *in his blood* is intended to modify *faith (faith in his blood)* since this idea does not occur elsewhere in Paul's writings or elsewhere in the New Testament (so Dunn 1988a; Moo 1996; Schreiner 1998). Instead, the blood is the means by which Christ became the sacrifice that atones for sin and satisfies God's wrath (so also Rom 5:9; Eph 1:7; 2:13; Col 1:20; Heb 9:12, 14). It is the initiative of God to effect atonement, and Paul first tells us the purpose and then the reason for Christ's atoning sacrifice. First we are told that God did this to *demonstrate his justice* or "righteousness" and then that he did so *because in his forbearance he had left the sins committed beforehand unpunished.* This is a well-known difficult passage to interpret. The key question is whether "righteousness" here means God's saving activity or his judging activity. Those who take the former view (Nygren 1949:160-61; Kümmel 1967:1-13) would translate this, "to show his saving grace through his forgiving sins committed beforehand when he was patient." Kümmel argues that "righteousness" refers to God's saving faithfulness rather than his justice and that "left unpunished" actually means to forgive.

While this interpretation is viable for the first verb (it refers to saving righteousness in vv. 21-22), it does not fit the second verb, which means to "pass over" or "let go unpunished" in a context like this (see Cranfield 1975:211-12). His failure to judge the former sins to the extent that he should might call his justice into question, but, Paul explains, in reality it simply shows his *forbearance,* meaning his patience or self-restraint. Moreover, God's justice is part of his saving righteousness. As in Deuteronomy, blessings and cursings are alike part of God's covenant. Therefore, the idea is that God has proven his justice in two ways: first, he has made an eternal decree that Christ has borne our sins on the cross and procured atonement for us; second, in so doing he has allowed the sins committed under the old covenant to go unpunished (that is, allowing the sacrificial system to suffice rather than punishing them to the full extent they deserved, namely, by eternal death) in order to prepare for Christ. If a person ever needed proof of the absolute righteousness and justice of God, this is it. Also, if one ever needed proof of why Christ is the only path to salvation, this is it. All time, before and after the Christ-event, points to Jesus' atoning work on the cross. A God who would do all that for the salvation of sinful humanity would hardly turn around and let people come to him on their own terms any way they wished. There is only one way to satisfy his justice, and that is the cross! The only other option is eternal hellfire.

Paul then adds that this *demonstration* has occurred *at the present time,* meaning that it has occurred in this present when "the time had fully come" (Gal 4:4) and has incredible relevance for people in the present. In other words, the *present* refers both to the immediately preceding present of Jesus' life and death and the present situation of the Roman church. God is still proving his righteousness in the present age of salvation (compare 8:18; 11:5; 13:11). The purpose of this is *so as to be just and the one who justifies those who have faith in Jesus.* As Moo explains (1996:241-42), the two purpose clauses (*to demonstrate* in v. 25 and *so as to be just* in v. 26) are "parallel modifiers of 'set forth' (NIV, 'presented'), the former focusing on how the propitiatory sacrifice of Christ enabled God to maintain his righteous character in postponing punishment of sins in the past, the latter showing how this same sacrifice preserved God's righteous character as he justifies those who, in this age of salvation, place their faith in Jesus." Consequently, the *and* is intensive, meaning that God is just "even (especially) when justifying" the repentant sinner. The switch from God's just character to his action in acquitting (justifying) the sinner is powerful and demonstrates that his essential attributes (just) are also relational (justifies).

Justification Only by Faith (3:27-31) Building on the centrality of *faith* in 3:22, 25, 26, Paul now highlights the necessity of faith for experiencing justification (for the meaning of the term, see 3:22). The term occurs four more times in this section. Paul demonstrates how justification by faith removes any possibility of boasting (v. 27) and then points out that justification can only occur by faith and not by *observing the law* (v. 28). Therefore God is the God of the Gentile as well as of the Jew (vv. 29-30). Finally, Paul points out that the centrality of faith establishes rather than nullifies the law (v. 31). The question-answer format of diatribe, used in 2:1—3:5, continues in this section.

In 3:21-26 Paul centered upon the gift of salvation made possible by Christ's atoning death that paid the penalty for sin so that God might acquit the repentant sinner. In verse 27 Paul asks the basic question resulting from that section, *Where, then, is boasting?* This refers to the Jewish boast that they are under the covenant and therefore are automatically the people of God (2:17-20) as well as to the covenant of works by which they believed they maintained that relationship with God (3:28). On the basis of verses 21-26 Paul states that all such boasting is *excluded* or rendered impossible by God himself (implied in the passive voice). Christ's atoning death has removed the possibility of anyone *boasting* of a right relationship with God based on achievement. As Moo points out (1996:247), this does not mean that keeping the law was wrong. In the old covenant it was the way of maintaining a right relationship with God. But the Messiah has now come, so the

---

3:28 The view that Paul is challenging the idea of human achievement or "works" is strongly questioned by the "new perspective on Paul" (see note on 3:20). Dunn (1988a:187-88) says that the phrase "works of law" here refers to "boundary markers," distinctive Jewish practices that distinguish Jews from Gentiles. Therefore this reflects the antitheses in 2:12-13, in which Jew and Gentile are equal in God's eyes, both needing to come to faith in Christ. But as stated above on 3:20, Paul is contrasting the Jewish tendency to focus upon external works in keeping the law rather than

relationship has changed. The error is in the view that keeping the law alone produces that proper relationship with God. Only the grace of God experienced by faith can suffice.

So Paul specifies this point when he says it is not *observing the law* (the original text adds "of works") but *faith* that is sufficient for experiencing salvation. This contrast between works and faith is at the heart of the argument here. The contrast is explicit between "the law of works" and "the law of faith." Many scholars argue that *law* refers in both cases to the Mosaic ordinances (in keeping with the use of *law* for the law of Moses throughout this section), thus contrasting a works approach to the law with a faith approach (Cranfield 1975:220; Stuhlmacher 1994:66-67). Thus the "law of faith" would mean that the law is finally fulfilled in Christian faith. But it is slightly better to see a play on words here, so that the "law of works" is indeed the law of Moses but the "law of faith" refers to "the principle of faith." The contrast is between the Jewish misuse of the law as a system of works to attain righteousness via human achievement and the priority of faith in Christian salvation. The Jewish works approach leads to boasting in their own attainment (2:17-20), but that is *excluded* on the basis of God's new "rule" of faith.

So Paul now draws his conclusion. Since faith rather than works predominates in the new covenant, justification (see 3:24) is now entirely *by faith,* and so righteousness is now attained *apart from observing the law* (v. 28). This has already been said in 3:20, which made it clear that the true purpose of the law is to make one "conscious of sin" rather than to solve the sin problem. This is made even more explicit in Gal 2:16, "a man is not justified by observing the law but by faith in Jesus Christ. So we, too, have put our faith in Christ Jesus that we may be justified by faith in Christ and not by observing the law, because by observing the law no one will be justified." In Gal 2:21 Paul adds, "if

upon internal faith in relating to God. As Schreiner says (1998:204), "Those who detect a polemic against works righteousness are substantially correct, and have not imposed Reformation theology onto Paul. . . . [Sanders] fails to see that legalism can operate at a more subtle level. People can confess God's grace, deeply believe in it, and yet believe that human works play a vital role in obtaining salvation. Paul vigorously opposed such a synergism, contending that entrance into the covenant was by faith alone."

righteousness could be gained through the law, Christ died for nothing!" So it is clear that works have no part in the process of justification (cf. Eph 2:8-9).

The antithesis between works and faith in described another way in vv. 29-30, arguing that God is the God of the Gentiles as well as of the Jews. This is the logical conclusion of 2:1—3:8. Since Jew and Gentile stand equally before God as sinners in need of grace, and since both are justified in the same way, namely, by faith, then it stands to reason that God is the God of both groups. If works were indeed the basis of salvation, then God would have been the God only of the Jews. But since that is not the case, and both Jew and Gentile alike come to God via faith, then both have the same God. The form of the question expects the answer yes: *Is he not the God of Gentiles too?* Certainly the Jewish people were the chosen ones, elect to be the focus of God's special lovingkindness. But there is a clear strain in the Old Testament that shows God always wanted them to draw the nations to himself (e.g., Gen 12:1-3; Ex 19:5-6; Is 42:6; 49:6). Thus Paul anchors this in the Jewish Shema or creed, "The LORD our God, the LORD is one" (Deut 6:4). So if there is only *one God,* then he must also be the God of the Gentiles. The belief that there was only one God was the heart of Judaism, but the Jews thought that he only had a true relationship with his chosen people. Gentiles could only come to God by accepting the Torah and the Jewish religion. But now a salvation-historical change has occurred. Relationship with God is based no longer on Torah but on faith in the Son of God. Therefore Gentiles now have equal access to salvation and therefore to God. In one sense Paul's argument would be accepted by most Jewish readers in his own day. God was the God of all. It was the implications for Jewish particularism that were the problem, and that was where the redemption established by Christ made the difference. Christ died for all, so the Gentile is just as acceptable as the Jew to God. Moreover, since the Jew is just as guilty of sin as the Gentile (2:1—3:8), all stand equally before the judgment seat of God,

---

3:30 As most scholars now agree (Murray 1968; Cranfield 1975; Dunn 1988a; Moo 1996; contra Godet 1969; Stowers 1989), the variation of prepositions—the Jews are saved *by faith,* and the Gentiles are saved *through . . . faith*—is most likely stylistic.

and the atoning sacrifice of Christ is just as efficacious for both groups. God expects only one response to his offer of salvation—not works but faith. Paul makes that explicit in verse 30—God *will justify the circumcised by faith and the uncircumcised through that same faith.* There is no longer any salvific advantage in circumcision. It is now faith and faith alone that leads to justification. Circumcision is now one of the many "works" that fail to suffice. In the old covenant it functioned as the sign of the covenant people. But now in light of Christ, it has lost that function and been replaced by faith.

Paul concludes in verse 31 that faith does not *nullify* or negate the law but rather *upholds* or establishes it. He uses his strongly worded *not at all* or "by no means" to give this special emphasis. The exact meaning of this negate-establish contrast is greatly debated in light of Paul's strong demand that salvation is by faith alone apart from works. How then can he say that this upholds the law?

1. Some (Käsemann 1980; Wilckens 1978) argue that we must see *law* here in another light, perhaps as referring to the law as testifying to the validity of faith (seen in "the law of faith" in v. 27 as well as in the emphasis on Abraham and David testifying to the priority of faith in chap. 4 below). While this is attractive, it is not likely because in chapters 3—4 it is the Scriptures as a whole that testify, and "the law" does not equate with Scripture as a whole (see "the Law and the Prophets" in 3:21 and "Scripture" in 4:3). In this context *the law* refers to the Mosaic ordinances, and they are not really pictured as witnessing here.

2. Some (Grundmann 1971:649) believe that the law is seen as convicting sinners of sin and therefore as pointing the way to the necessity of faith, as seen in the statement of 3:19 that through the law "every mouth may be silenced and the whole world held accountable to God." This interpretation also makes sense, but again it does not fit the emphases of verses 27-31. The convicting power of the law is missing from this particular section.

3. The most likely view (Fitzmyer 1993b; Stott 1994; Moo 1996;

They connote the same thing, that faith is the only means by which anyone can experience salvation.

Schreiner 1998) states that this refers to the commands of the Mosaic law. Elsewhere, Paul equates faith in Christ with the fulfillment of the law (Rom 8:4; cf. 13:8-10). This is also in keeping with Jesus' statement that he has "not come to abolish [the Law and the Prophets] but to fulfill them" (Mt 5:17-20). In Christ the whole law has not been nullified but fulfilled, so in turning to Christ in faith, we actually keep the law in its entirety. Paul is countering a common Jewish argument that in the Christian system of salvation the law is destroyed.

It is impossible to overstate the importance of faith as the only basis of knowing God. Tragically, far too many will experience Matthew 7:22-23: "Many will say to me on that day, 'Lord, Lord, did we not prophesy in your name, and in your name drive out demons and perform many miracles?' Then I will tell them plainly, 'I never knew you. Away from me, you evildoers!'" Works will never suffice to produce salvation. We can never earn eternal life. This theme will carry over into chapter 4.

Righteousness by Faith Alone: The Model of Abraham (4:1-25)

Have you ever tried to convince people to change their minds when they were absolutely sure they were right? There is no more difficult thing to do. You have made all the right arguments, and still they are intractable. You know the type: "My mind is made up; don't convince me with facts!" All you can do is use an illustration, the kind of example that demonstrates the truth and shows absolutely why they must change their minds. This is what Paul does in chapter 4. He has established the inadequacy of the law to produce salvation and the centrality of Christ's atoning death as the only basis of justification (3:21-26). He has also proven that works play no part in the experience of salvation and that righteousness comes by faith alone (3:27-31). Jew and Gentile alike come to God via faith (3:29-30), but this establishes the

---

4:4 Several scholars (e.g., Dunn 1988a:201, 204; B. W. Longenecker 1991:211-12) argue once again that there is no true polemic against works righteousness because the Jews had no such concept (see notes on 3:20, 28). Dunn says (1988a:204) that the language of working and reward does not describe the Judaism of Paul's day and is not a polemic against a theology of self-achieved merit and reward. Rather, Paul is simply showing that righteousness comes "in terms of grace, not of payment due." It is the Jewish boasting in the law that is the problem in chapters 3—4. Yet as

law rather than nullifying it (3:31).

Now in chapter 4 Paul provides an "apologetic theology" (so Guerra 1988:251-52) when he anchors this truth in salvation-history by showing that this was the way by which Abraham was made right with God as well. Abraham was looked upon as the "father" of the Jewish nation and so was the natural choice for this section. Not only was Abraham justified by faith (4:3), but because that faith preceded circumcision and the law, he is *the father of all who believe* (4:11-12), the Gentile as well as the Jew. In one sense all of this chapter is Paul's exposition of Genesis 15:6, "Abraham believed God, and it was credited to him as righteousness" (4:3). The primary terms in the chapter are *believed* (vv. 3, 5 [NIV, *trusts*], 11, 17, 18, 24), its cognate *faith* (vv. 5, 9, 11, 12, 13, 14, 16, 19, 20) and *credited* (vv. 3, 4, 5, 6, 8 [NIV, *count against*], 9, 10, 11, 22, 23, 24). Parker points out (2000:59):

> Romans 4 is thus not a stand-alone text describing an important historical precursor, but the heart of the subject matter of which Paul writes. . . . The rhetoric thus leads readers via Abraham from the meaning of Jesus Christ for the universal crisis of human faith and unbelief to understand how they are personally implicated in the way of faith revealed in Jesus the Christ. Romans 4 is thus the hinge joining the general description of the human condition and faith with the believer's personal situation.

There are five parts to this chapter: (1) 4:1-8 explains how Genesis 15:6 means that Abraham was justified by faith apart from works. To prove this Paul also appeals to David (4:6-8), who pointed out in Psalm 32:1-2 that forgiveness is a gracious act of God (thus not earned by works). (2) 4:9-12 shows that Abraham was justified before he was circumcised and therefore is the father of all who have faith, Gentile as well as Jew. (3) 4:13-17 demonstrates that there was no human merit in

---

Schreiner says (1998:217-18), there is no mention of the law in 4:1-8, and Paul separates Abraham from the era of the law. It is far more likely that Paul is indeed criticizing a merit-based righteousness. Hagner (1993:118-25, 129-30) argues that while the Old Testament was certainly a religion of grace, the postexilic period turned to the law as an end in itself and produced many legalistic statements; thus there were Jewish legalists in Paul's day who fit the descriptions in Romans 3—4.

Abraham receiving the promise but only *the righteousness that comes by faith*. All who experience God's grace through faith are the seed of Abraham. (4) 4:18-22 returns to the first part, explicating the significance of Abraham believing God from the standpoint of his faith shown at the birth of Isaac. (5) 4:23-25 concludes the argument by applying *credited to him as righteousness* to all of us who believe and for whom Christ died.

Faith Not Works in Abraham and David (4:1-8) As an inference from 3:27-31, Paul begins with *What then shall we say . . . ?* The previous paragraph had stated that all boasting is excluded because faith rather than works is the only basis for justification. Paul uses Abraham as his model in verses 1-2. He asks, "What has *Abraham, our forefather, discovered in this matter?*" In other words, he asks how the points of 3:27-31 can be demonstrated in the life of Abraham. The great patriarch also *discovered* (literally "found") that justification is by faith alone. The Greek text adds that Abraham is "our forefather according to the flesh," probably referring to 3:29-30, with the "our" pointing to Jew and Gentile. He is not only the earthly progenitor of the Jewish people but also the spiritual progenitor of the Gentile people, since salvation comes by faith not works. In Paul *flesh* usually has a negative tone, and so this is saying in effect that the Jewish claim that Abraham is only their "fleshly forefather" is wrong, for this is the age of grace not works. Dunn (1988a:198) says that the verb *discovered,* "found," probably looks back to its use in the Septuagint (Greek) version of Genesis (thirteen times) where Abraham "found favor" (grace) in the eyes of the celestial visitors (Gen 18:3) and therefore of God. This prepares for the centrality of the grace of God in 4:4, 16 below. Abraham was justified by God's grace, not by fleshly works.

So Paul turns to the issue of works in verse 2 and returns to the basic issue of boasting from 3:27. The conditional sentence is rhetorical: *If, in fact, Abraham was justified by works,* he would have grounds for boasting. As several have pointed out, this is not saying that good works are wrong but only that works cannot be sufficient to lead to salvation. Abraham could not have performed sufficient works to earn salvation so Abraham could not *boast . . . before God* because his works could never provide an adequate basis for such a thing. The Jewish people looked upon Abraham as the primary example of the pious Jew who kept the law even before it was given. Dunn (1988a:200) points to the many passages in Jewish literature saying that Abraham "kept the commandments of God" (Cairo Genizah *Damascus Document* 3.2; see also *Jubilees* 17:15-18; 18:16; 19:8; and especially Sirach 44:19-21, "he kept the law of the Most High, and was taken into covenant with him; he established the covenant in his flesh, and when he was tested he was found faithful"). So for the Jews the covenant promise was based on Abraham's faithfulness, and Paul is saying this was inadequate. More was needed to make Abraham right *before God*. This is a message desperately needed today as well. People cannot seem to understand that no one can buy his or her way into heaven on the basis of being basically a "good guy." If Abraham could not achieve righteousness on the basis of his works, what makes us think we can?

To find that added ingredient, Paul turns to Genesis 15:6. It is *the Scripture* that proves the inadequacy of works to make Abraham righteous and the absolute necessity of faith. By the use of the singular *Scripture* here Paul may be implying that the whole of Scripture is behind the centrality of faith over works. He quotes Genesis 15:6, closely following the LXX (the Greek Old Testament). In Genesis 15 Abraham is given a vision by God in which he is promised an heir through whom he will have as many offspring as there are stars in the sky (Gen 15:1-5), and in spite of being old it says "Abram believed the LORD," resulting not only in righteousness but in the Abrahamic covenant (Gen 15:7-21). Wenham (1987:329) says that rather than being peripheral to Old Testament theology, "faith is presupposed everywhere as the correct response of man to God's revelation. It is in crisis situations that faith or the lack of it is revealed, and therefore commented on, e.g., Isa 7:9; Jon 3:5; Ps 78:22, 32."

The key of course is that this belief is *credited to him as righteousness*. The difficulty is knowing exactly what this means. Several (Robertson 1980:265-66; Stott 1994; Moo 1996; Schreiner 1998) have said that this does not mean that his faith was a righteous act and therefore produced righteousness as its natural wages. Rather it was a gift from God, something that did not inherently belong to him but was credited to his account. It was a new status that he did not deserve. This is important theologically. There is no true inherent righteousness in any of us. Sin has marred the image of God in us, and we cannot achieve it on our own. Only as an act of grace can it come back to us, and Abraham is the model for the way that can occur—through faith. To be sure, this is not how Jewish people understood Genesis 15:6. Uniformly it was felt that Abraham's faithfulness in observing God's commandments was the implication of "faith counted for righteousness." His faith was seen as a meritorious work (see Käsemann 1980:196). For Paul, though, faith was not a work but meant only trusting in God.

The faith-works contrast is further explained in 4:4-5. Paul now uses the metaphor of wages, saying that since they are earned by a person's work, they are not a *gift* (literally "according to grace") but an *obligation*. Here he is building on Genesis 15:6 and showing the implications for us. If Abraham was justified by faith not works, then that means salvation is a free gift from God rather than an obligation on his part. But, Paul argues, we have not earned it through our works; it is a free gift of his grace. To demonstrate this, Paul turns to the world of commerce. When one works, the employer is obligated to pay wages as part of the contract with the worker. The point is that if righteousness could be earned by a person's good works, then God is under debt to that person and no longer sovereign. We would control our own salvation, earning it by our works, a view certainly argued by Pelagius but rightly labeled heresy. Then also the boasting of 3:27 and 4:1 would be valid, for merit would be the basis of righteousness, but Paul has already shown that to be erroneous.

The important term from Genesis 15:6 is *credited* or "reckoned." The passive *was credited* is a divine passive meaning that God credits these things to us. If works were the basis, eternal life would be "reck-

4:5 It is important to understand that the "work–not work" theme of these verses does not reject the importance of good works. At this point it is good to compare Paul with James (2:14-26), who said "faith without works is dead" (v. 26). Many have seen a direct contrast between the two, but it is critical to understand that Paul and James are using their terms quite differently. Paul is speaking of works righteousness, that is, works that supposedly earn salvation, while James talks of the "good works" that follow salvation and are the necessary proof that salvation

oned" or "accounted" by God as a reward he is obligated to pay, but
the obverse is the truth. God works without obligation and gives graciously. Therefore verse 5 corrects the erroneous viewpoint of verse 4.
The person *who does not work but trusts the God who justifies the
wicked* (or "the ungodly") is a person of *faith* not works, and that faith
is *credited as righteousness.* The thrust is clear. Righteousness simply
cannot be attained by merit or personal achievement. It can only come
as a free grace-gift from a loving God, and it can only be received by
faith. There is no salvific credit in how big a church I pastor or how
many people I reach or how many books I write, nor is there salvific
value in how often I attend church or how many things I do in church.
None of that can make me right with God. Only faith in the gracious
gift of Christ and his atoning sacrifice can suffice. Note the magnificent
phrase, *who justifies the ungodly.* At first glance this does not seem
right. It should be the godly, the pious who are justified. Stott says it
well (1994:112-13):

> How can the righteous God act unrighteously, and so overthrow
> the moral order, turning it upside down? It is unbelievable! Or
> rather it would be, if it were not for the cross of Christ. Without
> the cross the justification of the unjust would be unjustified, im-
> moral, and therefore impossible. The only reason God "justifies
> the wicked" (4:5) is that "Christ died for the wicked" (5:6, REB).
> Because he shed his blood (25) in a sacrificial death for us sin-
> ners, God is able justly to justify the unjust.

On the basis of faith the *wicked,* "ungodly," can be right with God
and thus be justified freely by his grace. Faith in this sense is *credited
. . . as righteousness,* and that is the meaning of justification, namely,
God declaring us righteous by reckoning Christ's death to our account.

Paul now turns to David to supplement his example of Abraham.
His purpose is to give confirming evidence that justification does in-

---

has occurred. Moreover, Paul speaks of true faith in Christ while James speaks of a
purported "faith" that people claim but do not have. Here it is helpful to combine
the two into this diagram: Works ≠ Faith → Works, meaning that works cannot produce faith but are the natural byproduct of true faith. Paul stresses the first half of
this diagram and James the second half. The two do not contradict but rather supplement each other.

deed come apart from works by quoting Psalm 32:1-2 (again from the
LXX). Therefore *David says the same thing* (as Gen 15:6 in v. 3 regarding faith *credited as righteousness*) when he *speaks of the blessedness* of
the person justified apart from works. The emphasis is on the *blessed*
(on this see further below) state of those who come to God without
works and trust themselves to the grace and mercy of God rather than
boasting in their own achievements. The point is obvious: righteousness cannot be attained by works. No matter what the attainment—whether religious, moral, ethical or spiritual—nothing can ever
earn justification. Moreover, it is *God* and God alone who controls salvation, and therefore he alone can *credit righteousness*. The sovereignty of God is uppermost.

The connection between Genesis 15:6 and Psalm 32:1-2 is the term
credited (*count* in the NIV versions of Ps 32:2; Rom 4:8), and this is
probably the reason Paul chose this passage. The psalm itself is a
psalm of forgiveness, beginning with the blessing of forgiveness (Ps
32:1-2) and ending with the blessing of faith (Ps 32:10-11). Craigie tells
us (1983:268), "It is recorded that Ps 32 was Augustine's favorite psalm,
that he read it frequently, and that before he died, he had its words in-
scribed on the wall by his sickbed, to be both exercised and comforted
by them." David centers on the person who is *blessed,* meaning one
who is fortunate because he or she receives divine favor. Here that favor is forgiveness. The psalm centers on the negative side of justification apart from works. The particular "works" mentioned in the psalm
are "transgressions" and "sins." Not only can they not produce righteousness; they must also be "forgiven" and "covered." Thus the flip
side of God's crediting righteousness is God's not crediting sin to one's
account. Moreover, this is the first step to righteousness. First sins must
be forgiven, and then God *credits* our faith as *righteousness,* the very
meaning of justification. In a real sense this restates the thesis paragraph of 3:21-26. Sin is universal and produces an insurmountable barrier between us and God. Works cannot suffice to bridge that gap.
However, on the basis of Christ's sacrifice God has brought salvation to
us, and we accept it by faith. At that point Christ's atoning work has
covered our sins, and so our sin is never put to our account. Here too
the forensic side of justification again comes to the fore (so Moo

1996:266, who says Paul compares "justification to the non-accrediting or not 'imputing' of sins to a person"). Thus we are acquitted and pronounced "right" with God.

Faith and Circumcision (4:9-12) To illustrate the point of righteousness by faith not works, Paul turns once more (cf. 2:25-27; 3:30) to the issue of circumcision, noting that Abraham was justified *before* he was circumcised, not after. He then concludes that Abraham thus was the father of all, uncircumcised Gentiles as well as circumcised Jewish people. And since Abraham was justified solely by faith, faith alone can suffice to render one righteous in the eyes of God. Paul begins by quoting Genesis 15:6 once more, asking whether the *blessedness* of forgiveness (4:7-8) is *only for the circumcised, or also for the uncircumcised.* He responds to this question by reminding his readers that for Abraham *faith was credited . . . as righteousness.* Here Psalm 32:1-2 (Rom 4:7-8) is interpreted via Genesis 15:6; that is, the basis of forgiveness is faith. Cranfield (1975:234-35) points out that the first-century rabbis applied Psalm 32 exclusively to the Jewish people, but Paul rejects this interpretation by appealing to Genesis 15:6. He then applies this point to circumcision by asking a further question (v. 10), Was this righteousness credited *after he was circumcised, or before?* If it was after, then it came by the works of the law and the Jewish system was correct. If before, then Abraham's faith was the initiating mechanism and Christianity was correct. Paul's answer is clear and forceful: *It was not after, but before!* History certainly bore this out—his faith is credited for righteousness anywhere from thirteen years (he is eighty-six in Gen 16:16 and ninety-nine in Gen 17:1) to twenty-nine years (stated by the rabbis) before his circumcision (Gen 17:23-24).

So what was the relationship of circumcision to righteousness? Paul answers this by stating that Abraham's circumcision was a *sign* and a *seal* of his justification (4:11). This probably goes back to Genesis 17:11, which calls circumcision "the sign of the covenant," meaning that it was the external symbol that pointed to the internal reality of the covenant. The two terms *sign* and *seal* here are virtually synonymous, with the sign pointing to and the seal validating the reality of the covenant/justification. Circumcision is seen both as the distinguishing mark and the confirming act of God's covenant with his people. The key is that both sign and seal are external to the covenant. Circumcision does not stand for it but rather is an indicator of it. Moreover, the Jewish leaders of Paul's day took circumcision as the sign of the Mosaic covenant while Paul here argues that it originates in the Abrahamic covenant, and so faith precedes and supersedes the law. Abraham's faith meant that he was already justified when he was circumcised, and so circumcision was not the essence of the covenant but instead was useful for it.

The rest of this section (4:11-12) details two interconnected purposes for the faith of Abraham that led to righteousness. Paul could have subsumed them under one statement that Abraham was *the father of all who believe,* Jew and Gentile alike. But instead Paul separates them into two sections for emphasis. First, Abraham's faith happened so that he might be *the father of all who believe but have not been circumcised.* Since Abraham was justified by faith, he was the father of all who are justified by faith. Circumcision is not necessary for faith. The Jewish people had long claimed that they were the chosen people because Abraham was their father; they were willing to call Gentiles his children only so long as these Gentiles became Jewish proselytes. But Paul is making a more radical claim. Since Abraham was justified by faith apart from circumcision, he is also the father of all who are justified by faith. Thus the Gentiles are his children apart from the law and apart from circumcision. The result (so Cranfield 1975; Käsemann 1980; Moo 1996; contra Barrett 1957 and Dunn 1988a, who take it as purpose) is that *righteousness* is *credited to* the Gentiles in the same way that it was credited to Abraham. Righteousness cannot be earned by one's deeds, only given by God as his grace-gift. In that sense both Jews and Gentiles stand equally before God, and the sole basis is faith in the atoning sacrifice of Christ.

The second aspect of Abraham's heritage concerns the Jewish peo-

---

4:12 There is some debate about whether there are two groups here, the Jews (those who are *circumcised*) and the Jewish Christians (those who *walk in the footsteps of the faith*). This is certainly possible since both are introduced by "those who" (NIV, *who . . . but who also*). But as several point out (Cranfield 1975; Dunn 1988a; Moo 1996; Schreiner 1998), the not only–but also style and the context as a whole make it more likely that one group is in mind, Jewish Christians. Abraham is father

ple themselves. Abraham is also *father of the circumcised.* But here is the twist. It is no longer based on ancestry or legal observance but can be experienced only when they *walk in the footsteps of the faith that our father Abraham had before he was circumcised.* Since circumcision is one of the "works of the law," it can no longer provide assurance of being a member of the covenant people. Since the Messiah has arrived, only faith in him can suffice. To prove the necessity of this, Paul has appealed in this chapter to the model of Abraham, who was declared righteous on the basis of his faith *before* he was circumcised. Faith precedes circumcision both historically and spiritually. So the biblical model, Paul argues, is one of faith rather than works.

Faith and Promise in Abraham (4:13-17) Paul turns from the issue of circumcision to argue next that *it was not through law that Abraham and his offspring received the promise.* Moo identifies (1996:273) four stages in this chapter: faith "apart from works" in verses 3-8, faith "apart from circumcision" in verses 9-12, faith "apart from the law" in verses 13-16, and faith "apart from sight" in verses 17-21. Here the third aspect is primary, as Paul turns to *the promise* God had given in the Abrahamic covenant. The key term is *promise,* appearing four times in verses 13-22 (with the verb adding a fifth reference). The problem comes with the identification of *the promise,* namely, that Abraham would be *heir of the world,* since the Abrahamic covenant says only that he would have descendants (Gen 12:2; 13:16; 15:5; 17:5-6), be a source of blessing to the nations (Gen 12:3; 18:18; 22:18), and inherit the promised land (Gen 12:7; 13:15; 15:7; 17:8). It is likely that this is a summation of these from the standpoint of the universal effects of the coming of the Messiah. Abraham and his offspring would inherit the world through the victory of Christ over the world (in Rev 22:5 the saints "will reign for ever and ever"). Here the contrast in the two possible means *(through)* by which this would be accomplished is uppermost. This inheritance cannot be

---

only of those circumcised people who believe.

4:13 There are two issues here. First, does *law* refer to the Mosaic economy or to the general principle of law (so Sanday and Headlam 1902; Murray 1968)? However, in this context the Mosaic law is certainly uppermost. Second, does *the offspring* here refer to Christ (as in Gal 3:16) or to the church? Yet it is clear that Abraham's seed refers to all who believe.

achieved *through law* but only *through the righteousness that comes by faith,* in contrast to the Jewish view that the promises given to Abraham were mediated through the law.

The next two verses (4:14-15) clarify this point carefully. If the inheritance comes to *those who live by law,* Paul maintains, both faith and the promise given to Abraham and his offspring are nullified. In other words, if it were possible to be righteous and thus gain an eternal inheritance on the basis of personal achievement, then faith would be unnecessary. If works and obedience were sufficient, the need for God's promise would be removed. The language Paul uses is particularly strong. Faith would have *no value,* that is, be "emptied" of its purpose and role in God's plan of salvation. The promise would be *worthless,* that is, rendered null and void, robbed of its effectiveness. The tense of both verbs refers to an ongoing state of affairs. Paul made this point earlier in Galatians 3:18, "For if the inheritance depends on the law, then it no longer depends on a promise." Law and promise are antithetical; the inheritance must stem from one and not the other. Paul's whole point in chapter 4 is that Abraham exemplifies the fact that divine promise rather than the law is the sole basis, as in Galatians 3:18, "but God in his grace gave it to Abraham through a promise." Stott says it well (1994:131), "Law and promise belong to different categories of thought, which are incompatible. Law-language ('you shall') demands our obedience, but promise-language ('I will') demands our faith. What God said to Abraham was not 'Obey this law and I will bless you,' but 'I will bless you; believe my promise.'" This state of affairs is just as critical today as in Paul's day. Too many churches center on law rather than grace, and too many Christians are placing their trust in what they are doing rather than in the One on whom they are believing. The level of commitment on the part of the average Christian all too often seems to be going down rather than up.

In fact, Paul adds, the actual effect of the law is *wrath,* that is, God's wrath on sinners (4:15). At first glance this does not seem right. Why

---

4:15 Some have argued that this verse is parenthetical (Barrett 1957; Fitzmyer 1993b) and does not truly relate to the argument of verse 14, but it is far more likely that it is essential to the developing idea, telling why *(for)* the law cannot produce the in-

would God devise a mechanism that would produce not salvation but wrath? But this is the wrong way to look at the situation. God did not create the law in order to pour wrath upon humanity. Rather he gave the law as a means of maintaining a right relationship with himself. However, people cannot keep the law, and so they fall into sin; sin produces the wrath. Paul uses a legal argument to make his point: *where there is no law there is no transgression.* The purpose of the law is to point out transgression. As Fitzmyer observes (1993a:385), "The prescriptions of the law, because they are not observed, produce transgressions (Gal 3:19) and so promote the reign of sin." This then brings the wrath of God down upon the sinner. If there were no law, there would be no way to identify what connotes transgressing the law. But God indeed did give his law, so there is *transgression,* referring to the violation of specific written decrees. Yet note also that Paul carefully does not say there is no sin without law, simply that those sins cannot be identified as *transgressions.* From this standpoint also, God's *wrath* is not simply his anger against sin but his judicial wrath against the transgression of his law. This is a more serious situation. Sin in general does bring about God's wrath (Rom 1:18), but it is not deliberate transgression since the laws have not been given. However, once God's law is revealed, the sins are deliberate and therefore more serious.

In verse 13 Paul gave his basic thesis that the divine promise came to Abraham and us not by the law but through faith. Then in verses 14-15 the negative side (not through the law) was presented, and now in verses 16-17 the positive side (through faith) is developed. Because the law is inadequate to produce the promised inheritance, that *promise* must come *by faith.* Again, this goes back to Abraham and Genesis 15:6 in Romans 4:3, "Abraham believed God, and it was credited to him as righteousness." Only by the same faith-act can Abraham's descendants (the Gentiles as well as the Jews) attain righteousness in the eyes of God. The purpose of this divine demand is that salvation *may be by grace,* a concept introduced in 4:4 (cf. 1:5, 7; 3:24) and emphasizing

---

heritance (Cranfield 1975; Morris 1988; Schreiner 1998). The true result of the law is not righteousness and acceptance by God but transgression and wrath from God.

the divine side of the equation. By God's grace salvation is possible, and people participate in it via faith. Salvation cannot be obtained by human effort but is entirely the act of God on the basis of his grace. As Bruce says (1985:117), "What God provides by his free grace can be appropriated by men only through faith. What, on the contrary, is earned by works (not faith) is bestowed as a matter of merit (not grace)."

As an act of grace, the promise is *guaranteed* or "confirmed" (another legal term referring to something that is made absolutely certain) not just to the Jews but *to all Abraham's offspring.* This in one sense goes back to verse 14—not only is the promise not *worthless,* but it is just the opposite, absolutely secure or certain of fulfillment. Moreover, it encompasses all who come to God in faith, not only those *of the law* (Jewish Christians) but also those *of the faith of Abraham* (Gentile Christians). So this sums up the first three chapters: Jew and Gentile are equal both in sin and in salvation. It is of no value to be Abraham's physical descendant or to observe the law unless that is accompanied by faith, which alone can be "credited as righteousness" (4:4). Only then can Abraham be *the father of us all,* for that can solely be true when both Jew and Gentile approach the throne of God by faith. On the positive side, it also means that all people have an equal opportunity to come before God. Neither right of birth nor piety of action will suffice. All sinners are called to God on the basis of the sacrificial atonement of Christ, and all can respond through faith. People today are not really very different from those of Paul's time—it is the human desire to earn salvation via works or pedigree. To accept it by faith as a grace-gift goes against human pride.

Paul then anchors the universal fatherhood of Abraham in another citation from Genesis, this time from Genesis 17:5, *I have made you a*

4:17 There are several ways to construe the relationship between the first half of verse 17 and the last half. Following the excellent summary of Moo (1996:279-80), the options are: (1) they are consecutive, with the quote confirming "the father of us all" in verse 16 and the second clause developing the first of verse 17 (TEV; NIV; REB; NLT; Käsemann 1980; Morris 1988; Moo 1996); (2) the first clause confirms "to all seed" (NIV "to all Abraham's offspring") in verse 16, and the second clause depends on the first (Wilckens 1978); (3) the first clause is parenthetical, and the second confirms "father of us all" in verse 16 (KJV; NASB; Calvin 1979; Michel 1966;

father of many nations (v. 17, quoting the LXX). Therefore once again Paul is saying that Abraham is father of Gentiles as well as Jews. Genesis 17 is another passage on the Abrahamic covenant, so Genesis 17:5 probably refers to Abraham's natural descendants, as in Genesis 17:6, "I will make you very fruitful." Paul, however, is speaking of his spiritual fatherhood over Jewish and Gentile *nations*. So as Fitzmyer says (1993b:386), the "many nations" are "all those who become believers in Christ, who are reckoned as upright through faith." Paul then describes Abraham as *our father in the sight of God, in whom he believed.* This is probably a reference to Abraham's faith in God's promise regarding the birth of Isaac (going back to the citation of Gen 15:6 in Rom 4:3).

Concluding the section is a description of the God in whom Abraham believed. First, he is *the God who gives life to the dead,* referring first of all to the life he placed in Sarah's "dead" womb in spite of Abraham's "dead" body (v. 19 below) and then to God's power to raise the dead. The latter was a major Jewish emphasis (Tobit 13:2; Wisdom of Solomon 16:13; the Eighteen Benedictions) as well as Christian. The promise to Abraham was made by the one who had the resurrection power to grant life to the dead. Second, God is the one who *calls things that are not as though they were.* In one sense this means that God called the nations that did not yet exist out of his covenant to Abraham. However, most realize there is more to the phrase than this. It could be a reference to God creating the world out of nothing (so Barrett 1957; Bruce 1985; Cranfield 1975; Wilckens 1978; Dunn 1988a), but the language makes this difficult by saying God called them *as though* they existed. Also, the context of bringing life out of death makes it more likely that this refers to God's power to "call" that which does not exist (i.e., the dead) as if they did (by giving them life, so Murray 1968; Stott 1994; Moo 1996; Schreiner 1998). Moreover, this is

---

Murray 1968; Cranfield 1975; Schreiner 1998); (4) the first confirms "father of us all," and the second goes back to "all the seed" in verse 16 (Bruce 1985); (5) the first clause goes with verse 16, and the second clause starts a new paragraph (M. Black 1973). The first thing that must be said is that the two parts of verse 17 belong together and should not be separated (eliminating the third and fifth options). The only question is what part of verse 16 they allude back. Because of the repetition of *father,* the first option fits best. Verse 17 anchors the statement in verse 16 that Abraham is "father of us all."

true on the spiritual plane (so Käsemann 1980; Morris 1988, speaking of the spiritually dead called to life) as well as the physical. This promise is just as critical today as it was in Paul's. In Christ we have the absolute certainty of eternal life. For us death, while still the "last enemy" (1 Cor 15:26), is a transition to a far more glorious eternal existence with Christ. Yet it is critically important to realize that, as Paul stresses throughout, we can only attain that "life" through faith in Christ, not by personal piety or human achievement.

Abraham's Faith at the Birth of Isaac (4:18-22) Verse 18 in one sense belongs with verses 16-17, continuing the emphasis on Abraham believing and becoming *the father of many nations.* Yet at the same time it moves into a primary example of that faith—Abraham's *offspring,* in particular Isaac. Paul also adds that Abraham believed *in hope,* which was the natural result of faith. The original Greek has "against hope, in hope he believed." It probably means that Abraham had hope in God against the kind of hope that Abraham could humanly have. Abraham's hope centered on God's promise rather on his own physical situation. God had promised him an heir, and despite his and Sarah's advanced age, he believed that promise and had *hope.* Therefore, his faith became hope, and that led to his becoming *the father of many nations,* physically through Isaac and spiritually through the new covenant established by Christ (the main thrust here). Paul anchors this in another citation, this time from Genesis 15:5, the verse immediately preceding that quoted in 4:3. In the Genesis context, God is anchoring his covenant promise by having Abraham count the incredible number of stars, saying *So shall your offspring be.* Therefore, the *many nations* (those who come to faith in Christ from the *many nations*) are seen as the descendants of Abraham.

The most amazing fact of all is that Abraham accepted his physical situation *without weakening in his faith* (v. 19), another way of expressing the same idea as in verse 18: "against hope, he hoped." Schreiner (1998:237-38) brings out the interesting irony that Abraham's faith did not "weaken" even as his and Sarah's bodies were progressively weakening. The evidence was certainly sufficient to make him strongly doubt God's promise. His body was *as good as dead* because he was *about a hundred years old* (cf. Gen 17:1), possibly a reference to imminent death because of his advanced age but more likely a statement that he was no longer able to bear children. This is problematic since he was later able to have six children by another wife, Keturah. But when God gave him the ability to bear children, it remained with him afterward. Yet the further problem was that *Sarah's womb was also dead,* meaning that she was unable to bear children. Yet they recognized that God was a God "who gives life to the dead" (v. 17). Morris (1988:212) says it well: "To believe God's promise under those circumstances was more than a passive acquiescence in a conventional religious posture; it was the active exercise of a profound faith." Here also we have a critical model for Christians in every age. Moo (1996:284) quotes John Calvin here: "Let us remember that the condition of us all is the same with that of Abraham. All things around us are in opposition to the promises of God. . . . We must with closed eyes pass by ourselves and all things connected with us, that nothing may hinder or prevent us from believing that God is true."

Paul proceeds to restate verse 19 in two ways. First, Abraham *did not waver through unbelief* (v. 20). On the surface this seems to contradict the Genesis story. After God's promise in Genesis 17:16 that they would bear a son, "Abraham fell facedown; he laughed and said to himself, 'Will a son be born to a man a hundred years old? Will Sarah bear a child at the age of ninety?'" (Gen 17:17). Sarah also laughed in Genesis 18:12. But Paul is discussing the long-term faith that Abraham showed in God's promise. Genesis 17:17 was a momentary doubt at the outset, but from that time Abraham exhibited an incredible trust in God. Second, Abraham *was strengthened in his faith,* which could be a divine passive, "God strengthened him" (so Cranfield 1975; Wilckens 1978), but more likely is parallel to *weakening* in verse 19 and means he "grew strong with reference to his faith" (Moo 1996; Schreiner 1998). This is another important model for us. Through adversity our trust in God's promises becomes stronger. In a sense, the difficulties of life are like weights in a gym. The more we struggle against them, the more our faith is strengthened.

There were two results of Abraham's growing strength in trusting God. He *gave glory to God* by refusing to consider his own resources and ability but instead throwing himself entirely into God's hands. If he had considered only the earthly circumstances, he would have been guilty of unbelief (v. 19); instead he looked to God's resources, placed himself at his mercy and thereby glorified him. This is also true today. Those who "conform . . . to the pattern of this world" (Rom 12:2) will not glorify God (Rom 1:21, 23), but those who seek God will by that very exercise of faith bring glory to him. As Schreiner says (1998:238), "faith glorifies God because it acknowledges that life must be lived in complete dependence on him." Also, Abraham was *fully persuaded that God had power to do what he had promised* (v. 21). As Abraham's faith grew stronger, so did the certainty that "he who promised is faithful" (Heb 10:23). This means a complete assurance that God will do what he has promised, similar to the definition in Hebrews 11:1: "faith is being sure of what we hope for and certain of what we do not see." Note the terms here—*fully persuaded, power, promised.* This is a summary of what it means to be a Christian: completely sure of God, whose promise is absolute and who is "able to do immeasurably more than all we ask or imagine, according to his power that is at work within us" (Eph 3:20).

Paul's conclusion (Greek "wherefore," v. 22) returns to the quotation of Genesis 15:6 in 4:3, *It was credited to him as righteousness.* The whole discussion of chapter 4 is framed with the Genesis quotation, thereby making the faith of Abraham the central point. Also, by repeating the point after his discussion of the Abrahamic covenant and the birth of Isaac, Paul is saying that faith characterized his whole life and therefore provides the required criterion for the child of God in every age. The argument of 3:21—4:22 has come full circle. *Faith* has occurred in this passage seventeen times, and throughout Paul is arguing that one cannot be right in God's eyes without belief in the salvific act of Christ. It is impossible to be declared righteous by God on the basis of human achievement or pious actions. The works of the law will never suffice, nor will church activity or good works in our day. God will always fulfill his covenant responsibilities, as Abraham discovered.

4:24 Fitzmyer (1992:388) points out that Paul is employing a Jewish midrashic technique in which the Old Testament story is "modernized" to fit a new situation, as in *Genesis Rabbah* 40:8, "All that is recorded of Abraham is repeated in the history of

Now we must fulfill our responsibility as well—faith in God's salvific work in Christ.

Conclusion: Abraham as the Model for Us (4:23-25) Paul concludes this section by showing that the story of Abraham's faith was not merely a historical event but was a paradigm for believers in every age. The key phrase from Genesis 15:6 for expressing this point is *it was credited to him* because it centers upon God's action in crediting Abraham's faith to his account as being right with God. As is argued throughout chapter 4, this is the major Old Testament model for the new covenant established by the atoning sacrifice of Christ. Thus redemption requires not "the works" of the law established by Moses but the "faith credited as righteousness" established by Abraham. When we exercise the same faith Abraham did, then for us too that faith is "counted as" righteousness. In fact, Paul says, that very faith "credited" on the part of Abraham was never meant by God just for him; God sent him that experience *for us,* that is, "for our sake."

The Christian is described in two ways. First, they are the ones *to whom God will credit righteousness.* This could refer to conversion (Cranfield 1975; Wilckens 1978; Moo 1996; Schreiner 1998) or to the last judgment (Schlatter 1995; Barrett 1957; Dunn 1988a; Fitzmyer 1993b). The key is the emphatic Greek term *mellei,* "about to." It could refer to the future converts on the basis of justification as a present reality in 4:25 and 5:1, or it could refer to the final consummation of salvation on Judgment Day. Morris (1988:214) takes it as both: "In one sense believers are justified now; they have received right standing with God and this is their present possession. From another point of view the consummation waits till Judgment Day and thus may be referred to as still future." This is certainly possible, but in the context the thrust of present conversion seems primary, for there is no real hint of future judgment in chapter 4 (it comes up in 5:9, but that is unlikely to influence the meaning here since 5:1 speaks of present salvation). So Abraham is the model for all who

---

his children." So Abraham's faith becomes the pattern for Christian faith, and his righteousness is the model for those who also will be "justified by faith" (NIV, *to whom God will credit righteousness).*

will experience faith "credited . . . as righteousness."

Second, they are the ones *who believe in him who raised Jesus our Lord from the dead*. In the original Greek there is a special emphasis on *believe in him,* signifying that God is the focus of faith. This is somewhat unusual, for Paul normally emphasizes belief in Jesus, but in this case the parallel with Abraham's faith in God leads to this thrust. Of course, Abraham did not believe in the God who would raise Jesus from the dead, but verse 17 stressed Abraham's faith in the God "who gives life to the dead," referring to Abraham's "dead" body given "life" through bearing the promised son, Isaac. Thus the parallel is apt, from physical life to ultimate resurrection life, and this promise galvanizes the faith of both Abraham and us. As Moo states (1996:288), "It is the God of the promise, the promise given to Abraham but ultimately fulfilled in Christ and Christians, in whom both Abraham and we believe." Jesus' resurrection is the heart of Christianity according to Paul (Rom 6:4; 8:11; 10:9; 1 Cor 6:14; 15:12-20; Gal 1:1; Eph 1:20; Col 2:12; 1 Thess 1:10). As he says in 1 Corinthians 15:14, "if Christ has not been raised, our preaching is useless and so is your faith."

The greatest truth ever given to mortal man is stated in verse 25, and it contains the essence of the Bible. Hodge (1950:129) says, "This verse is a comprehensive statement of the gospel." Paul here may well be quoting an existing creed developed by the early church to teach the reason for Christ's death and resurrection, *He was delivered over to death for our sins and was raised to life for our justification*. Behind it is probably the LXX form of Isaiah 53:12, "he was delivered on account of their sins." Isaiah 53 is distinctly in mind, for *delivered* is found there in verses 6 and 12, detailing how "the LORD has laid on [the Servant of Yahweh] the iniquity of us all" (Is 53:6; cf. also Is 53:5, 10, 11). Dunn points out (1988a:224) that *delivered* played a double role in the pas-

---

4:25 It is difficult to interpret the two "because of" (Greek *dia*) phrases in this verse. It is easy to see why sin "caused" Jesus' delivery to the cross but not so easy to see why our justification "caused" his resurrection. Those who argue for a causal sense (Godet 1969; Schlatter 1995; Morris 1988; Schreiner 1998) say that the resurrection was the basis and confirmation of the justification of the sinner. However, others (Hodge 1950; Murray 1968; Moo 1996) interpret this as saying Christ was raised "for the sake of" our justification. Still others (Michel 1966; Cranfield 1975; Käsemann

sion narratives, depicting both Judas' betrayal and God's handing Jesus over to his enemies (see especially the passion prediction—Mk 9:31; 10:33; and parallels). *Delivered* here is also a divine passive meaning "God delivered" Jesus to atone "for our sins" (here the more specific term "transgressions" is actually used). *For* here means "on account of," stating that human depravity was the reason for the cross. If Christ had not died, there could have been no forgiveness of sins.

The death and resurrection of Jesus compose a single event in salvation history, as seen especially in Matthew 27:51-53, which tells that the Old Testament saints were raised on the day of Christ's death but seen after his resurrection, thereby uniting the two aspects into a single whole. It is strange that Paul here says Jesus was *raised . . . for our justification,* since elsewhere he emphasizes Jesus' death as the basis of justification (Rom 3:24-26; 5:9; 6:3-9; 1 Cor 11:27; Eph 1:7; 2:13; Col 1:14, 20). However, the two aspects, his death and resurrection, are equally the basis for salvation. His death, as seen in the epistles, is the theological basis of justification, and his resurrection, as seen in Acts (2:31-36; 13:32-39), is the apologetic basis of salvation; that is, it proves the reality of the salvation produced in Christ.

So Paul has now summed up his points. In 3:21—4:25 his doctrine of salvation by faith alone, apart from works, is complete. At the heart of his doctrine is the fact that Christ's death was a "sacrifice of atonement" (propitiation, 3:25) that paid the price for our sins ("redemption") and resulted in God's legal decision to pronounce us "right" before him (justification, 3:21-26). The key is faith rather than observing the law, and this means that God is the God of the Gentiles as well as the Jews (3:27-31). To prove this, Paul turns to Abraham, the father of the nation and the one who precedes Moses (4:1-25), showing that faith has precedence over the law as the means by which one partici-

---

(1980); Wilckens 1978) take it in a final sense, saying that Christ was raised "in order to deal with" our justification. It is difficult to be dogmatic, for the *dia* is certainly repeated in the two parts. One of the first two options is the more likely, and perhaps it is slightly better to see a causal force repeated in the second (see Harris 1978:1184, where he calls the final sense "unusual" and believes a causal thrust makes perfect sense here).

pates in salvation. This issue is just as critical in our day as it was in Paul's, for people are always trying to get right with God on the basis of good works, such as an ethical lifestyle or involvement in church. Abraham is our example too—he "believed God, and it was credited to him as righteousness" (Gen 15:6 as quoted in Rom 4:3; cf. Rom 4:5-8, 9-10, 11, 22, 23-25). For us as well, belief in the saving work of Christ is the only basis of salvation.

☐ Righteousness and Sanctification: The New Life in Christ (5:1—8:39)

Self-help seminars are a current fad. Everyone wants to know how to do things right. Paul does exactly that in this section. He has just shown the necessity of faith in Christ as the only basis of salvation. Now he turns to the implications of salvation for the Christian life, answering the question, How then should we live? We are saved by faith, and now we must live by faith. But what does that look like? Exactly how do we live out the effects of our justification? Paul in these chapters explores the ramifications of this new life in Christ.

There is significant debate about whether chapter 5 belongs with 1:18—4:25 (Sanday and Headlam 1902; Murray 1968; Bruce 1985; Morris 1988; Wilckens 1978; Dunn 1988a) or with 6:1—8:39 (Nygren 1949; Cranfield 1975; Käsemann 1980; Stott 1994; Fitzmyer 1993b; Moo 1996; Schreiner 1998). In favor of the former is the number of terms common to chapters 1—4 and 5 (*righteous, righteousness, boast, wrath, blood*) and the centrality of justification themes in both. Many see chapters 1—5 centering on justification and chapters 6—8 centering on sanctification. However, there seems to be a significant shift of focus between chapters 1—4 and chapters 5—8, with the former centering on the necessity of faith for salvation and the latter on the effects of that salvation on the lives and experiences of believers. Moo (1996:292-94) gives four reasons for this: (1) the opening in 5:1, *since we have been justified through faith,* sums up the previous section and prepares for a new topic. (2) There is a shift in style from a polemical tone in chapters

---

5—8 A slightly different chiasm is suggested by Rolland (1988:396-400): A 5:1-21; B 6:1—7:6; C 7:7-25; C' 8:1-11; B' 8:12-21; A' 8:22-39. The strength of this would be the

1—4 to a confessional style employing the first-person plural in 5:1-2. (3) There is a shift from chapters 1—4 to chapters 5—8 in the relative frequency of some key terms, like *faith/believe* (thirty-three times in 1—4 and three in 5—8), *life/live* (twice in 1—4 and twenty-four times in 5—8); forms of *righteous* occur twenty-six times in 1—4 and sixteen in 5—8, but in the latter section they denote not so much justification by faith but either the result (eternal life) or the ethical aspect of living rightly. (4) There is a close connection between 5:1-11 and 8:18-39, with several words repeated in both *(love, justify, glory, peace, hope, tribulation, save, endurance)*, resulting in a chiastic structure in this section (see figure 2).

A   Assurance of future glory (5:1-11).
   B   Basis for assurance—work of Christ (5:12-21).
      C   The problem of sin (6:1-23).
      C′ The problem of sin and the law (7:1-25).
   B′ Basis for assurance—work of Christ through the Spirit (8:1-17).
A′ Assurance of future glory (8:18-39).

Figure 2. A chiastic diagram of Romans 5:1—8:39

The six sections of the chiastic structure detail how the one who is justified will live, and they describe further the shift from the law to the new life in Christ. Some believe that the central theme is hope, but that theme is confined to 5:2-5 and 8:24-25. It is certainly an important element, showing that both present (right living) and future (hope in final glory) blessings result from our justification by faith. If there is a single central theme (always uncertain in light of the complex issues Paul discusses), it would be the new life Christ has made available through the cross. In fact, Richard Longenecker (1999:67-68) believes that 5:1—8:39 is the central section of the letter and fulfills the "spiritual gift" Paul promises in 1:11. In this sense the focus of the letter is not just the ethnic question of Jewish and Gentile togetherness in the church but rather the even more critical issue of the walk of both groups "in Christ" and "in

contrast between the reign of sin and that of the Spirit. However, the outline above on the whole makes better sense of the parallelism in this section.

the Spirit." Unity is achieved via the reconciliation of both in Christ.

The Blessings of Justification—A New Peace and Hope in Christ (5:1-11) After detailing the meaning and process of justification by grace through faith, Paul now proceeds to the consequences of justification—reconciliation and peace with God. An atmosphere of joy predominates as Paul celebrates the privileges of being a Christian and part of the new covenant. Three concepts dominate the section: peace/reconciliation (vv. 1, 10, 11), hope (vv. 2, 4, 5), and boast/joy (vv. 2, 3). A number of scholars believe that hope is the central theme (Godet 1969; Dunn 1988a; Moo 1996; Schreiner 1998), while others make peace the unifying theme (Cranfield 1975; Käsemann 1980). It is best to see not one but a cluster of themes standing equally here. Fitzmyer says (1993b:394), "The emphasis in the paragraph is on God's love, on Christ Jesus as the mediator of that love, and on reconciliation as the effect produced by that love." This comes closest, for *love* appears at critical junctures (vv. 5, 8), but it is best to see all these concepts clustering together to produce the basic theme: the blessings that result from justification. There are two sections: (1) verses 1-5, centering on the hope we have in Christ, and (2) verses 6-11, centering on the reconciliation that has resulted from Christ's death for us. The first section has two parts: *(a)* verses 1-2, tracing the process of salvation from justification to peace and grace and then to boasting in our new hope, and *(b)* verses 3-5, showing why we boast in suffering because suffering leads to endurance, character and hope. The second section also has two parts: *(a)* verses 6-8, which demonstrate the love of God as shown in Christ's death for us, and *(b)* verses 9-11, which trace the reconciliation and salvation resulting from Christ's death for us.

Peace and Hope in Christ (5:1-5) Whenever something particularly joyous occurs (say a promotion or an incredible gift), one of the first things we do is think of the difference it will make in our lives. This is what Paul does here. The beginning statement, *since we have been justified through faith,* is a summary of the message of 1:18—4:25. Since Paul is addressing the Roman church, he presents this justification as a past experience, obviously referring to their conversion. This is at the heart of the gospel message: we who once were sinners destined for final judgment (1:18—3:8, 23) have been redeemed through Christ's blood and justified or declared right with God on the basis of our faith (3:21—4:25). Note the centrality of *we* in verses 1-11. Mc-Donald (1990:87-88) calls this a "rhetorical bridge" that brings Paul together with his readers in a united experience. As one group, they have all experienced the blessings of justification. Paul has described the basis and nature of justification in the preceding chapters, and now he begins to probe the results of that blessed gift. The first blessing enumerated is *peace with God,* intended in the Old Testament sense of the Hebrew *shalom,* a "sense of general well-being, the source and giver of which is Yahweh alone" and "approximates closely to the idea of salvation" (Beck and Brown 1976:777). In the early church it was connected to the eschatological promise of the peace God would bring with his kingdom in the last days (see Is 32:17; 48:20-22; 52:7; 53:5; Jer 37:26; Ezek 34:25). On the basis of the added *with God,* it approximates the "reconciliation" of verses 10-11 below. Our sins have been forgiven (4:7-8) and our guilt removed (4:25), and we have been made right with God. This peace comes to us *through our Lord Jesus Christ.* The emphasis on Christ as Lord was also seen in 4:24 and highlights his exaltation to cosmic Lord as the result of his death and resurrection. He is both the means of our salvation and the Lord of our life. There is no possibility of experiencing the peace brought about by salvation except through him. Moo notes that Romans contains no extended christological discussion, but yet in chapters 5—8 every blessing the Christian experiences comes through Christ (peace, 5:1; access to grace, 5:2; boasting in God, 5:11; eternal life, 5:21 and 6:23; thanks for deliverance, 7:25; the absolute love of God, 8:39). Thus "christology, we might say, is not the topic of any part of Rom. 5—8, but it is the basis for everything in these chapters" (Moo 1996:300).

The second result of justification is *access by faith into this grace in which we now stand.* By *access* Paul could mean cultic "access to the sanctuary as the place of God's presence" (Käsemann 1980:133; this is the connotation in Eph 2:18), but more likely here the word has a connotation of royalty, signifying entrance into the audience chamber of the King of kings (Dunn 1988a; Fitzmyer 1993b). There is a twofold basis for this entrance: Christ (whose death made it possible, vv. 6-8) and faith (the means emphasized in 3:21—4:25). It is interesting that Paul says *this grace,* referring to the grace of God highlighted in 3:24 ("justified freely by his grace") and 4:16 ("the promise comes . . . by grace"). However, there it referred to the character of God, while here it refers to the realm of grace that we experience in Christ, namely, the *grace in which we now stand.* In fact, the perfect tenses here, *have gained* and *now stand* ("have stood" in the Greek), express the idea of a "given state of affairs" to which a person belongs (Porter 1994:22). We now not only have access to but actually *stand* or have our being in God's realm. As in Philippians 3:20, "our citizenship is in heaven." This grace includes our new status as justified and also all the blessings enumerated in 5:1-11.

Yet we not only have peace and access to grace, but we also have an entirely new basis for "boasting" (*rejoice* in the NIV). In 3:27 Paul said that all "boasting" in the law is "excluded" on the basis of the principle of "faith" (see also 2:17, 23). In 4:2-3 he noted that Abraham had nothing "to boast about" because he believed God rather than depended on his works. Yet here there is ground for boasting, namely, *in the hope of the glory of God.* The earlier passages forbade bragging over human achievement while here pride is encouraged regarding what God has accomplished on our behalf. Pride is sin when it centers on self but valid when centered on the accomplishments of another (like your children or especially your God!). The basis of this pride in God, *the hope of the glory of God,* is almost certainly not the present glory of the believer (seen in Jn 17:22; Rom 8:30; 1 Cor 11:7; Heb 2:10; 1 Pet 4:14) but the final glory that will be ours at the eschaton (Rom 8:17, 18, 21; Eph 1:18; Col 1:27). Our *hope,* as in verses 5:4, 5 and 8:20, 24 is a glorious trust in and anticipation of the promises God has given regarding the future. In light of this, Cranfield (1975:260) calls *the glory of God* "that illumination of man's whole being by the radiance of the divine glory which is man's true destiny but which was lost through sin, as it

---

5:2 "Boast" is variously explained. Many translate this "rejoice" (NIV; Cranfield 1975; Schreiner 1998; Moo 1996) or "confidence" (Morris 1988) because Paul elsewhere criticizes human boasting (Rom 2:17, 23; 3:27; 1 Cor 1:29; 3:21; Gal 6:13). While these are certainly part of the verb's meaning and may be part of its use here, the thrust of boasting in God for all his gifts should not be ruled out. As Dunn says

will be restored . . . when man's redemption is finally consummated at the parousia of Jesus Christ." The hope that every sacrifice will be rewarded is the basis for the Christian life with its mandate to live separately from the world; for every earthly glory surrendered, God will recompense an eternal glory (Mt 6:19-21; Mk 10:29-31).

The second half of this section (vv. 3-5) turns to the primary challenge to the joy of our salvation, namely, our *sufferings* or "afflictions," probably including trials in general and persecution in particular (Rom 8:35; 12:12; 2 Cor 2:4; 7:4; Phil 1:17). It is common to see these specifically as the eschatological sufferings of the end time (Mk 13:19, 24), especially since the already/not yet tension is predominant here (so Dunn 1988a:250). While the end-time suffering (inaugurated now in the church) is part of the meaning, the term here almost certainly refers to affliction in general (1 Pet 1:6-7). Paul says Christians should *rejoice* or "exult" in their difficulties (note the parallel in Jas 1:2-4), not meaning that they should be happy in their troubles (see Heb 12:11) but that they should delight in what those troubles will do in their lives, as is made clear in the list that follows. The New Testament teaching on trials is quite illuminating. In Hebrews 12:5-11 trials are looked at from the standpoint of God, a loving Father who must "discipline" his children. 1 Peter 1:6-7 looks at trials from the standpoint of who we are, namely, "of greater weight than gold." If gold must be purified "by fire," how much more do we need the purifying effects of "all kinds of trials" to be made pure. Finally, James 1:2-4 looks at trials from the standpoint of their results; through them we learn "perseverance" and thereby become "mature and complete, not lacking anything." In all three passages the true goal of trials is to increase our "faith," meaning a God-centered, God-dependent way of life. The list here follows a similar pattern.

Paul shows the results of our afflictions, beginning with *because we know*, indicating the reasons that we can rejoice in suffering. What fol-

(1988a:248), "Paul's point is not simply that there is a boasting which is proper, but that such boasting is only possible for the person who stands in God's grace, so that his boasting is of the God on whom he totally depends without being able to claim any special privilege (contrast 2:17, 23)."

lows is a chain of qualities similar to that in Romans 8:29-30 and especially to the chain attached to trials in James 1:3-4. It is indeed possible that the two passages (as well as 1 Pet 1:6-7) belong to the same catechetical tradition in the early church. In fact, the very first quality produced by suffering is the same as in James 1:3—"endurance" (*perseverance* in the NIV), an "independent, unyielding . . . perseverance in the face of aggressive misfortune . . . made possible by Christian hope (Rom 8:25)" (Radl 1993:405). It is often connected with faith in God during hard times (2 Thess 1:4; 3:5; 1 Tim 6:11; 2 Tim 3:10), especially in Revelation (1:9; 2:2, 3, 19; 3:10; 13:10; 14:12). It is clear that in adverse circumstances believers are expected to display a steadfast hope that enables them to remain faithful to God and to run the race of life in the way that God has "marked out for us" (Heb 12:1). Endurance then will produce proper Christian *character* (Greek *dokimē*), a term also found in James 1:3 and 1 Peter 1:7, connoting a proven character produced by "testing." The Greek word for *testing* occurs only in Paul's writings in the New Testament but is part of a word group used of testing or purifying gold by bringing it to the boiling point, thus allowing the lighter minerals (gold is one of the heaviest of metals) to rise to the surface where the goldsmith can skim them off. This is the message in 1 Peter 1:7, where our faith is *refined* or "tested" in the crucible of life to make it purer. In the context of Romans 5:3-5 (as in James and 1 Peter) trials "test" the Christian and give them both endurance and a proven character. This was certainly the case with Abraham as discussed in Romans 4, and it was also true for Paul (read 2 Cor 11:16-33, where Paul uses "boast" three times to describe the effects of his own sufferings). Finally, tested character will produce *hope,* used already in 4:18 to describe how Abraham "in hope believed" and therefore became "the father of many nations" through Isaac. There is a circularity in this. Hope makes it possible to endure, and at the same time the process of enduring and the godly character it produces increases our hope by making us continually reflect on the future realities guaran-

---

5:5 Many take *has poured out* entirely of the conversion experience, but it is more likely that it refers to a constant "state of affairs" (the normal thrust of the perfect tense) beginning with conversion and daily experienced by the Christian. The same

teed by God. So the four—*sufferings, perseverance, character, hope*—interrelate and define the Christian approach to life in this world. Bieringer (1995:305-25) shows that hope is at all times active rather than passive; that is, it must always be demonstrated in the kind of victorious living that results from the experience of Christ and brings glory to God in difficult times.

Paul then elaborates on the meaning of *hope* by saying that it *does not disappoint us* (v. 5). Since *hope* begins and ends this section (vv. 2, 5), it is probably the major theme (Godet 1969; Moo 1996; Schreiner 1998). Christ has died for us, and to be justified by faith is evidence of God's love (vv. 5, 8) and proof that we are delivered from his wrath (v. 9). That is the basis of our hope. *Not disappoint* means literally "will not put us to shame" and alludes to Old Testament passages that teach that the child of God does not need to fear "shame" or judgment because of relationship to God (Ps 22:5; 25:3, 20; 31:1; 71:1; Is 28:16; 50:7; 54:4). Thus there is a connection with verse 9, which says that, because we have been justified, we need not fear the wrath of God. Here we have hope *because God has poured out his love into our hearts. His love* ("the love of God" in the Greek) is probably not our love for God (so Augustine) but God's love for us (so Calvin 1948 and nearly all today). This is the first time Paul has mentioned God's love in Romans, but it will become a major theme. Interestingly, in many places it is God's wrath that is poured out (Ps 65:9; Hos 5:10; Rev 16:1-17 [nine times]), but here Paul has already explicitly stated that the believer has no fear of that. The verb refers to a flood of love that God has poured into our lives. Two further points are critical. First, this love is poured out *into our hearts,* meaning we realize God's love as an inner, spiritual experience at the deepest level of our being. Second, the means by which we experience this is *the Holy Spirit whom he has given us.* In several passages it is the Holy Spirit who is "poured out" (Joel 2:28; Ezek 36:25-27; Acts 2:17-18, 33; Tit 3:6), but here the Spirit is the means by which God's love is poured into our lives. The Holy Spirit is the supreme gift

---

is true of the gift of the Holy Spirit. While the Spirit is certainly given at conversion (Rom 8:1-2), here the Spirit is continually active in us.

---

that makes it possible for us to know the gift of God's love. As Augustine says, "It is not by ourselves but by the Holy Spirit who is given to us that this charity, shown by the apostle to be God's gift, is the reason why tribulation does not destroy patience but rather gives rise to it" (Bray 1998:130). The Holy Spirit fills us with the love of God and gives us the strength to endure.

Love and Reconciliation in Christ (5:6-11) Paul now elaborates on his statement in verse 5 that God's love has been poured out into our lives. There our hope is grounded in the depth of his love. In verses 6-8 this depth is plumbed, as the divine love is exemplified especially in the sacrificial death of Christ. The *gar* ("for," omitted by the NIV) that begins the verse shows that this section continues the basis for our hope that was discussed in verse 5. There is an ABA pattern in these verses; Christ's death for sinners (A, vv. 6, 8) is set in bold relief by comparing it with the deepest example of human love, namely, dying for a good person (B, v. 7). The emphasis in the first part is on *still,* which appears twice in the Greek for emphasis, *when we were still powerless.* The point is that all of us were *still* in a state of sin when Christ died for us. Fitzmyer says (1993b:399) that this "stresses the persistence of the condition. In the face of such persistent weakness and helplessness stands God's action in Christ."

Two terms are used to characterize that sinful condition. *Powerless,* or better "weak," often refers to physical incapacitation but here refers to the complete inability of every sinful person to accomplish anything of eternal consequence. This does not mean that human beings are incapable of good (Calvin 1979:194-95) called this "common grace," the ability of the natural person to do good since all are made in the image of God), but it conveys that they can do nothing that will make them right with God. In 1:18-19 Paul described the total depravity of the non-Christian, and this is connected to that doctrine, describing the

---

5:6 Dunn (1988a:254) says there is no theological overtone in "weak" (NIV *powerless*) but simply a contrast between the human condition and the power of God. This is possible and could connote the helpless nature of human beings, but what are they helpless to do? It certainly points to moral inability, and in connection with *ungodly* must refer to the spiritual condition.

5:7 Many argue that the two sentences are synonymous, perhaps with the second

helpless condition of the unsaved to earn salvation. *Ungodly* is a stronger term and refers to "living without regard to proper religious beliefs and practice" (Louw and Nida 1988:533). It appeared in a similar context in Romans 4:5 to describe those whom God "justifies," the "wicked," or ungodly. Here it is used to depict those for whom *Christ died.* The language of Christ "dying for" us is quite common (four times in 5:6-8; 14:15; Jn 11:50, 51; 1 Cor 15:3; 2 Cor 5:15) and connotes substitutionary atonement, describing Christ's vicarious death "for" us or in place of us (see Harris 1978:1196-97, who states that *hyper* means both representation and substitution). Moreover, this sacrificial death of Christ occurred *at just the right time,* which could mean "at that very time when we were weak" (Käsemann 1980; Moo 1996) but more likely modifies "Christ died for the ungodly," paralleling "when the time had fully come" in Galatians 4:4 and meaning the perfect time in history for God to carry out his plan of salvation (Barrett 1957; Cranfield 1975).

In contrast to Christ's death for the ungodly, Paul goes on to say, human love at its highest level will sometimes move a person to die for a *righteous* or *good* person (v. 7). He presents the concept in an ascending pair of statements. First, the "righteous" person would be a morally upright individual, perhaps a zealot (Dunn 1988a), one for whom we have respect but no particular attachment (Moo 1996). The "good" person is one with whom we have close relations, possibly a "benefactor" (Cranfield 1975; Schreiner 1998) or a relative who has done us significant "good." Paul's point is in part that we might be slightly more willing to die for a good person than for a righteous one, but it is more important to emphasize the astonishing love of Christ. The highest example of human love is a rare willingness to die for a righteous person and the slightly more common impulse to die for a good person. On the other hand, Christ died for the ungodly who de-

---

sentence a scribal correction of the first (Barrett 1957; Käsemann 1980) or by explaining the first further (Bruce 1985; Murray 1968; Morris 1988). Others believe there is some development, interpreting the *righteous* person as morally just and the *good* person as someone close to us, perhaps a dear friend or a relative or a benefactor (Sanday and Headlam 1902; Cranfield 1975; Clarke 1990; Moo 1996; Schreiner 1998). This latter fits the context better.

served nothing and wanted nothing to do with him.

This is especially seen in the fact that God not only loves us but *demonstrates his own love for us,* that is, has concretely "proven" this love in the greatest possible way (v. 8). This justly famous verse is the apex of biblical statements on divine love. Anyone who loves another person tries to give concrete proof of that love via certain actions, perhaps buying presents or flowers or surprising them with a romantic getaway. God proved the depths of his love in a way none of us would want to do, by giving his Son to die for us. Yet it is far more than that: he did so *while we were still sinners,* that is, when we were his enemies, godless sinners. This is the primary point Paul is making. Christ did not die for righteous people or for friends; he died for sinful human beings in all their degrading depravity, for those who "suppress the truth by their wickedness" (1:18) and do "not think it worthwhile to retain the knowledge of God" (1:28), who are "filled with every kind of wickedness, evil, greed and depravity" (1:29). Therefore we deserved to experience the wrath of God and eternal judgment, but Christ took our punishment upon himself and paid the penalty in our place, thereby procuring redemption on our behalf (3:21-26).

The second half of this section (vv. 9-11) describes the natural conclusion (*oun,* "therefore," omitted by the NIV) to this act of divine love. We are justified, saved from his wrath and reconciled to him. The result of Christ's atoning death is that *we have now been justified by his blood,* the message of 3:21—4:25. There have been several ways of signifying the means of justification in this section: "by his grace" in 3:24, *in his blood* in 3:25 and 5:9, "by faith" in 3:28, his resurrection in 4:25, and *through his life* in 5:10. The emphasis on his blood here emphasizes the sacrificial, atoning aspect of his death, bringing out the idea of the ransom price behind "redemption" language (see on 3:24). Moreover, it is a present reality (now) and force in our lives. Paul's point, however, is that since our justification is a fact, *how much more* (first in the Greek for emphasis) is it true that we are *saved from God's wrath through him!* This uses a Jewish hermeneutical technique called "from the weightier to the lighter," that is, from the more difficult to the less (Cranfield 1975; Moo 1996; Schreiner 1998; Dunn 1988a shows it is used four times—vv. 9, 10, 15, 17). Since God has done the more difficult, justified the ungodly, how much more can he achieve the easier, delivering those who have been declared innocent from his wrath. *Saved* in this context refers not to spiritual salvation but to being "delivered" from wrath, namely, God's wrath at the last judgment (see 2:5, 8 on final wrath; 1:18; 3:5; 4:15; 9:22; 12:19 on present wrath). Moo (1996:310-11 n.) has a good summary, pointing out that Paul often uses this term "to depict the final deliverance of the Christian from the power of sin, the evils of this life, and especially judgment (e.g., 1 Cor. 3:15; 5:5; Phil. 2:12)." Paul pictures the Christian as *having been saved, as looking forward to being saved,* and even as *in the process of being saved* (cf. 2 Cor 2:15; 2 Thess 2:10).

The following verse (v. 10) repeats the argument from a different perspective. Here *the death of his Son* has resulted in our being *reconciled* to him. Reconciliation is the natural result of justification. After God has declared us righteous on the basis of Christ's sacrificial death, he establishes a new relationship with us. The language moves from the legal to the personal. Cranfield (1975:267) says reconciliation language was never used in the religious language of the Hellenistic world because it was too deeply personal, but Paul (Rom 5:10, 11; 11:15; 2 Cor 5:18-20) uses it to show the new personal relationship established by God's justification. Here those who are *God's enemies* have been both justified and *reconciled . . . through the death of his Son.* That is the thrust of being *reconciled,* to bring *enemies* into proper relationship with each other. Note the two directions—hostility from the unbeliever due to sin and hostility from God due to his judgment on sin. But as a result of Christ's death, that hostility has been removed from both sides, and a new relationship has ensued. So if this exceedingly difficult thing has taken place, how much easier it is for God to have *saved* us *through his life.* As in verse 9, *saved* must mean deliverance from his final wrath. But what does *through his life* connote? Most likely it refers to his resurrection as the means of reconciliation (cf. 4:25; 8:34). Christ's death and resurrection are a single event in salvation history and together constitute the basis of our salvation (see on 4:25).

The concluding idea of this section is once again that of boasting, thus framing the paragraph with the theme of boasting or exulting—we *rejoice in God through our Lord Jesus Christ.* The natural reaction to all

that God has done for us *through* . . . *Christ* (see vv. 1, 2, 9, 10 for the
centrality of Christ as the means of salvation) is joy. Paul says here that
God *not only* has saved us from his future wrath (vv. 9-10) *but . . . also*
has given us the joy of our present *reconciliation*. We have both future
hope (vv. 2, 5, 9-10) and present salvation. What joy! And that joy is *in
God*, showing that the highest action anyone can perform is worship,
and this worship is a continuous activity. The Christian life is God-centered, and Christ is the instrument whose death on the Cross made this
possible. God has given us salvation, and thus we have received an entirely new relationship *(reconciliation)* from him.

New Life as Christ Overcomes Adam's Sin (5:12-21) Paul has established the fact of justification and its results—present salvation and future hope. Now he turns to the primary barrier between people and
God—the sin and guilt inherited from Adam. The point is that Christ
has overcome the power of sin and death by becoming the victor over
those evil forces. The effects of Adam's sin have been reversed for
those who have experienced salvation; the universal consequences of
the Fall are overcome by the universal consequences of the cross.

This section is organized around a series of comparisons—*just as . . .
so also* (vv. 12, 18, 19, 21) and *if . . . how much more* (vv. 15, 17). There
are probably four subsections—verses 12-14, 15-17, 18-19, and 20-21.
Murray (1968:179) shows that this passage contrasts two opposed
complexes—sin/condemnation/death versus righteousness/justifica-
tion/life—and these are "antithetical at each point of the parallel." It
provides a natural transition from the justification of 3:21—5:11 to the
new life in Christ of 6:1—8:39. There is some link, in fact, to the universality of sin passage in 1:18—3:20, so that one could see 5:12-21 as
introducing 6:1—8:39 in the same way that 1:18—3:20 introduced
3:21—5:11. Paul begins to establish the comparison in verse 12 but fails
to complete it because the readers needed clarification regarding the
reign of sin and death (vv. 13-14). Having made this clarification, he

---

5:12 There is some discussion of whether *just as* introduces a true comparison with
the second half *and in this way death came to all men* (so Barrett 1957; Lenski
1945), but the *and* makes this unlikely. Instead, the comparison is not completed

then makes four comparisons in verses 15-19 before drawing the section together by discussing the contrast between sin and grace (vv. 20-21).

Commentators debate whether *therefore* (literally "because of this") in verse 12 refers back to 1:18—5:11 (Dunn 1988a; Stuhlmacher 1994), to 5:1-11 (Sanday and Headlam 1902; Cranfield 1975; M. Black 1973, Fitzmyer 1993b), to verses 6-11 (Lenski 1945), to verses 9-10 (Moo 1996), or just to verse 11 (Morris 1988). While we cannot be certain, the immediately preceding section (vv. 1-11) provides the best scenario. On the basis of the new salvation and reconciliation given by God through Christ, Paul wants us to understand more specifically how sin was nullified in Christ. So he begins by saying that *sin entered the world through one man*. The *one man* is Adam, and the *world* is all humanity. The Jewish concept of corporate solidarity is central: Adam represents all humanity. As Christ was the means of salvation (5:1, 6, 8, 9, 10, 11), so Adam was the means by which sin came into the world. As Sanday and Headlam state (1902:132), sin here is personified as "a malignant force let loose among mankind." Moreover, while sin came through Adam, *death* came *through sin*. The progression is clear— Adam to sin to death. The universal presence of these hostile powers is the basic tragedy of life. Sin is also seen accompanying death in 1 Corinthians 15:56, "the sting of death is sin." However, as Moo demonstrates (1996:320), this refers not just to physical death but also to "spiritual" death, "the estrangement from God that is the result of sin and that, if not healed through Christ, will lead to 'eternal death.'" Moreover, *in this way* that sin produced death, it also brought death to every person.

The most debated portion is the last clause of verse 12, *because all sinned*. For the most part, debates about the imputation of sins (see below) center on these four Greek words. The introductory *eph hō* (in whom, because) has led to several different interpretations (see Cranfield 1975; Morris 1988; Fitzmyer 1993b): (1) "in whom all sinned," referring back to *one man* and meaning that all humankind sinned in

---

until verse 18 (with vv. 15-17 preparing the way), and Paul digresses to discuss the reign of sin and death in this fallen world.

Adam (Augustinian/natural headship, but the antecedent would be too far away); (2) "because all sinned," taking the *all sinned* to be every person sinning after the example of Adam (Pelagian, but this is contradicted by the context); (3) taking *eph hō* as sequential (Schreiner 1998, "upon the basis of which") with death being the antecedent, thus "on the basis of this death all sinned"; (4) taking it as sequential (Murray 1968, "in whom") or causal (Bruce 1985, "because") and *sinned* in a corporate sense, so that all sin by virtue of their solidarity with Adam (federal headship); or (5) taking it as consecutive (Fitzmyer 1993a:332-36, "with the result that") or causal (Sanday and Headlam 1902; Cranfield 1975—"because all sinned"), taking all the sins of humankind as a whole, thus meaning that all people inherit corruption from Adam and then participate in that sin (mediate imputation and Arminianism). These last three views are the most likely, and it is difficult to choose among them. The federal view (see Morris 1988; Moo 1996) has the advantage of seeing all of verse 12 as corporate, but it has to take *all sinned* with verses 18-19 as corporate while Paul does not explicitly say that here. Mediate imputation reads *all sinned* in a more natural way but then has to see the individual (*all* read as "every person" sinning) in a context that is primarily corporate. Still, this is more the natural meaning of *all sinned,* which usually refers to the individual sins of people (so Fitzmyer 1993b; Wilckens 1978; Schreiner 1998). Schreiner's option makes sense in the context, but the result is theologically difficult, with death the basis for universal sin. On the whole, the mediate imputation view is best. All people have inherited corruption from Adam (the first part of v. 12) and then have participated in that sin (here). Therefore, they are guilty from two directions—the sinful

---

5:12 The imputation-of-sin debate flowing out of this passage has been immense. The following solutions have been proposed: (1) Pelagius—every person is born innocent and has no connection with the sin of Adam; that is only an example here. (2) Arminian (Wesley)—we inherit both depravity and guilt but still participate in that guilt when we sin. (3) "new school" theory—we are born with a sin tendency, but this does not become sin until we *consciously* transgress God's law. (4) Mediate imputation—we inherit the principle of corruption, and this determines our guilt; i.e., the condition leads to legal guilt not vice versa. (5) Realistic theory—Adam possessed the total human nature, and so all people *actually* sin because every person was a part of Adam. (Jonathan Edwards: we were all ideally present in Adam and

nature inherited from Adam (passive sin) and their personal participation in that via their own sins (active sin). In fact, this is the basic difference of Christianity from all other religions, the nature of total depravity and the universal guilt of all people under sin. It is this that necessitated the cross, for this guilt is so severe that no human effort could ever assuage it.

Paul now breaks his thought (note the dash in the NIV) and turns to the question of sin/death and the law on the basis of verse 12. The issue of the universality of sin and death needs to be explained further. In verse 12 Paul has already based the universality of death in the fact that *all have sinned*. But this needs more explanation, so Paul adds that the universal reign of death is grounded in (*gar,* "for") the fact that *before the law was given, sin was in the world*. As Barrett points out (1957:111), Paul is answering a possible misinterpretation: If death is connected to sin, there must not have been any deaths before sin came since "where there is no law there is no transgression" (4:15). So Paul clarifies here that sin existed before the law of Moses came. The effects of the Fall were seen even before the Mosaic law showed them to be transgressions of divine law. Sin was present before there was legislative proof of it. But the problem still remains, namely, that *sin is not taken into account when there is no law*. The verb meaning *taken into account* is a commercial metaphor that indicates that sin is registered on God's official ledger as transgression, as in Revelation 20:12, "the dead were judged according to what they had done as recorded in the books." Paul is saying that while there was sin, it was not officially known as such. As in 4:15 it was the Mosaic law that made sin a deliberate transgression against God and

---

sinned when he sinned.) (6) Federal headship—as the father of mankind, Adam was the representative head of the race; therefore the covenant of works (the pre-Fall condition) extended to Adam and belonged to the race, so that Adam's disobedience meant his descendants are born depraved and guilty. (7) Natural headship (Augustinian)—Adam is the head of the race, and so the whole race sinned together in Adam as its head; the nature of every person is corrupt and guilt is imputed *seminally* and immediately. Reformed theologians tend to take positions 5-7 and Arminian theologians positions 2-4. On the whole, it must be said that the entire debate reads too much into verse 12. However, with the interpretation of *because all sinned* here, I believe a combination of 2 and 4 best solves the issue.

showed humankind what it was. Yet people were still guilty before the law came. While there was no official registry of their sin, the sins committed were still quite real.

Paul goes on to say that the proof of this is the fact that *death reigned from the time of Adam to the time of Moses, even over those who did not sin by breaking a command, as did Adam.* As Bruce says (1985:130), "sin was all-pervasive, and mortal in its effect, even in the absence of any positive commandment for them to transgress as there was for Adam." We know the universal presence of sin on the basis of the universal presence of death. There was still moral transgression even if there was no official law that identified it as such, and the fact of death (God's legal punishment on sin) proves that this was the case. Death is personified here as a power that rules over humankind. So the period from Adam to Moses cannot be called "the age of innocence," for as Calvin points out (1979:202-3) Cain was punished, the world was destroyed by a flood, Sodom was wiped from the earth and plagues were inflicted on Egypt. Sin was still punished, and guilt was still present. Some have thought that *those who did not sin by breaking a command* is a reference to infants or the mentally challenged, but that is highly unlikely. This refers to those who lived between Adam and Moses. In short, sin is universal, and all stand guilty before God. As already stated, this is the major difference between Christianity and other world religions. All others have a basic works-righteousness orientation: those who have more "good karma" than bad are all right. Only Christianity realizes it is much more complex, for our sinful nature has made it impossible for any of us to be right with God. Intervention from above is needed, and that is what Paul proceeds to point out.

5:13 There are two different ways of looking at Paul's digression in verses 13-14. Some (Murray 1968; Moo 1996; and others who opt for the federal headship position) take the first clause in verse 13 as concessive and emphasize the contrast between verses 13 and 14 ("Though sin was in the world before the law, sin is not taken into account when there is no law; nevertheless, death reigned from the time of Adam to the time of Moses"). Others (Cranfield 1975; Käsemann 1980; and others who hold the mediate-imputation view) emphasize the first clause and see the second as concessive ("sin was in the world before the law, but sin is not taken into account when there is no law; nevertheless, death reigned from the time of Adam to the time of Moses"). In the first view the reign of death over those who had not

Paul returns to his Adam/Christ typology in the last clause of verse 14, saying that Adam *was a pattern [or type] of the one to come*. "Type" is a technical Jewish term referring to a figure or event of the past that provides a pattern or model for the new age inaugurated by Christ. The term meant the "mark" or impression left by a sharp blow, as with a "stamp" made by a die or molded figure. In the New Testament this was a historical event that prefigured the New Testament reality. Adam is a type of Christ in the sense that the universal effects of his act prefigure the universal effects of Christ's act (so Moo 1996:334). The *one to come* is a title for the coming Messiah (see the cry of the crowd at the triumphal entry, "blessed is he who comes in the name of the Lord," Mk 11:9 and parallels).

The rest of the passage explicates this typological relationship (vv. 15-17, 18-19, 20-21). Point by point, what Adam has done is turned aside by what Christ has done. In another sense humanity is broken up into two groups, those who live with the effects of Adam's sin and those who live with the effects of Christ's atoning sacrifice. The corporate solidarity is complete, with Adam the head of his "race" and Christ the head of his "race." The first antithesis is in verse 15, literally "not as the transgress, so also the grace." This is stated well in the NLT, "and what a difference between our sin and God's generous gift of forgiveness." The term for sin here is different from that for *transgression* in verse 14 (there meaning "false step" or "lapse"), and it is debated how great a difference in meaning there is. Most likely, the word in verse 15 goes back to the basic meaning of *sin* in verse 12 (rather than the legal concept of v. 14) and refers to the universal presence of sin throughout the history of the human race. The trespass of Adam is countered by

---

sinned is central, while in the second the presence of sin in the world before the law is central. In one sense the debate is overdrawn. Neither side truly relegates the concessive clause to an insignificant place (as both sides claim). It is rather a matter of emphasis. However, if we allow the conjunctions to guide us, the *gar (for)* beginning verse 13 shows that it provides the clarification for verse 12, not for the second clause. Then the *de (but)* beginning the last half of verse 13 notes a problem to the statement of the first clause of the verse, and the *alla (nevertheless)* of verse 14 answers the whole of verse 13 and not just the second clause. So the conjunctions favor the second option over the first.

the gift of Christ, and so God's grace-gift is greater than people's sin.

Paul proceeds to provide a lengthy explanation giving three contrasts developing this theme. First, Adam's trespass brought death while the grace-gift of Christ brought abundance (v. 15). This essentially reproduces the teaching of verse 12, substituting *the many* for *all*. But the contrast is not really *the one* and *the many* but *the one* (Adam) and *the one man, Jesus Christ. The many* are the recipients of his grace; divine grace alone has overcome the sin of Adam. Sanday and Headlam (1902:140) note two aspects of the application of grace to Christ: that active favor toward humankind, which moved him to intervene for their salvation (2 Cor 8:9), and that active favor shown by the Father and Son acting together (Rom 1:7). This act of grace is further defined as *the gift that came by the grace of the one man, Jesus Christ.* The term *gift* is a strong Hellenistic word denoting the best gifts and is chosen to highlight the gift of what Christ has done for *the many*. This gift is further defined in verse 17 as *the gift of righteousness* conferred upon those who have put their faith in Christ. So *the many* are not all humanity but those who have become believers. The contrast between the two groups is obvious. For *the many* who are of Adam there is only one consequence, death. For *the many* who have come to Christ there is the proliferation of terms for the incredible grace-gift of Christ, and this gift did *overflow* or "abound" to their benefit. This overwhelming gift is the true meaning of Christmas, the gift of the one who was born to become "obedient to death—even death on a cross" (Phil 2:8).

The second contrast (v. 16) centers on the results—the trespass brought judgment and condemnation, while the free gift brought justification and righteousness. The verse begins with a terse statement, literally "the gift is not as through the one who sinned," meaning there is a completely different result. As a result of Adam's trespass, *the judgment . . . brought condemnation. Condemnation* (used only three times in the New Testament—Rom 15:16, 18; 8:1) refers to the sentence of judgment leading to the execution of that sentence on the sinner. This terrible result is nullified by the "free gift" of Christ that *brought justification,* a term that means not only the justification of the sinner but the righteousness that flows from that. However, the contrast is rightly between the judicial results, the sentences of condemnation and of justification. Yet there is another contrast, for the condemnation came via *one sin,* that of Adam, but the gift of justification *followed many trespasses,* that is, the sins of all humanity. So Christ's gift is all the more powerful and comprehensive. Cranfield says it well (1975:286): "That one single misdeed should be answered by judgment, that is perfectly understandable: that the accumulated sins and guilt of all the ages should be answered by God's free gift, that is the miracle of miracles, utterly beyond human comprehension."

The third contrast (v. 17) continues the results—death reigned through sin, but the recipients of grace and righteousness reign in life through Jesus Christ. The condemnation of verse 16 led to the reign of death, and the justification of verse 16 led to the grace of God that enables believers to reign in life. Moreover, the presence of both *grace* and *gift* shows that this develops further the emphases of verse 15. This verse sums up and concludes the contrasts between the effects of Adam and Christ (so Käsemann 1980; Fitzmyer 1993b; Moo 1996), but it also encapsulates the message on the universal reign of death in verses 12-14 (Dunn 1988a). Here, however, that universal reign is answered and overturned by the incredible grace of God. The aorist tense of *reigned* is global, incorporating the age of Adam into a single sweeping whole. Sin and death hold sway over all humanity because of *the trespass of the one man.* Yet once more that power has been nullified. Grace overturns sin, and life triumphs over death because the *one man, Jesus Christ* has overturned the act of the *one* (Adam). Paul's language virtually stumbles over itself to demonstrate *how much more* God's gift has accomplished. *Grace* from verse 15 has become *God's abundant provision of grace,* pointing to the over-reaching bountifulness (so Barrett 1957, "excess") of God's grace as the source of life. The *gift* is now clarified as *the gift of righteousness,* probably referring to both the new status bestowed as well as the act of justifying (as in v. 16). Salvation-history is here portrayed as the actors switch from God, whose act of grace makes salvation possible, to Christ whose gift procures salvation, to the believers who *receive* the gift and *reign in life.* This reign, the overturning of death's reign, is future. Death reigned in the past, but for the believer life controls the future. Many take this as an apocalyptic concept referring to eternal life after the establishment of "a new heaven and a new earth" in Revelation 21, but it is more likely inaugurated eschatology, meaning that life reigns from the moment one becomes a follower of Christ and will be consummated at the eschaton.

The next series of contrasts (vv. 18-19) returns to the language of verse 12 (just as . . . so also) and completes the thought begun there. At the same time, the introductory *consequently* shows that Paul intends for this to function as a summary of his thought. He has already developed in verses 15-17 the basic argument of the one/many contrast between Adam and Christ; now here he elaborates his thesis and draws it to a conclusion. There are three further contrasts. The first (v. 18) not only completes the contrast begun but not completed in verse 12 but also restates verses 16-17. It centers again on the results of the deeds, with the *one trespass* (so NASB and NIV but probably better "one man's trespass," so NRSV, NLT) producing *condemnation for all* and the *one act of righteousness* producing the *justification that brings life for all.* The *for all* stresses the universal effects of Adam and Christ (as in v. 12, compare *the many* in v. 15). The *act of righteousness* could refer to the act of justifying people (so Sanday and Headlam 1902; Morris 1988) but more likely refers to the righteous act of Jesus' sacrificial death (Murray 1968; Cranfield 1975; Dunn 1988a; Schreiner 1998). Moo (1996:342-44) shows why *for all* does not mean universal salvation, as some have interpreted it. In verses 15 and 19 Paul uses *the many* to show that salvation is given only to those who *receive God's abundant provision of grace* (v. 17) by faith (3:21-4:25). So when he uses *all men* here, he does not mean every human being but rather is saying "that Christ effects those who are his just as certainly as Adam does those who are his." While all are in Adam, it is clear in Romans that only those who believe are in Christ.

The second concluding contrast (v. 19) restates the first using different language, with Adam's *disobedience* making many people *sinners* while Christ's *obedience* makes many people *righteous*. The word order in the verse emphasizes *the one* and *the many,* concluding the emphasis in this section as both Adam and Christ affect the many who are corporately identified with them. Now the antithesis shifts to *disobedience/obedience*. These terms show that both the trespass of Adam and the righteous act of Christ were done in relation to God's divine command. While *obedience* could refer to Jesus' whole life (so Godet 1969; Murray 1968; Cranfield 1975), it is more likely that it refers to the obedience of the cross (Phil 2:8, so Käsemann 1980; Dunn 1988a; Moo 1996). The translation *were made* is somewhat weak, for as M. Black shows (1973:84), it has a strong legal connotation and means to "appoint" or "constitute" someone into a certain class or category. Moreover, the results center on a state of being into which the people are placed, *sinners* versus *righteous,* so it is best to say that those in Adam's sin were "constituted as belonging to the class of sinners" and Christ's atoning sacrifice "constituted his followers as belonging to the class of the righteous." In this sense too the adjective *righteous* does not just connote the legal act of being declared righteous by God but also refers to the ethical result of righteous living. The adjective often in Romans refers to those who live righteously (1:17; 3:10; 5:7) and so has a double meaning—those who are declared righteous will live righteously (see also on justification language in 3:24).

The final section (vv. 20-21) returns to Paul's digression of verses 13-14 and the question of the law. Those who complained about the law earlier might have another critique, namely, that the law cannot be so easily set aside as having no part to play. So Paul returns to that issue. First he elaborates on the purpose of the law. In verse 13 the law pointed out that sin is transgression against God's standards. Here *the law was added so that the trespass might increase.* The meaning of *was added* is disputed. Some (Sanday and Headlam 1902; Barrett 1957; Dunn 1988a) give a negative thrust (as in Gal 2:4, the only other place it occurs in the New Testament), meaning that the law is "inferior" or "an afterthought." However, it is generally agreed that this does not fit the context, so some take it simply as the "entrance" of the law into salvation-history (Murray 1968; Cranfield 1975) or with a slight negative connotation, that it was added into a world dominated by sin and has no power to change the situation—it is subordinate to the grace of God (Morris 1988; Moo 1996; Schreiner 1998). This latter is probably the best understanding. So the purpose of the law was not to solve the problem of sin but actually to cause it to increase! Some have interpreted this to mean that the law made sin more attractive by highlighting it. For instance, Origen said it "promotes the lusts of the flesh and leads men captive, inclining them to desire and excesses, so that sin might abound in them"; and Augustine believed that through it "sin abounded . . . because desire grew more ardent in the light of the prohibition" (Bray 1998:149, 150). But that does not fit here. The point is not so much an increase in the number of sins but in the seriousness of sin (so Cranfield 1975; Wilckens 1978; Moo 1996; Schreiner 1998). The law showed people that moral sin transgresses the laws of God.

The final two antitheses respond to this increase of sin, but this time the contrast is not between Adam and Christ but between sin and grace. First, "where sin abounded, grace superabounded" (NIV, *increased/increased all the more*). While Paul could have been concerned only with the place of Israel under the law (so Cranfield 1975; Moo 1996; Schreiner 1998), this statement sums up the exalted language of the whole section (see *much more* and *increase* in vv. 15, 17) and thus highlights the overflowing grace and love of God as well as the extent to which they cover sin. So Paul includes Israel under the law and both Jew and Gentile under grace. Grace triumphs over evil. Stott (1994:157, quoting Cranfield 1975:830) says, "If its [the sin of Adam] 'increase' is its spread and intensification across history, reaching a 'hideous climax' in the rejection of Christ at the cross, then God's abounding grace will refer to 'the divine self-giving of the cross.'" Second, the reign of sin in death is contrasted to the reign of grace bringing eternal life (v. 21). Paul is saying that the sphere within which sin reigns in humanity is death, the basic point of verse 12 (better than instrument, "by death," or accompaniment, "with death"). Sin not only enslaves us but kills us. But once more the grace of God is triumphant. Through the cross, God's grace reigns in the life of every believer, producing eternal life in place of death. Again, the superabundance of God's grace is evident. There is no death/life dualism, for *death* here is the temporal experience of physical death, while God provides *eternal life* for the believer. Moreover, grace reigns *through righteousness,* probably here not so much the righteous living of the Christian as the new gift of righteousness (vv. 17, 19) God attributes to the believer on the basis of Christ's justifying work (though Schreiner 1998:296-97 is probably right in saying that the gift must produce righteous living).

And this is all made possible by *Jesus Christ our Lord*. Christ is Lord over life, and only he has conquered death for all of us.

Sanctification: Liberated from the Power of Sin (6:1-23) When missionaries move to a new country, they attempt to enter that new culture. They take language classes, spend as much time as they can with the people, and slowly alter their patterns of life to match those of the new culture. This is what Paul is talking about in this chapter. The new believer has entered a new realm of existence and therefore begins the process of changing old habits and patterns to fit the new way of life he or she has chosen. But here the analogy of the missionary is insufficient, for the believer has also changed citizenship and joined the commonwealth of heaven (Phil 3:20; Eph 2:19). The believer has experienced justification (been declared righteous by God) and now enters a life of sanctification (the process of being set apart for God via living by the Spirit). At the outset, a misconception must be corrected. It has been thought by many that the process of sanctification begins at some point after justification has occurred. This chapter will show that to be a false premise. In actuality, justification is the first moment of sanctification; it launches the process. In the same way that accepting Jesus as savior begins the process of knowing him as Lord, the gift of justification begins the process of sanctification.

Let us recapitulate the development of Paul's thought thus far. In 1:18—3:20 the universality of sin and guilt was proven; all stand equally before God without excuse for their wickedness. In response to this human dilemma, Christ became the atoning sacrifice that made it possible for people to be justified and redeemed from their sins (3:21-26). Abraham became the primary example of this (4:1-25); his faith was "credited to him as righteousness." Thus it is clear that we participate in the grace-gift from God via faith. The results are explored in 5:1-11—peace, hope, eternal salvation—all made possible because Christ died for us and reconciled us with God. Finally, the cosmic process is explored, as Christ is contrasted with Adam in 5:12-21. Through Adam sin came and brought death to all humankind, but Christ has reversed that and brought life to the "many" who come to faith. Sin no longer reigns, for grace reigns and brings with it eternal life. Chapter 6 now explores the process by which sin is defeated in the life of the believer. It tells how the grace of chapter 5 accomplishes the triumph over sin. The saints are no longer under the power of sin but have entered a new realm, the kingdom of grace. Moo captures it well (1996:352): "By using this imagery of a transfer of realms, or 'dominions,' with its associations of power and ruling, Paul makes clear that the new status enjoyed by the believer (justification) brings with it a new influence and power that both has led and must lead to a new way of life (sanctification)."

Romans 6:1-23 has two major sections centering on the rhetorical questions of verses 1 and 15. The first section (vv. 1-14) reiterates that we have died to sin and are now alive to God in Christ. The second (vv. 15-23) explains that we have been liberated from enslavement to sin and are now slaves to righteousness. It is clear, however, that the believer is not totally free from sin, for while sin is no longer our master, it is still a power in our lives. Thus sanctification is a process by which we grow in our dependence on God, in our holiness, as we live more and more in the new life Christ has made possible.

Dying to Sin Through the New Life in Christ (6:1-14) One possible misunderstanding that could arise from 5:20-21 is that the best way for grace to increase is for sin to increase, so Paul asks the question, *Shall we go on sinning so that grace may increase?* Here Paul returns to the dialogue style he used in chapters 3 and 4. The introduction (*What shall we say, then?*) is found also in 3:5; 4:1; 7:7; 8:31; and 9:14, 30 to forestall a potential false conclusion from what he has been saying. In 3:20 Paul emphasized the incredible abundance of grace available to the sinner through Christ. Yet some who have not availed themselves of this grace could misunderstand and think that the more sin they commit, the more grace they can experience. The problem is obvious: sin continues to reign in their lives. The NIV's *go on*

6:2 Cranfield (1975:299-300; 1994:40-43) lists four possible understandings of *died to sin* and *raised* in Christ (v. 4): (1) The juridical sense: at justification we die to sin in God's sight on the basis of Christ's sacrificial death. (2) The baptismal sense: in baptism we ratify God's decision and his seal on us in that we die to sin and are raised in baptism. (3) The moral sense: we die daily to sin by putting to death our sinful natures. (4) The eschatological sense: when we die physically, sin is once and for all defeated, and we are raised with Christ to the resurrection life. It must be said that *sinning* is more literally translated "continue in sin." The singular *sin* in the Greek stresses that they remain under the power of sin (this is more the emphasis than just multiplying the number of sins), and so they cannot experience grace on the basis of Paul's message in 5:12-21. This is the very issue addressed in 3:8, where Paul responds to those who have "slanderously reported" him as saying, "Let us do evil that good may result." The point in both places is the same: one cannot live in both realms (that of sin and of grace) simultaneously.

Paul's response, the same as in 3:4, 6, 31; 6:15; 7:7, 13; 9:14; 11:1, 11, means "certainly not!" Paul radically rejects any such possibility. The answer is given in a series of small paragraphs, verses 2-5, 6-10, and 11-13, with verse 14 concluding the section. First, Paul uses the metaphor of baptism to affirm that in Christ we have passed from death to life (vv. 2-5). He begins with two further questions. The first is a marvelous play on words utilizing the fact that sin brought death, which reigns over this age (5:12, 14, 15, 17, 21). But in response Paul says *we died to sin*, meaning that death was defeated when we *died to sin* at our conversion. Therefore the Christian is no longer under the power of sin, a fact stated again in verses 6 (sin is *done away with*), 11 *(dead to sin)* and 14 (sin is no longer our *master*) below. Of course this does not mean that sin no longer affects the believer, for Christians do yield to sin. But sin has now become a force tempting us rather than a power controlling us (as in the old self/new self passages; cf. v. 6 below). Paul's natural question in light of this is, *how can we live in it any longer?* As already stated, this means that believers can no longer be under the power of sin. They experienced the decisive power of God when Christ's atoning work on the cross was put to their account by God. At that moment they died to sin, and it lost its power over them. Again it must be emphasized that sin still is at war against us (see the

---

theologically each of these is basically correct, but not all are intended by Paul here. The fourth is not in the context, and the third would require a different understanding of *live in* sin (i.e., individual sins rather than the principle or power of sin). So the best is a combination of the first two: with the experience of justification at our conversion and with the pledge to live for him that seals our salvation contract at our baptism (see 1 Pet 3:21), we die to sin and no longer live under its power.

rest of this chapter), but it no longer is an internal force controlling us. Christ is the internal power in our lives, and sin is now an external power trying to defeat us. We belong to the realm of grace and no longer live in the realm of sin.

The second question reminds them of their experience of baptism (v. 3). The opening *or don't you know* tells us that this was based on preexistent Christian teaching on baptism and points to common knowledge about the meaning of baptism as dying and rising with Christ. Paul is using this common knowledge about the meaning of baptism (more than metaphorical, contra Dunn 1988a; Morris 1988) to help the Roman Christians understand what it means to *die to sin* (v. 2). First, he tells them they have been *baptized into Christ Jesus,* probably a reference to the early creedal statement that one is baptized "in the name of the Father and of the Son and of the Holy Spirit" (Mt 28:19; cf. also Acts 8:16, 19:3, 5; Gal 3:27), meaning "into union with" the Godhead. While some see a referential sense ("baptized with respect to Christ," so Godet 1969; Cranfield 1975; Wilckens 1980), the majority see this as a union with or incorporation into Christ ("baptized into Christ," so Murray 1968; Morris 1988, Stott 1994; Moo 1996; Schreiner 1998). Paul's main point is that since baptism signifies our complete union with Christ, it also means we were baptized into his death; that is, we united with him in dying to our old nature. This is Paul's main point. We can no longer live under the power of sin (v. 2) because in our baptism we signified that we have died to that power in our union with Christ's death and entered the

---

6:3 Some (e.g., Käsemann 1980:160-63) have argued that Paul is drawing this teaching from the mystery religions, specifically from the Isis cult, whose initiation rite also depicted a dying and a resultant born-again state. Especially when Paul describes baptism as "buried with" Christ (v. 4), Käsemann sees a direct connection and concludes, "In the pre-Pauline community outside Palestine baptism was really understood as a mystery event which incorporated one into the fate of the cultic god, Christ" (1980:162). However, the influence of the mystery religions in general on baptism has been disproven by G. Wagner (1967) and Wedderburn (1983:337-55) among others, and the influence of the Isis cult in particular has been shown to be unlikely by Dunn (1988a:308-10). The background for this is undoubtedly seen in the Christian understanding of baptism.

6:4 Moo (1996:361-65) notes three different approaches to the meaning and significance of *buried with* Christ: (1) it is a metaphor for the believer's total break with the

new realm of the justified. Our power to defeat sin comes from the presence of Christ in our lives. He gives us the strength to defeat temptation (1 Cor 10:13).

Paul concludes this argument in verse 4 *(therefore),* saying that we were *buried with him through baptism* and then also were united with him in his resurrection. If one follows the basic connotation of *baptizō* as "immerse" and sees the imagery as building on the idea of immersion in water (as I do), then the *death* would signify the going down into the water and our being *raised* like Christ would signify the coming up out of the water. There is a great deal of debate about whether baptism is understood sacramentally here, that is, as an actual presence of Christ in baptism (so Légasse 1991). This is unlikely, however, for as Moo points out (1996:363-64) the subject of baptism is dropped after this verse. Its purpose is not to tell *how* we are buried with Christ but to tell that we are buried with Christ. The emphasis is not on baptism but on our death and resurrection in Christ. A further question is what Paul means when he says we are buried *through baptism.* In some sense it is the instrument or means by which burial with Christ is accomplished. This is seen also in 1 Peter 3:21, where we are told that "baptism . . . now saves you," with the process further defined as "the pledge *for* a good conscience" (better than the NIV, "of a good conscience"). It does not mean baptism is the instrument of our salvation; rather it seals the salvation experience and is the means by which the faith experience is mediated to us. In other words, conversion and baptism are spoken of here as a unified experience, a being with

---

old life and a new life in Christ (Bruce 1985); however, this occurs *through* (means) rather than "in" (place) baptism, and nowhere else in the New Testament is the going down and coming up given symbolic significance. (2) Burial symbolizes a complete break with the past, but baptism is the mediator of that break (Sanday and Headlam 1902; Dunn 1988a); however, the "with Christ" is a problem for the metaphorical view (it does not mean "as Christ was buried, so are we"). (3) It describes the participation of the convert in Christ's own burial as mediated by baptism (Beasley-Murray 1962). This could mean that we were "in him" at his own burial (a second Adam Christology similar to 5:12-21), but more likely this takes place at our conversion. I would combine the second and third; there is both a metaphorical and salvation-historical aspect to the imagery here. While the "with Christ" points to the presence of Christ in our conversion (we die "with" him), there is still the metaphor of going down and coming up in the imagery.

Christ. Dunn (1988a:314) speaks of "baptism as the psychologically climactic expression of commitment to and self-identification with the last Adam." Baptism is not the means of salvation; in Paul our faith in Christ's atoning work is the means. But it represents our death to sin and rising in Christ, and it is a very real participation in what Christ has accomplished.

Baptism is not merely a participation in his death but also a participation in his resurrection. As stated in 1 Corinthians 15:20, 23, Christ was raised as the "firstfruits" of our new life, a resurrection that occurs in two stages, first to our new life in Christ now (here) and second to our final resurrection at the second coming (1 Corinthians 15). Christ's death and resurrection are a single event in salvation history, signifying not only the destruction of the old eon but also the inauguration of the new age. The result of this (Greek *hina,* "so that," NIV, *in order that*) is that *we too may live a new life,* or better that "we should walk in newness of life." In other words, our daily lives should be characterized by the new realm Christ has brought about, as seen in a new moral stance and new priorities to live for God rather than for the things of this world. We are to live in the Spirit rather than the flesh (Rom 8).

The theme of union with Christ's death and resurrection is summed up in verse 5. Paul says that *if* (Greek *ei,* assuming the reality of the condition) we are united with Christ in his death, then of course we will be united with him in his resurrection. But there are several difficulties: first is the meaning of "united in the likeness of his death" (the literal translation), in particular "likeness." It can mean a "copy" of a thing or the "form" (not identity but likeness) of it. In Romans (1:23 [idols in the likeness of mortal man etc.]; 5:14 [sin in the likeness of Adam]; 8:3 [Christ sent in the likeness of sinful people]) it means form rather than copy, and that is probably the meaning here as well. We have not experienced his death but have died *like* he did; ours is a spiritual death. While some (Barrett 1957; Fitzmyer 1993b) believe that the form was baptism, Paul has left the analogy of baptism and is now concluding his argument. The form is our participation in his death and the resultant death to the age of sin and our old way of life. We have been united with his death. If that is true, then *we will certainly also be united with him in his resurrection.* The major issue here is the meaning of *will . . . be.* Does it refer to the immediate future, the present experience of newness of life in verse 4 (Godet 1969; Murray 1968; Fitzmyer 1993b; Cranfield 1975), or to the distant future, the final resurrection with Christ (most others). In reality, this is not an either-or. It is best to take this in an inaugurated sense, where our present resurrection to a new life in Christ (v. 4) is an anticipation of our final resurrection with him (vv. 8-10). This is a message desperately needed today, when studies are showing that the majority of members in our churches are far more secular than they are godly. Our perspective on the true meaning of Christianity has been jaded by our secular age. We no longer belong to it and must understand that in Christ we have died to these things and have a whole new existence that we need to be celebrating.

The next paragraph (vv. 6-10) clarifies and expands the meaning of dying and living with Christ. Verses 6-7 center on our death with Christ and its consequences with respect to sin (returning to the theme of v. 2). As in verse 3, Paul begins with theological truths that they already *know* from past teaching. The idea of dying with Christ is now restated with a new metaphor: *our old self was crucified with him.* The *old self* is a Pauline image found also in Ephesians 4:22-24 and Colossians 3:9-11 (cf. the "new creation" in 2 Cor 5:17) and has often been thought of individually, that is, of our death to self and the new life of Christ experienced at conversion (so Barth 1933; Morris 1988; Stott 1994; Fitzmyer 1993b). But it is more likely intended as a salvation-historical concept that should be understood corporately of humanity "in Adam," that is, under the power of sin (see Ridderbos 1975:63-64; Moo 1996; Schreiner 1998). This is the same concept we saw earlier, referring to the old eon we were once part of. This former way of life was "crucified with Christ" when we were crucified with Christ (Gal 2:20) and can be thought of as no longer in control of our lives; it is only working through our "flesh" (Rom 7:5; 8:3-8, 12-13). We are now in Christ rather than in Adam and so belong to the "new self" (Eph 4:24; Col 3:10), which is the realm of the new life. As Moo says (1996:375), "What we *were* 'in Adam' is no more, but, until heaven, the temptation to live in Adam always remains." This is seen by comparing Ephesians 4:22-24, where Paul says we must put off the old person "which is being corrupted by its deceitful desires," which means it is still a present reality. There is an already-not yet tension in which the old person has been crucified and yet must still be resisted. We are no longer under the dominion of sin but are still at war against it (see Schreiner 1998:318).

The purpose (*hina,* "in order that") of the crucifixion of the old self is that *the body of sin might be rendered powerless* (see NIV note; better than "do away with" in the text). When the old self is crucified with Christ, sin loses its power over us. The *body of sin* does not mean the physical body (contra Murray 1968; Gundry 1987:30-31; Morris 1988); rather this phrase refers to the whole person (a common use of the term) as dominated by sin. While the verb can mean that the sinful nature has been "annihilated" or "destroyed" (so Murray 1968; Schreiner 1998), it more likely means "rendered ineffective" (Fitzmyer 1993b; Moo 1996). As in verse 2 sin has lost its power over the believer; it has been nullified as a force. Yet again one must ask how Christians so readily fall into sin. The answer again has to be the flesh. While sin has lost its ability to overpower, it has not lost its ability to deceive. This is the true teaching about Satan in the New Testament. He does not overpower but lives entirely by deception (see Rev 12:9; 20:3, 8, 10). While he is the "god of this age" (2 Cor 4:4), he is the god only of the people of this age, not of the believer. Yet he is still "a roaring lion looking for someone to devour" and can only be defeated by disciplined dependence on God (1 Pet 5:8-9).

The second purpose is that *we should no longer be slaves to sin.* Those in Adam are further defined as *slaves to sin.* They are in chains to the passions described in 1:18-32. This power over us ends when we are crucified and buried with Christ, thereby liberated and beginning a new life in him. This is true (v. 7) *because anyone who has died has been freed from sin.* This is the same verb that means "justified" in 3:20, 24 and so could mean that the one who dies in Christ is "acquitted" from sin (so Cranfield 1975; Fitzmyer 1993b; Stott 1994), but it could also mean more simply that dying in Christ has *freed* us from the power of sin (so Calvin 1979; Bruce 1985; Moo 1996). While the latter is more likely, it is probably also true that we should not see the meaning as exclusively one or the other. The justification of believers frees them from the enslavement of sin (so Barrett 1957; Schreiner 1998).

After developing the significance of dying with Christ (vv. 6-7) Paul develops further the significance of living with him (vv. 8-10). The *if* clause virtually means *since we died with Christ* and assumes the reality of the experience of the believer described in verses 6-7. On that basis, then, *we believe that we will also live with him.* The future tense here has the same difficulties as *will be united* in verse 5. Does this describe our present life with him or the final resurrection life in eternity? There are likely both similarity and development in the two verses. Both refer to the inauguration of newness of life (v. 4) in Christ now as a harbinger of the final resurrection life to come, and yet verses 4-5 relate more to the present experience and verse 8 to the future reality.

How can the Christian find the strength to overcome the world and the pressure of sin? This strength comes from the knowledge that the future is absolutely secure in Christ and the realization that he has conquered death and sin once for all on our behalf (vv. 9-10). For the third time (cf. vv. 3, 6), Paul in verse 9 appeals to what the Roman Christians already *know*, namely that since *Christ was raised from the dead, he cannot die again.* He has conquered death, and it no longer *has mastery* (literally "has lordship") *over him.* During his life, he was under the old eon of sin and death (he did not sin but was "tempted . . . as we are," Heb 4:15), but after his resurrection that authority of death over Jesus was broken completely. This means that we know that we *will . . . live with him* (v. 8) because he has been raised as a guarantee of our own final resurrection. The daughter of Jairus, the widow's son and Lazarus were all raised from the dead only to have to die again. Not so Jesus! And as a result we too will conquer death, for he was raised as our "firstfruits" (1 Cor 15:23), the absolute promise of our future inheritance. Moreover, his resurrection not only conquered death; his death also conquered sin, for *the death he died, he died to sin once for all.* The logic goes back to 5:12-21. Adam's sin brought death into the world, so Christ's death conquered sin and his resurrection conquered death. This tells us how we can *die to sin* (v. 2) and like Christ be raised to *a new life* (v. 4). Christ has conquered sin *once for all* on our behalf, and therefore the *body of sin* has been *done away with* or nullified (v. 6). And because sin and death have been conquered, life has new meaning. So Paul adds, *the life he lives, he lives to God* (better "for God"). No longer under the dominion of sin and death, Christ can devote eternity to living for God. Not that he failed to do so while on earth, but now he is unencumbered by the strictures of his incarnate life under the burden of this world. As Hendriksen puts it (1981:200), Jesus after his resurrection returned to the life he had with the father before he came into this world.

The final paragraph (vv. 11-14) develops the implications of Jesus' victory over sin and death for the life of the believer. Here Paul departs from the teaching style he has been using and turns to commands, using a series of four present-tense imperatives in verses 11-13 to tell the Roman Christians in effect, "become what you are in process of becoming" (see Moo 1996:380; Schreiner 1998:321). In other words, they are on the path to spiritual maturity but must make certain that they continue to "walk the walk." There are four steps to this:

1. They are told, *count yourselves dead to sin but alive to God in Christ Jesus.* We have died to sin (v. 2) but now must "consider" (better than NIV's *count*) ourselves on a daily basis to be *dead to sin.* Christ is cited as the model in verse 10; he *died to sin* and *lives for God,* so we must follow in his steps (note *in the same way;* cf. 1 Pet 2:21). We were baptized into Christ (v. 3), buried with him (v. 4), united with him (v. 5) and crucified with him (v. 6), and we died with him (v. 8), so we must in every way emulate him in our lives, described here as dying to sin and living for God. Note also that while we have died to sin in Christ when we transferred from the realm of sin and death into the realm of life (vv. 7-8), we must still on a regular basis consider ourselves dead to the power of sin in our lives (note the present tense here). It is an act of the will on our part. We are now under a new power, that of Christ in us, and so can resist the power of sin and therefore live for God. But it takes a mental decision, a disciplined mindset that can switch from the world to God.

The means by which we can do this is *in Christ Jesus,* a major Pauline theme that occurs more than 150 times in Paul and seldom elsewhere in the New Testament. It has been long debated whether the phrase signifies more our mystical union with Christ or our corporate solidarity in the body of Christ, the church. More recently the focus has shifted to a "plurality of metaphors" that focus on our general union with Christ, especially in terms of sharing in his death and resurrection, describing "the life of faith under Christ's lordship in a world where other powers and temptations were present" (see Seifrid 1992a:434-35). It is our union with Christ and his power that allows us to defeat sin in our lives.

2. Paul commands, *do not let sin reign in your mortal body* (v. 12). Since we are dead to sin (vv. 2, 11), we must control our total self so that sin cannot "lord it over" us. As in verse 6, *mortal body* probably refers to the whole person and not just to the physical body, with *mortal* added to emphasize our finite condition in this sinful world. Our own fallen condition makes us depend so completely on the strength Christ provides. The present prohibition can mean, "stop letting it rule" or "at no time let it rule," but in this context of ongoing activity the latter is more likely. In 5:12-14 sin and death "reigned" in this world because of Adam's trespass, but believers now have left that realm and joined themselves to Christ. Therefore, we have the promise that "sin will not be your lord" (v. 14; NIV, *sin shall not be your master*), but we must still use the strength that Christ alone can give to put this promise into practice in specific situations. The purpose of this refusal to allow sin to reign is *so that* (we will not) *obey its evil desires.* In this context these are not only bodily lusts but also the general self-centered desires that lead us to sin, as in 1:24 and 7:7-8.

3. Paul gives an example of not letting sin reign by saying, *do not offer the parts of your body to sin, as instruments of wickedness* (v. 13). As before, the idea of bodily *parts* or "members" probably does not refer to the parts of the physical body but rather to the various faculties or capacities of a person (note the parallel with *yourselves* in the next clause). It is also common to see a military image here as in the offering of one's weapons in service to a tyrant (so Calvin 1979, Käsemann 1980; Dunn 1988a; Fitzmyer 1993b; Stott 1994; Schreiner 1998), or possibly the presentation of one's services to a ruler (Moo 1996) or of one's tools to the master workman (Cranfield 1975). Of these, the military image seems closest to the language. We are not to become spiri-

tual mercenaries who present our resources for the use of the tyrant sin; our spiritual weapons should never become weapons to be used in the service of evil. The rule of this tyrant has been broken, and we have been liberated from its power. Marcus gives this military image in verses 12-14 an excellent paraphrase (1988:394): "Let sin be dethroned in your mortal body! May God vanquish it! And you, for your part, remove your bodily members from the battle line where they serve Sin as weapons of its unrighteousness, and present them for duty to God as weapons of his righteousness! For sin will no longer be your master." In this passage he sees a great deal of Holy War imagery evoking a conflict with cosmic powers (Marcus 1988:390-93).

4. Rather than serve evil, we must yield our services to our true master, God. This is done in two stages. First, *offer yourselves to God, as those who have been brought from death to life.* The message of verses 2-11 was that the Christian no longer belongs to the world of sin and death, having transferred to the realm of life. For this reason (*as those who* is literally "because you") we are now citizens of the heavenly realm and belong to God. So now that we are soldiers of a new king, we must offer ourselves completely to God. Second, *offer the parts of your body to him as instruments of righteousness.* This is the opposite of verse 12, where the uncommitted Christian serves *wickedness.* All our faculties are to become weapons given over to service in God's army. As the classic hymn says, "Onward, Christian soldiers!" *Righteousness* here could be legal (a power to which believers yield themselves, so Barth 1933; Käsemann 1980; Dunn 1988a; Schreiner 1998) or moral (upright behavior that pleases God, so Fitzmyer 1993b; Moo 1996). In this context the former is closer to the thrust (the power of sin must be conquered by the power of divine righteousness), but as in 3:21-26 the one actually leads into the other. God's righteousness must take control of our lives. One of the great tragedies of the church today

---

6:14 The *law* here is clearly the Mosaic law (contra Murray 1968, who says it is law in general), but the question remains why Paul says *not under law* rather than "not under sin." Some see this as a legalistic misuse of the law to "scale God's throne" to salvation (so Barrett 1957), others that we cease to be under its condemnation (Cranfield 1975; Stott 1994) or under its social power to divide Jew and Gentile (Dunn 1988a). None of these capture the emphasis here. The key is that the law is

is the large number of members who sit in church and do very little for the Lord. They are more than wasting their lives. They are serving the wrong master! A key calling of every church must be the task of awakening the "dead" members and helping them to discover the joy of serving God with all their hearts and souls.

Verse 14 provides both the reason for the commands (*gar,* "for") and a conclusion that sums up the basic message of the section, *sin shall not be your master* (or "not have lordship over him"; see v. 9). The future tense refers not just to the eschatological future (when Christ returns to defeat evil once for all) but to the immediate future as well. The power of sin over God's people is over because of the cross. We have a new *master* ("lord," *kyrios,* related to this verb, *kyrieusei*), Jesus Christ. Though some believe this is imperatival (you must not let sin rule, e.g., Fitzmyer 1993b), that is unlikely because Paul has just used imperatives in verses 11-13 and is now returning to indicatives. So the statement is best seen as a promise—you can be sure sin no longer rules (e.g., Cranfield 1975; Dunn 1988a; Moo 1996; Schreiner 1998). Christ has broken the power of sin, so believers can know that it no longer has absolute sway over them. Once more, this does not mean sin cannot gain some control over our lives; rather, it means we will never again be helpless pawns under its power. We are "more than conquerors" (Rom 8:37) and so can resist its allures (1 Cor 10:13). The basis of this promise is then provided, *because you are not under law, but under grace.* This returns to the issue of the law in 5:13, 20, and Paul is thinking of the law as the instrument of sin (3:20; 4:15). It is of the old eon, a power that caused sin to increase (5:20) and that was broken by Christ. The grace of God has broken the power of sin and the law through the cross and the resurrection. As Stott says (1994:181), "To be 'under grace' is to acknowledge our dependence on the work of Christ for salvation, and so to be justified rather than condemned,

---

connected to the power of sin in chapters 5—6, as in 5:20, "the law was added so that the trespass might increase" (cf. 4:15). So to be under the law is to be part of the Adamic realm, under the control of sin. The best solution is to think of law and grace as "contrasting salvation-historical 'powers'" (so Moo 1996; cf. Stott 1994; Schreiner 1998). Christ has freed the believer from the power of sin and the law.

and thus set free." Out of the indicative of God's grace (v. 14) comes the imperative of living the sanctified life (vv. 11-13).

Freedom from Enslavement of Sin to Become Slaves of Righteousness (6:15-23) Paul now turns to a second metaphor, that of slavery. In verses 1-14 he used the image of the two realms of sin/the law and grace; here he uses that of emancipation from slavery, but with a twist. The great Christian paradox is that we are freed from the slavery of sin to become slaves to God. The difference is the hostility of the old master versus the love and grace of the new. The first ends in death, the second in eternal life. This section begins with another rhetorical question (compare v. 1) on the issue of sin and then offers four responses. Paul begins with (1) a general statement that everyone is enslaved to something (v. 16) and then (2) reminds them that they have been emancipated from slavery to sin (vv. 17-18) and so should become slaves to righteousness, leading to holiness (v. 19). He concludes by reminding them (3) that sin results in death (vv. 20-22) and (4) that following God results in holiness and eternal life (vv. 22-23).

1. The rhetorical question that begins this section (*shall we sin because we are not under law but under grace?*) is quite similar to the one in 6:1. In verse 1 the potential error was sinning more to experience more grace, while here it is sinning freely because grace has replaced law. Paul anticipates a possible misunderstanding of his statement in verse 14 that we "are not under law, but under grace." Some might interpret the absence of law to mean they are free to do whatever they want, and the presence of grace to mean God will understand and forgive whatever they do. People today often have this same low opinion of the seriousness of sin, thinking that forgiveness is easy to obtain. Paul responds as he did in 6:1, *By no means!* This assumption is terribly wrong.

Once more Paul appeals to a commonly known truth (cf. vv. 3, 6, 9), this time to a frequent occurrence in the ancient world, selling oneself into slavery to avoid debt. It has been estimated that 85-90 percent of the population of Rome and the Italian peninsula either was or had been slaves (Rupprecht 1993:881). So the metaphor here yielded a powerful image. Paul's point is that if you *offer yourselves* (the present tense means to do so on a continual basis) to a thing, you become *slaves to the one whom you obey.* This returns to the earlier discussion of sin as an enslaving power (6:6-7) and adds the point that the mark of slavery is constant obedience. Therefore, to surrender yourself (*offer* is the same verb as in 12:1, to "offer your bodies as living sacrifices" to God) to the power of sin is to become its slave. The obedience is voluntary and continual and means in effect that you become the willing slave of a sinful lifestyle. Aageson (1996:78-80) points out that the semantic domain of *slave* here especially centers on the image of sin as the controlling force in one's life. So Paul challenges his readers to choose their slavery—to *sin* or to *obedience* (to God). Which controlling agent do they prefer? His use of *obedience* rather than *God* is probably to underscore the ethical responsibility of the believer to obey God rather than sin. There is no choice—everyone is going to be a slave to something, and there are only two possibilities, sin or God. Neutrality is impossible. In fact, to choose neutrality is to choose sin because it constitutes a refusal to serve God. As Moo says (1996:399), "One is never 'free' from a master, and those non-Christians who think that they are 'free' are under an illusion created and sustained by Satan. The choice with which people are faced is not, 'Should I retain my freedom or give it up and submit to God?' but 'Should I serve sin or should I serve God?'"

Moreover, the choice has consequences. To choose sin is to find *death,* and to choose obedience is find *righteousness. Death* here is physical death, the current state of being spiritually dead and (mainly) the future experience of eternal death, the "second death" of Revelation 2:11 and 20:6. *Righteousness* here could be final righteousness, eternal life (so Cranfield 1975; Schreiner 1998) or present life in Christ via justification (Stott 1994) or the right living that is the hallmark of the Christian (Fitzmyer 1993b; Moo 1996). As in the case of *death,* it is certainly possible that *righteousness* is comprehensive and embraces all three ideas (Murray 1968).

2. However, Paul is not discouraged about their situation. In verse 17 he shows he does not think that the Roman Christians have given themselves over to sin, saying, *thanks be to God* that they had followed God with all their hearts. By giving thanks to God, Paul also makes it clear that it was the grace of God that enabled them to leave a life of sin and

find righteousness. So their choice was God rather than sin; they *used to be slaves to sin* (before their conversion), but no longer. But as was said in verse 16, they have *obeyed* God, submitting to his salvific work, obviously in terms of their faith commitment to Christ. Moreover, they did so *wholeheartedly,* meaning they were radically converted, giving themselves completely over to God. What they obeyed is *the form of teaching to which you were entrusted,* a clumsy and difficult expression. The verb often speaks of tradition being "handed down" to a person or group. But in this case it is the reverse, as the believer is "handed over" by God to his revealed truths. Schreiner (1998:335) says, "It denotes being delivered over to another power, as a slave is handed over from one master to another." God in this sense has transferred them from the realm of sin to the realm of obedience to the truth. The *form of teaching* could refer to the pattern, which consists of Christian teaching (apposition, so Cranfield 1975), but more likely means that the teaching shapes or molds the believer (source, so Gagnon 1993:685-87; Schreiner 1998). Some older commentators said it contrasts Paul's teaching with earlier Christian teachers (Godet 1969), but Paul hardly thought his gospel different from the apostolic norm. More likely, the contrast is with the *form* of the law or Jewish teaching (Käsemann 1980; Dunn 1988a; Moo 1996). So the message is that the truth of the gospel will mold us as God gives us over to it.

Paul restates verse 17 and sums up the teaching of chapter 6 thus far by saying we *have been set free from sin and have become slaves of righteousness* (v. 18). Both verbs are divine passives, indicating that God is the driving force in the transfer of the believer from the kingdom of sin to that of righteousness. First, we are liberated from the realm of sin, the first time the concept of freedom is found in Romans (so Dunn 1988a, but see 6:7, "anyone who has died has been freed from sin [justified]"). Those who come to faith in Christ receive their papers of manumission from the hostile enslaving power of sin. Yet again the great Christian paradox is found: we have been freed from slavery to become a willing slave once more, but this time to a loving, compassionate God (see above, introduction to vv. 15-23). Dunn points out (1988a:345) that "man exists only as a creature, only in relation of dependency on a superior power; his vaunted freedom and independence is illusory. If not enslaved to God, then enslaved to sin. . . . The only real freedom for man is as a slave of God, a life lived in recognition of his creaturely dependence." So now we have been freed from enslavement by sin in order to become *slaves of righteousness,* meaning again both God's declaration that we are right with him and the ethical right living that results from our new status (see on v. 13 above). God has called us into a new relation with him and transferred us from the realm of sin into his own kingdom, making it possible for us to live above sin and find righteousness in our lives.

Paul recognizes that his slavery metaphor is not quite sufficient and so says (v. 19), *I put this in human terms because you are weak in your natural selves* (literally "due to the weakness of your flesh"). While some believe Paul is speaking in a moral sense of sinful tendencies to self-deception (Cranfield 1975; Dunn 1988a) or apologizing for such a negative image (Fitzmyer 1993b), it is more likely that he is describing the inability of human beings to understand such deep truths without such an analogy (so Barrett 1957; Morris 1988). No simple "human" metaphor like slavery is completely adequate to such a task, but people need such word-pictures in order to grasp these theological realities.

Then he goes on to restate the basic truth of chapter 6 again: having repudiated their non-Christian *slavery to impurity and to ever-increasing wickedness* they must now embrace *slavery to righteousness leading to holiness.* This uses the same language as in verse 13, *offer the parts of your body,* a military metaphor related to offering one's services to an army. Before these people belonged to the army of evil, serving the master of sexual *impurity* or "uncleanness" (the word normally has a sexual connotation in Paul, so Schreiner 1998:336) and of *wickedness* or "lawlessness" in general (sin as setting oneself against the laws of God). Moreover, this is *ever-increasing wickedness* (literally "lawlessness to lawlessness"). This is the other side of the slavery metaphor: people willingly throw themselves into sin; it is not a hostile takeover. Still, the result is enslavement. But for believers this is not so. They have willingly joined God's army and as such are commanded (another imperative similar to vv. 11-13—these are the center points of the chapter) to become *slaves to righteousness* (see v. 18). Their new status

with God and the lifestyle that results lead to *holiness* or "sanctification," referring to the ongoing process of being set apart for God. In
the Greek there is a contrast between lawlessness and holiness, so the
emphasis is on the process of setting oneself either against God or to
God. Stott (1994:185) calls this "being changed into the likeness of
Christ."

3. The command to become *slaves to righteousness* is based on (*gar,*
"for") a further contrast between the results of enslavement to sin (vv.
20-21) and the results of enslavement to God (v. 22). So the readers are
reminded once again (see vv. 16-18) of what it was like before their
conversion. At that time they believed they were *free,* but in reality
they were slaves to sin, and the only thing they were actually free from
was *the control of righteousness.* This strikes at the basic delusion of
unbelievers that they are free because they have no controls over their
choices; they can do anything they want, unlike the Christians who
have all those terrible restrictions. They make this claim because they
are ignorant of the reality of sin and its total control over them. All they
are free from in reality is doing anything right in the sight of God. This
of course does not mean that non-Christians are incapable of good.
Calvin's doctrine of "common grace" recognizes the many good things
that unbelievers do. But in the final analysis none of this constitutes
righteousness before God. As Origen said, "Here *free* means *alien,* and
rightly so. For no one can serve sin and righteousness at the same time,
as the Savior said: *No one can serve two masters*" (Bray 1998:171, italics
his).

Not only is there very little true freedom under the power of sin, but
the results are even worse (v. 21). So Paul asks them to reflect further
on their pagan past: *What benefit did you reap at that time* (see below
for the shorter form of the question)? The major benefit (literally "fruit")

6:20 Käsemann (1980:185) calls *righteousness* "the sphere of a lordship which God's
creature is supposed to represent on earth but which is abandoned in pagan fashion
in favor of the lordship of sin." While this may well be an aspect of the emphasis
here, Moo (1996:406) is closer to the meaning when he argues that the context
makes it more likely that "ethical" righteousness is in view. It is "our actions rather
than our status" that are emphasized.

6:21 There are two ways to translate this passage: the traditional way as in NIV (favored by Sanday and Headlam 1902; Lenski 1945; Murray 1968; Schreiner 1998;

is stated clearly: these are *things you are now ashamed of*. When people plant sin, they gain a harvest of shame. While this shame does have a psychological dimension of embarrassment for sin (so Calvin 1979; Murray 1968; Schreiner 1998), it goes beyond that to illuminate the shame of the deeds and the judgment of God for those deeds. One only has to look at the state of things on the average university campus (drinking binges, orgies) or at the normal New Year's celebrations to see how true this observation is. The shame behind sinful deeds is even recognized by Hollywood, as seen in the themes of movie after movie. Yet there could be another connotation as well, for *shame* in the Bible also connotes shame before God and judgment to come, leading to disgrace and despair (Bultmann 1964a:189-90). But the major *result* is the judgment aspect of shame, eternal *death*. The only *result* or destiny the sinner can rightfully contemplate is the "second death" of Revelation 20:6, 14—first physical death and then everlasting punishment in the lake of fire.

4. However, the past shame (v. 21) has been replaced with present (*now*, v. 22) *holiness*, leading to its own outcome, *eternal life*. The basis of this incredible truth is our conversion when we were *set free from sin* (repeating v. 18). The evil empire of sin was "rendered powerless" (v. 6) by the cross, and we have been liberated from its control. This is the basic theme of the whole chapter: sanctification is defined first as a life of freedom from the dominance of sin and second as a process of becoming more like Christ. The former is the basis of the latter. Here the "fruit" is not shame but *holiness* (see on v. 19). Unlike the pagan, we plant righteousness, and the harvest is holiness or sanctification. Our allegiance to God results first in a way of life that is increasingly God-directed and God-centered (see Mt 6:19-21, "treasures in heaven" rather than "treasures on earth") and second in a destiny of *eternal life* with God. As

---

NASB; NRSV; TEV) or with a shorter question—"And what was the result? It was not good, since now you are ashamed of the things you used to do, things that end in eternal doom" (NLT; so also Michel [1966]; Cranfield 1975; Morris 1988; Dunn 1988a; Moo 1996; NEB; NJB). The grammar could fit either, but the shorter question seems preferable because it establishes a parallelism with verse 22 (so Moo 1996) of status (slaves of sin, slaves of God) followed by result (shame, sanctification) and outcome (death, eternal life).

Chrysostom said, "Note how Paul says that some things have already been given, while others are still hoped for, but that the former point to the latter. Thus if we can come to holiness now, we can be assured of sharing eternal life in the future" (Bray 1998:173). Holiness both makes us a slave of righteousness and is the evidence that we have truly become slaves of righteousness (Schreiner 1998:341).

Paul concludes the chapter as well as verses 20-22 in verse 23, the justly well-known *for the wages of sin is death, but the gift of God is eternal life in Christ Jesus our Lord.* With the image of wages, Paul adds another metaphor to those he has already used—baptism, the transfer from one kingdom to another, the old self, rendering a force powerless, joining an army, slavery, and harvest imagery. This is close to the harvest theme, for it denotes payment for services rendered. In fact, we again have a military image (Käsemann 1980; Schreiner 1998) denoting the *wages* paid soldiers for serving their country. So sin is a ruler giving to his army what they have earned, namely eternal death (as in v. 21). This is certainly the worst *wages* ever paid anyone, but it is also true that this is earned by a lifetime of rejecting God and deliberately choosing sin. As Dunn says (1988a:349), death is "sin's final payoff" (shame, 6:21, could be called an earlier payoff). In fact, *death* here is both the physical death that ends this earthly life and the eternal death that follows, though the latter is primary. While death is typified as *wages,* eternal life is seen as a *gift.* The contrast is deliberate (see also 5:21). One is judged by works (Rev 20:12-14) but cannot earn eternal life on the basis of works (see 3:20, 27-28; 4:2-5, 14; Eph 2:8-9; 2 Tim 1:9; Tit 3:5). Eternal life is God's gracious gift. Moreover, this is all possible only *in Christ Jesus our Lord,* a formal title stressing his lordship that appears also in 1:4, 7; 5:1, 11, 21; 7:25; 8:39; 13:14; 15:6, 30. Here it says that the gift of eternal life is only possible *in Christ* and his lordship over salvation.

Freedom from Condemnation Under the Law (7:1-25) The Mosaic law has been mentioned often thus far. Paul has made it clear that no one can be justified by keeping the law (3:21, 27-28) and that righteousness comes only by faith, not the law (4:13-16). Moreover, the actual purpose of the law was not to save but to identify sin. As a result sin actually increased through the law (5:20), and death reigned as a result of sin and the law (5:14, 21). Finally, believers have been liberated from sin, for they are "not under law, but under grace" (6:14, 15). This last idea is now developed further in chapter 7; that is, the Christian is no longer under the law's condemnation and so must live a life of freedom from it. There are two sections here. First, 7:1-6 elaborates the "not under law" of 6:14 and explains in more detail what this means, namely, that the bondage of the law has been broken. This is also the theme of chapter 6 as a whole, but 7:1-6 explains that the bondage has been broken by death, illustrating it with the metaphor of marriage (vv. 2-3), also a lifelong commitment broken only by death. The believer has died to the law in order to *belong to another* (v. 4), Christ, with the result that the believer is now dead to the law of sin and death.

The second section (vv. 7-25) takes up the dichotomy introduced in verse 6: the *old way* of the law (= vv. 7-13) and the *new way of the Spirit* (= vv. 14-25, paving the way for chap. 8), explaining how the law functions both positively and negatively. The view of some that this is an "apology" for the law is partly true in the sense that Paul is clarifying his negative portrait in verses 1-6. But the negative effects of the law still continue. The law is not sin (v. 7); it is holy, righteous, good (v. 12) and spiritual (v. 14), but it also produces coveting (v. 8) as well as sin and death (vv. 9-11). So Paul seeks to show that while the law was a positive force, it had very negative effects. Verses 7-12 explain that the law is not evil but has become the agent of evil (v. 13 is a transition to the second half); then verses 14-25 depict the human struggle to achieve goodness on its own, leading naturally into the work of the Spirit in chapter 8. Life in the flesh is described in chapter 7, and life in the Spirit is depicted in chapter 8.

Liberated from the Law to Join Christ (7:1-6) There are two equal ideas in verse 1: (1) the lifelong bondage of the law and (2) liberation only via death. Paul stresses his concern over this issue of the law by addressing the Roman believers as *brothers* here and in verse 4 for the first time since 1:13: "With 'brethren' and then 'my brethren' Paul puts his arm around the Roman Christians in order to draw as near to them as possible with the great assurance that the justified are, indeed, delivered from the law" (Lenski 1945:443). Paul begins with *do you not know,* a phrase found also in 6:3 (cf. also 1 Cor 6:2, 9, 16, 19), and like there, it is used to correct a possible misunderstanding by appealing to basic Christian knowledge. They should be aware of the meaning of "not under law" in 6:14 because they are people *who know the law,* meaning as elsewhere in Romans the Mosaic law rather than Roman law or law in general. The Roman Christians were not necessarily Jewish in background, but they were knowledgeable of the law. Some were Jewish Christians, others had been God-fearers (Gentiles who had worshiped in synagogues before finding Christ; cf. Acts 10:2; 13:16, 26), and still others had been taught about the law since becoming Christians. The point is that they knew this truth. Paul asks them to remember that *the law has authority over a man only as long as he lives.* This is the same verb as that used in 6:9, 14, speaking of the "lordship" of death and sin over people. The three—the law, sin and death—are interconnected throughout chapters 5—7. The law of sin and death reigns over humankind, and only death can free one of that obligation. But Paul's whole point in these sections is that the believer has been transferred from that domain to God's kingdom as a result of Christ's sacrificial death. The way the Christian is freed from that deadly rule is faith in the act of Christ, which constitutes dying to the realm of sin and death.

To illustrate this principle of lifelong control, Paul uses the metaphor of marriage (vv. 2-3), saying that a woman is *bound to her husband by the law [a reference to the laws of the Torah] so long as he lives and is only released from the law of marriage* by his death. Note how frequently law is used here, three times in verses 2-3 and eight times in verses 1-6. The topic of Paul's discussion is the law, and marriage is simply an illustration of its lifelong nature. Thus it is going too far to use this verse in debates over the possibility of exceptions to the lifelong nature of marriage (e.g., Mt 5:32; 19:9; 1 Cor 7:15). This is an illustration rather than a dogmatic statement (i.e., it builds on the basic rule of marriage rather than the total meaning of it; see Moo 1996:413 n.). Paul is saying that the Mosaic law mandates a lifelong commitment to one's husband, with *release* or removal from the bond only upon his death. In Jewish law only the husband could break a marriage (Deut

24:1), while in Roman law either partner could break the marriage bond. Paul uses a strange term for *married, hypandros* or "under the power of a man," showing that he is reflecting the Jewish teaching here. This is also supported by the phrase *released from the law of marriage,* literally "released from the law of her husband," meaning the law that bound her under her husband's authority (so Dunn 1988a:360). He elaborates his point (v. 3) by saying that any remarriage while the husband is still alive constitutes adultery, while a remarriage after his death does not. Note that here she is said to be free from the *law* rather than from her husband, thus emphasizing the legal aspect rather than the marriage aspect, proving again that verses 2-3 are an illustration rather than the point of the discussion.

Yet difficulties emerge when we try to interpret this allegorically. If the woman is the believer and the husband is the law, then it seems the law has died to set her free to belong to Christ in a new union (so Origen, Augustine, Chrysostom). But this approach clashes with verse 4, which says the believers have *died to the law* in order to *belong to* Christ. Therefore some others have taken the first husband to be the "old self" (6:6) and the wife the new self that is freed to join Christ (Godet 1969; Sanday and Headlam 1902). Earnshaw (1994) believes that the death of the first husband in verse 2 illustrates the death of Christ (v. 4) and the marriage to the second husband demonstrates union with Christ in his death. Dodd (1932:119-20) is frustrated enough to say that the illustration is "confused from the outset" because "'law' plays a double part," so it "has gone hopelessly astray." This is hardly necessary. The key is to realize (with Lenski 1945; Hendriksen 1981; Cranfield 1975; Käsemann 1980) that it is more of an illustration than an allegory and is tied more to verse 1 than to verse 4. It communicates one primary meaning, that death removes one from the bondage of the law. Verse 4 is a conclusion to verses 1-3 rather than an interpretation of the allegorical details of verses 2-3. Moo (1996:413-14) agrees but adds that the "striking parallels between vv. 2-3 and v. 4" still demand some understanding in which the wife and husband are identified with the Christian and Christ. Therefore there is still a sense in which "severance from the law enables one to enter into a new relationship" with Christ.

Paul concludes ("therefore," v. 4; *so* in the NIV) that like the woman in verses 2-3, the believer has *died to the law* and been united with Christ. At first glance it seems a simple statement that the law has been "put to death" (a divine passive that means God has put it to death) and that we now *belong to another,* similar in wording to verse 3 and meaning that the Christian is free to join Christ in marriage. But what does it mean to *die to the law?* The traditional view has always been that we have died to the condemnation of the law. This is true but does not go far enough. This is similar to 5:21—6:23 (especially 5:13, 20; 6:14); the reign of the law has been destroyed, and we have transferred from that kingdom to the kingdom of Christ. It is the law as a whole to which we have died. Moo (1996:414-17) brings up a key problem. Calvin (1979:247-48) distinguished between the law in its "office" (with its regulations and condemning power) and the law as "rule of life"; it is the first from which we have been set free, and this has become a staple feature of Reformed theology. Thus many have interpreted the situation here as a misunderstanding or perversion of the law as an instrument of justification. But that is not the thrust here. This is more the inability of the law (8:3) to combat sin. So this is a salvation-historical issue and means that the power of sin and the law has ended and the believer belongs to a new realm. Thus, as Moo says, these two uses of the law as well as the idea of "the third use of the law" (the law as a positive authority in the Christian life) cannot be found in this passage. This, however, does not mean the law has no value or place, for it teaches us how God deals with his people and what holiness means. Still, the Mosaic law as a whole has been "fulfilled" by Christ (Mt 5:17-20) and no longer plays a part in the process of salvation. God has revealed his righteousness "apart from law" (3:21), and it is faith not law that brings one to salvation.

The body of Christ is the means by which this new relationship is effected—he "bore our sins in his own body on the tree" (1 Pet 2:24).

7:4 Fitzmyer (1936:458) points to two misunderstandings of *the body of Christ.* Theodore of Mopsuestia took it as both the physical and mystical body of Christ, whereas Tertullian understood it as the church as Christ's body (as do Dodd 1932;

As a result, we have not just married *another,* but this one to whom
we have been united is the one *who was raised from the dead,* referring probably to Christ's resurrection as our "firstfruits" and implying
that our second marriage will be eternal. The purpose of it all is to
bear fruit to God. Several read in this a further metaphor in which
fruitfulness is the child born of the marriage to Christ in verses 2-4 (so
Godet 1969; Sanday and Headlam 1902; Barrett 1957; M. Black 1973),
but there is no hint here of such an allegorical meaning. Instead, it
simply means that as a result of union with Christ, Christians must
live fruitful lives. Paul discussed fruitfulness in 6:21-22, where he
stated that there was no "fruit" from their bondage to sin, but now
that they have been set free their fruit was "holiness." So the proper
fruit is a sanctified life, probably including the "fruit of the Spirit" in
Galatians 5:22-23.

Paul sums up the implications of this paragraph in verses 5-6, where
he contrasts life in *the flesh* with the new life in the Spirit. Ridderbos
(1975:94-95) says that "flesh" refers to "man in his sin and depravity"
(Rom 7:14; 8:6-7; Gal 5:19; 6:8; Eph 2:3), that general proclivity to sin
that is characteristic of the carnal nature. So here the non-Christian is
seen as living "in the sphere of" sin or under its power. Before they
found Christ, Paul reminds them, every decision they made was determined by the power of the flesh over them. This is because *the sinful
passions aroused by the law were at work in our bodies, so that we bore
fruit for death.* The choice is clear—bear fruit for God (v. 4) or fruit for
death (v. 5). Note how Paul has summed up his primary concepts—sin,
law and death—under the flesh. All are powers that dominate and destroy those who fail to find Christ. This verse culminates Paul's teaching on the relation of the law to sin. Dunn (1988a:364-65) says that
Paul has "redefined [the law's] role with increasing sharpness." In 3:20
the law makes us "conscious of sin"; then in 4:15 it produces "wrath."
In 5:13, 20 it causes "trespass" to "increase," meaning that through it
people are made aware of their sins, which "transgress" God's laws. Fi-

---

Nygren 1949). However, there is no hint in this context for such an ecclesial interpretation, and there is no connection with the "eucharistic 'body of Christ'" (so
Wilckens 1980).

nally, here Paul says that sin is directly aroused or stimulated by the law. *Sinful passions* is literally "the passions of sins," with sins adjectival ("sinful") rather than source ("passions from sin") and probably referring to the sinful deeds committed by human passion. The fact that these are committed *in our bodies* does not mean that they are sexual in nature, for *bodies* refers to our total person, not just our physical body (see on 6:13). These are the self-centered desires that are the basis of sin. The law is *at work* or powerfully active in our lives; here it is an operative or agent of sin because it tells us God's demands. This then stimulates our natural tendency to reject the way of God and go our own way. The result of this (*eis to, so that,* probably result rather than purpose in this context) is that *we bore fruit for death* when we were without Christ.

But all is different in the present, for *now* we have died *to what once bound us* (v. 6), primarily the law but possibly also sin, described in 6:16, 20 as an enslaving force (the same verb *bound* is used in 1:18 to describe people who "suppress the truth by their wickedness"). Obviously, the time when we *died* to it was at our conversion when we were "united with [Christ] . . . in his death" (6:4, 5) and "our old self was crucified with him" (6:6). As a result we were "freed from sin" (6:7) and the law. Here Paul says *we have been released from the law,* using language from 7:2 on marriage to say that we have been delivered from its power. The Christian is no longer under law but under grace (6:14). The old age of legalistic restrictions is passed, and we are no longer bound to law but *serve in the new way* (or "newness") *of the Spirit.* This does not mean that the law was evil, for Paul will say in 7:14 that "the law is spiritual." Rather, as he already said in chapters 5 and 6 above, the law could not solve the sin problem; it highlighted sin and revealed transgression but could not produce salvation from it. Indeed, as Paul says here, it became an agent of the very thing it was written against. Christ came to fulfill the law (Mt 5:17-20), so in him the entire law was summed up. To have faith in him was the essence of

---

7:6 There are several interpretations of the contrasted "newness of Spirit" and "oldness of letter" (literal translation): (1) the Spirit versus a misunderstanding and misuse of the law (Cranfield 1975); (2) the pre-Christian life versus the Christian life (Barrett 1957; Bruce 1985); (3) the law versus the gospel (Murray 1968); (4) the new

the law and the only solution to the sin problem. The contrast between *the Spirit* and *the written code* is used for the second time (see 2:27-29) and means that the old covenant of the law has given way to the new covenant of the Spirit. There is now a "newness" that characterizes both the new covenant reality and the life of the people who inhabit it. In this new freedom, however, we are back to the basic paradox that characterized 6:16-18; we have been set free from the enslaving power of sin to be made slaves of God. The new life in the Spirit will not be explicated until chapter 8, for in the rest of chapter 7 he will develop the first issue, life under sin and the law.

The Place of the Law in the Life of the People of God (7:7-25) This is certainly one of the most difficult and debated portions of the book, and its meaning depends on two preliminary issues. First, there is the question of Paul's switch to first-person singular forms in this section. There are four different theories regarding the identity of the speaker (see Fitzmyer 1993b; Moo 1996 for more extensive bibliography): (1) autobiographical—Paul is relating his own experience with the law and sin, either as he was growing up or more generally of his life as a whole (Hodge 1950; Dodd 1932; Murray 1968; Bruce 1985; Gundry 1980; Cranfield 1975; Morris 1988; Schreiner 1998); (2) Adam (especially vv. 7-12)—he is speaking of Adam's experience in the garden (Theodore of Mopsuestia, Michel 1966; R. N. Longenecker 1964:88-95, Garlington 1990c:208-10; Stuhlmacher 1994); (3) Israel—the *I* refers to Israel before and after receiving the law, especially her struggle with the law (Chrysostom; M. Black 1973; Käsemann 1980; Wright 1991:197-98; Karlberg 1986; Stott 1994; Seifrid 1992b; Moo 1996; Trudinger 1996); (4) general humanity—this refers not to anyone in particular but to all people who wrestle with God's demands on them (Dunn 1988a; Fitzmyer 1993b). The second is unlikely because there is no type of Adamic Christology developed here (compare 5:12-21), and there is little evidence that Paul intended the *I* to stand for Adam or to depict Adam as under the law. The third is very possible and definitely does

covenant (Spirit) versus the old covenant (the letter of the law; Käsemann 1980; Fitzmyer 1993b; Moo 1996; Schreiner 1998). Of these, the fourth is the most likely, for the emphasis throughout, as we have seen, is on the salvation-historical idea of realms or spheres of influence.

fit the centrality of the law in this passage and the Jewish nature of 7:7-25, but it does not quite do justice to the whole passage (see the discussion in the next paragraph). The centrality of the law in chapter 7 does not prove that Paul has Israel in mind because the law is also central in chapter 8 (vv. 2, 3, 4, 7), a passage that no one doubts describes the Christian life. The best is a combination of the first and fourth views. Morris (1988:277) says, "In this chapter he keeps on using the first person singular pronoun though he has not done this since the opening of his letter. . . . Moreover, words like, 'What a wretched man I am! Who will rescue me from the body of this death?' (v. 24) are impossibly theatrical if they apply to the people, but not to Paul himself." Yet it is equally unlikely that he is speaking only of himself, for the language broadens out to include all humanity. Therefore it is best to say with others (Cranfield 1975; Morris 1988; Stott 1994; Schreiner 1998) that Paul uses his own experience to describe the basic human situation. Garlington (1990c:199-202) follows Dunn (1988a) in interpreting this section via the doctrine of the two ages, i.e., the contrast between the old and new creations. Paul is being both autobiographical and typical as he describes the plight of all of us.

The second issue is similar. Is Paul describing Christians (Augustine, the Latin Fathers), non-Christians (Origen and the Greek Fathers; Kümmel 1967; Käsemann 1980), or the non-Christian in verses 7-13 and the Christian in verses 14-25 (Calvin 1979; Barrett 1957; Murray 1968; Cranfield 1975). The third makes most sense of the text, as we will see (see further the introduction to vv. 14-25), and is consistent with the switch from past tense verbs in verses 7-13 to present tense verbs in verses 14-25. While it is true that aspect theory takes past tense as background (prolegomena) and present tense as foreground (main emphasis, see Porter 1994:23-24), this analysis will still fit, for Paul's Jewish background was the prolegomena to his Christian life. So the idea of the Jewish person under the law (#3 above) is true of verses 7-13. Therefore, Paul describes every person, first on the basis of his Jewish past

---

7:8 There is some debate regarding the relationship between sin and the law. Does Paul mean that sin used the Tenth Commandment to make people lust all the more (Barrett 1957; Murray 1968; Käsemann 1980), or does he intend it more generally,

and then on the basis of his Christian present.

The Unbeliever and the Law: Sin and Death (7:7-13) Paul begins with the same rhetorical question *(What shall we say, then?)* that is used in 3:5, 6:1 and 9:14. He wants to clarify his message and avoid potential misunderstandings. In 5:20, 6:14 and 7:1-6 his theme was the inability of the law to deliver anyone from sin. Some might deduce that the law was inherently evil *(Is the law sin?)*, thus producing an unbridgeable barrier between Judaism and Christianity. Most likely his opponents had made just this charge against him. Paul responds with his characteristic *indeed* ("certainly not"; see 3:4, 6, 31; 6:2, 15), showing his abhorrence at the very thought. Still, he must clarify the connection between the law and sin very carefully. So he responds to this false charge in two related ways, showing that while the law is not sin, it is still related to sin. (1) Generally, he says he would never have *known what sin was* apart from the law. Here *known* is experiential and not just intellectual. People do not just realize what sin is but actually come to participate in it through the law (as stated in 7:5). (2) Specifically, Paul then turns to a single example of sin from the tenth commandment, coveting. When the law specified, "Thou shalt not covet" (Ex 20:17; Deut 5:21), Paul not only became conscious of his sin but was more attracted to it. While some narrow this to sexual lust, it almost certainly encompasses all types of sinful desires. In fact, covetousness was widely regarded as the core of the Ten Commandments and of the Torah in Judaism (cf. 4 Maccabees 2:6; Jas 1:15; so Cranfield 1975; Fitzmyer 1993b).

The progress from the law to sin and death is traced in verses 8-12. First, sin establishes a bridgehead. *Seizing the opportunity* is a military metaphor for establishing a base of operations in enemy territory (cf. Gal 5:13; 2 Cor 5:12; 11:12; 1 Tim 5:4). Sin is an active force taking the initiative and going to war by using the law as a weapon against us. Building on verse 7, this means that coveting grabbed at the chance that the law gave it and made *the commandment* its base of opera-

that the law against sin caused resentment and rebellion (Cranfield 1975)? In light of the repeated *every kind* of desire, the former is the more likely here.

tions. As a result it *produced* in Paul *every kind of covetous desire.* It is clear that sin is the evil force, and the law is simply the means by which the temptation work its influence. Morris (1988:280) gives two good illustrations of this phenomenon. Augustine's *Confessions* tells us that as a boy he and his friends would steal pears not because they liked them but simply for the joy of breaking the law. Also, Mark Twain said that, like a mule, a person will do the opposite of what they are told "just for the sake of meanness."

Moo (1996:437) shows how the last part of verse 8 initiates a chiastic pattern portraying "'dead' sin coming to 'life' at the same moment as the living 'I' dies" (see fig. 3). When he says, *apart from law, sin is dead,* Paul could hardly mean that there was no sin before the law, for he stated in 5:13 that "before the law was given, sin was in the world." So most believe that it is inactive or inert (compare Jas 2:17, 26 for this use of *dead*) in the sense that without the law people do not know that sin is a transgression of God's laws. Cranfield (1975:351) compares sin to the serpent in the Garden who could not attack until the commandment of Gen 2:17 had been given. It was motionless until given the opportunity.

"Apart from the Law" (v. 8b)	"When the commandment came." (v. 9b)
"sin is dead" (v. 8c)	"sin sprang to life again" (v. 9c)
"I was alive" (v. 9a)	"I died" (v. 9d)

Figure 3. Chiastic pattern in Romans 7:8-9 (from Moo 1996:437)

Once given that chance, however, sin produces death (vv. 9-11).

7:9 There are four views to be considered: (1) Käsemann (1980:196) sees a connection with 5:12-21, arguing that this depicts the fall of Adam into the "Primal I" as further dramatizing the dilemma of mankind as a whole. This would fit the *alive apart from law,* which would be Adam in the Garden, with the commandment being the order not to eat of the tree of the knowledge of good and evil. However, I have already discussed (see the introduction to this section) the difficulty of taking Adam as the *I.* (2) Or perhaps it is Israel before the law was given on Sinai—existing but not complete (Moo 1996). This is attractive, for it fits the centrality of *law* here but runs into difficulty with the idea of *I was alive,* which often in Paul refers to spiritual life and probably does here in light of its connection with *I died* in verses 9-10 (cf. Schreiner 1998:362, who cites Rom 6:11; 10:5; 12:1; 2 Cor 4:11; 5:15; 13:4; 1 Thess

Paul begins, *Once I was alive apart from law.* This is the first time in his epistle that Paul uses the emphatic *I,* and he most likely refers to his own experience as typical of every person. Still, one wonders when Paul would ever have been without law in a culture where the Torah was central from infancy on. Moreover, Paul himself talks about the zealous piety that characterized his life (Gal 1:13-14; Phil 3:4-6). So it is probably best to say that Paul was giving the other side to his "fault-less" behavior (Phil 3:6) as a Jew, that period, especially early in his life, when he lived as a Jew without a sense of conviction from the law, a time when "he had not realized the force of the law's demands" (Morris 1988:281). Most important, his experience is typical of all peo-ple who "live" (that is, think they are spiritually all right) apart from conviction of their sins. Yet *when the commandment came* (referring to the whole law and not just the tenth commandment), *sin sprang to life and I died.* Sin was previously dormant because there was no con-science or conviction of sin. But with the coming of the law, sin took advantage of the bridgehead (v. 8) and *sprang to life.* When that hap-pened, death was the natural result (5:12-14). There may be double meaning in *I died,* referring both to the death of his naive presumption that he was all right and to the spiritual death that characterizes every sinner. This is not the death to sin described in 6:2, 4-6, but the death that results from sin. In one sense there could be an echo of Adam's experience here as well. In the garden he too was innocent and with-out law, but when the serpent seduced him, death came upon all hu-mankind.

The great dilemma is that *the commandment* was supposed to *bring life* in the sense of making people right with God and helping

5:10). It is not as likely that Paul would be saying that Israel was "alive" before the law. (3) It could also be taken with Calvin (1979) as describing Paul's life before conversion (perhaps before the equivalent of his bar mitzvah—so Dodd 1932; Michel 1966; Barrett 1957; Bruce 1985), with *apart from law* meaning Paul did not properly understand sin and failed to realize the extent to which he was a sinner. This is closer to the meaning, but one has to wonder if any Jewish child would say he was *apart from law* in this sense. (4) Thus it is best to see that Paul is using him-self as the example of all humanity *apart from law.* Paul takes his experience of the interplay of the law and sin in his life to be typical of everyone (so Cranfield 1975; Morris 1988; Dunn 1988a).

them to experience life as he intended. Its true purpose was life-giving, but it "was found" or "proved to be" (NIV, *actually brought*) death-bringing. Sin has twisted the true purpose of the law and brought about spiritual death (again with a possible echo of the effects of the Fall). Let us trace the process (v. 11). Sin is seen as dormant without the law to turn it into transgression. The true purpose of the law is to be a positive force that restrains sin and produces life. But as soon as it appears, sin springs into action and uses it as a base of operations (*seizing the opportunity,* as in v. 8) to attack us. The attack takes the form of deception; it is not the law that is at fault but sin, which uses the law to seduce people like the serpent did in the Garden (*deceived* is used in 2 Cor 11:13; 1 Tim 2:14 of the seduction of Eve by the serpent). So in actuality the law has "aroused" sinful passions (7:5) rather than curtailing them. Throughout the New Testament this is the way Satan leads people to sin. He does not overpower them but tricks them (cf. Rev 12:9; 20:3, 8, 10). He is the greatest con man who ever lived. So the law has not reduced coveting but *produced in me every kind of covetous desire* (7:8). Moo (1996:439) explains that the law could only have produced this type of life if it had been perfectly obeyed. God of course knew that, because of the power of sin, no such possibility existed, but he provided Christ as the final fulfillment of the law to effect this final salvation and life. Still, the final result is that *the commandment put me to death.* Its purpose was life, but its true result was the dominion of death. For Adam and Eve it was physical death that entered the world and reigned over humankind (5:12-14), but for us it is also spiritual death. Again, the only hope is faith in

---

7:11 Cranfield (1975:352-53) sees three parallels with Genesis 3 here: (1) the serpent distorted and misrepresented the divine commandment by centering on only the negative aspect and ignoring the positive (Gen 2:16-17; 3:1); (2) he made Eve believe God would not punish disobedience with death (Gen 3:4); (3) he used the commandment itself to "insinuate doubts about God's good will and to suggest the possibility of man's asserting himself in opposition with God (v. 5)." However, it is also important to remember that Paul is not referring to Adam here but using Adam and Eve as an example of the experience of all of us.

7:13 There is some debate about whether verse 13 belongs with verses 7-12 (Godet 1969; Murray 1968; Dunn 1988a; Fitzmyer 1993b; Stott 1994) or with verses 14-25 (Michel 1966; Cranfield 1975; Morris 1988; Moo 1996; Schreiner 1998). This almost

the atoning sacrifice of Jesus.

Paul has just shown us that the law was used by sin to achieve its nefarious purposes. So now he can go on to sum up the actual characteristics of the law (*so then,* v. 12). Rather than sinful, *the law is holy;* rather than evil, *the commandment is holy, righteous and good.* Though the law was an instrument of sin, Paul wants to make certain that no one misinterpret to understand that the law was unholy (compare v. 7). Sin is the true culprit. Calling the law *holy* points to God as its true originator. Holiness is a key attribute of God expressing his transcendent Otherness. With regard to people *holy* means "grasped by God" and thus "set apart" to God. With respect to the law or other immaterial objects, *holy* is used to stress their sacred character. So also *the commandment* (again, synonymous with the law) is *holy,* but now we see two other aspects. It is also *righteous,* which at first glance contradicts 3:20 and 5:20-21, which say that the law cannot produce righteousness. However, those statements dealt with the function of the law while here Paul is describing its character. There may be double meaning here as well—the commandments are *righteous* in terms of partaking of God's nature, and they are "just" (the term means both) in terms of being fair to his people. Finally, *the commandment . . . is good* is an expression of God's goodness, producing what is best for all people. So, far from being evil (though it is an instrument of evil), the law is a sign of God's justness and goodness.

The twofold thrust in verses 7-12 (the law is good but still stimulates evil) produces a key question: *Did that which is good, then, become death to me?* It would be easy to conclude that the law, though good (v. 12), meant death. This in a sense restates the question of

always means that the verse is a transition between the two sections. It concludes the first section and launches the second. For this reason the NIV makes verse 13 a separate paragraph in itself. Still, it is likely that it belongs more to the first section. The rhetorical question that parallels the style of verse 7 could be an indication of a new paragraph, but it could also be in inclusio with verse 7, framing the paragraph with rhetorical questions. Moreover, it is the final verse using past tenses (vv. 7-13), while verse 14 begins the present-tense section (vv. 14-25). It also responds to the basic issue arising from verses 7-12: how can the law that is good produce death? So it most likely should be seen as part of the first section, though its theme (sin using the law to accomplish evil) is explicated further in verses 14-25.

verse 7, *Is the law sin?* by asking further, Is the law death? In fact, verses 10-11 come close to saying just that, that death came *through the commandment.* With his characteristic *Certainly not!* (see v. 7) Paul forcefully dispels this erroneous thought. The villain is not the law but sin, which used the law as its agent in producing death. Once again (as in v. 11) the law is the instrument *(through what was good)* used by sin to produce death. In a sense Paul is laying down a two-fold model of that which produces death—sin is the actual basis, and the law is the instrumental basis. So the blame for producing death falls squarely on sin. There are two divine purposes regarding sin here. First, God wants to "reveal" (the meaning of *recognize*) to everyone the true nature of sin. As NEB says, its "true character" is "exposed." Second, God uses *the commandment* to prove to all that sin is *utterly sinful,* a strong idiom that means it is shown to be "exceedingly sinful" or "completely evil." Through the law, the depth of its perversity is finally realized. Sin is *recognized* not only to be sin but to be extremely so. In other words, it is absolutely opposed to God and opposed by God. This shows the law to be *good,* in that it exposes the deep underside of sin. Grundmann says it well (1964: 311, from Morris 1988): "The function which we assert the law to have in the divine plan for the world is finally achieved when sin is unmasked in its demonic character as utter enmity against God. The state of the world and each individual since Adam has a demonic character as directed against God."

The Believer and the Law: Defeat (7:14-25) The central issue is still the law in this section. Here it is important to realize that while the believer has "died to the law" (7:4) and is "released" from it (7:3), the law is still present in a secondary way as fulfilled in Christ (Mt 5:17-20). Morris (1988:285-87) and Moo (1996:445-47) do an excellent job of summarizing the arguments for regenerate or unregenerate humanity here:

1. Favoring the view that this describes regenerate humankind: *(a)* the present tense and the emphatic *egō* (six times in this section) indicate Paul is speaking of his present experience; *(b)* it is believers who *delight in God's law* (v. 22), try to obey it (vv. 15-20) and serve it (v. 25); *(c)* the description of the unbelievers in 1:18—3:20 is quite different from this; they do not "seek God" (3:11) or "submit to God's law"

(8:7); *(d)* Paul's view of himself before conversion as a persecutor, zealous for the law and blameless is different from this; *(e)* the Christian life is the subject of chapters 5—8, and this seems to move in that direction; *(f)* Only a Christian has the "inner being" (v. 22), elsewhere found only in 2 Corinthians 4:16 and Ephesians 3:16; *(g)* the will is directed toward the good here, which does not fit the unregenerate; *(h)* when he calls himself *a slave to God's law* (v. 25), that fits a true follower; *(i)* the tension between will and action here is in keeping with Paul's view of Christian experience (cf. 8:23; 1 Cor 9:27; 1 Tim 1:15; Gal 5:16-17); *(j)* verse 25, *thanks be to God—through Christ Jesus our Lord,* seems to be the cry of a believer; *(k)* after describing the deliverance by God in Christ, the passage concludes by reiterating the divided state of the ego, showing that this struggle is that of a believer.

2. Favoring the view that these verses describe unregenerate humanity: (a) the connection of *egō* with the flesh (vv. 14, 18, 25) favors Paul's developing life in the flesh (7:5); *(b) egō* is constantly *sold as a slave to sin* (vv. 14, 25) and *a prisoner of the law of sin* (v. 23), which is unlike Paul (6:14, "sin shall not be your master"); (c) the entire picture here is much too negative for Paul, who depicts the struggle with sin (6:12-13; 13:12-14; Gal 5:17) but never a defeat by sin; *(d)* the Christian life is characterized by peace, not constant inner conflict; *(e)* Christ does not appear until verse 25, and the Holy Spirit is never mentioned, so the people are constantly on their own (*I myself,* v. 25) without Christ or the Spirit; *(f)* The statement that *nothing good lives in me* (v. 18) is not that of a believer; *(g)* the cry, *What a wretched man I am! Who will rescue me from this body of death?* (v. 24) does not fit a Christian; *(h)* the natural thrust of the language fits an unbeliever, for it describes a need to obey the Mosaic law, while the believer has already been released from the commands of the law (6:14; 7:4-6); *(i)* "now" in 8:1 marks a transition to a new thrust, namely, life in the Spirit, setting the life of the true child of God over against that of an unbeliever (7:14-25).

There are obviously good arguments on both sides; in fact, one could become virtually certain of each side simply by concentrating on the arguments for one and ignoring the opposite arguments. Thus, some (e.g., Schreiner 1998:390-92) believe Paul describes neither believer nor unbeliever here but simply depicts the inability of the law to transform people, whether Christian or not. Still, it is more likely that the contrast between life under the flesh in 7:14-25 and life under the Spirit in 8:1-17 is a comparison not of the unsaved and the saved but of the Christian trusting the flesh and the Christian living in the Spirit. This contrast describes Paul (and us) trying to defeat sin in his own strength and finally learning to surrender to the Spirit. It is simply too difficult to take *I* rhetorically as an unbeliever or as Israel without seeing Paul speaking of himself in some fashion. And the struggle with its victory in verses 24-25 is too close to that of a Christian. Very few Christians have read this section without thinking of their own struggle against sin. The centrality of the law in this passage seems inconsistent with Paul's characterization of the believer (e.g., *I delight in God's law,* v. 22), but it would fit Paul's own keeping the law (cf. Acts 18:18; 21:22-26) as fulfilled by Christ (Mt 5:17-20).

There are three subsections here. Verses 14-17 describe the futility of the natural person trying to do good but falling under the power of sin. Verses 18-20 describe the problem of sin living in *me.* Finally, verses 21-25 describe the opponents in the inner war—sin versus Christ.

Paul begins this section with a positive statement (v. 14)—*we know that the law is spiritual. We know* points again to a commonly accepted truth that Paul wants to deepen (see 2:2; 3:19). The law is not only holy, righteous and good (v. 12) but also spiritual, that is, the work of God's Spirit. This means that its origin is divine rather than human. In contrast, Paul says, *I am unspiritual* (literally "fleshly"), the first of six times in this section that *egō* is stressed. Basically, the term refers to his own humanity and is not particularly negative. But here the contrast with *spiritual* means it refers to the carnal nature, that power within that leads one to choose sin. It depicts the individual as belonging to this world and under the power of sin and death. This is shown in Paul's further description of "fleshly" as *sold as a slave to sin.* We can

---

7:15 When Paul says, *I do not understand what I do,* it could well be that he means "I do not approve of what I am doing" (see Cranfield 1975; Moo 1996) or perhaps that he does not fully "comprehend" the power of sin (Schreiner 1998). Rather than

picture the terrible image here, with the *I* in chains on the block and handed over to sin, its new master. This very negative picture goes back to 6:16-23 and is at the heart of the debate concerning whether Paul is describing the believer or the unbeliever. Moo (1996:454) speaks for the latter, arguing that the depiction of slavery to sin's power is incompatible with the picture of Romans 6, with the Christian having "died to the power of sin" (v. 2) and thus no longer "slaves of sin" (vv. 18, 22). On the other hand, Cranfield (1975:357-58) states that this simply describes our "continuing sinfulness"—our "very best acts and activities are disfigured by the egotism that is still powerful within" us. At the outset it must be said that Moo correctly notes that this is the most difficult challenge for any theory that Paul is describing a Christian here. But still, the arguments above for verses 14-25 depicting a believer are too strong. The answer probably lies in the imagery. The believer has been set free from the enslaving power of sin, but sin uses the flesh to make a counterattack and gain a bridgehead (vv. 8, 11) once more in the life of the believer. The slavery metaphor is hyperbole designed to emphasize this control by sin. This is not the "normal" Christian life; that is found in chapter 8. Paul is establishing a "straw man," a picture of Christians who try to live for Christ in their own strength. Dunn (1988a:389) describes it as "the [pious] saint who is most conscious of his sinfulness," citing parallels in Qumran (1QS 11:9-10, "As for me, I belong to wicked mankind, to the company of ungodly flesh. My iniquities, rebellions, and sins, together with the perversity of my heart, belong to the company of worms and to those who walk in darkness"). So Paul is demonstrating how powerful is the malevolent force that wars against him.

The dilemma is further defined in verse 15, beginning with Paul's statement, *I do not understand what I do.* This is in contrast with verse 14, which began, *We know.* Now Paul does not know or approve of what he is doing. There is a single thread running through these verses—conflict and self-guilt. He wants to do right but cannot seem to

---

ignorance, then, we could see conscience. This would lead into verse 15, where he says "I hate [my actions]," as well as into verses 18 ("I know that nothing good lives in me") and 19 ("the evil I do not want to do—this I keep on doing").

do so. We are now at the heart of the paradox of the struggle between living for God and living for self: *what I want to do I do not do, but what I hate I do.*

There are three different Greek words for "produce, do, practice" that are introduced in verse 15 and then occur again and again in the rest of the section. While some regard them as building on each other (Sanday and Headlam 1902; Cranfield 1975), it is better to see them as synonymous, as the NIV does in its consistent translation as *do* (so Barrett 1957; Murray 1968). They refer to the human actions of the individual who wants to do good but cannot seem to do so. Another central term is *want* (seven times in vv. 15-21); volition is part of the centrality of *mind* in this passage (vv. 23, 25). The will is part of the mind. Here Paul distinguishes his actual desire from that which is effectively carried out. He volitionally planned to do *the good* but actually carried out what he *hated.* This moral failure is caused by the power of sin within and by the human "fleshly" propensity to surrender to that power. It is neither sin nor the flesh that causes us to do what we hate but both working in concert. Sin provides the temptation; the flesh surrenders to it. Every one of us can identify with this struggle. It is at the heart of the Christian life, this war against evil and the human desire to give in to what we know is wrong.

Paul's desire to do good, even though he fails to follow through with those intentions, proves that *the law is good* (v. 16). The point is the desire to do what is right, not the failure to do it. Even when he does what he does not want, the fact that he does not want to do it constitutes implicit agreement to the moral goodness of the law. Theoretically he cannot oppose the law if he desires to do what is right. This is part of his response to the implication that the law might be evil in verses 1-6. The answer is: even though it is an instrument of evil, it is not sinful but "good." Beginning in verse 7, he has stated unequivocally that the law is not sin and in fact is spiritual (v. 14), holy and right-

---

7:18 Moo (1996:458-59) takes "flesh" (NIV *sinful nature*) here not in a moral sense but in an anthropological sense, that is, as the material or physical side of life seen also in verse 23, "the law of sin at work within my members," and in verse 25 where the mind and the flesh are set in opposition to one another. So there is a mind-body dualism in this passage. In this sense it could refer to the "dividedness" of the Jews

eous (v. 12), and good (vv. 12, 14). The reason this is so is given in verse 17: *As it is, it is no longer I myself who do it, but it is sin living in me.* The law is good, but I am not. However, it is not the real *I (egō)* but a separate force that is at fault. The logic is inescapable. Sin is that external force, a power or realm at war with us. Using the law and the flesh as its instruments, it first establishes a base of operations in us (vv. 8, 11), gains control over us (v. 5) enslaves us (v. 14) and finally kills us (v. 9). The law has prohibited sin, and yet it is *living in me.* Since it has established a bridgehead in our lives, it has made its home in us. It is therefore no longer an external force but an internal reality. Morris (1988:293) says it well: "This is not the honored guest, nor the paying tenant, but the 'squatter,' not legitimately there, but very difficult to eject." Let me expand this metaphor further—the squatter (v. 17) is an invading army (vv. 8, 11) trying to destroy us!

The next paragraph (vv. 18-20) further develops the bondage of the I to the power of sin. As Moo says (1996:458), this shows that the indwelling presence of sin is the central point of the section. Verses 15-16 lead up to it, and verses 18-20 expand on it, showing further the powerlessness of the I under the flesh. Paul repeats some of what he said in verse 14 *(I know . . . in my sinful nature)* in order to explain further his relation to sin. First, he knows *that nothing good lives in me,* meaning of course the sin that *lives in* him according to verse 17. The law is good, but that is the external power, and the internal controlling force has nothing to do with *good.* This is because the internal mechanism that is making the decisions is "the flesh" (NIV, *sinful nature;* see 7:5), the attachment to this world and the tendency to seek that which pleases the self. It is the flesh that has allowed sin to gain control. This leads to the second thing Paul knows—as a result, *I have the desire to do what is good, but I cannot carry it out.* The *I* has given way to the *flesh* or propensity to sin and chosen to do that which it detests. The battle between the will and the resultant action are ongoing. This neg-

---

under the law. While this is possible, it does not fit the emphasis on the "flesh" in 7:5, 14 (and, as will be seen, in v. 25 as well), where it refers to that aspect of the being that is susceptible to sin. It is difficult to deny a moral aspect to flesh here. There is a dualism, but it is a moral one—the desire to do what God demands in the law, but a fleshly weakness to overcome sin.

ative view of the flesh may stem from the Greek repugnance toward the flesh but more likely is connected to the Jewish doctrine of the two "natures" or *yetzerim.* The Jews believed every person has an impulse or inclination to do good *(yetzer tōb)* and an impulse to do evil *(yetzer hara')* and that every decision was made on the basis of interaction between these two forces. The flesh is the impulse toward evil. Murray (1968:263) finds three propositions here: (1) the flesh is wholly sinful—no good thing dwells in it; (2) the flesh is still associated with Paul's own personhood—it is his flesh and dwells i*n him;* (3) sin is also associated with his person—it is in his flesh that sin operates.

In order to emphasize his point more, Paul now recapitulates the thought of verses 15-17 on the defeat of the will by sin (vv. 19-20). Like Paul, we all want to do good but end up doing evil instead. The sense of futility can be overwhelming. This repeats verse 15 but adds clarity by specifically identifying what is willed *as the good* and what is actually practiced as *the evil.* Is Paul saying that he is totally controlled by the evil? At first glance there seems to be absolute pessimism here. However, we must realize that Paul is speaking both relatively and circumstantially, preparing for the other side of the issue in 7:25 and chapter 8. In every decision we make, the *egō* is involved, introducing self-seeking tendencies into the process. So, like Paul, we *keep on doing* the evil we do not want to do whenever the decision is made according to the flesh. That is the key. As we will see, life in the Spirit (that is, making decisions by the Spirit rather than the flesh) produces victory. But when the flesh is dominant, defeat is the result. So Paul repeats verses 16-17 in verse 20. The fact that he does what he does not want to do shows that it is not the I but sin indwelling him that is the culprit. The evil power that has established a base of operations in him (vv. 8, 11) has caused him to do evil.

The final section (vv. 21-25) describes the war between good and evil in Paul and us and forms a conclusion *(so,* better "therefore") to

---

7:22 Opinions differ about whether *inner being* refers to a Christian (Murray 1968; Cranfield 1975; Morris 1988) or to a non-Christian (Fitzmyer 1993b; Moo 1996). Those who argue the latter take it as speaking psychologically of our higher nature, in a Hellenistic sense referring to the mind or spirit as opposed to the physical body. Those who take it as describing a Christian note its use in 2 Corinthians

this section. To sum up the issue Paul says, *I find this law at work*. There is a great deal of debate about whether *law* refers to the Mosaic law (the meaning in vv. 21, 25; so Wilckens 1980; Dunn 1988a; Wright 1991:199-200; Schreiner 1998) or a general "principle" (Hodge 1950; Cranfield 1975; Käsemann 1980; Morris 1988; Fitzmyer 1993b; Moo 1996). If the former, we would translate, "I find with respect to the law for me who would do good that for me evil is present." However, verse 23 uses *law* for *another law*, namely, the *law of my mind* rather than the *law of sin*. While an argument can be made that the *law of my mind* is the Mosaic law (so Schreiner 1998), it is more likely that *law* in verses 21, 23 refers to the "principle" or "rule" that operates in the individual. This "rule" is spelled out in what follows. In this sense it is the other law of verse 23 that imitates the true law (Barrett 1957—"counterfeit law"). The rule that Paul has discovered is, *When I want to do good, evil is right there with me*. Once again, the battle between the will to do good and the force of sin/evil within us is presented. When we try to make the morally correct decision, the tendency toward evil counters our will and forces the wrong decision.

The war within is clarified further by the antithesis in verses 22-23, summarizing his emphasis throughout this chapter but especially the battle between good and evil in verse 21. On the positive side, Paul *delights in God's law* in his *inner being*. The verb means to "rejoice in" something and reflects the basic Jewish (and Christian) devotion to God's law. Once again, Christians rejoice in the law as divine covenant and as fulfilled in Christ (Mt 5:17-20). While *God's law* could refer to the whole Old Testament as divine revelation, the Mosaic law was often called "the Torah of God," and it is likely that *God's* was added partly to distinguish it from the *law* of verses 21, 23. The sphere within which this delight occurs is the *inner being,* used elsewhere in Paul of a Christian (2 Cor 4:16; Eph 3:16) and referring to the mental and spiritual aspect of our being. This idea of mental activity controls the rest of

---

4:6 and Ephesians 3:16 and connect it to the new man described in Romans 6:6. The decision is doubtless connected to the decision above regarding whether Paul is speaking of a believer or an unbeliever in 7:14-25, so that would favor Paul speaking of a believer here.

the chapter (*the law of my mind*, v. 23; *I myself in my mind*, v. 25). As we meditate on the law and its purpose, we are filled with joy at what God has done. Mentally, we joyfully know that the law is spiritual, holy, righteous and good (vv. 12, 14, 16) and desire to live by its precepts (vv. 15, 18, 19, 21).

However, the problem is that there is *another law at work in the members of my body*. This other principle or power (the *law of sin* below) is dynamically active in the person. Sin was first conceived as a power or realm (6:2-14), then as an enslaving master (6:16-22), and now as a law or controlling force at work in us. Paul then switches metaphors and looks at sin as an invading army *waging war against the law of my mind* (see also vv. 8, 11). The *law of my mind* parallels *God's law* in verse 22 and is the sphere within which God is at work, in the thinking process as well as the volition. The mind is the place where spiritual growth occurs (see 12:2 on "the renewing of your mind") and where the battle takes place. The warfare is carried out in the conscious realm, and entails *another law/law of sin* battling against both *God's law* (the work of the Spirit within; see 7:6) and *the law of my mind* (the "new self," cf. Rom 6:6). The believer has become a battleground with sin as the aggressor and *God's law* placed on the defensive. More than that, sin is the victor here and makes *me a prisoner of the law of sin at work within my members*. There is a difference of opinion whether *my members* refers to the physical body (because of parallels with *mind*) or to the whole person (the thrust it had in 6:13, 19; 7:5). While a good argument can be made for this referring to the physical body as controlled by sin, it is still better to see it more broadly of every aspect of our being attacked by the power of sin (including the mind and the body). Imagine that the enemy (sin) has

---

7:24 There is some question about whether we should translate *this body of death* (stressing the body as the place death operates; so NRSV; NIV; NJB; TEV; NLT; Cranfield 1975) or "the body of this death" (stressing the death that results from the battle with sin; so KJV; NASB; Murray 1968). While both death (vv. 10, 11, 13) and body (6:6, 12; equivalent terms in vv. 18, 23) occur in the context and are emphasized, the emphasis on body in the immediate context makes the former the better option.

7:24 Moo (1996:466 n.) argues that Christians would not have said *Who will rescue me . . . ?* because they would know the identity of the deliverer. This, however, presupposes that the Christian is thinking spiritually rather than from a self-centered or

made war against, triumphed over, captured and then enslaved the individual—a very serious portrait indeed! In this sense there is a dualism, with two opposing forces at work in us and the side of evil winning. But the extreme pessimism once again must be understood in light of Paul's purpose. This section describes a Christian trusting in the flesh, and chapter 8 shows that victory only comes in the Spirit. Origen writes (Bray 1998:198), "It appears that in this passage Paul is teaching us that the mortification of the flesh . . . is not something which happens overnight but rather is a gradual process, because the force of habit is such and the attraction of sin is so great that, even though our mind may want to do what is right and has decided to serve the law of God, yet the lusts of the flesh continue to urge him to serve sin and obey its laws instead."

So Paul concludes, *What a wretched man I am! Who will rescue me from this body of death?* (v. 24). Many have a hard time applying this abject distress to a believer because of the severity of the misery and the utter defeatism inherent in it. But this is also the natural result of the frustrations expressed throughout the passage, and it does describe the state of the "carnal Christian" (see 1 Cor 3:1, 3) or what has come to be called the "backslidden" condition. *Wretched* means to be in complete anguish and distress but does not mean total hopelessness and despair (so Cranfield 1975). The cry that follows has a sense of hope, especially in light of the next verse, for Paul tells us exactly who will rescue us. The question is rhetorical (like those in 6:1, 15; 7:7, 13), pointing forward to its answer in verse 25. So the sense is not of absolute defeat but rather of temporary defeat soon to be turned around. The *body of death* here looks at the total person (see discussion of "body" in 6:6, 12) as inhabited by sin and death. This is

worldly perspective. The fact is, many Christians live this kind of defeated life. That is the tragedy of it all.

7:24 Does the *rescue* of verses 24-25 refer to the parousia (emphasis on *this body,* so Murray 1968; Cranfield 1975 on the basis of *body* meaning the physical body) or present spiritual victory (emphasis on *rescue me;* so Barrett 1957 on the basis of the present perspective of the whole passage). In light of the present battle fought throughout and the meaning of *body* as the total person rather than just the physical body, the thrust is most likely the present deliverance from sin.

flesh (v. 18) and *members* (v. 23) under siege and conquered by sin, resulting in death (7:10-13). The death is probably both physical (see 5:12-14) and spiritual. Believers long to be released from the hostile power of sin at work in their total beings. Paul's question reverberates with all too many Christians who are living lives of tragic self-centeredness and spiritual defeat. Packer (1999:76) says it well: "The 'wretched man' outburst is the mark of a healthy believer who loves God's law and aims to keep it perfectly, but finds that something within him whose presence is known only by its effects, namely indwelling sin, obstructs and thwarts his purpose; for it betrays him time and again into doing things which at the moment of action seem good but in hindsight appear bad."

But it does not have to be this way, for the answer comes quickly in the form of a thanksgiving, *Thanks be to God—[rescue comes] through Jesus Christ our Lord!* The brevity with which Paul states this triumphant cry is in keeping with his style for important points. The only solution to the distress of spiritual defeat is to acknowledge and depend completely upon the lordship of Christ. Until Christ is made Lord of our lives, defeat will always be a reality. But in Christ there is both strength to resist and the power to be victorious. All the studies (Gallup, Barna and others) of the church at the dawn of the twenty-first century have reported the growing secularity that dominates. On the whole, you cannot tell a Christian from a non-Christian in terms of lifestyle, morals or priorities. This means that more Christians than ever are only partially committed to Christ. One of the important tasks of the church today is not just reaching the unchurched but waking up the dormant Christians who come but do nothing for the Lord. This passage describes those people. We must help them change their priorities and make *Jesus Christ their Lord.* This brief note of victory is in a sense a preview of coming attractions, for it points forward to chapter 8, where the means for accomplishing this is more fully explained.

Yet the problem still persists, for Paul concludes his argument by re-

---

7:25 Many have tried to explain away the reinsertion of the two-nature motif after the note of victory as a rearrangement of the original order (in which second half of v. 25 was placed before the first; so Moffatt; Dodd 1932; Michel 1966) or as a sec-

capitulating *(so then)* his teaching regarding the two natures of every person. There is no triumphal end to this chapter. Rather, the war continues, and the believer has to choose between surrendering to the lordship of Christ and thus gaining victory (v. 25) or choosing to obey the *law of sin* and thus facing spiritual defeat (v. 25). Again, the battle takes place in the *mind,* where Paul is consciously *a slave to God's law,* meaning he wants (note the emphasis on volition seven times in vv. 15-21) to serve God's law (cf. v. 22) with all his heart. But the *mind* is opposed by the *flesh,* and he becomes *a slave to the law of sin.* Here we have the paradox on slavery reversed from that in 6:22, where we have been set free from slavery to sin in order to become slaves to God. Now we try to serve God but end up serving sin. The spiritual self is defeated by the carnal self. At first glance this seems to end on a note of absolute defeat, as if there is no hope in the spiritual battle (and so many conclude that this cannot describe a Christian). But that is not so. The two options are presented in v. 25—choose to follow Christ or allow sin to dominate. Dunn (1988a:398-99) calls this the battle of two epochs, the old Adamic epoch in which sin dominates and the new epoch of Christ. While we in one sense have died to the old realm (6:1-7), we still live in this world and so are still subject to its power through the flesh. Paul wants us to know that the conflict is real, and we cannot escape it. The answer is hinted at in verse 25a and then explicated fully in chapter 8, namely life in Christ and the Spirit. Calvin summarizes the teaching here (1979:274): "the faithful never reach the goal of righteousness so long as they dwell in the flesh, but that they are running their course, until they put off the body."

New Life in the Spirit (8:1-39) We have all enjoyed those movies or sporting events that show a team snatching victory from the jaws of defeat (like *Hoosiers* or *Remember the Titans*). It is thrilling to see this happen, but many of us are thinking, "Yes, but it doesn't happen to me!" In the spiritual realm, it should be the normal Christian life. The

ondary gloss from a later scribe (Bultmann 1947; Käsemann 1980; Wilckens 1980). But there is no text-critical evidence whatsoever for either view, and we must interpret it as it is. As it stands it makes perfect sense.

defeatism of chapter 7 is turned around by the victory made possible by chapter 8. The twin issues of sin and the law have dominated chapters 6—7, and the last part of this section (7:14-25) has traced the frustration of attempting to live the Christian life according to the flesh. Here the solution is given—living our lives according to the power of the indwelling Spirit. It is often argued (e.g., Cranfield 1975) that 8:1-11 relates not to 7:7-25 but rather to 5:21-7:6, but yet the flesh/Spirit dualism of this passage carries on and culminates the battle with the *flesh* (twice in 7:14-25 and ten times in 8:1-13) in 7:14-25. The key term in this section is *Spirit,* found twenty-one times in this chapter (fifteen in vv. 1-17) and a total of thirteen times in the rest of the book (*spirit* in vv. 15, 16 does not refer to the Holy Spirit). Here the Spirit becomes the active force in believers' lives and enables them to defeat the flesh and live in victory. Moo (1996:468) sums up the thrust of the chapter with the word *assurance,* for the chapter enumerates "those gifts and graces that together assure the Christian that his relationship with God is secure and settled." The tension of the eschatological battle with sin is alleviated by the blessings poured out through the Spirit.

There are four sections in this chapter. Verses 1-11 describe the victorious life made possible in the Spirit. Verses 12-17 rejoice in the privilege of adoption as God's children and heirs. Verses 18-30 reassure believers of the new hope that the pain of present groaning will lead to the present experience of God's sovereign control and to final glory. Verses 31-39 affirm the absolute certainty of our security in God and conclude not just chapter 8 but the whole book thus far.

The Victorious Life in the Spirit (8:1-11) Sin and the law have produced condemnation and defeat in 5:21—7:25. In the midst of this, however, there have been glimpses of the life of victory and hope that is available as a result of justification (5:1-11): the result of the work of

---

8:2 There is considerable debate about whether *law* should be understood metaphorically as a "rule" or "authority" (as in 7:21, 23; so Sanday and Headlam 1902; Murray 1968; Cranfield 1975; Käsemann 1980; Fitzmyer 1993b; Moo 1996) or whether it refers to the Mosaic law (as in the rest of chap. 7; so Wilckens 1980; Dunn 1988a; Snodgrass 1988:99; Schreiner 1998). If the latter, it means the Mosaic law has no value apart from the Spirit; without the Spirit it becomes the law that leads to sin and death. If the former, it means the emphasis is on the Spirit's power to liberate us from sin and death. Each is viable and would fit the context ("principle" in 7:21, 23

Christ as the second Adam (5:15-21) and the fact that at conversion we have died to sin in Christ (6:1-11). In him we are free from the power of sin as we give ourselves over to God in obedience and right living (6:12-22). This passage acts as a conclusion to that section, for victory is only assured when the Spirit of Christ is in us and we yield to his presence.

There are four sections here: (1) verse 1 states the basic result of being *in Christ,* the absence of *condemnation;* (2) verses 2-4 tell how this occurs, as the *Spirit of life* liberates from *the law of sin and death;* (3) verses 5-8 describe the conflict between the flesh and the Spirit; (4) verses 9-11 describe the victory wrought by the Spirit in us and relate the promise of life via the Spirit, both now and at the final resurrection.

Paul begins by returning to the condemnation brought about by sin in 5:12-14 and 7:1-6, saying, *there is now no condemnation for those who are in Christ Jesus.* The emphasis on *now* returns to the idea of the two epochs in salvation-history. The *now*-ness of this new age of salvation (cf. 3:26; 5:9, 11; 6:19, 21) means that the condemnation of the old era is no longer. The term *condemnation* occurs only in 5:16, 18 elsewhere in the New Testament, the passage on Christ overturning the results of Adam's sin (5:12-21). So clearly this means that the condemnation resulting from sin has been removed for those who are *in Christ Jesus* (3:24; 6:11, 23; cf. 7:4), that is, are united with him in his death and resurrection. For them his atoning sacrifice has led to God's judicial forgiveness. In short, the forensic *condemnation* of the sinner by God has been removed by the forensic *justification* of the sinner in Christ. Moo says it well (1996:473), "Paul's judicial 'for us' language and his 'participationist' 'in him' language combine in perfect harmony."

The reason (*because,* v. 2) for this is the liberation from sin and death that Christ has effected and the Spirit has produced. Through his sacrificial death the condemnation of the believer has been removed.

---

and Mosaic law in 7:22, 25). There are several reasons for favoring the metaphorical use over the literal use of law: (1) 7:6 strongly separates the "Spirit" from the "written code." (2) Verse 3 says clearly that the law is "powerless" to do such a thing. (3) The closely parallel "law of sin" in 7:23 is the principle of sin. (4) This seems to recapitulate the "two powers/kingdoms" theme of chapters 6—7, the realm of the Spirit versus the realm of sin and death. However, there are equally compelling reasons pointing to the Mosaic law as the reference: (1) The positive view of the law is in keeping with Paul's defense of it in 7:14-25. (2) The teaching about the law in chap-

The antithesis is between *the law of the Spirit of life* and *the law of sin and death*. Now Paul introduces the leading character of the chapter, the Holy Spirit, looking back to 7:6, "the new way of the Spirit." In the Spirit we not only have a new way but a new value in the Mosaic law. Both genitives are subjective: sin and death have "used" the law to produce evil, but the Spirit "uses" the law to produce life. The Christian is not free from the law but from the law as used by sin and death. It is important to remember that this positive view of the law in the life of the Christian is the result of messianic fulfillment. The law is intact and fulfilled in Jesus (Mt 5:17-20; see on 7:4, 6, 22). The Jews believed that when the Messiah came he would bring "the Torah of the Messiah," the final Torah of the new age. This is what Paul is referring to. The power of sin and death are broken in the reign of the Spirit. *The Spirit of life* refers to "the Spirit who gives life," showing that the liberation of verse 1 is a liberation to true life now and eternal life in the future (inaugurated eschatology). Schreiner (1998:400) sees an allusion to Ezekiel 37:5-6, 9-10, 14, where the "breath of God" (the Spirit) produces life. Again Christ is the means by which this liberation has been accomplished. Finally, Paul shifts to the second person, *you,* to make the message more direct to the readers. He wants to be certain that *you* realize this essential truth of being set free from sin and death. This adds further depth to the *no condemnation* of verse 1. The Christian was once under bondage to sin, and the just penalty of that was death. Now both of these powers have been nullified by the Spirit, and so life in the Spirit is one of glorious freedom. That it is the *Spirit* rather than Christ who does this and produces life may mean that the emphasis here is more on the Christian life than on conversion. There are five liberations in the larger context: a freedom from slavery to sin (6:16-22), a freedom from being taken prisoner (7:23), a freedom from con-

---

ters 7—8 center on the law and the flesh (chap. 7) versus the law and the Spirit (chap. 8). (3) There is no actual contradiction between verses 2 and 3 (see above). (4) This teaches the flip side of 7:6; there the law was an instrument of sin, here an instrument of the Spirit. (5) The "two kingdoms" aspect is still present in the law used by the Spirit and the law used by sin and death. (6) In verse 4 the "righteous requirements of the law" are "fully met in us," culminating the positive view of the law in verse 2. In a very difficult decision, I must side with the Mosaic-law interpretation here as making slightly better sense of the passage.

demnation (8:1), a freedom from the power of sin and death (8:2), and a final liberation of both creation and the individual at the eschaton (8:21, 23). Cranfield (1995:220-25) argues that this is not just a "set free from" in a liberation sense but also a "set free for" in glorious Christian freedom to live for Christ. In the Spirit we are free to resist sin (here), to address God as father (8:15), to engage in Christian prayer (8:27) and to obey God's law (8:3-4).

Yet this new life in the Spirit is grounded (*gar,* for) in Christ and conversion. In verses 1-3 there is an ABA pattern, with the life in the Spirit framed by the effects of the cross. The new life cannot begin until the *condemnation* under sin has been removed. To accomplish this God *condemned sin* through the *sin offering* of Christ. Recapitulating the emphasis in chapter 7, Paul tells us first that *the law was powerless to [remove condemnation] in that it was weakened by the sinful nature* (literally, "the flesh"). We have already seen that the Mosaic law brings wrath by making people recognize that their sins are transgressions (4:13-15; 7:7) and so causes sin to increase (5:20). The law aroused the "sinful passions" and brought forth death (7:5; 8-11). From this standpoint, the law would indeed be *powerless* to remove condemnation since it actually produced condemnation. Again, the law in itself did not do this; rather it was sin (on which see 7:5) that accomplished this by using the law as its instrument (7:11, 14, 17-20). Calvin says on this (1979:280), "The corruption then of our nature renders the law of God in this respect useless to us; for while it shows the way of life, it does not bring us back who are running headlong into death."

What the law could not do because of sin, *God did by sending his own Son in the likeness of sinful man to be a sin offering.* The sending language is used often of the mission of a royal envoy (see especially John, where it is used over thirty times), but here that envoy is some-

---

8:2 While the NIV has "set *me* free," there are good reasons to believe that the better reading in the Greek is "set *you* free." The first person is supported by codices Alexandrinus and Bezae, the Majority Text, and several minuscules and versions; the second person is supported by codices Sinaiticus and Vaticanus as well as several other witnesses. The manuscript evidence is fairly even, but the fact that "you" is the less likely reading (it interrupts the first-person narrative of chap. 7, continued in 8:4, so it is more likely a later scribe changed "you" to "me") favors a switch to "you" as the probable reading (see Metzger 1971:516).

thing more, God's *own Son.* The use of *his own* emphasizes the deep relationship between Jesus and his Father, and as Fitzmyer says (1993b:484-85) implies the preexistence of Jesus. It is debated whether *the likeness of sinful man* means outward appearance or complete identity. The former is unlikely, for the New Testament as a whole indicates that Jesus was fully human, so "likeness" here is similar to "in the form of" in the incarnational hymn of Philippians 2:6, 7. But Paul has also added it was *sinful* flesh, so there must also be some fine nuances here. The New Testament is too clear on Jesus' sinless nature, so this can hardly be saying he participated in human sin. Schreiner catches the balance (1998:403), "This does not mean that the Son himself sinned . . . but that he participated in the old age of the flesh, and that his body was not immune to the powers of the old age: sickness and death." So the stress is on Jesus' identity with our own situation under *the flesh.* However, he did not sin but instead bore our sins on the cross. The result is that as the *sin offering,* Jesus *condemned sin in sinful man* (literally, "concerning sin, he condemned sin in the flesh"). Christ was in the likeness of sinful flesh so that he might become the perfect *sin offering* and accomplish what the law could not do, namely, condemn sin in the flesh. In verse 1 the condemnation of sin was removed for believers, and now we see the flip side: condemnation was taken away from us by the same act in which it was placed on sin—the cross. The judicial side of the term is highlighted in both verses. God as a result of Jesus' sin offering both condemned sin and justified the believer. In so doing the power of sin was broken (so Käsemann 1980; Cranfield 1975; Schreiner 1998; contra Moo 1996).

The purpose for God sending his Son to be the sin offering was to fulfill *the righteous requirements of the law* (v. 4). This could be primarily forensic, meaning that Christ judicially fulfilled the law's demands

---

8:3 There is discussion regarding whether "concerning sin" means simply that Christ came "with reference to sin" (so Murray 1968; Barrett 1957; Cranfield 1975) or has sacrificial overtones (Sanday and Headlam 1902; Wright 1980:453-59; Dunn 1988a; Moo 1996; Schreiner 1998). But the phrase occurs so often in the LXX for the sin offering (Sanday and Headlam—over fifty times in Leviticus alone) that it likely has this connotation here as well. God sent his Son to be *a sin offering* (the NIV translation).

on the cross (so Calvin 1979; Hodge 1950; Fitzmyer 1993b; Moo 1996), or it could be fulfilled when Christians obey God and live out the law's requirements (Murray 1968; Cranfield 1975; Morris 1988; Schreiner 1998). However, this is no either-or. In the context, Paul has just finished speaking of Christ's *sin offering,* and the whole of 8:1-17 describes the new life in the Spirit. The true purpose of the law is fulfilled when justification launches sanctification, that is, when Christ's sacrificial death enables these requirements to be *fully met in us* (in the Greek this is a divine passive meaning "God fulfills" it). Note that it is fulfilled *in us,* which means that we participate in the results. The idea of fulfilled is similar to that in Matthew 5:17, which says Christ came to "fulfill" the law, that is, caught it up in himself and lifted it to a higher plane (thus completing it). So here the true requirements of the law are completed in both the sin offering of Christ and the life of obedience that follows. Moo (1996:483) speaks of an "interchange" here—"Christ becomes what we are so that we might become what he is." This of course does not mean sinless perfection. Chapter 7 demonstrates the struggle we all go through. However, the message of this section is that we can experience progressive sanctification in the Spirit, that is, grow in righteous living. This can only occur when we live not *according to the flesh but according to the Spirit.* What Christ has done for us on the cross (v. 2) is worked out in Spirit-empowered living, and both together fulfill the law. There are two choices—to live by the flesh or the world's standards or to live in obedience to the Spirit's leading. This flesh/Spirit opposition will dominate the next few verses. As in chapter 6, we are back to the idea of the two powers or realms; there it was sin versus grace, and here it is flesh versus Spirit. There the solution was to die with Christ; here it is to live in the Spirit. The two are interdependent.

8:5 Moo (1996:486-87) argues that the contrast is between the unconverted and the converted in verses 5-8, not between two different approaches to the Christian life (the flesh and the Spirit). He points out that being *in the flesh* (v. 8) cannot describe a believer, and that the third-person language here is descriptive rather than hortatory. Moreover, in verse 9 Paul says, "You are not controlled by the flesh but by the Spirit," clearly separating the two groups.

The next paragraph (vv. 5-8; compare 5:12-21) develops the antithesis between the flesh and the Spirit (vv. 5-6) followed by a diatribe against the flesh (vv. 7-8). It tells us why we must live according to the Spirit (v. 4). Both contrasts deal with the mindset of two groups of people: the converted and the unconverted. The NIV translates, *those who live according to the flesh,* but the Greek says, "those who are according to the flesh." In actuality, Paul describes the ontological rather than the functional, that is, who they are rather than what they do (contra Dunn 1988a). Verse 4 describes the walk, verses 5-8 the nature behind that walk. Those of the flesh (again, describing the fallen nature) *have their minds set on what that nature desires* (literally, "the things of the flesh"). This includes the thinking process and the will (indeed, the whole person); it goes back to 1:21, 28 and the fact that depravity is especially manifest in the mindset of "those who are according to the flesh." Note that they deliberately choose not on the basis of what is right but on the basis of self-centered desires. Everything they do is controlled by the concerns of this world. In contrast, those who are characterized by the Spirit *have their minds set on* "the things of the Spirit" (NIV translates *what the Sprit desires*). They are directed by the Spirit and both think and choose that which is in accordance with the Spirit. Hendriksen says (1981:248), "Those who live according to the Spirit, and therefore submit to the Spirit's direction, concentrate their attention on, and specialize in, whatever is dear to the Spirit. In the conflict between God and sinful human nature the first group sides with human nature, the second sides with God."

The second antithesis (v. 6) describes the results of the mind of the flesh and the mind of the Spirit. The two genitives could be subjective (the flesh's mind) or objective (the mind set on fleshly things); the latter is slightly more likely, for the emphasis is on the person's mindset. *Mind* here refers not just to the thoughts but to the desires, outlook and worldview of the person. When the mindset is grounded in the flesh, *death* in its broadest sense is the result. This is not just final death in eternal punishment but a state of death that rules over the unsaved throughout their lives (cf. 5:12-15; 7:10-13), ending in the "second death" of Rev 2:11 and 20:6. Morris (1988:306) says that "to be bounded by the flesh is itself death. It is a cutting off of oneself from the life that is life indeed." Those who center on the Spirit, however, experience *life and peace. Life* is eternal life in 2:7, 5:21, and 6:22-23 and present life in Christ in 7:10 and 8:2. Here it is both. *Peace* with God is the result of justification (5:1). While it could refer to the tranquility of the soul (a peaceful heart, so Dodd 1932; Morris 1988), it more likely refers to the state of being reconciled to God, of being in right relationship with him.

Paul now explains why (*dioti, because,* omitted from the NIV) the fleshly mind must be in a state of death (vv. 7-8): *the sinful mind is hostile to God.* The term *hostile* does not just describe a person who has become an enemy of God; rather it describes a fierce, active enmity toward all that God is and stands for. The entire mindset is directed against the things of God, and this opposition is the chief characteristic of the state of death. It desires that which pleases self rather than that which pleases God, and its actions oppose that which God demands. This of course does not mean that secular persons are incapable of doing good but does mean that they do not seek the things of God. The basis of that hostility is its refusal to *submit to God's law. God's law* could be the Mosaic ordinances (as in vv. 3-4) or God's demands in general (as in 7:21, 23, though in 7:22 "God's law" refers to the Mosaic law), but in the larger context of chapters 7—8 it most likely refers to the Torah. The hostile mind of the carnal person is completely incapable of placing itself under (the meaning of *submit*) God's law. Paul intensifies this refusal by saying it is grounded in the very nature when he adds, *nor can it do so.* Because of the nature of sin, it is completely incapable of following God's law, again a reflection back to 1:18-32. This of course is total depravity, the domination of the will by the sinful nature. Once more, this does not imply that unbelievers are incapable of doing good or recognizing what is good; instead, it means they cannot choose good for God's sake. When they do good, it is due to the situation rather than to any desire to please God or follow him. Sin controls every aspect of their lives. In fact, that is the very point of the next verse. Because sinners are incapable of submitting to God's law, they *cannot please God.* They are "in the flesh" (compare 7:5); that is, they have the flesh as the sphere of their existence. Thus it is impossible for them to be pleasing to God. The verb *please* refers to a desire to please God and denotes that unbelievers exemplify an attitude of indifference, a lack of desire to bring pleasure to God, indeed an inability even to want to do so (contra Paul in 1 Thess 2:4; see Schneider 1990:151).

Verses 9-11 turn from the unsaved to the situation of the Roman Christians (note the shift to *you*): *You, however, are controlled not by the flesh but by the Spirit* (literally "in the Spirit"). Unbelievers can never please God, for they belong to the realm of sin and death. Believers belong to the realm of the Spirit, so they have life and peace (v. 6). The criterion for being a true believer is clearly stated: *if the Spirit of God lives in you.* The *if* form does not mean Paul is uncertain about their condition. He considers this a factual description—they know Christ and therefore have the Spirit living in them (note the contrast with 7:18, 20, where sin "lives in" a person). In successive clauses they are in the Spirit and the Spirit lives in them. This is an important doctrine. When people come to faith in Christ, they are immediately indwelt by the Holy Spirit. In fact, as will be seen in verse 16, this is the basis of the believer's assurance. When we have the Holy Spirit and feel his presence, we are truly the children of God. Jesus himself promised the disciples in John 14:17 that "you know [the Holy Spirit], for he lives with you and will be in you." To make his point more emphatic, Paul then says the opposite: those who do not *have the Spirit of Christ* do not *belong to Christ.* Notice that in the first half of the verse he is *the Spirit of God* and in the second half *the Spirit of Christ.* There is a hint of Trinitarian doctrine here, as the Spirit is sent both by God the Father and by God the Son.

In verse 10 Paul shifts from the Spirit in the believer to Christ in the believer (v. 10). The sacrificial atonement of Christ provided the basis for the work of the Spirit, so the focus shifts back to Christ's work. When Christ dwells within, two things happen. First, *your body is dead because of sin.* This could mean that the Christian has died to sin, as in

---

8:10 There are three contrasting pairs here: *flesh/spirit, dead/alive and sin/righteousness.* Because of the connection with the human body in verse 10, many take *pneuma* as the human spirit (so Hodge 1950; Sanday and Headlam 1902; Wilckens 1980; Fitzmyer 1993b; Stott 1994; NIV; NASB; JB; NEB; NLT). However, the Holy Spirit is central in this section and is certainly the meaning of *pneuma* in verses 9 and 11 sur-

6:2-11. However, this is not death *to* sin (as in 6:2, 11) but death *because of* sin, so it must refer to the fact that as sinners we still must face the death of the (physical) *body* (cf. 5:12). This is proven by the emphasis on the resurrection of *mortal bodies* in verse 11. The body faces death, but that will lead to resurrection. While sin has been nullified on the cross and we have victory over sin in Christ and the Spirit, we still struggle against sin (7:14-25) and face the terrible consequences of sin, physical death. In this sense it may be best to translate this clause, "although your body is dead because of sin" (so Cranfield 1975; Moo 1996; Schreiner 1998). The rest of the verse is difficult to interpret but should probably read, "yet the Spirit produces life because of righteousness." Thus the contrast is between the Holy Spirit and our physical bodies. While death still controls our mortal bodies, there dwells within us a new power, the Holy Spirit who represents the new life in God that is ours. As above, *life* must be understood via inaugurated eschatology, that is, the presence of God's life in us now and the guarantee of eternal life to come. Schreiner (1998:415), as in 8:2, sees Ezekiel 37 behind this teaching, stating that Paul saw the valley of dry bones fulfilled in the promise of resurrection life through the Spirit. The basis of this is *righteousness,* certainly to be seen as forensic here, that is, the justification (see on 3:21, 24) of the believer, producing righteousness. So while our bodies will die, the Spirit is the presence of God's life in us and gives us the promise that death will lead to resurrection.

This promise is elaborated in verse 11. Now the *Spirit of life* (v. 2) is called *the Spirit of him who raised Jesus from the dead.* So life leads to resurrection, and the Spirit is the means by which this is accomplished. Jesus was the "firstfruits" (1 Cor 15:20, 23) that guaranteed the resurrection of the believer (see also Rom 6:5). Since the Spirit who raised Jesus *is living* (literally "dwells") *in you,* it is the natural conclusion that this same Spirit *will also give life to your mortal bodies.* The indwelling of the Spirit engenders resurrection life. In fact, this is stated twice in

rounding this verse. Also, he is "the Spirit of life" in 8:2, and the human spirit is never called "life" in the New Testament. So it is best to see this also as the Holy Spirit (so Calvin 1979; Barrett 1957; Cranfield 1975; Bruce 1985; Dunn 1988a; Morris 1988; Moo 1996; Schreiner 1998; KJV; NRSV; REB).

this verse for emphasis. There is a syllogism inherent in this:

Major premise: The Spirit dwells in us.

Minor Premise: The Spirit is life.

Conclusion: Then life dwells in us.

Paul's point is that death will be overcome by final resurrection. However, that is not just a future hope but a present reality made possible by the Spirit "making its home" (so Moo 1996:493) in us. We have a *mortal body* now that is subject to death, but awaiting us is a "glorified body" (1 Cor 15:40-44) that will be ours for eternity. Augustine speaks of the "four states" of the believer (natural, legal, evangelical and glorified) and sees the fourth here: "This state is not attained in this life. It belongs to the hope by which we await the redemption of our body, when this corruptible matter will put on incorruption and immortality. Then there will be perfect peace, because the soul will no longer be troubled by the body, which will be revived and transformed into a heavenly substance" (Bray 1998:213).

The Adoption of the Believer as God's Heir (8:12-17) This is certainly one of the most remarkable paragraphs in the New Testament. Life in the Spirit brings the Christian into a new family relationship with God, and Paul explores this imagery in this section. Believers have been adopted as God's children and so can cry out to their new Father and know that they are joint heirs with Christ. Verses 12-13 are a transition, and while some place it with verses 1-11 (Stott 1994; Moo 1996), it is better to see this as leading into a new section. The mode of address changes drastically, from first plural *we* in verse 11 to second plural *you* in verse 13 to third plural *they* in verse 14 and back to *you* in verse 15. Paul obviously wants to drive the message home to them in a powerful way. In essence verses 12-13 are a call to what has been labeled "the mortification of the flesh" (or "putting the flesh to death"). Stott (1994:228) provides a good definition: "Mortification is neither masochism (taking pleasure in self-inflicted pain) nor asceticism (resenting and rejecting the fact that we have bodies and natural bodily appetites). It is rather a clear-sighted recognition of evil as evil, leading to such a decisive and radical repudiation of it that no imagery can do it justice except 'putting to death.'" Paul is drawing an inference *(therefore)* from verses 5-11; since we have the Spirit in us, we have a new

obligation, and this obligation is *not to the flesh, to live according to it.*
The *obligation* (see 1:14) has no debt or duty to obey the flesh. Here
we have a new metaphor for sin and the flesh, a kind of loan shark demanding payback. In the ancient world, debts often led to slavery, so
this may be connected to sin as enslavement in 6:16-22. While we live
fleshly lives and are subject to fleshly temptations (7:14), we owe the
flesh nothing and do not have to *live according to it.* This means that
the Christian has been set free from sin and the flesh by Christ (6:18,
22), achieved by dying to it in Christ (6:2-4, 11).

Paul fails to complete the thought in verse 12 (by discussing our obligation to the Spirit) but instead digresses to give a warning concerning the flesh, undoubtedly because of the seriousness of the problem
of fleshly temptation, as 7:14-25 has shown. He makes this more direct
by shifting to *you: if you live according to the flesh, you will [certainly]
die* (the Greek construction, "about to die," stresses the certainty of it).
The death here is not the physical death of verse 10 but the broader
spiritual and eternal death that is the lot of those who reject God and
Christ (compare Gal 6:8, "the one who sows to please the flesh . . . will
reap destruction"). Paul wants his readers to understand the seriousness of giving in to the dictates of the flesh. It is absolutely imperative
to refuse to surrender to the flesh; one's eternal destiny is at stake.
Whether one is a Calvinist (Moo 1996:494-95, who centers on security
passages like 5:9-10; 8:1-4, 10-11) or an Arminian like myself, the warning is very real. The answer to passages like this (or others like Jn 15:1-
6; Heb 6:4-6; 2 Pet 2:20-22) from the perspective of eternal security is
that such can indeed happen to members of the church who seem to
be Christian, and their apostasy proves that they never were believers.
Moo says (1996:495), "In a way that we cannot finally synthesize in a
neat logical arrangement, Paul insists that what God has done for us in
Christ is the sole and final grounds for our eternal life at the same time
as he insists on the indispensability of holy living as the precondition
for attaining that life." That balanced statement can fit both Calvinist
and Arminian perspectives. The answer of course is the Holy Spirit,
through whom *you put to death the misdeeds of the body.* The verb *put
to death* is used in 7:4, where the believer has "died to the law through
the body of Christ." Here the believer dies to the flesh. While in 7:14-25

believers who try to live the Christian life in their own strength utterly fail, in the Spirit they are able to mortify the flesh and find victory (8:37, "more than conquerors"). The Christian grows in holiness and defeats sin only when following the Spirit's leading and depending on the Spirit's empowering. It is interesting that Paul says *the misdeeds of the body,* almost equating the body with the flesh. Most likely (as in vv. 10, 11), this refers to the physical body as the arena in which these misdeeds occur. But when Christians heed the Spirit and die to these fleshly deeds, they *will live,* parallel to *die* in verse 13 and referring to eternal life (in this case not present life but future life).

The basis for this life (*because,* v. 14) is the new relationship with God that the Spirit brings us. This paragraph (vv. 14-17) is justifiably one of the most often quoted teachings of Paul. *Those who are led by the Spirit of God* defines further how Christians *put to death* the flesh and its deeds, namely, through the guiding power of the Spirit (compare Gal 5:16-18). Yet it goes beyond mere guidance. The Spirit must take control of every aspect of our life and direct it toward God rather than toward the world (as in the case of 7:14-25, when we take charge of our own lives). This is almost a definition of the victorious Christian life: the extent to which the Spirit is governing our actions determines the extent to which we are progressing in our sanctification. The theme is that those led by the Spirit constitute *sons of God. Sons* in verses 14-15 and *children* in verses 16-17 are synonymous, referring to the new filial relationship with God made possible by the atoning sacrifice of Christ and the work of the Spirit. Byrne (1979:9-70) has an extensive study of the Old Testament background of the sonship concept, showing that it is grounded in the idea of Israel as "the sons of God" (Ex 4:22; Deut 14:1; Is 43:6; Jer 3:19; Hos 11:1). Hosea 1:10, in fact, is quoted in Romans 9:26. Israel's privilege of being chosen out of the na-

---

8:14 *Those* translates the Greek *hosoi,* "as many as," and is probably deliberately ambiguous, with both an inclusive force ("all those who") and an exclusive force ("only those who") at the same time (so Dunn 1988a).

8:14 Some (Käsemann 1980; Dunn 1988a) see a charismatic enthusiasm in the experience of being *led by the Spirit,* but the language does not really support this (so Fee 1994:563). This deals with a controlling force in the believer's life rather than with an emotional response. The proper response here is obedience rather than ecstasy.

tions to be God's special children is replicated in God's newly chosen people, the Gentiles, who along with all Jews who have faith in Christ become the new children of God, the true Israel. One issue is whether this means the leading of the Spirit has salvific force, that is, becomes a basis of salvation. Yet that goes beyond the statement here and is unlikely in light of Galatians 4:5-6, where Paul says that God sends the Spirit upon our becoming "sons." It is evident in this chapter that we receive the Spirit upon conversion, so the leading of the Spirit is a sign of salvation rather than a basis of salvation. Still, it can be said that the lack of evidence of the Holy Spirit in a person's life should make us doubt the salvation of that person.

Paul clarifies this new sonship by contrasting two kinds of spirit, the spirit of slavery that produces *fear* and the *Spirit of adoption* that cries out, *Abba, Father. Received* points back to their conversion when they received the Spirit. Paul is saying that at that moment enslavement ended and sonship began. The enslaving power of sin and the law has already been dealt with (6:6, 16-22; 7:6, 25). It refers to the unregenerate state, the power of sin to dominate and the power of the law to arouse sin. While this would apply to the fleshly Christian of 7:14-25, Paul is describing the person without the Spirit, whose sin leads to death and thus who knows only *fear,* that is, general anxiety for the uncertain future as well as a more specific fear of final judgment before God. It is common today to link this especially with the law under the old covenant, but it is probably broader, referring to the law for the Jewish Christian and the power of sin for the Gentile Christian (1:18-32). Instead, we have received the *Spirit of adoption,* namely the Spirit "that 'goes with' or 'pledges'" adoption (Byrne 1979:100). The adoption metaphor is peculiarly Pauline (Rom 8:15, 23; 9:4; Gal 4:5; Eph 1:5) and comes from Hellenistic practice (though still reflecting the Old Testa-

---

8:15 Since the *Spirit of adoption* is the Holy Spirit, many have concluded that the "spirit of slavery" (NIV *a spirit that makes you a slave*) must also be the Holy Spirit, concluding that it is the Spirit's work under the old epoch of the law, in which people were enslaved to the law (Calvin 1979; Dunn 1988a). However, it is unlikely that Paul would have said the Holy Spirit was behind the enslaving power of the law, and the consensus today is that *spirit* in the first instance is rhetorical, simply meaning that those without Christ are enslaved to sin and know only *fear.*

ment idea of sonship). It depicts the transformation of the believer's status "not only from slave to freedman (see on 6:16) but also from freedman to adopted son" (Dunn 1988a:452). This is a wonderful metaphor for conversion, for under Roman law the adopted child had "all the legal rights and privileges that would ordinarily accrue to a natural child" (Moo 1996:501). Moreover, the emphasis is on the present status of the believer rather than a future expectation (contra Barrett 1957). The future side is found in the inheritance language of verse 17.

The Spirit produces not fear in us but a sense of membership in God's family and the joy that goes with that wonderful new security. Note that we *cry* out our new relationship, with the verb pointing to strong emotion and probably deep-seated joy. This also goes back to the idea of prayer as "crying out" to God (Ps 3:4; 17:6; 87:2, 10, 14; see Grundmann 1965:899, 902-3). *Abba, Father* was indeed a confessional prayer, seen also in Galatians 4:6, where it is the Spirit in our hearts that cries out this prayer. It stemmed from Jesus and was certainly a major confessional prayer in the early church, connoting a new intimacy with God that had never been seen before. When we cry this, we are noting our new relationship to God as our loving father and also are celebrating our adoption into the sonship of Jesus. Several (Bruce 1985; Moo 1996) have noted Luther's comment (from his Galatians commentary): "Although I be oppressed with anguish and terror on every side, and seem to be forsaken and utterly cast away from thy presence, yet am I thy child, and thou art my father for Christ's sake: I am beloved because of the Beloved. Wherefore this little word, Father, conceived effectually in the heart, passeth all the eloquence of Demosthenes, Cicero, and all the most eloquent rhetoricians that ever were in the world."

8:15 *Abba* is highly debated. Jeremias (1967b:57-65, followed by Cranfield 1975 and many others) brought out the tremendous intimacy entailed in the word. It was particularly used by small children (whose first words were *abba* or *imma*) and was hardly ever used in Jewish prayers addressed to the God on high. This was misused by some to make God our "Daddy," and the reaction of course was inevitable. Barr (1988a and 1988b) challenged this assumption, noting that there are examples in ancient Jewish prayers where *Abba* was used; he thus tried to overturn Jeremias's thesis. However, while some have abandoned the intimacy aspect of *Abba,* it is clear that Barr overstated his case. While it does occur in Judaism, it is rare, and Jesus made it the prime characteristic of his prayer life (the only recorded prayer without

When we receive the Spirit we are not only cognizant of our adoption into God's family but are also assured of our very salvation. Paul switches from the aorist tense of verse 15 (connoting the moment of conversion) to the present tense (connoting the continuing life in the Spirit), emphasizing the ongoing witness of the Spirit within. This is one of the two well-known passages on the assurance of the believer (with 1 Jn 5:10-11). The Spirit makes us aware that we have indeed been adopted as God's children and that this incredible new intimacy is a reality in our lives. Note that Paul uses *pneuma* in two ways here for emphasis: the Holy Spirit testifies to our human spirit. Moreover, the actual word for *testify* means "to testify together with," so there is not a single witness but a double witness: both the Holy Spirit and our own spirit testify to us that we belong to God's family (so Dunn 1988a; Fee 1994; Moo 1996; Schreiner 1998; contra Cranfield 1975; Morris 1988). There is no reason to be uncertain about our salvation. Those who have come to faith need to listen to this double witness.

Paul now turns to his second point: we are not only the children of God but are also the *heirs of God* (v. 17). In fact, the eschatological themes introduced here, the future promises for the people of God, are elaborated in verses 18-30. In a sense, the inheritance noted here is spelled out in what follows. The inheritance theme is certainly a major biblical emphasis. In the Old Testament it was first the land of Canaan that was Israel's inheritance (Gen 15:7; Num 34:2; Deut 1:7-8, 38; Josh 23:4; Ps 78:55). In the later writings Israel itself becomes God's inheritance/possession (Is 19:25; Jer 10:16; 16:18; 51:19), and Yahweh becomes Israel's inheritance (Ezek 44:28). In later Judaism and the early church the kingdom blessings become associated with the inheritance

---

father is the cry of dereliction, "My God, my God, why have you forsaken me?" Mt 27:46). Moreover, in Mark 14:36 in Gethsemane, Jesus cried out *"Abba,* Father," and this is probably the basis of its use in the early church. Dunn (1992a:618-19) points to two significances of its use in Galatians 4:6 and Romans 8:15: (1) this Aramaic address had become established in Greek-speaking churches, meaning it was part of the living tradition of the church; and (2) it linked the believer particularly with the sonship of Jesus and so had to have been a peculiar characteristic of Christian worship. Christ established a new level of intimacy between the believer (as a child of God) and God himself.

of Israel (*Psalms of Solomon* 14:10; *1 Enoch* 40:9; 4 Maccabees 18:3), in particular the kingdom and eternal life (Mk 10:17 and parallels; Mt 25:34; Gal 5:21; 1 Cor 15:50). In the New Testament and especially Paul, the emphasis is on the close connection between sonship and inheritance (Gal 3:29; 4:7; Rom 8:17; cf. Foerster and Hermann 1965:769-81; Byrne 1979:68-69). Paul here combines the latter two; sonship leads to the inheritance of all the kingdom blessings, especially life in its fullest and final sense. In Romans 4:13-15 Paul linked this with Abraham's "inheritance" now given to all who come to God through faith in Christ (also Gal 3:18, 29). *Heir of God* probably means that we receive our inheritance *from* God (genitive of source), though several take this to mean we inherit God himself (Murray 1968; Cranfield 1975; Schreiner 1998). Because we are his adopted children, we are also his heirs. Yet we are not only heirs of God but also *co-heirs with Christ*. In the Roman world the adopted child's inheritance depended to some extent on the willingness of the natural heir to include the adopted child. This means that Christ as well as the Father gives us our inheritance.

Possibly following Jesus' statement in Mark 10:29-30 (those who have sacrificed home and family will receive "a hundred times as much in this present age . . . and with them, persecutions"), Paul adds, *if indeed we share in his sufferings in order that we may also share in his glory*. If we are truly united with Christ as sons and heirs, we are also united with him in his path to glory, which is suffering. Paul calls this "the fellowship of sharing in his sufferings" (Phil 3:10), and Peter says that Jesus as the paradigm for us also received glory through suffering (1 Pet 1:11, one of the major themes of his book). Once again, the theme is simple and yet profound: suffering is the path to glory! Paul is unequivocal here. Christians should expect to suffer (note the conditional *if*). Most likely Paul is thinking of more than just persecution, as his list of his own sufferings in 2 Corinthians 11:23-29 demonstrates.

8:19 While there have been an enormous number of interpretations throughout history regarding the meaning of *creation,* there is a strong consensus now regarding its meaning. Michaels (1999:104-12) makes a strong case for the translation "creature" or "created thing" (compare 1:25; 8:39) on the grounds that Paul is speaking of the "resurrection of the body" here. But there are several difficulties with this. It cannot refer to believers, for they are a separate category in verse 23. Also, it is unlikely

Still, persecution was certainly uppermost, and it too is seen as expected in John 15:18—16:4 among other passages. Believers experience the glory of Christ as they share in his sufferings. The *glory*, like "life" above (8:2, 6) is probably comprehensive, the glory we share now in being God's children (2 Cor 3:18, "ever-increasing glory") but especially the final glory we will have in his eternal kingdom.

New Hope of Glory in the Spirit (8:18-30) Paul has given us the best news possible in 8:1-17. We do not have to struggle in constant defeat (7:14-25) because the power of sin and death has been nullified. As a result of Christ's sin offering, the age of the Spirit is here. We have passed from death to life in its fullest sense, and we have been adopted as God's children and heirs. However, we must share Christ's sufferings, for only that can bring us to share in his glory. The basic fact of suffering as the path to glory in verse 17 is now expanded into a major section covering creation as well as the Christian. Moo (1996:508) shows that while *glory* occurs only three times, it frames the paragraph (vv. 18, 30) and seems to be the central concern. Both creation (v. 22) and the believer (v. 23) *groan* in the midst of their infirmities as they *wait eagerly* for *redemption.* Paul has taken us to the issue that is one of the primary problems for every Christian: how can God be sovereign when suffering is the lot of everyone, believer or unbeliever? Paul's response is twofold: Christians must walk the path of their Lord, which is suffering (vv. 17-18), and present suffering will inexorably lead to final glory (vv. 18-30).

There are two ways of outlining the passage. (1) One can identify three *groanings:* of creation (vv. 19-22), of the believer (vv. 23-25) and of the Spirit (vv. 26-28), with a conclusion on God's sovereignly bringing us to glory (vv. 29-30). (2) One can identify three sections based on the grammatical flow: verses 18-25 discuss the hope of future restoration; verses 26-27 describe the intercessory prayer of the

---

that any of God's created beings are in view, human or angelic, for verse 20 says creation is subjected "not by its own choice," while both the angelic and the human orders did indeed make choices. Thus it is most likely the subhuman creation that is in view (see Murray 1968; Cranfield 1975; Dunn 1988a; Morris 1988; Wilckens 1980; Fitzmyer 1993b; Moo 1996; Schreiner 1998).

Spirit; and verses 28-30 explain that God is sovereignly working all for our good and our glory. Most take the latter literary approach, but the former may catch the flow of thought better, and that will be the approach here.

1. The Theme: Suffering to Glory (8:18) After talking about the necessity of sharing in Christ's sufferings as a participation in his glory (v. 17), Paul places the whole issue in perspective. *Consider* does not mean mere personal opinion but "a firm conviction reached by rational thought on the basis of the Gospel" (Cranfield 1975:408). While suffering is the lot of the Christian, it is *present sufferings,* which are temporary rather than permanent. Peter talked of trials as "for a little while" (1 Pet 1:6, 5:10), and the letter to Smyrna said they would suffer "for ten days" (Rev 2:10), probably a symbol for a short period. Paul in 2 Corinthians 4:17 says, "our light and momentary troubles are achieving for us an eternal glory that far outweighs them all." The suffering (trials in general as well as specific persecution) of God's people is literally "the sufferings of the present time," a phrase used in Romans (3:26; 8:18; 11:5; 13:11) for the present age of salvation anticipating the final glory; the trials are only part of this present age and only for this present period. It is *not worth comparing with the glory that will be revealed in us.* This continues the already-not yet tension of the book. We are already God's children but do not yet see him face to face. We are already heirs but have not yet received our full inheritance. We are already glorified but have not yet been accorded our final glory. In the "not yet" time of this life we struggle in the midst of suffering and sacrifice. Paul uses the same language here (literally "about to be revealed") that he used in 8:13 ("about to die"), and as there the emphasis is on the divine guarantee, *will [certainly] be revealed.* Moreover, *revealed in us* is probably better translated "revealed for us" (an unusual preposition, *eis,* is used here), meaning God is preparing this glorious future for us.

2. The Groaning of Creation (8:19-22) Interestingly, Paul decides to demonstrate his thesis of verse 18 by addressing the issue of creation

---

8:20 Cranfield (1975:413) shows the incredible diversity of interpretations for *frustration:* (1) synonymous to "decay" in verse 21 and referring to the mortality of all created things; (2) subject to "vain men" (abstract for concrete); (3) subject to man's idolatry in abusing it; (4) denoting a heathen deity and meaning subjection to celes-

first, probably to show that the future glory was far more comprehensive than just applying to believers. All of God's creation will be transformed, beginning with this world and then encompassing especially God's own people. The *eager expectation* with which creation longs for our revealed glory means literally "stretching the head" or "straining the neck" to see what is coming. While there may be no sense of anxiety here (so Schreiner 1998; Cranfield 1975 calls it "confident expectation"), there is a longing to see the final transformation come to pass. It is interesting that creation longs for the revelation of *the sons of God* here rather than its own, recognizing that the primary thrust is on the future glory of God's people. Creation will participate in those results in verse 21. This is truly an apocalyptic event (*apokalypsis,* revelation), the final unveiling of our status as royalty (the children of the King of kings) at the eschaton. We are already "sons of God" (vv. 14-16), but the final manifestation of that glorious reality is in the future. It is a spiritual reality now, but then it will be a visible event.

Verses 20-21 tell us why creation desires to see the revelation of the sons of God. Creation has been unable to realize its God-intended potential because it *was subjected to frustration* or "futility." Most believe this goes back to the Adam account, particularly Genesis 3:17-18 ("cursed is the ground because of you"). Creation cannot fulfill the purpose for which God designed it. *Was subjected* is a divine passive pointing to God as the actor, as shown in the following *not by its own choice, but by the will of the one who subjected it.* That cannot be Adam, for as Schreiner says (1998:435), "Subjecting the world to frustration connotes control over the world, whereas Adam lost dominion over the world by succumbing to sin." Besides, God is sovereign throughout this passage. It is true, of course, that Adam's transgression was the cause of the curse falling upon inanimate creation as well, and it was the serpent who led them into sin. However, it was God who proclaimed the curse and carried out the punishment.

---

tial powers (cf. Gal 4:9); (5) as in its use in Ecclesiastes, noting the futility and absurdity of all things. However, the simplest understanding is best: *creation* is frustrated because it cannot fulfill its God-given destiny.

Even with the curse, however, there was still the *hope that the creation itself will be liberated from its bondage to decay*. *Hope* is one of the main terms of this section (vv. 20, 24 [three times], 25), and it refers to the future-oriented *expectation* of verse 19. There is little uncertainty in the New Testament concept of hope, for it is grounded in the sovereign God of the covenant who is at work in this world, as in Hebrews 10:23, "Let us hold unswervingly to the hope we profess, for he who promised is faithful." Moo (1996:516) believes Paul is drawing on the *protevangelium* (Gen 3:15), "he [the seed of the woman] will crush your [the serpent's] head" (cf. Rom 16:20, where it is interpreted as the church in spiritual warfare). This would be in keeping with the Genesis 3 background to this passage as well as verse 19, where the expectation of release for creation is tied into the revelation of the sons of God. This release is called a liberation, linked with the earlier liberation of God's people from slavery to sin and death (6:18, 22; 8:2) as well as from the law (8:2). Dunn (1988a:471) says Paul deliberately "ties them all together as mutually reinforcing features of the age of Adam." Here the enslaving force is *decay*, possibly "destruction" (thus a reference to the destruction of the earth in 2 Pet 3:10), but more likely "corruption" (the progressive decay of the natural order). The stronger idea of the annihilation of the cosmos does not really fit the context as well (the emphasis is on liberation, not destruction). So while the created order is characterized by death and disorder, it also knows that the future holds liberation from the effects of sin. This wondrous state is best described in Revelation 22:1-5, where the final Eden is described with "the river of the water of life, . . . flowing from the throne of God and of the Lamb down the middle of the great street of the city. On each side of the river stood the tree of life, bearing twelve crops of fruit, yielding its fruit every month." This is what the original Garden of Eden would have become if Adam and Eve had not sinned, and it is indeed

---

8:20 There is discussion about whether *in hope* modifies what precedes ("by the will of the one who subjected it, in hope"; so KJV; RSV; Godet 1969; Dunn 1988a; Fitzmyer 1993b) or what follows ("in hope that the creation itself will be liberated from bondage"; so NIV; JB; NLT; Lenski 1945; Michel 1966; Cranfield 1975; Moo 1996; Schreiner 1998). The decision depends to some extent on whether the conjunction is *because* (seen in codices Sinaiticus and Bezae and a few other witnesses) or *that*

a confident hope! This liberation will occur as the disintegrating creation is *brought into the glorious freedom of the children of God*. As in verse 19, the release of creation is tied to the liberation of the people of God. But here *glorious freedom* should probably be translated "the freedom of the glory of the children of God," for the emphasis in this section is on the future glory that awaits God's children (8:18), namely, that final vindication when we share in his glory.

In light of this, Paul concludes (v. 22), *we know that the whole creation has been groaning as in the pains of childbirth.* Elsewhere when Paul uses *we know* (2:2; 3:19; 6:6; 7:14), he refers to a generally known teaching among the churches. This catechetical truth is the *groaning* of all creation (every part of inanimate creation; see on v. 19), which "groans together" (the compound *syn-* meaning with every part in complete accord) *right up to the present time,* referring to the continuous nature of this pain to the very present (better than a reference to the "now"-ness of salvation as Barrett 1957; Käsemann 1980; Dunn 1988a). *Groaning* is a key word in this section (vv. 22, 23, 26) and refers to the cry of agony and travail that accompanies the pain of decay (v. 21). Yet this is a positive agony of frustration, for the following metaphor qualifies it as *the pains of childbirth,* possibly connected to the "birth pains" that inaugurate the eschaton in Mark 13:8 and parallels. This is the pain of birth, not death (though the image is used of destruction in 1 Thess 5:3), and signifies a new life to come (see Jesus' use of this image for "grief will turn to joy" in Jn 16:20-22). Tsumura (1994:620-21) shows that the Old Testament background for this lies in a combination of Genesis 3:17 (the earth as cursed) with Genesis 3:16 (the "pains in childbearing" that were Eve's lot). Creation participates in the living hope of God's faithful who know that their present travail is a portent, not just of better things but of final glory and joy.

3. The Groaning of the Christian (8:23-25) Since Paul consistently tied

---

(seen in p[46], codices Alexandrinus, Vaticanus and Ephraemi, the Majority Text, and other witnesses). There is no question that *that* has better manuscript testimony, though some have opted for *because* since it is the more difficult reading (so Cranfield 1975; Dunn 1988a). However, *that* makes more sense in the context and is to be preferred (so also Metzger 1971:571). Therefore, *in hope* probably goes with the following rather than the preceding.

the liberation of creation to the future manifestation of his people's glory (vv. 19, 22), it is natural for him to turn to the similar *groaning* in anticipation on the part of his children. Here the groaning is probably an inward nonverbal sighing "within ourselves" rather than a verbal groaning "among ourselves" (so Godet 1969; Cranfield 1975; Dunn 1988a; Moo 1996). If creation experiences the frustration of finite limitations, how much more we who brought about this terrible state of affairs. This is even more true because we *have the firstfruits of the Spirit,* a metaphor that stems from the offering of the first part of the harvest to God (Ex 23:16, 19; Lev 2:12, 14; Deut 26:10). In the New Testament the direction is reversed, for God first has made Jesus the "firstfruits" of our promised resurrection (1 Cor 15:20, 23). Here God has given us the Spirit as the foretaste of the glory that is awaiting us. The Spirit's work in the believer is both a present reality and "a deposit guaranteeing our inheritance until the redemption of those who are God's possession" (Eph 1:14; cf. also 2 Cor 1:22; 5:5). It is an anticipation of the finished work at the return of Christ. Yet this presence of the Spirit in our lives makes it all the more difficult to endure our current afflictions, for we know what awaits us and long for that time. So we *wait eagerly for our adoption as sons, the redemption of our bodies.* If creation eagerly awaits this event (v. 19), how much more we who have the Spirit. As several point out (Dunn 1988a; Moo 1996; Schreiner 1998), the already-not yet tension continues. We already have the first installment of our final *redemption* (see on 3:24 for this term) in the Holy Spirit, but we do not yet know its full reality: the release of our suffering and the fullness of the glory we will share with Christ. We have already been adopted as God's children, but the complete promise has not yet been totally realized. We yearn for that eternal transformation of our finite bodies (Phil 3:21). As Chrysostom says, "If the firstfruits are enough to free us from our sins and give us righteousness and sanctification . . . consider how wonderful the whole inheritance must be. If the creation, devoid as it is of a mind and reason . . . nevertheless groans, much more should we groan as well" (Bray 1998:227).

8:26 There are several suggestions for the antecedent of *in the same way,* some saying it refers back to the Spirit in verse 23 (Dunn 1988a), others the groaning of the believer in verse 23 (Sanday and Headlam 1902; Cranfield 1975; Morris 1988) and

If we share the groaning of creation, we even more intensely share its hope (v. 20), especially since *in this hope we were saved* (v. 24). Our past conversion began a life of hope in our final redemption, so our present Christian life in the Spirit should be even more centered on this future hope. By its very nature, hope is not a present reality, so Paul is preparing them for the (perhaps lengthy) interim period before it is realized. So while we groan in the midst of this troubled life, we do so in expectation and hope. Yet Paul has to clarify this by reminding us that hope deals with what is not yet here. If we can see it and experience it, it *is no hope at all*. The present reality is antithetical to future hope, because no one *hopes for what he already has*. That is not logical; if it is here, it cannot be the subject of hope. Therefore we must *hope for what we do not yet have,* for only then can *we wait for it patiently.* This is the third time Paul has used the verb *wait eagerly* (vv. 19, 23), so there is great stress on the connection between hope and eager anticipation. But now he adds the idea of patient endurance (literally "eagerly wait with endurance"; cf. 5:3-4). In the midst of our earthly travails, we must often bear a terrible load of sorrow. Even as we know the final result and the glory that awaits us, the troubles of the present are almost more than we can bear. It is one thing to realize at the deepest level of our being that it is worthwhile to wait for the eternal reality in the midst of our transitory afflictions, but it is another thing to experience the untimely death of a spouse or a child or go through a debilitating illness. It is another thing still to pass through a terrible time of persecution in which we see friends and loved ones (or we ourselves) imprisoned and martyred. But that is when the Lord is closer than ever, when we can at an even deeper level "share in his sufferings" and the accompanying glory (v. 17). Thus hope triumphs over despair, for not only is the Spirit of Christ near to us in present suffering, but he also guarantees the future triumph in the midst of it.

4. Groaning, the Spirit and Prayer (8:26-28) This begins with the words *in the same way,* probably referring back to the hope provided by

others the hope that sustains us in verse 24 (Hodge 1950; Murray 1968; Moo 1996; Schreiner 1998). The idea of groaning is attractive because it unites the sections, but so does *hope* (vv. 20, 24), and the idea of the Spirit groaning is too far away in the

the Spirit in verses 23-25. As the Spirit gives us hope, *the Spirit* also *helps us in our weakness*. The verb *helps* is significant, used in the LXX to show how the seventy elders appointed to serve as judges over Israel were to "come to the aid of " or "share the burden" of responsibility with Moses (Ex 18:22; Num 11:17). So this means more than the Spirit helping us as we struggle with our infirmities; the Spirit also shoulders our burden along "with" us *(syn-* meaning "together with," so Moo 1996 contra Cranfield 1975). The other primary place the verb occurs in the LXX gives this idea as well, for there God says of David, "My hand will sustain him, surely my arm will strengthen him" (Ps 89:21). When David lacked strength, God provided it by taking over the burden of his "weakness," a term that describes the human condition in the period between Adam and the Lord's return. While some take this specifically to be weakness in prayer (Cranfield 1975; Schreiner 1998), it is better to take this more generally of our human frailty (Dunn 1988a; Fee 1994:578; Moo 1996).

Paul gives one specific instance of this weakness: *we do not know what to pray for as we should* (better than NIV). As Cranfield points out (1975:421), this is not discussing how we should pray or the general content of our prayer but rather the specific content, the very thing we are praying for, namely, our troubles. *As we should* connotes praying according to divine necessity, that is, praying according to the will of God (note the parallel with the Spirit interceding "in accordance with God's will" in v. 27). O'Brien (1987:67-68) says there are two aspects of this: we do not know what to ask for in accordance with the will of God, and even when we know what we want we cannot know whether it is in line with his purposes. When I pray for healing, financial aid, social relationships and so on, I do not know what is the actual will of the Lord in the circumstance. This is a very important qualification, especially for

---

verse. Yet it is the Spirit helping us that is the main thrust in the first of verse 26, so the antecedent is probably the Spirit providing hope in verses 23-24, with the Spirit providing help here in verse 26.

8:26 Some scholars (Käsemann 1971:122-37; 1980:239-41; Fee 1994:580-85) interpret the *intercedes for us with groans that words cannot express* as praying in tongues. They argue that the language is similar to glossolalic prayers in 1 Corinthians 14:14-15 and Ephesians 6:18 and that tongues best explain how the Spirit *groans* with our Spirit, namely, as he inspires the charismatic prayer. However, most (Cranfield 1975; Wilckens 1980; Dunn 1988a; Morris 1988; Moo 1996; Schreiner 1998) do not see a

those who think that faith always gets its request from God. God is clearly sovereign over our prayers and knows when to say no to them. In fact, from the perspective of true faith, God's no is actually a yes, for it is an affirmation of his love in giving us what we need rather than what we want. This is essentially the message of Hebrews 12:5-11, in which trials are said to be the result of a loving Father who disciplines us "for our good, that we may share in his holiness" (v. 10). Let me give a personal example. I have had chronic asthma virtually since I was born (I had my first attack when I was eight days old). I spent two childhood summers inside because my doctor (erroneously) told me I could not play outside. I have prayed all my life for healing, and some real prayer warriors have also prayed for me. God has never healed my asthma, and at this very moment I am on a two-week heavy dosage of prednisone for a severe attack. I still pray for healing (with only a grain of mustard seed faith!) but know that this has all been God's will and that I will only understand what it has contributed to who I am and what I have become when I get to heaven. I do know that God's will has been done and (by faith) that it has all been for the best. So Christ's Gethsemane prayer (Mk 14:36 and parallels) is the model for all our petitions: "*Abba,* Father, everything is possible for you. . . . Take this cup from me. Yet not what I will, but what you will."

But the most wonderful thing about our finite prayers is that we are not alone. What a joyful truth this is! When we feel that somehow God has forgotten us, when we complain as Israel did in Isaiah 40:27 ("My way is hidden from the LORD; my cause is disregarded by my God"), at that very moment the Spirit is closer to us than at any other time. As we groan in our infirmities, *the Spirit himself intercedes for us with groans that words cannot express.* Far from being unaware of our troubles, at

---

reference here to speaking in tongues. For one thing, glossolalia is a charismatic gift given to those chosen by the Spirit (1 Cor 12:11, 30) while these are the prayers of all believers. Moreover, "without words" does not necessarily mean apart from human speech (i.e., tongues) but is closer to inaudible speech, that is, unspoken groanings. Also, while some believe it likely that the Spirit is interceding through our prayers (e.g., Murray 1968; Morris 1988; Stott 1994; NEB "through our inarticulate groans"), that is not stated here. These are the Spirit's groans not ours (see Hendriksen 1981:275-76), and they would naturally not be uttered in audible words. This groaning is metaphorical and expresses the Spirit's deep concern for our needs.

that very moment the Spirit is entreating or petitioning God more deeply than we ever could! Far from being an uncaring God, the Spirit is groaning along with us! These intercessory groans are an expression of the Spirit's deep love and concern for us, and they are the Spirit's own, words that in a sense are "too deep for human utterance." Our own prayers are insufficient, for they are finite and ignorant of God's true plan. But that is the very source of our greatest comfort. While we do not know, the Spirit does, and he is praying for us more deeply than we are praying for ourselves. Moo quotes Luther here (1996:526 n.): "It is not a bad but a very good sign if the opposite of what we pray for appears to happen. Just as it is not a good sign if our prayers eventuate in the fulfillment of all we ask for. This is so because the counsel and will of God far excel our counsel and will." O'Brien goes a step further (1987:70, 73): Our very weakness in prayer is part of the main idea of verses 18-30, the glory to come. Our inadequacy points forward to the intercessory power of the Spirit, and that very intercession is a foretaste of the future glory that will be ours.

The value and effect of the Spirit's prayer for us is further clarified in verse 27. God is described as the one *who searches our hearts,* referring to him not just as the one who judges our innermost thoughts (1 Sam 16:7; 1 Kings 8:39; Ps 26:2; 44:21; Jer 17:10) but also as the one who knows our deepest needs and hears our heartfelt groanings. As Dunn says (1988a:479), the thrust is of comfort rather than warning or caution. "Paul assumes an openness and honesty before God expressed in this fumbling and confusion which has not tried to cloak or conceal itself either in strict silence or in idle words, but has confessed its dependence on God in this humbling wordless groaning." And if God knows our hearts, how much more he *knows the mind of the Spirit,* that is, the intention and meaning of the Spirit's petitions for us. This is based on the fact that *the Spirit intercedes for the saints in accor-*

8:28 The key difficulty in this verse is the implied subject of "all things work together for good." This is hardly a statement of chance or blind luck, as if somehow everything worked out fine in the end. The question is whether the Spirit or God (as in the NIV) is the implied force behind the guarantee. From verses 26-27 it could well be the Spirit, saying that on the basis of the Spirit's intercession for us, the third member of the Trinity made certain that it all worked out (so M. Black 1962:169-72; Bruce 1985; Fee 1994:588-90; NEB). But from verses 29-30 the subject could also be

dance with God's will. It is hard to know whether the conjunction tells the reason (*because*, so Moo 1996; NIV; NRSV; NLT) or the contents of the Spirit's prayer-intention (*that*, so Cranfield 1975; JB). Providing the reason may be slightly better, but both produce a similar meaning, that God knows the Spirit prays in keeping with his will. This is how we know that God's will is going to be accomplished, for the Spirit's intercession undergirds our prayers. That takes away a great deal of pressure regarding asking for the wrong thing.

The result (v. 28) is one of the most famous passages in Scripture. Paul begins with the by now familiar *and we know* (cf. 2:2; 3:19; 6:6; 7:14; 8:22) pointing to common knowledge of a key truth. This truth is not only a traditional early church teaching but it is experienced on a regular basis in their lives. While many believe this starts a new paragraph, it follows so closely with the previous section on the Spirit's intercession that it is more likely a continuation of that thought. The progression of these verses is illuminating. We do not know how to pray. But as we struggle in prayer in the midst of our difficulties, the Spirit is groaning in intercession more deeply than we are, and he does know the will of God. Therefore, God hears our prayer as well as the Spirit's intercession, and so he acts. As a result of that action, the entire situation turns out for the best. Moreover, we must take *all things* seriously. While the phrase most closely refers to "*all* [a word not present in NIV] our present sufferings" (v. 18), it may even include our sins as turned around by God for good; that is, in his sovereignty he overcomes our errors (so Cranfield 1975; Moo 1996). The sovereignty of God responding to the Spirit's cry on our behalf turns everything around for the best. The verb *works* could mean that all events "work together with" each other in producing the good, but that is too complex and not fitting with God's sovereignty in this context. Finally *good* must be understood in terms of the already-not yet tension of the

God, and indeed several ancient manuscripts (p[46] as well as codices Vaticanus and Alexandrinus) place *God* after the verb (so Sanday and Headlam 1902). However, it is more likely that later scribes added *God* to clarify the uncertainty and that the original had "all things" for its subject (the verb normally is intransitive, that is, without an object). Still, of the two options, it is better to take God as the active force. An intercessor does not normally provide the response, and it is better to see God as answering the petition of the Spirit.

whole chapter. It is the present *good*, that which is in accordance with God's will and with our new life in the Spirit, and it is also the final joy and peace that we will have with Christ in eternity. Moreover, *good* does not mean we will always get what we want; rather we will be given what is best for us.

This is promised to *those who love him, who have been called according to his purpose*. In the Greek, the two frame the promise, with "to those who love him" at the beginning of the verse. The question is whether this is restrictive (it works only for Christians when they love God) or comforting (by nature all Christians love God and are called). The latter is far more likely, for this is a passage of encouragement rather than warning. Paul only occasionally speaks of Christians loving God (1 Cor 2:9; 8:3; Eph 6:24), but this is a wonderful way of describing that relationship with God that results in all things working out for the best. It is a love relationship that results from the new family intimacy between God the father and we his children (cf. vv. 15-16). Yet Paul qualifies this further by concluding the passage on the note of divine calling. The Spirit prays in accord with his will, and we live our lives in accord with our calling on the basis of his *purpose* or will (regarding whether this means an effectual calling, see on v. 29). One could say that the first looks at it from our side (our love for God) and the second from God's side (his will for us). God's will is a result of his love for us and his plan for us. This divine plan guarantees the best for us. Obviously, this is a major passage on the security of the believer and must be understood this way (in keeping with vv. 35-39 below). As we place our hope in God, we can be certain that we are "shielded by God's power" (1 Pet 1:5), and that he is ensuring that in all our trials and troubles all things work for our good.

5. Conclusion: From Foreknowledge to Glory (8:29-30) What is the way by which *all things work together for good?* It is the process by which salvation in its fullest orb is worked out in the life of the believer. This is more than the process that leads to conversion; it is salvation in its fullest sense, the entire life of the Christian, including justification and salvation. The *for* that begins the five stages gives the reason why all things work together for good. As Moo says (1996:531, from Byrne 1979:114), it also tells the *purpose* (v. 28) for which God works in our lives, namely, to realize in us "the hope of glory." It is common to call these five steps "the golden chain," since they describe how God brings his people to himself and to their final glory. Each stage is important:

a. *Those God foreknew he also predestined.* The verb is connected to the Hebrew *yada* (Gen 18:19; Ps 1:6; 18:43; Jer 1:5) for God's loving knowledge of his people, but it adds the idea of "knowing beforehand," referring to God's eternal foreknowledge of all events. This is the key term in the Calvinist-Arminian debate over the doctrine of election. The majority of commentators (Murray 1968; Cranfield 1975; Hendriksen 1981; Bruce 1985; Morris 1988; Stott 1994; Moo 1996; Schreiner 1998) take "foreknew" as virtually equivalent to "predestined" on several grounds: (1) The relational love inherent in "foreknew" goes further than mere knowledge of choices and means "to determine to enter a relationship," that is, God's choice or election (as in Rom 11:2; 1 Pet 1:2, 20); (2) it relates to his preordained plan from verse 28; (3) it is a foreknowledge that determines rather than just knows what is to happen; (4) the emphasis is on the second verb, *predestined,* and the first verb simply prepares for it; (5) it connotes that God knew his people, not just about what they would decide to do; (6) since it refers to a prior intimate knowledge of believers, it by nature becomes synonymous with God's choice "before the creation of the world" (Eph 1:4; 1 Pet 1:20). This is very impressive, even persuasive, for it fits the emphasis on divine sovereignty throughout this passage (leading into chaps. 9—11). Yet one wonders if it is the most natural understanding of the verb. For one thing, none of the other five stages are virtually equivalent (even *predestined* and *called* are different stages); rather, each one prepares for the next. Why should the first two be synonymous? Moreover, God's knowledge here is certainly of believers, for they are the subject of 8:9-39. But that does not mean God determines their decisions beforehand. Also, the other passages using *foreknowledge,* especially 1 Peter 1:2 ("chosen according to the foreknowledge of God the Father," where the choosing is based on the foreknowing; see below on 11:2), also probably separate it from predestination. And the passages on knowing "before the creation of the world" more naturally would connote God's foreknowledge of who would make a faith decision. Therefore, it is better to link this with the emphasis on faith decision in 3:21—4:25 (seventeen times) and interpret it as God's knowledge regarding those who would respond in faith to his call (see Godet 1969; Lenski 1945; Cottrell 1975:57-62; Marshall 1969:93; Osborne 1975:178). Marshall says (1969:93), "But justification in Paul is always *by faith,* and therefore the completion of this chain of blessings applies only where men have faith." So it means that on the basis of divine foreknowledge of each one's faith decision, God chooses those who turn to Christ to be his children. Several have taken this corporately of the choosing of the church rather than individuals (Shank 1970:45-55; W. W. Klein 1990:163-64), but it is hard to see why such a distinction should be maintained. God has chosen individuals who form the church. The corporate includes the individual.

b. Predestined to be conformed to the likeness [= image] *of his Son, that he might be the firstborn among many brothers.* Marshall (1975:140-42) believes that election language in the New Testament does demonstrate that God takes the initiative and calls people to himself, but this is not effectual. Rather, it places people in a position to accept or reject that call. In this context, in fact, the election deals more with sanctification than with justification, with conformity more than conversion. The purpose of predestination here is for Christ-likeness. It is debated whether this deals with present spiritual growth (Hodge 1950; Käsemann 1980; Fitzmyer 1993b) or with final conformity to Christ's eschatological glory at the end of this earthly order (Murray 1968; Barrett 1957; Byrne 1996; Dunn 1988a; Moo 1996). Yet in light of the already-not yet teaching throughout, Cranfield (1975:432) says it best, "Paul is here thinking not only of their final glorification but of their growing conformity to Christ here and now in suffering and in obedience" (so also Sanday and Headlam 1902;

8:28 Theologians constantly debate the question of whether the *call* here is effectual (meaning it cannot be resisted; so Augustine; Moo 1996; Schreiner 1998) or it implies choice on the part of the individual (so Origen; Chrysostom; Theodoret). Neither side is implied in the text. It is certainly speaking of a Christian being called here, but Paul is clearly not speaking of the process of coming to salvation (i.e., conversion) in this context. That is outside this text (it may be inferred from v. 29) and must be decided

Schreiner 1998). Kinghorn (1997:66-67) calls this a shared union with Christ and believes it is the essential core of true holiness, a corporate event in which believers become members together in the family of Christ. Life in the Spirit is stated well in 2 Corinthians 3:18, "And we, who with unveiled faces all reflect the Lord's glory, are being transformed into his likeness with ever-increasing glory, which comes from the Lord, who is the Spirit" (also Col 3:10). It is difficult to imagine a verse that more closely catches the thrust of verses 29-30. Humanity was created in the image of God (Gen 1:26-27), but as a result of Adam's sin that image was lost. Christ through his atoning sacrifice has restored that image, and in him we are conformed once more to it. In this progressive conformity, then, Christ will become *the first-born among many brothers* and sisters. Schreiner (1998:453-54) sees the *many* as a fulfillment of the Abrahamic covenant, as "all peoples" are blessed in Abraham (Gen 12:3). As Israel was the firstborn of God (Ex 4:22), Christ is the firstborn who brings many other children into God's family (so Rom 8:15-18).

c. *Those he predestined he also called.* Again the issue is whether this is an effectual call (= irresistible grace, for which see Pyne 1993:211-15) or a call to faith decision. On the basis of the above argument, it is more likely the latter. Fitzmyer (1993b:524) says it means "called by God's plan to be followers of Christ his Son and now stand in that vocation." It is definitely an elective call, but it is resistible, as seen also in the next stage of justification, in light of the centrality of "justified by faith" in 3:21—4:25. God calls us to salvation, but we must respond.

d. *Those he called, he also justified.* Many from the time of Luther have called this the central theme in Romans, perhaps in all of Paul. While that is an overstatement, there is no denying the centrality of the theme of justification in the soteriology of Romans. Yet once more, the

---

on the basis of the whole counsel of God. Fitzmyer (1933b:524) takes this not as individual predestination but as corporate, the complement to *those who love him.* For myself, I believe faith decision is too essential to the New Testament (see for example the Gospel of John) to allow for the doctrine of irresistible grace (see Osborne 1975). See especially the discussion of verse 29 below (a major argument for the effectual calling position) as well as the discussion of chapters 9—11.

emphasis is on the balance between the divine and the human in "justified by faith" (3:30; 4:11-13, 16, 25). As Moo says (1996:535), "Paul's focus on the divine side of salvation in no way mitigates the importance of human response. It is, indeed, God who 'justifies'; but it is the person who believes who is so justified."

e. *Those he justified, he also glorified.* The final stage is another of the major themes of this section, glory (vv. 18, 21). Again, there is an inaugurated sense, for the final glory we will enjoy in eternity with Christ has already begun in that we have been adopted as God's children and joint heirs with Christ. It is difficult to think that Paul would leap from the emphasis on justification to final glory here with no thought of the present glory of the believer (again, see 2 Cor 3:18; Col 3:10). Those who take this as future fail to note that the tense of glorified is aorist, the same as the other verbs in the series. So it describes a process that has already begun and will be consummated at Christ's return. God is in control, and the believer's security is anchored in his divine intention to bring his people to glory, a process that is firmly established in the fact that the Holy Spirit is our "seal" and "deposit" guaranteeing our future inheritance (Eph 1:13, 14).

The Security and Victory of the Believer in the Midst of Earthly Struggles (8:31-39) The incredible comfort of this chapter now culminates with a beautiful summary of both the problems and the blessings experienced by God's people. The theme is similar to that of 1 Peter 1:3-12, where Peter tells his discouraged readers to place their sufferings in perspective by meditating on the blessings of salvation. As stated in the introduction to this chapter, this section culminates not only chapter 8 but also 3:21—8:30 and indeed the entire book. The conclusion is one of the absolute security and victory of the believer because of the love of God in Christ. There is a very elegant style, and several believe it to be a liturgical quote (e.g., Käsemann 1980) or a poetic section modeled after Greek rhetoric (Cranfield 1975; Snyman 1988). But that is unlikely, for there is too little evidence of actual poetic strophes, and it seems more like elevated Pauline style (see Dunn 1988a; Moo 1996; Schreiner 1998). Yet the beauty of its style remains. Fitzmyer (1993b:529) sees the setting as a law court, with a prosecutor making accusations and the Lord defending his followers.

That may be somewhat overdone, but there is a judicial element, seen in phrases like *against us, bring a charge against those whom God has chosen, condemns, interceding, victors* (NIV, *conquerors*). There are two main sections, each with two subsections, verses 31-34 on judicial victory in Christ (with vv. 31-32 on the gift of God's Son and vv. 33-34 on the victory in Christ) and verses 35-39 on the inseparable love of the Godhead (with vv. 35-36 on the love of Christ and vv. 37-38 on the love of God).

1. Judicial Victory Through the Gift of the Son (8:31-34) In 3:5, 9; 4:1; and 9:30, *what, then, shall we say* introduces an important qualification to the argument, often introducing a section and concluding a logical argument as here. So *in response to this* refers to the whole movement from guilt to sacrificial death to justification to sanctification and the life of the Sprit. The conclusion in this instance brings together the thought of 3:21—8:30 in the key affirmation, *If* (a condition of fact meaning "since") *God is for us, who can be against us?* The idea of God at work literally "on our behalf" brings in the basic gospel message of the book; Christ has died on the cross on our behalf, and the Spirit intercedes on our behalf. Dunn (1988a:500) believes the idea stems from the Old Testament idea of Jewish monotheism in the sense that it is not any God but the one covenant God who is *for us* and brings in the confident confessions of the Psalms (e.g., Ps 23:4; 56:9, 12; 118:6-7). God is faithful to his covenant people (including the Gentiles), and so those who are *against us* will come to nothing. The triumphant and joyous cry intimated in this question is obvious. There are none whom we may fear, and all their opposition is ultimately doomed. There is no better example than in the book of Revelation. In Revelation 13:7 God allows ("was given") the beast to "make war against the saints and to conquer them." The persecution and martyrdom found in that book is an extreme instance of opposition, needless to say. But in Revelation 12:11 the saints conquered the dragon "by the word of their testimony; they did not love their lives so much as to shrink from death." The implications are enormous. Every time Satan conquers the saints by killing them, they conquer him by being killed. Their seeming defeat is their great victory!

The absolute proof that *God is for us* is seen in the incredible truth

that he *did not spare his own Son, but gave him up for us all.* There is
a great deal of Old Testament background behind the idea of God
not sparing Jesus but handing him over, from Abraham's sacrifice of
Isaac (Gen 22:12, 16) to Isaiah 53:6, 12 ("the Lord has laid on him the
iniquity of us all," with the LXX reading this as a vicarious delivery of
the suffering servant). It also echoes Romans 4:25 ("he was delivered
over to death for our sins") and so sums up the Pauline gospel. The
main point is that this was a sovereign act of God for us. It was not
something we could do for ourselves or that could be accomplished
by the law. Only God could provide such a gift and produce such a
salvation. Such love is beyond human comprehension (cf. 5:8); God
did not just allow the cross but deliberately "delivered" his Son to the
cross for our sake.

Paul's point is that if God would do all this for us, *how will he not
also, along with him, graciously give us all things.* The verb connotes
the idea of a grace-gift (cf. 1 Cor 2:12; Gal 3:18) and refers to the kingdom blessings awaiting God's people. Thus *all things* could be restricted to the blessings of salvation (Cranfield 1975; Morris 1988;
Fitzmyer 1993b) or to the final blessings at the eschaton (Dunn 1988a),
but the phrase most likely refers to both present and future blessings
inclusively (Barrett 1957; Hendriksen 1981; Käsemann 1980; Stott 1994;
Moo 1996; Schreiner 1998). In the midst of the implacable opposition
of our enemies (v. 31), God is actually giving us *all things* for our good
(note the parallel with v. 28).

This theme is restated in verses 33-34, where the *against us* of verse
31 is echoed in, *Who will bring any charge against those whom God
has chosen?* The punctuation of these verses has been debated (see
Moo 1996:541 n. for a good summary), but the NIV is basically correct.
Each verse begins with a rhetorical question followed by a response.
The *charge against those* introduces a courtroom atmosphere, but it is
also questioned whether the future tense of the verb means this is a
charge at the last judgment (perhaps by Satan or our enemies, so Bar-

---

8:32 There is a question whether the idea of God not sparing his own Son is an allusion to Genesis 22:12 and 16—Abraham not sparing Isaac—and to the Jewish tradition of the Aqedah, that Abraham's willingness to sacrifice Isaac had atoning value.
Many believe this likely (Irenaeus; Origen; Cranfield 1975; Wilckens 1980; Dunn

rett 1957; Dunn 1988a; Moo 1996; Schreiner 1998) or whether it refers to the constant opposition of opponents throughout history (Calvin 1979; Cranfield 1975; Fitzmyer 1993b; Stott 1994). It is amazing how often this comes up in chapter 8, and the answer has always been that it has both meanings. However, in the context of present opposition and persecution in the last half of this chapter, the present form "charges" is more likely. This means that all those people who *will* seek to harm believers in the near future (and Satan the great "accuser" ["day and night"] of Rev 12:10) will ultimately be frustrated in their attempts to thwart the plan of God with his people (compare Job 42:2). They are the elect, the special people chosen as God's covenant possession, and he is watching over them. The basis for this security is indeed God's sovereignty, for *it is God who justifies.* Behind this verse is Isaiah 50:8-9, "Who then will bring charges against me? . . . It is the sovereign LORD who helps me. Who is he that will condemn me?" The switch to the present tense at the very least shows that this is in the foreground of the sentence (see Porter 1994:23) and may well indicate God's continuous sustaining presence among his people (so Dunn 1988a; contra Schreiner 1998). In this sense *justifies* may move from the act of declaring righteous to the process of God making us righteous through his Spirit (see on 3:24). But the main idea is forensic. In God's law court people will accuse us, but God the righteous judge will at all times declare us innocent.

Those who accuse us will also try to *condemn* us, a word virtually synonymous with *charge* of verse 33. The response is also connected with *justify,* for the death and resurrection of Jesus provided the basis of the justification of the saints (4:25). All attempts to condemn the followers of Christ fail because his death has covered their sins (3:25, "sacrifice of atonement"). The fourfold list of Christ's accomplishments ascends upward from his death to his resurrection to his exaltation to his intercessory work on our behalf. Paul's argument seems to get increasingly excited, as he says in effect, *Christ Jesus . . . died,* but even *more than*

1988a; Schreiner 1998) while others doubt the connection (Barrett 1957; Käsemann 1980 finds it possible but uncertain). It is probably best to see an echo of Genesis 22 but not of the Aqedah legend, for that was late (post-200, so Fitzmyer 1993b; Moo 1996).

that, he *was raised* by God *to life.* In this Paul intends all the imagery of the "firstfruits" from verse 23—Christ's resurrection is the harbinger and guarantee for our own, so we have nothing to fear from our enemies. At the same time, Jesus was not only raised but also exalted *at the right hand of God,* an allusion to Psalm 110:1, which is the most quoted Old Testament passage in the New Testament (thirteen times, five in Hebrews alone; in Paul, see also Eph 1:20; Col 3:1). This was the primary Old Testament type for the exaltation of Jesus, with the right hand symbolizing the place of majesty and power. Finally, Christ's intercessory work is the climax of this second "golden chain" (see vv. 29-30). In verse 26 the Spirit was our intercessor before God, and now Christ *is also interceding for us* (once again "on our behalf," as in vv. 27, 31). In Hebrews 7:25 this intercession is Jesus' high priestly work, and here there is also a distinct reference to the cross as intercession.

2. The Inseparable Love of God and Christ (8:35-39) The love of God for his own in 5:8 was the basis for the salvific actions of 5:6-10. That whole section was linked to the love of God "poured into our hearts by the Holy Spirit" in 5:5, so this is an extension of that passage (these are the only two places *love* has occurred in Romans thus far). That divine love which was shown on the cross and poured out in the Holy Spirit will naturally prove unbreakable. Since this love was shown by Christ, it is *the love of Christ* that is highlighted here. The idea of separation probably looks back to the charges and condemnation of verses 33, 34, and the following list of trials elaborates these problems. It is likely that the list itself reflects the very difficulties Paul went through in his ministry—*trouble or hardship or persecution or famine or nakedness or danger or sword*—with all found in 2 Corinthians 11:26-27, 12:10 and others passages (Moo 1996; see complete list in Cranfield 1975), and the last (the sword) a constant threat for Paul. Indeed, tradition holds that he was martyred by the sword. Paul wants his readers to consider that many of them will suffer similar agonies for Christ, but they do not need to be afraid. The love of Christ is with them all the way. This list is similar to Old Testament lists of disasters, such as 2 Chronicles 6:28 and 20:9. These remind us that the lot of God's people will not be an easy one, and suffering is to be expected, both generally as one inhabiting a fallen world and specifically as one suffering for Christ. But there is no need for despair, for the God who is in charge is one who loves us completely.

To anchor this Paul quotes Psalm 44:22 (from the LXX), a lament psalm that begins with a litany regarding the victories Yahweh won for the nation (Ps 44:1-9) and then decrying his delivery of them to their enemies (Ps 44:10-22) and concluding with a plea for him to "rise up and help us" (Ps 44:23-26). This verse concludes the lament section and says that in spite of the fact that his people "have not forgotten his name" (Ps 44:20 LXX), *For your sake we face death all day long; we are considered as sheep to be slaughtered.* The list in verse 35 is parallel primarily to *face death all day long,* while the final item, the *sword,* parallels *sheep to be slaughtered.* So the suffering of Christians in Paul's day (and ours) is not a new thing but in keeping with what the saints have always endured. As 1 Peter 4:12-13 says, "Do not be surprised at the painful trial you are suffering, as though something strange were happening to you. But rejoice that you participate in the sufferings of Christ" (compare Rom 8:17).

In contrast (*but,* translated *no* in NIV to show that Paul is responding negatively to the question in v. 35) to the suffering, those who place their trust wholly in God are not defeated. Rather, *in all these things we are more than conquerors.* This is one of the beloved passages in Scripture because it promises that in every area where there is opposition and trouble (*all these things* summarizing the lists in vv. 31-36 but possibly also encompassing all the pressures Christians face), the believer is an overwhelming victor in Christ (the verb literally means "hyperconquer"). In response to verse 35, this says, "Not only can nothing separate us from the love of Christ, but as a result of that love, absolute victory over them is ours." The means by which this occurs is spelled out: *through him who loved us.* Christ's love (including his intercessory work) gives the strength and produces the victory. Once more we are reminded of our own inadequacies and Christ's adequacy. Whenever we center on our own strength (7:14-25), we are completely defeated. When we rely entirely on Christ and his Spirit, we are utterly victorious. As Calvin says (1979:329), "the Apostle speaks not here of the fervency of that love which we have towards God, but of the paternal kindness of God and of Christ towards us, the assurance of which, being thoroughly fixed in our hearts, will always draw us from the gates of hell into the light of life, and will sufficiently avail for our support."

From the love of Christ, Paul now turns to the love of God (vv. 38-39), emphasizing the inseparability of that love as well. The message is virtually the same as that of verse 35 but with the opposite order; this verse begins with the list of troubles and then proceeds to the affirmation of God's love. *I am convinced* points to Paul's absolute certainty that nothing can come between him and the God who loves him. He wants to impart to his readers a similar conviction in the face of adversity. The list of afflictions is organized for the most part in a series of pairs, except for *powers* and the concluding *anything else in all creation*.

a. *Neither death nor life*. This reflects the same idea as in Philippians 1:21, "for to me, to live is Christ and to die is gain." Death has been often discussed in chapters 5—8 as "the great hostile power . . . the fullest measure of sin's power over this age" (Dunn 1988a:506). Here the contrast is between the two forces at work in the believer (though this is likely simply life in the abstract rather than spiritual life).

b. *Neither angels nor demons*. This takes us from daily life to the spirit realm. The second term is literally "rulers," and while it can apply to any kind of angel or even to civic powers, here it is probably drawn from passages where Paul links them with "principalities and powers" to designate fallen angels (Eph 1:21; 6:12; Col 1:16; 2:15). These powers have already been conquered by Christ on behalf of the church (Eph 3:10; 6:10-12; Col 2:15) and cannot overpower Christians, only deceive them.

c. *Neither the present nor the future*. This brings in the temporal realm. Nothing that can happen to us today or at any time in the future can separate us from God's love. This was certainly true of Paul's life, where the present saw one crisis after another (2 Cor 11:23-29) and the future was even more difficult (Romans and 2 Corinthians were written in the period reflected in Acts 20:1-3; read the rest of Acts as well as the prison and pastoral epistles to trace his "future").

d. *Nor any powers*. This is a single entry, and probably it is intended to sum up the celestial beings. While some have thought of these as "miracles" (the term is used this way in the Synoptic Gospels, in Acts, and in 1 Cor 12:10, 28-29; 2 Cor 12:12), that is unlikely in this context.

It is difficult to know why Paul would add this since the point has already been made. Perhaps spiritual warfare was especially on his mind, or perhaps he wanted to be sure the readers noted it since cosmic powers were not mentioned in verses 31-37.

e. *Neither height nor depth.* There are two possible meanings for this: some (M. Black 1973; Käsemann 1980; Fitzmyer 1993b) note the use of these terms in Greek literature for the heavens above and the subearthly realm and for the beings that inhabit them and so see these as celestial powers. But such a use is not found elsewhere in the New Testament (so Moo 1996), so it is more likely that the emphasis is spatial and refers either to anything above the earth or below it or perhaps anything in heaven or hell. Schreiner (1998:465) argues against such specific connotations and believes this refers metaphorically to the boundless nature of God's love (compare Eph 3:18 for this use of "height and depth"). Either way it means that nothing in this world can separate us from God's love.

f. *Nor anything else in all creation.* Paul wants to make absolutely certain he has left nothing out and so sums up the issue—absolutely nothing in the created world we inhabit can threaten the relationship between God and his children.

This inseparable love of God is ours *in Christ Jesus our Lord,* with the *in Christ* theme once again emphasizing both our union with Christ and our membership in his family (see on 3:24; 6:11, 23; 8:1). But this longer formula adds a stress on his Lordship. Cranfield (1975:444) points out that this final section of the first half of the book (5:1—8:39) is framed by this formula (5:1; 8:39) and that it is also used to conclude several sections (5:21; 6:23; 7:25). Jesus is cosmic Lord, and this guarantees the love of God even further. There is no question that 8:31-39 is a magnificent passage on the security of the believer. It is indeed one of the most powerful in all of Scripture.

Moo (1996:546-47) states clearly the one issue of controversy in this passage. Does Christ's Lordship encompass only all external forces or does it also include the internal ones as well, namely, "the believer's own free and responsible choices"? He believes this does indeed include the believers themselves, as seen in the broad *who* in verse 35 and the list of verses 38-39 (including *anything else in all creation;* see also Gundry-Volf 1990:57-58; Schreiner 1998:466). Others, however, have argued that this does not include the believer, for the lists in this section are all pressures outside the person. Godet (1969:333) says it is "the moral life that is in question, and in this liberty has always its part to play. . . . What Paul means is, that nothing will tear us from the arms of Christ against our will." Sanday and Headlam add (1902:221), "no external power can bar them from it; if they lose it, they will do so by their own fault" (see also Marshall 1969:93-94; Osborne 1975:179). The answer lies outside the passage, and each of us will find that solution that fits our conclusion regarding how the entire canon treats the doctrines of eternal security and warning—whether those passages on security (e.g., Jn 6:35-51; 10:27-30; Rom 8; Eph 1:13-14; 2:8-9; 4:30; Phil 1:6; 2:13; 1 Pet 1:5) or those on the possibility of apostasy (e.g., Jn 15:1-6; Rom 11:18-21; 1 Cor 9:24-27; Heb 6:4-6; 10:26-31; Jas 5:19-20; 2 Pet 2:20-22) will prevail. Each of us must try to harmonize both sets of passages, and each should recognize that there is no final answer and that both security and responsibility are essential to a balanced theology (see also the discussion at the end of chap. 10 below). But this whole debate is outside the interests of Paul here. He wants us to realize the extent to which God's love keeps us secure from all dangerous forces arrayed *against us* (v. 31). This passage is a linchpin in the blessings of security, and Arminians especially should embrace this wonderful truth (since they too often fail to recognize it sufficiently).

DEFENDING GOD'S COVENANT: REJECTION OF THE JEWS AND INCLUSION OF THE GENTILES (9:1—11:36)

Suppose that you were a young Jewish Christian in A.D. 57 (the year Paul wrote Romans), and that you had just read the first eight chapters for the first time. You would be shocked at what had been said about your people, the Jews. You had been steeped in Jewish lore—that you were the covenant people, that God had chosen you out of the nations for his special possession, and that he would "never leave you nor forsake you" (Deut 31:8; see also Gen 28:15). He was your God, and you were his people (Deut 7:6; 29:12-13; Jer 11:4-5). God was always faithful to his promises. The statements you read in this epistle would be highly disturbing. First, the gospel is now for "everyone who believes, first for the Jew, then for the Gentile" (1:16). But the Jews alone were the special people, you would cry. Then you would read that your people are also the focus of God's judgment (2:2-3) and even are "storing up wrath against yourself for the day of God's wrath" (2:5). The Gentiles are now seen equally as a people of circumcision (2:25-29). The shock is double—the rejection of the Jews and the inclusion of the Gentiles. Moreover, you would then read that the law, the heart of the covenant relationship, is insufficient. Righteousness comes "apart from law" (3:21) and apart from circumcision (4:9-12). In fact, the law, far from solving the sin problem, caused trespass to increase (5:20) and even established a bridgehead for sin (7:8), stimulated sin (7:9) and produced death (7:13). The natural question you would have for Paul is whether he had established a contradiction between the covenant God of the Old Testament and the God of his gospel, a God who could turn his back on his covenant promises to Israel and turn to the Gentiles. Has he contradicted his claim that in his system "a righteousness from God is revealed" (1:17)?

This is the issue that Paul addresses in chapters 9—11. These chapters are not an afterthought or excursus in Romans (contra Augustine; Sanday and Headlam 1902; Dodd 1932 and Beker 1990:44-49 see it as inconsistent with Pauline thought) but are an integral part of his developing argument. In fact, Beker (1990:44, in spite of its "inconsistency"; see above) calls chapters 9—11 "the climax of the theme of the letter." Paul was well aware of the Jewish reaction to his gospel, and as he did with his rhetorical questions (3:3-4, 5-6, 31; 6:1-2, 15; 7:7, 13), he meets the possible misunderstanding head on and answers it. Moreover, as Moo (1996:548) shows, Paul was also responding to controversy in the Roman churches over Judaism and the Gentile question. He had for years been fighting against the Judaizers and others regarding the place of the law and Jewish ritual in the church. The Romans were involved in this debate, and Paul had to address these issues. When Christ came, the law was intact in him but yet fulfilled, and both the law and the rituals were no longer essential. By rejecting the gospel, the Jewish people had forfeited their rights and become God's enemies (11:28). By accepting the gospel, the Gentiles had become a new covenant people. Both peoples are now equal before God, both sinners and in need of grace. The Jewish people no longer have a special place but have to repent and turn to Christ in faith just like the Gentiles. At the same time, as Guerra demonstrates (1990:224-25), Paul was controversial because he seemed to favor the Gentiles over the Jews, and so the Roman Christians might think he would increase the tensions between the two communities in the church there. So Paul wrote to convince them that his ministry was pro-Jewish as well as pro-Gentile, and that it stemmed from the Scriptures themselves.

Cranfield (1979:446-49) adds that Paul's message builds on the theme of hope in the Spirit, so this was a natural place to discuss the relation of Israel to that hope; since God's seeming purpose for Israel has been frustrated by the exclusion of the majority of the nation, what does that say for the claim that nothing can separate us from God's love in Christ? Paul responds that God is entirely just, for all stand equally before him in need of grace, both the Jews and the Gentiles. Finally, it must be noted that the situation behind these chapters is not just the issue of a possible failure of God (9:6) but even more the failure of God's mission to the Jews (Fitzmyer 1993b:549). Could God be faithful to his promises if he did not oversee his mission and save his people? These chapters explore the theological reasons that this is so. Paul defends the God of the covenant by showing that he has not turned away from his covenant people but actually uses this state of affairs to guarantee his people a future place (11:25-32). At the same time, this section has become best known as the battleground for the debate over predestination, for Paul's chief argument for the justice of God is that he is absolutely sovereign and can choose whomever he pleases (especially 9:1-29).

Paul's method in these chapters is to provide a logical defense for God's actions. It is common to see five sections framed by Paul's sor-

---

9:1-5 Some scholars (Gaston 1982:417-18; Gager 1983:117-19) have argued that Paul was not discussing the rejection of Israel. They assert that Paul believed Israel was still under the covenant in Christ. Instead, Paul was criticizing Israel here for refusing to extend the covenant privileges to the Gentiles. This, however, is highly doubtful. It is true that there is no statement that all of Israel has been rejected, but their unbelief is strongly condemned (9:32; 10:16-17, 21), and only a remnant has been saved (10:1-6), while the rest of the people were hardened (11:7-10). They have been "bro-

rowful lament over the state of his people (9:1-5) and his closing doxology over the riches of God and his "unsearchable . . . judgments"
(11:33-36). The three main sections are: (1) Romans 9:6-29, which emphasizes the centrality of election. God's promises have not failed because he has sovereignly chosen to fulfill his purposes this way. (2)
Romans 9:30—10:21, which portrays the rejection of Israel as a result of
her own intransigence. The unbelief of the Jews and their refusal to accept God's righteousness through faith in Christ has led to this state of
affairs. (3) Romans 11:1-32, in which the sad state of Israel's rejection is
seen as temporary. There is a righteous remnant (11:1-10), and while
some of the branches of Israel have been broken off from the olive
tree and the Gentiles have been grafted in (11:11-24), there is a future
salvation for national Israel (11:25-32). Integrating the whole is an incredible abundance of Old Testament quotations and allusions. Moo
points out (1996:550) that a third of all Paul's Old Testament quotations
in his writings occur in these chapters, undoubtedly to show that his
gospel is in keeping with God's word and promises in the Old Testament. Aageson (1987:54, 66) argues that Paul throughout this section
uses a "correspondence" theory in applying the Old Testament passages to the Gentile problem at Rome; that is, Paul shows how the Old
Testament situation corresponds to the current Jew-Gentile difficulties.

☐ Sorrow over Israel's Curse (9:1-5)

Paul's deep lament for his people contains a marvelous recapitulation
of her covenant privileges that makes his *unceasing anguish* (v. 2) all
the more profound. What makes it all so deeply sorrowful is that they
have seemingly forfeited all these blessings. What makes it particularly
agonizing is that they are his kindred people; he would take their curse
upon himself if he could (v. 3). It seems evident that Paul has been ac-

---

ken off" the olive tree and the Gentiles grafted in (11:17). Moreover, 10:1 says that
Paul's deep desire is "that they may be saved," and the rest of that chapter develops
this theme. So it can be said that the covenant promises are no longer the privilege
of Israel, and that inclusion in the people of God now comes by faith and not by national identity. Since most Jews have rejected the gospel, God has turned to the
Gentiles, and Jewish people can only enter the covenant the same way the Gentiles
do, by faith in Christ's atoning sacrifice (see Schreiner 1998:481-82).

cused of anti-Semitism for becoming God's missionary to the Gentiles. He goes to unprecedented lengths in verse 1 to establish the veracity of his concern for his Jewish kindred, making three statements about this truthfulness. Three doublets *(speak the truth/am not lying; in Christ/in the Holy Spirit; great sorrow/unceasing anguish)* control verses 1-2. The first emphasizes his trustworthiness—*I speak the truth in Christ . . . I am not lying* (compare 2 Cor 11:31; Gal 1:20). Paul adds the atmosphere of an oath to the truthfulness of his claim. By anchoring his claim in the *in Christ* theme (see on 8:39), Paul emphasizes that his feelings are anchored in his union with Christ. In a sense Christ is the first witness to the truthfulness of his concern for Israel. The other two are his conscience and the Holy Spirit. Paul's conscience, that inner awareness of right and wrong (see on 2:15), provides a valid testimony not because it is infallible but because it comes *in the Holy Spirit,* or better "by the Holy Spirit." The Spirit is the means by which Paul's conscience witnesses rightly to his feelings, not just that they are rightly his but also that they are right. Note that the whole is framed by *in Christ* and *in the Spirit.* Paul wants his readers to understand that he is not speaking on his own but is controlled by both Christ and the Holy Spirit in his feelings for the Jewish people.

The focus of this solemn affirmation is Paul's lament over his people, Israel (vv. 2-3). The third doublet heightens this deep-seated grief: *I have great sorrow and unceasing anguish in my heart.* This statement is in keeping with the prophets, particularly Jeremiah, who was called the "weeping prophet" for his tears over apostate Israel (see Jer 4:19; 6:24; 9:10 and so on). As several bring out (Dunn 1988b; Fitzmyer 1993b) Paul may be alluding to Isaiah 35:10 and 51:11, the only two Old Testament places where *sorrow* and *anguish* (sighing) are combined. If so, it will anticipate 11:25-32, for those passages celebrate the time when the remnant will return and all sorrow will cease. However, that is certainly secondary here at best, for Paul is describing his personal grief over Israel's current state. Indeed, Paul could *wish that I myself were cursed and cut off from Christ for the sake of my brothers.* There has been some discussion about whether this was a prayer, not just a wish, and whether Paul thought the wish was attainable (see the lengthy coverage in Cranfield 1979:454-57, who translates "I would pray [if it were permissible]"). The word normally has a prayer connotation, and Paul is then saying he would ask God for this if it would bring Israel to Christ. The Greek is anathema, and in Galatians 1:8, 9 (also 1 Cor 12:3; 16:22) it is translated in the NIV as "eternally condemned." In the LXX the Greek phrase can refer positively to a gift dedicated to God (Judg 16:19; 2 Maccabees 2:13; Lk 21:5) or negatively to something intended for destruction (Lev 27:28; Deut 7:26; Zech 14:11). This latter is the obvious use here. So to be *cursed* here has connotations of everlasting punishment. Even worse, Paul adds his willingness to be eternally separated literally "from the Messiah" (the definite article indicating Jesus' messianic office). Paul cares so deeply for his people that he would be willing to take their curse upon him. It is likely that there is an allusion here to Exodus 32:32, where after the golden calf incident Moses pleaded with God, "But now, please forgive their sin—but if not, then blot me out of the book you have written." Paul identified with Moses' deep-seated concern for Israel.

Paul's desire is stated clearly—*for the sake of my brothers.* This is the same preposition (Greek *hyper*) used in 8:31, 32 with a substitutionary thrust. Paul was willing to take the curse "on behalf of" Israel if it would lead them to repentance. The term *brothers* leads into a list of terms and phrases (vv. 3-5) describing Israel's special relationship to Paul (v. 3) and even more to God (vv. 4-5). He often uses *brothers* to describe his special family relationship to other Christians, but this is the one place he uses it also of the Jews. This does not indicate that he believes they are Christians, for the next phrase shows he is thinking of his brothers and sisters in ethnic Israel. They are also *those of my own race,* literally "my kindred according to the flesh," with "flesh" probably having double meaning, not only referring to physical descent but also adding negative overtones of fleshly existence as seen in 7:5, 18, 25 and 11:14.

The covenant relation of the Jewish people with God is explored in a series of six statements (v. 4). Scholars (Cranfield 1979; Dunn 1988b; Moo 1996; especially Schreiner 1998, who develops their relationship to one another) generally recognize that the list in verse 4 is composed of two sets of three, with each related to its corresponding member in the other list (see fig. 4). Paul is not only establishing the special relationship of God with Israel but is also describing the problem addressed in this entire section. If God has made such a special covenant with Israel, how can so few have been saved? Have his promises failed (v. 6)? The list is introduced by the general title, *the people of Israel*. This is the covenant name for the nation, naming them as his chosen people (Gen 32:28; 35:9-12; Ps 25:22; 130:7-8). In fact, they were called Jews by others, but they called themselves Israelites in conscious reflection of their elect status as God's special people. So Paul uses this phrase to introduce his theological reflection on their salvation-historical relationship to God.

the adoption as sons	=	the receiving of the law
the glory	=	the temple worship
the covenants	=	the promises

Figure 4. God's covenant relationship with the Israelites as described in Romans 9:4

First, Paul speaks of their *adoption* as God's children, probably a direct allusion to the adoption theme of 8:15-17, 23. This is surprising in light of the emphasis on their unbelief, but the purpose is to establish their status as the children of God (se Ex 4:22-23; Is 1:2; Hos 11:1; 12:9). For Paul this relationship was ongoing; though endangered by her rejection of the gospel, this status was still very real. There is no guarantee for the salvation of individual Israelites, for that is dependent on faith, but there is a guarantee of God's special favor toward the nation as his covenant people. Second, Paul reflects on their *divine glory,* a reference to the Shekinah presence of God among his people, as in the pillar of fire by night and the cloud by day (Ex 13:21-22) as well as in the giving of the law (Ex 24:15-17) and his dwelling presence in the temple (1 Kings 8:11). This glorious presence of God among his people was a sign of his gracious love. Piper (1983: 33-34) believes this is

---

9:4 There is a question whether the Greek *nomothesia* means God's action in giving the law (Sanday and Headlam 1902; Murray 1968; Käsemann 1980; Moo 1996; Schreiner 1998) or Israel's act of receiving the law (Hodge 1950; Cranfield 1979; Piper 1983; Wilckens 1980; Fitzmyer 1993b). In favor of the first is the use of it else-

a promise of Israel's future glory (anticipating 11:25-32), but that does not fit this context dealing with the present status of the nation. Third, Paul describes *the covenants,* summing up the covenants God made with Noah (Gen 9:9), Abraham (Gen 12:1-3; 15:1-21), Isaac and Jacob (Gen 26:3-5; 28:10-15), Moses (Ex 19:5-6; 24:7-8), and David (2 Sam 23:5). While some think it should be restricted to the Abrahamic covenant (Dunn 1988b) or perhaps the Mosaic (Barrett 1957), the plural probably indicates all the Old Testament covenants. The purpose is to further heighten the special place of Israel in God's plan.

The second set of descriptions repeats the first, adding theological depth. Paralleling their *adoption* is their *receiving of the law* (better "giving of the law"), since both reflect Sinai when their sonship resulted in the giving of the law, showing that God indeed made them his special people. The Torah was the sign of his favor to the Jewish people, the core of their wisdom and knowledge (the term means "instruction"). Paralleling *glory* is *the temple worship* (actually "worship"), since the Shekinah glory was especially manifest in the temple services (the term is used primarily in Old Testament and New Testament texts for the temple ritual). The true purpose of the temple was to facilitate worship, and the sacrificial system had as its goal the enabling of the people to be ritually clean so they could worship God there. Finally, paralleling *the covenants* is *the promises,* possibly centering specially on the Abrahamic promises (all the other occurrences refer to this—4:13, 14, 16, 20; 9:8, 9; 15:8) but probably including all the covenant promises given by God to his people.

In verse 5 Paul relates two more privileges that function to culminate the others. *Theirs are the patriarchs* reminds the readers that the key covenants came to the nation through the patriarchs (see above on *covenants).* The heritage of the nation descended from them, and through them they became God's special people. Schreiner (1998:486, following Piper 1983) believes this also includes the promise of eschatological salvation, anticipating 11:28, "as far as election is concerned,

where for giving the law (Ps 9:21; cognate in Heb 7:11, 8:6), and in favor of the second is the contemporary use of it (2 Maccabees 6:23; 4 Maccabees 5:35; 17:16). It is a difficult decision, but in a context centering on the blessings God had given Israel, the former is slightly better.

they are beloved on account of the patriarchs." Next, Paul relates, *from them is traced the human ancestry of Christ* (literally "from whom is the Messiah according to the flesh"), with *from* indicating ancestry and the antecedent of *whom* being Israel rather than the patriarchs. This is a fitting climax, for the Messiah is the culmination and greatest of God's gifts to his people. So in these final two items Paul presents the first (the patriarchs, particularly Abraham the "father" of the nation; cf. Jn 8:33, 37, 39) and the last of the great benefits. The presence of an article before *human ancestry* stresses a limitation on the ancestry, and this was expressed in the "fleshly" nature of the relationship (see v. 3; so Murray 1968; Cranfield 1979; Dunn 1988b; Moo 1996). God sent the Messiah, but Israel greeted him with unbelief.

Paul concludes with a note of doxological worship indicating the main thing the Jewish people failed to realize, the deity of the Christ— *who is God over all, forever praised! Amen*. Yet this was the greatest gift of all, that God himself became incarnate and became the suffering servant for his people (Phil 2:6-8). As God, he is *over all*, indicating cosmic lordship over all creation. As God, he controls the universe, world history and all beings, good or evil, inhabiting his creation. Paul wants his people to understand the one whom they are rejecting. He is not only Messiah but God himself. Therefore, he alone is worthy of eternal praise, and Paul in 10:1-13 calls on the Jews to do just that. The *Amen* forms a normal closing affirmation of the validity of the worship (so also 1:25; 11:36; 15:33; 16:27).

□ God's Sovereignty in Election (9:6-29)

The list of privileges God has accorded Israel now leads to the basic

---

9:5 Interpreters throughout history have debated whether the doxological ending affirms the deity of Christ. The key is the punctuation. If we place a period after *Christ,* Paul is praising God, as in the RSV: "of their race, according to the flesh, is the Christ. God, who is over all, be blessed forever" (so also REB; TEV; Dodd 1932; Barth 1933; Wilckens 1980; Stuhlmacher 1994; Käsemann 1980; Dunn 1988b). If we place a comma there, it becomes an important witness to the deity of Christ, as in the NIV (so also KJV; NASB; JB; NRSV; NLT; Calvin 1979; Godet 1969; Hodge 1950; Lenski 1945; Murray 1968; Bruce 1985; Morris 1988; Fitzmyer 1993b; Stott 1994; Moo 1996; Schreiner 1998). However, both on textual grounds (see Metzger 1973:95-112) and for exegetical reasons (see Harris 1992:144-72) the christological

question, Have his promises failed? (v. 6). This problem was exacerbated by the fact that the Jewish people had not come to faith while the Gentiles had streamed into the church. So Paul's opponents, both Jewish and Jewish Christian, had rightly raised this serious question. Paul responds in two ways, first from the standpoint of God's sovereignty (vv. 6-29) and then from the standpoint of Israel's responsibility (vv. 30-33). His message is that God had never guaranteed automatic acceptance into his family on the basis of national identity. This was a serious misunderstanding on the part of Jewish particularism, that is, the belief that they alone were God's elect people and were born into his family. It is not Israel but God who is sovereign over salvation. Nevertheless, as Cranfield states (1979:448, 472), the key concept is not just God's determinate will but also his *mercy*. This verb, *have mercy on*, only occurs once elsewhere in Romans outside of chapters 9—11 and five times in the rest of the Pauline corpus but is found seven times in Romans 9—11 (the noun is found two of the three times in Romans here). God's elective will is "connected with the nature of God's mercy and as mercy not just for one people but for all peoples to show that Israel's disobedience, together with the divine judgment which it merits and procures, is surrounded on all sides by the divine mercy" (Cranfield 1979:448).

There are three sections here, verses 6-13 on national Israel versus true Israel, verses 14-23 on the righteousness of God and his freedom to destroy whom he wishes, and verses 24-29 on God's call of Gentiles as well as Jews (for a chiastic structure with vv. 6-9 paralleling vv. 27-29 and vv. 10-13 paralleling vv. 25-26, see Aletti 1987; Dunn 1988b).

---

interpretation is best. Doxologies are normally connected to their preceding context (and in this case *who is* naturally refers to *Christ*), and if Paul intended to praise God rather than Christ, one would have expected him to include *God* in the doxology (compare 2 Cor 11:31). Moreover, in the vast majority of Old Testament cases (the only exception is Ps 67:19-20; see Gen 14:20; Ex 18:10; 1 Kings 8:15; Ps 27:6; Zech 11:5 among others) *blessed* occurs first in the praise. Here it occurs after *God,* most likely emphasizing the praise of Jesus as God. Most who doubt this argue that Paul does not call Jesus God, but Titus 2:13 does so (they doubt Paul wrote the pastorals), and in Philippians 2:6 and Colossians 1:15 Paul says that deity was the essence of Jesus. Therefore this too is most likely praising Jesus as God.

National Israel and True Israel (9:6-13) In answering the question whether God's word has failed (v. 6), Paul responds that the problem is with Jewish misunderstanding of their identity. They had equated their national heritage with their spiritual standing before God, and that was seriously flawed. It is not birthright but spiritual commitment, "promise" rather than ancestry. Paul uses two examples in response, the choice of Isaac over Ishmael (vv. 7-9) and the choice of Jacob over Esau (vv. 10-13). In both it was God's sovereign choice. Paul begins (v. 6) by denying the possible conclusion arising from the combination of God's promises in verses 1-5 with the reality that Israel largely lay outside the church—*it is not as though God's word* (= the Old Testament promises described in vv. 1-5) *had failed.* If God had given such extravagant privileges to the Jewish people and yet had failed (meaning "come to nothing") to bring them to himself, it could mean these promises had failed. On the contrary, Paul will argue, his promises are still valid, and God is keeping them. So he begins by denying their basic belief that being the people of God was their birthright. There is national Israel, and there is true Israel. As Paul argued in 3:21—4:25, one can only enter the true covenant people by faith. This has led some to believe that Paul was including the Gentile church (the church is called "the Israel of God" in Gal 6:16) in true Israel here (Käsemann 1980; Wright 1991:238 calls it "a worldwide family"). But that is unlikely, for the entire context narrows this to the Jewish people rather than the church. So true Israel refers to those Jews who put their faith in Christ.

Verses 7-8 restate the main thesis of verse 6 (not everyone descending from Israel is true Israel) in two different ways. First, just because they are descendants of Abraham does not mean they are actually children of Abraham. Since Abraham was the father of the nation (Mt 3:9; Lk 13:16; Acts 13:26; Rom 4:1, 12), this is a natural example. The message is once again that birthright is inadequate for actual sonship. Only

9:6-13 Scholars disagree about whether Paul is describing individual election (Piper 1983; Moo 1996; Schreiner 1998) or corporate, salvation-historical election dealing not with salvation so much as roles in history and with groups rather than individuals (W. W. Klein 1990:197-98). However, as I have said regarding 8:29-30, this is a false disjunction since election was both individual (Isaac and Jacob here) and corporate (Jacob symbolizes Israel and Esau Edom). God calls individuals to be part of his church.

faith is sufficient. To anchor this point biblically, Paul quotes Genesis 21:12 : *It is through Isaac that your offspring will be reckoned*. The context in Genesis was Abraham's distress at sending Ishmael and Hagar away. God then reminded him that his posterity was promised through Isaac not Ishmael. *Reckoned* is literally "called," and there is probably double meaning here; not only is the true offspring "recognized" in Isaac's lineage, but this also reflects God's "call." So God has "chosen" or elected those of the true lineage (Isaac) rather than the false one (Ishmael). As Schreiner says (1998:496), "Thus the thesis of v. 6a is defended. God's promises have not and cannot fail, because they are based on his call." Paul then proceeds to interpret the quote *(in other words)* to make sure his readers understand. Now the contrast is *the natural children* versus *the children of the promise*. It is through God's "promises" (v. 4) and not through "the flesh" (vv. 3, 5) that true Israel is found. Ishmael was the result of a purely fleshly union, while Isaac resulted from promise. Several (Cranfield 1979, Dunn 1988b; Wright 1991:238-39, Fitzmyer 1993b; Moo 1996) note a strong connection with Romans 4 and the grace of God; Wright and Moo cleverly label this "grace rather than race." The verb "reckoned as" (NIV, *regarded as*) is reminiscent of the Genesis 15:6 quote that dominates that chapter (faith "reckoned [NIV credited] . . . as righteousness"), and *God's children* often in Romans designates those who have come to faith (8:16, 17, 21). Finally, *the promise* could well hearken back to the grace of God shown in 4:13-20. So this likely refers to the grace of God shown his covenant people in bringing them to salvation and further answers the question about whether his promises have failed.

Verse 9 concludes this section (vv. 7-9) by elaborating on the meaning of *the promise,* indicating that the key idea in the section is the promises of God fulfilled in the Jewish mission. In effect, this says that the Genesis 21:12 quotation in verse 7 should be considered one of the

---

9:7 There is debate about whether Ishmael was excluded from the covenant blessings (Schreiner 1998) or still had a positive part to play on the basis of God's mercy (Cranfield 1979). The same question could be asked of Esau in verses 10-13. This has implications for one's definition of God's elective will, but many think it goes beyond the context of either Genesis or Romans. Were Ishmael and Esau completely excluded from God's grace? In Genesis this is not true (see the blessing of Esau in

covenant promises since Isaac's birth was a direct act of God and was foreseen by a divine promise (Gen 17:15-16; 21:12). Paul then amalgamates two of the promises (Gen 18:10, 14) in his own compilation, with *at the appointed time* (about this time) from Genesis 18:10 ("I will surely return to you *about this time* next year, and Sarah your wife will have a son") and *Sarah will have a son* from Genesis 18:14 ("I will return to you at the appointed time next year, and *Sarah will have a son*"), though in another sense both parts here are found in both verses. Paul's point is that God's promises were seen in the choice of Isaac over Ishmael, and they are also seen in his choice of some Jews over others. In both instances his promises have not failed.

The second illustration (vv. 10-13) concerns Jacob and Esau and provides an even stronger example *(not only that)*. While the previous example emphasized the father and son (Abraham and Isaac), this one dwells more on Rebekah, stating that her children (Jacob and Esau) had the same father, Isaac. In the earlier example there were two mothers involved, Sarah and Hagar, but in this one the two had the same mother as well as father. Moreover, both Sarah and Rebekah were childless, and their children came as a result of the direct intervention (and promise) of God. But now both sons were of the patriarchal heritage, and still God chose between them. Paul wants to make certain his readers understand the "grace rather than race principle," so he turns to an even better example, since here both sons were of the promised line. This is even more unusual because Esau was the older twin and therefore had more right to the patriarchal blessing. So the centrality of

Gen 27:38-40), but there is no hint of blessing in Romans. It could be argued that in the case of "Esau I hated" (v. 13) rejection is indeed the connotation, and as a type of those Jews excluded from God's people here in Romans 9, an exclusion sense would also be the implication. Therefore, it does seem that the covenant promises should be restricted to Isaac and Jacob.

9:12-13 It is going too far to make this a test case for a doctrine of predestination (as do Piper 1983; Moo 1996; Schreiner 1998), for Genesis itself stresses also Esau's works in selling his birthright (25:29-34) and in his anger (27:41-45). But that has little bearing on Romans 9, for Paul is emphasizing God's predetermined will and not the actions of either Jacob or Esau. Moo is somewhat correct when he says of this passage (1996:587), "Attempts to avoid this [Calvinistic] theological conclusion [regarding 9:7-13], whether by leaving room for human faith in v. 12 or by restricting the issue to the roles of nations in salvation history, are, I think, unsuccessful." But

God's choice is even more definitive here than in verses 7-9. It was not birthright (race) but the divine will (grace) that led to the choice of Jacob over Esau.

Paul then explains his example more explicitly in verses 11-12, which form a single sentence. *Before the twins were born or had done anything good or bad,* God had made his choice. This is "before the creation of the world" language (compare Eph 1:4; 1 Pet 1:20) and refers to God's predetermined will. It is commonly understood that verse 12 is the conclusion of this clause (note the dashes in NIV), so that Paul is saying, "Before they were born, *she was told, "The older will serve the younger."* In other words, the choice was made not on the basis of who they were or what they had done, but because God had willed it so. It is not works but divine will that is the basis of the choice. The quote is from Genesis 25:23 LXX, a promise made by God to Rebekah just after the twins were conceived but before they were born. When she asked, "Why is this happening to me?" (Gen 25:22), God tells her, "Two nations [Israel and Edom] are in your womb, and two peoples from within you will be separated; one people will be stronger than the other, and the older will serve the younger." It is a salvation-historical prophecy, but Paul is using it of the two individuals themselves to demonstrate his thesis. It is not birthright but divine will that determines destiny. God is sovereign, not man.

Paul qualifies this in two directions in verses 11-12. First, he tells us that the choice of Jacob over Esau occurred *in order that God's purpose in election might stand.* The whole idea of God's *purpose* goes back to

---

there is a broader issue, namely, whether such a theological conclusion should be made this quickly in the passage at all. Paul is not developing a systematic theology here but addressing one issue. Thus he is using these examples to demonstrate his thesis rather than to establish dogma (see on 8:29-30 for this issue), so it is incorrect to draw too many implications this soon for his theology of predestination. A tentative conclusion, of course, is helpful to understand what Paul is implying here, but it must be reworked as more data comes in. The question of whether "not of works" (v. 12, cf. Eph 2:8, 9) allows faith or does not is foreign to this context. Paul is indeed stressing God's predetermined choice rather than human responsibility (that will come in 9:30-33). However, the theological implications for the larger issue will emerge from the whole of 8:28—11:36 and must not be determined from one part of that whole, so a definition will emerge as the passage progresses (see the summary at the end of chap. 10).

8:28, where it referred to God's plan for our lives. In the phrase "elective will" *(election)*, then, Paul refers to that predetermined purpose that God had set for his people, in this case for Jacob and Esau. God's promises, far from failing, *stand* or "remain certain." They are firmly established and have indeed come to pass. It was not the actions of either Jacob or Esau (note the deception used by Jacob to get his way) but the will of God that controlled the situation. Second, Paul says this took place *not by works but by him who calls,* another way of saying the same thing. Jacob and Esau were equally sinners, Esau's secular outlook paralleled by Jacob's trickery. Neither by good works nor by evil works was God's will carried out, but on the basis only of the elect *call* of God. *Not by works* is an essential component of Pauline theology, seen in Romans 4:2, 6; 9:11, 32; 11:6; Ephesians 2:9; 2 Timothy 1:9; and Titus 3:5. Grace not works is the basis of salvation.

The conclusion comes in verse 13, where Paul quotes Malachi 1:2-3, *Jacob I loved, but Esau I hated.* The introductory *as it is written* adds emphasis to this, showing that it functions as a summary of the issues. In Malachi this explains why God is blessing Israel (Jacob is given the name "Israel" in Gen 32:28) and punishing Edom (Esau is called "Edom" in Gen 25:30, 36:1), so there is a corporate aspect in Malachi. Here in Paul, however, it is used to explain further the process of predestination, that is, God choosing one group from among the Israelites and rejecting another. So the statement encompasses both a corporate and an individual emphasis. Sanday and Headlam (1902:246-47) say that Paul anchors Genesis in subsequent history, showing that God's choice of Jacob/Israel over Esau/Edom continued through Old Testament history and implying that this can be seen typologically in God's choice of believing Jews over the rest of the nation. Still, what does it mean to say that God loves Jacob but hates Esau? That seems overly harsh. Fitzmyer (1993b:563) says this is a Near Eastern idiom meaning God loved Esau less than Jacob, but that does not seem to fit the context. It is better to see this as an illustration of acceptance and rejection (so Calvin 1979; Hodge 1950; Cranfield 1979; Dunn 1988b; Morris 1988; Moo 1996, Schreiner 1998). God has chosen one group over another. In Genesis and Malachi it meant that he had decided to accept Israel and reject Edom; here it means he has chosen the believers and rejected the unbelievers among Israel. But it is entirely God's choice. Some (Käsemann 1980; Dunn 1988b; Schreiner 1998) bring up the issue of double predestination here, that is, the idea that God has chosen some for eternal life and others for eternal punishment. That can certainly be an implication, but as Schreiner says (1998:501), this cannot be stated without emphasizing human responsibility as well (9:30-33). That will be my thesis regarding this section as a whole, but here the emphasis is on divine choice.

It is appropriate here to sum up Paul's argument in verses 6-13. He wants to show that God's promises have not failed, and his response to those who doubt is predicated on divine election. God is sovereign, and if he wishes to choose Isaac over Ishmael (vv. 7-9) or Jacob over Esau (v. 10-13), that is his divine prerogative. While this certainly has implications for the doctrine of predestination, it cannot of itself constitute that doctrine. That must come from this whole section interacting with the rest of Scripture.

The Freedom of God to Choose (9:14-23) Paul has proffered God's sovereign choice as the answer to the failure of all Israel to be saved. God is truly faithful to his promises, and that is seen in his predetermined will. But that can lead to the accusation that God is unjust. So Paul returns to his diatribe method of asking rhetorical questions (stating potential complaints) and then answering them (see chaps. 2—3). His argument reiterates the message of verses 7-13—God is completely free to choose whomever he wishes. As a defense of God's elective will, this can leave the modern reader unsatisfied because it never addresses the issue of human choice and the part it plays in the process. But we must remember that Paul is addressing a first-century audience, not a modern one, and his answer is theologically satisfying. The issue of human choice will be addressed later (9:30—10:21).

This section has three parts: verse 14 introduces the question of the justice of God; then verses 15-18 respond that God's justice is actually divine mercy at work, using Old Testament quotations to illustrate this from the story of Moses and Pharaoh. Finally, verses 19-23 use a series of questions to probe further the question of God's right to bring glory to himself in whatever way he wants.

Whenever Paul uses *what then shall we say?* (4:1; 8:31; especially

3:5; 6:1; 7:7, which are the closest parallels), he is always introducing potential misunderstandings in order to qualify his argument carefully. Here the possible erroneous conclusion is *Is God unjust?* Paul's response is immediate, *Certainly not!* (see 3:4, 6, 31; 6:2, 15; 7:7, 13). What follows is theodicy (a defense of God's righteousness). Many could conclude from Paul's presentation about God's accepting certain ones and rejecting others from within Israel that God has ceased to be just. A sovereign who would ignore the merits of a person and make a choice only on the basis of his own will (9:12) cannot be a righteous God because rightness depends upon keeping his promises to his covenant people. Moo asserts (1996:591-92) that the issue for Paul is not so much God's faithfulness to his people as God's "faithfulness to his own person and character. And the course of Paul's argument suggests that, in Paul's answer at least, it is ultimately this standard, revealed in Scripture and in creation, against which God's acts must be measured."

The first half of Paul's response (vv. 15-18) turns to the third biblical illustration (after Isaac and Jacob in vv. 7-13), that of Moses and Pharaoh. In this case he uses God's own statements, first to Moses (v. 15) and then to Pharaoh (v. 17), to demonstrate that God is free to show mercy on or harden whomever he wishes. In effect Paul is saying, "If you don't want to accept my arguments, then consider what Scripture itself has to say on this point." The two parts parallel each other, with a citation (vv. 15, 17) followed by a conclusion (vv. 16, 18). The first citation is taken from Exodus 33:19, in which Moses at Sinai asks Yahweh to "show me your glory" as proof to Israel that his "presence" is with them. God replies that he would indeed pass in front of him and proclaim his name, "Yahweh," to ratify his covenant. He adds, *I will have mercy on whom I have mercy, and I will have compassion on whom I*

9:17 There is a question about whether verse 17 is related more to verse 14 (as a second illustration; so Cranfield 1979; Morris 1988; Moo 1996; Schreiner 1998) or to verse 16 (as a further development of the point about God's mercy; so Sanday and Headlam 1902; Piper 1983; Dunn 1988b). While a case can be made for both, all four verses begin with *for (gar)*, and they fall naturally into two pairs, with the first of each (vv. 15, 17) telling why God is just and the second (vv. 16, 18) providing a conclusion. From this perspective it is better to see verse 17 related to verse 14 rather than to verse 16.

have compassion. In the Exodus context this means that God has decided to show mercy and compassion on Israel even after the golden-calf incident. For Paul the key point is the affirmation of God's mercy. That concept will dominate this section. God's elect will stems from his mercy and compassion. This tells us that God's will is not capricious. It is free but not arbitrary. Cranfield says this well, claiming that Paul understood this Exodus text

> to be affirming emphatically the *freedom* of God's mercy (and therefore the fact that God's mercy is not something to which men can establish a claim whether on the ground of parentage or of works), and at the same time making it clear that it is the freedom of God's *mercy* that is being affirmed, and not of some unqualified will of God behind, and distinct from, His merciful will. (1979:484)

So Paul concludes *(therefore)* that it is not *man's desire or effort* (literally "willing or running") but *God's mercy* that is the basis of his compassionate acceptance of people. This is an important clarification for verse 12, which said it is "not by works but by him who calls." God's call is an act of mercy. The "willing" is the ability of people to decide on a course of action, and the "running" is the action that results from the decision. As Dunn (1988b:553) and Moo (1996:593) state, the two "sum up the totality of man's capacity."

The negative side of God's elective will is stressed in verses 17-18, beginning with a citation of God's message to Pharaoh in Exodus 9:16. In the Exodus context, the sixth plague (of boils) has just occurred, and God is telling Moses how to confront Pharaoh with the demand to "let [God's] people go," warning that God could have wiped him and his nation from the earth but did not because he had a *purpose* for Pharaoh. His very existence on earth is due to the sovereign purpose of God. God then pro-

---

9:17 The wording of the quotation here differs somewhat from the LXX (see especially Cranfield 1979; Schreiner 1998). Two differences are important for us: (1) Paul uses the stronger *for this very purpose* rather than the LXX "on account of this" in order to emphasize God's sovereign purpose. (2) He uses *I raised you up* instead of the LXX "you have been preserved," probably to show that Pharaoh's very place in history is due to God's own purposes. The effect is to emphasize the sovereign control of God over Pharaoh.

vides two intentions. First, he intends to *display [his] power* in Pharaoh. Some believe this is God's saving power (Cranfield 1979; Morris 1988; Dunn 1988b) and others his judging power (Käsemann 1980), but more likely both are intended in Exodus as well as in Romans. God's saving power was experienced by Israel (extended by Paul to believing Israel) and his judging power by the Egyptians (extended by Paul to unbelieving Israel). Second, God intends that his "name might be proclaimed in all the earth." In Exodus that was accomplished through the plagues and the exodus of Israel from Egypt (cf. Josh 2:9-10; 9:9). For Paul the rejection of the gospel by the Jewish people led in part to the proclamation of the gospel throughout the (Gentile) world (so Moo 1996).

So now Paul concludes that God can show mercy whenever he wants and can *harden whom he wants to harden.* God's mercy and justice are interdependent aspects of his character and flow out of his holiness. By having mercy and hardening side by side, verse 18 effectively concludes the paragraph (vv. 14-18) and not just verse 17. It is said often in Exodus that God "hardened Pharaoh's heart" (Ex 4:21; 7:3, 13, 14, 22; 8:15, 19, 32; 9:7, 12, 34, 35; 10:1, 20, 27; 11:10; 14:4, 8, 17), and this means that God made him "stubborn" and unyielding, impenitent in every way. The point here is that God did it to accomplish his own purposes. It is amazing how much ink has been spilled on the issue of whether God's hardening was the result of Pharaoh's hardening of his own heart (see Ex 7:14, 22; 8:11, 15, 28; 9:33; 13:15 for Pharaoh's responsibility). While that is a very real question with regard to Exodus, it is not an issue here. Paul centers on the predominant Exodus theme, that God hardened Pharaoh's heart to accomplish his sovereign purposes. Beale (1984:149) finds three purposes in the hardening of Pharaoh's heart in Exodus 4-14: to demonstrate the uniqueness of Yahweh's omnipotence to the Egyptians; to

---

9:18 The larger question is whether God hardened Pharaoh's heart as judgment for Pharaoh hardening his own heart. Fitzmyer says (1993b:568) that the hardening expresses "divine reaction to persistent human obstinacy against him, a sealing of a situation arising, not from God, but from a creature that rejects divine invitation." On the other hand, several (Piper 1983:139-55; Beale 1984:129-54; to some extent Moo 1996:596-99) argue strongly for a virtual double predestination sense here (Beale calls it "unconditional reprobation"), that God predestined Pharaoh to harden his heart. They point out that God told his intentions to harden before the act occurred (4:21; 7:3; cf. 14:4, 17) and note the many passives (7:13, 14, 22; 8:11, 15) that may

make Yahweh's acts a memorial to Israel and its later generations; and to bring Yahweh glory. These are similar to the message in Romans 9. So this is the negative side of mercy and must be taken seriously. For Paul this illustrates his point regarding the justice of God (9:6, 14). God has freedom to show mercy to some in Israel and to harden others. In the larger context of Romans 9—11 he shows mercy to those who turn to him in faith and hardens those who refuse to do so, but that aspect is not developed until 9:30-33. Here the thrust is the divine right to act in accordance with his sovereign will.

The final paragraph of this section (vv. 19-23) employs a diatribe style in which Paul quotes an imaginary objector *(one of you will say to me)* who complains that if God indeed hardens people at will, why should he *blame* anybody for doing so, since neither the believer nor the unbeliever can *resist his will?* One cannot find fault with those who do what they are forced to do. Once again God is being charged with injustice for acting apart from his covenant promises. *Resist* means to refuse to act in accordance with the will of another, here the will of God. So the opponent is saying that God's elect will has rendered it impossible to do so, and therefore God has no right to attach blame to any creature who has no such ability to resist that divine will. If all resistance is predetermined, then no fault can be assigned.

Paul challenges the legitimacy of this complaint. He is saying not that there is no answer, but rather that there is no right to ask such a thing. While some think *O man* is equivalent to "my dear sir," it is far more likely that there is a deliberate contrast between *man* and *God* to indicate that the objection comes from a purely human perspective (so Cranfield 1979; Dunn 1988b; Fitzmyer 1993b; Schreiner 1998; contra Barrett 1957; M. Black 1973). Finite humanity has neither the right nor the understand-

---

indicate God as the implied subject. So Pharaoh hardening his heart was the result of God's prior hardening. However, when one considers the flow of Exodus 4—14, the two sides are interdependent. It is doubtful that the issue of priority (God versus Pharaoh) is part of the plot development of the narrative. The causal relationship between Pharaoh's guilt and God's sovereign choice must be held in tension. Moo says it well (1996:599): "God's hardening does not, then, *cause* spiritual insensitivity to the things of God; it maintains people in the state of sin that characterizes them." God is sovereign, but Pharaoh was responsible. For the larger picture, including the important issue of "foreknowledge," see the discussion of 8:29.

ing to *talk back to God* in this way. As a created being, the creature cannot tell the creator how to act, nor can the creature question the way the creator has decided to operate. Morris (1988:364) comments, "'Little, impotent, ignorant man' (Wesley) is set over against the great God whose purpose runs through the whole creation and who moves people and nations." To anchor this Paul cites part of Isaiah 29:16 LXX *(Shall what is formed say to him who formed it)* and then adds a portion that may reflect Isaiah 45:9 *(Why did you make me like this?)*. Both passages in Isaiah are part of the metaphor of the potter and the clay, so this is a natural introduction to verse 21. Isaiah was also speaking of God's judgment upon his people Israel. Once more, the creature has no place criticizing the creator. It is like a small child "talking back" to their parents. In most families that provides grounds for punishment, which is also true in the family of God.

Building on the potter-clay image of Isaiah, Paul asks the same question of his opponent (v. 21): *Does not the potter have the right* to take a *lump of clay* and fashion both *noble* and *common* pottery (literally, "honor" and "dishonor"). The *lump of clay* is Israel, and the *noble purpose* is becoming a member of God's family. The idea of vessels for honor and dishonor is quite common in both Judaism and the New Testament (Job 10:9; 38:14; Ps 2:9; Is 29:16; 41:25; 45:9; 64:7; Jer 18:1-6; Sir 33:13; Sirach 27:5; *Testament of Naphtali* 2:2, 4; 1QS 11:22; 2 Tim 2:20), with a possible allusion here (so Cranfield 1979; Moo 1996) to Wisdom of Solomon 15:7, "For when a potter kneads the soft earth and laboriously molds each vessel for our service, he fashions out of the same clay both the vessels that serve clean uses and those for contrary uses." The common theme is that the Creator controls his creation and has the sovereign right to form whatever he wishes in his created order. On the issue of corporate versus individual emphases here, see the discussion of the introduction to 9:6-13. It is likely that Paul has in

---

9:19 Several (Cranfield 1979; Dunn 1988b; Fitzmyer 1993b; Moo 1996) point to the perfect tense of *resist* as gnomic or present in force, meaning "resist at any time."
9:22-23 The grammar of this passage is quite difficult. There is an *if* clause but no *then* clause, and this has caused commentators to see different structures in the sentence. Some (e.g., Stählin 1967:426) see verse 23 as the *then* clause: *If God . . . bore with great patience the objects of his wrath . . . [then he did it] to make the riches of his glory known.* However, that does not quite fit and weakens the overall argument (so Piper 1983; Schreiner 1998). The majority feel Paul simply has left the *then* clause

mind the individuals that make up the group. The same is true regarding the question of whether Paul has individual salvation in mind (so Murray 1968; Piper 1983; Moo 1996; Schreiner 1998) or not (so Cranfield 1979; Dunn 1988b; Fitzmyer 1993b, who take this corporately of the national future of Israel). All of chapter 9 is a unit, and the single issue is how to understand (in light of God's promises to Israel) that so many in Israel have not found salvation. Thus this passage must be part of that larger issue and address the question of individual salvation. So once again the theological issue is the predestination of individuals to damnation. This cannot be decided by this passage alone, though it certainly does provide strong evidence for double predestination. There is no question that Paul is arguing for the sovereign authority of God to do just that. Still, the question of foreknowledge (8:29) and human responsibility (9:30-33) must be considered before a final decision is reached. So this issue will continue to be a focus throughout chapters 9—11. Morris (1988:366; see similar statements in Hodge 1950; Murray 1968) provides a middle ground: "[Paul] is saying that God created people, that people became sinners, and that God then dealt with them as sinners." This approach avoids a theology that has God creating sinners in order to punish them.

This theme is carried on in verses 22-23, where the *potter* is explicitly identified as God and the reason for his choice of some to honor and others to dishonor is unveiled—to make both his power (v. 22) and his glory (v. 23) known. As in the case of Pharaoh in verses 17-18, God *bore with great patience the objects of his wrath*. That can certainly be seen in Exodus 4—14 and in the incredible number of times God interacted patiently with Pharaoh during the plagues without simply wiping him out. The verb *bore (phero)* means to "bear patiently, endure, put up with" (Bauer et al.) someone, and Paul makes it more explicit by adding *with*

---

unstated, and so many translate *what if* (KJV; NASB; NIV; NEB; NRSV) or simply leave out the *if* clause (JB; NLT). The second issue is whether the participle *choosing* (literally "willing") should be translated "although" (Sanday and Headlam 1902; Lenski 1945; Fitzmyer 1993b; NRSV; JB) or "because" (Calvin 1979; Murray 1968; Cranfield 1979; Moo 1996; Morris 1988; Schreiner 1998). Both make sense of the passage, but the causal is slightly better in a context that is emphasizing God's sovereign choice: "Because" he wants to make his power known, he is patient toward *the objects of his wrath*.

great patience, meaning "longsuffering" or "endurance." He is piling up terms to show the unbelievable patience of God. In the Old Testament God is "slow to anger" (Neh 9:17; Ps 103:8; 145:8; Prov 14:29; 15:18; 16:32; Joel 2:13; Jon 4:2; Nahum 1:3), and in the New Testament he often employs his patience to bring people to repentance (Rom 2:4; 1 Tim 1:16; 2 Pet 3:9). A special example is in the book of Revelation, where one of God's purposes in pouring out the seals, trumpets and bowls is to bring the people to repentance (Rev 9:20-21; 14:6-7; 16:9, 11; see Osborne 2002 on these passages). However, it is difficult to know whether Paul hints at a positive as well as a negative purpose here. The negative side certainly seems uppermost, since they are called *objects* (literally "vessels") *of his wrath—prepared for destruction,* where the focus is on the final judgment. Both *wrath* (Rom 2:5, 8; 5:9; Eph 5:6) and *destruction* (Phil 1:28; 2 Thess 2:3; 1 Tim 6:9) are often used for the last judgment. Yet it is wrong to dichotomize the two aspects, for it is God's present patience even in his wrath that necessitates his final wrath at the eschaton. Morris (1988:367) says "Paul seems to be saying that God is working out a single purpose of mercy and this is to be discerned in his wrath as well as his long-suffering." In other words, wrath and mercy are interdependent. Cranfield (1979:495) notes the parallel with 2:4 (God's patience leading to repentance) and 3:26 (God showing his justice in the present time) along with Ephesians 2:3 (Christians described as having once been "by nature objects of wrath"), concluding that here too they are *prepared for destruction* on the basis of unbelief, not that they have been predestined to unbelief. This makes more sense than a double predestination thrust. Once again (as throughout chaps. 7—9) there is an inaugurated thrust, with present wrath culminating in final destruction. Yet the present wrath is part of God's mercy, and, as in 10:1-15 and 11:25-32, the present *objects of his wrath* are also the object of God's patient call to salvation. The final *destruction* is the result of unbelief and not just God's predetermined will.

9:24 It is difficult to know for sure whether this continues verses 22-23 (NASB; NIV; NRSV; NLT; Murray 1968; Cranfield 1979) or begins a new sentence (NEB; Käsemann 1980; Dunn 1988b; Moo 1996; Schreiner 1998). Syntactically, it is closely connected with verse 23 (it begins with a relative pronoun modifying the "vessels [NIV objects] of mercy"). But at the same time it does move into a new area of meaning (Dunn

There are three purposes here. First, God wants *to show his wrath,* meaning his present anger toward sinful, unbelieving humanity (1:18; 2:5, 8; 3:5); in all these verses the wrath is God's reaction to sin and not a predestined phenomenon. Thus Paul is emphasizing God's righteous anger but not saying that God created people purely for wrath. Second, God wants *to make his power known,* referring to the acts of power in the Egyptian plagues that *proclaimed [the name of God] in all the earth* (vv. 17-18). This proclamation of the divine name is mission oriented and part of the gospel presentation (as in 10:1-15; cf. 10:8, "the word of faith we are proclaiming"), and even the demonstration of his wrath is part of that. His *power* is both his saving power and his judging power (see on v. 17). The third purpose is the primary one (for the two purposes in v. 22 point forward to v. 23, so Cranfield 1979), namely, *to make the riches of his glory known to the objects* (literally "vessels") *of his mercy.* Now we move from wrath to mercy (see vv. 15-16). In chapter 9 the "vessels of mercy" are believing Jews and "the vessels of wrath" are unbelieving Jews. The *riches of his glory* refer to the blessings of salvation (the thrust of "riches" in Rom 2:4; 11:12; Eph 1:7, 18; 2:7) by which God's *glory* is revealed to his people. The glorious God has revealed his glory through his mercy in bringing the saints to himself and justifying them. Moreover, in the same way that he "prepared" the vessels of wrath for destruction, he has *prepared* the saints *beforehand for glory.* Once again this is God's predetermined will in producing salvation in his elect (on this see 8:29). Note that the first use of *glory* in this verse is God's glory, and this second use refers to the glory the saints have in him. Once more this is our present glory (the already) as an anticipation of our final glory (the not yet), with the greater emphasis here on the glory we will have in eternity.

The New Community—The Remnant and the Gentiles (9:24-29)

In a collage of Old Testament citations, Paul concludes this section by

says a "pause for breath" is indicated) and introduces the next topic, the inclusion of the Gentiles. So it is best to see this as explaining further who the "objects of mercy" (v. 23) are and yet beginning a new paragraph in which both the Gentiles (vv. 25-26) and a remnant from among the Jews (vv. 27-28) are called to constitute the new community of God.

showing how God had previously foretold his turn from the apostate nation to the righteous remnant and to the Gentiles. Moo (1996:610) shows how Paul has progressively moved through the Old Testament canon in chapter 9, from the patriarchal narratives in verses 6-13 to the exodus in verses 14-18 to the prophets here. Now he simply has quote after quote without commentary; he wants the citations themselves to carry the message and to prove that the Old Testament is in agreement with his claim in verse 24 that God has *called* both Jews and Gentiles to himself. This shows that all along Paul has been moving toward this moment. Not only is God just in excluding some Jews from his people, but also he is just in turning to the Gentiles. So people become his children not on the basis of their rights as a covenant people (birthright in vv. 3-4, 7-8) but on the basis of the divine call (the flip side of 3:21—4:25, where it is on the basis of faith).

The thesis is stated in verse 24. *Called* looks back to 8:28, 30 and means the call to salvation. The two major questions in chapter 9 center on whether the promises of God have failed (v. 6) and whether God is unjust (v. 14). In both cases the issue is the exclusion of the majority of the Jewish people, but here we see the second issue, why God would call people *not only from the Jews but also from the Gentiles.* That was a huge issue in the first century. A brief look at the theology of "people" in Luke-Acts will illustrate this. In Luke the "people" (a semitechnical term for the people of God) are on the side of Jesus until the leaders finally talk them into demanding Jesus' death at the trial before Pilate. In Acts the "people" support the church until it turns to the Gentiles after the council of Jerusalem. So this caused great debate within the early church.

The first two citations are from Hosea 2:23 and 1:10, respectively (vv. 25-26), in order to confirm the second element from verse 24, those *called . . . from the Gentiles.* The first is a free rendition of Hosea 2:23; Paul changes the "I will say" of Hosea to *I will call* and reverses the order of the clauses (so that *I will call* can be first in the citation). The effect is to provide a close match with the themes of 9:6-23, namely, the call of God to belong to his people. Also, the verb *call* frames the two Hosea quotes, beginning the first and concluding the second. The major problem is that in Hosea the Gentiles are not part of the message; the statement is addressed to the northern tribes who have incurred God's wrath for their sin, and so God led Hosea to name his two children Lo-Ruhamah ("not loved," 1:6) and Lo-Ammi ("not my people," 1:9). The two passages, Hosea 2:23 and 1:10, promise the remnant that God would indeed remove his judgment and reinstate his people. Those who were rejected as God's people and the object of his love have been returned to their place and forgiven. As Dunn notes (1988b:571), the theme is "that those once rejected can be taken back again." For Hosea it was the northern kingdom, but for Paul it is the Gentiles. Moo explains the hermeneutic behind this (1996:613), "that Old Testament predictions of a renewed Israel find their fulfillment in the church." For Paul the church is the true Israel, meaning that salvation for the Gentiles is the proper next stage of salvation history.

The second citation, Hosea 1:10 (this time a quote of the LXX), provides a similar message. Those who have been called *not my people* will have a new status as *sons of the living God* (cf. 8:15-16). God's effectual call has resulted in a radical new birthright and status as a member of God's family. *The very place* in Hosea was the land of Israel, but for Paul it refers to the Gentile mission. God's call has become worldwide, and all peoples are included. Yet there is more than this. Segal (1990:58-59) points out that in verses 25-26 Paul's great innovation is not so much that the Gentiles are brought into the salvation process (many Jews allowed that) as that the Jews and Gentiles "form a single community, which is called 'being in Christ.'" All barriers are removed in a new oneness in Christ. For us in the twenty-first century this signifies a willingness to move out of our comfort zone as well. For instance, suburban churches should have a major ministry presence in the inner city. Missions should center on the world-class city, and ethnic churches should especially minister to their old enemies (e.g., tribal ministries in Africa). Never before has tribalism been so proven to be a worldwide phenomenon (in the old Czech Republic as well as in Africa). The church is called to be a solution to the old animosities and to bring the love and forgiveness of Christ to all peoples.

Then the emphasis shifts to the call of a remnant from Israel (vv. 27-29) and confirms the first part of verse 24, those *called . . . from the Jews*. While much of the nation has been excluded, a portion remains the focus of God's call, and this is entirely in keeping with Old Testament prophecy. This time the quotations are from Isaiah, who *cries out concerning Israel,* emphasizing Isaiah's (and Paul's) tremendous concern for the chosen people. The quotation itself intersperses Hosea 1:10 (from which is taken *the number of the Israelites;* Isaiah has "your people, O Israel") with Isaiah 10:22-23, probably to draw the two (vv. 26 and 27) together into a single message, namely, that the church is made up of Gentiles and a remnant from the Jews. In Isaiah this was part of an oracle (Is 7—12) asking the people of Israel whether they want to trust in Assyria or God; because they have placed their trust in Assyria, they will be destroyed, but not all (see Oswalt 1986:55-56). God was still in control, and a remnant would be spared. Verses 22-23 sum up the twin themes of judgment and mercy in that section of Isaiah. There would be a remnant but only they would *be saved.* Paul uses this in a slightly different way to show why God has chosen only a few from among Israel and in this way to bolster what he has already said in verses 6-13. So those taken from the innumerable multitude of the Jewish people to constitute true Israel (vv. 6-7a) are now linked with the Old Testament concept of the *remnant,* those among Israel who had remained true to God and had not apostatized like the rest of the nation. For Isaiah this meant that God was still faithful to his promises, for the apostate nation had forfeited its right to be numbered among the people of God; their doom was certain. Paul picks up on this completely, for in his day the nation had apostatized again by rejecting God's Messiah. Once more only a *remnant* is *saved,* but that is in keeping with God's promises. As Hofius says (1990:23-27), Romans 9—11 asserts the righteousness of God as demonstrated in justification through Christ. Israel has rejected God's righteousness, but God has not rejected them in a final sense. He has preserved a remnant now (see 11:1-10) and will bring Israel back to himself (see 11:25-32).

A serious warning is given in the second half of the quotation, *the Lord will carry out his sentence . . . with speed and finality.* The *sentence* (literally "word" or "decree") is probably divine judgment on those who remain unrepentant, but it is less certain what *speed* and *finality* mean. The first has more the idea of completeness and finality, but the second is disputed. It occurs only here in the New Testament and only six times in the LXX. It basically means to "cut short," but Morris notes three options (1988:372): shortening the promise (fulfilling it in a limited way), shortening the nation (only a remnant saved, so Calvin 1979; Wilckens 1980; Dunn 1988b; Fitzmyer 1993b), or shortening the time (swift judgment, so Murray 1968; Morris 1988). However, there is a fourth option, that it refers to the decisiveness and finality of the execution of the sentence (so Cranfield 1979; Moo 1996; Schreiner 1998). This fits the context better, so it is best to translate "with completeness and finality," referring to the decisive action of God by which he will carry out his will. Both mercy and judgment are connoted, with God's mercy upon the remnant who believe (v. 28) and his complete judgment upon those who do not (v. 29). God is completely faithful to his promises in both instances, for they flow out of the blessings and cursings that characterize the covenant.

The final citation (v. 29) is from Isaiah 1:9 LXX and again confirms the mercy of God upon Israel. Isaiah begins his book by rebuking Israel for its rebellion against God (1:2, 5) and its corruption (1:4). So God has sent desolation upon it (1:7-8), and unless God had mercifully left survivors, they would have been wiped out like Sodom and Gomorrah (1:9). Paul takes this as a prediction or "foretelling" of the Jews in Paul's day. The point for Isaiah and Paul is that Israel deserved to be utterly destroyed for its rebellion, and only God's mercy kept it from the same oblivion as Sodom and Gomorrah (Gen 19). God has *left us descendants,* literally "a seed," referring to the *remnant* of verse 27. Once again there is hope for the future based on the faithful promises of God (answering the question of v. 6) and his justice (answering the question of v. 14).

☐ Israel's Responsibility for Rejecting God's Offer of Salvation (9:30—10:21)

Whenever we human beings are punished for wrongdoing, we commonly try to shift the blame—"It's his fault!" The people of Israel had done the same thing, questioning the justice of God rather than facing honestly their unbelief. The question that dominates chapters 9—11 is the justice of God in light of the contradiction between his promises to his covenant people and the fact that so few of them had been converted. In these chapters Paul answers the question from two perspectives, first from the sovereignty of God to choose whom he wishes (9:6-29) and second from the responsibility of Israel to accept God's gift of salvation by faith (9:30—10:21). As Schreiner says (1998:531), "We learn from this that Paul viewed divine sovereignty and human responsibility as complementary rather than contradictory truths." Israel cannot blame God for its predicament, for God has been completely faithful to his covenant promises, while Israel has been unfaithful in keeping its part of the bargain, namely, in accepting God's Messiah by faith.

Moo notes (1996:616-17) that this section is dominated by two concepts, *righteousness* (six times here but nowhere else in chaps. 9—11) and *faith/believe* (twelve times here and only in 11:20 in the rest of the section). Righteousness is a gift from God attained only by faith (9:32; 10:3, 4). Also, the section is framed by two passages (9:30-32; 10:19-21) contrasting the exclusion of Israel (they sought it by works) and the inclusion of the Gentiles (they obtained it by faith). Israel has *stumbled* (9:33) because they *sought to establish their own* righteousness (10:3), were guilty of unbelief (10:14), and were both *disobedient and obstinate* (10:21). They failed to understand that their own law had at all times been intended to point to Christ and to faith in him (so Cranfield 1979:505). There are three sections here: 9:30—10:4 (righteousness by faith, not by works); 10:5-13 (salvation by faith not by the law); and 10:14-21 (Israel's guilt for rejecting the gospel).

Righteousness by Faith, Not by Works (9:30—10:4) Righteousness was the key concept in 1:16-17 and 3:21-26, where it referred in a forensic sense to the judicial act of God in declaring us innocent and in "right" standing with him. Paul introduces this idea once more to explain why the Gentiles rather than Israel have come into God's family. In her ignorance Israel is *zealous* (10:2) for the wrong thing, namely,

---

9:31 *Law of righteousness* has been variously interpreted: (1) *Law* could mean "principle" as in 3:27; 7:21, 23; and 8:2 (so Sanday and Headlam 1902; Murray 1968) so that Israel was seeking a right relationship with God; but the whole context of legal righteousness based on the law in 10:4-5 makes this unlikely. (2) It could be "righteousness obtained from the law" (so Chrysostom; Calvin 1979; RSV; NJB), but then one would expect Paul to have the order "righteousness of the law," and he does

their own (10:3) works righteousness centered on the law rather than God's righteousness that can only come via faith. But Christ is *the end of the law* (10:4); the law is no longer a valid approach to God. Paul begins the section with two questions (9:30, 32). First, he opens with his characteristic *what then shall we say?* (3:5; 4:1; 6:1; 7:7; 8:31; 9:14), indicating another response to the question of God turning from Israel to the Gentiles. Paul begins with the Gentiles. In verses 30-31, there are two contrasts between the Gentiles and the Jews:

1. The Gentiles *did not pursue righteousness* while the Jews *pursued a law of righteousness.* Paul is hardly saying that no Gentiles sought moral righteousness; rather, he is echoing 1:18-32 on the depravity of their minds and especially the fact that they never sought a right standing with God. Again the emphasis is not on ethical living but on relationship with God. The Jews, however, sought *a law of righteousness,* a deliberately chosen phrase that means they sought the law as a path to righteousness. The imagery of "pursuing/attaining" (compare Phil 3:12-14) invokes the picture of a racecourse, running toward a goal (so Käsemann 1980; Fitzmyer 1993b; Schreiner 1998; contra Dunn 1988b; Moo 1996). It connotes an energetic pursuit. So the Gentiles did not seek right standing with God yet found it while the Jews sought it with all their strength and failed.

2. The Gentiles *obtained . . . righteousness* while the Jewish people did not. They attained it *by faith.* The contrast between faith and law that dominated chapters 4—7 continues here. The only possible way to find that right relationship with God is to realize it only "comes by faith." The proper response is not keeping the law or living in the right way but only turning to God in faith on the basis of Christ's atoning sacrifice. We have now come full circle. Since it is only possible to gain a right standing with God by faith, it does not matter who has run after it, for we cannot attain it by our own efforts. It is a gift

---

not. (3) It might refer to "the righteous law," but that would not fit the use of "righteousness" throughout this section. (4) The best option is to take this as the pursuit of "the law that promises righteousness" or "produces righteousness," because this fits the grammar of the phrase and the thrust of the context (so Godet 1969; Cranfield 1979; Dunn 1988b; Morris 1988; Moo 1996; Schreiner 1998).

of God attainable only on the basis of faith.

The second question *(Why not?)* seems to bring back the imaginary opponent who asks why Israel has not attained right standing with God (v. 32). The answer sums up chapters 4—8, *they pursued it not by faith but as if it were by works.* There is actually no verb here, so some have "they live not by faith but by works" (so Käsemann 1980). But that does not fit the context well, so the idea of pursuing or trying to attain is best. The faith/works antithesis has been often emphasized (3:20, 27-28; 4:2, 6; 9:11), and as elsewhere their pursuit of righteousness is not at fault but rather their trying to attain it by works. It was not wrong to pursue the law, but to make it the locus of salvation in light of the Christ-event meant that they rejected God's Messiah and the salvation he made possible. Because of Christ's atoning sacrifice, salvation could only be attained by faith not works (for the debate with Sanders, Dunn and others on this, see the discussion on 3:20 as well as Schreiner 1998:539-40). The interesting *as if it were* may have be added to heighten the contrast between faith and works (Murray 1968; Morris 1988), or perhaps to emphasize the illusion of their perspective on the law (Cranfield 1979; Dunn 1988b).

Because the Jewish people sought righteousness by the works of the law, they *stumbled,* which can mean they fall into sin (Rom 14:21) but here (and 1 Pet 2:8) means they "take offense" at Christ, leading to divine judgment (seen in the Isaiah quote in the next verse). The *stumbling stone* is not the Torah (so Barrett 1982:144-45) but Christ, in keeping with the use of the stone passages throughout the New Testament (Mk 12:10-11 and parallels; Acts 4:11; 1 Pet 2:6-8, so Cranfield 1979, Wilckens 1980; Dunn 1988b; Harrisville 1980; Schreiner 1998). Jesus was the first to call himself "the cornerstone" (Mk 12:10), a positive messianic image since the stone passages were seen as messianic in first-century Judaism (see Jeremias 1967a:272-73; Dunn 1988b:583-84). However, verses 32-33 employ another image, that of judgment and destruction. The early church used stone imagery to describe how the Jews rejected Jesus ("the stone you builders rejected," Acts 4:11; 1 Pet 2:7) but God made him the chief cornerstone of his church (many believe the early church developed a "stone *testimonium*" collection of Old Testament parallels for this purpose).

The citation in verse 33 conflates Isaiah 8:14 and 28:16, both of which describe the Assyrian threat. Isaiah 8:14, the source of the first two lines, is a warning that God will judge Israel, "a stone that causes men to stumble," and Isaiah 28:16, the source of the last two lines, is a promise that God will deliver Israel, "a precious cornerstone for a sure foundation." The verse provides an excellent summary of the message about Israel in this section—those who "believe" (NIV, *trusts*) will be saved and those who *stumble* will be destroyed. For those Jews who have rejected their Messiah, Christ has become *a stone that causes men to stumble and a rock that makes them fall,* with both "stumbling" and "offense" (NIV, *fall*) referring to destruction at the last judgment. For those Jews (and Gentiles) who believe in him, there will be no *shame,* meaning not so much a lack of embarrassment as vindication at the last judgment (*shame* in both Old Testament and New Testament often refers to eschatological judgment, so Käsemann 1980; Dunn 1988b; Schreiner 1998).

The second half of this section (by using "brothers and sisters" [NIV, *brothers*] Paul shifts to another aspect of his topic [so Moo 1996]) begins by reiterating Paul's deep concern for his own Jewish people (cf. 9:1-5), stating his *heart's desire* or "deepest will" (with *heart* indicating the depth of his being, see Dunn 1988b) for the Jews. The term has the idea of "good pleasure," "wish," or "desire." Moreover, it is also his *prayer to God;* the result of his heartfelt concern is prayer on behalf of his people. The focus of this prayer for Israel is *that they may be saved.* This echoes the quotation of Isaiah 28:16 in 9:33. Since only those who "believe" will not *be put to shame* at the last judgment, Paul prays that they may indeed turn to Christ in faith and *be saved,* thus preparing for 11:25-26, which says that although "Israel has experienced a hardening . . . all Israel will be saved" (see on that passage). Paul's prayer will be answered.

The reason *(for)* for Paul's prayer is his personal testimony that the Jewish people are *zealous for God.* By using the legal term *testify,* he gives special stress to the truth of what he is saying. *Zeal* means a passionate desire to serve and worship God; Paul spoke of his own zeal for Torah and God in Galatians 1:13-14 and Philippians 3:4-6. Cranfield (1979:514) calls it "fervent, strenuous, tenacious, concentrated zeal" and points out that "orthodox Judaism puts much that passes for Christianity, and even much true Christianity, to shame both in respect to the seriousness of its zeal and by the fact that its zeal is truly zeal for God." This was obviously a major characteristic of every aspect of Judaism, from the Pharisees to the Essenes, in the first century. In fact, we could say that the time from 400 B.C. to A.D. 100 was the first such extended period of zeal for God in the history of the nation (note the regular periods of apostasy in the time of the wilderness wanderings as well as of the time of the Judges and the divided monarchy in the Old Testament). However, its zeal was *not based on knowledge,* here undoubtedly meaning they did not "perceive" (for the term see 1:28) that righteousness could be attained only by faith in Christ rather than the works of the law.

This ignorance is explained further in verse 3: *they did not know the righteousness that comes from God* but instead *sought to establish their own.* In biblical times, ignorance was more than a lack of knowledge; it referred to active rejection of a truth (see on 1:28). Here Paul sums up the message of 9:30-32, which itself sums up the many passages in Romans on attaining right understanding with God only by faith (3:21—4:25; 5:1, 2) and not by works (3:20, 27-28; 4:2, 6; 9:11). Righteousness of God is often perceived to be the thesis of the whole book

---

10:3 Those who have sought a "new perspective" on the law (see note on 3:20) argue that this is not a diatribe against the "works of the law" (the individual view) but rather a diatribe against the Jewish refusal to allow the Gentiles to share in their "righteousness" by erecting "boundary markers" against Gentile inclusion (the corporate or national view, using circumcision, food laws, ceremonial requirements and so on; so Dunn 1988b:587-88; B. W. Longenecker 1991:219). But Schreiner is certainly correct (1998:544) in pointing out that in the text Israel *sought to establish their own* standing with God rather than to set barriers against the Gentiles. It is Israel's attempt to establish its own righteousness that is the issue. Moo (1996:634-36) gives four reasons for this interpretation: (1) The genitives ("of God"/"of their own") are connected and probably should be seen as genitives of source, meaning they sought a righteousness that came from their own efforts. (2) *Their own* is connected to Old Testament references on "one's own" righteousness; cf. Deuteronomy 9:4-6; Isaiah 64:5; Ezekiel 14:14, 18:22-26; 33:12, 13, 18. (3) The idea of "self-righteousness" fits the context; cf. 9:31-32; 10:5. (4) The only other time Paul has this contrast (Phil 3:4-6), there is also a faith versus law antithesis.

10:4 There is a great amount of controversy over the meaning of *end of the law.* Both terms are debated. Does *end* mean (1) that Christ is the fulfillment of the law

(see on 1:17; 3:21) and is the key here. The Jewish people certainly understood that God was righteous and that they needed to be in right relationship with him. But they had rejected the only basis for that right standing, namely, Christ and his atoning death. Thus they could never be "justified" and so could never find that right relationship with God. Instead of doing it God's way and allowing him to work his salvation in them, they tried to stand in *their own* righteousness, the righteousness of the law. As a result, they *did not submit to God's righteousness,* which was no longer connected to the law but now depended upon Christ. The global aorist *did not submit* summarizes their ongoing rejection of Christ. Only in Christ and his atoning sacrifice can there be any declaration of *righteousness,* but many of the Jewish people have clung stubbornly to the law.

A law-based righteousness is no longer sufficient because *Christ is the end of the law*. This means that Christ has become the culmination or climax of the law in the sense that it has pointed to him and been finalized in him. The law has not ceased to have any value; in 7:12, 14 Paul says the law is "holy, righteous, good" and "spiritual." As part of Scripture, it is also "profitable" (so Moo 1996). So Christ has not abolished the law (cf. Mt 5:17-20) but has replaced it as the standard for righteousness. In this sense he has culminated the law as the focal point of its purpose.

(Cranfield 1979 names Clement of Alexandria and Eusebius; Barth 1933), (2) that he has put a temporal end to the law (Sanday and Headlam 1902; Dodd 1932; Michel 1966; Godet 1969; Käsemann 1980; Fitzmyer 1993b; Linss 1993; Stott 1994; Schreiner 1998), (3) that he is the culmination of the law (Moo 1996), or (4) that he is the goal of the law (Howard 1969:332-33; Badenas 1985; Rhyne 1985; Barth 1933; Cranfield 1979; Fitzmyer 1993b; Bechtler 1994). At the outset, it must be said that there is no hint in Paul or the New Testament that Christ has abolished the law. The closest is Hebrew 8:13, saying it is "obsolete" and "will soon disappear." But that is not total replacement. Matthew 5:17-20 says that the law is intact in Christ, which could support the fulfillment interpretation; but that is difficult to uphold in Paul. More possible is the idea of goal, for Paul often emphasizes that the law points forward to Christ (Gal 3:19—4:7). Probably best is a combination of (2) and (3), that Christ provided a temporal end but in the sense of "culmination" rather than replacement. The law did point to Christ, but it has been caught up in him rather than replaced by him. There is indeed a salvation-historical movement from law to gospel, but there is continuity and not just discontinuity between them. As for the meaning of *law,* it is almost certainly the Mosaic law rather than the principle of law in general or the Old Testament as a whole (as I have argued throughout this commentary).

Paul is saying, then, that Christ has put an end to any attempt to achieve righteousness by means of the law (so Morris 1988; Schreiner 1993b). Salvation is attained by faith in him alone, and the works of the law in that sense are at an end. In 6:1-6 we have "died to sin" so that we can "live a new life," and in 7:4 we "died to the law through the body of Christ" so that we can "belong to" God. The slavery to the law of sin and death has been broken, and we are now slaves to God (6:15-22). There has been a salvation-historical switch from the covenant of the law to the covenant of grace *so that there may be righteousness for everyone who believes.* The works of the law have been replaced by faith as the only standard for righteousness. Jew and Gentile alike can be made right with God the same way—only by believing in Christ. The problem of faith and works is the same today as it was in the time of Paul. Every church has many in it trying to buy their way into heaven by church attendance, by activity in charity organizations and by doing their best in general. It is just as important today as in the first century to make the message as clear as possible—examine your heart before you rationalize your life. You are playing games with your eternal destiny!

Salvation by Faith, Not by the Law (10:5-13) It is clear that those who try to get right with God by obeying his laws are doomed to failure, for no one can keep the law perfectly. Verse 5 says in effect that only the person who perfectly heeds the law will be saved, and this obviously cannot happen. So righteousness can only come from faith (vv. 6-8). Thus verses 5-8 unpack the meaning of righteousness only for those who believe in verse 4 (so Cranfield 1979, Fitzmyer 1993b; Stott 1994, Moo 1996; Schreiner 1998). Verse 5 concentrates on the

---

10:5 There are three different interpretations of this passage: (1) Some (Hendriksen 1981; Cranfield 1979) believe it is Christ who perfectly *does these things* in the law and so makes it possible for people to live by faith (vv. 6-8). But that is unlikely, for there is no hint in the context (before or after this verse) that Paul has shifted to Christ here. (2) Several scholars (Howard 1969:333-37; Kaiser 1971:19-28; Stowers 1994:308-10) take *the righteousness that is by the law* as closely connected to the righteousness by faith (vv. 4, 6). In this sense there is no contrast between verse 5 and verses 6-8. They argue that Christ is the goal of the law (v. 4), and so verse 5 demonstrates how a person can indeed keep the law in Christ. Moreover, both Leviticus 18:5 (v. 5) and Deuteronomy 30:12-14 (vv. 6-8) center on keeping

works of the law and verses 6-8 on faith, emphasizing that human achievement has nothing to do with faith. Human effort can neither bring about the incarnation nor produce the resurrection (v. 7). Only *the word of faith* can accomplish anything (v. 8). Then verses 9-13 explain how faith works; only confession and belief can result in justification and salvation (vv. 9-10), and only faith can keep one from the last judgment (v. 11). Therefore both Jew and Gentile alike must *call on the name of the Lord* in faith to be saved (vv. 12-13).

Paul begins by telling why (*for* actually begins v. 5 but is omitted in NIV) righteousness comes only by faith (v. 4). *The righteousness that is by the law* cannot produce salvation because to do so it must be lived perfectly, which no person under sin can possibly do. To show this Paul cites Leviticus 18:5, a passage where Yahweh commands Israel not to be like the Canaanites but to obey his decrees and live by them. As such it does not seem to fit the argument here, for it advocates keeping the law as a means of enjoying the covenant blessings. However, Wenham (1979:253) interprets *live by them* as "enjoy life through them," meaning the promise that those who keep the law will experience God's covenant blessings in this life (but probably not eternal life; contra Kaiser 1971:19-28). Paul, however, does read this as eternal life, but only if one *does these things* (i.e., keeps the law) perfectly (cf. 2:13; 7:10; so Moo 1996). So the Jewish people (and people today) who want a right relationship with God through doing must follow the law absolutely, a task rendered impossible by human depravity (so Rom 1:18—3:20). Eternal life can never be obtained by mere obedience or human achievement. In fact, that was proven by the reality that Israel did not keep the law and did not find the life promised in the law.

---

the law as part of the covenantal relationship with God. While attractive, there are good reasons for rejecting this (see Moo 1996:645-46; Schreiner 1998:551-54). First, the antithesis between doing (v. 5) and believing (vv. 6-8) strongly supports a contrast here. Second, the works of the law are set against salvation by faith throughout Romans, and to see them as complementary would overturn many of Paul's arguments. Third, the parallel in Philippians 3:6-9 (where "a righteousness of my own that comes from the law" is also set against "righteousness . . . by faith") makes it more likely that that contrast is seen here as well. Therefore, the correct solution is (3), to see verse 5 on keeping the law as contrasted to verses 6-8 on believing in Christ.

In contrast *(but)* Paul turns to Deuteronomy 30:12-14 to describe *the righteousness that is by faith* (vv. 6-8). He sees this passage on the renewal of the nation after exile fulfilled in Christ and the new covenant he provided. He introduces the passage by citing Deuteronomy 9:4 LXX (also Deut 8:17), *Do not say in your heart.* Several point out (Leenhart 1961; Cranfield 1979; Moo 1996; Schreiner 1998) that the context in Deuteronomy is important. In Deuteronomy 9:4-6 Moses warns Israel that their inheritance of the land is not due to their own righteousness but to the gracious gift of God alone. This is essentially the message here as well and provides a natural introduction to the next section. The first part of Deuteronomy 30:12 is *Who will ascend into heaven?* Paul interprets this as *to bring Christ down* (= "that is, the incarnation"). Paul's use of *that is* is similar to Qumran's *pesher* interpretation (so Cranfield 1979; Wilckens 1980; Fitzmyer 1993b), in which the Old Testament text is made to fit a contemporary situation. Paul's is somewhat different in that he does not view this as the actual meaning of the Old Testament text (as Qumran did) but is applying the Deuteronomy quote to Christ and to the issue of justification by faith (so Moo 1996). Ascending into heaven is an impossible quest. Moses meant that one did not have to climb up to heaven or cross the sea to obey the law. Paul is saying that one does not have to go to heaven to bring Christ down to earth so he can provide salvation to humankind. God has already done that for them. The incarnation is God's grace gift; it can never be the product of human achievement.

In the second instance, Paul alters Deuteronomy's "Who will cross the sea?" to *Who will descend into the deep?* (literally "abyss"). Some

---

10:6-8 The problem is that this Old Testament passage is similar in meaning to Leviticus 18:5, which focuses on obeying the law to find new life in God (Deut 30:10, 15). Moses warns the people that there is no excuse for failing to obey God's commands by pretending they have not heard them. In the Torah these commands are evident. So how can Paul use this to support faith, and how can he apply the passage to Christ? Several (Sanday and Headlam 1902; Hodge 1950; Fitzmyer 1993b; Barrett 1957:199 calls it "a rhetorical form") call these general allusions rather than a quote and claim that Paul is not exegeting the Old Testament passage but merely using it. But the use of *says* in verses 6 and 8 (used to introduce citations in 9:15, 17, 25 and often in chap. 10 [vv. 11, 16, 19-21]) favors a citation, and *that is* was a common Jewish introduction to the interpretation of a text. Still, on what basis does Paul apply this text so differently from how it was intended by Deuteronomy? It is differ-

think Paul substitutes Psalm 107:26 ("went down to the depths") for Deuteronomy 30:13 (Cranfield 1979; Fitzmyer 1993b), but it is better to realize that *sea* and *abyss* were interchangeable (the "abyss" was the unfathomable depths of the sea) and that Paul simply substitutes the one for the other (so Dunn 1988b; Moo 1996; Schreiner 1998). This of course fits the point that it is just as impossible to "go down to the abyss" (namely the grave) in order to *bring Christ up from the dead* as it is to ascend to heaven. Human effort can no more produce the resurrection than it can the incarnation. Both are the result of the grace of God rather than the will of man, and so they can only be accepted by faith. The Messiah has already appeared, has died on the cross for sins and has been raised to exaltation with God. The work has already been accomplished by God, and human effort was not part of it. All we are asked to do is accept God's gift by faith.

The final citation from Deuteronomy (30:14 LXX) begins with *But what does it* (the teaching on righteousness by faith, v. 6) *say?* This turns to the positive element. It does not mean that human effort can produce the incarnation or the resurrection (vv. 6-7); instead righteousness by faith does say that *the word is near you; it is in your mouth and in your heart*. In Deuteronomy (the law) and here (the gospel) this means that God has "drawn near to them in His word which could be taken on their lips and received in their hearts" (Cranfield 1979:526). In his revealed truth God could be experienced and understood; he is not distant but near and can be both shared (mouth) and worshiped (heart). Paul then applies this to *the word of faith we are proclaiming*. Behind this is the fact that Christ is the culmination of the law (see v.

---

ent in two respects—seen as fulfilled in Christ and seen as advocating faith rather than the works of the law, gospel over law. The best solution is provided by those who believe that Paul's approach is anchored in "the larger narrative structure of Deuteronomy" (Schreiner 1998:557-58; cf. Thielmann 1994:209-10; Seifrid 1985:23). In the section in which Deuteronomy 30:12-14 occurs, the blessings and curses of the covenant are uppermost (Deut 27:1—29:1). Then in Deuteronomy 29:2—30:1 Israel is first warned about disobeying the covenant and then charged with doing just that. Thielmann tells us how the final section begins with a prophecy ("When all these things have happened to you," referring to the exile) and then tells how God will turn the nation around to love him and live (Deut 30:2-10). Paul sees this promise fulfilled in Christ and the new covenant age he inaugurated. So Paul sees Deuteronomy 30 fulfilled typologically in Christ and the age of salvation he made possible.

4), so that in the gospel itself the law is finalized. Schreiner (1998:559) points out that this *word of faith* refers both to the content of our faith (so Käsemann 1980; Fitzmyer 1993b) and to the act of trusting (so Sanday and Headlam 1902; Cranfield 1979). It is also closely connected to verse 9 and involves both confession *(with your mouth)* of the deep truths regarding the lordship of Christ and the salvation he produced and the deep conviction *(in your heart)* that believes in Christ.

The second half of this section (vv. 9-13) is closely tied to verses 6-8 and explains how "righteousness that is by faith" works. It is commonly thought that verses 9-10 compose a pre-Pauline creedal confession used by him to define further the meaning of faith. It is debated whether the term which begins verse 9 should be translated "that" (so providing the meaning of *the word of faith,* so NIV; Murray 1968; Barrett 1957; Käsemann 1980; Schreiner 1998) or "because" (telling why "the word is near you," so NRSV; NLT; Cranfield 1979; Moo 1996), but the explanatory "that" seems better because the issue of faith is central to the whole context. These verses sum up the response to the gospel, telling how people come to faith, with the very order reflecting the *mouth/ heart* order of Deuteronomy 30:14 in verse 8. Salvation is in the future tense *(will be saved)* and could be seen as final salvation at the eschaton (so Barrett 1957; Cranfield 1979; Dunn 1988b; Morris 1988; Schreiner 1998) but is better seen as a logical future describing what is the case beginning at conversion (namely after confessing and believing) and extending into the future (so Moo 1996). So again (as often in chaps. 6—10) there is an inaugurated sense: salvation is present now and will be consummated at the return of Christ (with the latter aspect emphasized in v. 11 below).

Salvation is experienced in the twin responses of confessing and believing. The content of the confession *(Jesus is Lord)* is at the very heart of early Christian confession (Acts 2:36; 10:36; 1 Cor 8:6; 12:3; 16:22; 2 Cor 4:5; Phil 2:11; Col 2:6), for the lordship of Jesus was an essential aspect of early Christian worship from the start (as proven in the Aramaic *marana tha* ["Our Lord, come!"] in 1 Cor 16:22, showing that the confession stems from the Palestinian period). Cranfield (1979:529) shows that "for Paul, the confession that Jesus is Lord meant the acknowledgement that Jesus shares the name and the nature, the holiness, the authority, power, majesty, and eternity of the one and only true God." At the heart of true Christian worship is the realization that Jesus is more than a mere Rabbi, more even than a Messiah. He is fully God and Lord of all (see Heb 1:3; 1 Pet 3:22). It is reflected in the most-often-quoted Old Testament passage of them all, Psalm 110:1 ("The LORD says to my Lord: 'Sit at my right hand until I make your enemies a footstool for your feet'"), cited in Mark 12:36-37 = Matthew 22:44-45 = Luke 20:42-44; Acts 2:34-35; Hebrews 1:3, 13; 5:6, 10; 6:20; 7:3, 7, 17, 21; 8:1; 10:12-13; 12:2; and others. Psalm 110:1 is so prominent because it provides the primary Old Testament underpinning for the exaltation of Christ. It has sometimes been argued that it is possible to know Jesus as Savior without knowing him as Lord. That is impossible according to this passage. To know Jesus as Savior begins the process of knowing him more and more as Lord. Without lordship there is no saviorhood. Belief is intimately connected to Jesus' lordship, belief *that God raised him from the dead*. The resurrection of Jesus is at the heart of Romans (4:24; 6:4, 9; 7:4; 8:11, 34; 10:9; 13:11) and was in a sense his investiture into lordship. It was at the heart of early Christian preaching (Acts 3:15; 4:10; 13:30) and belief, for without the resurrection all belief was empty of meaning and power (1 Cor 15:14).

Verse 10 amplifies these ideas and draws together the ideas of righteousness and salvation from verses 6 and 9. It also reverses the order of verses 8 and 9, with heart/belief first and mouth/confession second, thus forming an ABBA chiasm for emphasis. As in verse 9, the two pairs are virtually synonymous, for confession is the expression of belief, and righteousness/justification is part of the experience of salvation. Paul is summing up his argument thus far in verses 5-9; faith is the only way to have a right relationship with God, and it includes both the mouth and the heart, both confession and belief. To try to get right with God any other way is inadequate and impossible. In Christ, God has graciously provided the only way to him, so all anyone can do is accept his grace-gift by faith.

Finally, in verses 11-13 Paul applies this whole truth of justification by faith alone to the question of who can be saved. The answer is, anyone who believes, whether Jew or Gentile. He begins with another Old Testament quotation to confirm (literally "for" rather than *as*) his earlier citation of Deuteronomy 30:12-14. This one is taken from Isaiah 28:16, used earlier in 9:33. The introductory formula, *the Scripture says,* is more formal than *says* in verses 6-8 (possibly introducing the conclud-ing citations [vv. 11, 13] of the string beginning in v. 5) and is used elsewhere in 4:3, 9:17, 10:11 and 11:2. Paul has added the word *any-one* (literally, "everyone"), not found in the Isaiah passage but used here to stress the universal thrust of the gospel (note "everyone who believes" in v. 4). As in 9:33 it refers to vindication at the last judgment ("never be put to shame" = not face eternal punishment).

The universal scope of the gospel is further explained in verses 12-13. There are three consecutive *for* clauses, each of which adds further nuances to the meaning. First, *there is no difference between Jew and Gentile.* In 3:22-23, this was used negatively to explain that there is no distinction between Jew and Gentile in terms of sin. Both alike stand judged by God because of their depravity. Here it is used positively to say that both alike can be justified on the basis of faith. The Jewish peo-ple thought that they had a special covenant promise that distinguished them from the Gentiles and gave them special privileges. They had ne-glected the Abrahamic covenant, which said that their special place was so that "all peoples on earth will be blessed through you" (Gen 12:3; 18:18; 22:18; 26:4; 28:14). Moreover, they had rejected God's Messiah and so lost their covenant relationship with God. Yet God is gracious and gives them the same promise as he gave to the Gentiles without distinction—Jesus died for everyone, so anyone may be saved through faith in him (e.g., 3:22, 29-30; 4:11-12, 16-17; 5:6-11, 18-19). *Jew and Gentile* stand equally before God in need of justification by faith.

Second, *the same Lord is Lord of all and richly blesses all who call on him.* In 3:29-30 God is God of both Gentiles and Jews, and at first glance one could think this is the case here, especially since in Joel 2:32 (quoted in v. 13) the "LORD" on whose name they call is Yahweh (as also in Ps 99:6; 105:1; 1 Sam 12:17-18; and others). But that does not work here, because in verse 9 the Christian confession is "Jesus is Lord," and Christ is the focus of faith in verse 11, so that is certainly the thrust here. Moreover, in the New Testament the universal lordship of Christ is frequently asserted (see passages noted in v. 9). Jesus then is Lord of Jew and Gentile alike, so both are the recipient of his loving grace. This grace is seen in his riches poured out upon his followers. Elsewhere in Paul God's riches are "lavished" on his people (Eph 1:7; cf. Rom 2:4; 9:23; 11:33; Eph 1:18; 2:7; 3:16; Phil 4:19; Col 1:27; 1 Tim 6:17), but here it is Christ's riches (as also in 2 Cor 8:9; Eph 3:8). Here these riches are the outpouring of his kindness and grace in providing salvation for *all who call on him*. Building on the use of *call on him* in secular Greek to "invoke" the gods in prayer, Cranfield (1979:532) believes this refers to specific prayer to the exalted Christ. However, it should not be narrowed to prayer but includes prayer, worship and a general dependence on Christ for grace and mercy in every area of life (so Godet 1969; Käsemann 1980; Dunn 1988b; Moo 1996). Here it begins with calling on the Lord in faith for salvation (as in v. 13) and continues with the lifelong calling on the Lord that results.

Third, Paul draws this together by citing Joel 2:32 (LXX 3:5), *Everyone who calls on the name of the Lord will be saved.* As in verse 9, *will be saved* refers to the present experience of salvation as a proleptic promise of future salvation at the end of history. What draws this together with verse 12 is *call on,* expressing the way faith is confirmed in turning to Christ for the riches of his grace in redeeming and justifying the sinner. The major emphasis is the other connecting term, *everyone* (vv. 4, 11, 12), pointing to the universal thrust of the gospel. In Joel it is part of the prophecy regarding the pouring out of the Spirit on all people at the Day of the Lord (2:28-32) and refers to the promised deliverance of all who repent and turn to God. While in Joel "all" refers to all Israel, here it refers to all people, Jew and Gentile alike. So salvation (as in vv. 1, 9, 10) refers to universal salvation available to anyone *who calls on the name of the Lord.* As Schreiner argues (1998:562), Paul may intend the larger context of Joel here as well, referring to the gift of the Spirit and eschatological blessings poured out in "the last days" (note the use of Joel 2:28-32 by Peter at Pentecost, Acts 2:16-21). Since the last days have dawned, this is the time when Jew and Gentile alike enjoy the salvific blessings God has promised his people, both justification and sanctification (as in Rom 8).

Israel's Guilt for Rejecting the Gospel (10:14-21) While the promise is the same for Jew and Gentile, the people of the old covenant, Israel, have not responded with faith. Paul begins by tracing the process that conversion takes (vv. 14-15). As often in the New Testament, this list goes in reverse order, beginning with the final step, to *call on* the Lord, and then listing the underlying steps. Thus the order is the sending of the witness, leading to the preaching of the gospel, leading to hearing the message, leading to believing the truth, leading to calling on the Lord. Paul's purpose is to show that this process has been followed in the case of Israel; yet many have not responded in faith although they have heard the message (v. 16-17). So the section concludes with a series of Old Testament passages that prove that Israel has not listened because the people are obstinate, so God has turned to the Gentiles (vv. 18-21).

The list of steps to conversion takes the form of a series of rhetorical questions (see 5:3-5; 8:29-30 for similar lists and 3:1, 9, 27; 4:1, 9; 6:1, 15; 7:1, 7, 13, 24; 8:24, 31, 35; 9:14, 22, 30 for similar rhetorical questions). The questions are equivalent to saying "one cannot unless," so that the item that follows (e.g., belief) is a precondition for the preceding (e.g., calling on the Lord). While it is common to assume that the subject is the Jewish people, it is best to see these as tracing the process every believer must follow (*they* is indefinite), which is then applied to the Jews in verse 16. The list builds on the promise of verse 13 that those who *call on* the Lord *will be saved* and goes backward through the steps leading to the cry of faith resulting in salvation. The necessary basis for a call to God, of course, is belief, as has been said so often previously (seventeen times in 3:21-4:25 alone as well as 10:4, 6, 8, 9, 10, 11 in the immediately preceding context). This is a full-fledged faith that includes belief in the lordship of Christ and his resurrection (10:9). The precondition for belief is hearing the gospel. While some have said that it is Christ who is heard in the preaching (Murray 1968; Cranfield 1979; Dunn 1988b), it is more likely that it is the gospel about Christ (so Sanday and Headlam 1902; Moo 1996), in keeping with the *word of Christ* in verse 17 (see below).

10:15 Some believe that *beautiful* should be translated "timely" or "at the appropriate time," thus lending an eschatological emphasis (so Käsemann 1980; Dunn 1988b; Fitzmyer 1993b; Moo 1996). However, while the Hebrew term can mean either "beautiful" or "timely," it most likely means "beautiful" there (see Oswalt 1998:365),

Hearing is impossible unless there is *someone preaching to them*. The emphasis on the proclamation of the gospel in Paul is widespread. From the start he viewed preaching Christ as the heart of his commission (Gal 2:2; 1 Thess 2:9) and the mainstay of his apostolic ministry (1 Cor 1:23; 15:11-12; 2 Cor 1:19; 4:5; Col 1:23). For the sake of preaching he disciplined himself absolutely (1 Cor 9:27), so preaching the gospel is the core of all ministry (1 Tim 3:16; 2 Tim 4:2). Still, preaching is impossible *unless they are sent*. Without the calling and commissioning by God there is no power or validity in any ministry. A preacher is a "herald" (the meaning of the noun behind *preach*), and a herald has no authority without the sending agent. In fact, an *apostle* is really a "sent one" (the noun cognate of *sent*), an emphasis especially seen in John 17:18 and 20:21 ("as the Father has sent me, I am sending you") in light of the number of passages in John on Jesus as the Sent One (5:23, 24, 36; 8:16, 18, 29, 42 among others). Combining this with 2 Timothy 2:2, there is a powerful passing of the baton from Jesus to the preacher to "reliable [people] who will also be qualified to teach others." But the basis of it all is the authority of being sent as Christ's herald. Finally, Paul anchors this process in a citation from Isaiah 52:7. This is a paraphrase of the original (more of the MT than the LXX), probably to emphasize the act of preaching rather than the proclamation of peace (important in 1:7; 2:10; 5:1; 8:6 but not the point here). The purpose is to demonstrate that both the sending and the preaching are in fulfillment of the prophetic mandate. *How beautiful are the feet* shows that itinerant preaching of the gospel is the highest of callings. As Dunn brings out (1988b:622), Isaiah 52:7 was already understood as messianic in Jesus' time (see 11QMelch 15-19), and that adds force to its use here. The mission of the gospel is in this sense a continuation of Jesus' own ministry. The same must be said for the church today. While the proclaimed word is being de-emphasized of late, and many churches prefer to think of the pastor as a CEO of a business rather than the shepherd of a church, the biblical emphasis could not be more clear. Pastors are to feed their flocks (Jn 21:15-17) and will

---

and since Paul is working with the Masoretic Text, that is the more likely use here as well (so Schreiner 1998). Moreover, the term means "beautiful" in its other New Testament uses (Mt 23:7; Acts 3:2, 10).

be judged by the quality of their handling the word of truth (2 Tim 2:15). Even more, all believers are to be repositories of God's Truth and thereby dispensers of it.

However, while the message clearly went out to Israel, *not all Israelites accepted* (literally, "obeyed") *the good news* (v. 16). As most agree, Paul is actually saying that the majority of Jews have rejected the gospel—"only a few" (NIV, *not all*) have responded. There is a play on words here—they have not "heard" (Greek *akouō*) and so have refused to "obey" (Greek *hypakouō*). Adam "disobeyed" when he sinned (5:19), and obedience is synonymous with belief (1:5; 6:16-17; 15:18; 16:26). So in the case of Israel, the chain has been broken by disobedience/ unbelief. Without active obedience there is no belief. To anchor this, Paul quotes Isaiah 53:1 LXX, *Lord, who has believed our message?* This echoes John 12:38, which also describes Jewish unbelief. Isaiah 52:7 (v. 15) and 53:1 (v. 16) had much the same purpose. God had sent his message of redemption to Israel, but they rejected it. So once again Israel is following the same pattern as before, rejection of the divinely commissioned message.

In verse 17 Paul sums up the process of salvation from verses 14-15 to show that it is still offered to Israel. Even though many in Israel have refused it, the chain is still at work. While at first glance this verse seems out of place, it actually makes perfect sense. In verses 14-15 the process by which the gospel leads to faith is presented, and then Paul states Israel's failure to believe in verse 16. Thus he shows the exact place in the chain where their failure has occurred, namely, in *hearing the message.* They heard in one sense (v. 18) but did not truly hear, for there was no faith response. Both the other aspects—sending and preaching—have been done successfully, but the hearing that leads to faith has not occurred. In this sense verse 16 (Israel has not believed) leads naturally to verse 17

10:17 This verse interrupts the narrative flow and seems out of place because it recapitulates the message of verses 14-15 but does not quite fit verse 16. So some have suggested that Paul would have done better if he had placed it after verse 15 (Barrett 1957), and others have even called it a gloss (Bultmann 1947:199). However, this is unnecessary, for it makes perfect sense where it is. Israel failed at exactly the point noted here, namely, *hearing the message* of the gospel. So Paul in verses 14-15 sums up the gospel, then details Israel's unbelief in verse 16, and finally in verse 17 highlights the one aspect of the chain where Israel failed.

(explaining why it has not believed—it has not heard). *Faith comes from hearing the message.* This parallels Jesus' challenge: "If anyone has ears to hear, let him hear" (Mk 4:9, 23 and parallels; Mt 11:15; Lk 14:35; Rev 2:7, 11, 17, 29; 3:6, 13, 22; 13:9). The Jewish people had ears to hear but did not listen. Moreover, Paul adds, *the message is heard through the word of Christ.* This is "the word about Christ" rather than "the word from Christ" and means the proclaimed word of preaching (vv. 14-15). Indeed, as Acts proves so well, the proclamation of the gospel to the Jewish people was very thoroughly done. In virtually every town that Paul visited on his missionary journeys, he went to the synagogues first, proving his mission principle in Romans 1:16, "first for the Jew, then for the Gentile." Israel was given the "word about Christ" but did not hear it with ears of faith and as a result stood before God guilty of unbelief.

Israel not only heard but understood, as Paul proves by citing several Old Testament passages in verses 18-21. His purpose is to show their deliberate rejection of the gospel and to justify God's judgment of them. Each quote begins with *I ask,* a style used also in 11:1, 11 to make the rhetorical question more personal. Paul asks, *Did they not hear?* Then he answers, *Of course they did.* He wants to clarify his statement in verses 16-17 that Israel failed to truly hear the gospel. In one sense they not only heard it but understood it. To anchor this, Psalm 19:4 LXX is cited. There is a problem in that in the psalm the *voice* that has *gone out into all the earth* is not special but natural revelation; that is, it is nature speaking rather than the gospel. The best solution is found in Moo (1996:666-67, following Hays 1989:175), who says this constitutes an "echo" of the Old Testament text in an analogous direction. He uses the language of the psalm to say that in the same way that God has revealed himself in nature to *the ends of the world,* he has also revealed himself even more clearly through the gos-

---

10:18 Those (e.g., Stuhlmacher 1994; Schreiner 1998) who restrict the preaching *to the ends of the world* to the Gentile mission are wrong. In Acts as well as in Paul the Jewish people are part of the universal mission, and certainly in the echo from Psalm 19:4 Israel as well as the Gentiles are intended. Schreiner's further comment (1998:583) that "the Reformation was propelled by scholars who believed in and preached passionately the doctrine of grace; it probably would not have occurred if Luther, Calvin, and Zwingli were semi-Pelagian" is highly offensive to Arminians. This common assumption that all Arminian theology is semi-Pelagian must be jetti-

pel via the universal mission of the church (this is made more viable when we realize that the second half of Ps 19 moves from natural to special revelation). Yet this introduces a second problem. Does Paul really believe that the gospel had reached the ends of the earth? That is highly unlikely, especially since he yet planned to visit Spain (Rom 15:24, 28). He knew that the mission of the church was incomplete. What this actually means is that the preaching of the gospel to every nation was in process of completion (Bruce 1985:209 calls this "representative universalism"). And if the worldwide mission was being successfully accomplished, the mission to Israel was as well. As in the great commission of Matthew 28:20, the mission to "all nations" means to Jew and Gentile alike. Therefore the people of Israel have no excuse; they have heard.

Paul now turns to the question of Israel's understanding (vv. 19-21). By using the name *Israel,* he emphasizes its religious history, for that was the covenant title for the nation and referred to "its long line of prophets, and its religious privileges and its Divine teaching" (Cranfield 1979:538, following Sanday and Headlam 1902). The Jewish people "knew" (the meaning of the verb) what they were hearing. They knew about the messianic prophecies and about God's intention to bring the nations to himself. They knew that judgment would come upon them if they turned from God. All this is clear from the Old Testament revelation. So Paul turns to a series of quotations, beginning with *first, Moses says*, probably meaning that Moses was the first in a long line of witnesses (though it could be that his was the first of the three here) to testify regarding Israel's knowledge. The quotation is from Deuteronomy 32:21 LXX, part of the farewell Song of Moses. The only change to the LXX is replacing *them* with *you* to strengthen the force of the passage and to contrast the Jews with the Gentiles *who are not a nation* (see Reinbold 1995:124-26). The song celebrates God's covenant faithfulness to Israel in spite of her corruption and idolatry. So since the Jews made God "jealous" with "worthless idols" (Deut 32:21), God *will*

soned once for all. To be semi-Pelagian is to proclaim a salvation by works, but that is exactly what true Arminian theology does not do! Faith is not a work (Eph 2:8-9), and faith-decision does not mean we control the salvation process in any way. In reality, it is the Holy Spirit's convicting presence that makes faith-decision possible,

make you envious by those who are not a nation . . . angry by a nation that has no understanding. As Bruce brings out (1985:210), the mention of their jealousy by a "no people" (the Hebrew in the MT) was probably linked in Paul's mind to the similar language in the prophecy from Hosea 1:10, which had been used in 9:25 ("I will call them 'my people' who are not my people"). Paul saw in both of these passages a prophecy of the Gentile mission. When God turned to the Gentiles, one of his purposes was to provoke Israel to jealousy. Moreover, the Jews should have known this from their own Scriptures. If Israel was angered in the wilderness wanderings, how much more now, for this is the messianic age. The purpose of the jealousy is to make them turn back to God. This will become a central theme in 11:11, 14.

Second, Isaiah prophesies *boldly,* underlining the incredible nature of the truth, citing Isaiah 65:1, *I was found by those who did not seek me; I revealed myself to those who did not ask for me.* Paul reverses the two verbs, possibly to emphasize Gentile conversion *(found)* as resulting in a new relationship with God *(revealed* myself). In the Isaianic context this does not refer to the Gentiles but is God's response to a rebellious nation that had complained he had turned against his people and forgotten them (Is 63:7—64:11). God responds that in their apostasy they had not even called on his name (Is 65:1-2). Paul takes this passage and applies it to the Gentiles. The language of Isaiah 65:1 is particularly apt for the Gentiles (Calvin [1979:405-6] believed it was originally meant for the Gentiles in Isaiah), and so Paul is using another principle of analogy here (as he did in v. 18) to show its aptness for the Jewish people. Indeed, by their apostasy, unbelieving Jews have lost their place in the olive tree (11:17) and now must come to God along with the Gentiles as repentant sinners. This takes us back to the beginning of this section (9:30, so Murray 1968; Moo 1996; Schreiner 1998), where it is the Gentiles who did not "pursue righteousness" but have "obtained it."

Note that in verses 20 and 21 Paul cites in succession Isaiah 65:1

---

and it is God who does the work of salvation, not we ourselves. So Arminians have a very similar view of grace to that of Calvinists; it is entirely the provenance of God and his elect will. But within that there is still faith-decision, as God's grace does the work of salvation within us.

and 2, and applies the first to the Gentiles and the second to the Jews. In Isaiah 65:2 and here there are two elements—God's continuous concern for his people *(all day long I have held out my hands)* and Israel's obstinate response *(to a disobedient and obstinate people)*. Since *all day long* is placed first by Paul (it was at the end of the first line in the LXX) and the stretching out of the arms signifies a fervent appeal, some believe the emphasis here is on God's graciousness (so Cranfield 1979; Morris 1988; Dunn 1988b; Fitzmyer 1993b). Yet in the context the emphasis is on the disobedience and guilt of Israel (so Godet 1969; Murray 1968; Michel 1966). Thus it is best to realize that both are equal emphases here (so Moo 1996). God in his gracious love has always sought his people, yet they have in their obstinacy rejected him.

Conclusion We are now in a better position to discuss the relationship between divine sovereignty (9:6-29) and human responsibility (9:30—10:21). Schreiner (1998:574-75) believes that responsibility is "subsidiary" to sovereignty and that both "Israel's disobedience and the Gentiles' faith were predetermined by God." The former is correct, but the latter must be questioned. There is a better way to portray the relationship than that of double predestination. Sovereignty and responsibility are interdependent, and in a sense we could say that God has "decreed" human choice. To understand this, we must begin with the Fall. God could have created an Adam and Eve who could not have sinned. Then there would never have been the endless wars and atrocities like the Holocaust. There would never have been children dying of malnutrition or leukemia. But without choice there would never have been love, for love demands choice. God did not create evil, but he did create choice, and with choice comes the possibility of evil. The best defense of this is that of Alvin Plantinga, whose "free will defense" is summarized by Stackhouse (2001:74-75): "God deems the cost of evil to be worth the benefit of loving and enjoying the love of these human beings. So, the Free Will Defense concludes, theists can simultaneously affirm that God is good, that God is all-powerful, and that evil exists" (see also Gooch 1987 for an attempt to blend sovereignty and freedom).

So sovereignty demands free will. But how does this work at the level of salvation, specifically in terms of the relationship of predestination to faith-decision? For instance, Moo says (1996:679 n.), "Paul's conception of God's grace (see particularly 4:3-5) would seem to rule out anything outside God's own free will as a basis for his actions. To make election ultimately dependent on the human decision to believe violates Paul's notion of the grace of God." That in fact is correct. But it is not the "human decision to believe" that is the basis for salvation but rather the Holy Spirit's convicting work. Faith is not a "work" but a passive opening of oneself up to the work of the Spirit within. Let us begin with the issue of foreknowledge in 8:29-30. The decision there was that foreknowledge preceded predestination, that God knew who would respond positively to the Holy Spirit's convicting work and chose them to be his children. God's predetermined will is exactly correct, as is the priority of sovereignty over human choice. It is God who demands free choice, and only he can make it possible to overcome total depravity with that choice. This is the theme of 9:1—10:21, that God has made his sovereign choice to judge Israel but that this choice is based on his foreknowledge of Israel's choice to reject the gospel. In fact, this is the theme of 11:1-32, seen in 11:2, "God did not reject his people, whom he foreknew," that is, those in Israel who opened themselves up to the gospel. Marshall (1969:94-95) makes three points: (1) Though God chose Israel, this does not mean the whole nation accepted his gracious offer; he elected them, but that did not guarantee the salvation of everyone. (2) Israel did not fail to obtain salvation because God had rejected them but because they themselves had refused to obey him. (3) The Gentiles as well will be warned that if they do not remain true, like Israel they too will be removed from the olive tree because of unbelief (11:17-21). He adds, "Loss of faith will mean loss of salvation." This viewpoint seems to balance the material in 8:29—10:21 better. God is entirely sovereign, but every individual is accountable to respond positively to God's call to salvation, a response made possible only by the Spirit's convicting work. Israel was elected as the special people of God but lost her place because of unbelief. Then God sovereignly chose to turn to the Gentiles, but Israel is still a focus of his gracious salvific work (11:25-32). God is sovereign, but out of that sovereignty he decreed the free choice of every human being on the basis of the Spirit's convicting and enabling work.

☐ God's Faithfulness: A National Future for Israel (11:1-32)

All children at some time wonder if their parents really love them and ask, "If they do, why are they so mean to me?" This is always at a time when they have been severely disciplined. That is also the situation with Israel. Moreover, the response of parents is quite similar to Paul's answer: (1) Your Father has a perfect right to do what he knows is best (9:6-29), and (2) you have gotten just what you deserve for your actions (9:3—10:21). Chapters 9—11 primarily are a defense of the faithfulness of God in dealing with his covenant people. Chapters 9—10 deal with the negative side: why has he rejected Israel? But Paul has been very careful with his language, never saying that all of Israel has been rejected: In 9:6-7, "*not all* who are descended from Israel are Israel"; in 9:21, "*some* pottery for noble purposes and *some* for common use"; in 10:16, "*not all* the Israelites accepted the good news"; and in 11:17, "*some* of the branches have been broken off." In other words, there are still Israelites who have become part of the new covenant people. That is the topic of this chapter. The theme is stated in verse 2, *God did not reject his people, whom he foreknew.*

There are three subsections in this apology to prove the faithfulness of God to his people: (1) At the present time there is a remnant of Jews who have found Christ and are *chosen by grace* (11:1-10). (2) The removal of *some of* Israel from the olive tree and their replacement by the Gentiles is not permanent and means responsibility for the Gentiles (11:11-24). (3) His faithfulness means that Israel has a national future and will indeed be saved (11:25-32).

The Election of a Remnant from Israel (11:1-10) The language of this chapter is drawn closely from 8:29—10:21, especially the terms for the process of election—*foreknew* (v. 2), *chosen by grace* (v. 5), *elect* (v.

11:1 There are three ways of thinking about this list: (1) It could be a "motivation" (Sanday and Headlam 1902; Dunn 1988b; Fitzmyer 1993b) for Paul's refusal to allow the possibility of God's cutting off his people; speaking as a Jew, Paul found such an idea repugnant. (2) It could provide a "reason" for the argument from the standpoint of Paul's calling as apostle to the Gentiles (Cranfield 1979); the fact that God chose an Israelite to be the bearer of such an important office proves that he had not abandoned his people. (3) It could provide a reason but more from the standpoint of Paul's experience as a Jew under God's grace (Luther 1972; Calvin 1979; Hodge

7) and *hardened* (v. 7). So this is the other side of the coin from 9:6-29. There God chose for eternal punishment; here he has chosen a remnant for himself. He has not rejected all his people, only those among his people who were guilty of unbelief (10:3, 14, 16-21). Yet he has also graciously chosen out of his people a group who have not rejected his Son. There are two sections here, a positive one on the chosen remnant (vv. 1-6) and a negative one on those *hardened* (vv. 7-10). This forms a viable summary of the whole. Israel now consists of two groups: the chosen, *who have not bowed the knee to Baal* (v. 4), and the hardened, who have been condemned by God. Yet on the whole God has not rejected his people, for he has preserved a remnant, and they are his focus, proving that he is faithful to his promises (9:6, 14).

When Paul begins with "therefore I say" (NIV, *I ask then*), he is signaling a major point, as in 10:18-19 and 11:11. Here he is drawing a conclusion from chapter 10. As in the other three, the "I say" is followed by a rhetorical question expecting a negative answer, *Did God reject his people? By no means!* (see also 3:3-5; 9:14). It has just been shown that Israel had not believed the gospel even though the people had clearly heard and understood it (10:16-21). The emphasis on the disobedience and guilt of the Jewish people could easily lead someone to the conclusion that God had rejected *his people*. In 9:25-26 and 10:19 Paul quoted from Hosea 1:10, 2:23 and Deuteronomy 32:21 where apostate Israel is called "not my people" and used these quotations to contrast Israel with the Gentiles. So the opponent is asking whether God has made Israel a not-my-people. Paul denies this outright and, as in chapter 9, repudiates the view that God has failed to keep his covenant obligations to his people. Paul then reminds his readers, as in 9:1-4, of his deep Jewish roots—*I am an Israelite myself, a descendant of Abraham, from the tribe of Benjamin.* This is similar to 2 Corinthians 11:22 and Philippians 3:4-6,

---

1950; Barrett 1957; Käsemann 1980; Wilckens 1980; Stott 1994; Moo 1996; Schreiner 1998). Some (Murray 1968; Morris 1988) try to accept all three, but they seem mutually exclusive. The best is the third, for it is likely that Paul uses his own conversion as proof that one who is completely Jewish can indeed be of the elect. Luther (1972:421) states that Paul was so opposed to the gospel that he of all the Jews should have been cut off. So his conversion is evidence par excellence that God has not abandoned Israel.

where Paul uses an even longer list to establish his right to counter his opponents. His purpose is to use himself as a supreme example of a Jew who has become one of the elect. If he, one of the primary persecutors of Christians and a leader among the Jews, could find Christ, then God has not rejected his people. The three designations he has used here are interesting. He uses *an Israelite* because this was the primary covenant name for the chosen people (see on 9:4). He uses *descendant of Abraham* because of the centrality of Abraham as an example of justification by faith in chapter 4 (also 9:7, 8). The mention of *tribe of Benjamin* is more difficult. Paul could have named this designation because the tribe had a great history—it was "beloved of the LORD" (Deut 33:12); Saul had come from it; and rabbis believed it was the first to cross the Red Sea and would be the basis of unifying the twelve tribes (so Michel 1966; Käsemann 1980; Fitzmyer 1993b). But it is probably added simply as part of the list of Paul's ancestry (so Calvin 1979; Cranfield 1979; Dunn 1988b). Paul is typically Jewish, and he is evidence that God's people are still becoming believers.

So the basic premise is now stated outright: *God did not reject his people, whom he foreknew* (v. 2), closely reflecting Psalm 94:14 and 1 Samuel 12:22 (which have identical wording in the LXX). Several other Old Testament passages also contain God's promise that he would not cut off his people (e.g., Lev 26:11; Deut 31:6; Ps 37:28). So Paul is alluding to one of the basic covenant promises. By changing the future "will not cut off" of the Old Testament passages to the global aorist "has not cut off" (NIV, *did not reject*), he points especially to the unchanging nature of the promise—God still has refused to reject his people. By adding *whom he foreknew,* Paul brings in all the theology of election from 8:28-30. This theme will dominate the section (see the introduction to this section). It is debated whether this refers to the special election of a portion out of Israel (Calvin 1979; Hodge 1950; Schreiner 1998) or the general election of the nation as a whole (Cranfield 1979; Dunn 1988b; Moo 1996). However, in light of the Old Testament citations (as well as Amos 3:2; Hos 13:5 on God "knowing" his people) the latter is more likely here, with special election coming to the fore in verse 5. Although many in Israel have turned their backs on God (note especially the context of 1 Sam 12 here), God has not turned his back on them. They are still his people. Romans 8:35-39 is especially apt here—nothing can separate us from the love of God and of Christ!

The next section (vv. 2-4) introduces the idea of a remnant chosen from within the apostate nation as the recipients of God's covenant love. It begins with the rhetorical question, *Don't you know . . . ?* (compare 6:3, 16; 7:1). This assumes that the readers are familiar with the two passages from 1 Kings 19 *about Elijah.* He was the great prophet who single-handedly opposed Ahab and Jezebel and their plan to introduce Baal worship into Israel. More than any other, he was the prophet who performed miracles, but his purpose was to rescue his people from idolatry. Thus when it says here, *he appealed to God against Israel,* it refers to his complaints against their apostasy. The verb can mean "to intercede, plead" but here has a negative connotation of praying "against" his people. The passages cited are from 1 Kings 19:10, 14 (v. 3), 18 (v. 4). They are part of a section (1 Kings 19:1-18) describing the events after the great victory against the prophets of Baal on Mt. Carmel (1 Kings 18). Immediately afterwards, Jezebel threatens to kill Elijah, and in one of life's great ironies, this prophet who had been the focal point of that great victory runs for his life into the wilderness. There he is cared for by God (vv. 4-8) and then travels forty days and nights to Mount Horeb (where Moses saw the burning bush, Ex 3:1). There he pours out his complaint, which has shifted from Jezebel to the people of Israel and their desertion of him: *Lord, they have killed your prophets and torn down your altars; I am the only one left, and they are trying to kill me.* Elijah's complaint appears twice in 1 Kings 12:10, 14 to emphasize his discouragement and Israel's sins. The differences with the LXX (inverting the first two clauses, slightly altering the others) probably come from Paul quoting from memory rather than for any theological purposes (so Cranfield 1979; Dunn 1988b). Paul uses this to show that the failures of Israel in his own day are no different from those in the past. The nation is still turning against God and his chosen leaders.

After Elijah's lament, God responds, *I have reserved for myself seven thousand who have not bowed the knee to Baal* (v. 4 = 1 Kings 19:18), an abbreviation of the LXX, probably also from memory. Although the majority of the nation has turned against God, he has been faithful to his covenant by reserving for himself a faithful remnant (*reserve* is a major remnant term in the Old Testament, a cognate of *remnant* in v. 5). Here is another example of the balance between sovereignty *(reserved for myself)* and responsibility *(not bowed the knee)* in this passage. God *foreknew* (v. 2) that they would be faithful and so *reserved* them *for himself*. But the emphasis is on sovereignty and election. Some (Michel 1966; Cranfield 1979; Dunn 1988b; Morris 1988) see significance in the number seven thousand, since seven is the number of completeness. However, it is difficult to see why this must be so. Paul is quoting an Old Testament text, and there is no indication he sees numerological meaning in the number (so Moo 1996). At best the emphasis is on the paucity of the number (Schreiner 1998).

Paul applies this to *the present time* when there is also *a remnant chosen by grace* (v. 5). He sees a typological connection between the time of Elijah and the *present* situation of his own day. This might be true in terms both of Israel and of Paul himself, who could well see himself as a type of Elijah figure (so Käsemann 1980; Dunn 1988b; Morris 1988; Moo 1996). Like Elijah, Paul was standing firm and presenting the gospel to an apostate nation, yet finding hope in God's preservation of a remnant. Park (1997:14-17) points out that the remnant idea came into prominence especially among the eighth-century prophets. First was Amos, who foretold the doom of Israel, with only a remnant spared (Amos 5:3), called "the remnant of Joseph" (Amos 5:15), alluding to Genesis 45:7 and saying that only those who seek the Lord will be delivered (Amos 5:4-6, 14-15). There will also be an eschatological remnant who will inherit the Davidic kingdom (Amos 9:11-12). The remnant theology comes into full fruition in Isaiah, again in a context of judgment for the unrepentant nation and salvation for the faithful remnant. The latter is the result only of the mercy of Yahweh (Is 37:32; 46:3), who will purge and purify them so that they will be holy (Is 4:2-3) and redeemed (Is 11:11). He will open a highway for them (Is 11:16) and will be their crown (Is 28:5). The whole concept is bound up with faith and faithfulness to Yahweh (Is 7:3, 9; 10:20-23). This theme is particularly fitting for Paul in response to the situation of Israel in his *present* day. As in Isaiah's time, they have been *chosen by grace.* Each aspect is important for Romans. Election is stressed in 8:33; 9:11; 11:5, 7, 28; and 16:33 (with equivalent terms like "predestined" in 8:29, 30; and "called" in 1:1, 6, 7; 8:28; 9:24-26). *Grace* as opposed to works is emphasized in 3:24; 4:16; 5:2, 15, 17, 20-21; 6:14; and 11:5, 6. It is quite clear that there would be no salvation apart from grace. If all humanity received its just desserts, there would be nothing except eternal damnation. Yet God's lovingkindness and mercy have led him to choose a remnant. Morris says (1988:401-2, following Lagrange), "it was not the number so much as the permanence of God's plan for Israel that mattered in the time of Elijah, and it is this that mattered for Paul too. He put his trust in God's grace, not in numbers."

The grace-not-works concept is spelled out clearly in verse 6: *if by grace, then it* (namely, election) *is no longer by works.* As several say (Michel 1966; Käsemann 1980; Dunn 1988b; Schreiner 1998), the *no longer* is logical, not temporal. It does not mean that in the old covenant salvation came by works. The "not by works" theme is found in 3:20, 27-28; 4:2, 6; and 9:11, 32. The message is that human achievement can never make a person right with God because the law of sin and death is in control, and every individual is unable to be good enough. "I have the desire to do what is good, but I cannot carry it out" (7:18). In fact, as Moo states (1996:678), we are not just dealing here with "the works of the law" per se but with all human works of any kind. "Because of their sin but also simply because of their creaturely status, people can make no claim on God." Paul anchors this by saying, *if it were, grace would no longer be grace.* If divine election/grace were based on human merit, it would be man-centered rather than God-centered and would cease to be grace at all. It is a sovereign act of God that must by necessity be his choice, and as such human effort can have no place in it (on the connection of grace with faith-decision, see the comments at the end of chap. 10).

Paul now clarifies his teaching (note the introductory *what then?*) regarding the remnant in verses 2-6 by separating God's work with *the elect* from those God has *hardened* (verses 7-10). He has just dealt with the positive side of the remnant concept, the remnant God has chosen to save. Now he turns to the negative side, those whom he has chosen to harden. This is the same issue as in 9:6-29, so in a sense Paul is recapitulating the themes he stated there. Moo (1996:679-80) distinguishes three entities—corporate Israel, the elect and the hardened. Yet as he admits, the *elect* do not include the Gentiles in the context of verses 1-10. So it is better to say there is one entity, Israel, made up of the elect and the hardened. In 2:17-18 Israel relied on the law, knew God's will and approved what is superior, but failed to teach themselves; in 9:31 she "pursued a law of righteousness" without attaining it; and in 10:2 she was "zealous for God" but without knowledge. Here Israel *sought* salvation *earnestly* but *did not obtain* it. This in fact is the reason for Paul's deep sorrow in 9:2-3, where he said "I could wish that I myself were cursed and cut off from Christ for the sake of my brothers [and sisters]." However, only the elect attained right standing with God, and that was a source for joy. Paul uses the same term for *elect* as in 9:11 and 11:5, and it places "special emphasis on the action of God as that which is altogether determinative of the existence of the elect" (Cranfield 1979:548). God is in control. On the other side are *the others* who *were hardened* (a divine passive), making clear the point that again divine action is emphasized. This points back to 9:14-18, which concludes, "God has mercy on whom he wants to have mercy, and he hardens whom he wants to harden" (v. 18). While the two verbs for harden in 9:18 and here are different, they are synonymous in referring to a spiritual callousness toward the gospel. The verb here is a medical term for a stone in the bladder or the hardening when bones are knit together (Cranfield 1979; Schmidt and Schmidt 1967:1025-26). Thus it connotes a refusal to listen and consider God's call to salvation.

Three Old Testament texts (v. 8 conflates two passages) are used to support this harsh reality. As Moo notes (1996:681), Paul "follows Jewish precedent in using each of the three main divisions of the Hebrew canon: the 'law' (Deut. 29:4), the prophets (Isa. 29:10), and the 'writings' (Ps. 69:22-23)." The first is drawn from Deuteronomy 29:4, which begins the concluding charge of Moses to the people of Israel before they enter the promised land. Deuteronomy 29:1-8 summarize themes from the book, with verses 4-5 looking back to Deuteronomy 8:2-4 on God watching out for Israel during the wilderness wanderings (see Craigie 1976:356). In that context the point was a positive one: they had not understood the events of the wanderings because "to this day the LORD has not given you a mind that understands or eyes that see or ears that hear" (Deut 29:4), but that would come in time as God continued to lead his people. Paul changes the thrust by altering the opening to the positive *God gave them* and turning the rest into negatives *(not see . . . not hear)*. As a result Paul uses the passage to anchor a far more negative issue—spiritual hardening. It seems likely that Paul has in mind Isaiah 6:9-10, that oft-cited passage on God hardening Israel ("Be ever hearing, but never understanding; be ever seeing, but never perceiving"), quoted in Mark 4:12 and parallels; John 12:40; and Acts 28:26-27. This is also seen in Paul's inclusion of a phrase from Isaiah 29:10, *a spirit of stupor* (Isaiah, "deep sleep"). The actual term is fairly rare and is found only here in the New Testament and only in Isaiah 29:10 and 60:3 in the LXX, meaning a spirit of "torpor" or "stupefaction" (Sanday and Headlam 1902; Cranfield 1979; Dunn 1988b), that is, an inability to comprehend spiritual truth. The tone here comes more from Isaiah 29:10 and 6:9-10 on the hardening of Israel's heart, for Isaiah 29 also centers on divine judgment against Israel (Dunn 1988b:641 shows how often this chapter is used in the New Testament to support the theme of Jewish blindness).

The third text is taken from Psalm 69:22-23 LXX. Psalm 69 was used often in the early church to support Jesus' life and especially his passion (Mk 3:21; 15:23, 36 and parallels; Jn 2:17; 15:25; Acts 1:20; Rom 15:3; Phil 4:3; Heb 11:26; Rev 3:5; 16:1). This makes it especially apt for Paul to apply the portion of the psalm on David's "enemies" (Ps 69:19) to the enemies of Christ (so Moo 1996; Schreiner 1998). The emphasis is not on details like the table or their back but on the general tenor of the quote. What links this with the Deuteronomy 29 citation in verse 8 is the idea of the *eyes darkened so they cannot see,* so the accent is on *a snare and a trap, a stumbling block and a retribution.* Paul is asking God to confirm their hardness and rejection, to condemn them for their unbelief. The *stumbling block* first appears in 9:33 (also 14:13, 16:17), where it is part of the stone imagery ("a stone that causes men to stumble and a rock that makes them fall"); so this asks God to cause their failure and destruction. The theme of darkness is seen in 1:21 of the total depravity of the Gentiles and in 2:19 of the Jewish pretense that they were "a light for those who are in the dark" when in fact they were equally guilty. So all these images are part of the theme of absolute depravity that turns upon itself. The final part asks that *their backs be bent forever,* perhaps requesting eternal punishment, though several (Cranfield 1979; Fitzmyer 1993b) prefer the translation "continually," thus meaning as long as they remain closed to the gospel. Morris concludes (1988:405), "Paul sees catastrophe as inevitable for unbelieving Jews as they continue to reject the gospel."

God's Future Place for Jews and Gentiles (11:11-24) Since Paul is "apostle to the Gentiles" (v. 13), he feels he has to place in perspective all that he has said in chapters 9—11 thus far. Fitzmyer (1993b:608-9) believes Paul in this passage sees three purposes in the failure of Israel: to bring salvation to the Gentiles, to make Israel jealous and to bring about their eventual share in salvation (a coming from death to life). In the present, Israel is separated into a remnant minority and a hardened majority, but that is not God's plan for the future. He still has a salvific intent, beginning with his turning to the Gentiles.

There are two parts in this section: (1) In verses 11-16 the rejection of Israel has as its purpose the coming of salvation to the Gentiles, namely, "the reconciliation of the world" (v. 15); yet the further purpose is to make Israel jealous and bring them to salvation. (2) In verses 17-24 God has removed many Jewish branches from the olive tree and replaced them with Gentile branches; but that should produce humility not pride, for the Gentiles are also responsible to God and can in turn be removed.

Three of the four stages of this section are found in verse 11:

Israel has been rejected, but this state is not permanent (v. 11a).

11:9-10 The basic tenor of the quote is widely agreed on. However, it is strongly debated how much meaning should be attributed to details such as *May their table become a snare and a trap* or *May . . . their backs be bent forever.* Some (Cranfield 1979; Moo 1996; Schreiner 1998) believe there was no allegorical thrust in details like the *table* or the *backs.* Rather, they were simply part of the Old Testament text that implied judgment on the hardened Jewish people. On the other hand, many see significance in such details, seeing in the table a symbol of the Jewish sacrificial cultus (Käsemann 1980; Dunn 1988b), the bounties of God's providence (Murray 1968), the centrality of table fellowship for the Pharisees (Michel 1966), a misuse of Scrip-

The immediate purpose of rejection is to bring salvation to the Gentiles (vv. 11b, 12).

The more distant purpose is to make Israel jealous through the Gentiles (vv. 11c, 14).

This will eventually bring Israel back to God (vv. 14-16).

As in 11:1-10 this section begins with *I ask* followed by a rhetorical question expecting a negative answer. Again this device is used to counter a possible misunderstanding stemming from what has just been said (v. 11). In verse 9 the psalm citation asked God to make "their table" a "stumbling block," meaning to cause them to fall, and the strong language could make one think that fall would be irredeemable. So Paul asks, *Did they stumble so as to fall beyond recovery?* The question is whether God's rejection of his people is final and irrevocable. The answer is, *Not at all!*

In fact, not only is it retrievable, but it is also an important stage in salvation history, for *because of their transgression, salvation has come to the Gentiles*. The word *transgression* looks back to the "trespass" of Adam in 5:15-21 (six times) and the consequent sinfulness of humanity (4:25). Some (Barrett 1957; Fitzmyer 1993b) translate it "false step" and link it with the verb *stumble* in the first half of the verse. However, that is doubtful (see Cranfield 1979; Dunn 1988b). It is rather showing that the sin of rejecting the gospel on the part of the Jews has a positive result, namely, that God has turned to the Gentiles. So it is part of God's plan of salvation. This was certainly the case during the missionary journeys. When the Jews revealed their "jealousy" and kicked Paul out of the synagogues, he would turn to the Gentiles (Acts 13:45-46; 18:6-7; 19:8-10). So the great commission was fulfilled partly through Jewish opposition.

tures by the Jews (Morris 1988), trusting in the law (Sanday and Headlam 1902; Barrett 1957), or the false security, well-being and community of the Jews (Stott 1994). The bent back has been variously seen as slavery, grief, fear, oppression, weakness or even blindness (see Cranfield 1979). While some of the options are attractive (especially dealing with the sacrificial cultus or the law as a whole), there is no indication in the context that we are to allegorize the details, and no way to prove which might be correct. On the whole, it is best to be cautious and see only a general sense in the quote.

However, this does not complete the picture. God also used the success of the Gentile mission *to make Israel envious*. In a very real sense, this jealousy worked in two directions. It caused the Jews to persecute the church intensely (Acts 13:45; 17:5), but here its purpose is to make the Jews want back what they had lost, namely, their right relationship with God. This probably goes back to the Deuteronomy 32:21 quotation in 10:19, "I will make you envious by those who are not a nation." God is using the Gentiles to remind Israel of what they have lost and to stimulate their return to him. Origen said it well: "Consider the wisdom of God in this. For with him not even sins and lapses are wasted, but whenever someone rejects freedom of his own accord, the dispensation of divine wisdom makes others rich by using the same failing by which they have become poor" (Bray 1998:291).

Clearly the main point for Paul is the return of Israel to God. He seems to consider the Gentile mission, as dear as it is to his heart, as a step to the really important thing, the *fullness* of the evangelization of his Jewish people. It is clear that Paul in verses 12-16 is addressing his Gentile readers explicitly, not only because he says so in verse 13 but also with his use of the third person for the Jews in these verses. He wants the Gentiles to understand why the conversion of the Jewish people is so important. He uses two *if* clauses to highlight the benefits of Jewish rejection of the gospel. The two are virtually synonymous and center on *salvation* for *the Gentiles* from verse 11. The basis is Israel's *transgression* (the same term as in v. 11) and her *loss,* a rare term that means "inferior," "weaker," "defeated" and infers that their rejection of Christ is their defeat (so Murray 1968; Cranfield 1979; Fitzmyer 1993b). At the same time it produces *riches for the*

11:11 Moo (1996:686) believes that *they* of verse 11 and *their* of verse 12 refer not to the hardened segment of Israel (vv. 7-10) but to Israel as a whole and therefore verse 7. So it is Israel as a whole that has failed to attain the right relationship with God it was seeking; and it is not the hardened who will be saved. However, by the use of *stumble* here in verse 11, Paul is clearly linking it with verse 10 and therefore with verses 7-10. The hardened are not those who have committed the unpardonable sin but those who are currently rejecting Christ.

11:12 *Fullness* (Greek *plērōma*) can have several different meanings in a context like this. Cranfield's list (1979:558) is quite helpful: (1) complete conversion or restoration; (2) fulfillment, consummation or perfection; (3) obedience in terms of fulfilling

world and *for the Gentiles,* respectively (the two are synonyms here). These *riches* are kingdom blessings, all the wealth of being children and heirs of God (8:14-16). They include salvation as well as sanctification, the "riches of his kindness, tolerance and patience" (2:4) as well as the "riches of his glory" (9:23). More difficult to understand is the last part, *how much greater riches will their fullness bring!* While the statement could connote the idea of both "fulfilling God's will" and the conversion of "the full number" of Jews, it is best to see it as looking forward to the salvation of "all Israel" in 11:25-32. The "defeat" of God's people through unbelief is the sad situation for the present, but there is a glorious future ahead for Israel when "the full number" will come to Christ. Paul's point here is that the current unbelief is wonderful in the sense that it brought God's *riches* to bear on the Gentiles, but *how much greater* will the *riches* be when Israel also returns to God. Donaldson (1993:92-94) sees strong implications for the whole motif of Israel's rejection, arguing that Paul does not see so much a spatial displacement of the nation as a temporal delay of Israel's salvation. In other words, offering *riches . . . for the Gentiles* has as God's ultimate purpose the final salvation of the Jewish people. The turning to the Gentiles is a temporal delay in God's plan of salvation centering on the parousia of Christ as the deliverer of the nation. Israel's rejection opens up not space but time for the divine will to operate.

In verses 13-14 Paul goes on a slight tangent (many scholars believe this is parenthetical) and returns to his own deep-seated concern for his people (see 9:11-5; 10:1; 11:1-2). His own calling to minister to the Gentiles has a deeper purpose, to bring the Jewish

---

God's will; or (4) the full, complete number. Of these the two most likely would be the restoration of Israel as fulfilling or completing God's will for his people (so Hodge 1950; Lenski 1945; Murray 1968; Hendriksen 1981) or the conversion of the full number of the Jewish people (so Godet 1969; Barrett 1957; M. Black 1973; Cranfield 1979; Bruce 1985; Käsemann 1980; Dunn 1988b; Fitzmyer 1993b; Schreiner 1998). A few (Morris 1988; Moo 1996) believe both may well be intended. While the latter may be true, the parallel with verse 25 ("the full number of the Gentiles") makes the quantitative ("full number") more likely (see also Rev 6:11, "until the number . . . was completed").

people to salvation by arousing their envy. So he makes explicit that he is *talking to you Gentiles* when he explains this ultimate goal. Several (Godet 1969; Sanday and Headlam 1902; Dunn 1988b; Fitzmyer 1993b; Moo 1996; contra Cranfield 1979) believe this indicates Gentiles were in the majority at Rome. Paul wants them to understand the inner motivation behind his ministry. He has not forgotten his Jewish heritage; indeed, part of his reason for ministering to the Gentiles is to use it as a wedge for the salvation of Israel. Paul is *the apostle to the Gentiles;* this was the commission he received in the Damascus Road vision (Acts 26:17-18), which was then confirmed by Ananias (Acts 9:15) and a temple vision (Acts 22:21). He considered it one of the great apocalyptic "mysteries" (Eph 3:3-6, 6:19-20; Col 1:26-27). It was the core of his life, but even then a critical aspect of his larger strategy was to use this ministry to the Gentiles to awaken a longing for God and Christ among his countrymen.

So he goes on to say that *I make much of my ministry* (literally, "glorify my ministry"), probably meaning that he esteems and takes great pride in his ministry to the Gentiles, zealously working very hard at it (so Godet 1969; Dunn 1988b; Moo 1996). He "glories" in it, though, not only to see Gentiles come to Christ, but also *in the hope that I may somehow arouse my own people to envy and save some of them.* We have seen this jealousy earlier in 10:19 and 11:11. Paul's desire once again was to *arouse* or "provoke" Israel, to force them to envy as they saw God pour out upon the Gentiles the blessings that used to be theirs. This would then drive them to reconsider Christ and discover the *riches* to be found in him. Paul reveals here that by "all Israel" (11:26) he does not mean that every single person will be saved (Paul is not a universalist). But his modest hope is that *some of them* will find faith in Christ. He had no delusion that somehow every single Jewish person would be converted but did trust that through

---

11:15 *Life from the dead* has occasioned a great deal of discussion. (1) Many (Calvin 1979; Hodge 1950; Godet 1969; Lenski 1945; Murray 1968; Leenhardt 1961; Morris 1988; Stott 1994; Fitzmyer 1993b) take this in a metaphorical sense for the conversion of the world (Godet 1969; Morris 1988; Lenski 1945) or Israel (Calvin 1979; Fitzmyer 1993b) because Paul does not use "resurrection from the dead," his usual phrase for the final resurrection, and because the parousia is not mentioned in the context. (2) Most of the Greek Fathers (Origen; Theodore of Mopsuestia; Chrysos-

him *some* would come to Christ.

Verse 15 returns to the point of verse 12 (Israel's *rejection* leads to the world's *reconciliation*) yet at the same time anchors verses 13-14 (the return of Israel will bring incredible blessings to the world). As Dunn says (1988b:657), "the ultimate success of the Gentile mission depends on Israel's acceptance." In the only other occurrence in biblical Greek of the word here translated *rejection,* it means "loss" ("not one of you will be lost," Acts 27:22). However, it may well have its other sense here of being "thrown away" (by God, with *their* actually being an objective genitive, God rejecting "them"), in opposition to *acceptance* in the second clause. In other words, God rejects them in order to accept them later (so Murray 1968; Cranfield 1979; Wilckens 1980; Dunn 1988b; Moo 1996; Schreiner 1998). So while in verse 12 the Jewish people are the active agents, in verse 15 God once again is the central figure. Jewish unbelief produces *the reconciliation of the world,* referring to the act of bringing the world into right relationship with God (see on 5:10). Building on 5:9-10, *reconciliation* may well imply the accomplishment of this by the death of Christ and its acceptance by the world, that is, by both Jews and Gentiles (Cranfield 1979 sees this as an either-or, but Dunn 1988b rightly sees it as a both-and). Yet the main thrust of the verse is certainly in the final conclusion, that God accepting them back means *life from the dead.* This could refer to a literal resurrection of the believer at the eschaton but more likely is used figuratively of the conversion of Israel as *life from the dead* (reflecting the same idea as 6:13). Paul may be thinking once more of the valley of dry bones in Ezekiel 37:2-14. The restoration of Israel is a spiritual resurrection from the dead.

Finally, Paul illustrates the return of the Jewish people from the dead by using two metaphors. The first comes from Numbers 15:17-21, in which God commanded that the Israelites, after entering the prom-

tom), as well as many other commentators (Sanday and Headlam 1902; Barrett 1957; Bruce 1985; Nygren 1949; Cranfield 1979; Käsemann 1980; Dunn 1988b; Wilckens 1980; Moo 1996; Schreiner 1998) take it literally as a reference to the final resurrection from the dead, arguing that in the relation with verse 12 this must be something more than the "salvation" of verse 11 and the "riches" of verse 12, namely, the physical resurrection of believers. Since the restoration of Israel will be at the end of history (v. 25), the *life from the dead* must follow that and occur at the eschaton. They

ised land, take the *firstfruits* of the cake of dough they used for baking their bread and offer it to the Lord. This looked forward to the grain offering that would be given once they were in the land. Paul's point, that from these firstfruits *the whole batch is holy,* is not made in Numbers, and several explanations have been offered, such as parallels with Leviticus 19:23-25 (the consecration of the fruit trees; so Cranfield 1979) or with the temple as making all of Jerusalem holy (so Dunn 1988b) or a Pauline principle like "a little yeast works through the whole batch of dough" (1 Cor 5:6; so Moo 1996). It is probably best to see Paul as simply using rabbinic logic to make his point. When firstfruits consecrated a harvest, then the harvest was set apart for God. The second metaphor is similar and more easily understood: *if the root is holy, so are the branches.* The holiness of the firstfruits/root makes certain the holiness of that which they affect, the batch/branches. The difficulty is ascertaining the point that Paul is making. Of the possibilities (see below), the more likely is that of Abraham and the patriarchs. Abraham's faith is the center point of Paul's argument for justification by faith (chap. 4), and he appealed to Abraham as his ancestor in 11:1. Because Abraham and the patriarchs were set apart by God to convey his blessings on the nation as a whole, the nation is still special in

---

argue further that *from the dead* nearly always refers to physical resurrection (Schreiner [1998] lists only Rom 6:13; Eph 5:14 as exceptions out of forty-seven passages) and that Paul's apocalyptic perspective favors the literal view. However, one of those exceptions provides the nearest parallel; Romans 6:13 has, "offer yourselves to God, as those who have been brought from life to death." Moreover, the solution is closely related to the ongoing discussion about whether Paul, in using salvation terminology in recent chapters, is thinking of present or final salvation. In these chapters it has been decided often that there is an inaugurated aspect reflecting tension between the already and the not yet (see on 6:5; 8:2, 10, 30; 9:22-23; 10:9-10). So there may well be double meaning here, spiritual life now and final resurrection life at the eschaton. However, the figurative most likely predominates, for the return of Israel (better than *the world* in this context) to salvation in Christ (more a present than a final thrust) is seen as a return of *life from the dead.* Paul's thrust throughout this section is on rejection versus belief, and that better fits a figurative use of *life from the dead* similar to that in 6:13.

11:16 It is difficult to say whether verse 16 provides a conclusion to verses 11-15 or an introduction to verses 17-24. The use of *branches* may favor the latter (so Sanday and Headlam 1902; Murray 1968; Käsemann 1980; Wilckens 1980; Moo 1996), but the theme of *firstfruits* may favor the former (so Cranfield 1979; Dunn 1988b; Morris

God's eyes. It is important to understand that this does not mean they were set apart for salvation (in terms of individual salvation); rather they were set apart as the special people of God (so Moo 1996). Israel still remains the focus of God's love.

The second half of this section (vv. 17-24) develops the root and branches metaphor into a picture of the current relationship of Jews and Gentiles to God. As Dunn explains (1988b:660-61), there are two reasons for the image of the olive tree: Israel is sometimes called an olive tree (Jer 11:16; Hos 14:6), and the olive tree was widely culti-vated in the Mediterranean, so the procedures for cultivating it were well known. Still, as is generally agreed, the olive tree here repre-sents the whole people of God and not just Israel. Paul begins with a lengthy *if* clause (v. 17) that assumes the reality of the condition (Is-rael broken off and the Gentiles grafted in) and then concludes with a warning (v. 18, the *then* clause, *do not boast*). First, *some of the branches have been broken off*. It is important to note that *some of* in-dicates only those Jews who have rejected the gospel. This is the point of chapters 9—11 thus far (see the introduction to 11:1-32). The majority have turned away from Christ, but many Jewish people have turned to Christ and remain part of the olive tree. The emphasis is on

---

1988; Schreiner 1998). All agree that it is transitional. On the whole it is probably better to see verse 16 concluding the first section, for the themes fit that better, and to see the idea of *branches* as a catchword uniting it with the second section. So it il-lustrates the theme of Israel's return from the dead (v. 15) and prepares for the olive tree and branches illustration of verses 17-18.

11:16 There are three main interpretations of the *firstfruits* and the *root:* (1) the pa-triarchs, since the *root* would be natural for them and verse 28 says Israel is "loved on account of the patriarchs" (so Calvin 1979; Sanday and Headlam 1902; Murray 1968; Morris 1988; Käsemann 1980; Wilckens 1980; Moo 1996; Schreiner 1998); (2) Jewish Christians, the "remnant" (v. 14) from whom the whole nation is to be saved (so Barrett 1957; Hafemann 1988:51); or (3) Jesus Christ as the basis of salvation (so many church vathers like Clement of Alexandria, Origen and Theodore of Mopsues-tia). Since the *firstfruits* would easily fit the Jewish Christians and the *root* the patri-archs, some (Bruce 1985; Cranfield 1979; Harrisville 1980; Fitzmyer 1993b) think the metaphors each have a different meaning, but that is unlikely. Paul places them side by side, and they complement each other. Both a remnant idea and that of the patri-archs can make sense, and it is a difficult choice. However, it is hard to see the Jew-ish Christians as the root of the nations, and Paul's use of the patriarchs in verse 28 makes it slightly more likely that he has the patriarchs in mind here as well.

individuals, not the corporate nation. This is also seen in the fact that Gentiles have been grafted in *among* the Jewish Christians (not "in place of" them). Moreover, these Gentiles have been *grafted in* as *a wild olive shoot*. Davies (1984:158-63; also Moo 1996) points out that the wild olive tree was quite unproductive, and normally grafting used a cultivated shoot rather than a wild one. So Paul has deliberately turned the imagery around to make his point that the Gentiles have nothing to boast about. They are a wild olive shoot and have done nothing to warrant God's turning to them. It is only by God's grace (the passive verbs point to God as the one who performs the action) that the Gentiles can be productive as God's children. So the engrafted Gentiles *share in the nourishing sap from the olive root.* The olive tree was famous for the amount of sap it produced, so this is an apt picture of the bounty that the Christian has in Christ.

Since the privilege is a gift from God and has no basis in merit, the Gentiles are warned, *do not boast over those branches.* Like Israel, they could become proud of their election and forget the true source of it. The verb *boast over* describes the Gentiles comparing themselves to the Jews and feeling superior (see Bultmann 1965:653-54), so the idea is that the Gentiles believe they are more privileged than the Jews and lord it *over* them. It is generally agreed that the *branches* here are all Jews and not just the unbelieving ones (so Sanday and Headlam 1902; Cranfield 1979; Dunn 1988b; Moo 1996). Many Gentiles began to feel they were now the chosen ones and that the Jewish Christians were inferior (see chap. 14). The Jewish people have already been condemned about such boasting (2:17, 23), and now it is the turn of the Gentiles. All the glory must go to God. This is a very important principle. Pride is one of the basic human sins, and the tendency of all too many is to feel superior to others because of gifts God has given them. It is also common for this to be seen along racial or ethnic lines, for one group to feel their brand of Christianity is superior. This type of paternalism was a problem in missions in the nineteenth and twentieth centuries, when missionaries often proclaimed the superiority of Western civilization as much as the gospel. So Paul tells the Gentiles the truth: *you do not support the root, but the root supports you.* In verse 16 we learned that the root was

Abraham and the patriarchs. So the Gentiles are reminded that they are not the source of blessing to the Jews; rather, they have received the blessing that has come down to them because of what Abraham has accomplished (see chap. 4). The direction of the privilege is obvious, from Abraham to the Jews to the Gentiles. In fact, the Gentiles are Abraham's offspring (4:11-13, 16-18; 9:7-8) and dependent entirely on what they have received from him.

The proper response is not pride of place but responsibility and warning. Paul again chooses a typical opponent. The basic response of the proud Gentile is, *Branches were broken off so that I could be grafted in* (v. 19). Note the centrality of I (the pronoun *egō* is present in the Greek for emphasis). In other words, the Gentiles are saying that God removed the Jewish people just so he could turn to them. Paul responds with a qualified yes: *Granted* (this is true). *But . . .* It is only a half truth, for while God did indeed turn from the Jews to the Gentiles, he turned to the Gentiles "to make [Israel] envious" (10:19; 11:11). Moreover, *they were broken off because of unbelief,* not because God preferred the Gentiles. In contrast, the Gentiles *stand by faith,* not works. This is the basic point of chapters 4—11 as a whole. There is no ground for boasting because salvation is entirely *by faith,* not human merit (3:27; 4:2). There can be no pride when one becomes a part of God's family. One of the basic lessons (and a difficult one to learn by hyperachieving people today!) is that we are nothing and God is everything.

Paul concludes, *Do not be arrogant, but be afraid. Arrogant* means to "think highly of yourself" (cf. Rom 12:16; 1 Tim 6:17), to have an over-inflated view of your own worth. Instead, there are grounds for fear, *for if God did not spare the natural branches, he will not spare you either.* It is common today to read *fear* in the Bible as *reverence,* but this is another passage where the meaning is closer to the modern meaning of fear, for the danger is rejection. There are three overtones in *fear* passages—fear, awe and reverence. These are not mutually exclusive, but it goes too far to read worship into warning passages (like many do in Phil 2:12 or 1 Pet 1:17). Porter (1993:292), after discussing Romans 3:18 and 11:20, says, "The link between fear and reverence as an appropriate response to God and fear or terror for disobedience is well illustrated by these passages." However, the emphasis here is on the terror side, for the danger is that God *will not spare* the Gentiles in the same way that he rejected the Jews. Since the *wild olive shoot* is not as valuable as the cultivated ones (see on v. 17), why should it expect more mercy? Moreover, cultivated branches are stronger than grafted ones (so Dunn 1988b; Stott 1994), so the weaker branches should be even more cognizant of the dangers. The danger is final judgment, so this is a serious warning indeed. The proper response is the kind of fear noted in Philippians 2:12, "work out your own salvation with fear and trembling." Yet it is not a descent into pure terror but a reasoned sense of responsibility that leads us to work hard at our walk while depending on God, since "it is God who works in you to will and to act according to his good purpose" (Phil 2:13).

In light of all the privilege and responsibility that the Gentiles have received (vv. 17-21), Paul asks them to *consider . . . the kindness and sternness of God* (v. 22). Schreiner (1998:608) calls this a "restatement and elaboration" of the meaning behind *fear* in verse 20. The removal of unbelieving Jews from the olive tree is divine "severity" (NIV, *sternness*) while the grafting in of the Gentiles is his *kindness*. The term for *kindness* refers to God's goodness and mercy (see on 2:4), shown in his acts in bringing the Gentiles to himself. His *sternness* refers to "the inflexible hardness and severity" of God as Judge; cf. Wisdom of Solomon 5:20, 22; 6:5; 12:9; and 18:15, where God is "a sovereign monarch who judges justly but does not have to give account to any for his acts" (Köster 1972:107-8). The Jewish people *who fell* into unbelief (v. 20) experienced the severe judgment of God, with the imagery of falling stressing their own responsibility for their actions (so Dunn 1988b; see Rom 11:11; 1 Cor 10:12; Heb 4:11; Rev 2:5). There is

---

11:22 Several (Murray 1968; Gundry-Volf 1990:198-99; Moo 1996; Schreiner 1998) argue that the imagery of *provided that you continue . . . otherwise, you also will be cut off* does not constitute a warning that Christians can lose their salvation. The response is that this does not refer to true believers but to those who are members of the Christian community (the visible church) and seem to be part of the true church (the invisible church). When they fall away, they show they have never truly belonged. This is certainly viable and is in fact the best Calvinist response to passages like Hebrews 6:4-6; 10:26-31; 2 Peter 2:20-22; and others. But does it suffice in passages like this? Paul has been speaking individually throughout, and the Jews who

a distinct contrast between the Jews who *fell* and the Gentiles who *stand by faith* in verse 20. Those who depend on their own merit will fall, and only those who stand on God will find salvation. But the Gentiles must *continue in his kindness,* that is, persevere in their walk with God, as in Colossians 1:23, "if you continue in your faith." The emphasis here is on God's *kindness* (three times in this verse!). Faith is not a work that we accomplish (Eph 2:8-9) but a privilege given to us by God, and we are responsible to maintain our relationship with him. *Otherwise,* Paul goes on to warn, *you also will be cut off.* This is the flip side of the security promised in 8:28, 35-39. God faithfully performs his work of kindness in bringing us into his family and protecting us securely with his power (1 Pet 1:5), but we must *continue* to persevere in his *kindness,* lest we lose it all. As Moo states (1996:706), "ultimate salvation is dependent on continuing faith; therefore, the person who ceases to believe forfeits any hope of salvation (cf. Rom 8:13; Col 1:23; Heb 3:6, 14)."

Paul now turns back to the Jewish people (v. 23). Those among Israel who have rejected the gospel are still the focus of God's salvific love. In fact, one of the major purposes for the Gentile mission was to make the Jews jealous (10:19; 11:11, 14) to experience God again and to draw them to Christ. Therefore, *if they do not persist in unbelief, they will be grafted in.* This is the opposite of verse 22. The Gentiles must *continue* in their faith, while the Jews must not *continue* (same verb) in their unbelief. Those who have been *broken off* from the olive tree (v. 17) but come to faith in Christ will then follow the Gentiles as grafted branches. While they have lost their place in the true people of God and cannot regain their forfeited position, *God is able to graft them in again.* As Jesus said regarding the salvation of the wealthy, "With

---

were *cut off* were not all of true Israel but were those individuals who did not believe. Similarly, those Gentiles who have experienced the *kindness* of God would naturally in this context be not all Gentiles but those who have believed. It is difficult to relegate this warning only to those who are in the church but have not yet believed. That is not hinted at anywhere in the context. Therefore it seems a valid warning that any believing Gentile who falls away (as many Jews have) will also be *cut off.* Gundry-Volf is correct that those who are cut off may indeed be grafted in again, but so long as they are cut off they are headed for divine judgment and eternal death (compare Jas 5:19-20).

man this is impossible, but not with God; all things are possible with God" (Mk 10:27). The Greek is stronger than the NIV: "God has the power to graft them in again." The emphasis on divine power is also found in 4:21 ("God had power to do what he had promised") and 9:22 ("choosing to show his wrath and make his power known"; cf. also 1:4, 20; 9:17). All is made possible not by human worth but by divine grace seen in divine power. The Gentiles are not to think that they are in and Israel is out. In fact, God has brought the Gentiles into his family as part of the process of bringing Israel back (11:11, 14), so there is no room for pride.

The metaphor of the olive tree is continued in verse 24 to illustrate the point. In doing so, he repeats his "how much greater" argument of 11:12. If God had the power to graft a wild olive branch, the Gentiles, onto the olive tree to which they did not naturally belong, *how much more readily* would he be able to graft the Jewish people *into their own olive tree.* This is similar to verse 21 in continuing the contrast between the wild and the natural olive branch. There are two contrasts: the wild branch is less productive than the natural branch, and it is against nature to graft one into a natural olive tree. In both, the natural branch is superior. The point is that if God has the power to bring the "wild" Gentiles to himself, he certainly has the power to bring the "natural" Jews to himself. Yet it is important not to take the metaphor too far. This does not mean God cares more for the Jewish people than for Gentiles, nor that Jews have an advantage over Gentiles. Just the opposite—Paul is responding to some Gentiles who believed that they had an advantage over Jews and were boasting (v. 18). Since Paul spent so much time on Gentile boasting (vv. 17-24), it is likely that this was a real problem in the Roman church. Some there must have felt that they were superior to their Jewish-Christian

---

11:24 Many place *by nature* with the olive tree, as in the NIV's *an olive tree that is wild by nature* (NRSV; NASB; Barrett 1957; Käsemann 1980; Schreiner 1998), but several rightfully point out that this is tautologous, since it is unnecessary to say a wild olive tree is naturally wild (so Cranfield 1979; Moo 1996); these translate "the wild olive tree you belonged to by nature." Thus the emphasis is on the grafting of the Gentiles rather than on the tree.

11:24 Moo (1996:709-10) provides a valuable summary of the issues here, focusing on the olive tree as depicting the basic unity of God's people. Stemming from the

brothers and sisters and that God cared only for them. This is always a huge mistake. We are equally sinful, and we are equally the object of God's love.

Future Salvation for Israel (11:25-32) This provides a natural conclusion for the whole of chapters 9—11, not just for chapter 11. The question all along has been the justice of God and the destiny of Israel. In chapter 9 the issue was the possible failure of God's promises to Israel and his justice and faithfulness. Paul answered that God is sovereign (9:6-29) and that Israel had failed to believe (9:30—10:21). Then in chapter 11 the theme of God's faithfulness continues in terms of the national future for Israel. There is currently a remnant (vv. 1-10), and even the "stumbling" of Israel unleashed the power of God, which led to a three-stage salvific purpose—the conversion of the Gentiles led to making Israel envious, which will lead to the salvation of Israel (vv. 11-24). This section then concludes the process by detailing the certainty of this future salvation of God's people after the Gentile mission (vv. 25-26) and then grounding it in Old Testament promises (vv. 26-27), the irrevocable nature of God's call (vv. 28-29) and God's mercy to the disobedient (vv. 30-32). Thielmann (1994:179-80) argues that there is no contradiction between the rejection of Israel in 9:6-13 and her future salvation in 11:25-32, as some have said (e.g., Sanders 1983:192-98). Rather, Paul teaches that Israel's salvation is based not on human ethnicity but on divine choice (9:6-13).

Paul begins with *for* (omitted in NIV), showing that the regrafting of the natural branches (v. 24) is made certain by the knowledge of the great *mystery* God has revealed to him. The introductory *I do not want you to be ignorant* was used earlier in 1:13 (cf. 1 Cor 10:1; 12:1; 2 Cor 1:8; 1 Thess 4:13) and points to important information (so Cran-

---

Old Testament, the image shows that Jew and Gentile together are the true people of God. There is no actual transition from one to the other, and there is no truth in the notion that the church has replaced Israel. Rather, there is continuity from Old Testament Israel to New Testament church composed of both Jews and Gentiles. Two issues are part of this: (1) there is no basis for anti-Semitism, for the Jewish people are equally the object of divine love as are Gentiles, and (2) all cultures and races become one in Christ. There is no possibility of racism, for every race and ethnic group is brought into both unity and equality in Christ.

field 1979). A *mystery* is an apocalyptic concept for a salvation-historical event that has not been known but has now been revealed by God in these last days for the sake of his people. The primary mystery for Paul is Jesus Christ himself and his work of salvation (Rom 16:25; Eph 1:9; 6:19; Col 2:2; 4:3; 1 Tim 3:16) and then the Gentile mission itself (Eph 3:3-6; Col 1:26-27). It is debated whether Paul received this from God through general study of the Old Testament (Cranfield 1979) or special prophetic inspiration at this time (Michel 1966; Bruce 1985). But there is no reason to choose between them, and both personal meditation and divine insight were probably involved (Dunn 1988b; Moo 1996). Here the mystery centers not on present but final salvation (as also 1 Cor 15:51) and on the Jews rather than the Gentiles. Paul's purpose is to counter the problem of conceit, better translated, "lest you be wise in your own estimation" (so Dunn 1988b). Some Gentiles, as seen in verses 11-24, thought that they had displaced the Jews in God's family. As Moo (1996:715) suggests, this was not so much "a sense of superiority engendered by spiritual giftedness or accomplishments" as it was "an attitude of ethnic pride and exclusiveness." Paul counters this by revealing God's *mystery,* namely that *Israel has experienced a hardening in part until the full number of the Gentiles has come in. And so all Israel will be saved.* It is generally agreed that all three parts constitute the *mystery.* While scholars have often debated which is the central point of the revelation, it is doubtful whether Paul saw one element as more critical than another.

11:25 The mysteries were well known in the Roman world of the first century, associated with the mystery religions. These centered on secret initiation rites and rituals and were private associations that people joined, such as the Eleusinian mysteries centered on Attica (the most popular of the cults) or the Egyptian cult of Isis or the Iranian cult of Mithra (see Aune 1993:792-93). However, Paul's use of *mystery* came not from Hellenism but entirely from Judaism, beginning with Daniel (2:17-30) and then found frequently in intertestamental apocalyptic (e.g., *2 Baruch* 81:4; *4 Ezra* 14:5; *1 Enoch* 51:3; 103:2; see O'Brien 1993:622). Kim (1997:420-22) believes Paul came to realize this mystery soon after his conversion by reflecting on the significance of his Damascus Road vision via Isaiah 6 and 49.

11:25-26 Scholars debate the central point of the mystery. Some (Cranfield 1979) believe it is the future salvation of Israel because the others point to it. Others (Moo 1996; Schreiner 1998) argue that it is the comment that Israel will be saved after the

1. Paul begins by saying that Israel's *hardening* is partial and temporary. Paul has taught the divine hardening of Israel in 11:7-10 and probably linked it to the hardening of Pharaoh in 9:14-18, concluding with "he hardens whom he wants to harden" (9:18). The *in part* could modify *Israel* (so Barrett 1957; Käsemann 1980; Morris 1988), thus indicating that only some of the Jews have been hardened; or *hardening*, indicating a partial hardening (so Hodge 1950; Dunn 1988b); or *experienced*, indicating it has partially come on Israel (so Michel 1966; Cranfield 1979, Moo 1996). Since it is adverbial in force, *in part* must modify the verb (partially *come*), meaning that the present is a time of hardening in which most of the Jewish people will remain closed to the gospel.

2. Yet it is also a temporary hardening that will continue until the "fullness of the Gentiles" has arrived (the literal translation of the Greek). It is difficult to know whether "fullness" means completing the Gentile mission (Munck 1967:133-35), the complete blessing God intends for the Gentiles (Murray 1968) or the full number of Gentiles God has destined (most commentators). The third translation best fits the parallel of the "fullness" of Israel in 11:12. This concept was well known in Israel, as evidenced in Revelation 6:11, which discusses the completion of the number of martyrs before God will vindicate the saints (cf. also *4 Ezra* 4:35-37; *2 Baruch* 23:4). So the great revival of the Jewish people will take place at the end of history after the times of the Gentiles.

3. At that time *all Israel will be saved. And so* means that by bringing the Gentiles to himself, "in this manner" God would reach the

time of the Gentiles, since that is the only new element here. In reality, however, there is no indication Paul is elevating one element over another. The whole constitutes the revelation, and each part leads to the next.

11:26 *And so* could be (1) temporal, "and then" (emphasizing temporal order; so Barrett 1957; Käsemann 1980), but that is an unlikely meaning for the Greek; (2) connected to *as it is written* (meaning "and so Israel will be saved, as written"; so Stuhlmacher 1994); (3) emphasizing results, "and so" (so Fitzmyer 1993b); or (4) manner (Israel will be saved in this way; so Sanday and Headlam 1902; Cranfield 1979; Dunn 1988b; Moo 1996). The last is the most natural and fits the context well. Through the process of bringing the Gentiles to himself, "in this way" God will win Israel as well.

11:26 The primary debate here is the meaning of *all Israel*, seen as (1) all the elect, comprising Jews and Gentiles alike (many of the church fathers as well as

Jewish people. This in fact is the process outlined in verses 11-14 (see the introduction to vv. 25-32). The conversion of the Gentiles would arouse the Jews to envy and bring them to Christ. *All Israel* refers not to the Jewish people down through the ages but to the nation at the end of history who *will be saved*. The text clearly does not detail how this will come about but rather promises the event itself, with the Isaianic quote in verses 26-27 indicating that it will be connected to the parousia of Christ. Some have suggested a "special way" in which Gentiles are saved by faith in Christ and Jews by their faithful adherence to Torah, but this is certainly foreign to Paul with the centrality of faith over the works of the law as well as to the New Testament emphasis on Christ as the only way to God (Jn 14:6; Acts 4:12; see the excellent critique of this in Hafemann 1988:38-58; Moo 1996:725-26). The promise of Israel's future salvation has developed throughout this section (11:1-24). At present there is a remnant who have come to Christ, but the majority in Israel have been hardened (vv. 1-10). Yet the purpose of this hardening has unleashed a powerful act of God whereby he first has brought the Gentiles to himself and grafted then into the olive tree. But even this act has been purposed to make the Jewish people jealous and cause them to want to regain their covenant relationship with God (vv. 11-24). The result is that after the Gentile mission is complete (v. 25), Israel will experience a national revival and come to Christ.

Paul now anchors this in Old Testament fulfillment (vv. 26-27), conflating Isaiah 59:20-21 LXX and 27:9 LXX. Isaiah 59 centers on the sinful-

---

Calvin 1979); (2) the elect from Israel (Lenski 1945; Hendriksen 1981); or (3) the nation of Israel (Barrett 1957; Cranfield 1979; Dunn 1988b; Moo 1996). The first is unlikely since the context is discussing Jews and Gentiles separately, and in verse 25 "Israel" refers to the Jewish people. The second is possible but would be tautologous since by definition the elect will be saved. The third is most likely, but the question is whether this would lead to universalism, that every Jewish person will be saved (so Barth 1933). But as Moo says (1996:722), *all Israel* does not mean "every Israelite" but is rather a corporate designation. Paul has already talked about God rejecting many Jews, and this interpretation parallels "the full number of the Gentiles" in verse 25. So this refers to a great number of Jews rather than every Jewish person. Another issue is how Israel will come to salvation. A few (e.g., Stendahl 1976; Mussner 1976) believe there is a "special way" (German *Sonderweg*) to salvation, the Gentiles by faith and the Jews by faithfully observing Torah.

ness and injustice of Israel confessed to Yahweh, with the result that
Yahweh puts on his armor (Is 59:17) and repays his enemies (Is 59:18)
while forgiving the repentant. *The deliverer* ("redeemer") in Isaiah is
Yahweh, while here it is Christ. Moreover, Paul changes Isaiah's "come
to Zion" to *come from Zion*. The question is whether Paul is assimilat-
ing this to another Old Testament passage on redemption coming
"from Zion" (probably Ps 14:7; so Bruce 1985; Cranfield 1979; Fitzmyer
1993b; Schreiner 1998) or makes the change himself, probably bringing
in the motif of the "heavenly Zion" from which Christ will return (Heb
12:22; cf. Gal 4:26; Rev 3:12; 21:2; so Käsemann 1980; Dunn 1988b;
Moo 1996). Of the two, the latter seems more likely, for it is certainly
the parousia that Paul has in mind (compare 1 Thess 1:10; contra Fitzmyer 1993b).

When Christ returns, he *will turn godlessness away from Jacob.* In
the context of Romans 11, this must be the unbelief of verse 23 and the
hardness of verse 25. This refers to the conversion of the people (*turn*
can also mean "remove," so Dunn [1988b:683] via Bauer et al. 1979). In
so doing Christ would renew *my covenant with them,* which is from
Isaiah 59:21 but might also include the new covenant of Jeremiah
31:31-34 (so Murray 1968; Morris 1988; Schreiner 1998; contra Moo
1996), in which God will "put my laws in their minds" and "forgive
their wickedness" (the passage is quoted in Heb 8:8-12). The old covenant led to the new covenant of grace established by Christ (in his first
advent), and here that new covenant is finalized with respect to Israel.
Here once more we have the already-not yet tension so endemic to Ro-

---

Needless to say, this has been highly criticized (especially Hvalvik 1990; see the
extensive bibliographies in Moo 1996 and Schreiner 1998) as both exegetically and
theologically impossible.

11:26 There is also debate over the meaning of *will be* saved. Does this have a di-
achronic sense and mean the Jewish people will be converted in every period of history (so Sanday and Headlam 1902; Munck 1967:135-36; Dunn 1988b; Fitzmyer
1993b)? It is far more likely that this should be understood synchronically to refer to
a conversion of the nation at the end of history (so Cranfield 1979; Gundry-Volf
1990:183-85; Moo 1996; Schreiner 1998). The progression of thought requires this. It
occurs after the "full number of the Gentiles has come in," referring to the end of the
Gentile mission, and *will be saved* seems in this light to point to an event after this.
So the present hardening and time of Gentile mission anticipate the future promise
of a full harvest of the Jewish people as well.

mans. The new covenant was inaugurated in Christ's first coming (especially in his death and resurrection; see Rom 4:25), and it is seen now in the Gentile mission. But it will be consummated in the restoration and conversion of Israel at the second coming.

To Isaiah 59:20, Paul then adds a final clause from Isaiah 27:9, *when I take away their sins*. Isaiah 27 (like Is 59) centers on the deliverance of Israel and forgiveness of her sins. There God's judgment of the nation leads to her repentance, a perfect picture of Israel here in Romans 11. In both passages the divine condemnation or *hardening* has redemptive purposes; "the hardening of Israel is temporary and intended to lead to her ultimate deliverance" (Moo 1996:729; contra Schreiner 1998). The Jewish people will realize who Christ is, repent of their transgressions and hardness, and be restored to the covenant. It is impossible to know exactly how this will take place at the parousia. Paul tells us the what but not the how. We will have to leave the method up to God, especially since the other passages on the return of Christ detail the resurrection of the saints (1 Thess 4:13-20; 1 Cor 15:51-57) and the destruction of God's enemies (1 Thess 5:1-10; 2 Thess 2:8-12; Rev 19:17-21) rather than the conversion of Israel. All we can know is that it will happen, not how it fits into the other details.

Verses 28-32 are a single unit (Schreiner makes them a separate section [1998:624]). These verses (just as vv. 25-27) discuss the theological meaning but not the method of the conversion of Israel: Through the love of God, those who were once enemies and disobedient to God will receive mercy and be called to him. Yet these verses also function as a summary of chapters 9—11, reiterating that God has called not only the Gentiles but the Jews to himself. They begin with two parallel clauses containing three word-pairs: *gospel/election, enemies/loved* and *on your account/on account of the patriarchs*. Paul starts with, *as far as the gospel is concerned, they are enemies on your account*. The *gospel* could be Christ as the content of the gospel (Dunn 1988b) or the progress of the gospel in the world (so Cranfield 1979), but it more likely refers to both aspects (Schreiner 1998). Because the Jews rejected the gospel and op-

---

11:29 *Gifts and . . . call* could be separate ("the gifts and the call"; so Cranfield 1979; Morris 1988), one entity ("the benefits of the call"; so Calvin 1979; Käsemann 1980), or with the calling a special kind of gift ("the gifts, especially the call"; so Michel

posed its proclamation to the world, they became *enemies* of God (cf. 5:10) and of the church and therefore the object of God's wrath and judgment. The idea of *enemy* is both active (they hate God) and passive (they are considered by God to be his enemies; compare Is 63:10; Jer 30:14; so Käsemann 1980; Moo 1996; Schreiner 1998).

Verses 28-32 thus summarize the themes of chapters 9—11: Israel rejected the gospel (9:30—10:21) and thus was rejected by God (9:6-29). Moreover, this was done "for the sake of" (NIV, *on your account*) the Gentiles. This goes back to 11:11-15, in which the "rejection" of the Jews meant "salvation" and "reconciliation" for the Gentiles. When the natural branches were broken off, the wild shoots were grafted in (v. 17). This is part of God's plan of salvation—the rejection of the Jews led to the inclusion of the Gentiles, and that in turn will lead to the jealousy of the Jews and through that to their conversion as well. This latter part is the message of the second clause—*as far as election is concerned, they are loved on account of the patriarchs.* Election is the major theme of chapter 9, and it speaks of God's control of salvation history. God has chosen to reject some and to accept others, as in the quotation of Exodus 33:19 in Romans 9:15, "I will have mercy on whom I have mercy, and I will have compassion on whom I have compassion." God's gracious choice of Israel is a hallmark of biblical truth (11:5-6). Throughout the Old Testament, Israel is the chosen people because of God's unswerving love for them (2 Chron 9:8; Ps 102:13; Is 14:1; 41:8-9; 44:1), so even though many have rejected Christ and become his enemies, God's love is still upon the nation. It is interesting that this love is with them *on account of the patriarchs.* This does not mean the patriarchs have done anything to merit the divine love or to produce it for the people; God's love is by grace, not works (11:6). Rather, the patriarchs are mentioned because the covenant promises were given to the nation through them (Gen 12:1-3; 13:14-17; 15:1-21; 17:4-19; 22:16-18; 26:3-5; 28:10-15). They were the source of God's covenant blessings, and it is those promises that are the basis of his elect will.

This in fact is the thrust of verse 29, *for God's gifts and his call are*

1966; Moo 1996). It is not easy to choose between these (Dunn [1988b] believes Paul would accept all three), and so the third may be slightly better because of the emphasis on the call in this section.

irrevocable. The *gifts* most likely are those enumerated in 9:3-5, the privileges and blessings Israel has experienced as the covenant people. The greatest of these gifts (see below) is their *call* to be God's special people. They are the chosen people of God, and the elect will of God is *irrevocable,* a strong term meaning God will never "regret" or feel "remorse" for his call. The reverse of this is seen in Matthew 21:29, where the son who had refused to work in the vineyard "changed his mind and went," and also in Matthew 27:3, where Judas was "seized with remorse" and returned the thirty pieces of silver. So this means that God will never change his mind and regret the promises he had made to Israel. God's faithfulness to his covenant promises is everlasting; even though many of his people have turned their back on God, he will never turn away from them. The unchanging faithfulness of God is found often in the Old Testament (Num 23:19; 1 Sam 15:29; Job 12:13; Ps 33:11; Jer 4:28). This of course does not mean that he will never reject those who have rejected him (see in v. 28 on *enemies*). Rather, he will be faithful to the nation even though he will have to condemn many within it. As Moo says (1996:731-32), the choice of Israel "does not mean salvation for every single member of the nation, but blessings for the nation as a whole."

Paul now tells how this love has manifested itself in spite of the disobedience of many in Israel. Verses 30-31 are a carefully constructed *just as . . . so . . . too* sentence explaining the same point made in verses 11-15: God has used the disobedience of Israel to save the Gentiles and now is using the mercy shown the Gentiles to save the Jews. The Gentiles *were at one time disobedient,* referring

---

11:31 There are two ways to translate this verse, depending on whether we see "for mercy to you" (literally translated) modifying "disobeyed" or "received mercy" (both are possible). The majority take it with *received mercy* and so translate it similarly to the NIV, *so they too have now become disobedient in order that they too may now receive mercy as a result of God's mercy to you* (so also KJV; NASB; NRSV; NJB; Godet 1969; Sanday and Headlam 1902; Michel 1966; Lenski 1945; Murray 1968; Cranfield 1979; Morris 1988), with some taking the last clause as "because of God's mercy to you" (Hodge 1950; Fitzmyer 1993b). This has the advantage of producing a similar order as in verse 30, with the dative phrase modifying the last verb, and also centers on Jewish conversion as a result of the Gentile mission (as in vv. 11-15). However, a

back to 1:18-32 and the description of their total depravity. The pagan world was under God's indictment because of the Gentiles' willful refusal to follow God (see "suppress the truth" in 1:18, "without excuse" in 1:20 and "know God's righteous decree" in 1:32). Yet even though they deserved nothing, they *now receive mercy,* referring to the new era in which God has turned to the Gentiles. Paul considered this a *mystery,* an apocalyptic era in which God revealed a new reality, namely, the mission to the Gentiles (Eph 3:3-6; Col 1:26-27). This new reality was so astounding to Paul that it took three revelatory events to enable Paul to accept it (Christ on the Damascus Road [Acts 26:17-18] as confirmed by Ananias [Acts 9:15-19] and a vision in the temple [Acts 22:21]). Yet even this was only made possible *as a result of [Israel's] disobedience.* This reiterates a major emphasis of this chapter (vv. 11-12, 15), that Jewish unbelief led God to turn to the Gentiles and graft them into the olive tree (v. 17).

Paul then turns from the situation of the Gentiles to that of the Jewish people. Here I depart from the NIV and see a three-part message: "So now they also have disobeyed for the sake of (God's) mercy to you, so that they also may now receive mercy." The first two parts sum up the message of verse 31 and therefore of chapter 11, that Jewish disobedience has resulted in the Gentile mission. Paul has reversed the order of verse 30 in verse 31 in order to create a chiasm. But there is a final step, and that is the theme of verses 25-32—Jewish conversion. While Jewish disobedience has led to God's *mercy* shown to the Gentiles, Gentile conversion leads first to Jewish envy (10:19; 11:11-15) and then to their conversion (11:15-16, 25-32). Yet this is not the case in the present. Israel has *now become disobedient,* and the present is the time

---

significant minority (NLT; Calvin 1979; Barrett 1957; Käsemann 1980; Wilckens 1980; Dunn 1988b; Moo 1996; Schreiner 1998) prefer to see it modifying "disobeyed" (NIV *become disobedient*) producing a chiasm with verse 30,

"you have received mercy because of their disobedience" (v. 30)
"they have disobeyed for the sake of mercy to you" (v. 31)

This fits the more natural order of the Greek, since "for the sake of mercy to you" follows the verb "disobeyed" and precedes the clause "so that they may now receive mercy." Moreover, this produces a message that is equally at home with Paul's teaching in chapter 11 (see above) and so is to be preferred.

of the Gentile mission. However, Paul has probably added another *now* in the final clause, and this complicates the message. It is possible to take this as adding a second implication: while one portion of Israel is *now* disobedient, another portion is *now* being converted. But it is better with most commentators (Cranfield 1979; Morris 1988; Moo 1996; Schreiner 1998; with Michel 1966; Käsemann 1980; Dunn 1988b taking it as referring to an imminent "End" of history) to see this as referring to the imminent future as an "eschatological now"; that is, the conversion of Israel can occur at any time. It is also difficult to know whether this refers to the process of the Jewish mission (as in 1:16, "first for the Jew"; so Cranfield 1979) or to the final conversion of Israel (as in 11:25-26) as at any time in the *now* future (so Moo 1996; Schreiner 1998). The first view makes more sense; it is simplest to take this in an inaugurated sense, so that the ongoing Jewish mission is a proleptic anticipation of the final harvest at the end of the age.

Summing up the message on God's mercy to both Jew and Gentile, Paul says (v. 32), *For God has bound all men over to disobedience so that he may have mercy on them all.* As throughout chapters 9—11, the emphasis is on the sovereign initiative of God in "confining" or "shutting all people up" in disobedience. Dunn (1988b:688-89) points out that the closest parallel is Galatians 3:22-23 ("the whole world is a prisoner of sin," reminiscent of Ps 31:8; 78:50, 62), with an echo of the threefold "handed over" (NIV, *gave over*) in Romans 1:24, 26, 28. By using *disobedience* Paul also creates a balance in God's punishment of imprisoning people in the very *disobedience* they have preferred for themselves. In this sense it sums up the previous emphasis on God's sovereignty (9:6-29) and human responsibility (9:30—10:21). Still, God's purpose was not condemnation but *so that he may have mercy on them all.* While some have taken this to mean universal salvation (Dodd 1932; Cranfield 1979; Dunn 1988b; Wilckens 1980 say it is a possible conclusion), this is impossible in light of the constant emphasis on final punishment at the eschaton (1:18; 2:5-11; 6:21, 23; 9:22, 28).

11:31 The second *now* in the last clause of verse 31 is disputed because it is missing in p[46], codex Alexandrinus, two corrections of codex Bezae, the Majority Text and several others. However, it is found in codices Vaticanus and Sinaiticus, the original codex Bezae and several others. While the manuscript evidence is fairly balanced

Therefore, it is likely that the *all* here is corporate, meaning that God's mercy will be shown to Jew and Gentile alike (so Calvin 1979; Murray 1968; Cranfield 1979; Stott 1994; Fitzmyer 1993b; Moo 1996; Schreiner 1998).

☐ Concluding Doxology (11:33-36)

The theme of Gentile and Jewish conversion lifts Paul to the heights of religious ecstasy. God's mercy is so great that human language is inadequate to describe it. So he concludes with a hymn that forms a doxology of praise to the great God who has done all this for unworthy humanity. It forms a conclusion to his message in chapters 9—11 and possibly to chapters 1—11 as a whole (so Fitzmyer 1993b). As Paul meditates on human sinfulness and divine grace, as he thinks about the depths of divine mercy that has reached down to Gentile and Jew alike in spite of their terrible depravity and unbelief, he can only exclaim in wonder about the unbelievable depth of God's riches and the inscrutable nature of his judgments. Indeed, no one can know *the mind of the Lord*. The nine-line hymn is constructed in a series of threes: three exclamations (v. 33; the first names three divine attributes), three questions (vv. 34-35) and a threefold prepositional formula (v. 36; see Deichgräber 1967:61-64; Dunn 1988b; Fitzmyer 1993b).

Paul begins with an awestruck exclamation regarding *the depth of the riches of the wisdom and knowledge of God*. Although the NIV makes it seem that there are two attributes listed after *depth of riches,* the term *riches* is also an attribute; the line should read "the depth of the riches and wisdom and knowledge of God" (contra Murray 1968; Schreiner 1998). The *depth* of God refers metaphorically to the inexhaustible immensity of his attributes. No one can comprehend the vastness of who he is. There are three areas of his depth here, which Moo (1996:741) labels his "communicable attributes" because human beings share them to an extent and because they describe God interacting with his creation. The *riches* of God refers back to 2:4, 9:23, 10:12 and

---

(perhaps slightly stronger evidence for its inclusion), it is also the more difficult reading, since on the surface it seems to contradict the *now* in the first clause. Therefore, it is likely that it should be seen as original (see also Cranfield 1979; Dunn 1988b; Fitzmyer 1993b; Moo 1996; Schreiner 1998).

11:12 and to his rich mercy and grace (in 2:4, "the riches of his kindness, tolerance and patience") shown to unworthy humanity in bringing salvation to them. His *wisdom* refers to his plan of salvation as expressed in 3:21—8:39, the accomplishment of his wise will in the atoning sacrifice of Christ and the offer of salvation to the world, Jew and Gentile alike. The *knowledge of God* (specifically his knowing us, not our knowing him) could mean generally his omniscience and as such be virtually synonymous with his *wisdom,* but in Romans it may well be meant specifically of his foreknowledge (8:29; 11:2) of us. Thus *knowledge* would refer to his predetermined will, a central theme of chapters 9—11. All three—*riches, wisdom* and *knowledge*—relate primarily to his saving knowledge and plan.

The two exclamations that follow develop further God's incredible *wisdom and knowledge.* The two are parallel in structure as well as meaning. *His judgments* are *unsearchable* or "inscrutable," and *his paths* or "ways" are *beyond tracing out.* The word *judgments* refers not negatively to final judgment or condemnation (as in 2:2; 5:16) but rather to God's decisions in general, especially his decision to bring salvation to humankind (thus they certainly include "sternness" as well as "kindness"; see 11:22). His decision to make "some pottery for noble purposes and some for common use" (9:21) is "inscrutable" or "unfathomable, impossible to understand" (see Job 42:3; Ps 147:5; Is 40:28). Many quote *2 Baruch* 14:8-9, "O Lord, my Lord, who can understand your judgment? Or who can explore the depth of your way? Or who can discern the majesty of your path? Or who can discern your incomprehensible counsel? Or who of those who are born has ever discovered the beginning and the end of your incomprehensible counsel?"

11:33 Let me apply this to the central debate on election and eternal security explored in chapters 8—11. Theologians pretend to know more than they actually do and make absolutist statements about their decisions. One scholar recently even said that all Arminians are going to hell because by definition they have to deny the sovereignty of God. Such hubris is a sin in itself. While we must all work out our understanding of such important issues as predestination to the best of our abilities, we must do so humbly, recognizing our partial knowledge. On these issues there are important passages on both sides, and each of us must respect the other and be "iron sharpening iron" as we discuss the issues. It is time to quit fighting over such ultimately unknowable doctrines, for "we know in part and we prophesy in part" (1

God knows us, but we do not understand God. The only solution is to trust his greater judgment as we encounter the mysteries of life. The *paths of God* would be the action side of his *judgments*. When God's decisions are acted out, they also are *beyond tracing out* or "incomprehensible." God's sovereign actions (especially in salvation history here) can never be truly understood by mere human beings, believers as well as unbelievers. The mysteries Paul has explored in these chapters will only be comprehended when we get to heaven. For now we must simply accept God's greater wisdom.

The three rhetorical questions (vv. 34-35) build on this theme of the inscrutable nature of God's ways. The first two allude to Isaiah 40:13 LXX, part of the well-known turning point of Isaiah that begins "Comfort, comfort my people" (40:1) and describes how God would reveal his glory and rescue his people. In the midst of confusion and doubt, God is faithful to his promises. Paul may well have in mind the whole of that section. In the same way that deliverance seemed impossible in the days of Isaiah, so too God has now promised to save Israel in a far more significant way. The answer is quite clear—no one *has known the mind of the Lord*, and no one *has been his counselor*. God is indeed inscrutable, and human beings can only watch in awe as he performs his will. Paul also quotes Isaiah 40:13 in 1 Corinthians 2:16, where Paul concludes, "but we have the mind of Christ." At first glance the two passages seem to contradict each other, but Paul in 1 Corinthians is actually saying that no one can know God's mind except through the revelation of the Holy Spirit in Christ, and that is compatible with this (see Schreiner 1998:635-36). The point is that God's knowledge of salvation history is absolute while ours is finite, so none of us can be his *counse-*

Cor 13:9). This does not mean we cannot take a strong stance on the issue (this commentary does—see comments at 8:29-30 and the conclusion to chap. 10), but the positions must be held heuristically and with respect.

11:34 Some (Käsemann 1980; Fitzmyer 1993b; Moo 1996) have seen a chiastic order in which the first question *(mind of the Lord)* parallels *paths beyond tracing out,* the second *(counselor)* parallels *unsearchable . . . judgments,* and the third *(given to God)* parallels *the depth of the riches.* But that stretches the language and fails to fit the development of thought. It is more likely that the questions build on the general idea of verse 33, namely, the unknowable mind of God.

lor. We all depend on his knowledge and his will, so we live lives of Christ-dependency (the true meaning of *faith*).

The second Old Testament text alluded to is Job 41:11 (apparently a Pauline paraphrase of the Hebrew text), quoted as *Who has ever given to God, that God should repay him?* In Job this is toward the end of Yahweh's speech (Job 38—41) where Yahweh declares that he is sovereign over everything, for "everything under heaven belongs to me" (41:11). As Schreiner points out (1998:637), Job has been doubting the justice and wisdom of God (note the parallel with 9:6, 14), and here God responds that he alone has the wisdom to "superintend the world." Paul is faithful to Job, for *given* means to "give beforehand" so that God would be obligated to *repay.* No one has ever been able to *give* something to God so that God owes them anything. Rather, all accept God's gifts as a free act of grace on his part. *Wisdom* and *knowledge* (v. 33) are beyond us (v. 34) and come to us as a free gift from God (v. 35).

All of this (vv. 33-35) is grounded *(hoti, for)* in the fact that God is the source *(ek, from),* instrument *(dia, through)* and goal *(eis, to)* of *all things* (compare 1 Cor 8:6 of God, and Col 1:16-17 of Christ). While there is strong background for this in Stoic writings of the first century, it is likely that the basis for this is in Hellenistic Judaism, whose writers borrowed from the Stoics (so Cranfield 1979; Dunn 1988b; Moo 1996). This clearly undergirds the sovereignty of God over all things in creation, a fitting climax to chapters 9—11. God is in charge and determines all things, so no one can know his mind. He reveals all truth, so no one can be his counselor. He is the giver and thus the controller of salvation-history. Therefore, only one conclusion is possible: *to him be the glory forever.* The One who has made salvation possible and who has brought both Jew and Gentile to himself is the one who deserves *glory* above all else. As the Westminster Catechism says, God created humanity to "glorify him and to enjoy him forever." It is indeed our privilege to magnify his name and to enjoy his loving presence. The *amen* affirms the validity of the doxology (cf. 1:25; 9:5).

LIVING LIFE IN THE SPIRIT (12:1—15:13)
When we get up every morning, we go to a mirror and examine our-

selves to see where we need to make changes in order to make our-selves presentable to others. What good would it be to look in the mirror, shrug our shoulders and go outside without changing a thing? That is the point James makes in James 1:23-24. To look into the Word of God (the mirror of our soul) and ignore what it shows is the height of folly. When we are changed by the gospel, we must show this change in our daily conduct. That is exactly what Paul is saying in the rest of Romans. In 1:18—11:36 Paul has developed the meaning of the gospel and created his own soteriology—the Christian has been res-cued from a life of sin that would have led to everlasting punishment and has been transferred to the realm of righteousness by the atoning death of Christ, i.e., been justified by faith. Now Paul turns to the prac-tical difference it must make in our conduct. Chapters 1—11 are prima-rily in the indicative and reflect right belief, while chapters 12—15 turn to the imperative and reflect right conduct. Actually, this is not the first time Paul has made this point. He has mentioned "the obedience that comes from faith" in 1:5, "persistence in doing good" in 2:7, "live a new life" in 6:4, "slaves to righteousness" in 6:18, and "live according to the Spirit" in 8:5-6. What Paul foreshadowed in chapters 1—11 he now spells out clearly—what life in the Spirit looks like.

This movement from indicative to imperative was a common prac-tice for Paul, as reflected also in Galatians, 1 Thessalonians, Ephesians and Colossians. Moreover, these are not just general issues but address specific problems, like spiritual gifts (12:3-8), relation to persecutors (12:14-21), relation to government (13:1-7), and the strong and the weak (14:1—15:12). It is common to regard these as issues that reflect the situation of the early church as a whole, but more and more it is thought that several of these are more specific to the Roman church (see Cranfield 1979; Moiser 1990; Fitzmyer 1993b; Moo 1996; Schreiner 1998). This section is divided into two subsections: 12:1—13:14 (exhor-tation to live the Christian life) and 14:1—15:13 (the problem of the strong and the weak over meat offered to idols). As Towner points out (1999:153-54), the unity/disunity theme dominates and ties the section together, with the exhortation to harmony bracketing the section (12:16, 15:5) and *one another* a major motif (12:5, 10, 16; 13:8; 14:13, 19; 15:5, 7).

☐ Exhortation to Live the Christian Life (12:1—13:14)

Moo (1996:747) points out the eschatological nature of these injunctions; since Christians have been transferred from the realm of darkness to that of light, they must live accordingly (as seen in the frames for this section, 12:1-2 on not conforming to the world and 13:11-14 on putting aside the deeds of darkness). There are six sections here: 12:1-2 on yielding oneself as a living sacrifice, 12:3-8 on ministering in the church by using one's spiritual gifts, 12:9-21 on love for insiders and outsiders, 13:1-7 on submission to government, 13:8-10 on loving one's neighbor, and 13:11-14 on living as a child of light.

The Christian Life as Total Transformation (12:1-2) The transition from the meaning of the gospel to its implication for Christian conduct is certainly one of the most beautiful and powerful portions of Scripture. The introductory *therefore* shows that this instruction is the natural conclusion to what precedes, probably the whole of 1:18—11:36 rather than just the immediately preceding paragraph (so Sanday and Headlam 1902; Cranfield 1979; Morris 1988; Schreiner 1998; contra Käsemann 1980). Paul's strong verb "I exhort" (better than NIV, *urge*) refers to an authoritative proclamation that demands serious adherence. It is common for Paul to use it in teaching contexts (Moo [1996:748] points to thirty-one uses of "exhort" in Paul versus nine times for "beseech"). The phrase *in view of God's mercy* points back to the mercy of God in 11:30-36 but also sums up the emphasis of all of chapters 1—11. It is true that *mercy* occurs in Romans only in chapters 9—11 (9:15, 23; 11:31) and not in chapters 1—8, but most believe that *mercy* sums up the grace and compassion of God throughout the epistle (see especially Cranfield 1979:595-96). As Stott says (1994:320), "the gospel is precisely God's mercy to inexcusable and undeserving sinners, in giving his Son to die for them, in justifying them freely by faith, in sending them the life-giving Spirit, and in making them his children." The total commitment of ourselves to God

---

12:1 Many churches see a once-for-all sense in the aorist infinitive *to offer* here and therefore argue for a "second work of grace," a crisis spiritual transformation that occurs only once. But that is to misunderstand the aorist force. It can only have an idea of one-time action in certain contexts, and the aorist infinitive rarely has this force.

is based on the totality of his mercy to us.

The response of the believer to this mercy is absolute surrender, expressed in sacrificial imagery, *offer your bodies as. . . sacrifices.* This metaphor is a powerful one, picturing us at God's altar baring our necks to be sacrificed for him (compare 6:3-6 on dying with Christ). The Old Testament also has several passages in which sacrificial language is used metaphorically, e.g., "sacrifice thank offerings to God" (Ps 50:14, 23) or "may the lifting up of my hands be like the evening sacrifice" (Ps 141:2). In the New Testament we find the "sacrifice of praise" (Heb 13:15) or the "spiritual sacrifices" (1 Pet 2:5). As Daly (1997:234-37) argues strongly, sacrificial language in the New Testament is always ethical, that is, meant to be lived out practically in daily life. The content of the sacrifice is *your bodies,* which could be the physical body as dedicated to God (so Sanday and Headlam 1902; Lenski 1945; Murray 1968; Gundry 1987:35-36) but more likely is the whole person (so Calvin 1979; Barrett 1957; Cranfield 1979; Fitzmyer 1993b; Moo 1996; Schreiner 1998), for that better fits the context of the dedication of every aspect of our beings to God. There are three aspects of our sacrifice: (1) it is *living,* denoting not only the dynamic nature of the sacrifice (its ongoing force; so Hodge 1950; Dunn 1988b; Moo 1996) but also the spiritual state of the "new life" in Christ and the Spirit (6:4, 8-11, 13; so Cranfield 1979; Morris 1988; Thompson 1991:79; Schreiner 1998). (2) It is *holy,* meaning that the person is wholly dedicated, "set apart" from the world and belonging to God. (3) It is *pleasing to God,* building on the Old Testament concept of the sacrifice as pleasing God (Ex 29:18, 25, 41; Num 15:7-14; Ps 51:19) and common in the New Testament as well (2 Cor 5:9, "we make it our goal to please him"; cf. Eph 5:10; Phil 4:18; Col 3:20; Heb 13:21). Each of these is a critical aspect of the Christian life—we must strive at all times to experience the new life of the Spirit so we might be sanctified or set apart to God and bring him pleasure.

Instead, it draws its force from the main verb, the present-tense *I urge,* and it is followed by two present-tense imperatives in verse 2—*conform* and *be transformed.* Thus its force is more of a continuous action. The process of presenting ourselves to God is an ongoing one.

Finally, this sacrifice of our total self to God is a *spiritual act of worship*. This means that our whole life must be considered one of worship. Every moment is an act of serving and celebrating God in our lives. This is a strong cultic term describing the corporate experience of worship, but here it is applied metaphorically to the daily life of the believer. This is especially seen in the addition of *spiritual,* which combines the idea of rational thinking with spiritual living to describe the "reasonable" nature of serving God at all times. As Schreiner brings out (1998:646), there is an eschatological aspect as well; the transfer of realms from the law to grace is connected to the inauguration of the new age in Christ, a time of spiritual worship as daily conduct. This of course does not replace the corporate worship of the people of God in the church service. But it does mean that the corporate service is a launching of daily worship. The two are inseparable parts of a larger whole—serving God in every area of life.

Paul then moves from the what of the Christian life (v. 1) to the how (v. 2). He develops the negative means for offering ourselves to God and then the positive means. Negatively, *do not conform any longer to the pattern of this world*. It used to be said that *conform* is an outward, shallow act and *transform* is an inward, powerful act (see Sanday and Headlam 1902; Lenski 1945; Morris 1988), but that has been disproven (see Cranfield 1979; Dunn 1988b; Schreiner 1998). It means to pattern oneself after another and is stated well by the Phillips translation, "stop letting the world squeeze you into its mold." The forces of this "age" (the time in which sin reigns; cf. 5:21; 7:17, 20, 23) are forcing the believer to conform to its ideals. There are so many areas where this is true—consumerism, power politics, the success syndrome, sexual immorality, the pleasure principle and so on. First Peter 4:4 traces the

---

12:1 *Spiritual* has several possible meanings: (1) logical or reasonable, meaning that the worship is consistent with the demands of God, appropriate to the Christian calling (so Godet 1969; Cranfield 1979; Schreiner 1998); (2) rational, meaning that it makes good sense and is the natural thing to do for a thinking person as opposed to irrational animal sacrifices (so Hodge 1950; Sanday and Headlam 1902; Morris 1988; Fitzmyer 1993b); (3) spiritual in the sense of an act of inner worship that honors God (so Michel 1966; Bruce 1985; Barrett 1957); or (4) "understanding worship," that is, "the service rendered by those who truly understand the gospel and its implica-

process—"they think it strange that you do not plunge with them into the same flood of dissipation, and they heap abuse on you." The result is that we all too often cave into the pressure and follow our worldly friends into sin.

The positive solution is to *be transformed by the renewing of your mind.* There is an inherent passive sense in which the transforming power is the Holy Spirit, who penetrates to the core of our being and reshapes us into a "new creation" (2 Cor 5:17; the transliteration of the Greek word is the English *metamorphosis*). This is an apocalyptic concept (so Dunn 1988b) of the new being in Christ as a harbinger of the final new person we will be in eternity. The Spirit "changes" us and enables us to offer ourselves completely to God. This takes place in *the mind,* which is renewed or changed (literally "made new again and again") by the Holy Spirit. Moo (1996:756-57) calls this a "'re-programming' of the mind," a lifelong process in which the mind is taken from the world and more and more made to "have in mind the things of God" (Mk 8:33). It is startling how much there is in Scripture on the mind (see Osborne 1984:55-70). In Romans 1:18-32 the focus of Paul's diatribe against depravity is clearly the mind. In 7:23, 25 the mind is the sphere of battle between the desire to serve God and sin at the same time. In 8:5-7 this war continues in the mind but now between sin and the Spirit. Thus it is clear that the mind is where spiritual growth occurs, and in the mind decisions are made that determine one's spiritual direction and destiny. Paul's focus is inner, spiritual transformation, and the locus is in the thinking process. In other words, the ongoing conduct of the believer is based on input from the world (v. 2) or from God (v. 2). This will determine whether one lives the victorious Christian life (8:1-8, 37) or a life of spiritual defeat (7:14-25). In fact, that is

tions" (Peterson 1993:275, on the grounds that *spiritual* is too inward and *reasonable* too mentally focused). The use of the term in normal Greek had a definite sense of mental activity as the power of reason, and it also had this use in Hellenistic Judaism. So there must be an aspect of rationalism inherent in it. At the same time, the entire passage has overtones of the spiritual aspect of holiness and worship. So it is probably best to see (with Dunn 1988b; Moo 1996) all these involved in the meaning, though the translation "reasonable worship" is probably best as catching all three.

one of the major purposes of Christian fellowship, providing a counter to the mind-control of the world.

The purpose *(eis to, so that)* is that we may *test and approve what God's will is.* The verb means to "examine" something in order to live according to it, that is, both discernment and practice. *God's will* is meant generally to connote the direction and guidance for life that must come from God. It is a moral and ethical concept that defines proper Christian thoughts and conduct before God. There are three areas that we are trying to "prove," namely that God's will is *good, pleasing and perfect.* This means that as we seek to please God and obey his will, we discover that his will is best for us, pleases us and is *perfect* for us (or perhaps "matures" us). In short, as we please him (v. 1), he pleases us (v. 2). In this sense we are God's "show and tell" that his will works out for the best in our lives.

Minister to One Another in the Church (12:3-8) When our thinking has truly been transformed and renewed by the Spirit, it is impossible to have an exaggerated view of our own worth. Instead, we will humbly use all our gifts and strengths to minister to each other. This is Paul's concern here as he calls for *sober judgment* regarding our place in God's community. So he begins with *the grace given to me,* probably a reference to his Damascus Road experience (Acts 9) where he encountered God's gracious call to be his apostle to the Gentiles; thus he is appealing to his apostolic authority. In this sense his *I say* is not simply a gentle request but an authoritative requirement for *every one*

12:2 The vast majority of commentators take the three adjectives (*good, pleasing* and *perfect*) as appositional to *God's will* and believe that Paul is asking the readers to do that which is *good* and *perfect* in order to *please* God. Thus Paul is saying that to please God, they must do his will, that is, maintain good and perfect ethical behavior. However, does this fit the context well? While it is true that *pleasing* nearly always connotes pleasing God in the New Testament, Titus 2:9 uses the term of slaves seeking to "please" their masters. In other words, the individual context must decide whether the term means to "please God" or "please a person." In the near context, it is true that it is used of pleasing God in verse 1. However, the question is whether verse 2 continues the thought of verse 1 or adds to it. In verse 1 we have the what of the command ("offer your bodies as living sacrifices"), and in verse 2 we have the how (not conformed but transformed). In verse 1 the sacrifice of ourselves pleases God, but in verse 2 the focus changes. First, after we are transformed by God, we

without exception. Since their minds have been renewed, their *judgment* must be changed as well. If they are conformed to this world (v. 2) they will *think . . . more highly* of themselves than they *ought,* but if the Spirit has *transformed* them (v. 2), they will *think with sober judgment.* As Moo points out (1996:760), the meaning of *think* is not so much the intellectual process itself as the way one views something. It connotes the way the Christians consider themselves with respect to others in the church. So to think too highly is to have an overly inflated view of our own importance. To think soberly is to have the divine perspective—we are slaves to God (Rom 6:16, 18, 22) and to one another (Gal 5:13), so we place ourselves under others rather than above them (compare Phil 2:3-4).

The basis of this proper estimate of ourselves is *the measure of faith God has given* (literally, "God has measured the measure of faith"). There are two ways of looking at this. The *measure* could be the "standard" by which we judge ourselves, namely, our shared faith; thus we look at ourselves on the basis of that common faith God's grace has allotted to each of us (so Cranfield 1979; Wilckens 1982; Morris 1988; Fitzmyer 1993b; Harrisville 1980; Moo 1996). On the other hand, it could be that different "measure" or "apportionment" given to each believer as God wills and as accepted by *faith* (so Michel 1966; Murray 1968; M. Black 1973; Käsemann 1980; Dunn 1988b; Schreiner 1998). It is a difficult decision, for *faith* (as that given equally to all believers) favors the first and *measure* (referring to the different things apportioned) favors the second. The answer must be found in the context, specifically in verses 4-8 and the spir-

---

are to *test and approve* or discover and live out his will in our daily practice. This is then followed by three adjectives that are either in apposition to *will* ("approve the will of God, namely, what is good, pleasing and perfect") or in attributive relationship to it ("approve God's good, pleasing, and perfect will"). The appositional view could favor a God-directed thrust—in doing his will, we do what is good and perfect in God's eyes and therefore please him. The attributive view favors a people-oriented thrust—God's will is good, pleasing and perfect for those who follow it. I prefer the attributive interpretation, for the context of verse 1 is what we do for God, and of verse 2 is what he does for us. He transforms us by renewing our minds, and thus his will is good for us, is perfect for us and thereby is pleasing to us. In short, we discover that God's will is best for us and completes our lives. In verse 1 we please God, and in verse 2 he pleases us.

itual gifts given to each believer. Murray shows (1968:118-19) how this relates to "distinct endowments distributed among the members of the Christian community," called "the measure of faith in the restricted sense of the faith that is suited to the exercise of this gift." This makes best sense of the whole context: different members in the church having *different gifts* (vv. 4-6) provides a good parallel with *the measure of faith* sufficient for each to discover his or her gift and therefore *function* (v. 4) in the community. This is also in keeping with the near parallel in 2 Corinthians 10:13 ("the field God has assigned to us"; cf. 1 Cor 7:17; 12:7-11, all texts written near the time when Romans was composed). So Paul is saying that we will have a proper humility when we examine ourselves in keeping with the different gifts God has apportioned to us. There can be no pride, for all gifts are equally important to God and must be received by faith.

The tendency to arrogance is especially seen in the area of spiritual gifts, for they bring attention to the individual and can lead to false pride, especially in a central community like the church in Rome. So in verses 4-6 Paul develops a theology of spiritual gifts akin to that in 1 Corinthians 12:12-26. He chooses for his binding metaphor one of his most important pictures of the church, the body. The basic metaphor is easy to understand. The human body is composed of *many members* that *do not all have the same function*. The body is a whole mechanism and yet depends on each one of its members to function properly. If all the body parts tried to function other than the way they were intended, the body would be crippled. And also if any one member failed to function properly, the body would be crippled. That is exactly Paul's point. The church as a body parallels this exactly. *We*, the *many* members of the church, do indeed *form one body*, and as such are dependent on each other. Yet together *each member belongs to all the others.*

12:4-5 Dunn (1988b:722-23) gives valuable insight into the background of the *body* concept: (1) It flows out of the corporate expression of the gospel, that is, the communal character of salvation. (2) There may be some background in the Hellenistic idea of the *polis* (city) as a "body" or in the concept of Christ as the "eschatological Adam" (cf. 5:12-21) or the eucharist as a communal celebration, but the major origin/background must be the experience of community in worship and fellowship as a whole. (3) Therefore, the major point is not its origin but its meaning in the experience of the church as the body of Christ (v. 5; cf. Eph 1:22-23; Col 1:18).

There is unity and diversity in the church. We are not meant to be "rugged individualists"; rather we are intended to think of ourselves as part of *one body.* Vertically, we are "not our own" but belong to Christ (1 Cor 6:19-20). Horizontally, we belong to each other. This is the principle of the many and the one. We are many members but form one body and so are interdependent. Our *different gifts* are the way we blend into one body. That is, each of us has a critical part to play in the oneness that is the church; we need each other. In the eyes of God no one gift is more important than any other; there is no place for pride, for none of us can function properly without the whole. Studies have shown that in the average church, 15 percent are truly active both in terms of working in the church and in terms of giving. If only 15 percent of our body parts functioned, we would be virtually comatose. In the same way, our churches are crippled by the unwillingness of so many members to use their gifts to minister to each other (Eph 4:12). Yet this is only possible when we recognize we are *one body . . . in Christ.* It is only in union with him that we can gain the humility and the strength to function in unity.

Diversity is stressed in verses 6-8. First, we are reminded that as part of the *one body,* we each have different gifts that have come *according to the grace given us,* meaning that they are grace-gifts or charismata and that God is the true source of them. Note the three emphases: (1) we all have gifts; (2) the gifts vary among us; and (3) all gifts come from God. What follows is a representative list, only two of which are found in other lists of gifts (prophecy, teaching). So they stand for all the spiritual gifts God graciously grants his people. It is also important to remember that these ministries function at two levels: several are qualities we all should exemplify (serving, encouraging, giving, showing mercy), but when they become spiritual gifts they become foci of

---

12:6 There is some question whether the first half of verse 6 is part of the sentence in verses 4-5 (so NRSV; Dunn 1988b), making the list of gifts that follows purely descriptive ("if serving, on their service"), or whether it begins a new sentence (so NASB; NIV; NJB; NLT; Sanday and Headlam 1902; Murray 1968; Barrett 1957; Cranfield 1979; Fitzmyer 1993b), making the list of gifts imperatival ("if serving, let them serve"). The latter makes more sense, for Paul is exhorting the believers throughout this section.

our Christian ministry and are distributed as the Spirit wills (1 Cor 12:11). Stott makes the interesting observation that in Romans 12 God the Father is the source of the gift, in Ephesians 4 it is God the Son, and in 1 Corinthians 12 it is God the Holy Spirit. So these indeed are "gifts of Trinitarian grace" (1994:328).

1. *Prophesying.* It is popular today to link this with preaching or teaching, but that was not its use in the early church (note that *teaching* is the third on the list here and thus a different gift). This was one of the important offices in the early church (second on the lists in 1 Cor 12:28; Eph 4:11 after apostles). Prophets were the divinely chosen means by which God gave specific revelations to the church regarding specific needs (so Cranfield 1979; Käsemann 1980; Grudem 1982; Dunn 1988b; Moo 1996; Schreiner 1998). It is important to realize that these revelations are not canonical but occasional, as in the case of Agabus, whose two revelations are in the canon only because Luke wrote them down in Acts 11:28 and 21:10-11. Prophets are to exercise their gift *in proportion to [their] faith,* meaning either according to the standards established by true doctrine ("the faith" as the content of our faith; so Cranfield 1979; Morris 1988; Stott 1994; Fitzmyer 1993b; Moo 1996) or according to the faith God has given them to use their gift properly (so Sanday and Headlam 1902; Barrett 1957; Murray 1968; Dunn 1988b; Schreiner 1998). On the basis of the discussion regarding "measure of faith" in verse 3, the latter is more likely. Paul is then saying that they must use their prophetic gift to serve God and the church rather than to serve themselves.

2. *Serving.* This could be the kind of *serving* associated with the specific ministry of a deacon (so Cranfield 1979; Moo 1996). But more likely this refers to ministry in general, not just the purview of the pastoral office but of all believers. In Ephesians 4:12, the pastors "prepare God's people for works of service, so that the body of Christ may be built up." This would refer to a wide range of services, like

---

12:6-8 On the basis of the grammar of the passage, the list breaks down into one group of four and one of three (the four are preceded by *if* while the three have no introductory particle). It might be that the four are official ministry gifts while the three are general gifts Christians exemplify in the church, but that does not fit the use of general "ministry" (NIV *serving*) in the first part and the presence of *leadership*

discipleship, youth work, children's ministry and so on. Paul is saying that those called to ministry are to give themselves wholly to that task, realizing that it is a high calling and a privilege to serve the church in any way.

3. *Teaching.* This gift is also mentioned in 1 Corinthians 12:28 and Ephesians 4:11 (cf. also Acts 2:42, where it is one of the four pillars of the early church). In the pastoral epistles the teaching office is stressed more than any other thing as the essential component of church ministry. In 1 Timothy 3:2 one of the criteria for leadership is "able to teach," and in 2 Timothy 2:2 the proper process is passing on the sound doctrine to others who also "teach others." Teachers are different from prophets in the sense that they explain the traditional biblical truths while prophets give specific messages from God. Like prophets, teachers are to dedicate themselves to their ministry. The pastor is also a teacher according to Ephesians 4:11 and the pastorals. It was a critical area in the early church because of the problem with false teachers, and it is even more critical today (there are now thousands of cults worldwide). Studies have shown that biblical illiteracy is on the rise in churches, and theology is on the wane. We desperately need to ground people in the Word and turn them into Berean Christians who "examine the Scriptures every day" (Acts 17:11) and care deeply for biblical truth.

4. *Encouraging.* This is better translated "exhorter" because of its place after *teaching,* and in keeping with its use in 12:1, where NIV translates it as *urge* (contra Morris 1988; Stott 1994). Of course, exhortation includes comfort and consolation but cannot be restricted to these ministries (the word means "exhort, encourage" and even "admonish" [my preference for Heb 3:13]). It refers to the practice of verbal care in general. Cranfield (1979:623-24) says the purpose of teaching was to instruct or explain truth while that of exhortation was "to help Christians to live out their obedience to the gospel." So it con-

---

in the second. So the use of *if* may be simply stylistic variation. Perhaps the best solution is in Schreiner (1998:658-59), who says that the first four denote the sphere in which the ministry is conducted while the last three address the manner in which it is exercised.

cerns the "pastoral application" of these truths to the practical lives and needs of believers.

5. *Contributing to the needs of others.* The steward of this gift could be one who shares his own possessions with others (so Godet 1969; Murray 1968; Cranfield 1979; Dunn 1988b; Morris 1988) or an official who distributes the church's resources (as in Acts 6:1-7; so Calvin 1979; Käsemann 1980). Yet the more common use of the language would favor the former. Paul is asking those who give to the needy to do so *generously* or perhaps "simply" in the sense that there should be no self-serving ulterior motives (so Godet 1969; Cranfield 1979; Moo 1996). When Christians give to help others, the goal is simply to provide for their needs rather than to gain credit from others or from God (cf. Acts 2:44-45; 4:32-34).

6. *Leadership.* It is interesting that this category appears so far down the list. One would expect it to be near the prophets and teachers at the head of the list. However, it is doubtful that Paul has any hierarchy of gifts in mind, so it is not necessary to try to read the term in a secondary (but possible) sense of someone who "comes to the aid" of others (as do Michel 1966; Cranfield 1979; Dunn 1988b, based on its placement between the one who gives to the needy and the one who shows mercy). Everywhere else in Paul's writings (and commonly elsewhere in literature) the Greek word refers to leadership (see 1 Thess 5:12; 1 Tim 3:4-5, 12; 5:17; Tit 3:8, 14), and that is more likely here. The concept may be broader than just church leadership and include managing the home (so 1 Tim 3:4-5, 12), but in this context of church ministry it more likely refers to those in charge of the church. Still, in the modern framework this would fit many aspects of church leadership, not just the pastoral staff. At any rate, they are to *govern diligently,* meaning with "zeal" or "eagerness." *Leadership* demands a willingness to work hard, to give our best effort.

7. *Showing mercy.* Most agree that this is a general category of caring for people in difficult circumstances, whether it be economic troubles, illness, old age, depression or any other misfortune. This is very close to *contributing to the needs of others,* though that probably implies financial aid while this is helping others in any way. Those "able to help others" (1 Cor 12:28) should *do it cheerfully,* a term used in

2 Corinthians 9:7 in the phrase "cheerful giver." In short, those who help the needy must never do so in a grudging or gloomy manner but must feel the joy of the Lord in their hearts, recognizing the great privilege of helping others. Cranfield (1979:627) says it well—this comes "naturally to one who knows the secret that in those needy and suffering people whom he is called to tend the Lord is himself present (cf. Mt 25:31ff), for he will recognize in them Christ's gracious gift to him and to the congregation . . . of an opportunity to love and thank Him who can never be loved and thanked enough."

Exhortation to Love (12:9-21) The several similarities between verses 9-21 and 1 Corinthians 12—14 make some scholars believe a situation may have arisen in the Roman church (or Paul may have anticipated a problem) similar to one he had recently addressed in Corinth, namely, a group of charismatic enthusiasts who had elevated the importance of their gift and thought of themselves more highly than they should (v. 3 above). So as in 1 Corinthians 13 Paul had to address the need to love one another. Another possibility is that Paul wanted to establish the necessity of love in light of the following problem of the weak and the strong discussed in 14:1—15:13. While there may be some connections between conflicts in the two churches, they do not explain why Paul goes on to discuss several aspects of love, not only the internal need for love in the community (vv. 9-13) but also the external need to love your enemies (vv. 14-21). So several scholars believe Paul is more interested in summarizing the church's catechetical instructions regarding love (so Wilckens 1982; Dunn 1988b; Fitzmyer 1993b; Moo 1996). There is truth in both approaches. Paul probably has the Roman situation in mind but also wants to address issues related to love in general. He draws his material from several traditions, not only from the Old Testament but also from Jesus' teaching (see vv. 14, 17, 18, 19, 21; cf. Thompson 1991:90-110). The style is very clipped, with few conjunctions or finite verbs and a difficult structure to unlock. Several elaborate schemes involving chiasm (D. A. Black 1989 for vv. 9-13 or Schreiner 1998 for vv. 17-19) have been suggested. It is probably best to see a loose structure revolving around the two issues of internal (vv. 9-13) and external (vv. 14-21) needs. Yet there are loosely related sayings as well (e.g., vv. 11-12, 15-16) with only a partial relation to the major themes, so Paul has combined general ethical teaching with the two topics of relations with those inside and those outside the church.

Love in the Community (12:9-13) Verse 9 has a strange structure, for the first clause has no verb, and the other two contain participles. Most assume rightly that these should be taken as commands. The first is a kind of title for the section, *Love must be sincere* (literally "unhypocritical"). This means that love in the community must be genuine and not mere pretense. The term "unhypocritical" was often used of an actor's mask, with which people could pretend to be various characters. Paul wants to make certain no one puts on a "mask" of love and pretends to care for others. John calls love for one another "a new command" (Jn 13:34), not because it had never been said before ("love your neighbor as yourself," Lev 19:18) but because it is now part of the new covenant and bound up with Jesus' love for us. This new love existing first between the Father and Son and then between the Godhead and us is the basis of a new degree of loving relationships in God's community. Thus Paul could say, "And now these three remain: faith, hope and love. But the greatest of these is love" (1 Cor 13:13). In a nutshell it could be said that love is selfless giving, with selflessness being the attitude and total giving the resultant action.

The rest of the section tells how we can accomplish selfless giving. First, we must *hate what is evil* and *cling to what is good.* The fact that the verbs are participles might indicate Paul is bringing out the implications of "genuine love" (so Moo 1996), but the meaning is probably more general and simply indicates further expectations of Christian conduct (so Cranfield 1979; Fitzmyer 1993b). These attitudes are frequent in Scripture, as in Psalm 97:10 ("Let those who love the LORD hate evil") or Amos 5:15 ("Hate evil, love good"; note its opposite in Ps 52:3, "You love evil rather than good"). The true Christian characterized by love must abhor and detest all wickedness, as in Romans 13:12, "put

---

12:10 There are two ways to translate the second sentence: (1) As in the NRSV, "outdo one another in showing honor" (Chrysostom; Morris 1988; Dunn 1988b; Fitzmyer 1993b; Moo 1996); or (2) as in the NIV, *honor one another above yourselves* (so Sanday and Headlam 1902; Bruce 1985; Barrett 1957; Cranfield 1979; Schreiner 1998; compare Phil 2:3, "consider others better than yourselves"). The one emphasizes

aside the deeds of darkness" (cf. 1 Cor 13:6; Col 3:8; 1 Thess 5:21-22; 1 Pet 2:1). At the same time, it is essential to hold onto goodness with every ounce of strength we have. 1 Peter 2:12 says, "Live such good lives among the pagans that, though they accuse you of doing wrong, they may see your good deeds and glorify God on the day he visits us." *Good* here connotes both an attitude of goodness and the good deeds that flow out of that.

If love is truly genuine, it will center especially on the brothers and sisters of the Christian community, because we are *devoted to one another in brotherly love.* The language Paul is using here centers on the church as a loving family. *Devoted* occurs only here in the New Testament but was used in the Greco-Roman world for the tender affections of family life. The Greek word this comes from *(stergō)* "means to love, feel affection, especially of the mutual love of parents and children" (Günther and Link 1976:539). The same is true of *brotherly love,* so Paul is piling up terms to demonstrate the family dimensions of love in the community. Believers are to feel the absolute devotion that families naturally have for each other. In the same way, then, Christians should *honor one another above yourselves.* This is better translated "surpass one another in showing honor" and means we should all strive with all our strength to show honor or respect to each other. In other words, each of us should not be centering on our own personal status in the community but instead should go out of our way in esteeming others. This is desperately needed in an age of personal achievement when most of us feel unappreciated. To go out of our way to affirm others is one of the most powerful ministries we can have.

The next set of commands centers on Christian service. As we minister for God, we should *never be lacking in zeal* (v. 11), or more literally, "in zeal not lazy or timid." *Zeal* was just used in verse 8 (there translated *diligently*) to describe *leadership;* it is the opposite of "laziness." By using these opposite terms, Paul emphasizes the great energy

---

strong effort, the other preference for one another. The difficulty is that the verb occurs only here in the LXX or New Testament. It basically means to "go before someone and show the way" (Bauer et al. 1979:706). However, the idea of "preferring others" is not well attested for this verb (it does fit its cognate in Phil 2:3), and so the first must be judged slightly better.

needed to put our spiritual gifts to work. This was the problem with
the Hebrew Christians, who were "slow to learn" or indolent in their
spiritual lives (Heb 5:11; 6:12), and it was also a failure on Timothy's
part, as he failed to use the "gift of God" he received at his commissioning service because of his "timidity" (2 Tim 1:6-7). The flip side of
this is to *keep your spiritual fervor*. This is better translated "set on fire
by the Spirit" (Moo 1996) or "aglow with the Spirit" (Dunn 1988b), with
the verb picturing something boiling or on fire. It tells how we maintain our love and honor above in the sight of God. There are many
passages describing similar ideas of being taken over by the Spirit,
such as 1 Corinthians 12:13 ("we were all given the one Spirit to
drink"), Ephesians 5:18 ("filled with the Spirit") and 1 Thessalonians 1:6
("joy given by the Holy Spirit"). With the idea of "fire," see Matthew
3:11 ("he will baptize you with the Holy Spirit and with fire") and
1 Thessalonians 5:19 ("do not put out the Spirit's fire"). The Spirit must
have absolute control of each of us. There may be imagery of Pentecost, where the Spirit came with "tongues of fire" (Acts 2:3), and in Acts
18:25 it is said that Apollos was "fervent in the Spirit" (so Barrett
1998:888). When the Spirit takes over, we are set aflame for God and
thus will be *serving the Lord*. Some (Moo 1996; Schreiner 1998) believe
that Paul is correcting misunderstanding of the charismata as he does
in 1 Corinthians 12—14, thus saying, "when you are on fire for the
Spirit, make sure you are serving the Lord." That may be so, but his
statement goes beyond addressing potential problems to summarizing
the true meaning of Christian service. When we are aglow with the
Spirit, the result is always *serving the Lord*. And when we do serve
Christ, we must be filled with the Spirit to be ultimately successful. In a
sense, every aspect of verses 9-13 is Christian service, so this encompasses the whole list.

Paul continues with three spiritual exhortations in verse 12, and these
admonitions are interrelated. The combination of hope, endurance and

---

12:11 There is a question whether it is "your spirit" (thus the NIV *spiritual fervor;* so
Sanday and Headlam 1902; Barth 1933; Murray 1968; Fitzmyer 1993b; Schreiner
1998) or "be set on fire by the Spirit" (Chrysostom; Calvin 1979; Käsemann 1980;
Cranfield 1979; Dunn 1988b; Stott 1994; Moo 1996). On the basis of Romans, either
is possible (*Spirit* is used twenty times in chap. 8 plus 9:1, while *spirit* is intended in

prayer is frequent in Romans. In 5:3-5 Paul explains the chain of suffer-ing-perseverance-character-hope, and in 8:23-27 he names prayer and hope in the midst of infirmities. So first we are to *be joyful in hope* (which could also be "because of hope" or "by means of hope"; Dunn 1988b; Schreiner 1998 argue that these distinctions should not be pressed). Our hope in God's control of the future makes it possible to re-joice in all circumstances. This is emphasized both in 1 Peter 1:6-7 ("In this [our salvation] you greatly rejoice, though now for a little while you may have had to suffer grief in all kinds of trials"; cf. Jas 1:2-4) and in Hebrews 10:23 ("Let us hold unswervingly to the hope we profess, for he who promised is faithful"). In God our hope is actualized, and our fu-ture is secure. However, like all biblical writers Paul knew that this does not mean life will be easy or simple, so he adds, *patient in affliction.* Hope is needed because life is filled with difficulties. *Patient* is actually the word "endure," which in 5:3-5 leads to hope. In the midst of suffer-ing, perseverance in the midst of hope is the only proper response. En-durance is a key trait of the true believer in Revelation (2:2-3, 19; 3:10; 13:10; 14:12) as well as in Paul's writings (Rom 5:3-4; 8:24-25; 15:4-5; 1 Cor 13:7; 2 Cor 1:6; 6:4 and so on). When God keeps us secure, this does not mean that he protects us from life's problems. As Jesus said in Mark 10:29-30, those who have to sacrifice family or home will receive a hundred homes and family members (= the church"), but *with them* will come *persecutions.* Trials are a necessary part of the Christian life, for they stimulate faith (1 Pet 1:6, Jas 1:2-3), and so Paul calls us to *be faith-ful in prayer.* For him faithful prayer is the antidote to the worries of life (Phil 4:6-7). The verb here means to "persist" or "continue in" prayer (the term is also used with prayer in Acts 1:14; 2:42; 6:4; Eph 6:18; Col 4:2). A diligent prayer life is the only way to handle the vicissitudes of life. With-out it (and the concomitant faith in God—prayer is faith in action), we would be overwhelmed by the seemingly random problems that sur-round us like an invading army (the imagery behind "whenever you face

1:9 and the nearest parallel, 11:8). Perhaps Sanday and Headlam (1902) and Schreiner (1998) are correct in seeing a double reference to both human and divine "spirit/Spirit." However, clearly the Holy Spirit is the common use in Romans, and both the "set on fire" (NIV *spiritual fervor*) image and the parallel with *serving the Lord* would favor a reference to the Holy Spirit here.

trials of many kinds" in Jas 1:2).

The final set of instructions returns to the issue of relationships in the community (vv. 9-10). If they truly *love* each other and are *devoted to one another,* they will *share with God's people who are in need* (v. 13). This is also related to two spiritual gifts above—contributing to the needs of others and showing mercy (v. 8). Here he uses the verb cognate of the noun *koinōnia,* which means to have fellowship by sharing. Here as elsewhere it refers to sharing financially in the needs of others. Probably the two most important passages are Acts 2:42, 44-45 and 4:32, where the early church was "one in heart and mind" and "shared everything they had" (cf. also Rom 15:26-27; 2 Cor 8:4; 9:13; Gal 6:6; Phil 4:15; 1 Tim 6:18; Heb 13:16). This in the New Testament was considered a natural outgrowth of true community, and it is so desperately needed today. Probably Paul did have in mind the collection for the poor he was soon to take to Jerusalem (15:25-28; cf. 1 Cor 16:1-4; 2 Cor 8-9; so M. Black 1973; Dunn 1988b; Moo 1996), but the command goes beyond that to become a general attitude all believers should have toward one another. In Paul's teaching there is a set of three concentric circles on this ministry of helps (see Schreiner 1998): primarily to one's own family (1 Tim 5:4, 8) then to fellow believers (here) and third to the larger community outside the church (Gal 6:10). Closely connected to this is the need to *practice hospitality. Hospitality* is a natural outgrowth of love (Heb 13:2; 1 Pet 4:9) and a requirement for leaders in the church (1 Tim 3:2; 5:10; Tit 1:8). In the first century, inns were both very expensive and somewhat dangerous as well as filthy (in one Greek play the characters compared inns on the basis of which had the fewest cockroaches), so Jesus' mission (Mk 1:29; 6:10-11; 14:3 and parallels) also demanded hospitality (cf. 2 Jn 10-11; 3 Jn 10). In our day this is needed because most people are lonely and need someone who cares. In our individualistic society there are too few willing to share their homes.

Love Shown to Persecutors (12:14-21) After dealing with spiritual responsibilities in the community, Paul turns to relations with outsiders, primarily those who persecute the faithful. So he begins, *bless those who persecute you.* Actually, this continues the thesis of the section dealing with sincere love (v. 9), here shown to oppressors. Paul may well be drawing this from Jesus' own teaching, "Love your enemies and pray for those who persecute you" (Mt 5:44 = Lk 6:27-28). The trait is exemplified in Jesus' own prayer on the cross, "Father, forgive them, for they do not know what they are doing" (Lk 23:34), paralleled by Stephen's similar prayer (Acts 7:60). The idea of blessing them might entail a prayer that God's favor rest on them (so Dunn 1988b; Fitzmyer 1993b), but it may also connote acts of blessing, which fits better the tenor of verses 17-21. Undoubtedly, however, it intends both forms, for the following *bless and do not curse* definitely means to ask for divine blessing rather than calling down curses on them (yet see the discussion of v. 19 below). Most likely this blessing means a prayer for their conversion, but it may also imply something akin to 1 Timothy 2:2, asking for prayer for governmental authorities "that we may live peaceful and quiet lives in all godliness and holiness." Primarily, of course, it is asking God's blessings to shower down upon them as proof of divine love and concern. This is a radical command and certainly counter to our natural inclinations. Roman law centered on "an eye for an eye," while this demands the opposite. But that is exactly what makes it endemic to the revolutionary nature of kingdom living. When we love our enemies, this becomes one of the most powerful tools for converting the lost (cf. 1 Pet 2:12).

Verse 15 probably returns to relationships inside the Christian community, although in this context it may well include unbelievers as well (see Cranfield 1979; Dunn 1988b for the possibility that this primarily speaks of non-Christians). It may also be loosely linked with verse 14 in the sense that persecution was certainly a major cause of weeping. It flows out of the love and sharing of verses 9 and 13 and means that true *koinōnia* is sharing in the joys as well as the sorrows of others. Closely parallel is 1 Corinthians 12:26, "If one part suffers, every part suffers with it; if one part is honored, every part rejoices with it." As Stott says (1994:333), "Love enters deeply into [people's] experiences and their emotions, their laughter and their tears, and feels solidarity with them, whatever their mood."

This is continued in verse 16: *live in harmony with one another.* As in verse 15, Paul would be promoting harmony primarily in the Christian community but may also include outsiders. The command may be related to tensions between Jews and Gentiles in Rome, but with the added *associate with people of low position* it has a wider purpose as well. *Harmony* literally means "think the same thing" and occurs also in Philippians 2:2, "being like-minded, having the same love, being one in spirit and purpose." This is certainly not demanding that everyone think the same things, but it is calling for a unity of heart and attitude. Also, Paul is thinking more relationally than doctrinally, although it would certainly apply to the "sound doctrine" of the pastorals (1 Tim 1:10; 6:3; 2 Tim 1:13; 4:3; Tit 1:9; 2:1). As Moo rightly asserts (1996:782), this is not so much "think the same thing *among* one another" as "think the same thing *toward* one another." In other words, we should maintain the same attitude toward all, whatever their social, racial or economic status (see below). We all have different gifts in the church (vv. 3-8), but no gift should gain over any other. When our minds have been renewed (12:2) and we have learned to think soberly (12:3), that transformed mindset will produce true harmony with one another.

Yet harmony is impossible until believers gain a proper perspective about themselves, so Paul adds, *Do not be proud*. This repeats the injunction of 11:20, "Do not be arrogant" (compare 1 Tim 6:17) and builds on 12:3, "Do not think of yourself more highly than you ought." In fact, there is an ABA pattern here:

Do not be proud (literally "think too highly of yourself").
Be willing to associate with people of low position.
Do not be conceited (literally "wise in your own eyes").

The idea of associating with the lowly is framed by the problem of conceit, for pride is the greatest barrier to both unity in the church and caring for the lowly. When we have too high a view of ourselves (see 12:3), we think we are always right and never listen to the ideas of others. An important solution is to "associate with the lowly," which

---

12:16 *Lowly* could mean "lowly things" (Sanday and Headlam 1902; Michel 1966; Murray 1968) as well as "lowly people" (Käsemann 1980; Cranfield 1979; Fitzmyer 1993b; Schreiner 1998), though there is a good possibility that both may be intended (Barrett 1957; Dunn 1988b; Morris 1988; Moo 1996). The term could be either masculine or neuter. "Lowly people" is best in the context, but both fit equally well.
12:17 There is some debate regarding what Paul is saying. Some (Cranfield 1979; Morris 1988) believe that since Romans 1 says the minds of unbelievers are dark-

means both "lowly people" and "lowly things." As Jesus taught, true leaders are known for their servant attitude (Mk 9:35; 10:43-44 and parallels). Christ exemplified the simple lifestyle (he had "no place to lay his head," Mt 8:20) and was known for preferring the lowly over the haughty (Mt 11:19). We too must eschew a lifestyle centered on the things of this world and a preference for the rich and powerful. We must seek "things above" rather than of the earth (Col 3:1-2) and "treasures in heaven" rather than of the earth (Mt 6:19-21). This will only happen when we "have in mind the things of God" rather than mere human thoughts (Mk 8:33).

Paul now returns directly to relations with persecutors (vv. 17-21). With *do not repay anyone evil for evil,* he gives the other side of verse 9, *hate what is evil.* When evil is done to us, we are not to exact vengeance. Then we are no better than the perpetrator of the evil. In verse 14 we are not to *curse* them; here we are not to retaliate in kind. Such an eye-for-an-eye attitude was rejected by Christ (Mt 5:38; Paul probably alludes to this saying here) and the early church (1 Thess 5:15; 1 Pet 3:9). Christ was the perfect model when he did not "retaliate" or make "threats" but instead "entrusted himself to him who judges justly" (1 Pet 2:23). So we too should do the impossible—refuse to get even with those who hurt us. The positive side of this is, *Be careful to do what is right in the eyes of everybody.* Instead of vengeance, seek good works. The verb actually means "think beforehand" and means to give careful thought and attention, to plan before evil happens so as to do what is "good" in the face of it. Moreover, we must do what *everybody,* including the oppressors themselves, know is right. This may allude to Proverbs 3:4, "Then you will win favor and a good name in the sight of God and man." In the face of evil we are commanded to maintain such exemplary conduct that our very persecutors will have no grounds for criticism. In the eyes of 1 Peter 2:12, our slanderers will "see [our] good

ened, the standard of what is right must be the gospel. When their lives exemplify such high standards, the pagans will be drawn to the gospel. Others (Käsemann 1980; Wilckens 1982) interpret, "do what is right to everybody" rather than *in the eyes of everybody.* However, the Greek here says to "do what is good in the eyes of everybody," and it is best to translate it this way (so Murray 1968; Dunn 1988b; Fitzmyer 1993b; Moo 1996; Schreiner 1998).

deeds and glorify God on the day he visits us." In other words, our goodness will first convict them and then convert them.

It is natural that, in light of the encouragement to *do what is right in the eyes of everybody,* Paul would then extol us to *live at peace with everyone* (v. 18). Here again (cf. vv. 14, 17) we have a reflection of Jesus' teaching, especially Mark 9:50, "be at peace with each other," but also Matthew 5:9, "blessed are the peacemakers" (so Dunn 1988b; Fitzmyer 1993b; Moo 1996). The necessity of establishing peaceful relations with others is a frequent biblical theme (Ps 34:14; Rom 14:19; 2 Cor 13:11; 1 Thess 5:13; Heb 12:14). However, Paul realizes that we do not always control the situation and so prefaces his command with, *if it is possible, as far as it depends on you.* All we can do is pursue peace; if the other does not wish peace but prefers conflict, there is nothing we can do. This is especially true in the persecution setting that surrounds this section. We cannot *live in harmony* unless our neighbors want it as much as we do. Calvin gives two caveats (1979:472-73): (1) we should not seek peace so much that we refuse to undergo hatred for Christ; (2) courtesy should not descend to compliance, leading us to "flatter the vices of men for the sake of preserving peace."

Verse 19 sums up what has already been said about not cursing others (v. 14) or retaliating (v. 17): *Do not take revenge, my friends* (literally "beloved"). As stated earlier, the desire to get even is normal when we are wronged. In fact, Cranfield (1979:646) says Paul inserts "beloved" because "he was enjoining something very hard even for Christians." The problem of vengeance was so acute in the ancient world that Israel established cities of refuge (Ex 21:12-14; Num 35:6-34; Deut 4:41-43; Josh 20:1-9) as places of asylum for those who had accidentally killed someone, to protect them from retaliation. The Torah stipulated that a murderer was to be executed by an "avenger of blood" (Num 35:19-21; Deut 19:12), a family member of the victim chosen to execute the guilty party. In accidental death, the perpetrator needed to be protected from this "avenger." In fact, such cities were evenly dis-

---

12:19 Schreiner (1998:673) gives the options for the interpretation of *wrath.* It could be (1) the believer's own wrath, but that is negated here and in Eph 4:26-27; (2) the wrath of our enemies, but that is unlikely in this context of divine vengeance; (3) the

tributed in Israel for easy access (not more than a day's journey from anywhere, Deut 19:3). But things are different now because of the advent of Christ. Instead of vengeance, we must *leave room for God's wrath* (literally, "give place to wrath," certainly God's in this context). The wrath of God has been discussed in 1:18; 2:5, 8; 3:5; 5:9; and 9:22; in most passages it refers to the last judgment, but here it is the ongoing justice of God bringing retribution for the suffering of his people. Once again, the already-not yet tension of the book is operative. God will choose the appropriate time for *wrath* to take place, whether now, later or at the final judgment.

To prove the point, Paul quotes Deuteronomy 32:35 (neither MT or LXX but possibly another Greek text similar to the Targumim; so Wilckens 1982; Moo 1996), *It is mine to avenge; I will repay*. We must free ourselves from bitterness and find the strength to forgive those who do not deserve forgiveness. Only God has the right to avenge wrongs, and only he can do it perfectly. This is one of the most difficult quandaries a believer faces. The person deserves judgment, but to "repay . . . evil for evil" (v. 17) will render us no better than the one who so deeply hurt us. The answer is right here—leave the vengeance to God. The means by which we can do this is called the imprecatory prayer or prayer for vengeance such as is exemplified in Revelation 6:10, "How long, Sovereign Lord . . . until you . . . avenge our blood" (see also the imprecatory psalms—Ps 12; 35; 52; 57—59; 69; 70; 83; 109; 137; 140). These psalms are not the product of an ethics that has long since been shown sub-Christian. Actually, they put into practice the injunction here by asking God to do what he has promised here—avenge and repay the hurt. However, it is important to realize that this prayer is not an end in itself but a means to a larger end, namely, leaving the hurt and the justice with God. This then will allow us to forgive those who do not deserve it and to free ourselves from a life of bitterness.

When we have put the desire for vengeance behind us, we are ready to act on the next aspect of God's requirement, doing good (vv.

---

wrath of the state, but that is the subject of the next section rather than this one; (4) the wrath of God, which is by far the most likely here.

9, 14, 17). Paul turns to Proverbs 25:21-22 LXX, *If your enemy is hungry, feed him; if he is thirsty, give him something to drink.* As Cranfield notes (1979:648), food and drink stand for good works of every kind. Rather than returning evil for evil, we are to show love for our enemies concretely via acts of kindness. When we do this, it will *heap burning coals on his head.* Scholars are divided on whether the *coals of fire* here and in Proverbs refer to shame and remorse caused by the good deeds (Augustine; Godet 1969; Cranfield 1979; Käsemann 1980; Moo 1996) or to the judgment of God coming down on the oppressors as a result (Chrysostom; Stendahl 1962:343-55; Piper 1979:115-19; Schreiner 1998). In actuality, this is not an either-or. Both options fit the biblical imagery as well as the context. Fire is a frequent image of judgment in Scripture (e.g., Ps 140:10; Is 1:31; Heb 10:27), and good deeds as causing "burning pangs of shame" (so Fitzmyer 1993b; Moo 1996) among the oppressors fits well with the immediate context. The problem is that the one (shame) is favored by context, the other (judgment) by the imagery. Critics are doubtful regarding the judgment interpretation because it could lead people to do good for a negative purpose (to bring judgment on their enemies), while others doubt the shame interpretation as not fitting the "fire" metaphor. Actually, the two work well together (another example of double meaning) and may well supply the missing aspect in 1 Peter 2:12 (see on vv. 9, 14 above), in which oppressors view the good deeds and "glorify God on the day he visits us." Paul here would be telling us that the good deeds cause the oppressors to feel shame for their slander and bring them under conviction (Rom 12), leading many to be converted (1 Pet 2); but those who refuse to respond with repentance will then come under divine judgment (Rom 12). Augustine says it well: "The evil man who is overcome by good is set free, not from an exterior, foreign evil but from an interior, personal one, by which he is more grievously and ruinously laid waste than he would be by the inhumanity of any enemy from without" (Bray 1998:323).

Paul sums up his discussion (v. 21) with an injunction not to *be overcome by evil* but to *overcome evil with good.* Throughout this section Paul has told us to *hate . . . evil* and *cling to . . . good* (v. 9), *bless* rather than *curse* your persecutors (v. 14), refuse to retaliate (v. 17),

seek peace (v. 18), and refuse to seek vengeance (v. 19). Most importantly, when we give food and drink to our enemies (v. 20), we will
overcome their evil with good. If we seek vengeance, the evil that has
been done to us will conquer us and turn us into replicas of our enemy. There may also be a double meaning here: we are conquered
both by the *evil* act perpetrated against us and by the *evil* bitterness of
our own heart. John speaks of overcoming the world (Jn 16:33), and in
Revelation 2—3 each of the seven letters ends with a promise to "the
one who overcomes" (2:7, 11, 17, 26; 3:5, 12, 21). So by returning good
for evil, the believer becomes a victor in the race of life. Cranfield concludes (1979:651), "it is the victory of the man who has been justified
by faith, who is borne up by the grace of God in Christ, who is indeed
confident, but confident in the knowledge of the victorious power of
the gospel, and not in any sense of his own moral superiority."

Submission to Government (13:1-7) How do we relate to our increasingly secular government and culture? Is it correct to say with
some that when a government begins to turn evil, the Christian is obligated to oppose it and to refuse to support it? We must remember that
when Paul was writing this, Nero was on the Roman throne. While he
had not yet turned into the evil anti-Christian emperor he was to become, there were definitely signs of anti-Christian activity in the empire. So Paul is not writing this under the kind of government many of
us have grown up under, and he still calls upon people to submit. This
section comes out of the blue without any thematic preparation. Some
(Munro 1983:56-67) believe it was a later interpolation into the letter,
but that is unnecessary. Probably the discussion of persecutors in 12:9-
21 brought this to Paul's mind. It develops the message of 12:9, 14, 17
and 21 to respond to evil/oppression with good. As Fitzmyer points
out (1993b:662), there had not yet been any official persecution in
Rome. Claudius had expelled Jews and Christians for rioting in A.D. 49,
but that had been local. Still, there were signs of unrest, and Acts tells
us of ongoing local problems in most of the cities Paul evangelized.

Several commentators (Barrett 1957; Bruce 1985, Wilckens 1982;
Dunn 1988b; Moo 1996; Schreiner 1998; Towner 1999) also see a link
with the "do not conform any longer to the pattern of this world" of

12:2. Some in the early church may have interpreted that to mean that Christians no longer have any connection to this world, including the state. While remaining apart from this world, believers are still a part of this world, and the responsibilities to government are clearly spelled out in Jesus' teaching, to which Paul is undoubtedly indebted. In Matthew 17:24-27 Jesus said that while the children of the kingdom in one sense are exempt from duties such as taxes, they will pay them anyway as a witness. In Matthew 22:15-22 he said further that his followers are responsible to "give to Caesar what is Caesar's." Paul is probably reflecting on this (see further Thompson 1991:112-17), and the similarities between this passage and 1 Peter 2:13-17 probably mean both were reflecting early Christian catechetical tradition on these issues. Towner (1999:159-60) believes a major purpose is to tell the Christians how they can be a transforming influence in society. Since God has entered this world, his people must reform it. Paul's purpose is not disengagement or radical separation but transformation.

The organization of the passage is fairly simple, consisting of two parts: verses 1-4 are on submission to government, and verses 5-7 are a clarification and example of the basic command. The major question is the relation of the three *for* clauses (vv. 1, 3, 4). All agree that verses 3-4 form a single idea, but is verse 3 parallel to or subordinate to verses 1-2? On the basis of content, it is more likely that the three form stepping stones, with each one explaining further the one before (see the exposition below). Verses 1-2 say that those who refuse to submit will be judged by God and the state, verse 3 clarifies the judgment by the civil authorities, and verse 4 sums up the ministry for good and the judgment of evil by the state. So the organization is: command to submit (v. 1) followed by three statements telling why we should submit (vv. 1-2, 3, 4); then a second command that qualifies and summarizes the first (v. 5) followed by an example of submission—paying taxes (vv. 6-7; see also Stein 1989).

13:1 Since *authorities* occurs in verses 1-2 and *rulers* in verse 3, some believe this is equivalent to Paul's "principalities and powers" in 1 Corinthians 15:24; Ephesians 3:10; 6:12; Colossians 1:16; 2:10, 15, where it refers to demonic forces. Thus here it would refer to governing authorities and also to spiritual powers, perhaps the powers that are behind the earthly rulers (so Luther 1972; Cullmann 1956:50-70; Morrison 1960; Wink 1984:46-47). However, while Paul does use the terms that way on occasion, the context here hardly allows for that, and virtually all commentators reject the

When Paul says to *submit . . . to the governing authorities,* he is telling the Romans to "place themselves under" (the meaning of *submit*) those whom God has placed over them. *Submit* is used throughout New Testament writings for social relationships, asking *every* Christian (*everyone* is emphatic) to accept the authorities of society (governor-citizen, husband-wife, slave-master); in other words, all should take their places willingly in the social strata of the day. Two caveats are necessary: (1) submission does not mean inferiority, for in Ephesians 5:21 we are told to "submit to one another"; rather, it means a willing subordination. (2) In Acts 4:19 and 5:29 Peter told the Sanhedrin, "We must obey God rather than men"; the power of government over Christians is not absolute but is always qualified by our greater allegiance to God and his will. As stated in the introduction to this section, this does not depend on how "good" a government is, for Paul was writing this in the time of Nero. Nevertheless, there is a higher governing Authority.

The first reason *(for)* for submission is that *God has established* every single governing authority (probably the individual rulers themselves and not just the principle of government) in existence. This is rather startling, for *the authorities that exist* must include evil governors as well as good. However, this is the teaching of the Old Testament (Prov 8:15-16; Is 45:1; Dan 2:21, 37; 4:17; 5:21), of Judaism (Wisdom of Solomon 6:3; Sirach 10:4; 17:17; *1 Enoch* 46:5) and of the New Testament (1 Pet 2:13-14). In fact, even the "beast" in Revelation 13:5, 7 "was given" (a divine passive) his authority from God (so also Schreiner 1998). The message of Revelation is certainly in keeping with Romans 13—God is in charge and will remove unworthy rulers in his own time. He will indeed judge them but will do so at a time of his choosing. The saints are to submit to these authorities and let God take care of the rest (in a persecution setting, note Rev 13:10, "If anyone is to go into captivity, into captivity he will go," a call for passivity). Since

possibility. Four objections are decisive (from Moo 1996; Schreiner 1998): (1) When *authorities* refers to celestial beings, it always is coupled with *rulers.* (2) Neither *rulers* nor "minister" (NIV *servant*) in verses 3-4 can have such a double meaning; rather, the words refer to Roman officials. (3) The command to pay taxes (vv. 6-7) demands that they be earthly rulers since no taxes are ever paid to angelic beings. (4) Paul would never command Christians to submit to demonic forces (or any celestial being; cf. Col 2:8-15; Heb 1-2). Thus the *authorities* here are human.

all rulers *have been established by God,* they bear his authority. This means they are "appointed" by him and rule in his stead. This does not mean that God's people stand idly by. But evil in government calls for prophetic warning rather than active revolt; that is, we must call them to accountability and tell them of judgment to come if they do not follow God and govern righteously (as indeed Jesus and the apostles as well as Jeremiah and Amos did with Israel's leaders).

If civic leaders govern as God's viceroys, then it is logical that "those who refuse to obey the laws of the land are refusing to obey God" (v. 2, NLT; literally, "what God has instituted"). There is a play on words between "appointed" and "instituted," so we might paraphrase, "God has *ordained* them, so when we rebel against them we are actually rebelling against the *ordinances* of God." Moreover, to "refuse to obey" is not simply an individual act of opposition but a settled attitude of rebellion. Such people will *bring judgment on themselves,* referring either to divine judgment (Cranfield 1979; Wilckens 1982; Stein 1989:332; Moo 1996) or to the judgment of the governing official (Calvin 1979; Sanday and Headlam 1902; Godet 1969; Schreiner 1998). Actually, it is unnecessary to choose, for the ruler's judgment is God's judgment (so Nygren 1949; Murray 1968; Dunn 1988b; Morris 1988), so in the already-not yet perspective seen so often in Romans, it is best to see immediate judgment (from the secular authorities) leading to final judgment (God's).

Building upon the idea of God working through the secular authorities, Paul then adds that *rulers* are a *terror* for wrongdoers but not for *those who do right* (vv. 3-4). Peter says this another way: "governors . . . are sent by him to punish those who do wrong and to commend those who do right" (1 Pet 2:14). Since they are appointed by God to carry out his judgments, they are objects of fear not for the righteous but only for the wicked. Government is a friend to those who are good but

---

13:3 Cranfield (1979:664-65) says there are three possible explanations for why Paul idealistically assumes that the state will truly credit the good and punish evil: (1) Paul has had such good experiences that he cannot conceive the Romans would become an evil government (but he has experienced the bad too; cf. Acts 16:22-23, 37; 2 Cor 11:25-26); (2) he emphasizes the true duty of the ruler while knowing many fail (but he is realistic elsewhere, as in 8:35-39); (3) under God's guidance government will one way or another do his work. Though Cranfield prefers the third, the

the enemy of evildoers. So Paul asks the obvious question: *Do you want to be free from fear of the one in authority? Then do what is right* and be "commended." There are two options—terror for the one who does wrong and commendation for the righteous. We must choose. *Commend* is literally "praise," and once again it is probably given both by the secular authority and by God. Some (Winter 1994:25-30; Towner 1999:165-67) believe Paul is encouraging the Christians to practice "benefaction" in verses 3-4, that is, to perform civic deeds as well as give gifts that would ensure the continued welfare of the city. While the context here is certainly larger than the concept of benefaction, the idea of civic duty is certainly a major part of the passage. Christians today as well as then should show that they are exemplary citizens in the eyes of those around them.

The government is primary, for it is *God's servant* or "minister" (Greek *diakonos*) for *good.* Actually, verse 4 begins and ends with the twofold work of government as God's servant for good and his servant for wrath. Here *servant* is used in its more common meaning to designate a government "official" rather than its religious use for a "minister," but still it refers to the ruler as a servant of God doing his work. This is especially seen when Paul says the authority is "an avenger for wrath against the evildoer." *Avenger* (NIV, *agent*) is a cognate of *vengeance* or "revenge" in 12:19. Since only God can avenge, the state does so only because it is his *servant* in bringing revenge upon evil people. So those who *do wrong* should rightly *be afraid,* for the ruler *does not bear the sword for nothing.* The power of the sword was reserved for Roman officials. This was why the Sanhedrin had to deliver Jesus to Pilate, for only the Roman government could execute a person. So while *bear the sword* primarily connotes the death penalty, it also generally describes the duty of the state to punish people who commit crimes in general. Modern debates over capital punishment

---

second seems better here and in 1 Peter 2. Paul centers on God's will for the state. If it fails, it will be accountable to God.

13:4 Most agree that the sword does not refer to *ius gladii,* the "law of the sword" that gave the governors the right of execution, for that was restricted to Roman citizens serving in the military. However, the sword still represents generally the power over life and death (so Murray 1968; Dunn 1988b; Schreiner 1998).

were foreign to the ancient world for the most part. Paul means that those who do wrong will receive their just desserts from the state.

After stating the reasons for submitting to government, Paul repeats the command (v. 5) and adds further material, arguing *it is necessary* to submit. This probably refers to the divine order of things, saying that it is God's will that they do so. Now there are two reasons for submission—*not only because of possible punishment but also because of conscience*. Paul had developed the *wrath* motivation in verses 2-4, but now he adds *conscience*. The unbeliever will primarily be motivated by the danger of facing the *wrath* of government, but the Christian will depend upon conscience, which in 2:14-15 referred to that inner awareness of right and wrong that God had "written on [the Gentiles'] hearts." Here *conscience* is still an inner awareness of God's will, but for the Christian it is based on the knowledge of God's will that is informed and transformed by the Spirit (cf. 12:1-2). Brown (1975:352-53, building on Pierce 1955) argues that conscience has primarily a negative function, referring to the pain we feel when we transgress the moral law, but at the same time it "includes the power of discernment and rational reflection which enables the mind to analyze situations and actions, to discern moral issues and principles, the capacity to hear and apply the Word of God to our lives." The negative force is primarily true here for unbelievers, while for Christians it functions positively, telling what God wants us to do.

The primary example of submission is paying taxes (vv. 6-7). *This is also why* points back to both the God-given authority of government (vv. 1-4) and the Christian conscience (v. 5) as the reasons for Christians to pay taxes. Paul says that officials are *God's servants,* using a different term from that in verse 4; this Greek word *(leitourgos)* may have religious connotations, appropriate to the context of the government doing God's work. Taxes were especially onerous in the first century because the Jewish people had to pay Roman taxes as well as the temple tax. Paul may also be responding to a particular situation in Rome. At the time this letter was written (A.D. 57) there was growing resistance to the indirect taxes (see on v. 7). Rome's increasing demands on its people culminated in a tax revolt in A.D. 58 (so Tacitus). Paul thus would be telling the Roman Christians that they were obli-

gated before God to pay these taxes as a sign of their submission to the
state (so Dunn 1988b; Thompson 1991:114-15; Schreiner 1998; contra
Moo 1996). This undoubtedly reflects the Jesus tradition, specifically
the pronouncements about paying taxes as a sign of Christian steward-
ship (Mt 17:24-27; 22:15-22). The reason for paying such taxes is that
the authorities *give their full time to governing* (literally, "devote themselves to this very thing"), meaning that they give themselves totally to
serving God in governing the people. Since they have dedicated themselves to doing God's work in running the nation, believers are obligated to support them both generally with submission and specifically
by paying taxes.

Paul concludes that the believers must *give everyone what you owe.*
The language is that of monetary obligations (literally, "pay back a
debt") and at first glance seems a general demand to repay all debts.
But in the context *everyone* must refer to government officials; thus
this is a reference to paying taxes. It probably alludes to Matthew
22:21, "Give to Caesar what is Caesar's" (with the same verb and a
context of paying taxes). There are four obligations in two pairs, with
the first pair referring to the specific obligations from verses 6-7 and
the second pair referring to the general obligations of verses 1-5
(Coleman 1997:309-10). In the first pair there are "direct taxes"
(*phoros,* "taxes"), meaning the direct tribute paid to Rome by a conquered nation, including the property tax and the poll tax collected by
such men as Levi/Matthew (Mk 2:14 and parallels). Roman citizens did
not have to pay such taxes. In addition, there are "indirect taxes" (*telos,*
"revenue"), referring to sales tax, customs duty, tolls and so on. Everyone had to pay these. Before God, Christians must honor such responsibilities. But there is also the general responsibility to give *respect* and
honor to those who deserve them, namely, to government officials.
Most agree that *respect* (literally "fear, awe, reverence") is the more intense feeling. Since Christians are told they do not have to fear government (v. 3), some think the "fear" here is directed to God and the
honor to government (so Cranfield 1979; cf. 1 Pet 2:17, "fear God,
honor the king"), but one cannot distinguish the state and God in this
context, so it is likely that both relate to government as an instrument
of God. We are to *respect* or "fear" government because it punishes

wrongdoing, and *honor* it as an instrument of God.

The teaching of Paul in this section has had an important and often negative effect on the history of the Western world. It has been used to justify the papal states of the middle ages as well as Hitler's government. Yet at the same time it teaches an important doctrine, that the Christian is duty bound to respect and submit to the secular government as an arm of the will of God. The difficulty is always how a Christian submits to a government that is not following God. Moo (1996:807-9) gives us a survey of the possible solutions (from the least to the most likely): (1) submission is not mandated because the text is a late addition (there is no evidence for this); (2) Paul was naïve because he was living in the early years of Nero's reign, a period of peace and stability (overstated and untrue); (3) Paul expected the eschaton to come soon and so only demanded submission for this "interim" period before the end of all things (there is no evidence for such an eschatological view here); (4) submission to the "authorities" (both secular and angelic) is mandated only so long as those powers are subject to God (unlikely; see discussion of v. 1); (5) Paul is addressing only a local situation and is not developing universal principles (the text says "every person" and "all authorities" and goes beyond a purely local situation); (6) submission is only demanded so long as the government functions as it should (Paul's language in vv. 1-2 is universal and not based on how good government is); (7) Paul demands submission but not blind obedience—the believer respects and submits in every way possible except when the government asks something contrary to God's will. This last is the proper understanding. For a valid response to evil in government, see the concept of prophetic warning in the discussion on verse 1 above.

Love as the Fulfilling of the Law (13:8-10) Paul introduces this section by repeating the idea that began verse 7, *Let no debt remain out-*

13:8 Barrett (1957:249-50) argues that we should translate, "Owe no one anything, *but* love one another," which has the effect of dividing the two into separate commands. But the normal translation of *ei mē* is "except," and that makes better sense here (see the exposition above).

13:8 Sanday and Headlam (1902:373) believe that *the law* here refers to law as a general principle. However, this is very difficult in the context, which uses the Ten

standing. Christians are to pay their debts in full. But Paul then introduces the only *debt* that can never be paid: *love one another* (so Sanday and Headlam 1902; Cranfield 1979; Moo 1996). In so doing he returns to the theme of 12:9-21, love. When we love one another, we give of ourselves so thoroughly that we come under debt to each other. And as long as love governs the relationship, the so-called debt continues. In other words, we say, "I owe you my very life," to the one we love. As for the question of whether the object of this love is believers or unbelievers, it is probably both, following the injunction of Galatians 6:10, "Do good to all people, especially to those who belong to the family of believers." In 12:9-13 the love was within the community, but in 12:14-21 it was extended to outsiders. So we are to love all around us (Mt 5:44, "Love your enemies") but have a special relationship with fellow Christians. In fact, by emphasizing *one another,* Paul shows he is thinking especially of Christian relationships. Indeed, this love *has fulfilled the law,* returning to the issue of the law in the earlier part of Romans. Paul probably turns to the question of the law in preparation for the issue of the law and meat offered to idols in 14:1—15:12. Both sides were exhibiting a lack of love (compare 1 Cor 13 in a similar situation of charismatic debates). He wants his readers to understand that the law has already been fulfilled in the new law of love that Christ has brought about. When we love others, the law is completed in us. While the verb *fulfill* could mean that the loving believer "does" or "performs" the law properly (so Murray 1968; Dunn 1988b; Schreiner 1998), the thrust is more likely eschatological fulfillment (so Cranfield 1979; Käsemann 1980; Moo 1996); in love the Christian sums up the purpose of the law and brings it to completion. No wonder the obligation is never ending; we can never love perfectly but can only continue to grow in it.

This idea of fulfillment in love is explained further in verse 9, where

---

Commandments for illustration. It must be the Mosaic law. Marxsen (1955:230-37) argues that "other" (NIV *fellow man*) should be taken with *law* to mean "the other law," that is, the Mosaic law as opposed to Roman law. While this is possible, there is no mention of Roman law earlier, so this is unlikely (so Cranfield 1979). It is far more naturally the object of the verb *loves.*

Paul shows that the second table of the Decalogue (i.e., the second half of the Ten Commandments) is *summed up in this one rule: 'Love your neighbor as yourself'* (from Lev 19:18). Those commandments named are, in order, the seventh (adultery), sixth (murder), eighth (theft), and tenth (coveting) commandments. The first half (table) of the Ten Commandments centers on relations with God, and the second half on relationships with others, so Paul chooses the second half to emphasize loving relationships. These are representative, however, for Paul adds *whatever other commandment there may be* to show that *love your neighbor* sums up all the laws, though he certainly means those laws that deal with social relations. This may well echo Jesus' teaching (Mk 12:29-31 and parallels), for he said the law is summed up in two commands, "love the LORD your God" (Deut 6:4, 5, summing up the first table) and "love your neighbor" (Lev 19:18, summing up the second table). As above, *neighbor* would refer to believers and unbelievers alike. This of course assumes that all people love themselves and asks that the same effort that goes into caring for ourselves dominate our relations with others. Paul is certainly aware that at times we are all disgusted with ourselves, but on the whole every one of us is deeply concerned for our own well being. We must show the same concern for others. This type of love *summed up* the law, further clarifying the idea of fulfillment in verse 8. This probably does not mean simply a new focus for the law but rather it means that in loving according to the "new commandment" (Jn 13:34; 1 Jn 2:8) we are replacing the law in the sense that we belong to the new covenant and therefore follow the new "law of Christ" (Mt 5:17-20; Gal 6:2; 1 Cor 9:19-21; so Moo 1996).

Finally, Paul explains more explicitly how love fulfills the law. What Paul has stated positively in 12:9-21 (love is doing good for others) is now stated negatively for effect: *Love does no harm to its neighbor.* We seek only the good for others and refuse to have any part in manipulating or hurting them. With believers we are "devoted to one another"

13:11 Cranfield (1979:680-81) argues that *hour* here is not eschatological, given the fact that elsewhere in Paul it always has its ordinary use: "it is time to do something." However, as others point out (Barrett 1957; Dunn 1988b; Moo 1996; Schreiner 1998) the context is supremely eschatological, and *hour* is used in Daniel (8:17, 19; 11:35,

(12:10) and with unbelievers we "bless and do not curse" (12:14). With respect to every neighbor we show constant love and avoid harm. In so doing we fulfill the law, which once again means bring it to completion, sum up its purpose.

Living in Light Due to Christ's Return (13:11-14) Concluding the ethical section of 12:9—13:14, Paul reminds the Romans of the urgency of ethical living in light of the imminent eschaton (the end of all things). This is a common theme in the New Testament. Every passage dealing with the impending return of Christ leads to a call to a new ethical standard. When Christ comes, he will hold us all accountable for our conduct and spiritual condition (see especially the parables of Mt 25). Therefore, we must be spiritually vigilant, always ready for that return (cf. 1 Thess 5:2-3; Heb 9:28; Jas 5:7-8; 1 Pet 4:7; Rev 16:15). We have talked often of the "transfer of realms" as the age of Adam gave way to the age of Christ and the age of sin gave way to the age of righteousness. Here we have the final transfer of realms, the culmination of all the promises, the eschaton. In the present we have a foretaste of the glory and peace awaiting us, but we still "groan inwardly as we await eagerly for our [final] adoption" (8:23). So Paul tells us, *Do this* (not just the love of vv. 8-10 but all the exhortations of 12:1—13:10; so Barrett 1957; Hendriksen 1981; Cranfield 1979; Moo 1996; Schreiner 1998), *understanding the present time* (literally "knowing the time"). The *present time* has been used in 3:26, 8:18 and 11:5 for the present age of salvation as anticipating the final age of glory that will be ours. So the *time* here is meant eschatologically for the knowledge that the time is short, that the return of Christ is imminent (compare Heb 10:25, "and all the more as you see the Day approaching").

In light of this sense of imminence, *the hour has come for you to wake up from your slumber.* This is similar to the hymn of salvation in Ephesians 5:14, "Wake up, O sleeper, rise from the dead, and Christ will shine on you." There the sleepers are unbelievers and here believers. There

---

40) and John (4:23; 5:25; 12:34; 1 Jn 2:18; Rev 3:3, 10) eschatologically. Since the *hour* is connected to the end of night and the coming of day (see on v. 12), it probably has a strong eschatological connotation here.

slumber is spiritual salvation while here it is moral lethargy. Paul also uses the image in 1 Thessalonians 5:6-8 of pagans who "sleep at night" while Christians belong to the "day." Thus Paul is charging many of the Christians with resembling pagans (compare 12:2, "Do not be conformed to this age"). They have been asleep spiritually. Moo (1996:820) points out that people then were governed by the sun and so got up at dawn. Moreover, in the hot Mediterranean climate they had to get much of their work done early in the morning before the heat of midday. So the image is particularly apt. There is no time for spiritual laziness because *our salvation is nearer now than when we first believed.* In this context this is certainly our final *salvation* that will come when Christ returns. The idea of its being *nearer* is not simplistic (of course it is nearer than when we were converted) but deeply theological, referring to the nearness of that day. Christians will be delivered and vindicated, but they will also be accountable for their conduct.

In verse 12 Paul returns to his image of nighttime: *The night is nearly over; the day is almost here.* In Scripture the *night* is often a metaphor for the time of darkness or sin (Ps 139:12; Is 21:11-12; Jn 3:2; 9:4; 11:10; 13:30; 1 Thess 5:2, 5, 7), and the *day* is "the day of the LORD," symbolizing judgment for the enemies of God (Joel 1:15; Amos 5:18; Rom 2:5, 16) and vindication for the saints (Joel 3:18; 1 Cor 1:8; 2 Cor 1:14; Eph 4:30; Phil 1:6, 10). The message is again one of imminence. The end of the age is fast approaching when good will triumph over evil once and for all. God's people must wake up and begin to live accordingly. There is only one way to prepare for that day: "Stand firm. Let nothing move you. Always give yourselves fully to the work of the Lord" (1 Cor 15:58). In light of this precious truth, Paul says, *let us put aside the deeds of darkness and put on the armor of light.* The imagery is that of taking off old clothes and putting on new ones, a favorite metaphor of Paul's (Eph 4:22, 24; Col 3:9, 10 of putting off the old self and putting on the new; cf. Eph 4:25; Col

13:13 Cranfield (1979:686) notes four possible understandings of *as in the daytime:* (1) time of respectable conduct in contrast to the debaucheries of the night; (2) an eschatological meaning connoting the coming age, thus "as if in the day (that is coming)"; (3) an inaugurated sense, with the coming day thought of as already here; or (4) *daytime* as a metaphor for the regeneration and enlightened state of the Chris-

3:12). In Ephesians 6:14 and 1 Thessalonians 5:8 the image is used of putting on God's armor. It is also possible, in light of the night-and-day contrast, that the picture is taking off the nightclothes and putting on the day clothes (Dunn 1988b; Moo 1996). Fitzmyer (1993b:683) says, "Christians cannot afford to remain in the unprotected condition of scantily clothed sleepers at a time when the situation calls for 'armor.'" *Deeds of darkness* refers to the sin that characterizes this present evil world (2 Cor 6:14; 1 Thess 5:4-5). We must throw off all such evil tendencies. Instead, we are to clothe ourselves with the *armor* or "weapons" of light; more likely armor is intended, that is, both defensive protection and offensive weapons (as in Eph 6:14-17). Darkness-and-light dualism is common in the Old Testament (Prov 4:14-19; Is 60:19-20; Amos 5:18), in Judaism (*1 Enoch* 10:5; *2 Baruch* 18:2; and "the sons of light" versus "the sons of darkness" at Qumran, e.g., 1QS 1:9-10; 3:13; and so on), and in the New Testament (Jn 1:5; 3:19-21; 2 Cor 4:6; Eph 5:8; Col 1:12-13). By having the *armor of light,* we are both protected from the powers of darkness and have the weapons to produce victory in the cosmic war. In the middle of this cosmic war we cannot pretend neutrality. Paul is calling for a wartime attitude of sacrifice and single-minded focus; there is no time for lazy, ineffectual soldiers.

Since we are soldiers in the midst of war (cf. 2 Tim 2:3-4), we must *behave decently, as in the daytime. Decently* literally means "of good appearance," but the idea of external looks was not really part of the meaning (so Dunn 1988b); it referred to "proper" or "appropriate" behavior (cf. 1 Cor 14:40, "everything should be done in a fitting and orderly way"). Using the imagery of "walking" *(behave),* Paul is saying that Christians should live such exemplary lives that when people observe them, their conduct is beyond reproach. *As in the daytime* has the same already-not yet tension we have observed often in Romans (e.g., 8:18, 19, 28; 11:26-27; 12:19). Christians walk in the present day

---

tian. Cranfield doubts (1) and (4) because *day* would have a different thrust from that in verse 12; he prefers the third interpretation as more forceful and in keeping with Paul's style. Several others (Dunn 1988b; Moo 1996; Käsemann 1980 probably) concur, seeing an already–not yet tension in the phrase.

in light of the final Day when we meet the Lord. In the present we experience all the blessings of being the children of the new covenant (cf. Eph 1:3), but we also are responsible to live accordingly. Consequently, Paul turns to a vice list of things we are to *put aside,* giving them in three pairs (the first two pairs could be labeled "sins of the night").

1. *Not in orgies and drunkenness.* These could be combined into a single vice, "drunken carousing" (Barrett 1957; Cranfield 1979; Dunn 1988b) but should probably be separated because of the listing in pairs. Still, they do go together to describe the wild parties and binge drinking so characteristic of unbelievers (every bit as prevalent today as in Roman times!). The use of plural nouns refers to the repeated nature of the sins. The wild parties of the emperors exemplify the excess that Paul had in mind.

2. *Not in sexual immorality and debauchery.* From the uninhibited parties, Paul turns to the sexual sins that are part of them. The first term describes the sexual sin itself and the second the lifestyle that results. The sins in the first two pairs obviously go together. Nothing stimulates sexual excess so much as drinking and wild parties.

3. *Not in dissension and jealousy.* We turn from the party life to social sins, with the two terms denoting the envy that characterizes the world and the quarreling that results. There was no better example of this than the political infighting that characterized Rome itself, with the jealousy and strife between patrician families. At the same time, this is as big a problem in the church as it is in society.

In conclusion, Paul returns to the image of *clothe yourselves* from verse 12, but now those new clothes are not the *armor of light* but *the Lord Jesus Christ* himself. In a sense then the *light* is Christ (Jn 8:12, "I am the light of the world"). There is probably a picture of baptism in this as in Galatians 3:27, "all of you who were baptized into Christ have clothed yourselves with Christ," but this includes conversion as a whole (Rom 6:3, those "who were baptized into Christ Jesus were baptized into his death") and goes beyond that into the spiritual life that results. The command here centers on the present and connotes the process of becoming like Christ (Eph 4:13, "the whole measure of the fullness of Christ"). It is not a once-for-all event (contra Lenski 1945, who misreads the aorist tense here) but a process of becoming (a global aorist). After we have been brought into God's family and put off the old self and put on the new (see on v. 12 above), we begin a lifetime of becoming more like Christ as well as of making him the *Lord* of our life. The negative side of this is that we *do not think about how to gratify the desires of the sinful nature* (literally "flesh"). This sums up the problem of sin discussed throughout verses 11-13, for all the vices of darkness could be labeled "the desires of the flesh." The war between the flesh and the Spirit dominated chapter 8 (eleven times) and is at the heart of the victorious Christian life. Only in Christ through the power of the Spirit can we conquer our sinful tendencies. So we must *think* carefully of the dangers when we *gratify* the flesh and consider carefully how to overcome this destructive power. Morris (1988:474) tells how this passage led to the conversion of Augustine. Discouraged by his inability to overcome sexual sin, he one day heard a child at play call out, "Take up and read." Picking up a copy of Romans, his eye fell on this passage. God convicted him of the reality both of his sin and of salvation, and he was converted.

□ Love and Unity in the Community (14:1—15:13)

One of the great difficulties in every church is deciding between unity and purity on specific issues. The Bible demands unity (Jn 17:20-23; Phil 2:2), but it also demands purity (as in the diatribes against false teachers in Gal 1—2; 2 Cor 11; Phil 3; the pastoral epistles; 2 Peter; and so on). The question is when to greet an issue with tolerance and when to be intolerant (see Osborne 1991:311-14 on this). A major example of how to handle a situation that demands tolerance when a church is greeting it with intolerance is found here. The Gentiles at Rome (the *strong,* probably including some Jewish Christians like Paul) were in conflict with a group of Jewish Christians (the *weak*) who had strong convictions about several issues, including avoiding meat (14:2), observing sacred days (14:5) and abstaining from wine (14:21). Each group tended to look down on the other (14:3), and Paul is calling for tolerance. Yet it is also true that the strong in this case are in the right, for God has indeed removed the food laws and other legal requirements (14:14). The Jewish Christians have a weak faith (14:2) that is unable to grasp the reality of the new covenant Christ has established. Nevertheless, God honors their level of faith and expects them to live up to it. The strong, therefore, are the major focus of this section. While the weak are to quit being judgmental (14:10), the strong must both accept their weaker brothers and sisters and respect their convictions. They are required to refrain from putting pressure on the weaker members and even from exercising their freedom when in the midst of the legalistic Christians (14:21). They must respect the right, indeed the necessity, of the weak believers to live at the level of their faith.

This section includes four subsections: Romans 14:1-12 describes the conflict and admonishes the two groups to stop fighting. Romans 14:13-23 admonishes the strong not to cause their opponents to stumble by overemphasizing their freedom. In 15:1-6 Paul tells the strong to understand and tolerate the weak. Finally, in 15:7-13 Paul asks both groups to accept the other on the model of Christ's acceptance of Jew and Gentile.

The Command to Stop Fighting (14:1-12) The basic situation is described in this section. While there are many possible divisions, it is probably best to see verses 1-4 as describing the problem, verses 5-9 as giving specifics and verses 10-12 as a concluding admonition. The NIV omits the opening conjunction "but" *(de),* which shows that Paul has the previous section in mind here. Probably there are two connections: the command to "love one another," which dominates 12:9—13:14 and the problem of the "flesh" that is endemic to 13:11-14 (see Dunn 1988b). The Roman Christians had separated into "fleshly" parties, which they labeled the weak and the strong, and love was ignored in

---

14:1—15:13 There is wide disagreement regarding the background to this section and Paul's purpose in writing it (see especially Cranfield 1979; Moo 1996; Reasoner 1999:5-22). (1) Some believe it is a general treatise on potential problems rather than a discussion of a specific problem in Rome itself (Sanday and Headlam 1902; Karris 1991:65-84). In this scenario the problem of meat offered to idols in Corinth made Paul wary, and he wanted to warn the Roman church regarding the issue. There are certainly similarities with 1 Corinthians 8—10 (the use of the "weak" and the "strong," the danger of being a stumbling block to others, the desire to please others), but the basic situation is quite different, for the vegetarianism, observance of holy days and abstinence from wine are found only here, while the issue of meat offered to idols is missing. (2) Others believe the "weak" were either Gentiles (Rauer 1923:164-69, 185-87; Käsemann 1980:368 believes it a Jew-Gentile syncretism like at

the squabbles. Most likely the "strong" party dominated (see introduction on the makeup of the Roman church), so Paul commanded them to *accept* those "who are weak in the faith" (NIV, *whose faith is weak*). By accepting them, Paul meant that the strong should consider the weak as fellow believers, as equals in the church. It does not mean that the weak had been kicked out of the church and needed to be received back, only that they were marginalized in the body fellowship.

The pejorative title "weak in faith" was probably used in the church to describe those whose ascetic tendencies (see introduction above) were looked down upon. Yet this does not mean that they were quasi-Christians (taking *faith* as saving faith as in 3:21—4:25); rather they had not understood that their *faith* (i.e., their relationship to God in Christ) meant complete freedom from all legalistic requirements. They were not Judaizers (replacing Christ with the law) but Jewish Christians who failed to realize that all Jewish rituals (food laws, holy days) had been replaced by Christ. If they had been Judaizers (considered heretics by the early church), Paul would have had to condemn them as he did in Galatians or Philippians 3. Their observance was not salvific but cultic; that is, they followed such regulations as part of their worship of Christ. These regulations were not a basis of their Christian faith but part of their religious observance. Thus by *faith,* Paul meant that they believed that they had to follow these practices in order to walk with Christ properly. In that sense, many Jewish-Christian congregations today would fit this scenario. Moreover, accepting the *weak* included the admonition that neither group pass *judgment on disputable matters,* namely, the issues of food (v. 2), holy days (v. 5) and drinking wine (v. 21). *Passing*

Colossae) or Christians in general (Lenski 1945; Murray 1968) who had adopted an ascetic religion. But the Jewish overtones are too strong to be ignored. (3) Most likely the weak were primarily Jewish Christians and the strong Gentile Christians with a few like Paul who sided more with the strong (Origen; Chrysostom; Cranfield 1979; Dunn 1988b; Moo 1996; Schreiner 1998). (4) Several commentators are basically agnostic, saying that the actual situation cannot be known (Morris 1988; Sampley 1995:41-52). (5) Reasoner (1999:218-19) believes it was a social situation, with the strong being upper-class Christians and the weak lower-class Christians. They all agree that Paul was addressing a local situation of conflict over legal restrictions. Of the options, (3) and (5) seem most likely, and it may be that nuances of each are correct, with the Gentiles having more status and the Jews less.

judgment refers to the debates splitting the community. This does not mean that discussion was forbidden (cf. the Berean Christians who "examined the Scriptures every day to see if what Paul said was true," Acts 17:11), but rather that acrimonious quarrels were outlawed. There was to be a larger unity in the midst of diverse beliefs. Reasoner (1999:65) speaks of the Roman belief in "conviviality," where people of diverse social strata and beliefs could meet together in mutual acceptance. This was obviously ignored in the church on this issue.

Paul turns to one of the major *disputable matters* causing dissension: one person has *faith . . . to eat everything,* while another is *weak* and *eats only vegetables.* Obviously the first one belongs to the "strong" party in Rome, with enough faith or understanding to eat all kinds of food without restriction. Those with a *weak* or deficient faith/understanding were vegetarians. Some (Dunn 1988b; Schreiner 1998) believe it is significant that the Greek does not use *faith* for this *weak* person (the NIV adds it), hinting that he is not exercising faith in this matter. Since most vegetarian groups in the ancient world were Gentile (e.g., the neo-Pythagoreans), some have insisted that this was a Gentile movement (see above), but the answer is more likely found in the dietary regulations of the Jewish-Christian community. Dunn (1988b:800) says that the Maccabean revolt had made such observance a test of Jewishness since dietary observance was linked to military success. The refusal to eat Gentile foods was a major test of faithfulness in the first century. Moo adds (1996:830-31) that while abstinence from meat was not part of the Torah, many Jews would abstain when unable to obtain kosher meat. Moreover, these Jewish Christians would have been ostracized by the larger Jewish community and forced to live in "strange parts of the city after their exile (by the decree of Claudius)" and so been unable to get kosher meat. Another interesting possibility is the suggestion that *eat everything* should be seen in light of 13:13 as an "orgy" of gluttonous consumption (Reasoner 1999:67-70). This is possible, for *orgy* can refer to excessive feasting as well as sexual orgies. If so, both parties were wrong. Still, there is too little indication that Paul

---

14:4 The majority take *stands or falls* to be a reference to the present spiritual life (Barrett 1957; Murray 1968; Käsemann 1980; Morris 1988; Fitzmyer 1993b), but a few

was castigating the strong here.

The dissension caused by this is explored in verse 3—the strong *look down on* or "despise" the weak while the weak *condemn* or "judge" the strong. Paul probably chose his verbs carefully. Those who had no convictions about dietary restrictions felt contempt for those who did; they understood that Christ had removed all food laws (Mk 7:19) and so felt disdain for the ignorant others. Those with strong convictions would naturally pass judgment on those they felt broke the laws of the Lord. The one committed the sin of pride, the other the sin of judgmentalism. So Paul reminds them that *God has accepted* the other. There is inclusio with verse 1, which began with the command to the strong to *accept* the weak. Now the weak are told that God has *accepted* the strong. Therefore both groups are warned to accept each other because God has accepted both (so Käsemann 1980). It is a sin to reject those whom God has accepted. This is a frequent problem in the church today. The closest parallel would be legalistic divisions over movies, cards, dancing and social drinking, but similar would be divisive quarrels over doctrines like the charismatic issue, the rapture/millennium and Calvinism-Arminianism. We must learn to agree to disagree over such noncardinal issues. It is not that they are unimportant doctrines (see the discussion of predestination at 8:28-30 and the conclusion to chapter 10). However, like the Christians in Rome, we must realize that God has accepted both sides, and so we must accept each other even while disagreeing.

Paul concludes the first section with a strong rhetorical question, *Who are you to judge someone else's servant?* As in verse 3, this is addressed especially to the weak who *judge* (the same term is used in vv. 3-4) the strong (compare 2:1, 3 of the proud Jews), but it encompasses both groups. *Servant* is the word used for household slave, and the master of the house is certainly God. In the Roman world, it was the worst kind of manners for a person to interfere with someone else's slave. How much more true is it when that master is God himself. Paul adds that the slave *stands or falls* only with respect to

(Moo 1996; Schreiner 1998) believe there is also a reference to the last judgment that alone will determine whether one ultimately *stands or falls*.

his own master, that is, all approval/acceptance or rejection comes from God himself, the eternal Master of us all, not from other Christians. The only approval that matters comes from our Master, and it would be wrong for anyone else to meddle. The error here concerns the weak who are passing judgment upon those with whom they disagreed. This constituted what James (2:1-13) calls "discrimination," and they became "judges with evil thoughts" (Jas 2:4). This is all the more true because it was absolutely certain that the strong also would *stand* or be approved, because *the Lord is able to make [them] stand.* As Peter says, they are "shielded by God's power until the coming of the salvation that is ready to be revealed in the last time" (1 Pet 1:5). The strong are not merely accepted but shielded by his power (*is able to* = "has the power"). God's presence in their lives is based not on their external conduct (what they eat) but upon their internal trust in God. Since the Lord, their master, is behind the strong, who are the weak to stand over them in judgment! This is a critical example of the importance of tolerance in our day as well. Christians must stop fighting over nonessential issues and realize that God accepts both sides. The difficult question, of course, is what constitutes a nonessential issue. The answer is twofold: these are doctrines that are not clear in Scripture (that is, passages seem to support both sides), and they have never been settled in the history of the church (that is, Bible-believing groups continue to follow both sides)—more on this below.

In verses 5-9 Paul gives further details of the dispute. It concerns not only food but also the observance of holy days. The weak *consider one day more sacred than another* while the strong *consider every day alike.* Literally, the weak were "judging one day more

---

14:5 The exact nature of these *days* is difficult, and it could be related to the Roman practice of calendrical observance, perhaps the Greek belief that days were under "lucky or unlucky stars" (Käsemann 1980:370) or some other Hellenistic practice. But that is unlikely, and a Jewish-Christian debate is more likely. At issue may be the Jewish festivals like Passover or Day of Atonement. Reasoner (1999:147-58) believes it was a Sabbath conflict in which the weak observed "the Lord's Day" (Rev 1:10) as a Christian celebration. He shows that the Romans thought Sabbath observance a superstition for the lazy and argues that the debate was over scrupulous demands for Sabbath worship. Yet this does not state what the strong would have believed, and it

important than another" while the strong were "judging each day the same." So the "judgmental" attitude persisted, this time on both sides. Apparently, the two sides were also divided over the observance of sacred days like the Sabbath, fast days and the Jewish festivals. Many Romans thought the observance of holy days like the Sabbath to be superstitious, but others were strongly attracted to it. In the Roman church the two sides were at odds over such requirements, but Paul says it should be an open issue: whatever conclusion is drawn, *each one should be fully convinced in his own mind.* In other words, both approaches were viable, and the only requirement was faithfulness to the Lord. This may go back to the "renewing of your mind" in 12:2. If the Spirit was indeed transforming the thought process of each believer, the two sides must think through the issue carefully and make a reasoned decision. Obviously, then, there is no single truth in matters such as this. Paul refuses to take sides but simply wants each group to respect the other. This could well be applied to similar issues today, though people would differ as to its application. I personally would apply it to debates regarding the rapture, the charismatic issue, women in the church and Calvinism-Arminianism among others. The Word of God is not explicit on these issues, and while each of us is indeed "fully convinced in [our] mind," Paul calls us to respect our opponents on these issues as well.

The key to Christian understanding is to make certain that all Christian observance is *to the Lord* (v. 6). Paul summarizes his arguments thus far by mentioning three examples—observing holy days, eating meat and abstaining from meat. Both the "weak" and the "strong" views at Rome are acceptable providing they sincerely worship the Lord in their practices. Paul's concern is that all such decisions be mo-

---

is unlikely they would have failed to observe a day of worship at all (for early worship on Sunday, see Acts 20:7; 1 Cor 16:2; Rev 1:10). If it is a Sabbath debate, it could have been between Saturday (Jewish = the weak) or Sunday (the strong) demands. This would fit the Gentile versus Jewish make-up of the larger issue, but there is too little evidence for such a debate. Most likely, it refers to tension over the observance of holy days in general, including the Sabbath (so Dunn 1988b; Moo 1996) as well as days of fasting (Cranfield 1979; Fitzmyer 1993b, due to the close connection between food and sacred days).

tivated by an overriding concern to glorify God in every area of life. Paul uses a special example of the prayer of thanksgiving at mealtime (the Jewish people offered two prayers then). Whether they eat meat or not, both sides thank God for their food, and so their meals are acceptable to God. Neither side should be criticized by the other but should be allowed to worship God as they believe they should *(fully convinced in [their] mind)*. This is an important passage for denominational differences. Paul does not believe one is preferred by God over another. Whom did God prefer—Luther or Calvin or Wesley or Menno Simons? Paul would say God loved and used them all. It is true that the issues in verses 5-6 are practices rather than beliefs, but the two cannot truly be separated. Practices always relate to beliefs (as in this chapter), so both apply here.

Paul anchors his admonitions theologically in verses 7-9, as he elaborates on the implications of *to the Lord* in verse 6. *Whether we live or die,* we do it not for ourselves but for God. The problem of both the weak and the strong is that the purpose of both systems is to prove the superiority of their movement rather than to glorify the Lord. Nothing in life, let alone in death, must be done to benefit ourselves or our movements. Religious debates, and conflict between movements, might indeed benefit ourselves, for example in talking people into joining our group, but such will never glorify God. Some (Fitzmyer 1993b; Schreiner 1998) believe this goes back to Romans 1:21—those who take part in such disputes do not glorify God but have the "futile thinking" and "foolish hearts" of the world. This is especially true of our death, for God alone determines that moment, and all we can do is surrender to his will and make certain that our lives are so centered on him that our death will be as well. Our goal at all times is not sectarianism but devotion to God. Paul concludes, *whether we live or die, we belong to the Lord.* We are his children (8:14-17) and his slaves (6:15-22), so we belong wholly to him. It is natural that the servant live to please the master (14:4), so we must place the glory of God over all sectarian debates.

As 1 Corinthians 6:19-20 says, "you are not your own; you were bought at a price." To place our own agenda ahead of the interests of God is one of the basic sins. This is Paul's point in verse 9. *Christ died and returned to life* for two reasons: so that we might belong to God (v. 8) and so that *he might be the Lord of both the dead and the living* (v. 9). His death was a ransom payment (3:24) that purchased us for God, and through it he became Lord of all, the dead as well as the living. The cross and the resurrection are a single event in salvation history, and together they constitute his final victory over sin and death. Thus he is in control of the living and the dead, and so everything both depends on and points to him. A lot more is at stake than just community harmony; if Jesus is truly Lord of the church, such friction should not be possible. Internal disputes constitute more than simply corporate tension. They endanger both the glory of God and the lordship of Christ. Once again, we must distinguish cardinal and noncardinal issues. Cardinal doctrines (e.g., the Trinity, the deity of Christ and substitutionary atonement) demand discipline and an intolerant "test of the spirits" (1 Jn 4:1-3) on the part of the church (examples—the Judaizers in Galatians and Phil 4 or the heretics in 1-2 Timothy), but noncardinal issues demand dialogue and tolerance (as here).

This section concludes with another set of admonitions (vv. 10-12). It begins with a diatribe (see 2:1-4, 17-24) that asks biting questions of the two groups in the reverse order of verse 3, namely, judging and despising each other. The weak tended to *judge* or "condemn" the strong for failing to follow their legalistic demands, while the strong tended to *look down on* or "despise" the weak for failing to rise above their unnecessary requirements. Both are equally wrong. Paul strengthens his challenge by pointing out that they are brothers and sisters in the Lord. How can they condemn a member of their own family? As Moo points out (1996:846), "Paul's direct and lively style creates the picture of the apostle shifting his gaze from the 'weak' to the 'strong' as he publicly chastises these representative Christians from the Roman community." They are setting themselves up as judges, and they have no right to do so, for only God is the judge and *we will all stand before God's judgment seat*. This is a two-fold warning—only God is the judge, and those who take that role upon themselves will in turn be judged. Paul elaborates on this point in 2 Corinthians 5:10, where at the judgment seat (here God's *bēma*, there Christ's *bēma*—the two are one) each one will "receive what is due for the things done while in the body, whether good or bad." This is another critical reminder to us not to judge each other when we differ over nonessential issues. Some prefer a high-church style of worship, others a low-church style. Some prefer hymns, others praise songs. God blesses all of these and more. Yet we continue to fight over such things. Warren Wiersbe says it well—"when Satan was thrown out of heaven, he landed in the choir loft!" We are not to condemn or feel contempt for those who differ in their worship tastes, for God does not prefer one over the other.

Paul anchors the point that God alone is the judge by citing Isaiah 45:23 LXX, although the opening (*'As surely as I live,' says the Lord*) does not occur there but is a common introductory formula (Is 49:18; Jer 22:24; Ezek 5:11; and others). Paul is probably drawing together the contexts of Isaiah 49 and 45 in addressing the issue. In Isaiah 49, by showing his love for his children and promising that they will be returned to their bereaved mother, God is addressing the complaint of Israel that he had forsaken his people (v. 14). In Isaiah 45 God promises his people that he will take over and sovereignly redeem his people and force the nations to bow before him. Dunn (1988b:815) calls this "one of the most powerful monotheistic passages in the scriptures." In both contexts God alone is in charge; he alone will judge the nations and his people. The warning to the judgmental Christians in Rome is obvious. They will either *bow before* the Lord and *confess to God* their error now, or they will face a much more severe judgment in the future. Some believe *confess* here means homage to God rather than confession of sins (so Dunn 1988b; Schreiner 1998), but the context of judgment in verses 10 and 12 make it more likely that there is implicit warning as well as promise in verse 11. To give proper homage to God, we must first confess our sins before him. When the Roman groups judged each other, they were replacing God and would therefore be indicted before him.

14:11 Some think the opening *As surely as I live* was inadvertently placed here by Paul because he was quoting from memory (Cranfield 1979), but that is surely unlikely of one who quoted Isaiah so frequently. Others believe it is added to show that Christ is Lord (Hodge 1950; M. Black 1973, linking it with Christ's return to life

Verse 12 continues this message, saying that we will all give an account of ourselves *to God*. As in verse 11 there is a twofold thrust pointing to reward and punishment. Every Christian (*each of us* is emphatic) as well as non-Christian will stand before God's *bēma* and answer for his or her life. This teaching is incredibly frequent in the Old Testament (2 Chron 6:23; Job 34:11; Ps 28:4; 62:12; Prov 24:12; Jer 17:10; Ezek 18:20; Hos 12:2), in Jewish literature (*1 Enoch* 41:1-2; *Psalms of Solomon* 2:16; 17:8; 2 Esdras *[4 Ezra]* 7:35; 8:33; *2 Baruch* 14:12), and in the New Testament (Mt 16:27; Rom 2:6; 14:12; 1 Cor 3:12-15; 2 Cor 5:10; 11:15; 2 Tim 4:14; 1 Pet 1:17; Rev 2:23; 11:18; 14:13; 20:12; 22:12), and many of the passages speak explicitly of the people of God. It relates both to reward and judgment. For the believer probably the most powerful image is 1 Corinthians 3:12-15, which states that our lives will be tested by fire to see what will go into eternity with us. This is behind Paul's warning here. If we judge each other, we will in turn be judged by God. If we allow God to be judge and establish unity in the church, there will be reward.

The Strong Are Not to Cause the Weak to Stumble (14:13-23) The first section ends with an admonition against judging your brother (vv. 10-12), and this section picks up this theme, beginning, *Therefore let us stop passing judgment on one another*. However, while the first section addressed both groups, this section centers on the strong. In verses 3 and 10 the ones guilty of judgment were the weak, while the strong were characterized as despising the weak. Here both groups are seen as judging, but in the second half of verse 13 Paul applies the admonition especially to the strong. The thesis is stated in verse 13—do not do anything that will hurt another believer (namely, the "weak") spiritually. Several have noted a chiastic pattern here. Perhaps the most comprehensive is Dunn (1988b:816 [see fig. 5, representing discussion]).

This section addresses the strong, who should be leading the way to establishing unity in the church by opening themselves up to the "weaker"

in v. 9), but in the context of verses 10-12 it is more likely that Paul is emphasizing God as the final judge (so Cranfield 1979; Moo 1996). Perhaps best is the thought that Paul is drawing together Isaiah 49:18 with 45:32 (Harrisville, 1980:22), for the contexts of both fit what Paul is saying here.

A Judging (v. 13a).
   B Stumbling block (v. 13b)
      C Clean/unclean (v. 14)
         D Destroying (v. 15)
            E Peace and unity (vv. 16-18)
            E′ Peace and unity (v. 19)
         D′ Destroying (v. 20a)
      C′ Clean/unclean (v. 20b)
   B′ Stumbling block (v. 21)
A′ Judging (vv. 22-23)

Figure 5. Chiastic structure of Romans 14:13-23 (based on Dunn 1988b:816)

brothers and sisters. Neither side should stand in judgment over the other, for God alone is the judge of all, and he has accepted both groups (vv. 3, 10). In a terrific play on words, Paul tells the strong that instead of "judging" (*krinō*) the weak, they must "decide" *(krinō)* not to *put any stumbling block or obstacle in . . . [the] way* of the "weak" Christians. Rather than negative judgment, they must be characterized by positive discernment. The two words are virtually synonymous. A *stumbling block* is that which causes someone to fall into sin. Similarly, an obstacle derives from the concept of "trapping something in a snare" and therefore is used in the LXX of falling into sin. So it came to mean "an obstacle in coming to faith and a cause of going astray," a transgression that leads to destruction, thus something that destroys faith and causes apostasy (Stählin 1971:345-47). Here it does not carry that strong a force but rather speaks of causing the faith of the weak to fail (though see v. 15 below). Thompson (1991:177) says that Paul like Matthew (9:42) "is concerned with the actions of people within his community which may lead to the spiritual ruin of their fellow members." While Paul does not specify how this was to come to pass, the danger has to do with food that the weak think is unclean (v. 14). Therefore, it probably means that the strong force the weak to accept

14:14 Moo (1996:852) notes three options for the *one who is in the Lord Jesus*: (1) "through my fellowship with the Lord Jesus" (Sanday and Headlam 1902; Murray 1968; Morris 1988; Fitzmyer 1993b); (2) "through my understanding of the truth revealed in the Lord Jesus" (Godet 1969; Wilckens 1982; Käsemann 1980); or (3)

their freedom to eat meat, causing the consciences of the weak to be defiled. We must remember the admonition of verse 5 that "each one should be fully convinced in his own mind." In other words, we must all respect the honest religious convictions of others. A good example would be the fundamentalist prohibition against movies, card playing and dancing. If other Christians have a conscience against such things, those who feel free in these matters should not put them down and mock them. To make them adhere to our freedom would be to hurt them spiritually. In short, the strong are not to flaunt their freedom in front of the weak and so hurt them spiritually.

Paul then shows his basic agreement with the argument of the strong by saying, *I am fully convinced that no food is unclean in itself* (v. 14). This refers to the Old Testament restrictions of some foods as "common" or causing defilement. Most likely these Jewish Christians believed that the Old Testament food laws in Leviticus 11 and Deuteronomy 14 were still mandatory, and they were "scandalized" (NIV, *distressed*) at the freedom of the strong to ignore such prohibitions. If the issue was meat offered to idols, we would expect that to be mentioned as in 1 Corinthians 8—10. Also, these were not Judaizers who made this essential for salvation, for Paul's tone would be quite different (as in Gal 1 or Phil 4) if that were the case. Here Paul shows his basic agreement with the strong that the food laws are no longer binding on Christians. He makes this statement *as one who is in the Lord Jesus.* On the basis of Jesus' explicit teaching (Mk 7:15, 19) as well as his general experience of Christ's teaching, Paul can draw this conclusion. Thompson argues (1991:194-99) that *in the Lord Jesus* refers explicitly to Jesus' teaching that the food laws are no longer binding. However, Paul wants the strong to understand a basic point: the exercise of one's freedom is not always the best thing to do. They may be right yet still wrong in their practice, because *if anyone regards something as unclean,* for that person *it is unclean.* The religious conscience of a person is all important, for it determines his or her walk with God. If a

---

"through the teaching of the Lord Jesus" (Michel 1966; Dunn 1988b; Cranfield 1979). I agree with Cranfield that these are not mutually exclusive. In Mark 7:19 we have the statement that Jesus "declared all foods 'clean,'" and this could be part of Paul's point here as well as the first two more general aspects.

person has an honest conviction about something (v. 5, "fully convinced in his [or her] own mind"), that conviction must be honored. Believers must be allowed to follow the Lord as they think best, even if that does not logically follow from biblical teaching. Once again, this principle fits current debates regarding movies, cards, dancing and social drinking.

Paul goes further in verse 15, switching to the second-person singular *your* for greater impact. The strong should not only refuse to argue with the weak on the issue but should not even exercise their freedom around the weak. Once again (cf. v. 10) Paul calls both sides *brothers* in the Lord. How can a brother or sister deliberately bring *distress* or "pain" to their own kin? This does not mean it simply upsets their conscience but more that it hurts them spiritually. As Cranfield says (1979:714), "The weak in faith will be grievously hurt, he will have the integrity of his faith . . . and obedience destroyed, and his salvation put at risk." Probably verses 14 and 15 together cause this—the weak are told they are wrong (v. 14) and then see the strong eat the forbidden foods (v. 15); this leads them to go against their conscience, eat what they believe is unclean, and thereby destroy their conscience. The progression is deliberate and quite emphatic—the weak see the freedom and are first terribly "hurt" (NIV, *distressed*) and then *destroyed*. Until the weak have the faith to eat such foods, they should never be talked into doing so. The word *destroy* is incredibly strong. Several point out (Cranfield 1979; Dunn 1988b; Moo 1996) that *destroy* means spiritual ruin, namely, "to turn away entirely from their faith" (Moo 1996:855). Schreiner (1998:734) calls this "eschatological destruction" caused by the loss of eternal salvation. Paul adds strength to this by adding *for whom Christ died*. Jesus gave himself as an atoning sacrifice for these people, and the strong glibly bring them to complete spiritual ruin just for the sake of their freedom! It is clear in Paul's mind that their convictions on these issues are intimately interwoven into their whole walk with the Lord. Hurting their conscience here might produce a domino

14:16 There is disagreement about whether the *good* should be seen generally for all God's covenant blessings or the gospel (Luther 1972; Lenski 1945; Cranfield 1979; Morris 1988; Dunn 1988b) or specifically for the knowledge of the strong (Calvin 1979; Godet 1969; Murray 1968; Barrett 1957; Bruce 1985; Fitzmyer 1993b; Moo

effect that would produce their complete spiritual downfall. It is not stated how such an extreme result could occur, but the implication is obvious—do not exercise freedom in any matter that can hurt the conscience of another Christian. To do so is to fail to "walk according to love," the essential characteristic of the true believer (12:9-21). Respect their convictions by freely (it is also a free act to refrain from an action) honoring their conscience and refraining from eating such foods. In other words, Paul felt free to eat unclean foods but would not do so when with Christians who were convicted against doing so. This is another essential principle for us today. When worshiping with a group of Christians who define their walk via certain conditions (see previous paragraphs), we must honor their convictions and refrain from those things that hurt them.

In conclusion to the first part of his argument (vv. 14-15) Paul points out that eating all foods is indeed a *good* thing in light of the freedom that Christ has inaugurated but that such freedom had to be used cautiously. If it ever led to fellow believers being hurt and ultimately destroyed spiritually, then the name of Christ could be "blasphemed" or slandered (NIV, *spoken of as evil*) by outsiders (Cranfield 1979; Schreiner 1998) or perhaps by the weak when they apostatize (so Moo 1996). Either way, the name of Christ is maligned by the spiritual ruin caused by the misuse of freedom on the part of the strong. What is good in itself can have terrible consequences if not used wisely. The dissension and the spiritual hurt it might cause would result in the church being reviled by many. Above all, believers must live on the basis of love by respecting the honest convictions of other Christians and honoring those convictions when in the presence of such "weak" brothers and sisters in Christ. This certainly has been proven true in our own day as well. Many non-Christians say, "Why should I be a Christian? You don't get along with each other, so why should I think becoming a Christian will bring peace or happiness?"

In verses 17-18 Paul tries to view the issue in its proper perspective.

___

1996). In the context of verses 14-15 the latter makes more sense, for Paul is referring to the misuse of the *good* knowledge of the strong to bring criticism on the church.

The issue of *eating and drinking* is not the essence of *the kingdom of God*. The Roman Christians should not be stressing peripheral matters. By mentioning *the kingdom of God* Paul returns to the Jesus tradition (this is the only place in Romans that it is mentioned) regarding the in-breaking of the kingdom in this world as proof that the last days are here. Freedom to eat certain foods and the strife occasioned by that insistence on freedom is not what the kingdom is all about. Instead, they should be centering on *righteousness, peace and joy in the Holy Spirit*, exactly what the dissension was endangering. Each of these is a critical aspect of Romans. *Righteousness* is the central theme of the book, referring to the justification of the believer by the atoning death of Christ and the righteous life that results (especially 1:17; 3:21-26). *Peace* is the primary result of justification (5:1) and of the presence of the Spirit (8:6). Paul's goal is to produce peace in the midst of the conflict (v. 19 below). This is the first appearance of *joy* in Romans, but Paul concludes this section with a prayer that "joy and peace" will "fill" the Roman church through the "power of the Holy Spirit" (15:13). It is *the Holy Spirit* alone that can turn the destructive conflict around so that righteous behavior will predominate and the church will find the peace and joy that is the primary proof that the kingdom of God has once again triumphed. Before this can happen, however, the "strong" at Rome will have to temper their demands and start caring more about the spiritual development of the "weak" Christians than about their precious freedom.

The necessary response is to seek to *serve Christ in this way*, meaning to serve him by the kind of kingdom-centered living that produces righteous deeds and community peace and joy. Such is only possible under the leading of the Holy Spirit, and when that happens, the weak and the strong at Rome will learn to live together in mutual respect and

---

14:17 Dunn (1988b:822) shows how seldom Paul emphasizes *kingdom* by comparing him with the Synoptics: *kingdom* appears infrequently (14 versus 105 times) while *righteousness* (57 versus 7 times) and *Spirit* (110 versus 13 times) show the true Pauline emphasis. Paul probably uses it here to stress the essence of Christianity.

14:18 There are several ways to interpret *in this way*: (1) it could mean "in this matter," referring to the point Paul has been making (Michel 1966; Dunn 1988b); (2) it could refer to the threefold "righteousness, joy and peace" that they were to pursue

love. And the servant of Christ will indeed be approved by the Master (v. 4). When the strong subordinate their freedom to these more important kingdom principles, then they will first be *pleasing to God,* alluding back to 12:1 where the presentation of the total self to God was also "pleasing" to him. This also is a self-sacrificial act. Second, they will be *approved* by those around them, probably the same who would "blaspheme" them for destroying the "weak" Christians in verse 16. The picture may be that people are "testing" them (also in the Greek word *dokimos,* "approved") to see if they deserve slander or approval. When they serve Christ properly and produce peace in the community by following the leading of the Spirit, they find approval.

The obvious conclusion *(therefore)* is that we *make every effort* to produce *peace* in the community. Literally, Paul commands us to "pursue the things of peace." The idea of "pursuing peace" occurs frequently in the New Testament (2 Tim 2:22; Heb 12:14; 1 Pet 3:11; cf. 2 Cor 13:11; Eph 4:3; 1 Thess 5:13; Jas 3:18) and is an essential component of life in the Spirit. The point here is that corporate peace takes tremendous energy, and the strong must "pursue" it with all the strength they have, especially since their tendency is to stress their freedom at the expense of peace. The way to peace is to pursue "the things that make for the edification of one another" (NIV, *mutual edification*). If the strong are seeking to "edify" or "build up" the weak rather than to satisfy their own freedom, peace will be a natural result. Paul states this well in Ephesians 4:12, where the saints are to "prepare God's people for works of service, so that the body of Christ may be built up." Cranfield correctly notes (1979:722; contra Barrett 1957; Moo 1996) that this refers to the strengthening of both the individual member and the corporate body as a whole. Paul has been switching between the second singular (vv. 10, 15, 20) and the plural to stress both

---

(Sanday and Headlam 1902; Cranfield 1979; Käsemann 1980; Morris 1988; Fitzmyer 1993b); (3) it could mean "in the Holy Spirit" (Wilckens 1982); (4) it could refer to the kingdom focus behind verse 17 (Moo 1996); or (5) it could mean recognizing the secondary importance of food and drink (Barrett 1957). Due to the neuter singular *touto,* "this," it is likely that it refers to the whole idea of verse 17 (Barrett 1957; Schreiner 1998), namely, the kingdom living that produces righteousness, joy and peace (the neuter singular in Greek is often holistic, summarizing the preceding idea).

the individual and the group. In this context it means that both the weak and the strong must seek to build up each other, with the greater responsibility on the strong (the focus of this section).

Once more Paul turns to the second-person singular (vv. 10, 15) for effect. Each member of the "strong" must make certain they *do not destroy the work of God for the sake of food*. The terms of verses 19 and 20 (build up/destroy) are polar opposites; they must "build up" rather than "tear down" God's building (so Moo 1996; Schreiner 1998). In verse 15 the danger was destroying the weak Christians, and here it is expanded to encompass the destruction of the *work of God* or the church as a whole (contra Murray 1968; Cranfield 1979 who see this also referring to God's work among the weak believers). The message is clear. It is true that *all food is clean* (probably the main slogan of the strong): the strong have a perfect right to eat all foods, for they all are clean in the sight of God (vv. 2, 14). However, it is one thing to have a right to do something, quite another to misuse that right to bring harm to another believer. This is exactly the subject of 1 Corinthians 9:4, 12, 15, 19-22. Paul as an apostle had certain rights but surrendered them for the sake of the Gospel. So as in verse 14, Paul immediately qualifies their freedom, saying it is wrong *to eat anything that causes someone else to stumble*. The strong must relinquish their rights to those foods the weak regarded as unclean, lest they bring them to spiritual ruin.

So Paul sums up the point and restates it positively (v. 21). It is wrong to hurt someone with your freedom (v. 20) and right to refrain from eating lest it harm a brother or sister in Christ (v. 21). The first part (not eating meat) restates the point of verse 2. The weak Jewish Christians would refuse to eat meat because they were uncertain whether it would be kosher. Cranfield says it well (1979:725): "The strong Christian who 'has the faith to eat any food' has more room in

---

14:20 Scholars are divided whether *it is wrong for a [person] to eat anything* refers to the weak (so Chrysostom; Murray 1968; Käsemann 1980; Wilckens 1982) or to the strong (so Sanday and Headlam 1902; Barrett 1957; Cranfield 1979; Dunn 1988b; Fitzmyer 1993b; Moo 1996). The parallel with verse 14 could favor the former, but the immediate context favors the latter. The focus is on the strong, and it is they who are causing the weak Christian to fall.

14:22 There are three possible understandings of the beatitude: (1) it could challenge the strong to make sure they do not have to blame themselves for causing the

which to maneuver than the weak Christian who 'eats *only* vegetables.' He has the inner freedom not only to eat flesh but also equally to refrain from eating it." The idea of avoiding wine is more difficult and is found only here. Probably the weak applied the same scrupulous attitude regarding meat to wine, for it might have been offered to the gods (compare meat offered to idols in 1 Cor 8—10). The strong should be willing freely to surrender meat and wine rather than hurt the conscience of their fellow believers. Paul then expands this by adding *anything else* to show the universal principle involved. The mature Christian will not do *anything* that could cause spiritual harm to another believer.

This section is drawn to a conclusion in verses 22-23. First, Paul commands them, *whatever you believe about these things keep between yourself and God*. Here faith is not just a belief that their view is correct but also the "confidence that one's faith allows one to do a particular thing" (Cranfield 1979:726). This is not saving faith or appropriating faith but faith as a type of Christian action. So here it relates to faith as a conviction regarding the three aspects—food, drink and holy days. The strong Gentile Christians have enough faith or understanding in the new covenant to realize that the food laws and other legal restrictions no longer apply. However, to trumpet these in such a way that the weak Christians might be damaged spiritually is wrong, so the strong must keep their beliefs *between [themselves] and God*. This probably means two things: do not exercise your freedom in these matters when in the company of weak Christians, and do not put pressure on the weak to assent to your views. God honors their deeper understanding and the Christian lifestyle that results from it, but he will not honor any spiritual damage that can accrue from an overzealous forcing of it upon weaker Christians.

In verses 22-23 Paul addresses the strong and the weak in turn. For

---

weak to fall (so Michel 1966; Wilckens 1982); (2) it might address both the weak and the strong to go with their conscience and not to castigate themselves for doing so (so Käsemann 1980; Fitzmyer 1993b); or (3) it might address only the strong, encouraging them that they can partake of the food and wine without condemning themselves (Cranfield 1979; Dunn 1988b; Moo 1996). The first does not quite fit the language of verse 22. Either of the other two is possible, but the language of "approving" what they eat best fits the strong who "approve" of the meat they partake.

the strong he adds a beatitude promising God's blessing on those who are not condemned by what they approve. He is telling them that they can be confident of God's blessing on them when they follow their conscience and *approve* of the meat and wine as they partake of it. In other words, their beliefs are correct, and there is no need for judgment on such practices. For the weak he warns them to be faithful to their own consciences. What would be right for one group is wrong for the other, for believers are responsible to God to live according to the level of their faith. So for the weak to eat meat would lead to divine condemnation because it would not be done in faith (like the strong) but in *doubt*, that is, eating without the faith that it is right before God. Paul's point is that *everything that does not come from faith is sin*. God expects every believer to live up to the level of faith he or she has attained. While it is true that all meat and drink are acceptable before God, those whose faith does not allow such would fall into *sin* if they partake. And it would be sin, for they would be going against their consciences. For instance, if some believe it is wrong to eat out or play sports on Sunday, God expects them to live up to their convictions. For them it *is* wrong to eat out on Sunday. It is true that the faith of the weak is deficient, but God honors their conviction and expects them to live by it. The strong should understand that and honor their convictions. To force them to change would be to lead them into sin and provide a stumbling block that could destroy them spiritually.

Bear the Burdens of the Weak (15:1-6) Paul continues to address the problem of the strong and the weak, and still he places the primary burden on the strong. Some scholars believe Paul turns to a general discussion of caring for others in church conflicts (e.g., Käsemann 1980), but the majority correctly recognize that Paul continues to address the problem of chapter 14 here. Shifting to the first-person plural in verses 1-4 for rhetorical effect, Paul begins by identifying himself with *we who are strong* (Greek *dynatoi,* the first time Paul has used this term) in faith and contrasting this with those who are *weak* or "powerless" in faith (Greek *adynatoi*). As in 14:2 the issue is the strength of one's faith to accept the new-covenant reality in which all foods are clean and there is no longer an obligation to observe the Jewish holy days (14:2, 5, 14). But many *weak* Jewish Christians are unable to grasp this truth, and this has caused innumerable problems in the Roman church, not only in the deficient faith of this group but also in the over-reaction of many of the *strong* Gentile believers. So Paul must once again counsel the strong to curtail their reactions, telling them to *bear with the failings of the weak,* using language reminiscent of Galatians 6:2, "carry each other's burdens, and in this way you will fulfill the law of Christ." In fact, this is a Christian "obligation" (NIV, *ought to*) meaning God requires them to do this. The *failings* are most likely the weak faith that forces them to obey the food laws and observe the holy days.

It is difficult to know exactly what Paul wants them to do. It is doubtful that he wants them to correct the error of the weak, for he has already told them to accept the others and not to hurt their faith (14:13-18). At the least he is telling the *strong* not to dominate the others but to shoulder their burdens in a positive way. It is more than tolerance (so Dunn 1988b). Moo says it as well as anyone (1996:866): "they are sympathetically to 'enter into' their attitudes, refrain from criticizing and judging them, and do what love would require toward them." In other words, Paul calls for sympathetic understanding and empathetic accep-tance. In doing so, the strong are *not to please [them]selves,* that is, not to flaunt their freedom to partake of meat and wine without any con-sideration for the convictions of the Jewish Christians. This is a call for restraint and understanding.

Instead of pleasing ourselves, Paul adds, *each of us* should live to *please his neighbor.* Certainly Paul was including both the weak and the strong (the weak were judging, and the strong were showing con-tempt; cf. 14:10), but primarily he is addressing the strong, who had the greater obligation (v. 1). This returns their attention to the section on loving your neighbor (13:8-10) and redefines love as a desire to please. They were to accept the weak as they were and to avoid look-ing down on them; to understand where they were coming from and try to bring them spiritual pleasure (as in Rom 12:1, 2, the "pleasing" will of God). Paul defines this pleasure in two ways—their *good* and their "edification" (14:19). This means to seek what is best for them spiritually (again 12:2), to make certain we do not bring them the type of spiritual harm that can destroy them (14:15). The goal is to help them grow in the Lord, to *build them up* in Christ. "Mutual edification" was also the goal in 14:19, referring to strengthening fellow believers in the Lord. So the strong were to understand the present spiritual state of the weak and help them to grow in the Lord from that position rather than to castigate them for their deficiencies and try to force them to adopt the "superior" stance.

Paul turns to the example of Christ (v. 3) to anchor his argument. *Christ did not please himself,* that is, live his life to fit what met his own desires. This in essence was the heart of the temptation narratives (Mt 4:1-11 = Lk 4:1-13), where Satan tempted Christ to seek his own glory rather than what God wanted. It is somewhat surprising that Paul quotes Psalm 69:9 (LXX 68:10), for we would expect a statement of Jesus' sacrificial lifestyle, especially his death for us. But for Paul the entire Old Testament pointed forward to Jesus, so to place these words on Jesus' lips was completely valid: *The insults of those who insult you have fallen on me.* In this statement, *you* refers to God and *me* to Jesus. This means that all the contempt that sinful humanity has heaped upon God has now been borne by Christ. The psalm itself was a lament psalm focusing on the trials of the righteous sufferer. It was applied to Christ and became one of the most often quoted of the psalms (Mk 15:35-36 and parallels; Jn 2:17, 15:25; Acts 1:20; Rom 11:9). Most likely these insults were especially borne by Jesus on the cross, and Paul considers this the supreme act of self-sacrificial giving (Rom 5:8, where Jesus' death "demonstrates [God's] love for us"). The Messiah willingly bore insult, and the Roman Christians (especially the strong) should consider this model and imitate it. If Christ endured such insults for them, could not the strong endure the loss of some of their freedoms for Christ? Moreover, in Psalm 69 the reproach came from friends as well as enemies, and there may be a hint here as well that the judgment of the weak against them should also be borne with equanimity by the strong. As Schreiner says (1998:748), Jesus was willing to suffer such indignity and death for the sake of the greater glory of God, and

_____

15:4 Most scholars understand *through endurance* to be attendant circumstances (so Cranfield 1979; Käsemann 1980; Dunn 1988b; Moo 1996), meaning that we experience hope "along with" endurance, but it is better to see the two as parallel *dia*

in the same way the strong should be willing to suffer the loss of their freedom so that God's name will be honored among his people.

Paul then swerves from his argument briefly to explain his use of the Old Testament text (v. 4). He wants his readers to understand that *everything that was written in the past was written to teach us.* While the Old Testament had been fulfilled by Jesus (Mt 5:17-20) and had been abolished as a salvific force (Eph 2:15), it still had a canonical function for the instruction of God's people. Since the Old Testament pointed to Christ, it still had a part in God's plan, and its principles were still essential. In 2 Timothy 3:16 "teaching" is the first of four purposes of the inspired Scriptures. So the Roman believers should listen closely to its message. The basic purpose of this is *so that . . . we might have hope.* This seems out of place in a section on internal problems, but we must remember that all of this is taking place in the broader context of living the Christian life in a difficult world, and *hope* has already been emphasized in 4:18; 5:2-5; 8:20, 24; and 12:12. In the midst of pressure from outside and now inside the church, they need the hope of the gospel more than ever. The basis of that hope is first in the work of Christ and second in the witness of the Scriptures to him, both stressed in verse 3. The means by which this is manifest in the church is first *through endurance,* that is, steadfastly enduring the difficulties of life. This is seen in the chain of 5:3-4, where suffering produces endurance and that in turn leads to proven character and then hope. Endurance in the midst of suffering (note the connection with the suffering of Christ in v. 3) is the path to hope. The second means by which we find hope is *the encouragement of the Scriptures,* which here probably means more the "comfort" or "consolation" that the Scriptures bring us in the midst of suffering. Paul's point is that the Roman church has experienced these things together, and they have found both endurance and comfort in Christ and the Scriptures together, not as separate groups in conflict. Hope is endangered when the church is fractured by dissension. The "strong" Gentile believers are "obligated"

---

phrases telling the means *through* which hope is secured (so Godet 1969; Lenski 1945; Schreiner 1998). This is more natural and makes good sense in the context.

before God (v. 1) to go beyond their differences and find unity with the "weak" Jewish Christians. They share both Christ and the Word and now must share each other.

This theme of unity becomes the subject of the prayer-wish (a type of liturgical prayer; cf. 2 Thess 3:5; 2 Tim 1:16; Heb 13:20-21) of verses 5-6. It combines prayer to God (the major purpose) and exhortation to the church (so Murray 1968). The two means of hope in verse 4 are now linked to *endurance and encouragement,* or "comfort," with God the source of both. This is emphasized because Paul wants the Roman Christians to focus on these needs rather than on their differences. Both sides must realize that they cannot endure or find comfort in their present problems without each other. So Paul prays that God will *give you a spirit of unity among yourselves.* Literally, Paul asks that they learn to "think the same thing" or find a harmony of mental outlook, the very thing he commanded of the Philippians in Philippians 2:2 and 5 and of the Corinthians in 2 Corinthians 13:11. It is of course certain that he is not asking for them to come to agreement on the issues, for that is his whole theme in 14:13-18 and 15:1-2, that they learn to live with their differences. So it must mean that they learn to focus on the major issues of agreement and "agree to disagree" in the areas of conflict. They need to cultivate an attitude of thinking "with one another," a phrase used ten times in Romans to describe the united fellowship of the saints (1:12; 12:5, 10, 16; 13:8; 14:13; 15:5, 7, 14; 16:16). The basis of this unity is that both sides *follow Christ Jesus* and center on the salvation he has wrought with his atoning sacrifice.

The core of this unity is to function as a church *with one heart and mouth* (v. 6). The first is a political term speaking of a government body making decisions "with one accord." It is used often in Acts of the church meeting "together" in harmony (1:14; 2:46; 4:24; 5:12) and

---

15:6 *The God and Father of our Lord Jesus Christ* was a liturgical title appearing often in salutations to epistles (2 Cor 1:3; Eph 1:3; Col 1:3; 1 Pet 1:3) but was also used elsewhere (2 Cor 11:31; Eph 1:17; Rom 15:6). The major difficulty is the idea of him as "the God of Jesus," but this is a reference to Jesus' incarnate state and is related to the separate offices within the Trinity. As Michaels says (1988:17), "The 'God . . . of our Lord Jesus Christ' (cf. Eph 1:17) is the God whom Jesus worshipped and who raised him from the dead, and the God whom the risen Jesus makes known." Moreover, Jesus is *Lord,* a title that unites him with the God of the Old Testament.

so brings in connotations of the earliest period of unity among the believers. In the "with one voice" (NIV, *mouth*) the inward harmony finds outward expression (so Cranfield 1979). But the true purpose of both the inward and outward unity is to *glorify the God and Father of our Lord Jesus Christ.* This is the heart of the entire book of Romans; as the Westminster Confession puts it so aptly, humankind was created to "glorify God and enjoy him forever." The glory of God is the supreme goal, and the Romans were endangering this purpose through their disunity. Moreover, if the church is truly praising and glorifying God, dissension will not occur. In fact, there might be a deliberate allusion to 1:21, where depraved humanity did not glorify him as God. In their conflict, the Romans were acting like the pagans. Unity is mandated by the larger purpose of glorifying God in everything we do. In the larger sphere of commonality, we can place our differences in perspective and find a respect and love for each other in the Spirit, whether we are Calvinist or Arminian, charismatic or not, dispensational or covenant, whether we baptize by sprinkling or immersion. We can find unity whatever our denomination or background so long as we worship the same Lord and focus on the same cardinal doctrines.

Mutual Acceptance of One Another (15:7-13) This section has two purposes—it concludes the section on the strong and the weak, but is also serves to draw the letter together as a whole, especially regarding Jew-Gentile relationships. Sass (1993) goes so far as to argue that this passage sums up the themes of the whole letter, including what God has done through Christ (vv. 8-9) and the Pauline gospel (vv. 9-12). This certainly shows that the conflict between the Jewish and the Gentile factions in the Roman Church was one of the major purposes in his writing the letter. The organization is simple, with the command for

---

15:7 Dunn (1988b:844-45) goes too far when he separates this section from 14:1—15:6 and calls it a "Concluding Summary" of the book as a whole. Moo points out (1996:874) that too many of the major themes are missing (justification, victory over sin, the law) and believes Paul here is setting "the local conflict in Rome against the panorama of salvation history in order to stimulate them to obedience." At best one could say this both concludes the section and several major themes of the epistle (Käsemann 1980; Fitzmyer 1993b; Schreiner 1998).

mutual acceptance (v. 7) followed by two reasons for acceptance: Christ has accepted them all, and Christ has confirmed God's covenant promises to both (vv. 7-8). Then four Old Testament citations show that the basis of unity is worshiping God together (vv. 9-12); the section concludes with a prayer for joy and peace (v. 13).

Paul now addresses both groups and draws the challenge to a close by commanding them to *accept one another,* the very theme with which he began the section in 14:1. In 14:3 the basis of this is that "God has accepted" them, while here the basis is *just as Christ accepted you.* So there are two differences with chapter 14: there Paul addressed only the strong while here the command is for both groups, and there it was God receiving them while here it is Christ. This moves from the horizontal to the vertical dimension and continues the theme that the internal relationship of the people of God is vital for their relationship with God. The command to *accept one another* is at the heart of the New Testament doctrine of the fellowship of believers, as seen in Acts 2:44 ("all the believers were together and had everything in common") and 4:32 ("all the believers were one in heart and mind"). For this to be possible, the saints must disregard their differences and *accept one another* (see v. 5 on "one another") as members of the same body, the same family of God. The basis of this is that Christ has received both groups into his family, so therefore both sides are brothers and sisters of one another. They must now reflect this reality in their relationships with each other. Moreover, this again must be done to the glory of God, restating the theme of verse 6. Christ has glorified God in bringing us into his family, and the glory of God is at stake in our own unity.

The heart of this demand that the Jewish and Gentile Christians *accept one another* is one of the primary themes in Romans, namely, that the inclusion of Gentiles in the church fulfills the basic covenant promise given to the patriarchs (vv. 8-9; so Moo 1996). As such, it unpacks the meaning of Christ accepting the church, describing it as a covenant reality. Paul's opening *I tell you* introduces a "solemn doctrinal declara-

---

15:8-9 There are two options for the syntactical structure of these verses: (1) Paul is saying two parallel things, that Christ has become a servant of the Jews and that the Gentiles are glorifying God (so Cranfield 1979; Wilckens 1982); and (2) that Christ has become a servant of the Jews for two purposes, to confirm the covenant prom-

tion" (Cranfield 1979:740) used to support the preceding statement. The message is that Jew and Gentile are equally the recipients of the work of Christ. First, Jesus is the *servant* or "minister" *of the Jews on behalf of God's truth.* As Jesus himself said in Matthew 15:24 (cf. 10:6), he had come "only to the lost sheep of Israel." Yet Paul is saying that this is a continuing ministry, for the perfect form *has become* indicates an ongoing service (so most commentators) or a continual state of being (aspect theory). This reflects the "to the Jew first" priority of Romans 1:16; Christ's work among his people is not finished (see 11:25-32). Many believe that *God's truth* here especially refers to his covenant faithfulness (*truth* = "faithful"; so Käsemann 1980; Dunn 1988b; Schreiner 1998), meaning that God keeps his covenant promises, as stated in the following clause. The purpose of God's faithfulness is *to confirm the promises made to the patriarchs.* The idea of confirming the promises means more than proving their reliability or truthful character; it also connotes the idea of fulfilling the promises in himself (so Michel 1966; Cranfield 1979; Käsemann 1980; Dunn 1988b). Both the certainty of the promises and their fulfillment in Christ are intended. God's covenant faithfulness and the reliability of the promises composed the primary issue in chapters 9—11 (see 9:6, 14; 11:1, 11). Paul is reminding them again that those promises are still valid. God has not forgotten his people.

Yet at the same time there is a second purpose in the ongoing nature of God's faithful work in Jesus, and this was also a significant emphasis in chapter 11, *that the Gentiles may glorify God for his mercy.* This is the second half of 1:16, "first for the Jew, *then for the Gentile.*" In 10:19—11:32 Paul presented a complex plan—God had rejected the Jew and turned to the Gentile in part to make the Jews jealous and eventually to bring them into the kingdom themselves. Here he summarizes the message. Those who originally were "objects of his wrath" have become "objects of his mercy" (9:22-23) and have been grafted into the olive tree (11:17) so that they might praise God for his mercy.

---

ises and to enable the Gentiles to glorify God (so Murray 1968; Barrett 1957; Morris 1988; Dunn 1988b; Moo 1996; Schreiner 1998). The grammar is quite difficult, but the latter fits the developing message better.

Both Jew and Gentile are included in God's plan of salvation, and both are the recipients of Christ's salvific work. Therefore, they are one in God and Christ and must become one in heart and mind in the church. J. R. Wagner (1997:482-84) makes the point that in effect Christ has become "servant" of the Gentiles as well as of the Jews, and the unity of the two groups in the church is based on the fact that Christ is servant of both.

Paul anchors this truth in a series of four quotations from the Old Testament that focus on the place of the Gentiles in God's plan and especially on the unity of Jew and Gentile in praising God (vv. 9-12). Paul wants them to understand unequivocally that the unity of the two groups was always part of God's covenant plan. The first three quotations are closely related to verse 9 since they describe the Gentiles praising God and rejoicing. They also stem from every part of the Old Testament—the law (v. 10), the writings (vv. 9b, 11) and the prophets (v. 12)—"to show that the inclusion of Gentiles with Jews in the praise of God has always been part of God's purpose" (Moo 1996:878).

1. Paul begins with ideas drawn from Psalm 18:49 (it is quoted in 2 Sam 22:50), in which David, after defeating his enemies, sits on his throne and thanks God for the victory, promising, *I will praise you among the Gentiles; I will sing hymns to your name.* In the psalm it is the defeated nations that hear God praised, and here that becomes the Gentiles. The point here is that the Jewish Christians are to follow David's model and praise God along with the Gentile Christians (so Dunn 1988b; Fitzmyer 1993b; Schreiner 1998). In the psalm, the defeated nations are invited to join in praise of the divine Warrior, Yahweh. Here the converted Gentiles join the Jewish Christians in worship.

2. Paul then turns to Deuteronomy 32:43, but this differs from the MT and follows the LXX. The quotation comes from the last verse of the Song of Moses, a cry of victory that calls upon the nations to rejoice with Israel that God has delivered them. The picture of the nations re-

_____

15:9 Because the original psalm had *Lord* added, and since David was typologically related to Christ, many think Paul intends this to be the words of Christ himself (so Sanday and Headlam 1902; Cranfield 1979; Wilckens 1982; Moo 1996), perhaps also reflecting Paul's own mission (Käsemann 1980). While this is very interesting, it is difficult to prove, and as one of four successive quotes, it should be seen more sim-

joicing with God's people in the Song of Moses is seen by Paul as fulfilled in the New Testament reality of Gentile and Jew worshiping together. Note the development—in the first quotation God is praised *among the Gentiles,* while here the Gentiles directly join in the praise with Israel—*with his people* (so Moo 1996).

3. This quotation comes from Psalm 117:1, a short psalm of praise extolling God's love and faithfulness. In the same way that the Gentiles praised God for his mercy in verse 9, so here they praise him for his steadfast faithfulness. The two lines are synonymous, as the Gentiles are told to *praise the Lord,* and *all . . . peoples* are called upon to *sing praises to him.* There is further development here. In the first two quotes the Gentiles participate in worship with the Jews, while here they worship on their own. Note the emphasis on *all* (in both lines); this is universal worship, with no group left out (cf. Rev 7:9, where the "great multitude" before the throne came from "every nation, tribe, people and language").

4. The final passage is the only one mentioning the author, possibly because the quotation from Isaiah concludes the list and contains a messianic prophecy. Isaiah 11:10 (again Paul follows the LXX) follows a prophetic passage on the "Root of Jesse" (a messianic title; cf. Jer 23:5; 33:15; Sirach 47:22) who will be filled with "the Spirit of the Lord" (Is 11:2, quoted by Jesus in Lk 4:18-19) and deliver his people (Is 11:1-9), leading to the return of the remnant from exile (Is 11:11-16). So this culminates the emphasis on God's plan of salvation in verses 9-12 by showing that it was prophetically predicted as a messianic act. The Messiah as *the Root of Jesse* would bring it to pass by "rising up" (NIV, *spring up;* possibly connoting Jesus' resurrection; so Käsemann 1980; Dunn 1988b; Moo 1996; contra Cranfield 1979; Schreiner 1998) and ruling *over the nations.* Christ became "Lord" (v. 6) over the nations, so that now *the Gentiles will hope in him,* echoing the "hope" that is the focus of verse 4. It is this *hope* that will bring unity between the war-

---

ply as supporting the inclusion of the Gentiles in God's plan. The *I* in this instance is David, corporately identified with the nation (so Schreiner 1998), providing the pattern for the Jewish Christians in the church at Rome. Just as the nation participated in David's victories in the psalm (and 2 Sam 22), so the nation/Jewish Christians now participate in worship with the Gentiles.

ring factions at Rome, for this is the basis of their worship and praise. Sharing the same hope in the Root of Jesse, they can overcome their differences.

Just as Paul finished the first section of this chapter with a prayer-wish (v. 6), he now concludes the second part with another, asking that *the God of hope fill you with all joy and peace* (v. 13). Most of the themes here summarize key emphases elsewhere. This is the God who brings people hope, stressed not only in verses 4 and 12 of this chapter but throughout the epistle (see on v. 4). In other words, the hope that the Gentiles have in the Root of Jesse (v. 12) is given them by God. Moreover, the *peace and joy* refer to the internal harmony and joyous spirit that come to the church through the Holy Spirit in 14:17. So this prayer-wish is already in process of being fulfilled as God is at work in the community. The key is that this only comes *as you trust him,* refer-ring to the active dependence on the power of God that alone makes all this possible. *Trust* or belief/faith is the key aspect in the work of salvation within (see especially 3:21—4:25) and means not just a mysti-cal trust but a total reliance on God. In addition, "faith" in 14:1, 2, 22-23 is that belief in God that enables one to understand his covenant prom-ises and appropriate the lifestyle he has for us. In this latter sense the weak and the strong had differing degrees of "faith," but Paul wants the larger fact of faith in Christ to bring peace and joy into their differ-ent degrees of "faith." This is only possible when they live *by the power of the Holy Spirit* and find his strength to forge a greater unity out of their differences. In chapter 8 the work of the Holy Spirit is seen as the enabling presence in the church and the individual. Without his em-powering, hope, peace and joy are beyond our reach. With him we do not just have hope but *overflow with hope,* meaning that our cup of hope is "full and running over." In 5:15 the grace of God and his gift of salvation "overflow," and this in a sense is the result of that; in our mu-tual salvation hope overflows to us all and gives us the spiritual strength to "accept one another" (v. 7).

Moo (1996:881-83) has an excellent discussion on the applicability of 14:1—15:13 to current issues. He makes two points: First, the specif-ics have limited relevance, for the actual situation was not just a differ-ence of theological opinion but limited faith on the part of the Jewish

Christians to appropriate the new covenant situation. Therefore, of the three issues—prohibition of meat and of wine and the observance of special days—only the issue of Sabbath observance today is a real parallel. However, the principles do apply more broadly to current issues on matters of *adiaphora*, that is, issues that are open biblically and on which we can "agree to disagree." He notes three points made by Paul: (1) as a realist, he knew that Christians actually live at different levels, and for the weak Jewish Christians these issues were indeed "sin" (14:14, 20); in the same way, the scruples of believers today are very real to them, and they should not violate their conscience. (2) Other believers are stronger and do not share these scruples; they must understand the weaker believers, respect their convictions and make sure to build up rather than tear down the others' "faith." They can practice their freedom whenever the "weaker" Christians are not there to be "harmed" (cf. 1 Cor 10:25-29) but curtail their practices whenever it will cause problems. (3) The "'bottom line' is the unity of the church" (Moo 1996:883). The weak are not to condemn the strong, and the strong are not to look down on the weak (14:10). Rather, the unity of the church must be preserved in all areas where it is a matter of openness (that is, where it does not impinge on a cardinal doctrine). There are two ways to contextualize biblical material, at the specific level (food laws, wine, holy days) or at the general level, in which the principles are applied to issues that parallel the biblical situation (see Osborne 1991:336-38). As discussed in this chapter, there are two areas that fit the general situation, first noncardinal doctrines (see on 14:3, 5, 9) and practical life situations (see on 14:13, 14). In both these areas Christians must learn to accept each other and forge a larger unity that recognizes and allows such differences.

PAUL CONCLUDES HIS EPISTLE (15:14—16:27)

Paul has concluded his letter addressing the situation at Rome and his exhortation regarding the Gospel and the place of the law in the Christian life. Now he returns to the material of his letter introduction (1:1-17) and addresses those issues once more but in reverse order, first of all discussing his travel plans (15:14-29 = 1:11-13), then asking for prayer (15:30-32 = 1:8-10), and finally offering an extensive list of greetings and salutations (16:1-27 = 1:1-7). Of course, he also includes aspects not found in his opening but emphasized in his epistle, such as a prayer for peace (15:33; cf. 14:17; 15:13), as well as new material like the warning against false teachers (16:17-19). This conclusion is the longest of Paul's letter closings, possibly because of his circumstances when writing the letter: his third missionary journey is nearly over, and he is on his way to Jerusalem with the collection for the poor (15:25-27). He plans to visit Rome on his way to the next stage of his mission plan, the evangelization of Spain; his hope is that the Roman church will sponsor that missionary journey (15:24, 28). The most unusual feature is the lengthy greetings to individuals, families and house churches in 16:3-16. No other epistle comes close. This is probably because Paul has addressed this pastoral letter to a church he had not yet visited. He most likely is greeting everyone he knows to establish a personal relationship with the church and to prepare the way for his visit. He may never have been there, but his authority and right to speak are firmly established in the number of leaders who were personal acquaintances.

☐ Paul's Travel Plans (15:14-33)

As his letter moves to a conclusion, Paul elaborates (from 1:11-13) his apostolic mission to the Gentiles (vv. 14-16), both in terms of his past ministry (vv. 17-21) and of his forthcoming trip to Jerusalem, Rome and then on to Spain (vv. 22-30), concluding with a request for prayer regarding his imminent trip to Jerusalem (vv. 31-33). It is interesting to compare Paul's desires here with what actually happened according to Acts 22 and following. He felt that his ministry in the eastern part of the Roman empire was finished, and it was time now to reach the west. In Acts 20:25, in his farewell to the Ephesian elders just a short time after completing this letter, he told them, "none of you . . . will ever see me again." So his goal was to deliver the gift to the saints in Jerusalem then proceed on a fourth missionary journey through Rome to Spain. By delivering the gift from the Gentile Christians to the Jewish Christians in Palestine, he hoped to forge a new unity between the two groups in the church and to establish a new era of peace out of the conflict between the two as seen in Galatians, Ephesians, Colossians, Philippians and Romans. His was a salvation-historical mission, hoping to produce a new era of peace in the church.

Paul's Past Ministry to the Gentiles (15:14-21) Paul wants the Romans to understand why he is coming to them and also why he has presumed to write an apostolic letter to a church he has never visited. Both purposes flow out of his sense that God has called him as apostle to the Gentiles. He is also certain that they will receive the letter in the spirit in which it was written, calling them "brothers [and sisters]" and complimenting them for the depth of their walk in Christ. Some have thought him insincere here, merely trying to flatter them, but that does not fit the tone of the letter as a whole. Rather, this is courtesy shown to a church with problems but still containing many mature Christians (see Cranfield 1979; Schreiner 1998). He is *convinced* of three things: first, that they are *full of goodness*, a term referring to their kindness and generosity and perhaps also their honesty in dealing with others (Käsemann 1980; Cranfield 1979 prefer the latter). Second, they are *complete in knowledge*, meaning they have a comprehensive knowledge of God and the gospel truths, including all Paul has talked about in this letter. As a result, they are *competent to instruct one another*, certainly referring to the problem of the strong and the weak in the previous section but going beyond that to general instruction in the Christian faith. *Instruct* is often used of "the word of admonition which is designed to correct while not provoking or embittering" (Behm 1967:1021), but here it may be more neutral, denoting imparting knowledge. Paul is saying that he knows that the Roman church has not only accepted but understood and acted upon the things he has told them in the letter.

Paul indeed expected that they knew much of what he had told them, but he felt led by the Lord to write them *quite boldly*, realizing they could be offended but intending *to remind* them of these truths again. Certainly Paul is being diplomatic, for no person could know all he told them. But some in the Roman church knew much of what Paul was saying, and he certainly assumes here the basic spiritual maturity of the members as a whole. We all need to be reminded of the basic truths again and again because it is human nature to have selective memories, especially in times of conflict. Both the strong and the weak, for instance, knew of the need for tolerance and unity in the church. But they forgot those in the heat of the moment, and many probably thought their issue was exempt from such considerations. So Paul had to *boldly* exhort them to remember those principles and follow them once again.

The reason that Paul had the boldness to write so forcefully was *because of the grace God gave [him] to be a minister of Christ Jesus to the Gentiles* (vv. 15-16). This is a statement of the authority behind the letter as a whole. Paul could write to a Gentile church he had never visited because God through his grace had made Paul "apostle to the Gentiles" (cf. Acts 22:21; 26:17-18; Rom 1:5; 1 Cor 3:10; Gal 2:9; Eph 3:2; Col 1:25). Yet it is interesting that Paul calls himself not an apostle but rather a *minister* to the Gentiles. Moreover, he uses a specific term that, while it can refer to a *minister* or servant, often connotes a priestly office (as in Is 61:6; Neh 10:40; Sirach 7:30), and in this context that fits very well. In his priestly work, he *proclaim[s] the gospel of God* to the Gentiles and then makes them *an offering acceptable to God.* Lohse (1995) shows the connection between the "gospel" in 1:3-4, 16-17 and here as a summary of Paul's message of justification in Christ. In short, he wins them to Christ through the gospel and offers them to God, who accepts them. The offering is not coming from the Gentiles; Paul metaphorically presents the Gentiles as an offering to God. The gospel is his *priestly duty,* and proclaiming it is the fulfillment of the Old Testament sacrifices. Moreover, the converted Gentiles are *acceptable,* a term that also means "well-pleasing," used also of the acceptability of "spiritual sacrifices" in 1 Peter 2:5. God is pleased with the offering of the Gentiles, but as with Old Testament sacrifices, it is essential that those offerings be *sanctified* or "set apart" for God. This can only be done by the Holy Spirit. As Moo says (1996:891), "it is ultimately God himself, by his Holy Spirit, who 'sanctifies' Gentiles, turning them from unclean and sinful creatures to 'holy' offerings fit for the service and praise of a holy God." Thus in the words of 1 Peter 2:9,

---

15:16 Some (Barth 1933; Cranfield 1979) believe that Paul is calling himself a Levite rather than a priest, with Christ the high priest whom Paul is serving as a Levite. This is certainly possible, since the term is often used of the levitical office in the LXX (Ex

they become "a chosen people, a royal priesthood, a holy nation."

Because of the grace God has shown Paul in bringing the Gentiles to God as an offering, he can "boast" (NIV, *glory*) *in Christ Jesus in [his] service to God* (literally, "the things concerning God," v. 17). While boasting in one's own works is wrong (3:27; 4:2), boasting in Christ is not. Paul is overjoyed and very proud of what God has accomplished *in Christ Jesus,* namely, the Gentile mission (vv. 15-16). Note the emphasis on God in Christ; compare 5:11, "in God through Christ" for Paul's variety of usage (so Dunn 1988b). It is interesting to see how often Paul speaks of boasting in that short period when he wrote the Corinthian and Roman epistles: he "boasts" over the Corinthian Christians (1 Cor 15:31), in the mutual relationship with the Corinthians ("you can boast of us just as we will boast of you," 2 Cor 1:12-14; cf. also 7:4, 14; 8:24); in the Corinthians willingness to give (2 Cor 9:2); in his own mission to the Corinthians (2 Cor 10:13-17; 11:10-21); and even in his weaknesses (2 Cor 11:31). Paul uses boasting language more than any other New Testament writer (fifty-five of the sixty times in the New Testament, with forty-two of them in Romans and Corinthians), but he was never proud of himself or felt superiority (like the Jews in Rom 3:17). Rather, he was proud of what Christ had done in him (as in v. 18 below; see the excellent survey in Zmijewski 1991:276-79).

The thought continues in verse 18, as Paul says he would not "be so bold" (NIV, *venture;* the cognate of *boldly* in verse 15 [so Moo 1996:891]) as to *speak of anything except what Christ has accomplished through me.* His boasting was entirely in Christ, and it would be presumptuous to do anything else. The verb *accomplish* means to "produce" or "bring about" and looks to Christ as the active agent in accomplishing everything. Paul was the instrument *(through me),* but Christ was the force that produced the results. Those results are *leading the Gentiles to obey God by what I have said and done* (literally "in word and deed"). Obviously Paul has the Gentile mission in mind, that which was given him by the grace of God (v. 15). The obedience of

---

38:21; Num 1:50; 3:6; 1 Chron 6:32-33; and so on). However, the context here does not support this interpretation, and it is best to see Paul using priestly imagery for his apostolic work.

the Gentiles here refers not only to their conversion but also to a lifetime of following Christ, the "obedience that comes from faith" that was the basic purpose of his mission also in 1:5. Obedience is stressed in 1:5; 5:19; 6:16; and 16:19, 26 and is the proper response to Christ and the Spirit. Paul centered not just on evangelism but discipleship; when people came to Christ, he wanted to ensure that they surrendered their lives fully to him. But he refuses to brag about his own accomplishments because he realizes none of this would have occurred without the Lord's intervention and guidance. Paul did indeed speak and act, but behind every word was the empowering presence of Christ. With the emphasis on God, the Spirit and Christ in Paul's mission in verses 16-17 and again in verses 18-19, there is an implicit Trinitarianism (so Murray 1968; Moo 1996).

The deeds are detailed in verse 19—*by the power of signs and miracles.* "Signs and wonders" is a common phrase for miracles, occurring first at the Exodus (Ex 7:3; 10:9-10; Deut 4:34; and so on) then elsewhere in the Old Testament (Ps 78:43; Jer 32:20-21) as well as in the New Testament (Acts 2:19; 4:30; 5:12; 6:8; 7:36; 2 Thess 2:9; Heb 2:4). It is used of Paul's miracles in Acts 14:3 and 15:12. In a sense the *signs* are the God-ward aspect pointing to his *power* behind it, and "wonder" is the human response to his powerful deed. The word *power* is found twice, first in the powerful miracle and then in the basis of the miracle, *through the power of the Spirit.* The Spirit both undergirds everything Paul does, including his miracles, and brings the Gentiles into the sanctifying presence of God (v. 16).

The result of the Spirit's work (*hōste,* "so that") is Paul's ministry of gospel proclamation *from Jerusalem all the way around to Illyricum.* Actually, the Greek says he has "fulfilled the gospel of Christ," which could mean that he had "fully proclaimed the gospel" in the sense of

---

15:19 Some think that there is chiasm in verses 18-19: *word—deed—signs and wonders—the power of the Holy Spirit* (Michel 1966; M. Black 1973). But the Holy Spirit is not just connected with the words of Paul (indicating the power of Paul's preaching), nor can the deeds be narrowed to signs and wonders. The deeds are everything Paul has done, and the Holy Spirit provides the power for the deeds as well as the words.

The movement *around* from Jerusalem to Illyricum has led to diverse interpretations. Some think of it as a ministry "round about" the vicinity of Jerusalem (Godet

effective communication (so KJV; NIV; Sanday and Headlam 1902; cf. Bowers 1987, who says it means he had a "complete" ministry of developing settled churches), but more likely means he had "completed" his ministry there (Godet 1969; Hodge 1950; Cranfield 1979; Morris 1988; Moo 1996). He is hardly saying he had evangelized every town and village; rather that he had finished his pioneer missionary work of bringing the gospel to every region. His strategy was to plant churches strategically in central cities and to use them as hubs to reach the rest of the area. That had been completed. The geographical designations of Jerusalem and Illyricum are also somewhat puzzling, since Antioch was the sending church for Paul's mission and neither place was directly connected to any of his journeys. But they could designate the extent of his mission, for Jerusalem would have been the southernmost point and Illyricum the northernmost point, as it was north and west of Macedonia (modern Yugoslavia and Albania). While no such trip to Illyricum is indicated in the New Testament, there is no reason to doubt that Paul could have gone there, perhaps during his trip through Macedonia to Greece in Acts 20:1-3. Also, while Paul is never said to have made Jerusalem a focus of his mission (especially to the Gentiles as indicated here), we do know he ministered there in Acts 9:27 ("preached fearlessly in the name of Jesus") and visited there in Acts 11:30, 15:1-21 and 18:22. This probably indicates simply the extent of his missionary work "from the borders of Jerusalem to the borders of Illyricum"). Paul is saying two things—all of this incredible ministry was only possible because of the power of the Spirit; he had finished his mission in the eastern part of the Roman Empire, and it was now time to turn to the west.

In verses 20-21 Paul then explains what he means by saying he had "completed" his mission. His desire has always been *to preach the gos-*

1969) or as related to the centrality of Jerusalem, referring to Paul's mission as a "circle" building on the table of the nations in Genesis 10 and fanning out from Jerusalem to the nations (Schreiner 1998). Others conceive it as an arc or "grand sweep" by which the gospel moved out throughout the Gentile world (Lenski 1945; Cranfield 1979; Käsemann 1980; Dunn 1988b; Fitzmyer 1993b). But it most simply means that Paul has moved "around" from place to place as he brought the gospel to the nations (Sanday and Headlam 1902; Cranfield 1979; Moo 1996). The first two are too complex for this one word, and the second does not fit as well as the third.

pel where Christ was not known. That led him to cities from Jerusalem to Illyricum. As several have noted (Cranfield 1979; Dunn 1988b; Moo 1996), "ambition" is probably too strong a translation, and the term more likely means to "strive after" or "be zealous" regarding a thing. So Paul has been zealous about his intention to reach the lost. His goal has been that of a pioneer missionary who is the first to proclaim the gospel in an area. As Stott says (1994:382), "His own calling and gift as apostle to the Gentiles was to pioneer the evangelization of the Gentile world, and then leave to others, especially to local, residential presbyters, the pastoral care of the churches." As he said to Corinth, "I planted the seed, Apollos watered it" (1 Cor 3:6). As several note (Michel 1966; Murray 1968; Käsemann 1980; Cranfield 1979; Schreiner 1998), *known* (literally, "named") does not mean knowing about Christ in general but rather that no one "names Christ in worship" or "confesses his name." Paul wants to go where no church has been established because he does not want to *build on someone else's foundation.* This is the same metaphor as 1 Corinthians 3:10, "I laid a foundation as an expert builder, and someone else is building on it." Moo uses an apt illustration (1996:896), "Paul . . . believed that God had given him the ministry of establishing strategic churches in virgin gospel territory; like the early American pioneers who pulled up stakes anytime they could see the smoke from another person's cabin, Paul felt 'crowded' by too many Christians."

This is then anchored in a citation from Isaiah 52:15 LXX, part of the best known of the Servant Songs (Is 52:13—53:12). Isaiah's message is that the One who is disfigured (v. 14) will "sprinkle many nations" (Is 52:15) so that *those who were not told about him will see, and those who have not heard will understand.* This passage is very apropos for Paul's purpose, for the "nations" who *have not heard* are the Gentiles, and the Servant of the Lord *(about him)* is certainly the Messiah. In the larger context, Isaiah 49:6 tells Israel, "I will make you a light for the

---

15:20 It is debated whether "in this manner" beginning verse 20 (omitted in the NIV) explains Paul's past mission (Cranfield 1979; Dunn 1988b; Fitzmyer 1993b; Moo 1996) or looks forward to his future plans in verses 22-23 (Sanday and Headlam 1902; Lagrange 1950; Käsemann 1980). This is somewhat of a false dichotomy. Verse 20 is transitional, both telling why he feels he has completed his mission in the east

Gentiles, that you may bring my salvation to the ends of the earth."
Paul undoubtedly saw this aspect of the Servant Songs as fulfilled in
the Gentile mission. So the goal of Paul's mission is that the Gentiles
who *were not told* (that is, where "Christ was not known") and *who
have not heard* will finally *understand* or "see," implying their conversion. What Paul has "completed" then is laying the groundwork for the
evangelism of the Gentile world in the eastern part of the empire; now
it is time for the local pastors to come and "water" what he has
"planted" (2 Cor 3:6).

Paul's Future Plans—Jerusalem, Then Rome and Spain (15:22-29)

Paul's vision has now turned to the west, to those lands that still have
not "heard." His exposition of that vision is framed with his desire to
visit the Roman church (vv. 22-24, 28-29), but his actual hope is to have
the Roman church support a mission to Spain (vv. 24, 28). However, in
the meantime he must first take the monetary gift the Gentile churches
have collected and deliver it to the Jerusalem saints (vv. 25-28). First, he
tells them why he has gone so long without visiting Rome—he has *been
hindered from coming* (see also 1:10, 13 above). It would appear from
the context that nothing negative has prevented a visit; rather the mission in the east "from Jerusalem to Illyricum" has forestalled his visit. It
is possible that *was hindered* is a divine passive indicating that it was
God's will that he not come yet (so Schreiner 1998). His work was not
yet complete, and he could not leave until it was. We must remember
that Romans was written at the end of the third missionary journey, and
if we peruse Acts 13—19, it is hard to find a time when Paul could have
pulled up stakes and sailed off to Rome. It is likely that he divided the
Roman Empire into east and west, and Rome to him was the gateway to
the west. It was so difficult to visit Rome (it took a lengthy sea voyage)
that he felt that God would not have him interrupt the needs of his ministry in the east in order to do so.

---

and providing the reason for the mission in the west.
15:21 A few (Michel 1966; Dunn 1988b) believe that Paul saw himself as the Servant
in the Scripture quoted from Isaiah proclaiming the message to the Gentiles, but the
majority correctly identify Christ as the Servant of the Lord. Paul's mission is to an-
nounce the gospel "about him," that is, the Messiah.

Still, he had long wanted to do so. *For many years* he had *been longing* to visit Rome. As the list in chapter 16 shows, he had many friends there, and since Rome was the capital of the empire, the churches in the east were frequently kept abreast of the situation in the churches there. So Paul was undoubtedly well acquainted (second hand) with the Roman church. What has made this upcoming visit possible is the fact that there was *no more place for [Paul] to work in these regions* (that is, in the eastern regions of the empire). As Schreiner states (1998:774), *place* here means "opportunity" (cf. Rom 12:19; Eph 4:27), and Paul could hardly mean he is forced to leave or that every town had been evangelized. Rather, his work there is finished, and the stage has been set for the work to go on throughout the region. His desire to plant the gospel in new regions now makes it possible for him to visit Rome on his way to the west.

So Paul says, *I plan to do so when I go to Spain.* It is certainly possible that Paul views Spain as the Tarshish of Isaiah 66:19, "I will send some of those who survive to the nations—to Tarshish" (so Aus 1979:237-46; Schreiner 1998), but why would Paul pick Tarshish over the others in the Isaianic passage (that is, "the Lybians and Lydians (famous as archers), to Tubal and Greece, and to the distant islands that have not heard my name"). Still, it is possible he saw himself playing a part in the fulfillment of that prophecy. We cannot know why Paul chose Spain; it is only mentioned in verses 24 and 28 in the New Testament. Still, he obviously felt it was God's will, and it is in keeping with his calling to plant the gospel in new territories. Spain was well known in Rome; colonies had been established there from the time of Julius

15:22 While some (e.g., Käsemann 1980) believe the hindrance was Paul's desire *not [to] be building on someone else's foundation* (v. 20), it is unlikely that that would keep Paul from visiting Rome (he shows no desire to minister there for any length of time). Rather, it had to be the needs of his mission in the east that prevented his visit.

15:23 Paul's mind is moving so fast here that he actually fails to finish his sentence. Verse 23 introduces two reasons (two causal participial clauses) for his plan to visit Rome (unstated but definitely the main clause), and verse 24 tells the time *when* he is going to come (on his way to Spain).

15:23-24 Cranfield (1979:766-68) does an excellent job of putting to rest the view of some (Munck 1959:49-55; Barrett 1957; Käsemann 1980; Aus 1979:232-62; Dunn 1988b) that Paul believed he was ushering in the parousia by taking the gospel to

Caesar. The Romans divided it into three provinces, and there was a developed Roman colony there. There is even the possibility that Paul actually got to Spain, as suggested in *1 Clement* (his epistle to Corinth written around A.D. 96) 5:7, "reaching the limits of the west he bore witness before rulers." However, it is difficult to know when Paul could have gone since he went back to the churches of Macedonia and Asia Minor after his Roman imprisonment (as seen in Phil 2:24 as well as the pastoral epistles) and on the basis of tradition was arrested (in 2 Tim 1:15 he was arrested in Asia, where he went after the first imprisonment), imprisoned and executed under Nero about four years later. The only way it would be possible is for Paul to have been executed after the Neronian period. In short, it is an interesting possibility but cannot be proven.

When Paul comes, he will just be *passing through* on the way to Spain. This is different from his purpose in 1:15, where he said he is "eager to preach the gospel also to you who are at Rome." The two are not at odds, however, for he planned a short stay *(while),* and certainly during that time planned to preach. His primary goal, however, was twofold: first to *enjoy your company,* that is, have a time of fellowship with them, and, second, *to have you assist me on my journey there.* It is generally agreed that *assist* is a term used often for missionary support (cf. Acts 15:3; 20:38; 21:5; 1 Cor 6:6; 2 Cor 1:16). This refers not only to prayer support and a commissioning for the mission but also to financial support and perhaps even to providing "companions who would know the country" (Käsemann 1980:398). Paul could be hoping to develop a team like the ones that set out

the nations, and that Spain was the last to be evangelized, thus completing the Old Testament expectations of the pilgrimage of the nations to Zion. First, there is no evidence that Paul thought himself so central a figure in salvation history that he could usher in the eschaton. Second, as Cranfield points out, Paul was not so geographically naïve as to think he had reached all the Gentiles. He would certainly have known of the Parthians (the tribes to the west of the Euphrates), the Germans (who had just defeated a Roman legion) and the British (conquered by Claudius's troops shortly before) as well as of Egypt and India (a major factor in Roman trade). So while Paul may have thought that when the Gentile mission was complete the End would come (Mk 13:10; Mt 24:14), he would hardly have thought that he himself could fulfill this or that the mission to Spain was the final link in the chain.

from Antioch on the first two missionary journeys. What Antioch was to the missionary journeys in the eastern empire Paul is hoping Rome would be for the western mission.

One important responsibility remains for Paul before he can come to Rome, delivering the collection for the poor he had been gathering for the past several months *in the service of the saints* (v. 25), with probably a purposive force, "in order that I might minister to the saints" (with the offering, so Cranfield 1979; Wilckens 1982; Moo 1996). This was actually the second such collection; Paul and Barnabas delivered the first about A.D. 48 after Agabus's prophecy regarding an empire-wide famine (Acts 11:27-30 = Gal 2:1-10, Paul's second visit to Jerusalem). At that time the "pillars" of the church—James the Lord's brother, Peter and John—affirmed Paul as apostle to the Gentiles and asked only that he "remember the poor," to which he added, "the very thing I was eager to do" (Gal 2:10). This charge probably had a great effect on him, and on the third missionary journey he spent a great deal of time collecting another gift from the Gentile churches *for the poor among the saints in Jerusalem* (v. 26).

Poverty seemed to be an ongoing problem for the Palestinian church, possibly because of several factors such as famines, the poverty of Judea in general and persecution (for the latter, see Acts 8:1-3; Jas 2:5-8; see Keck 1965:100-129). Paul's concern for the poor in general and his earlier experience made him focus on the collection during his third missionary journey, and he may have spent a great deal of time on it during his two- to three-year stay in Ephesus. From 1 Corinthians 16:1-4, written toward the end of that stay (around 56), he had already told the Corinthians about the collection, perhaps in an earlier letter (1 Cor 5:9), and he encouraged them to take weekly offerings and set the money aside for the collection. In 2 Corinthians 8—9, written several months later, they still had not done so, and Paul reminded

---

15:25 It is interesting that Luke never mentions the collection for the poor in Acts 20—21, even though he mentions the delegates who carried it. Most likely the collection was not an emphasis and did not fit his major purpose, which was to show how the Spirit was leading Paul to Jerusalem and to his God-given destiny.

15:26 The meaning of "the poor of the saints" is variously understood. Some (KJV, "the poor saints"; cf. Bammel 1968:909; Schlier 1964; T. E. Schmidt 1993:827) think it

them of the sacrificial giving of the much poorer Macedonian churches (2 Cor 8:1-5). They must have responded after the second letter, for Paul says here that *Macedonia and Achaia* (the province Corinth is part of) *were pleased to make a contribution*. Shortly after, Paul visited Corinth (2 Cor 2:3; 9:5; 12:20—13:1), where he wrote his epistle to the Romans (see the introduction to this commentary). The collection had to be going on for some time, for Acts 20:4 mentions delegates also from Galatia and Asia, and they most likely accompanied Paul with the funds they had collected (probably while Paul was in Ephesus, Acts 19). So this was a lengthy collection, possibly over a couple of years, involving most of the Gentile churches (see the excellent survey in McKnight 1993:143-44). Note also that he does not ask the Roman church to participate, probably because there is insufficient time and they are too far out of the way. The collection was taken among the Pauline churches. However, one wonders why he takes so much time talking about it. He obviously wants the Roman church to be involved by praying for it. Moreover, the example of unity between Jew and Gentile that it symbolizes (see below) is an important model for the Roman Christians, who had the same Jew-Gentile tensions (see 14:1 = 15:13).

Paul had several purposes in developing this collection for the poor: (1) In verse 26 he calls the gift a "fellowship" (NIV, *contribution*), indicating a unity of sharing between the Gentile and Jewish factions in the church. The gift from the Gentiles was intended to bind them with the Jews in Jerusalem and to show their love. In fact, Paul considered this an obligation (*they owe it to them,* v. 27). Undoubtedly, he wished to forge a new sense of unity with the gift. (2) In verse 27 he develops the principle of sharing—*if the Gentiles have shared in the Jews' spiritual blessings, they owe it to the Jews to share with them their material blessings*. This has often been called the principle of equality, as in 2 Corin-

---

epexegetical, that is, "the poor who are the saints." But that is difficult since it implies that all the saints are poor. It is better to take it with the majority of versions (NASB; NIV; NRSV; NJB; NLT) and scholars (e.g., Murray 1968; Cranfield 1979; Morris 1988; Dunn 1988b; Fitzmyer 1993b; Moo 1996) as partitive: *the poor among the saints*. Paul does not mean that all the saints were poor; he means that a sizable group among them were poverty-stricken.

thians 8:14, "At the present time your plenty will supply what they need, so that in turn their plenty will supply what you need. Then there will be equality." In other words, the Jews provide help from their spiritual heritage, and the Gentiles provide material help; in that way they find equality before the Lord. Such mutual sharing would go a long way in reducing the tensions. (3) McKnight (1993:146; so also Schreiner 1998) notes a further purpose: this could well have been intended as an "eschatological provocation" of Israel to conversion, functioning as part of the "envy" (Rom 11:11-24) that would bring Israel to salvation. They would see in the offering "the fulfillment of the promise that the Gentiles would bring gifts to Zion (Is 2:2-4; 60:6-7, 11; Mic 4:13)." (4) It was an act of joy. Paul emphasized that the Macedonians and Achaians *were pleased to do it*. He says it marvelously of the Macedonians in 2 Corinthians 8:2: "Out of the most severe trial, their overflowing joy and their extreme poverty welled up in rich generosity." It simply cannot be stated any better than that. It was a pleasure to give!

Paul uses very strong language regarding the gift in verse 28, where he repeats his plans to visit Rome on the way to Spain. Again note that he plans only a short time in Rome as a stop on the way to his true objective, Spain and the west. However, before that can occur, he explains a final time, he must deliver the gift to Jerusalem. Three aspects are highlighted: (1) he must *complete this task,* which could connote the fulfillment of his religious obligation (so Sanday and Headlam 1902; Morris 1988; Dunn 1988b) but probably simply means he must finish or carry out this task before he can go on to Rome. (2) Paul plans to "seal" the collection (NIV, *made sure*), a term used in Paul for the seal of the Holy Spirit (2 Cor 1:22; Eph 1:13; 4:30, the only other times Paul uses this term); *seal* means to authenticate or provide a mark of ownership. It probably indicates that Paul intends to be part of the group bringing the gift and plans to personally authenticate it. (3) The offering is a *fruit* that the Jewish Christians will *receive,* possibly meaning that it is the "harvest" from the spiritual legacy that the Jewish people have given the Gentiles (Murray 1968; Moo 1996) or the visible demonstration of the *fruit* of Paul's mission (Morris 1988; Fitzmyer 1993b; Cranfield 1979 takes both as possible).

Paul virtually breathes a "sigh of relief" (Käsemann 1980; Moo 1996) and expresses his certainty *(I know)* that God would indeed work everything out and he would arrive in Rome shortly (v. 29). This quiet certainty provided great strength to Paul on the tumultuous trip to Jerusalem, when his associates repeatedly told Paul that the Spirit had told them he should not go (Acts 21:4), especially after Agabus gave his famous prophecy that Paul would go to Rome in chains (Acts 21:10-12). This is an important passage for discovering the Lord's will, for there were two interpretations of Agabus's prophecy, the one by his associates that it was a warning not to go and the other (the correct one) by Paul himself when he said, "Why are you weeping and breaking my heart? I am ready not only to be bound, but also to die in Jerusalem for the name of the Lord Jesus" (Acts 21:13). The same assurance reflected here in Romans gave Paul the strength to interpret the prophecy as telling how God intended that he go to Jerusalem rather than warning him not to go (providing an important model for us in similar circumstances). So he knows that he will arrive in Rome *in the full measure of the blessing of Christ.* The *full measure* is the overwhelming fullness of the blessing Paul was sure would accompany his coming. Also, it most likely is double edged, referring to the blessing the Romans would receive from Paul and the blessing he would receive from them (so Sanday and Headlam 1902; Murray 1968; Morris 1988).

Request for Prayer (15:30-33) Paul's deep-seated concern for the situation surrounding his visit to Jerusalem and the effect of the collection for the poor saints there is especially seen in his request for prayer here. He asks for two things—protection from his Jewish enemies and the reception of the offering by the Jerusalem saints. The language he chooses is very strong. He does not ask but *urges* or "appeals" to them for prayer. Moreover, he does so on the basis of *our Lord Jesus Christ,* the authority of Christ and his lordship over the church. The second basis is *the love of the Spirit,* which could be his love for us (Fitzmyer 1993b) but is better seen as the love the church experiences as made possible by the Spirit ("love from the Spirit," most other commentators). Since the Roman Christians are one in Christ, and since they have that sense of brotherly love made possible by the Holy Spirit, they should pray for Paul and his mission. In so doing they will *join . . . in (his) struggle* (literally "agonize with me"), a wrestling metaphor that calls for intense effort in prayer (see also Col 4:12). Prayer becomes a partnership in ministry as the intercessors participate in the needs by bringing them before the Lord.

The first prayer request is *that I may be rescued from the unbelievers in Judea,* showing that Paul already knew that the Jews were lying in wait for him. A short time later he learned of a plot against him as he was about to board a ship for Syria (Acts 20:3), so he could have been aware of potential problems. Such Jewish opposition had always been a part of his ministry (Acts 9:29; 13:45; 14:2-5, 19; 17:5-9, 13; 18:12-17; 19:9). Of course, history tells how well founded this concern was, with the riot and demand for his death after he had arrived in Jerusalem (Acts 21:27-36). In fact, the prayers were efficacious. His arrest by the Romans saved him from the mob, and when another plot took place, Paul's nephew learned of it (miraculously it seems), and Paul was taken to Caesarea (Acts 23:12-24). God was firmly in control, and the prayer was answered (though in a way hardly expected). The second request was for the acceptance of the offering by the saints in Jerusalem. In one sense Paul's *service* or "ministry" could be taken as all that Paul did, including the sacrifices in the temple. But this term was used in verse 25 explicitly for the offering to the poor in Palestine, and that is probably what it means here as well. This was also a valid concern, for he had also been opposed by many Jewish Christians (as in Galatians and Phil 4), who could have rejected a gift from Gentile Christians. But this prayer was granted as well, for Luke tells us that Paul and his team were "received . . . warmly" and the Jerusalem saints "praised God" at the report of the Gentile mission (Acts 21:17, 20).

The purpose of the two prayer requests was *so that by God's will I may come to you with joy.* His deliverance from his Jewish enemies and the acceptance of the offering by the Jerusalem saints would fill him with joy as he arrived in Rome. Once again the irony of this is that it did indeed come to pass but not in the way Paul thought. All the tumult in Jerusalem, the two years in prison in Caesarea and the tumultu-

---

15:32 This could be a third prayer request ("Pray that I may be rescued, that the collection will be accepted, that I might arrive with joy"), but it is more likely that this is subordinate to verse 31 and indicates the purpose of the prayers (so Morris 1988; Moo 1996).

ous journey by ship to Rome (Acts 22—27) must have made him wonder many times if God had rejected this prayer request. Yet the key is *by God's will*, and that was certainly evident throughout those chaotic events. There is little doubt that Paul's arrival was *with joy*, for Luke tells us that a group of Christians came down to meet Paul on the way to Rome, and "at the sight of these men Paul thanked God and was encouraged" (Acts 28:15). Even though he was a prisoner about to start a capital trial, there was joy because God was in charge. And it was in many ways a triumphant two years in Rome. Paul told the Philippian church at the end of that time that through his imprisonment the entire Pretorian guard had heard the gospel and Christians everywhere had become more bold for their faith (Phil 1:13-14). Paul's second desire was that he might *be refreshed* during his time in Rome. Schreiner (1998:783) says this is "the fellowship and joy that exist when members of the church mutually minister one to another." In other words, this refers to fellowship with the believers there. There is no direct evidence that this occurred while Paul was in Rome, but the picture of Paul in Rome in Acts 28 and the prison epistles themselves show a person who does seem *refreshed* in his spirit. Undoubtedly he had many times of fellowship with the Roman church during that period.

Paul concludes with a further prayer-wish (see 15:5-6, 13), asking that *the God of peace be with you all*. The *God of peace* is a major motif in the Old Testament (e.g., Lev 26:6; Judg 6:24; Ps 29:11; Is 26:12) and in Paul's writings (2 Cor 13:11; Phil 4:9; 1 Thess 5:23). It connotes "the God who brings peace" and is linked with Paul's plea for peace in the Roman community in 14:17 and 19. The *peace* here probably includes both individual tranquility of the soul and corporate togetherness in the church. The concluding *amen* affirms the prayer and provides a formal conclusion (see 1:25; 9:5; 11:36).

□ Concluding Greetings (16:1-23)

Paul normally concludes his epistles with a series of greetings both to

---

15:33 Cranfield (1979:780) points out that this cannot be the concluding prayer of the epistle because all the others in Paul's epistles include the word *grace*. Thus this is the concluding prayer of this section (15:14-32, possibly 14:1—15:32).

individuals in the church and from individuals who are friends of the church (see the introduction to this commentary for including this chapter as the authentic ending of this epistle). This is by far the longest list of greetings in his epistles, possibly because he has never actually visited the church and wants to establish a more personal relationship. He commends Phoebe (vv. 1-2), greets his coworkers (vv. 3-16), warns them of false teachers (vv. 17-19), gives an eschatological promise (v. 20), provides a benediction (v. 20) and provides greetings from many leaders (vv. 21-23).

Commending Phoebe (16:1-2) This is the only place in the New Testament where Phoebe (a Gentile by name) is mentioned, but she was a leader in the church at Cenchrea (the port city of Corinth) and was probably the bearer of this letter to Rome. So Paul is authenticating her and the letter she carries. Moo says such commendations were common then (1996:913): "People who were traveling in an age with few public facilities often depended on the assistance of people they had never met; and this assistance was easier to be had if the traveler could produce a letter of introduction from someone known to the potential host/ assistant." She is first *our sister,* meaning a fellow believer. Then she is a "deacon" (NIV, *servant*) of the church in Cenchrea, which could refer to a general service to the church (NIV; NASB; Romaniuk 1990:132-34) or an official office in the church (NRSV; REB; NLT; Cranfield 1979; Dunn 1988b; Morris 1988; Moo 1996; Schreiner 1998). Most accept the latter, for the term referred to that office (Phil 1:1; 1 Tim 3:8, 12), and women at times did hold the office (1 Tim 3:11). Moreover, this is the masculine noun *(diakonos),* and if it did indicate a general "serving," one would have expected the feminine *diakonia.* In fact, some have concluded that she was the pastor of the congregation (Schüssler Fiorenza 1986:425-26; Jewett 1988:148-50), but there is too little evidence that this term was used of the position of pastor or "overseer" in the first century. Most likely she held the office of "deacon," but there is little evidence regarding what

---

16:1-23 Of the twenty-six people greeted here, nine are women. Of these, two hold offices (Phoebe the deacon and Junia the apostle), another (Priscilla) is a *fellow worker,* and four (Mary, Tryphena, Tryphosa and Persis) are said to *work hard in the Lord.* It has been common to see strong implications in this list for the issue of

this office entailed (Dunn 1988b thinks it a "ministry of hospitality," but it was certainly more than that). Most likely deacons dealt with the practical needs of the church, for example, caring for the needy (Cranfield 1979) and financial oversight (Moo 1996).

So Paul asks the Roman church to *receive her in the Lord,* meaning to welcome her and give her lodging. *In the Lord* adds a spiritual dimension; they receive her as fellow believers. The added *in a way worthy of the saints* builds on *in the Lord* and means simply to accept her the way the saints should. In other words, hospitality is generally expected of all saints (Rom 12:13; Heb 13:2; 1 Pet 4:9; but especially of leaders, 1 Tim 3:2; Tit 1:8). Moreover, they should *give her any help she may need,* which could be legal assistance (as in 1 Cor 6:12; so Michel 1966; Dunn 1988b; Fitzmyer 1993b), meaning she would be coming to Rome as a litigant in a case. But there is little hint in the context for this, and it is a lot to read into the term "help" (*pragma,* "matter"). So Paul is simply asking them to help her in any need she might have. Paul then commends her further, saying *she has been a great help ["patron"] to many people, including me.* Some think this means simply that she has "helped" people (NASB; NIV; NLT; Käsemann 1980), but the term often referred to a person of wealth who gave assistance to a group as a "patron" (similar to the way the women in Lk 8:1-3 "were helping to support" the apostolic band). In a sense this means she was a leader of the church there in a manner similar to Lydia at Philippi (so Bruce 1985; Fitzmyer 1993b), though not the leader or president (as argued by Schulz 1990:124-26). Dunn (1988b:888-89) provides a great deal of evidence of leadership positions held by women in both the Hellenistic and Jewish worlds (such as ruler of a synagogue or patron of a *collegium*). In short, she was a patron/leader in the church at Cenchrea and worthy of all the assistance the Roman church could render her.

Greetings to People (16:3-16) There are twenty-six people at Rome Paul wants to greet as well as three house churches (five if we consider

women holding offices in the church today (see France 1994 and Cotter 1994 among others). Against such a possibility, see Moo (1996:927) and Schreiner (1998:797). For the hermeneutical issues, see Osborne (1991:326-32).

the *households* of vv. 10, 11 to be churches). This may well be everyone he can think of. His purpose may partly have been to enlist their help when he came (so Käsemann 1980; Moo 1996), but it was also to show that he had extensive knowledge of the Roman church and so wrote his epistle from a standpoint of personal involvement (so Schreiner 1998). Most of these are Gentile names, with two (Mary and Herodion) of Hebrew origin. There are nine women, which demonstrates the high view that Paul and the early church had of women in the church. Two are named as holding offices (Phoebe the deacon and Junia the apostle), and another (Priscilla) is called a "coworker." Moreover, four (Mary, Tryphena, Tryphosa and Persis) are said to *work hard in the Lord.* Clearly, women made a real difference in the early church. Moreover, most of the twenty-five names (one is simply called *his [Rufus's] mother*) are from the class of slaves, freedmen and craftsmen, the lower classes (so Fitzmyer 1993b; Moo 1996). It is also possible that Paul did not know several people but rather mentioned also those he had heard of, as seen in the more impersonal greetings (Schreiner 1998 lists the houses of Aristobulus and Narcissus as well as Tryphena, Tryphosa, Asyncritus, Phlegon, Hermes, Patrobas, Hermas, Philologus, Julia, Nereus and his sister, and Olympas in this category). Several have suggested three groups of names (Stuhlmacher 1994; Schreiner 1998), and I will follow that organization here.

1. Those Identified in the Pauline Mission (16:3-7):

a. *Priscilla* (Greek *Prisca*) *and Aquila* (vv. 3-4) are called *my fellow workers in Christ Jesus,* with "coworker" possibly being a semitechnical term for early church leaders who deserve pay (1 Cor 9:14) as well as respect and obedience (1 Cor 16:16, 18; see Ellis 1993:183). These two are major figures from Paul's mission, seen in the fact that they are named first in 16:3-16 (the order of names often indicates status). That Priscilla is named first (four of the six times the two are mentioned in the New Testament) may indicate she has higher social status or that she had a more significant ministry in the church. Paul met them in Corinth after they had been expelled from Rome by the emperor Claudius in A.D. 49 over the riots between Jews and Christians. They were fellow Jews and were also tentmakers/leatherworkers. Since they were probably wealthy (in virtually every city they have a home large enough for a house church),

Paul stayed with them and worked alongside them (Acts 18:1-3). Aquila was Jewish (18:2), and Priscilla may have been as well. When Paul went to Ephesus, they traveled with him (Acts 18:18). He then stayed there a while and used their home for a house church (1 Cor 16:19). They also had a significant ministry and on one occasion took Apollos aside, corrected his misunderstanding about baptism and "explained to him the way of God more adequately" (Acts 18:26).

Yet now they are back in Rome, perhaps partly as an advance team for Paul's visit. Claudius died in A.D. 54, and this allowed many to move back to Rome. Some think their movements indicate wealthy entrepreneurs with businesses in more than one city, but that cannot be proven. It is just as likely that they were free to move because they had a mobile business. At any rate, they obviously had become members of the Pauline team and major leaders in the early church. Probably in every city they used their (large?) home for a house church. Paul says here that *they risked their lives for me,* which means they used their status and influence to help Paul in a time of crisis, possibly saving his life at risk of their own. The most likely reference is to the riot in Ephesus (Acts 19:23-41) about a year earlier, undoubtedly a dangerous situation (cf. 1 Cor 15:32, "I fought wild beasts in Ephesus," a metaphor for extreme opposition). He then adds that *not only I but all the churches of the Gentiles are grateful to them.* This gratitude could be for rescuing Paul or for all the significant ministry they had in Corinth, Ephesus and Rome. The latter seems more likely (so Sanday and Headlam 1902; Bruce 1985; Dunn 1988b; Fitzmyer 1993b; contra Cranfield 1979).

b. *The church that meets at their house* (v. 5). As at Ephesus, their home was used as a house church. They could well have used their home for a house church before they were expelled from Rome in A.D. 49. Christians did not construct separate buildings for worship until after Constantine. This means that the largest congregations probably consisted of about fifty people. At any rate, they have quickly established themselves again as major Christian leaders in the Roman church.

c. *My Dear Friend Epenetus* (v. 5). A close friend of Paul's (though Paul tries to speak positively about everyone on the list, so this could be a semiformal compliment; see Cranfield 1979; Moo 1996), Epenetus is not mentioned anywhere else in the New Testament; he was *the first convert* (literally "firstfruits"). This probably means he was converted by Priscilla and Aquila, for Paul left them at Ephesus while he completed the second missionary journey (Acts 18:19). As often happens, the early converts become leaders in the church (Cranfield 1979). It could also mean his conversion "sparked the conversion of many others in the province" and that he traveled to Rome with Priscilla and Aquila (Fitzmyer 1993b).

d. *Mary* (v. 6). She was probably a Jewish Christian, though sometimes Gentiles also had this name (the feminine form of *Marius*). Obviously, we have no way of knowing whether this is any Mary in the New Testament (e.g., the mother of Jesus, Mary Magdalene, Mary and Martha). That is unlikely, for one would expect Paul to say more if she was one of those who had known Jesus. The same is true of Mary the mother of John Mark (who wrote the Second Gospel), whose home was one of the earliest house churches (Acts 12:12). She is thus an unknown leader *who worked very hard* for the Roman church. The term *work* does not indicate any specific task (some have tried to read it as a semitechnical term for apostolic ministry as in 1 Cor 15:10 and others) but means that she labored mightily on behalf of the Roman church. Still, she is the first to be noted by Paul in this way (see also v. 12), so she did play an important role in the life of the church there.

e. *Andronicus and Junia* (v. 7; NIV has the masculine *Junias;* TNIV has the feminine *Junia*). These are Jewish Christians who have great stature in the early church. Paul calls them his *relatives,* which could mean his actual blood relations (so Murray 1968) but more likely refers to fellow Jews (so "kinsfolk" is a better translation). *Andronicus* is a Greek name and probably means he was a Hellenistic Jew. The name *Junia* is debated, but the feminine is most likely. She was probably the

---

16:7 The name Paul uses, *Iounian*, could be either the masculine form of the masculine *Junias* or the feminine *Junia*. The accent would be different, but ancient manuscripts did not use accents, so that does not help. Until the twelfth century it was commonly believed to refer to the wife of Andronicus (see Fitzmyer's lengthy discussion [1993b]). Then from the thirteenth century until the middle of the twentieth century the masculine was generally preferred (Godet 1969; Sanday and Headlam 1902; Lenski 1945; Barrett 1957; Murray 1968; Michel 1966), meaning that the two were a

wife of Andronicus (like Priscilla and Aquila in v. 3). It is difficult to know when they were *in prison with* Paul. The only one recorded imprisonment before Romans was written was the short stay in Philippi (Acts 16:24-34), but Paul in 2 Corinthians 11:23 mentions that he has been in prison "frequently." Many scholars believe he was in prison for a while in Ephesus (possibly referred to in 1 Cor 15:32; 2 Cor 1:8-9). If that was true, it would provide a plausible occasion. Clement (*1 Clement* 5:6) says that there were seven imprisonments in all, and we can hardly know which one this refers to. Yet two other possibilities must be mentioned: this could be metaphorical for "prisoners of the Lord," but that does not seem viable here. It could also mean that they were imprisoned like Paul was rather than imprisoned with him, and this is a real possibility. There is no way to know for sure whether they were actually with Paul or not (the Greek simply says "fellow prisoners").

Paul next mentions that they were *outstanding among the apostles,* and that too has occasioned debate. It could mean that they were highly esteemed "by the apostles" or "among the apostles." If the former, they were not apostles; if the latter, they were. While "by" is technically possible, the general consensus is that *among the apostles* fits much better; they were probably two of the group of apostles named in 1 Corinthians 15:5 and 7 (Jesus appeared "to the Twelve" and then later "to all the apostles"). It is hard to know what use of *apostle* is meant in 1 Corinthians 5:7 and here. There are the Twelve and a few others like Paul and Barnabas, but there is also a use of the term *apostolos* for wandering missionaries, a use it had in the second-century Didache (11:3-6). This could well be the use in Acts 14:4 and 14, where Paul and Barnabas were doing missionary work as "apostles" (cf. 2 Cor 8:23; Phil 2:25, where it is translated "representative" and "messenger," respectively), and that may be the meaning here (so Godet 1969; Cran-

---

missionary team. However, most recent commentators prefer the feminine (Cranfield 1979; Wilckens 1982; Dunn 1988b; Stott 1994; Fitzmyer 1993b; Moo 1996; Schreiner 1998; see especially the strong arguments in Thorley 1996). The problem with the masculine interpretation is the absence of evidence for *Junias* used as a shortened form of *Junianus*. In contrast, *Junia* was a very common name, so it is most likely this was a woman.

field 1979; Fitzmyer 1993b; Moo 1996). Still, this would have been an office in the church, and Junia with her husband is an *outstanding* example of such a leader. Finally, *they were in Christ before [Paul] was,* meaning they had been converted before him. If they were among the "apostles" of 1 Cor 15:7, that would mean they had probably been followers of the Lord himself. However, they could also have been among the Hellenistic Christians in Jerusalem at the time of Acts 6—7. So they had been leaders/apostles for some time.

2. Friends and Acquaintances of Paul (16:8-15). These for the most part are not described as leaders (with the exception of Urbanus in v. 9). They depict people in the church that Paul either knew or had heard of.

a. *Ampliatus* (v. 8). This was a frequent name used for slaves or freedmen. He was a dear friend of Paul's, who calls him "beloved in the Lord." Cranfield (1979:790) thinks it quite possible it is the same Ampliatus named on a tomb in the Catacomb of Domitilla (the niece of the emperor Domitian) in Rome, saying it was a person "specially esteemed."

b. *Urbanus* (v. 9). This is another slave name, and like Ampliatus he too may have been part of the imperial household (so Sanday and Headlam 1902; Cranfield 1979; Dunn 1988b). He is also a "coworker" of Paul's, making him a leader in the Roman church (see v. 3).

c. *Stachys* (v. 9). We know nothing about him, though again there was a slave in the imperial household of that name. Paul refers to him as "beloved," just as he does Ampliatus in verse 8.

d. *Apelles* (v. 10). This is another person we know nothing about, though this name also appears in inscriptions from the imperial household. When Paul calls him *dokimion,* it could mean he was *tested* in a trial and proven through it, or it could mean simply that he was *approved* or esteemed by the church. NIV includes both in its translation.

e. *The Household of Aristobulus* (v. 10). This is a fairly common name, but most believe it may refer to the Aristobulus who was the brother of Agrippa I and grandson of Herod the Great. He never held office but accompanied his brother when he lived in Rome. Agrippa I died in A.D. 44, and Aristobulus between A.D. 45 and 48. After his death his household would have probably joined the imperial household but kept their name (so Sanday and Headlam 1902; Cranfield 1979; Dunn 1988b; Moo 1996). Paul is greeting the Christian members of his household.

f. *Herodion* (v. 11). Paul calls him a "kinsman" or fellow Jew (see v. 7). He was probably a slave or freedman in Herod's family. Such often took their patron's name (especially if they were foreigners). The fact that Paul mentions him right after the household of Aristobulus is further evidence that the Aristobulus named here belonged to the Herodian family.

g. *The Household of Narcissus* (v. 11). These are *in the Lord*, and as in verse 10 (the household of Aristobulus), this probably refers to Christians in the household. It is commonly believed that Narcissus is the prominent freedman who had been an aide to Claudius and was quite wealthy. However, after the accession of Nero (A.D. 54), his mother Agrippina conducted a purge, and he was forced to commit suicide. As above, his household would have become part of the imperial family but still retained its distinctive name.

h. *Tryphena and Tryphosa* (v. 12). These were also either slaves or freedwomen (common names in the papyri) and were probably sisters (families often gave sisters, especially twins, names from the same root). Since their names meant "dainty" and "delicate," there could possibly be a play on words when Paul says they *work hard in the Lord*. They were probably respected leaders in the church.

i. *Persis* (v. 12). The name means "Persian woman" and was commonly used for slaves and freedwomen. She has a double commendation, combining the "beloved" of verses 5 and 8 and the "worked hard in the Lord" of verses 6 and 12. Yet the description goes beyond Tryphena and Tryphosa, for Paul says she worked "*very* hard," possibly indicating that she was an outstanding leader in the church (like Mary in v. 6).

j. *Rufus* (v. 13). He is *chosen in the Lord*, which could mean he was especially respected or "choice" (so Godet 1969; Fitzmyer 1993b) but more likely describes him as one of the Lord's elect children. There is a good chance (though it obviously cannot be proven) that this is the Rufus of Mark 15:21, which describes Simon of Cyrene (who bore the cross for Jesus) as "the father of Alexander and Rufus." Mark's naming of the sons indicates that they were well known to his readers, and if Mark had its provenance in Rome (as many believe), that would indicate he was a prominent Christian leader there.

k. *[Rufus's] Mother* (v. 13). Paul describes her as "his mother and mine." This may mean that they were especially close, but it could also mean that she had shown him motherly affection or hospitality at some point. She may have traveled a great deal, perhaps as a member of a household or business, and encountered Paul in this way (so Dunn 1988b), or perhaps Paul stayed with the family of Simon of Cyrene in Jerusalem (so Godet 1969, but less likely since there is no indication that Paul and Rufus had known each other before).

l. *Asyncritus, Phlegon, Hermes, Patrobas, Hermas* (v. 14). These names as well were commonly used for slaves and freedmen and were probably members (perhaps leaders) of a house church. By adding *and the brothers with them* Paul is greeting the whole house church of which they were a part.

m. *Philologus, Julia, Nereus and His Sister* (v. 15). This could well be a family, with the father Philologus, his wife Julia, and their children Nereus and his sister. Also, the first two could be brother and sister, thus two pairs of siblings. It is impossible to know for certain. These were common slave names, and some think that they were slaves in the imperial household. However, those named with them may mean that this was a house church and therefore a family whose home was used. This latter is slightly more likely.

n. *Olympas and All the Saints with Them* (v. 15). As stated above, these Christians met with Philologus's family as a house church (as in v. 14).

o. *A Call for General Greetings* (v. 16). Having completed his extensive greetings to everyone he knew or had heard of in Rome, Paul

---

16:17 There has been no mention of heretical movements in the letter thus far, and Paul does not include such a warning in the conclusion to any of his other letters. As a result, some think this was not originally part of Romans (e.g., Byrne 1996). However, there is no text-critical evidence that these verses were ever not a part of this letter, and while Paul does not have this elsewhere, he does write general warnings occasionally in his epistles, such as the exhortation to stand firm in 1 Corinthians 16:13-14 or to be likeminded in 2 Corinthians 13:11. In short, there is no valid reason

now concludes with a general request to all the believers to *greet one another with a holy kiss.* This was his common plea (1 Cor 16:20; 2 Cor 13:12; 1 Thess 5:26; cf. 1 Pet 5:14). Kissing as a sign of special affection when greeting another was common not only in Judaism but elsewhere in the ancient world (cf. Mk 7:45; Lk 7:45; 15:20; 22:48; Acts 20:37). It signified a greeting with honor and respect (see Stäh
lin 1974:138-40). In the apostolic church the kiss came between the prayers and the eucharistic service (so Justin), but there is no evidence that it had this liturgical function during the New Testament age, though it may well be that Paul expected his letter to be read publicly, concluded with a *holy kiss* (so Michel 1966; Dunn 1988b). The emphasis on the *holy kiss* stressed the solemnity and spiritual significance of the greeting. Tertullian called it "the kiss of peace," but it is erroneous to translate this "kiss of peace" as in NEB. In our day, it calls for a loving Christian greeting.

When Paul says *all the churches of Christ send greetings,* he is certainly using hyperbole, for he means all the churches he is connected with rather than all that exist. As Moo points out (1996:927), this is probably part of his "strategy to bring the Roman church into the sphere of churches that know and support him." Also, it conveys the fact that behind Paul are churches all over the Roman empire.

Warning Against False Teachers (16:17-19) Very much like his warning to the Ephesian elders in Acts 20:29-31 ("savage wolves will come in among you and will not spare the flock"; cf. also Eph 4:14), Paul warns the Roman Christians about false teachers before they ever appear in the community. It is certainly possible that Paul had just heard that such teachers were on their way (compare Phil 3:1-2 for a similar possibility) and wants them to be ready, though the general de-

for thinking Paul could not include such a warning in his conclusion here. More difficult is the fact that he provides no hint of heresy in the Roman church in his epistle before this. Most likely, he knows of false teachers (as in 2 Cor 10:13) and may have heard they were on the way to Rome. As Sanday and Headlam say (1902:429), Paul was writing against "such as he knew of as existing in other churches which he had founded, whose advent to Rome he dreads."

scription of them may mean Paul simply wanted the church to be always vigilant. Moo may be correct (1996:807) in saying that Paul's greeting from "all the churches" in verse 16 reminded him of the problems false teachers had caused in many of them, so he felt he needed to add a general warning here. There is no way to identify the exact group Paul has in mind. He seems to be characterizing the type of people they are (self-centered, using flattery) rather than their specific teaching. Three groups have been suggested—protognostics (Dodd 1932; Bruce 1985), Judaizers (Godet 1969; Lenski 1945; Stuhlmacher 1994; Schreiner 1998), or the strong and weak parties (Barrett 1957; M. Black 1973—the Judaizing movement behind the "weak"). However, it is virtually impossible to know and more likely that he is giving a general description to warn the Roman church to be ready for any false teacher who comes.

Paul is *urging* or "exhorting" the church (cf. 12:1) and calls them "brothers [and sisters]" in order to stress his relationship with them. This points to a serious admonition. He commands them to *watch out* or maintain constant vigilance regarding the dangerous heretics who may come at any time. The first problem with these people is that they *cause divisions* or "dissension" in the community. Their teaching is divisive and would further erode the cohesion of a community already experiencing problems over the "strong" and "weak" factions (14:1—15:13). Second, they *put obstacles* or "stumbling blocks" before the believers. As stated in 9:33 (cf. 11:9), these are forces that destroy one's faith and can lead to apostasy. This is in fact a primary characteristic of heresy. It is not just serious error but actually destroys the core doctrines of the Christian faith. Such people are not Christians because they espouse what is *contrary to the teaching you have learned.* Such teaching contradicts the cardinal doctrines of the faith. These are not issues like the security of the believer or predestination (on which see the discussion on chapters 8—11) but central tenets like the doctrine of Christ or of salvation. The only proper response is to *keep away from them;* that is, have nothing to do with them. This is more than just avoiding them, for that would imply a modicum of tolerance. This is a more direct opposition involving both censure and discipline. It could infer a type of excommunication such as found in Matthew 18:17

("treat [them] as you would a pagan or a tax collector") or 2 Thessalonians 3:14 ("do not associate with" them). Of course, such discipline should also be done "gently" with the purpose of bringing them to "repentance" (2 Tim 2:24-26). The goal is not primarily to remove them from the church (though that is certainly an aspect of it) but rather to wake them up and help them to get right with the Lord. Nevertheless, the purity of the church must be guarded zealously.

The reason (*gar*, "for") that the church must act strongly is that *such people are not serving our Lord Christ, but their own appetites* (literally, "their bellies"). All the false teachers in the early church passed themselves off as Christians and ministered out of the church. The danger was the kind of tolerance shown by Pergamum and Thyatira in Revelation 2:14-16, 20-25, for they allowed the false teachers to work within their church. Paul wants to make it absolutely clear that such pretension will not work. Those people were not ministering for the Lord but for themselves. The language of "serving their own bellies" is similar to Philippians 3:19 ("their god is their stomach"), and while it could point to a libertine background (they live for pleasure) or a Jewish background (pointing to the food laws), it is best to take it as a metaphor for a greedy, self-centered ministry (so Cranfield 1979; Stott 1994). They serve only their own interests, not the Lord's.

The second reason the church must be vigilant is that false teachers *deceive the minds of naïve people*. Satan is the great "deceiver" (Rev 12:9, 20:3), and they follow in his steps (the connection with Satan is made in v. 20). Paul has used this word in 7:11, where he says "sin . . . deceived me, and through the commandment put me to death." He pictures the false teachers as deliberately manipulating truth to suck in the "foolish" or "simple-minded" people. These are weak Christians (Eph 4:14 calls them "infants") who do not understand the deep things of God and are easily fooled by the *smooth talk and flattery*, that is, the smooth "eloquence" of the heretics. What they say sounds so plausible and convincing that the gullible are easily drawn into their pernicious lies. This happens all too frequently. One is astounded at the ease with which a Jim Jones or a David Koresh finds adherents. I was once asked by *Christianity Today* to write an article on why it is that the cults seem to draw so many of their followers from evangelical churches (Osborne

1979:22-23). I discovered two reasons: one, the lack of true fellowship and caring in many churches; the other, the lack of hermeneutical and theological awareness on the part of too many Christians. When they hear these cult leaders twisting Scripture, they cannot tell that truth is being compromised. The answer is clear. We must develop Berean Christians who "search the Scriptures daily to see if these things are true" (Acts 17:11). We need to stress theological truth and help our believers learn how to study the Bible for themselves and so know when God's Word is being misused.

In contrast to the falsehood of these evil people, the Roman Christians are known for their *obedience,* so Paul is *full of joy over [them]* (v. 19). The heretics cause only dissension, but the Roman church is known for following the Lord, so Paul is confident that they will be ready should the false teachers appear. In fact, this could be a challenge. The Roman Christians "have a reputation to live up to" (so Cranfield 1979:802) and so must maintain the theological purity of their church, that is, remain obedient to the truths of their faith. Paul wants to make certain his *joy* remains complete (contra the Philippian church in Phil 2:2). The only way they can do this is to be *wise about what is good, and innocent about what is evil.* There is a play on words here, for *innocent* is similar in meaning to *naïve* in verse 18 (so Calvin 1979; Moo 1996). They must be *innocent* with regard to evil but not unwary. The only way to do this is to be *wise* with respect to that which is *good,* that is, know how to discern good from evil, not only with respect to ethical conduct but also with respect to theological truth. This tells us unequivocally how important the teaching ministry of the church is. The preoccupation with trivial pursuits in all too many churches today is incredibly dangerous, for a lack of theological concern is the first step to the destruction of the true vitality of the church and an open invitation to heresy.

Promise of Victory and Concluding Prayer (16:20) This is a remarkable promise and probably is both specifically related to the false teachers in verses 17-19 and generally related to the victory of the church in every area, including the discord caused by the strong and the weak groups in the church (14:1-2). The one who will bring this about is *the*

God of peace, a title used in 15:33 and closely connected with Paul's plea for peace in the Roman community in 14:17 and 19. God *will soon crush Satan under your feet,* a concept that alludes to the protevangelium of Genesis 3:15, "he will crush your head, and you will strike his heel." The false teachers are Satan's emissaries, but their influence is both temporary and doomed. Paul also links heretics with demonic forces in 1 Timothy 4:1, "in later times some will abandon the faith and follow deceiving spirits and things taught by demons." John also links the two in 1 John 2:18, "as you have heard that the antichrist is coming, even now many antichrists have come." Yet at the same time this has an inaugurated thrust centering on the tension between the already and the not yet seen so often in Romans (e.g., 8:18, 23, 30). The crushing of Satan has already begun but will not be consummated and finalized until the eschaton, when Satan will be first bound (Rev 20:3) and then thrown into the lake of fire (Rev 20:10). The Jewish understanding of Genesis 3:15 was that the serpent, Satan, would be defeated by God and his angelic forces (*Testament of Simeon* 6:6; *Testament of Levi* 18:12; cf. *1 Enoch* 54:6; *Jubilees* 10:8-9), a view found in Revelation 12:7-9, where Michael casts Satan and his armies out of heaven. Paul states that Satan would be defeated now in the Roman church and finally at the end of history. Moreover, this would occur *soon,* the same view of imminence seen in 13:12, "the day is almost here" (see on that passage).

The prayer-wish *the grace of our Lord Jesus be with you* concludes all of Paul's letters in some form or another (in many it is at the very end). He asks that the same grace of God and Christ that formed the initial greeting (1:7) might continue in their lives. Only in Christ can they experience the peace and victory over Satan that is theirs by divine right.

Greetings from Paul's Coworkers (16:21-23) He now returns to his normal practice of adding greetings from his mission team and others after sending greetings to members of the church he is writing. These are the team members who happen to be with him in Corinth at the end of the third missionary journey as well as some of the leaders of the Corinthian church.

1. *Timothy* was the young man who had had joined Paul at Lystra on his second missionary journey (Acts 16:1) and became one of his most

trusted associates. In fact, Paul sent Timothy on a short visit to Corinth from Ephesus (1 Cor 4:17; 16:10-11; probably on the Macedonian trip of Acts 19:22). He had returned by the time Paul wrote 2 Corinthians (2 Cor 1:1) and then accompanied Paul on his trip back to Corinth in Acts 20:1-3, from which place Paul wrote this letter to Rome. Later, Paul sent him to Philippi (Phil 2:19-24) and then Ephesus (1-2 Timothy).

2. *Lucius, Jason and Sosipater* are fellow Jewish Christians ("kinsmen"). Lucius could be Luke, Paul's coworker and the author of Luke-Acts (but Paul always calls him Loukas) or perhaps the prophet in Syrian Antioch (Acts 13:1), but there is no way to know for certain. Jason may be the same person whose home Paul stayed in during his time in Thessalonica (Acts 17:5-9), and Sosipater is probably the same as "Sopater," the representative of the Berean church who accompanied Paul and the collection for the poor when he left Greece shortly after writing this letter (Acts 20:4).

3. *Tertius* is the "amanuensis" or secretary who wrote down this epistle as Paul dictated it. Paul, who had poor eyesight, often used such help in writing his letters (Gal 6:11; 1 Cor 16:21; 2 Thess 3:17). While many gave their amanuenses great freedom in writing their letters, the similarity of style in Galatians, Romans and the Corinthian correspondence probably means Paul dictated his (so Stuhlmacher 1994; Moo 1996; Schreiner 1998; Cranfield 1979 points out he could have written in either longhand or shorthand). A first-person greeting from such a secretary is unusual but not unheard of. Tertius probably knew some of the Roman Christians. As he is mentioned only here in the New Testament, we know nothing more about him.

4. *Gaius* must be the Gaius of Corinth mentioned in 1 Corinthians 1:14, one of the two (early converts?) Paul baptized there (rather than the Gaius of Acts 19:29; 20:4 or the one in 3 Jn 1). He may also be the Titius Justus (full name Gaius Titius Justus) who was Paul's host in Corinth after he left the synagogue (Acts 18:7, with Crispus the synagogue ruler who is converted in v. 8 being the other one Paul baptized in 1 Cor 1:14; so Murray 1968; Bruce 1985; Morris 1988; Dunn 1988b).

16:24 While some western manuscripts (D, F, G, Θ and others) place a prayer-wish after verse 23 ("May the grace of our Lord Jesus Christ be with all of you. Amen"),

Paul says he is (literally) "host to me and to all the church" in Corinth. This could mean that his home was large enough to house the entire assembly in Corinth (so Dunn 1988b; Schreiner 1998) or that he was host to believers traveling through Corinth (so Käsemann 1980; Moo 1996). It is difficult to know for certain. The first seems unlikely, for there were almost certainly more Christians in Corinth than could fit into a single home. It is likely that Paul stayed in his home while writing this epistle.

5. *Erastus* was an important official, the "steward" or "treasurer" of the city. This is further evidence of the many high officials in the Roman empire who became Christians (cf. the proconsul Sergius Paulus of Acts 13:6-12). It is hard to know if he is the same Erastus mentioned in Acts 19:22 (Paul's assistant whom he sent to Macedonia) or 2 Timothy 4:20 (probably the one of Acts). It is difficult to think of an important public official having the time to accompany Paul on his mission travels. Another interesting possibility is the Erastus named in an inscription who paid for a marble pavement in Corinth so that he could be named "aedile" or "commissioner of public works" for a year. Cadbury strongly doubts this identification (1931:42-58; so also Meggitt 1996), but Gill believes it quite possible (1989:293-301, the basis of the *director of public works*). In the final analysis, this cannot be more than an interesting possibility (NLT goes back to "city treasurer").

6. *Quartus* is not found anywhere else in the New Testament. He is a fellow believer or *brother* rather than Tertius's brother (so Bruce 1985, but Paul would certainly have said "his brother" if that were the case).

☐ Concluding Doxology (16:25-27)

This extended doxological ending is used by Paul to sum up the implications of the gospel as well. In fact, it recapitulates the central motifs of the letter and is especially close to the introduction (1:1-7), thereby framing the letter with the theme of the revelation of God's salvation in Jesus. Paul begins the same way he does in Ephesians 3:20 (cf. Jude

---

this verse is missing in the better manuscripts (p^{46}, p^{61}, ℵ, B, C, 0150 and others) and is likely a later addition.

24), *Now to him who is able to,* referring to the fact that only God has the power to accomplish these things. So when Paul says God is "able to strengthen" us (NIV, *establish*), he means that our strength comes only via his strength. This is the strength to live the Christian life and to overcome temptation and trials. The twofold basis of this strength is Paul's *gospel and the proclamation of Jesus Christ,* though all agree that these are not separate but a single item, for it means that his gospel is proclaiming Christ. He is saying that the basis of strength for serving the Lord is found in the very gospel he has presented (primarily in 3:21—8:39), because in his gospel he is "preaching Jesus Christ" (better the preaching "about" Jesus than the preaching "by" Jesus for the *proclamation of Jesus Christ*), who is the sole source for Christian strength. Paul's gospel is further linked with *the revelation of the mystery.* In it God has revealed or made known his hidden mystery, which, as discussed in 11:25, is a salvation-historical event unknown before but now revealed to God's people. Here that *mystery* is the coming of Jesus Christ himself, which is further described in three ways. First it is *hidden for long ages past,* meaning that full understanding was not given to Israel in the past. They knew that their Messiah was coming, but they did not know the full significance of his coming. This is said well in 1 Peter 1:10-11, relating how the prophets "searched intently and with the greatest care, trying to find out the time and circumstances to which the Spirit of Christ in them was pointing when he predicted the sufferings of Christ and the glories that would follow." They only knew partly what was to happen, and they longed to experience the reality. Second, the mystery is *now revealed and made known through the prophetic writings.* In one sense there is a contradiction,

---

16:25-27 The majority of scholars argue that this doxology was added to the original letter (Dodd 1932; Barrett 1957; M. Black 1973; Bruce 1985; Cranfield 1979; Käsemann 1980; Wilckens 1982; Dunn 1988b; Munro 1990; Fitzmyer 1993b; Byrne 1996), possibly by a final editor when he compiled the Pauline corpus. The text-critical evidence is problematic. This passage is completely missing in several western manuscripts (F, G, 629 and others), placed after 14:23 in the Majority Text and others (Θ, 0209 and others), after 15:33 in p[46], after both 14:23 and 15:33 in 1506, and after both 14:23 and 16:23 in A, P, 33, 104 and others. However, it is found in its present position in p[61], ℵ, B, C, D, 81, 365, and several other manuscripts, and Metzger (1994:470-73) argues for its authenticity on the strength of those who place it after 16:23. Most who doubt it,

because this says that the mystery was both concealed and revealed in the prophecies. The solution is that the truths were indeed both revealed and hidden in the prophecies. Part was revealed, but a great deal was hidden. The fact of his coming and many details were made known, but a lot was not, and other aspects were made known but not understood until Christ actually came. Paul reflects that tension here. For instance, the Jewish people (including the disciples) expected a conquering king rather than a suffering servant. Also, God had said in the Abrahamic covenant that all nations would be blessed, but the equal place of the Gentiles in the divine plan was not understood. Third, the mystery has come *by the command of the eternal God.* It is the divine will that is behind the mystery of the gospel, and it has come to pass as the result of his decree. Since he is the *eternal God,* this plan was set before the world began (cf. Eph 1:4; Heb 4:3).

The purpose of this eternally decreed mystery is *so that all nations might believe and obey him.* This is a major theme throughout Romans, that Christ has come for all nations and peoples. Jew and Gentile stand equally before him as sinners in need of the grace of God, and Christ died so that all might find justification through faith. This is exactly Paul's purpose in 1:5, "to call people from among all the Gentiles [nations] to the obedience that comes from faith." Moreover, the moral side of salvation is stressed throughout Romans. To believe on Christ is to live for him, to obey him. Justification is the first moment of sanctification. Right belief leads to right standing with God, which itself leads to right living for God.

Paul concludes his epistle with praise *to the only wise God,* which could mean "to the only and wise God" but more likely means "to God

---

however, do so on its non-Pauline character, arguing that phrases like *hidden for long ages past* or *the eternal God* or *mystery* are unlike Paul and similar to the language of later epistles like Ephesians or Colossians. However, that is only valid if one accepts the non-Pauline authorship of those epistles. Moreover, as Moo has shown (1996:937), the language is quite similar to the rest of Romans, especially to the opening verses (1:1-17). Therefore, many (Godet 1969; Lenski 1945; Murray 1968; Nygren 1949; Hendriksen 1981; Hurtado 1981:185-99; Stuhlmacher 1994; Morris 1988; Stott 1994; Moo 1996; Schreiner 1998) accept the authenticity of the doxology and place it here. While one cannot be certain, it is more likely that the doxology does indeed belong in its present spot at the end of Romans.

who alone is wise" (so Cranfield 1979). In 11:33 Paul talked about "the depth of the riches of the wisdom and knowledge of God." The wisdom of God is certainly a major biblical emphasis. Paul focuses on the divine wisdom especially in 1 Corinthians 1:17—2:16 and 3:18-20, where he contrasts the wisdom of God with the so-called wisdom of the world. Paul's point here is similar—God alone is wise, and his people must seek only him as the source of wisdom. Wisdom in Paul is similar to the meaning of wisdom in Proverbs, where wisdom means living life in God's world by God's rules. It is always God-centered. So Paul ascribes God *glory forever,* meaning he deserves eternal praise. As the Westminster Confession says, God created us to "glorify him and enjoy him forever." It is our sacred privilege to give him the glory forever. In fact, that is how Revelation 7:15 pictures our eternal destiny: we will be "before the throne of God and serve him day and night in his temple" (see also Rev 22:3). Heaven will in one sense be an eternal worship service, with the difference being that God will be physically present with us, and we will look on his face for the first time since Adam sinned. Moreover, this praise is only possible *through Jesus Christ.* This is a fitting end to this epistle that teaches that all salvation is possible only through Jesus Christ. It was his act of love (5:8), his atoning sacrifice (3:25), that has brought all this about, and our faith in him (3:21—4:25) that brings us justification to eternal life (4:25; 6:23).

Bibliography

Aageson, James W.

1987   "Typology, Correspondence, and the Application of
               Scripture in Romans 9-11." *Journal for the Study of the
               New Testament* 31:57-72.

1996   "'Control' in Pauline Language and Culture: A Study of Ro-
               mans 6." *New Testament Studies* 42:75-89.

Achtemeier, Paul J.

1985   *Romans.* Interpretation: A Bible Commentary for Teach-
               ing and Preaching. Atlanta: John Knox.

Aletti, Jean-Noël

1987   "L'argumentation paulinienne en Rm 9." *Biblica* 68:41-56.

Anderson, Chip

1993   "Romans 1:1-5 and the Occasion of the Letter: The Solu-
               tion to the Two-Congregation Problem in Rome." *Trinity
               Journal* 14:25-40.

Aune, David E.

1993   "Religions, Greco-Roman." In *Dictionary of Paul and His
               Letters,* pp. 786-96. Edited by Gerald F. Hawthorne, Ralph
               P. Martin and Daniel G. Reid. Downers Grove, Ill.: Inter-
               Varsity Press.

Aus, Roger

1979   "Paul's Travel Plans to Spain and the 'Full Number of the
               Gentiles' of Rom. XI:25." *Novum Testamentum* 21:232-62.

Badenas, Robert

1985   *Christ the End of the Law: Romans 10.4 in Pauline Per-
               spective.* Journal for the Study of the New Testament Sup-
               plement Series 10. Sheffield: JSOT Press.

Bammel, Ernst

1968   "πτωχός." In *Theological Dictionary of the New Testa-
               ment,* 6:885-915. Edited by Gerhard Kittel and Gerhard
               Friedrich. 10 vols. Grand Rapids, Mich.: Eerdmans.

Barr, James

1988a   "'Abba, Father' and the Familiarity of Jesus' Speech." *The-
                      ology* 91:173-79.

1988b   "'*Abbā*' Isn't 'Daddy.'" *Journal of Theological Studies* n.s.
                      39:28-47.

Barrett, C. K.

1957   *The Epistle to the Romans*. Black's New Testament Com-
                      mentaries. London: Adam and Charles Black.

1982   "Rom. 9:30-10:21: Fall and Responsibility of Israel." In *Es-
                      says on Paul*, pp. 132-53. Philadelphia: Westminster.

1998   *The Acts of the Apostles*. The International Critical Com-
                      mentary. 2 vols. Edinburgh: T & T Clark.

Bartchy, S. Scott

1992   "Slavery (Greco-Roman)." In *The Anchor Bible Diction-
                      ary*, 6:65-73. Edited by David Noel Freedman. 6 vols. New
                      York: Doubleday.

Barth, Karl

1933   *The Epistle to the Romans*. 1919. Reprint, London: Oxford
                      University Press.

1959   *A Shorter Commentary on Romans*. Richmond: John
                      Knox.

Bauer, Walter,
William F. Arndt,
F. Wilbur Gingrich
and Frederick
W. Danker

1979   *A Greek-English Lexicon of the New Testament and Other
                      Early Christian Literature*. 2nd rev. and aug. ed. Chicago:
                      University of Chicago Press.

Beale, G. K.

1984   "An Exegetical and Theological Consideration of the
                      Hardening of Pharaoh's Heart in Exodus 4-14 and Romans
                      9." *Trinity Journal* n.s. 5:129-54.

Beasley-Murray, George

1962   *Baptism in the New Testament*. Grand Rapids, Mich.: Eerd-
                      mans.

Bechtler, Stephen R.

1994   "Christ, the Τέλος of the Law: The Goal of Romans 10:4."

Beck, Hartmut,
and Colin Brown

Catholic Biblical Quarterly 56:288-308.

1976   "Peace." In *New International Dictionary of New Testament Theology,* 2:776-83. Edited by Colin Brown. 3 vols. Grand Rapids, Mich.: Zondervan.

Behm, Johannes
1967   "νουθετέω, νουθεσία." In *Theological Dictionary of the New Testament,* 4:1019-22. Edited by Gerhard Kittel and Gerhard Friedrich. 10 vols. Grand Rapids, Mich.: Eerdmans.

Beker, Johan
Christiaan
1980   *Paul the Apostle: The Triumph of God in Life and Thought.* Philadelphia: Fortress.

1989   "Paul the Theologian: Major Motifs in Pauline Theology." *Interpretation* 43:356-65.

1990   "Romans 9-11 in the Context of the Early Church." *Princeton Seminary Bulletin* Supplement 1:40-55.

Best, Ernest
1967   *The Letter of Paul to the Romans.* Cambridge Bible Commentary. Cambridge: Cambridge University Press.

Bieringer, R.
1995   "Aktive Hoffnung im Leiden, Gegenstand, Grund, und Praxis der Hoffnung nach Röm 5, 1-5." *Theologische Zeitschrift* 51:305-25.

Black, David Alan
1989   "The Pauline Love Command: Structure, Style, and Ethics in Romans 12:9-21." *Filologia Neotestamentaria* 2:3-22.

Black, Matthew
1962   "The Interpretation of Romans viii. 28." In *Neotestamentica et Patristica: Eine Freundesgabe, Herrn Professor Dr. Oscar Cullmann zu seinem Geburtstag überreicht,* pp. 166-72. Supplements to Novum Testamentum 6. Leiden: Brill.

1973   *Romans.* New Century Bible. London: Oliphants.

Bornkamm, Günther
1991   "The Letter to the Romans as Paul's Last Will and Testa-

ment." In *The Romans Debate*, pp. 16-28. Edited by Karl D. Donfried. Peabody, Mass.: Hendrickson.

Boughton, Lynne C.

1992   "Biblical Texts and Homosexuality: A Response to John Boswell." *Irish Theological Quarterly* 58:141-53.

Bowers, Paul

1987   "Fulfilling the Gospel: The Scope of the Pauline Mission." *Journal of the Evangelical Theological Society* 30:185-98.

Bray, Gerald, ed.

1998   *Romans*. Ancient Christian Commentary on Scripture, New Testament 6. Edited by Thomas C. Oden. Downers Grove, Ill.: InterVarsity Press.

Brown, Colin

1975   "Conscience." In *The New International Dictionary of New Testament Theology*, 1:351-53. Edited by Colin Brown. 3 vols. Grand Rapids, Mich.: Zondervan.

Bruce, F. F.

1985   *The Epistle of Paul to the Romans*. Tyndale New Testament Commentaries. Grand Rapids, Mich.: Eerdmans.

Büchsel, Friedrich

1967   "λύω, κτλ." In *Theological Dictionary of the New Testament*, 4:328-56. Edited by Gerhard Kittel and Gerhard Friedrich. 10 vols. Grand Rapids, Mich.: Eerdmans.

Bultmann, Rudolf

1947   "Glossen im Römerbrief." *Theologische Literaturzeitung* 72:197-202.

1951   *Theology of the New Testament*. Vol. 1. Translated by K. Grobel. New York: Scribner.

1955   *Theology of the New Testament*. Vol. 2. Translated by K. Grobel. New York: Scribner.

1964a   "αἰσχύνω, κτλ." In *Theological Dictionary of the New Testament*, 1:189-91. Edited by Gerhard Kittel and Gerhard Friedrich. 10 vols. Grand Rapids, Mich.: Eerdmans.

1964b   "Δικαιοσύνη Θεοῦ." *Journal of Biblical Literature* 83:12-16.

1965   "καυχάομαι, κτλ." In *Theological Dictionary of the New Testament*, 3:645-54. Edited by Gerhard Kittel and Gerhard Friedrich. 10 vols. Grand Rapids, Mich.: Eerdmans.

Byrne, Brendan
1979   *"Sons of God"—"Seed of Abraham."* Analecta Biblica 83.
               Rome: Biblical Institute.

1996   *Romans.* Sacra Pagina. Collegeville, Minn.: Liturgical Press.

Cadbury, Henry Joel
1931   "Erastus of Corinth." *Journal of Biblical Literature* 50:42-58.

Calvin, John
1979   *Commentaries on the Epistle of Paul to the Romans.* 1540.
               Reprint, Grand Rapids, Mich.: Baker.

Campbell, William S.
1992   *Paul's Gospel in an Intercultural Context: Jew and Gentile
               in the Letter to the Romans.* New York: Lang.

Carras, George P.
1992   "Romans 2, 1-29: A Dialogue on Jewish Ideals." *Biblica*
               73:183-207.

Clarke, Andrew D.
1990   "The Good and the Just in Romans 5:7." *Tyndale Bulletin*
               41:128-42.

Cosgrove, Charles H.
1987a   "Justification in Paul: A Linguistic and Theological Reflec-
               tion." *Journal of Biblical Literature* 106:653-70.

1987b   "What If Some Have Not Believed? The Occasion and
               Thrust of Romans 3:1-8." *Zeitschrift für die neutestamentli-
               che Wissenschaft* 78:90-105.

Cotter, Wendy
1994   "Women's Authority Roles in Paul's Churches: Counter-
               cultural or Conventional?" *Novum Testamentum* 36:350-72.

Cottrell, Jack W.
1975   "Conditional Election." In *Grace Unlimited.* Edited by
               Clark Pinnock. Minneapolis: Bethany House.

Countryman,
Louis William
1988   *Dirt, Greed, and Sex: Sexual Ethics and the New Testament
               and Their Implications for Today.* Philadelphia: Fortress.

Crafton, J. A.
1990   "Paul's Rhetorical Vision and the Purpose of Romans: To-
               ward a New Understanding." *Novum Testamentum*
               32:317-39.

Craigie, Peter C.
1976   *The Book of Deuteronomy*. New International Commen-
                     tary on the Old Testament. Grand Rapids, Mich.: Eerd-
                     mans.

1983   *Psalms 1-50*. Word Biblical Commentary 19. Waco, Tex.:
                     Word.

Cranfield, C. E. B.
1975   *A Critical and Exegetical Commentary on the Epistle to the
                     Romans: Vol. 1*. International Critical Commentary, new
                     series. Edinburgh: T & T Clark.

1979   *A Critical and Exegetical Commentary on the Epistle to the
                     Romans: Vol. 2*. International Critical Commentary, new
                     series. Edinburgh: T & T Clark.

1991   "'The Works of the Law' in the Epistle to the Romans."
                     Journal for the Study of the New Testament 43:89-101.

1994   "Romans 6:1-14 Revisited." *Expository Times* 106:40-43.

1995   "Paul's Teaching on Sanctification." *Reformed Review* 48,
                     no. 2: 12-29.

Cranford, Michael
1995   "Abraham in Romans 4: The Father of All Who Believe."
                     New Testament Studies 41:71-88.

Cullmann, Oscar
1956   *The State in the New Testament*. New York: Scribner.

Daly, R. J.
1997   "Is Christianity Sacrificial or Antisacrificial?" *Religion*
                     27:231-43.

Davies, W. D.
1984   *Jewish and Pauline Studies*. Philadelphia: Fortress.

Deichgräber, Reinhard
1967   *Gotteshymnus und Christushymnus in der frühen Chris-
                     tenheit*. Göttingen: Vandenhoeck & Ruprecht.

Denney, James
1970   "St. Paul's Epistle to the Romans." In *The Expositor's Greek
                     New Testament,* vol. 2, edited by W. Robertson Nicoll.
                     1904. Reprint, Grand Rapids, Mich.: Eerdmans.

Derrett, J. D. M.

1994   "You Abominate False Gods; but Do You Rob Shrines?
               (Rom 2.22b)." *New Testament Studies* 40:558-71.

De Young, James B.

1988   "The Meaning of 'Nature' in Romans 1 and Its Implications
               for Biblical Proscriptions of Homosexual Behavior." *Jour-
               nal of the Evangelical Theological Society* 31:429-41.

2000   *Homosexuality: Contemporary Claims Examined in Light
               of the Bible and Other Ancient Literature and Law.* Grand
               Rapids, Mich.: Kregel.

Dodd, C. H.

1931   "ἱλάσκεσθαι: Its Cognates, Derivatives and Synonyms in
               the Septuagint." *Journal of Theological Studies* 32:352-60.

1932   *The Epistle of Paul to the Romans.* Moffatt New Testament
               Commentary. New York: Harper and Brothers.

Donaldson, Terrence L.

1993   "'Riches for the Gentiles' (Rom 11:12): Israel's Rejection
               and Paul's Gentile Mission." *Journal of Biblical Literature*
               112:81-98.

Donfried, Karl P.

1991   "A Short Note on Romans 16." In *The Romans Debate,* pp.
               44-52. Edited by Karl P. Donfried. Peabody, Mass.: Hen-
               drickson.

Du Toit, A. B.

1989   "Persuasion in Romans 1:1-17." *Biblische Zeitschrift* 33:192-
               209.

Dunn, James D. G.

1988a   *Romans 1-8.* Word Biblical Commentary 38A. Waco, Tex.:
               Word.

1988b   *Romans 9-16.* Word Biblical Commentary 38B. Waco,
               Tex.: Word.

1992a   "Prayer." In *Dictionary of Jesus and the Gospels,* pp. 617-
               25. Edited by Joel B. Green, Scot McKnight and I. Howard
               Marshall. Downers Grove, Ill.: InterVarsity Press.

1992b   "Yet Once More—'The Works of the Law': A Response."
               Journal for the Study of the New Testament 46:99-117.

1998   *The Theology of Paul the Apostle.* Grand Rapids, Mich.: Eerdmans.

Earnshaw, John D.

1994   "Reconsidering Paul's Marriage Analogy in Romans 7.1-4." *New Testament Studies* 40:68-88.

Ellis, E. Earle

1993   "Coworkers, Paul and His." In *Dictionary of Paul and His Letters,* pp. 183-89. Edited by Gerald F. Hawthorne, Ralph P. Martin and Daniel G. Reid. Downers Grove, Ill.: Inter-Varsity Press.

Faber, Riemer A.

1995   "The Juridical Nuance in the New Testament Use of προσω–πολημψία." *Westminster Theological Journal* 57:299-309.

Fee, Gordon D.

1994   *God's Empowering Presence: The Holy Spirit in the Letters of Paul.* Peabody, Mass.: Hendrickson.

Fitzmyer, Joseph A.

1993a   "The Consecutive Meaning of ἐφ' ᾧ– in Romans 5:12." *New Testament Studies* 39:321-39.

1993b   *Romans: A New Translation with Introduction and Commentary.* Anchor Bible 33. New York: Doubleday.

Foerster, Werner,
and Johannes Hermann

1965   "κληρονόμος, κτλ." In *Theological Dictionary of the New Testament,* 3:767-85. Edited by Gerhard Kittel and Gerhard Friedrich. 10 vols. Grand Rapids, Mich.: Eerdmans.

France, R. T.

1994   "'It Seemed Good to the Holy Spirit and to Us'? Some Thoughts on Decision-making in the Church, and on Christian Disagreement, in the Light of the Decision of the Church of England to Ordain Women to the Presbyterate." *Churchman* 108:234-41.

1999   "From Romans to the Real World: Biblical Principles and Cultural Change in Relation to Homosexuality and the Ministry of Women." In *Romans and the People of God: Essays in Honor of Gordon D. Fee on the Occasion of His 65th Birthday,* pp. 234-53. Edited by Sven K. Soderlund and N. T. Wright. Grand Rapids, Mich.: Eerdmans.

Fryer, N. S. L.
1987   "The Meaning and Translation of ἱλαστήριον in Romans
               3:25." *Evangelical Quarterly* 59:99-116.
Gager, John G.
1983   *The Origins of Anti-Semitism: Attitudes Toward Judaism in
               Pagan and Christian Antiquity.* New York: Oxford Uni-
               versity Press.
Gagnon, Robert A. J.
1993   "Heart of Wax and a Teaching That Stamps: ΤΥΠΟΣ ΔΙΔΑ-
               ΞΗΣ (Rom 6:17b) Once More." *Journal of Biblical Litera-
               ture* 112:667-87.
Garlington, Don B.
1990a   "Ἱεροσυλείν and the Idolatry of Israel (Romans 2:22)."
               New Testament Studies 36:142-51.

1990b   "The Obedience of Faith in the Letter to the Romans. Part
               I: The Meaning of ὑπακοή πίστεως (Rom 1:5; 16:26)."
               Westminster Theological Journal 52:201-24.

1990c   "Romans 7:7-25 and the Creation Theology of Paul." *Trin-
               ity Journal* 11:197-235.
Gaston, Lloyd
1982   "Israel's Enemies in Pauline Theology." *New Testament
               Studies* 28:400-423.
Giesen, Heinz
1991   "ἐριθεία." In *Exegetical Dictionary of the New Testament,*
               2:52. Edited by H. Balz and G. Schneider. 3 vols. Grand
               Rapids, Mich.: Eerdmans.
Gilchrist, J. M.
1988   "Paul and the Corinthians—The Sequence of Letters and
               Visits." *Journal for the Study of the New Testament* 34:47-
               69.
Gill, David W. J.
1989   "Erastus the Aedile." *Tyndale Bulletin* 40:293-301.

Godet, Frédéric Louis
1969   *Commentary on Romans.* 1879. Reprint. Grand Rapids,
               Mich.: Zondervan.
Gooch, Paul W.
1987   "Sovereignty and Freedom: Some Pauline Compati-
               bilisms." *Scottish Journal of Theology* 40:531-42.

Grobel, Kendrick
1964   "A Chiastic Retribution Formula in Romans 2." In *Zeit und Geschichte: Dankesgabe an Rudolf Bultmann zum 80 Geburtstag*, pp. 255-71. Edited by E. Dinkler. Tübingen: Mohr.

Grudem, Wayne A.
1982   *The Gift of Prophecy in 1 Corinthians*. Washington, D.C.: University Press of America.

Grundmann, Walter
1964   "ἁμαρτάνω, F. Sin in the NT." In *Theological Dictionary of the New Testament*, 1:302-16. Edited by Gerhard Kittel and Gerhard Friedrich. 10 vols. Grand Rapids, Mich.: Eerdmans.

1965   "κράζω, κτλ." In *Theological Dictionary of the New Testament*, 3:898-903. Edited by Gerhard Kittel and Gerhard Friedrich. 10 vols. Grand Rapids, Mich.: Eerdmans.

1971   "ἵστημι." In *Theological Dictionary of the New Testament*, 7:638-53. Edited by Gerhard Kittel and Gerhard Friedrich. 10 vols. Grand Rapids, Mich.: Eerdmans.

Guerra, Anthony J.
1988   "Romans 4 as Apologetic Theology." *Harvard Theological Review* 81:251-70.

1990   "Romans: Paul's Purpose and Audience with Special Attention to Romans 9-11." *Revue Biblique* 97:219-37.

Gundry, Robert H.
1980   "The Moral Frustration of Paul Before His Conversion: Sexual Lust in Romans 7:7-25." In *Pauline Studies: Essays Presented to Professor F. F. Bruce on His Seventieth Birthday*, pp. 228-45. Edited by Donald A. Hagner and Murray J. Harris. Grand Rapids, Mich.: Eerdmans.

1987   *SŌMA in Biblical Theology: With Emphasis on Pauline Anthropology*. Grand Rapids, Mich.: Zondervan.

Gundry-Volf, Judith M.
1990   *Paul and Perseverance: Staying in and Falling Away*. Louisville: Westminster John Knox.

Günther, Walter,
and Hans-Georg Link
1976   "Love." In *The New International Dictionary of New Testament Theology*, 3:538-46. Edited by C. Brown. 3 vols. Grand Rapids, Mich.: Zondervan.

Gutbrod, Walter

1965   "Ἰουδαῖος." In *Theological Dictionary of the New Testa-
                    ment*, 3:369-71. Edited by Gerhard Kittel and Gerhard
                    Friedrich. 10 vols. Grand Rapids, Mich.: Eerdmans.

Haacker, Klaus

1990   "Der Römerbrief als Friedensmemorandum." *New Testa-
                    ment Studies* 36:25-41.

Hackenburg, Wolfgang

1991   "ἐπίγνωσις." In *Exegetical Dictionary of the New Testa-
                    ment*, 2:25. Edited by H. Balz and G. Schneider. 3 vols.
                    Grand Rapids, Mich.: Eerdmans.

Hafemann, Scott J.

1988   "The Salvation of Israel in Romans 11:25-32: A Response
                    to Krister Stendahl." *Ex Auditu* 4:38-58.

Hagner, Donald A.

1993   "Paul and Judaism: The Jewish Matrix of Early Christianity."
                    Bulletin of Biblical Research 3:111-30.

Harder, Günter

1976   "Nature." In *New International Dictionary of New Testa-
                    ment Theology*, 2:656-62. Edited by Colin Brown. 3 vols.
                    Grand Rapids, Mich.: Zondervan.

Harris, Murray J.

1976   "2 Corinthians." In *Romans Through Galatians*, pp. 301-
                    406. Expositor's Bible Commentary 10. Edited by Frank
                    Gaebelein. Grand Rapids, Mich.: Zondervan.

1978   "Prepositions and Theology in the Greek New Testa-
                    ment." In *New International Dictionary of New Testament
                    Theology*, 3:1171-1215. Edited by C. Brown. 3 vols. Grand
                    Rapids, Mich.: Zondervan.

1992   *Jesus as "God": Theios as a Christological Term in the New
                    Testament.* Grand Rapids, Mich.: Baker.

Harrisville, Roy A.

1980   *Romans.* Augsburg Commentary on the New Testament.
                    Minneapolis: Augsburg.

Hay, David M.

1989 *   "Pistis as 'Ground for Faith' in Hellenized Judaism and
                    Paul." *Journal for Biblical Literature* 108:461-76.

Hays, Richard B.

1989   *Echoes of Scripture in the Letters of Paul.* New Haven,

Conn.: Yale University Press.

Hendriksen, William
1981   *New Testament Commentary: Exposition of Paul's Epistle to the Romans.* Grand Rapids, Mich.: Baker.

Hill, David
1967   *Greek Words and Hebrew Meanings: Studies in the Semantics of Soteriological Terms.* Society for New Testament Studies Monograph Series 5. Cambridge: Cambridge University Press.

Hodge, Charles
1950   *Commentary on the Epistle to the Romans.* 1886. Reprint, Grand Rapids, Mich.: Eerdmans.

Howard, George E.
1969   "Christ the End of the Law: The Meaning of Romans 10:4ff." *Journal of Biblical Literature* 88:331-37.

Hurtado, Larry W.
1981   "The Doxology at the End of Romans." In *New Testament Textual Criticism: Its Significance for Exegesis. Essays in Honour of Bruce M. Metzger,* pp. 185-99. Edited by E. J. Epp and Gordon D. Fee. Oxford: Clarendon.

1996   "The Bible and Same-Sex Erotic Relations." *Crux* 32:13-19.

1999   "Jesus' Divine Sonship in Paul's Epistle to the Romans." In *Romans and the People of God,* pp. 217-33. Edited by Sven K. Soderlund and N. T. Wright. Grand Rapids, Mich.: Eerdmans.

Hvalvik, Reidar
1990   "A 'Sonderweg' for Israel: A Critical Examination of a Current Interpretation of Romans 11:25-27." *Journal for the Study of the New Testament* 38:87-107.

Jeremias, Joachim
1967a   "λίθος, λίθινος." In *Theological Dictionary of the New Testament,* 4:268-80. Edited by Gerhard Kittel and Gerhard Friedrich. 10 vols. Grand Rapids, Mich.: Eerdmans.

1967b   *The Prayers of Jesus.* London: SCM Press.

Jervell, Jacob
1991   "The Letter to Jerusalem." In *The Romans Debate,* pp. 53-64. Edited by K. P. Donfried. Peabody Mass.: Hendrickson.

Jewett, Robert
1988   "Paul, Phoebe, and the Spanish Mission." In *The Social World of Formative Christianity and Judaism: Essays in Honor of Howard Clark Kee,* pp. 142-61. Edited by J. Neusner et al. Philadelphia: Fortress.

Johnson, Luke Timothy
1982   "Rom 3:21-26 and the Faith of Jesus." *Catholic Biblical Quarterly* 44:77-90.

Kaiser, Walter C., Jr.
1971   "Leviticus 18:5 and Paul: Do This and You Shall Live (Eternally?)." *Journal of the Evangelical Theological Society* 14:19-28.

Karlberg, Mark W.
1986   "Israel's History Personified: Romans 7:7-13 in Relation to Paul's Teaching on the 'Old Man.'" *Trinity Journal* n.s. 7.1:65-74.

Karris, Robert J.
1991   "Romans 14:1-15:13 and the Occasion of Romans." In *The Romans Debate,* pp. 65-84. Edited by K. P. Donfried. Peabody, Mass.: Hendricksen.

Käsemann, Ernst
1971   *Perspectives on Paul.* Translated by M. Kohl. Philadelphia: Fortress.

1980   *Commentary on Romans.* Translated and edited by Geoffrey W. Bromiley. Grand Rapids, Mich.: Eerdmans.

Keck, Leander E.
1965   "The Poor Among the Saints in the New Testament." *Zeitschrift für die neutestamentliche Wissenschaft* 56:100-129.

Kertelge, Karl
1981   *The Epistle to the Romans.* New Testament for Spiritual Reading. New York: Crossroad.

Kim, Seyoon
1997   "The 'Mystery' of Rom 11.25-6 Once More." *New Testament Studies* 43:412-29.

Kinghorn, Kenneth C.
1997   "Holiness: The Central Plan of God." *Evangelical Journal* 15:57-70.

Klein, Günter
1991   "Paul's Purpose in Writing the Epistle to the Romans." In *The Romans Debate,* pp. 29-43. Edited by K. P. Donfried.

Peabody, Mass.: Hendrickson.

Klein, William W.
1990   *The New Chosen People: A Corporate View of Election.*
                        Grand Rapids, Mich.: Zondervan.

Klostermann, Erich
1933   "Die adäquate Vergeltung in Röm 1.22-31." *Zeitschrift für
                        die neutestamentliche Wissenschaft* 32:1-6.

Koester, Helmut
1972   "ἀποτομία, κτλ." In *Theological Dictionary of the New Tes-
                        tament,* 8:106-9. Edited by Gerhard Kittel and Gerhard
                        Friedrich. 10 vols. Grand Rapids, Mich.: Eerdmans.

Krentz, Edgar
1990   "The Name of God in Disrepute: Romans 2:17-29 [22-23]."
                        Currents in Theology and Mission 17:429-39.

Kruger, M. A.
1987   "ΤΙΝΑ ΚΑΡΠΟΝ, 'Some Fruit' in Romans 1:13." *Westminster
                        Theological Journal* 49:167-73.

Kümmel, Werner Georg
1967   "*Paresis* and *Endeixis*: A Contribution to an Understand-
                        ing of the Pauline Doctrine of Justification." *Journal for
                        Theology and the Church* 3:1-13.

Lagrange, Marie-Joseph
1950   *Saint Paul Epître aux Romans Études Bibliques.* Paris:
                        Gabalda.

Leenhardt, Franz J.
1961   *The Epistle to the Romans: A Commentary.* Translated by
                        H. Knight. London: Lutterworth.

Légasse, Simon
1991   "Être baptizé dans la mort du Christ: Étude de Romains 6,
                        1-14." *Revue Biblique* 98:544-59.

Lenski, R. C. H.
1945   *The Interpretation of St. Paul's Epistle to the Romans.* Co-
                        lumbus, Ohio: Wartburg.

Linss, Wilhelm C.
1993   "Exegesis of *Telos* in Roman 10:4." *Biblical Research* 33:5-
                        12.

Lohse, Eduard
1995   "Εὐαγγέλιον θεοῦ, Paul's Interpretation of the Gospel in
                        His Epistle to the Romans." *Biblica* 76:127-40.

Longenecker, Bruce W.
1991   *Eschatology and the Covenant: A Comparison of 4 Ezra
                        and Romans 1-11.* Journal for the Study of the New Testa-

ment Supplement Series 57. Sheffield: JSOT Press.

1993   "Πίστις in Romans 3:25: Neglected Evidence for the 'Faithfulness of Christ'?" *New Testament Studies* 39:478-80.

Longenecker, Richard N.

1964   *Paul Apostle of Liberty: The Origin and Nature of Paul's Christianity.* Grand Rapids, Mich.: Baker.

1971   *Ministry and Message of Paul.* Grand Rapids, Mich.: Zondervan.

1999   "The Focus of Romans: The Central Role of 5:1-8:39 in the Argument of the Letter." In *Romans and the People of God: Essays in Honor of Gordon D. Fee on the Occasion of His 65th Birthday,* pp. 49-69. Edited by Sven K. Soderlund and N. T. Wright. Grand Rapids, Mich.: Eerdmans.

Louw, Johannes P., and Eugene A. Nida

1988   *Greek-English Lexicon of the New Testament Based on Semantic Domains.* 2 vols. New York: United Bible Societies.

Luther, Martin

1972   *Luther's Works,* vol. 25. *Lectures on Romans: Glosses and Scholia.* Translated and edited by H. C. Oswald. Philadelphia: Muhlenburg.

MacGregor, George Hogarth Carnaby

1960-1961   "The Concept of the Wrath of God in the New Testament." *New Testament Studies* 7:101-9.

Manson, T. W.

1991   "St. Paul's Letter to the Romans—and Others." In *The Romans Debate,* pp. 3-15. Edited by Karl P. Donfried. Peabody, Mass.: Hendrickson.

Marcus, Joel

1988   "Let God Arise and End the Reign of Sin! A Contribution to the Study of Paulistic Parenesis." *Biblica* 69:386-95.

1989   "The Circumcision and the Uncircumcision in Rome." *New Testament Studies* 35:67-81.

Marshall, I. Howard

1969   *Kept by the Power of God: A Study of Perseverance and Falling Away.* London: Epworth.

| 1974 | "The Development of the Concept of Redemption in the New Testament." In *Reconciliation and Hope: New Testament Essays on Atonement and Eschatology Presented to L. L. Morris on His Sixtieth Birthday,* pp. 153-69. Edited by R. Banks. Grand Rapids, Mich.: Eerdmans. |

| 1975 | "Predestination in the New Testament." In *Grace Unlimited,* pp. 127-43. Edited by Clark Pinnock. Minneapolis: Bethany Fellowship. |

Martens, John W.

| 1994 | "Romans 2.14-16: A Stoic Reading." *New Testament Studies* 40:55-67. |

Marxsen, Willi

| 1955 | "Der ἕτερος νόμος Röm 13,8." *Theologische Zeitschrift* 11:230-37. |

McDonald, Patricia M.

| 1990 | "Romans 5.1-11 as a Rhetorical Bridge." *Journal for the Study of the New Testament* 40:81-96. |

McKnight, Scot

| 1991 | *A Light Among the Gentiles: Jewish Missionary Activity in the Second Temple Period.* Minneapolis: Fortress. |

| 1993 | "Collection for the Saints." In *Dictionary of Paul and His Letters,* pp. 143-47. Edited by Gerald F. Hawthorne, Ralph P. Martin and Daniel G. Reid. Downers Grove, Ill.: InterVarsity Press. |

Meggitt, Justin J.

| 1996 | "The Social Status of Erastus (Rom 16:23)." *Novum Testamentum* 38:218-23. |

Metzger, Bruce M.

| 1971 | *A Textual Commentary on the Greek New Testament.* New York: United Bible Societies. |

| 1973 | "The Punctuation of Rom 9:5." In *Christ and Spirit in the New Testament: In Honour of Charles Francis Digby Moule,* pp. 95-112. Edited by B. Lindars and Stephen S. Smalley. Cambridge: Cambridge University Press. |

Michaels, J. Ramsey

| 1988 | *1 Peter.* Word Biblical Commentary 49. Waco, Tex.: Word. |

| 1999 | "The Redemption of Our Body: The Riddle of Romans 8:19-22." In *Romans and the People of God: Essays in* |

Honor of Gordon D. Fee on the Occasion of His 65th Birthday, pp. 92-114. Edited by Sven K. Soderlund and N. T. Wright. Grand Rapids, Mich.: Eerdmans.

Michel, Otto

1966   *Der Brief an die Römer.* 4th ed. Göttingen: Vandenhoeck & Ruprecht.

1975   "Faith." In *The New International Dictionary of New Testament Theology,* 1:593-605. Edited by C. Brown. 3 vols. Grand Rapids, Mich.: Zondervan.

Moiser, Jeremy

1990   "Rethinking Romans 12-15." *New Testament Studies* 36:571-82.

Mollenkott, Virginia
Ramey, and
Letha Scanzoni

1978   *Is the Homosexual My Neighbor? Another Christian View.* San Francisco: Harper & Row.

Moo, Douglas J.

1983   "'Law,' 'Works of the Law,' and Legalism in Paul." *Westminster Theological Journal* 45:73-100.

1996   *The Epistle to the Romans.* The New International Commentary on the New Testament. Grand Rapids, Mich.: Eerdmans.

Morris, Leon

1965   *The Apostolic Preaching of the Cross.* 2nd ed. Grand Rapids, Mich.: Eerdmans.

1988   *The Epistle to the Romans.* Pillar New Testament Commentary. Grand Rapids, Mich.: Eerdmans.

Morrison, Clinton

1960   *The Powers That Be: Earthly Rulers and Demonic Powers in Romans 13:1-7.* Studies in Biblical Theology 29. London: SCM Press.

Munck, Johannes

1959   *Paul and the Salvation of Mankind.* Translated by F. Clarke. Atlanta: John Knox.

1967   *Christ and Israel: An Interpretation of Romans 9-11.* Translated by I. Nixon. Philadelphia: Fortress.

Munro, Winsome

1983   *Authority in Paul and Peter: The Identification of a Pasto-
        ral Stratum in the Pauline Corpus and 1 Peter.* Society of
        New Testament Studies Monograph Series 45. Cambridge:
        Cambridge University Press.

1990   "Interpolation in the Epistles: Weighing Probability." *New
        Testament Studies* 36:431-43.

Murray, John

1968   *The Epistle to the Romans.* 2 vols. in 1. The New Interna-
        tional Commentary on the New Testament. Grand Rapids,
        Mich.: Eerdmans.

Mussner, Franz

1976   "'Ganz Israel wird gerettet werden' (Röm 11,26): Versuch
        einer Auslegung." *Kairos* 18:241-55.

Nygren, Anders

1949   *Commentary on Romans.* Philadelphia: Fortress.

O'Brien, Peter T.

1977   *Introductory Thanksgivings in the Letters of Paul.* Novum
        Testamentum Supplements 49. Leiden: Brill.

1987   "Romans 8:26, 27: A Revolutionary Approach to Prayer?"
        Reformed Theological Review 46:65-73.

1993   "Mystery." In *Dictionary of Paul and His Letters,* pp. 621-
        23. Edited by Gerald F. Hawthorne, Ralph P. Martin and
        Daniel G. Reid. Downers Grove, Ill.: InterVarsity Press.

1995   *Gospel and Mission in the Writings of Paul: An Exegetical
        and Theological Analysis.* Grand Rapids, Mich.: Baker
        Books.

Osborne, Grant R.

1975   "Exegetical Notes on Calvinist Texts." In *Grace Unlimited,*
        pp. 167-89. Edited by Clark Pinnock. Minneapolis: Beth-
        any Fellowship.

1979   "Countering the Cultic Curse." *Christianity Today* 23.18
        (June 29): 22-23.

1984   "Mind Control or Spirit-Controlled Mind?" In *Renewing
        Your Mind in a Secular Age,* pp. 55-70. Edited by John D.

Woodbridge. Chicago: Moody Press.

1991   *The Hermeneutical Spiral: A Comprehensive Introduction to Biblical Interpretation.* Downers Grove, Ill.: InterVarsity Press.

2002   *Revelation.* Baker Exegetical Commentary on the New Testament. Grand Rapids, Mich.: Baker.

Oswalt, John N.

1986   *The Book of Isaiah Chapters 1-39.* The New International Commentary on the Old Testament. Grand Rapids, Mich.: Eerdmans.

1998   *The Book of Isaiah Chapters 40-66.* The New International Commentary on the Old Testament. Grand Rapids, Mich.: Eerdmans.

Packer, J. I.

1999   "The 'Wretched Man' Revisited: Another Look at Romans 7:14-25." In *Romans and the People of God: Essays in Honor of Gordon D. Fee on the Occasion of His 65th Birthday,* pp. 70-81. Edited by Sven K. Soderlund and N. T. Wright. Grand Rapids, Mich.: Eerdmans.

Park, Sang Hoon

1997   "שׁאר." *New International Dictionary of Old Testament Theology and Exegesis,* 4:11-17. Edited by W. A. VanGemeren. 5 vols. Grand Rapids, Mich.: Zondervan.

Parker, Thomas D.

2000   "'Abraham, Father of Us All,' in Barth's *Epistle to the Romans.*" In *Reading Israel in Romans: Legitimacy and Plausibility of Divergent Interpretations,* pp. 57-73. Edited by C. Grenholm and D. Patte. Harrisburg, Penn.: Trinity Press International.

Peterson, David

1993   "Worship and Ethics in Romans 12." *Tyndale Bulletin* 44:271-88.

Pierce, Claude A.

1955   *Conscience in the New Testament. A Study of "Syneidesis" in the New Testament, in the Light of Its Sources, and with Particular Reference to St. Paul, with Some Observations Regarding Its Pastoral Relevance Today.* Studies in Biblical Theology. London: SCM Press.

Piper, John

1979   *"Love Your Enemies'":Jesus' Love Command in the Synoptic Gospels and in the Early Christian Paraenesis. A History of the Tradition and Interpretation of Its Uses.* Society for New Testament Studies Monograph Series 38. Cambridge: Cambridge University Press.

1983   *The Justification of God: An Exegetical and Theological Study of Romans 9:1-23.* Grand Rapids, Mich.: Baker.

Pollard, Paul

1997   "The 'Faith of Christ' in Recent Discussion." *Concordia Journal* 23:213-28.

Porter, Stanley E.

1993   "Fear, Reverence." In *Dictionary of Paul and His Letters,* pp 291-93. Edited by Gerald F. Hawthorne, Ralph P. Martin and D. G. Reid. Downers Grove, Ill.: InterVarsity Press.

1994   *Idioms of the Greek New Testament.* Sheffield: Sheffield Academic Press.

Pyne, Robert A.

1993   "The Role of the Holy Spirit in Conversion." *Bibliotheca Sacra* 150:203-18.

Radl, Walter

1993   "ὑπομονή." In *Exegetical Dictionary of the New Testament,* 3:405-6. Edited by H. Balz and G. Schneider. 3 vols. Grand Rapids, Mich.: Eerdmans.

Räisanen, Heikki

1983   *Paul and the Law.* Tübingen: Mohr.

Raver, Max

1923   *Die "Schwachen" in Korinth und Rom nach den Paulusbriefen.* Biblische Studien 21, no. 2-3. Freiburg: Herder.

Reasoner, Mark

1999   *The Strong and the Weak: Romans 14:1—15:13 in Context.* Society for New Testament Studies Monographs Series 103. Cambridge: Cambridge University Press.

Reinbold, Wolfgang

1995   "Israel und das Evangelium: Zur Exegese von Römer 10, 19-21." *Zeitschrift für die neutestamentliche Wissenschaft* 86:122-29.

Rhyne, C. Thomas

1985   *"Nomos Dikaiosynēs* and the Meaning of Romans 10:4."

Catholic Biblical Quarterly 47:486-99.

Ridderbos, Herman N.

1975   *Paul: An Outline of His Theology.* Translated by J. R. de
              Witt. Grand Rapids, Mich.: Eerdmans.

Robertson, O. Palmer

1980   "Genesis 15:6: New Covenant Expositions of an Old Testa-
              ment Text." *Westminster Theological Journal* 42:259-89.

Rolland, Philippe

1988   "L'antithèse de Rm 5-8." *Biblica* 69:396-400.

Romaniuk, Kazimierz

1990   "Was Phoebe in Romans 16, 1 a Deaconess?" *Zeitschrift für*
              die neutestamentliche Wissenschaft 81:132-34.

Rupprecht, Arthur A.

1993   "Slave, Slavery." In *Dictionary of Paul and His Letters,* pp.
              881-83. Edited by Gerald F. Hawthorne, Ralph P. Martin, and
              Daniel G. Reid. Downers Grove, Ill.: InterVarsity Press.

Sampley, J. Paul

1995   "The Weak and the Strong: Paul's Careful and Crafty Rhe-
              torical Strategy in Romans 14:1—5:13." In *The Social World*
              of the First Christians: Essays in Honor of Wayne A. Meeks,
              pp. 41-52. Edited by L. M. White and O. L. Yarbrough.
              Minneapolis: Augsburg Fortress.

Sanday, William,
and Arthur C. Headlam

1902   *A Critical and Exegetical Commentary on the Epistle to the*
              Romans. International Critical Commentary. 1895. Re-
              print, Edinburgh: T & T Clark.

Sanders, E. P.

1977   *Paul and Palestinian Judaism: A Comparison of Patterns*
              of Religion. Philadelphia: Fortress.

1983   *Paul, the Law, and the Jewish People.* Philadelphia: Fortress.

Sass, Gerhard

1993   "Röm 15:7-13—als Summe des Römerbriefs gelesen."
              Evangelische Theologie 53:510-27.

Schelke, Karl Hermann

1993   "σωτηρία." In *Exegetical Dictionary of the New Testament,*
              3:327-29. Edited by H. Balz and G. Schneider. 3 vols.
              Grand Rapids, Mich.: Eerdmans.

Schlatter, Adolf von

1995   *Romans: The Righteousness of God.* Translated by S. S. Schatzmann. Peabody, Mass.: Hendrickson.

Schlier, Heinrich

1964   "ἀμήν." In *Theological Dictionary of the New Testament,* 1:335-38. Edited by G. Kittel and G. Friedrich. 10 vols. Grand Rapids, Mich.: Eerdmans.

Schmidt, Karl Ludwig,
and Martin Anton Schmidt

1967   "πωρόω, κτλ." In *Theological Dictionary of the New Testament,* 5:1025-28. Edited by Gerhard Kittel and Gerhard Friedrich. 10 vols. Grand Rapids, Mich.: Eerdmans.

Schmidt, Thomas E.

1993   "Riches and Poverty." In *Dictionary of Paul and His Letters,* pp. 826-27. Edited by Gerald F. Hawthorne, Ralph P. Martin and Daniel G. Reid. Downers Grove, Ill.: InterVarsity Press.

Schneider, Gerhard

1990   "ἀρέσκω." In *Exegetical Dictionary of the New Testament,* 1:151. Edited by H. Balz and G. Schneider. 3 vols. Grand Rapids, Mich.: Eerdmans.

Schreiner, Thomas R.

1993a   "Did Paul Believe in Justification by Works? Another Look at Romans 2." *Bulletin for Biblical Research* 3:131-58.

1993b   "Paul's View of the Law in Romans 10:4-5." *Westminster Theological Journal* 55:113-35.

1998   *Romans.* Baker Exegetical Commentary on the New Testament. Grand Rapids, Mich.: Baker.

Schrenk, Gottlob

1964   "δίκη κτλ." In *Theological Dictionary of the New Testament,* 2:178-225. Edited by Gerhard Kittel and Gerhard Friedrich. 10 vols. Grand Rapids, Mich.: Eerdmans.

Schulz, Ray R.

1990   "A Case for 'President' Phoebe in Romans 16:2." *Lutheran Theological Journal* 24:124-27.

Schüssler Fiorenza,
Elisabeth

1986   "Missionaries, Apostles, Co-Workers: Romans 16 and the Reconstruction of Women's Early Christian History." *Word and World* 6:420-33.

Scroggs, Robin
1983   *The New Testament and Homosexuality*. Philadelphia: For-
               tress.
Seifrid, Mark A.
1985   "Paul's Approach to the Old Testament in Rom 10:6-8."
               Trinity Journal n.s. 6:3-37.

1992a   *Justification by Faith: The Origin and Development of a
               Central Pauline Theme*. Supplements to Novum Testa-
               mentum 68. Leiden: Brill.

1992b   "The Subject of Rom 7:14-25." *Novum Testamentum*
               34:313-33.
Shank, Robert
1970   *Elect in the Son: A Study of the Doctrine of Election* Spring-
               field, Mo.: Westcott.
Snodgrass, Klyne
1986   "Justification by Grace—to the Doers: An Analysis of the
               Place of Romans 2 in the Theology of Paul." *New Testa-
               ment Studies* 32:72-93.

1988   "Spheres of Influence: A Possible Solution to the Prob-
               lem of Paul and the Law." *Journal for the Study of the New
               Testament* 32:93-113.
Snyman, A. H.
1988   "Style and the Rhetorical Situation of Romans 8.31-39."
               New Testament Studies 34:218-31.
Stackhouse, John G., Jr.
2001   "Mind over Skepticism." *Christianity Today* 45.8:74-76.

Stählin, Gustav
1967   "ὀργή, E. The Wrath of Man and the Wrath of God in the
               NT." In *Theological Dictionary of the New Testament*,
               5:419-47. Edited by Gerhard Kittel and Gerhard Friedrich.
               10 vols. Grand Rapids, Mich.: Eerdmans.

1971   "σκάνδαλον, σκανδαλίζω." In *Theological Dictionary of
               the New Testament*, 7:339-58. Edited by Gerhard Kittel and
               Gerhard Friedrich. 10 vols. Grand Rapids, Mich.: Eerd-
               mans.

1974   "φιλέω, κτλ." In *Theological Dictionary of the New Testa-*

ment, 9:113-71. Edited by Gerhard Kittel and Gerhard Friedrich. 10 vols. Grand Rapids, Mich.: Eerdmans.

Stein, Robert H.

1989   "The Argument of Romans 13:1-7." *Novum Testamentum* 31:325-43.

Stendahl, Krister

1962   "Hate, Non-retaliation, and Love: 1QS x.17-20 and Rom. 12:19-21." *Harvard Theological Review* 55:343-55.

1976   *Paul Among Jews and Gentiles and Other Essays.* Philadelphia: Fortress.

Stott, John R. W.

1994   *Romans: God's Good News for the World.* The Bible Speaks Today. Downers Grove, Ill.: InterVarsity Press.

Stowers, Stanley Kent

1989   "Ἐκ πίστεως and διὰ τῆς πίστεως in Romans 3:30." *Journal of Biblical Literature* 108:665-74.

1994   *A Rereading of Romans: Justice, Jews, and Gentiles.* New Haven, Conn.: Yale University Press.

Stuhlmacher, Peter

1988   "The Theme of Romans." *Australian Biblical Review* 36:31-44.

1991   "The Purpose of Romans." In *The Romans Debate,* pp. 231-42. Edited by Karl P. Donfried. Peabody, Mass.: Hendrickson.

1994   *Paul's Letter to the Romans: A Commentary.* Translated by S. Hafemann. Louisville: Westminster John Knox.

Thielman, Frank

1994   *Paul and the Law: A Contextual Approach.* Downers Grove, Ill.: InterVarsity Press.

Thompson, Michael B.

1991   *Clothed with Christ: The Example and Teaching of Jesus in Romans 12.1-15.13.* Journal for the Study of the New Testament Supplement Series 59. Sheffield: JSOT Press.

Thorley, John

1996   "Junia, a Woman Apostle." *Novum Testamentum* 38:18-29.

Tobin, Thomas H.

1993   "Controversy and Continuity in Romans 1:18-3:20." *Catho-*

lic Biblical Quarterly 55:298-318.

Towner, Philip H.
1999   "Roman's 13:1-7 and Paul's Missiological Perspective: A Call to Political Quietism or Transformation?" In *Romans and the People of God: Essays in Honor of Gordon D. Fee on the Occasion of His 65th Birthday,* pp. 149-69. Edited by Sven K. Soderlund and N. T. Wright. Grand Rapids, Mich.: Eerdmans.

Trocmé, Etienne
1992   "L'apôtre Paul et Rome: Réflexions sur une fascination." *Revue d'Histoire et de Philosophie Religieuses* 72:41-51.

Trudinger, Paul
1996   "An Autobiographical Digression? A Note on Romans 7:7-25." *Expository Times* 107:173-74.

Tsumura, David Toshio
1994   "An OT Background to Rom 8.22." *New Testament Studies* 40:620-21.

Wagner, Günter
1967   *Pauline Baptism and the Pagan Mysteries: The Problem of the Pauline Doctrine of Baptism in Romans VI:1-11, in Light of Its Religio-Historical "Parallels."* Translated by J. P. Smith. Edinburgh: Oliver and Boyd.

Wagner, J. Ross
1997   "The Christ, Servant of Jew and Gentile: A Fresh Approach to Romans 15:8-9." *Journal of Biblical Literature* 116:473-85.

Watts, Rikki E.
1999   "'For I Am Not Ashamed of the Gospel': Romans 1:16-17 and Habakkuk 2:4." In *Romans and the People of God: Essays in Honor of Gordon D. Fee on the Occasion of His 65th Birthday,* pp. 3-25. Edited by Sven K. Soderlund and N. T. Wright. Grand Rapids, Mich.: Eerdmans.

Wedderburn, A. J. M.
1983   "Hellenistic Christian Traditions in Romans 6?" *New Testament Studies* 29:337-55.

Wenham, Gordon J.
1979   *The Book of Leviticus.* The New International Commentary on the Old Tesament. Grand Rapids, Mich.: Eerdmans.

1987   *Genesis 1-15.* Word Biblical Commentary 1. Waco, Tex: Word.

Wesley, John
n.d.   *John Wesley's Notes on Romans.* Nashville: Methodist Evan-
                 gelistic Materials.

Wilckens, Ulrich
1978   *Röm 1-5.* Vol. 1 of *Der Brief an die Römer.* Evangelisch-
                 Katholischer Kommentar zum Neuen Testament 6.1. Neu-
                 kirchen-Vluyn, Germany: Neukirchener Verlag.

1980   *Röm 6-11.* Vol. 2 of *Der Brief an die Römer.* Evangelisch-
                 Katholischer Kommentar zum Neuen Testament 6.2. Neu-
                 kirchen-Vluyn, Germany: Neukirchener Verlag.

1982   *Röm 12-16.* Vol. 3 of *Der Brief an die Römer.* Evangelisch-
                 Katholischer Kommentar zum Neuen Testament 6.3. Neu-
                 kirchen-Vluyn, Germany: Neukirchener Verlag.

Williams, Sam K.
1979   "The 'Righteousness of God' in Romans." *Journal of Bibli-
                 cal Literature* 99:241-90.

Wink, Walter
1984   *Naming the Powers: The Language of Power in the New
                 Testament.* Philadelphia: Fortress.

Winter, Bruce W.
1994   *Seek the Welfare of the City: Christians as Benefactors and
                 Citizens.* Grand Rapids, Mich.: Eerdmans.

Wright, N. T.
1980   "The Meaning of περὶ ἁμαρτίας in Romans 8:3." In *Studia
                 Biblica 1978: Sixth International Congress on Biblical
                 Studies. Vol. 3, Papers on Paul and Other New Testament
                 Authors,* pp. 453-59. Edited by E. A. Livingstone. Journal
                 for the Study of the New Testament Supplement Series 3.
                 Sheffield: JSOT Press.

1991   *The Climax of the Covenant: Christ and the Law in Pauline
                 Theology.* Minneapolis: Fortress.

1999   "New Exodus, New Inheritance: The Narrative Structure of
                 Romans 3-8." In *Romans and the People of God: Essays in
                 Honor of Gordon D. Fee on the Occasion of His 65th Birth-
                 day,* pp. 26-35. Edited by Sven K. Soderlund and N. T.
                 Wright. Grand Rapids, Mich.: Eerdmans.

Wuellner, Wilhelm H.
1991   "Paul's Rhetoric of Argumentation in Romans: An Alterna-

tive to the Donfried/Karris Debate over Romans." In *The Romans Debate*, pp. 128-46. Edited by K. P. Donfried. Peabody, Mass.: Hendrickson.

Ziesler, J. A.

1972 *The Meaning of Righteousness in Paul: A Linguistic and Theological Enquiry*. Society for New Testament Studies Monographs Series 20. Cambridge: Cambridge University Press.

Zmijewski, Josef

1991 "καύχησις." In *Exegetical Dictionary of the New Testament*, 2:276-79. Edited by H. Balz and G. Schneider. 3 vols. Grand Rapids, Mich.: Eerdmans.

1993 "χρηστότης." In *Exegetical Dictionary of the New Testament*, 3:475-77. Edited by H. Balz and G. Schneider. 3 vols. Grand Rapids, Mich.: Eerdmans.